Mathematical Applications
For Management, Life, and Social Sciences

D. C. HEATH AND COMPANY
Lexington, Massachusetts   Toronto

Mathematical Applications

For Management, Life, and Social Sciences

RONALD J. HARSHBARGER
The Pennsylvania State University

JAMES J. REYNOLDS
The Pennsylvania State University

TO MY WIFE

Carol Harshbarger

AND TO

Wende Reynolds

PREFACE

The purpose of this text is to present mathematical skills and concepts and to apply them to areas that are important to students in the management, life, and social sciences. Although the text is intended for students who have completed two years of high school algebra or its equivalent, it begins with a brief review of algebra, which may be omitted or covered quickly by students with stronger backgrounds.

To paraphrase Alfred North Whitehead, the purpose of education is not to fill a vessel, but to kindle a fire. Although this is a desirable goal, it is not always an easy one to realize with students whose primary interest is not in mathematics itself. The applications included allow students to view the required mathematical concepts in a practical setting and to see examples and problems that are relevant to their intended careers. An Index of Selected Applications that lists exercises and/or discussion of selected applications follows the table of contents.

Other important features of the text are the following:

- *Chapter Warmups.* These warmups appear at the beginning of each chapter and permit students to test themselves on the skills prerequisite for that chapter. The warmups direct students who have difficulty with a particular skill to specific sections of the text for review.

- *Intuitive Viewpoint.* The book is written from an intuitive viewpoint, with emphasis on concepts and problem solving rather than on mathematical theory. Each topic is carefully explained, and examples illustrate the techniques involved. Exercises stress computation and drill, but there are enough challenging problems to stimulate students.

- *Linear Models.* A considerable number of concepts in business, economics, and the social sciences can be described by using linear models. Chapter 2 presents a thorough discussion of linear functions and their applications. The study of matrices (Chapter 3) and linear programming (Chapter 4) follow.

- *Nonlinear Models.* In Chapters 5 and 6 many of the applications that were discussed by using linear models are expanded, and new applications (especially from the life sciences) are introduced. This discussion of nonlinear models includes applications of quadratic, exponential, and logarithmic functions.

- *Probability and Statistics.* Chapters 8 and 9 provide an introduction to probability and statistics. These chapters prepare students for later courses in statistics and provide the basics of probability and statistics for those who require no additional mathematics or statistics courses. They may be omitted without loss of continuity in the text.

- *Calculus.* The study of calculus begins with limits (Chapter 10) and continues with derivatives of functions and integration. The derivative is introduced as a rate of change and then related to slope of a curve. Chapter 12 is devoted to applications of the derivative, including maximization and minimization of functions occurring in the management, life, and social sciences. Integration is introduced as an antiderivative; applications of it and the definite integral are discussed. The discussion of functions of several variables in Chapter 15 includes partial differentiation and maximization subject to constraints.

- *Selected Solutions to Exercises.* In addition to an answer section at the end of the text, a Guide to Selected Solutions to exercises has been prepared. The solutions included are one of each kind of difficult problem.

We would like to thank the many people who have helped us at various stages of this project. The encouragement, criticism, and suggestions that have been offered have been invaluable to us. We are especially indebted to Samuel Laposata, The Pennsylvania State University, and Frank Spreng, Brescia College, who provided ideas and encouragement, and to Frank Kocher, The Pennsylvania State University, who provided support and reviews throughout the book's evolution. Our special thanks are due John G. Christiano, Northern Illinois University; George W. Johnson, University of South Carolina; Robert G. Kuller, Northern Illinois University; Judith Q. Longyear, Wayne State University; and Lawrence E. Spence, Illinois State University, who reviewed the entire manuscript or parts of it and made many helpful comments. We would also like to express our appreciation to the editorial staff at D. C. Heath for its continued enthusiasm and support.

RONALD J. HARSHBARGER
JAMES J. REYNOLDS

CONTENTS

Index of Selected Applications

PART ONE
Algebra Review

ALGEBRA CONCEPTS

This chapter provides a brief review of the algebraic concepts that will be used throughout the text. You should already be familiar with its topics, but it will be to your advantage to spend some time reviewing them. You will also find this chapter useful as a reference as you study related topics in later chapters.

0.1 Sets and the Real Numbers

A *set* is a well-defined collection of objects. We may talk about a set of books, a set of dishes, or a set of students. We shall be concerned with sets of numbers. There are two ways to tell what a given set contains. One way is by listing the **elements** (or **members**) of the set (usually between braces). We may say that a set A contains 1, 2, 3, and 4 by writing $A = \{1, 2, 3, 4\}$. To say that 4 is a member of set A, we write $4 \in A$.

If all the members of the set can be listed, the set is said to be a finite set. $A = \{1, 2, 3, 4\}$ and $B = \{x, y, z\}$ are examples of finite sets. Although we cannot list all the elements of an infinite set, we can use three dots to indicate the unlisted members of such a set. For example, $N = \{1, 2, 3, 4, \ldots\}$ is an infinite set. This set N is called the set of **natural numbers.** Although they are not all listed, we know $10 \in N$, $1121 \in N$, and $15,331 \in N$, but $\frac{1}{2}$ is not a member of N (that is, $\frac{1}{2} \notin N$) because $\frac{1}{2}$ is not a natural number.

Another way to specify the elements of a given set is by *description*. For example, we may write $D = \{x \colon x$ is a Ford automobile$\}$ to describe the set of all Ford automobiles. $F = \{y \colon y$ is an odd natural number$\}$ is read "F is the set of all y such that y is an odd natural number." Thus $3 \in F$, $5 \in F$, and $7 \in F$ because they are odd natural numbers, and $6 \notin F$ because 6 is not an odd natural number.

EXAMPLE 1   Write the following sets in two ways:
(a) The set A of natural numbers less than 6.
(b) The set B of natural numbers greater than 10.
(c) The set C containing only 3.

Solution   (a) $A = \{1, 2, 3, 4, 5\}$ or $A = \{x \colon x$ is a natural number less than 6$\}$
(b) $B = \{11, 12, 13, 14 \ldots\}$ or $B = \{x \colon x$ is a natural number greater than 10$\}$
(c) $C = \{3\}$ or $C = \{x \colon x = 3\}$ □

Note that set C of Example 1 contains one member, 3; set A contains five members; and set B contains an infinite number of members. It is possible for a set to contain no members. Such a set is called the **empty set** or the **null set,** and it is denoted by $\varnothing$ or by $\{\ \}$. The set of living veterans of the War of 1812 is empty because there are no living veterans of that war. Thus

$$\{x \colon x \text{ is a living veteran of the War of 1812}\} = \varnothing.$$

Operations and Relations with Sets

DEFINITION	EXAMPLE
1. Sets X and Y are **equal** if they contain the same elements.	1. If $X = \{1, 2, 3, 4\}$ and $Y = \{4, 3, 2, 1\}$, then $X = Y$.
2. $A \subseteq B$ if every element of A is an element of B. A is called a **subset** of B.	2. If $A = \{1, 2, c, f\}$ and $B = \{1, 2, 3, a, b, c, f\}$, then $A \subseteq B$.
3. If C and D have no elements in common, they are called **disjoint.**	3. If $C = \{1, 2, a, b\}$ and $D = \{3, e, 5, c\}$, C and D are disjoint.
4. The **intersection** of two sets is a set containing the elements common to both sets. A intersection B is denoted $A \cap B = \{x \colon x \in A \text{ and } x \in B\}$.	4. If $A = \{1, 2, 5, 8\}$ and $B = \{1, 3, 5, 7\}$, $A \cap B = \{1, 5\}$.
5. The **union** of two sets is a set that contains all elements of both sets. The union of A and B is denoted $A \cup B = \{x \colon x \in A \text{ or } x \in B\}$.	5. If $A = \{1, 2, 5, 8\}$ and $B = \{1, 3, 5, 7\}$, then $A \cup B = \{1, 2, 3, 5, 7, 8\}$.

Table 0.1   SUBSETS OF THE SET OF REAL NUMBERS

	Description	Example
Natural numbers	$\{1, 2, 3, \ldots\}$ The counting numbers	
Integers	$\{\ldots, -2, -1, 0, 1, 2, \ldots\}$ The natural numbers, 0, and the negatives of the natural numbers.	
Rational numbers	All numbers that can be written as the ratio of two integers, a/b, with $b \neq 0$.	
Irrational numbers	Those real numbers that can *not* be written as the ratio of two integers.	
Real numbers	The set of all rational and irrational numbers (the entire number line).	

The universal set for our discussion in this text is the set of **real numbers.** Because there is exactly one point on a straight line for each real number, we can represent the real numbers along a line. Thus this number line is a picture, or graph, of the real numbers. Two numbers are said to be equal whenever they are represented by the same point on the number line. The **equation** $a = b$ (a equals b) means that the symbols a and b represent the same real number. Thus $3 + 4 = 7$ means that $3 + 4$ and 7 represent the same number. See Table 0.1.

We say that a is less than b (written $a < b$) if the point representing a is to the left of the point representing b on the real number line. For example, $4 < 7$ because 4 is to the left of 7 on the number line. We may also say that 7 is greater than 4 (written $7 > 4$). We may indicate that the number x is less than or equal to another number y by writing $x \leq y$. We may also indicate that p is greater than or equal to 4 by writing $p \geq 4$.

EXAMPLE 2   Use $<$ or $>$ notation to write
(a) 6 is greater than 5.
(b) 10 is less than 15.
(c) 3 is to the left of 8 on the number line.
(d) x is less than or equal to 12.

Solution   (a) $6 > 5$
(b) $10 < 15$
(c) $3 < 8$
(d) $x \leq 12$ □

There will be occasions when we are interested in the **distance** from a number to the origin (O) of the number line. The numbers 4 and -4 are both 4 units from the origin. We use the **absolute value** of a number to indicate its distance from O on the number line. The absolute value of any number $(\neq 0)$ is positive, and the absolute value of 0 is 0. We write the absolute value of the number a as $|a|$. Note: If any number except 0 has no attached sign, it is assumed to be a positive number.

EXAMPLE 3   Evaluate the following:
(a) $|-4|$ (b) $|+2|$ (c) $|0|$ (d) $|5|$

Solution   (a) $|-4| = +4 = 4$
(b) $|+2| = +2 = 2$
(c) $|0| = 0$
(d) $|5| = +5 = 5$ □

In performing computations with real numbers, it is important to remember the rules for computations with signed numbers.

Operations with Real (Signed) Numbers

PROCEDURE	EXAMPLE
1. (a) To add two signed numbers with the same sign, add their absolute values and affix their common sign.	1. (a) $(+5) + (+6) +11$ $(-3) + (-4) = -7$ $\left(-\dfrac{1}{6}\right) + \left(-\dfrac{2}{6}\right) = -\dfrac{3}{6} = -\dfrac{1}{2}$
(b) To add two signed numbers with unlike signs, find the difference of their absolute values and affix the sign of the number with the larger absolute value.	(b) $(-4) + (+3) = -1$ $(+5) + (-3) = +2$ $\left(-\dfrac{11}{7}\right) + (+1) = -\dfrac{4}{7}$
2. To subtract one signed number from another, change the sign of the number being subtracted and proceed as in addition.	2. $(-9) - (-8) = (-9) + (+8) = -1$ $16 - (+8) = 16 + (-8) = +8$ $\left(-\dfrac{7}{12}\right) - \left(-\dfrac{5}{6}\right) = -\dfrac{7}{12} + \left(+\dfrac{10}{12}\right) = \dfrac{1}{4}$
3. (a) The product of two numbers with like signs is positive.	3. (a) $(-3)(-4) = +12$ $\left(+\dfrac{3}{4}\right)(+4) = +3$
(b) The product of two numbers with unlike signs is negative.	(b) $5(-3) = -15$ $(-3)(+4) = -12$
4. (a) The quotient of two numbers with like signs is positive.	4. (a) $(-14) \div (-2) = +7$ $+36/4 = +9$
(b) The quotient of two numbers with unlike signs is negative.	(b) $(-28)/4 = -7$ $45 \div (-5) = -9$

Exercise 0.1

In problems 1–4, use $\in$ or $\notin$ to indicate whether a given object is an element of the given set.

1. x $\{x, y, a, b\}$
2. 3 $\{1, 2, 4, 6\}$
3. 12 $\{1, 2, 3, 4, \ldots\}$
4. 5 $\{x: x$ is a natural number, $x > 5\}$
5. Is $A \subseteq B$ if $A = \{1, 2, 3, 4\}$ and $B = \{1, 2, 3, 4, 5, 6\}$?
6. Is $A \subseteq B$ if $A = \{6, 8, 10, 12\}$ and $B = \{6, 8, 10, 14, 18\}$?
7. If $D = \{x: x$ is a natural number less than 4$\}$ and $E = \{1, 2, 3, 4\}$, is $D = E$?
8. If $A = \{2, 3, 4, 5\}$ and $B = \{5, 6, 7\}$, are A and B disjoint?
9. Graph the integers from -6 to 10 on a number line.
10. Graph the rational numbers $-\frac{1}{4}$ and $\frac{7}{4}$ on a number line.

In problems 11–16, insert the proper inequality sign.

11. $\sqrt{16}$ 5
12. $-\sqrt{15}$ -3
13. $\frac{3}{4}$ $\frac{5}{6}$
14. $-3 + \sqrt{4}$ -5
15. -4 -3
16. π 3

Evaluate each of the following.

17. $|-6|$ 18. $|+5|$

Compute the following.

19. $(-5) + (-3) + (-6)$ 20. $(-3) + (+4) + 2$
21. $-6 + (-3) + (-7)$ 22. $-3 + (2 + 1)$
23. $(+6) - (-7)$ 24. $(-3) - (-8)$
25. $(-8) + (-6) - (+3)$ 26. $-6 - (-3) - (-4)$
27. $(-2)(+6)(-5)$ 28. $(+3)(-2)(-6)(-1)$

29. $\dfrac{(-33)(16)}{24}$ 30. $\dfrac{6(-3)(-2)}{-9}$

0.2 Exponents and Radicals

An understanding of the properties of exponents is fundamental to the algebra needed to study functions and solve equations. Furthermore, the definition of exponential and logarithmic functions and many of the techniques in calculus require an understanding of the properties of exponents and how they relate to radicals.

We may use letters (such as x, a, m) to represent numbers. The expression

$$a \cdot a \cdot a \cdot a \cdot a$$

can be written

$$a^5,$$

which is the number a to the fifth power. The number a is called the **base** and 5 is the **exponent.**

Some rules of exponents, with examples, follow.

RULES OF EXPONENTS	EXAMPLES

1. $a^m \cdot a^n = a^{m+n}$

   1. (a) $2^3 \cdot 2^2 = 2^5$
      (b) $(4x + 3)(4x + 3)^8 = (4x + 3)^9$

2. (a) $a^m \div a^n = a^{m-n}$ $(m > n, a \neq 0)$

  (b) $a^m \div a^n = \dfrac{1}{a^{n-m}}$ $(m < n, a \neq 0)$

  (c) $a^m \div a^m = 1$ $(a \neq 0)$

   2. (a) $\dfrac{5^6}{5^4} = 5^{6-4} = 5^2$

      (b) $\dfrac{x^2}{x^5} = \dfrac{1}{x^{5-2}} = \dfrac{1}{x^3}$

      (c) $\dfrac{(2x + 1)^{10}}{(2x + 1)^{10}} = 1$

3. $(ab)^m = a^m b^m$

   3. (a) $(2x)^4 = 2^4 x^4 = 16x^4$
      (b) $(3xy)^3 = 3^3 x^3 y^3 = 27x^3 y^3$

4. $\left(\dfrac{a}{b}\right)^m = \dfrac{a^m}{b^m}$ $(b \neq 0)$

   4. $\left(\dfrac{x}{y}\right)^4 = \dfrac{x^4}{y^4}$

5. $(a^m)^n = a^{mn}$

   5. (a) $(x^2)^5 = x^{2 \cdot 5} = x^{10}$
      (b) $(2x^2 y^3)^4 = 2^4 x^8 y^{12} = 16x^8 y^{12}$

6. $a^0 = 1$ $(a \neq 0)$

   6. (a) $(4x)^0 = 1$, if $x \neq 0$.
      (b) $4x^0 = 4 \cdot 1 = 4$, if $x \neq 0$.

7. (a) $a^{-m} = \dfrac{1}{a^m}$ $(m > 0, a \neq 0)$

  (b) $a^m = \dfrac{1}{a^{-m}}$ $(m > 0, a \neq 0)$

   7. (a) $x^{-2} = \dfrac{1}{x^2}$

      (b) $(2x)^{-3} = \dfrac{1}{(2x)^3} = \dfrac{1}{2^3 x^3} = \dfrac{1}{8x^3}$

      (c) $\dfrac{1}{x^5} = x^{-5}$

      (d) $\dfrac{4}{x^{-4}} = 4x^4$

EXAMPLE 1   (a) Evaluate 2^4.   (b) Evaluate $\left(\dfrac{2}{3}\right)^3$.   (c) Evaluate 3^{-2}.

           (d) Evaluate $\left(\dfrac{2}{3}\right)^{-1}$.   (e) Evaluate 9^0.   (f) Evaluate $\left(\dfrac{1}{2}\right)^0$.

Solution   (a) $2^4 = 2 \cdot 2 \cdot 2 \cdot 2 = 16$

       (b) $\left(\dfrac{2}{3}\right)^3 = \dfrac{2}{3} \cdot \dfrac{2}{3} \cdot \dfrac{2}{3} = \dfrac{8}{27}$

(c) $3^{-2} = \dfrac{1}{3^2} = \dfrac{1}{9}$

(d) $\left(\dfrac{2}{3}\right)^{-1} = \dfrac{1}{2/3} = \dfrac{3}{2}$

(e) $9^0 = 1$

(f) $\left(\dfrac{1}{2}\right)^0 = 1$ □

EXAMPLE 2   Evaluate the following:

(a) $4^3 \cdot 4^2$ (b) $x^5 \cdot x^2$ (c) $x^6 \cdot x^{-3}$ (d) $x^{-8} \cdot x^3$ (e) $a^5 \cdot b^2$

(f) $x^8 \div x^3$ (g) $x^5 \div x^8$ (h) $(x^6)^3$ (i) $(3y^3)^2$ (j) $\left(\dfrac{x^2}{y}\right)^3$

Solution   (a) $4^3 \cdot 4^2 = 4^{3+2} = 4^5$

(b) $x^5 \cdot x^2 = x^{5+2} = x^7$

(c) $x^6 \cdot x^{-3} = x^{6+(-3)} = x^3$

(d) $x^{-8} \cdot x^3 = x^{-8+3} = x^{-5} = 1/x^5$

(e) $a^5 \cdot b^2 = a^5 b^2$ (Bases are different, so we do not add the exponents.)

(f) $x^8 \div x^3 = x^{8-3} = x^5$

(g) $x^5 \div x^8 = x^{5-8} = x^{-3} = 1/x^3$

(h) $(x^6)^3 = x^{6 \cdot 3} = x^{18}$

(i) $(3y^3)^2 = 3^2(y^3)^2 = 9y^6$

(j) $\left(\dfrac{x^2}{y}\right)^3 = \dfrac{(x^2)^3}{y^3} = \dfrac{x^6}{y^3}$ □

A process closely linked to raising numbers to powers is the process of extracting roots. When we seek the square root of a number, such as 9, we are looking for that number whose square equals 9, namely 3 or -3. We represent the square root of 9 by $\sqrt{9}$. The $\sqrt{}$ is called a radical.

Because there are two square roots of 9 [$3^2 = 9$ and $(-3)^2 = 9$] we introduce the convention of **principal root:**

1. *The principal nth root of a positive number is the positive root.* Thus the principal square root is $\sqrt{9} = 3$; $-\sqrt{9} = -3$ is also a square root, but not the principal root.
2. *The principal nth root of 0 is 0.* Thus $\sqrt{0} = 0$ and $\sqrt[3]{0} = 0$.
3. *The principal nth root of a negative number is the negative root when n is odd.* Thus the principal cube root of -27 is $\sqrt[3]{-27} = -3$.

When we are asked for the root of a number, we give the principal root. We have seen by definition that $(\sqrt{a})^2 = a$. If we define $a^{1/2} = \sqrt{a}$, we see that the rules of exponents could be extended to fractional exponents, for $(a^{1/2})^2 = a^{(1/2)2} = a^1 = a$. In general, we define $\sqrt[n]{a}$ as $a^{1/n}$. That is, $\sqrt[3]{x} = x^{1/3}$ and $\sqrt[5]{y} = y^{1/5}$.

Since the rules of exponents extend to fractional exponents, we can write $\sqrt[3]{x^2} = (x^2)^{1/3} = x^{2/3}$. Thus, in general, we define for rational numbers m/n

$$a^{m/n} = (\sqrt[n]{a})^m \qquad (a > 0).$$

We note that when m/n is in lowest terms, then

$$a^{m/n} = (\sqrt[n]{a})^m = \sqrt[n]{a^m}.$$

EXAMPLE 3   Write the following in radical form:
(a) $5^{3/4}$ (b) $y^{3/2}$ (c) $(6m)^{2/3}$

Solution   (a) $5^{3/4} = \sqrt[4]{5^3}$, or $(\sqrt[4]{5})^3$
(b) $y^{3/2} = \sqrt{y^3}$, or $(\sqrt{y})^3$
(c) $(6m)^{2/3} = \sqrt[3]{(6m)^2} = \sqrt[3]{36m^2}$, or $(\sqrt[3]{6m})^2$ □

EXAMPLE 4   Write the following without radicals:
(a) $\sqrt{x^3}$ (b) $\sqrt[3]{b^2}$ (c) $\sqrt{(ab)^3}$

Solution   (a) $\sqrt{x^3} = x^{3/2}$ (b) $\sqrt[3]{b^2} = b^{2/3}$ (c) $\sqrt{(ab)^3} = (ab)^{3/2}$ □

EXAMPLE 5   Compute the following:
(a) $a^{1/2} \cdot a^{1/2}$ (b) $a^{3/2} \div a^{1/2}$ (c) $(ab)^{3/2}$ (d) $\left(\dfrac{a}{b}\right)^{1/2}$ (e) $(a^{3/2})^{1/2}$

Solution   (a) $a^1 = a$
(b) $a^{3/2-1/2} = a$
(c) $a^{3/2}b^{3/2}$
(d) $\dfrac{a^{1/2}}{b^{1/2}}$
(e) $a^{3/2 \cdot 1/2} = a^{3/4}$ □

Although in this text we will limit our study to the real numbers, there are numbers that are not real. For example, there is no real number whose square equals -1. Thus $\sqrt{-1}$ is not a real number. In this text we will say that the square root (in fact, any even root) of a negative number is undefined. Thus $\sqrt{-9}$, $\sqrt[4]{-16}$, and $\sqrt[6]{-64}$ are undefined. Note, however, that odd roots of negative numbers do exist. For example, $\sqrt[3]{-8} = -2$, for $(-2)^3 = -8$. Note also that $a/0$ is undefined for any number a.

Exercise 0.2

Write in exponential form.

1. $2 \cdot 2 \cdot 2 \cdot 2$

2. $x \cdot x \cdot y \cdot y$

Simplify, using only positive exponents.

3. 2^{-3}

4. $x^{-4}, \qquad x \neq 0$

5. $xy^{-2}z^0, \qquad y, z \neq 0$

6. $(xy^{-2})^0, \qquad x, y \neq 0$

Simplify the following.

7. $x^3 \cdot x^4$

8. $a^5 \cdot a$

9. $x^{-5} \cdot x^3$

10. $y^{-5} \cdot y^{-2/5}$

11. $2^3 \cdot 2^4$

12. $a^3 \cdot x^2$

13. $x^8 \div x^4$

14. $a^5 \div a^{-1}$

15. $y^5 \div y^7$

16. $y^{-3} \div y^{-4}$

17. $(x^4)^{1/2}$

18. $(y^3)^{-2/3}$

19. $(xy)^{2/3}$

20. $(2m)^3$

21. $(2x^2y)^4$

22. $\left(\dfrac{2}{x}\right)^4$

23. $\left(\dfrac{x^2}{y^3}\right)^5$

24. $\sqrt{16}$

25. $\sqrt[5]{-32x^5}$

26. $(\sqrt{25})^3$

Determine if the following are real numbers.

27. $\sqrt[3]{-27}$

28. $-\sqrt{81}$

29. $\sqrt{-16}$

30. $\sqrt{15}$

Compute and simplify so only positive exponents remain.

31. $(3x)^{-2}, \qquad x \neq 0$

32. $3(4x)^{-3}, \qquad x \neq 0$

33. $(2x^2y)^{-3}, \qquad x, y \neq 0$

34. $(-3m^2y^{-1}) \cdot (2m^{-3}y^{-1}), \qquad m, y \neq 0$

35. $(2x^{-2}y) \div (x^{-1}y^2), \qquad x, y \neq 0$

36. $\left(\dfrac{x^{-2}}{y}\right)^{-3}, \qquad x, y \neq 0$

37. $(2a)^{1/3} \div (2a)^{2/3}, \qquad a \neq 0$

38. $y^{1/4} \cdot y^{1/2}$

39. Multiply $(2x + 1)^{1/2}[(2x + 1)^{3/2} - (2x + 1)^{-1/2}]$ and simplify.

40. Multiply $(4x - 3)^{-5/3}[(4x - 3)^{8/3} + 3(4x - 3)^{5/3}]$ and simplify.

In problems 41–44, rewrite so that all radicals are expressed as exponents *and* all x's appear in the numerator.

41. $4\sqrt{x} + \dfrac{5}{x^3}$

42. $\dfrac{2}{x} - \dfrac{\sqrt[3]{x}}{3} + 1$

43. $4\sqrt[3]{x^2} + \dfrac{2}{3x^4}$

44. $\dfrac{4}{5x^2} + \dfrac{7}{3\sqrt[5]{x^4}}$

45. Prove $\left(\dfrac{x}{y}\right)^{-n} = \left(\dfrac{y}{x}\right)^n$

0.3 Operations with Algebraic Expressions

An expression containing one or more numerals or letters is called an **algebraic expression.** Examples of algebraic expressions are $3x - y$, $2x^3 + 4$, $15 - x$, $ax + by + c$, and $15x$. Note that the last algebraic expression $(15x)$ is the product of a numeral (15) and a letter (x). Each numeral, letter, or product of numerals and letters is called a term. Thus $15x$ is an expression with one term, and $3x - y + 2z$ is an expression with three terms. *Note that each term is completely set off from the others by a plus $(+)$ or minus $(-)$ sign.* An expression with only one term (such as $15x$) is called a **monomial.** An algebraic expression with two or more terms is called a **multinomial.** If the multinomial has no letters under a radical sign $(\sqrt{\ })$ or in a denominator, it is called a **polynomial.** The expression $3x + 5by + 2 + 6$ is a polynomial with four terms. A polynomial with two terms is called a **binomial,** and one with three terms is called a **trinomial.**

In the term $15x$, we say that 15 is the **coefficient** of x and x is the coefficient of 15. We will frequently need to use the *numerical coefficient* in a term. The numerical coefficient in $15x$ is 15 and the numerical coefficient in $-5xy$ is -5. If no numeral appears as a coefficient in a term, the numerical coefficient is understood to be 1. That is, x means $1x$ and $-y$ means $-1y$. The letter in a term is frequently called a **literal factor** of the term. If a term contains no literal factors, it is called a **constant term.**

The expression $x^3 + 2x^2 - 3x$ is a polynomial in one variable (x) and $x^2 - 3xy + y^2$ is a polynomial in two variables $(x$ and $y)$.

The *degree of a term* containing one variable is the same as the exponent of that variable. For example, $14x$ is a first-degree term and $6x^3$ is a third-degree term. If two or more variables are in a term, the degree of the term is the *sum* of the exponents of the variables. Thus the degree of $4x^2y$ is $2 + 1 = 3$ and the degree of $6xy$ is $1 + 1 = 2$. The degree of a polynomial is the degree of the term in the polynomial having the highest degree. Thus the polynomial $4x^3 - 2x + 4$ is a third-degree polynomial and $2x^2 - 4x + 6$ is a second-degree polynomial. Second-degree polynomials are called **quadratic polynomials.**

Two or more terms that differ only in their numerical coefficients are called **similar terms,** or **like terms.** Thus $3x^2y$, $5x^2y$ and $16yx^2$ are like terms. $3x^2y$ and $3xy$ are not like terms because x is used twice as a factor in $3x^2y$ and only once in $3xy$. *We can add or subtract two like terms by adding or subtracting their numerical coefficients and assigning their common literal factors.* For example, $3x + 2x = 5x$. [Note that $3x = x + x + x$ and $2x = x + x$, so $3x + 2x = (x + x + x) + (x + x) = 5x$.]

This procedure can easily be extended to the operation of subtraction. For example, $8x - 3x = 8x + (-3x) = 5x$.

Performing the indicated additions and subtractions is called combining the like terms. We can simplify several terms by combining the like terms.

EXAMPLE 1   Combine: $-3x^2 + 4xy + 5x^2 + 7xy$.

Solution   The terms $-3x^2$ and $5x^2$ are like terms, so their sum is $2x^2$. The terms $4xy$ and $7xy$ are like terms, so their sum is $11xy$. Thus

$$-3x^2 + 4xy + 5x^2 + 7xy = 2x^2 + 11xy. \qquad \square$$

The procedures for adding and subtracting polynomials are based on the procedures for combining like terms. If, for example, we want to add $5x + 3y$ and $7x - y$, we combine their like terms to find the sum. Thus the sum of $5x + 3y$ and $7x - y$ is $12x + 2y$. We may indicate the sum as $(5x + 3y) + (7x - y) = 12x + 2y$.

EXAMPLE 2   Compute $(4xy + 3x) + (5xy - 2x)$.

Solution $$(4xy + 3x) + (5xy - 2x) = 4xy + 3x + 5xy - 2x = 9xy + x \qquad \square$$

We may subtract one polynomial from another by changing the sign of each term of the polynomial we are subtracting and proceeding as in addition.

EXAMPLE 3   Compute $(3x^2 + 4xy + 5y^2 + 1) - (6x^2 - 2xy + 4)$.

Solution   Removing the parentheses gives $3x^2 + 4xy + 5y^2 + 1 - 6x^2 + 2xy - 4$, which simplifies to $-3x^2 + 6xy + 5y^2 - 3$. $\qquad \square$

We multiply monomials by multiplying the numerical coefficients, finding the product of the corresponding literal factors, and writing these products together as the final product.

EXAMPLE 4   Multiply the following:
(a) $(8xy^3)(2x^3y)$ (b) $(12m^2n)(-3mn^2)(4kn)$

Solution   (a) $(8xy^3)(2x^3y) = 16x^4y^4$
(b) $(12m^2n)(-3mn^2)(4kn) = (-36m^3n^3)(4kn) = -144m^3n^4k$ $\qquad \square$

EXAMPLE 5   Simplify the following: $(3x^3y)(6y^2) - (2x^3y)(3y^2)$

Solution   The multiplications must be performed before the additions or subtractions:

$$(3x^3y)(6y^2) - (2x^3y)(3y^2) = 18x^3y^3 - 6x^3y^3 = 12x^3y^3 \qquad \square$$

To divide two monomials, we divide their numerical coefficients, find the quotients of the corresponding literal factors, and write the products of these quotients together as the final quotient.

EXAMPLE 6   Find the quotient: $-15x^2y^3 \div 3xy^2, \qquad x \neq 0, y \neq 0$

Solution
$$-15 \div 3 = -5$$
$$x^2 \div x = x$$
$$y^3 \div y^2 = y$$

Thus $-15x^2y^3 \div 3xy^2 = -5xy$. Note that we may write

$$-15x^2y^3 \div 3xy^2 \text{ as } \frac{-15x^2y^3}{3xy^2}. \qquad \square$$

We can divide a polynomial by a monomial by dividing the monomial into *each* term of the polynomial.

EXAMPLE 7   Divide $4x^3y^2 + 8x^2y^3 - 12x^4y^5$ by $4xy^2, \qquad x \neq 0, y \neq 0$.

Solution
$$(4x^3y^2 + 8x^2y^3 - 12x^4y^5) \div 4xy^2 = \frac{4x^3y^2 + 8x^2y^3 - 12x^4y^5}{4xy^2}$$

$$= \frac{4x^3y^2}{4xy^2} + \frac{8x^2y^3}{4xy^2} - \frac{12x^4y^5}{4xy^2}$$

$$= x^2 + 2xy - 3x^3y^3 \qquad \square$$

An important law in algebra is the Distributive Law, which is stated symbolically as $a(b + c) = ab + ac$. By the use of this law we can multiply a polynomial by a monomial. For example, $x(2x + 3) = x \cdot 2x + x \cdot 3 = 2x^2 + 3x$. We can extend the Distributive Law to cover polynomials with more than two terms. For example, $5(x + y + 2) = 5x + 5y + 10$. Thus we multiply a polynomial by a monomial by multiplying each term of the polynomial by the monomial.

EXAMPLE 8   Find the following products:
(a) $-4ab(3a^2b + 4ab^2 - 1)$ (b) $(4a + 5b + c)ac$

Solution   (a) $-4ab(3a^2b + 4ab^2 - 1) = -12a^3b^2 - 16a^2b^3 + 4ab$
(b) $(4a + 5b + c)ac = 4a \cdot ac + 5b \cdot ac + c \cdot ac = 4a^2c + 5abc + ac^2 \qquad \square$

The Distributive Law can be used to show us how to multiply two polynomials. Consider the indicated multiplication $(a + b)(c + d)$. If we first treat the sum $(a + b)$ as a single quantity, then two successive applications of the Distributive Law gives

$$(a + b)(c + d) = (a + b) \cdot c + (a + b) \cdot d = ac + bc + ad + bd.$$

Thus we see that the product can be found by multiplying $(a + b)$ by c, $(a + b)$ by d, and then adding the products. This is frequently set up as follows.

PROCEDURE	EXAMPLE
To multiply two polynomials:	Multiply $(3x + 4xy + 3y)$ by $(x - 2y)$.
1. Write one of the polynomials above the other.	1. $3x + 4xy + 3y$ $\ x - 2y$
2. Multiply each term of the top polynomial by each term of the bottom one, and write the similar terms of the product under one another.	2. $3x^2 + 4x^2y + 3xy$ $\qquad\ - 6xy - 8xy^2 - 6y^2$
3. Add like terms to simplify the product.	3. $3x^2 + 4x^2y - 3xy - 8xy^2 - 6y^2$

EXAMPLE 9   Multiply: $(4x^2 + 3xy + 4x)(2x - 3y)$

Solution

$$
\begin{array}{l}
4x^2 + 3xy + 4x \\
2x - 3y \\
\hline
8x^3 + 6x^2y + 8x^2 \\
 - 12x^2y - 9xy^2 - 12xy \\
\hline
8x^3 - 6x^2y + 8x^2 - 9xy^2 - 12xy \\
\end{array}
$$

      □

Since the multiplications we must perform often involve binomials, the following special products are worth remembering.

> A. $(x + a)(x + b) = x^2 + (a + b)x + ab$
> B. $(ax + b)(cx + d) = acx^2 + (ad + bc)x + bd$

It is easier to remember these two special products if we note the structure of the result and realize that we can obtain this result by finding the products of the First terms, Outside terms, Inside terms, and Last terms, and adding the results. This is called the FOIL method of multiplying two binomials.

EXAMPLE 10   Multiply the following:
     (a) $(x - 4)(x + 3)$ (b) $(3x + 2)(2x + 5)$

Solution   (a) $(x - 4)(x + 3) = \underset{\text{First}}{(x^2)} + \underset{\text{Outside}}{(3x)} + \underset{\text{Inside}}{(-4x)} + \underset{\text{Last}}{(-12)} = x^2 - x - 12$

     (b) $(3x + 2)(2x + 5) = (6x^2) + (15x) + (4x) + (10) = 6x^2 + 19x + 10$ □

Additional special products are as follows:

> C. $(x + a)^2 = x^2 + 2ax + a^2$ (trinomial square)
> D. $(x + a)(x - a) = x^2 - a^2$ (difference of two squares)
> E. $(x + a)^3 = x^3 + 3ax^2 + 3a^2x + a^3$ (binomial cubed)

EXAMPLE 11   Multiply the following:

(a) $(x - 4)^2$ (b) $(x - 5)(x + 5)$ (c) $(p + q)^3$

Solution   (a) By C, $(x - 4)^2 = x^2 + 2(-4)x + (-4)^2 = x^2 - 8x + 16$

(b) By D, $(x - 5)(x + 5) = x^2 - (5^2) = x^2 - 25$

(c) By E, $(p + q)^3 = p^3 + 3p^2q + 3pq^2 + q^3$ □

In later chapters we will need to write problems in a simplified form so that we can perform certain operations on them. We can often use division of one polynomial by another to obtain the simplification. The procedure for dividing one polynomial by another follows.

PROCEDURE	EXAMPLE
To divide one polynomial into another:	Divide $(4x^2 + 3x + 2)$ by $(x + 2)$, $x \neq -2$.
1. Write the division problem with both polynomials in descending powers of a variable.	1. $x + 2 \overline{)4x^2 + 3x + 2}$
2. Divide the highest power of the divisor into the highest power of the dividend to obtain the first partial quotient.	2. x divided into $4x^2$ is $4x$.
3. Write this partial quotient above the highest power in the dividend. Multiply the divisor by this quotient, write the product under the dividend, and subtract like terms.	3. $\begin{array}{r} 4x \\ x + 2 \overline{)4x^2 + 3x + 2} \\ 4x^2 + 8x \\ \hline -5x \end{array}$
4. To the remainder bring down the next term of the dividend to form a new partial dividend. Divide the highest power of the divisor into the highest power of the partial dividend and write this partial quotient above the dividend. Multiply the partial quotient times the divisor, write the product under the partial dividend, and subtract.	4. $\begin{array}{r} 4x - 5 \\ x + 2 \overline{)4x^2 + 3x + 2} \\ 4x^2 + 8x \\ \hline -5x + 2 \\ -5x - 10 \\ \hline +12 \end{array}$
5. Repeat step 4 until all terms of the dividend have been used. Any remainder is written over the divisor.	5. All terms have been used. The quotient is $$4x - 5 + \frac{+12}{x + 2}$$ or $$4x - 5 + \frac{12}{x + 2}.$$

EXAMPLE 12   Divide $(4x^3 - 13x - 22)$ by $(x - 3)$, $x \neq 3$.

Solution
$$
\begin{array}{r}
4x^2 + 12x + 23 \\
x - 3 \overline{)\smash{)}\ 4x^3 + 0x^2 - 13x - 22} \\
\underline{4x^3 - 12x^2} \\
12x^2 - 13x \\
\underline{12x^2 - 36x} \\
23x - 22 \\
\underline{23x - 69} \\
47
\end{array}
$$

(0x^2 is inserted so each power of x is present.)

The quotient is $4x^2 + 12x + 23$, with remainder 47, or

$$4x^2 + 12x + 23 + \frac{47}{x - 3}. \qquad \square$$

Exercise 0.3

Simplify problems 1–5.

1. $7x^2 + 8x + 4x^2 + 11x - 6$
2. $(16pq - 7p^2) + (5pq + 5p^2)$
3. $(3r^3 + 4x^2y^2 + 3x^2y^2 - 7x^3)$
4. $(4m^2 - 3n^2 + 5) - (3m^2 + 4n^2 + 8)$
5. $(4a + 2b) - (3a + 3c) + (6b + 2c)$

Compute problems 6–26.

6. $(5x^3)(7x^2)$
7. $(-3x^2y)(2xy^3)(4x^2y^2)$
8. $39r^3s^2 \div 13r^2s$
9. $-15m^3n \div 5mn^4$
10. $(3mx)(2mx^2) - (4xm^2)x^2$
11. $\dfrac{15y^3z^2}{3yz^2} - \dfrac{8y^4z}{y^2z}$
12. $8 - |4 - (q + 5)|$
13. $x^0 + [3x - (x^3 - 9x)]$
14. $4(x + 2y) - 4(4x + 3y)$
15. $2(x + y)$
16. $ax^2(2x^2 + ax + ab)$
17. $(3y + 4)(2y - 3)$
18. $(4x - 1)(x - 3)$
19. $(x + 1)(x^2 + 2x + 4)$
20. $(a - 2b)(a^2 - 3ab + b^2)$
21. $(18m^2n + 6m^3n + 12m^4n^2) \div 6m^2n$
22. $(16x^2 + 4xy^2 + 8x) \div 4xy$
23. $(3x^4 + 4x^3 + 2x^2 - 4x - 5) \div (x^2 - 1)$
24. $(u^3 + 3a^2 + 6a + 8) \div (a + 2)$
25. $(2x^3 + x^2 - 6x + 1) \div (2x + 1)$
26. $(4x^4 - 3x^2 - x + 1) \div (2x - 1)$

0.4 Factoring

We can factor monomial factors out of a polynomial by using the Distributive Law backwards; $ab + ac = a(b + c)$ is an example showing that a is a monomial factor of the polynomial $ab + ac$. But it is also a statement of the Distributive Law (with the sides of the equation interchanged). The monomial factor of a polynomial must be a factor of each term of the polynomial, so it is frequently called a common monomial factor.

EXAMPLE 1   Factor $-3x^2t - 3x + 9xt^2$.

Solution   1. $3x$ can be factored out, giving $-3x^2t - 3x + 9xt^2 = 3x(-xt - 1 + 3t^2)$; or

2. $-3x$ can be factored out (factoring out the negative will make the first term of the polynomial positive), giving

$$-3x^2t - 3x + 9xt^2 = -3x(xt + 1 - 3t^2).$$ □

If a factor is common to each term of a polynomial, we can use the above procedure to factor it out, even if it is not a monomial. For example, we can factor $(a + b)$ out of the polynomial $2x(a + b) - 3y(a + b)$. If we factor $(a + b)$ from both terms, we get $(a + b)(2x - 3y)$.

EXAMPLE 2   Factor $5x - 5y + bx - by$.

Solution   We can factor this polynomial by the use of grouping. The grouping is done so that common factors (frequently binomial factors) can be removed. We see that we can factor 5 from the first two terms and b from the last two, giving

$$5(x - y) + b(x - y).$$

This gives two terms with the common factor $x - y$, so we get

$$(x - y)(5 + b).$$ □

We can use the formula for multiplying two binomials to factor certain trinomials. The formula

$$(x + a)(x + b) = x^2 + (a + b)x + ab$$

can be used to factor trinomials like

$$x^2 - 7x + 6.$$

EXAMPLE 3   Factor $x^2 - 7x + 6$.

Solution   If this trinomial can be factored into an expression of the form $(x + a)(x + b)$, then we need to find a and b such that $x^2 - 7x + 6 = x^2 + (a + b)x + ab$. That is, we need to find a and b such that $a + b = -7$ and $ab = 6$. The two numbers whose sum is -7 and whose product is 6 are -1 and -6. Thus

$$x^2 - 7x + 6 = (x - 1)(x - 6).$$ □

A similar method of factoring can be used to factor trinomials like $9x^2 - 31x + 12$. Finding the proper factors for this type of trinomial may involve a fair amount of trial and error, because we must find factors a, b, c, and d such that

$$(ax + b)(cx + d) = acx^2 + (ad + bc)x + bd.$$

Another technique of factoring can be used to factor trinomials like those we have been discussing. It is especially useful in factoring more complicated trinomials, like $9x^2 - 31x + 12$. The procedure for factoring second-degree trinomials follows.

PROCEDURE	EXAMPLE
To factor a trinomial into the product of its binomial factors:	Factor $9x^2 - 31x + 12$.
1. Form the product of the second-degree term and the constant term.	1. $9x^2 \cdot 12 = 108x^2$
2. Determine if there are any factors of the product of step 1 which will sum to the middle term of the trinomial. (If the answer is no, the trinomial will not factor into two binomials.)	2. The factors $-27x$ and $-4x$ give a sum of $-31x$.
3. Use the sum of these two factors to replace the middle term of the trinomial.	3. $9x^2 - 31x + 12 = 9x^2 - 27x - 4x + 12$
4. Group the first two terms together, and the second two terms.	4. $= (9x^2 - 27x) + (-4x + 12)$
5. Factor the common monomial out of each group.	5. $= 9x(x - 3) - 4(x - 3)$
6. Both groups now have a common (binomial) factor. Factor it out.	6. $= (x - 3)(9x - 4)$
7. Check your answer by multiplying.	7. $(x - 3)(9x - 4) = 9x^2 - 31x + 12$

In the example just completed, note that writing the middle term $(-31x)$ as $-4x - 27x$ rather than as $-27x - 4x$ (as we did) will still result in the correct factorization. (Try it.)

EXAMPLE 4 Factor $9x^2 - 9x - 10$.

Solution The product of the second-degree term and the constant is $-90x^2$. Factors of $-90x^2$ that sum to $-9x$ are $-15x$ and $6x$. Thus

$$9x^2 - 9x - 10 = 9x^2 - 15x + 6x - 10$$
$$= (9x^2 - 15x) + (6x - 10)$$
$$= 3x(3x - 5) + 2(3x - 5)$$
$$= (3x - 5)(3x + 2).$$

Checking gives

$$(3x - 5)(3x + 2) = 9x^2 + 6x - 15x - 10$$
$$= 9x^2 - 9x - 10. \qquad \square$$

Some special products that make factoring easier are

The perfect-square trinomials:

$$(x + a)^2 = x^2 + 2ax + a^2$$
$$(x - a)^2 = x^2 - 2ax + a^2$$

The difference of two squares:

$$(x - a)(x + a) = x^2 - a^2$$

EXAMPLE 5   Factor $25x^2 - 36y^2$.

Solution   Because $25x^2 - 36y^2$ is the difference of two squares, the factorization is $(5x - 6y)(5x + 6y)$. These two factors are called binomial **conjugates** because they differ only in one sign.   ☐

EXAMPLE 6   Factor $4x^2 + 12x + 9$.

Solution   Although we can use the technique we have learned to factor trinomials, the factors come quickly if we recognize that this trinomial is a perfect square. It has two square terms, and the remaining term $(12x)$ is twice the product of the square roots of the squares $(12x = 2 \cdot 2x \cdot 3)$. Thus $4x^2 + 12x + 9 = (2x + 3)^2$.   ☐

Most of the polynomials we have factored have been second-degree polynomials, or **quadratic polynomials.** Some polynomials that are not quadratic are in a form that can be factored in the same manner as quadratics. For example, $x^4 + 4x^2 + 4$ can be written as $a^2 + 4a + 4$, where $a = x^2$.

EXAMPLE 7   Factor $x^4 + 4x^2 + 4$ completely.

Solution   The trinomial is in the form of a perfect square, so letting $a = x^2$ gives $x^4 + 4x^2 + 4 = a^2 + 4a + 4 = (a + 2)^2$. Thus $x^4 + 4x^2 + 4 = (x^2 + 2)^2$.   ☐

EXAMPLE 8   Factor $x^4 - 16$ completely.

Solution $x^4 - 16$ can be treated as the difference of two squares, $(x^2)^2 - 4^2$, so $x^4 - 16 = (x^2 - 4)(x^2 + 4)$. But $x^2 - 4$ can be factored into $(x - 2)(x + 2)$, so $x^4 - 16 = (x - 2)(x + 2)(x^2 + 4)$.   ☐

A polynomial is said to be factored completely if all possible factorizations have been completed. For example, $(2x - 4)(x + 3)$ is not factored completely because a 2 can still be factored out of $2x - 4$. Confining our attention to factors with integer coefficients, we can factor a number of polynomials completely using the following procedure:

> Look for: Monomials first.
> Then for: Difference of two squares.
> Then for: Trinomial squares.
> Then for: Other methods of factoring trinomials.

EXAMPLE 9   Factor completely: $12x^2 - 36x + 27$

Solution
$$12x^2 - 36x + 27 = 3(4x^2 - 12x + 9) \qquad \text{(Monomial)}$$
$$= 3(2x - 3)^2 \qquad\qquad \text{(Perfect square)} \qquad \square$$

EXAMPLE 10   Factor completely: $16x^2 - 64y^2$

Solution
$$16x^2 - 64y^2 = 16(x^2 - 4y^2)$$
$$= 16(x + 2y)(x - 2y)$$

Note that factoring the difference of two squares immediately would give $(4x + 8y)(4x - 8y)$, which is not factored completely (we could still factor 4 from $4x + 8y$ and 4 from $4x - 8y$). $\qquad\qquad \square$

Exercise 0.4

Factor the following completely.

1. $9ab - 12a^2b + 18b^2$
2. $8a^2b - 160x + 4bx^2$
3. $4x^2 + 8xy^2 + 2xy^3$
4. $12y^3z + 4yz^2 - 8y^2z^3$
5. $5(y - 4) - x^2(y - 4)$
6. $x(x - 3) + 5(x - 3)$
7. $6x - 6m + xy - my$
8. $x^2 + 4x + 4x + 16$
9. $x^2 + 8x + 16$
10. $x^2 + 6x + 8$
11. $7x^2 - 10x - 8$
12. $12x^2 + 11x + 2$
13. $x^2 - 10x + 25$
14. $4y^2 + 12y + 9$
15. $10x^2 + 19x + 6$
16. $6x^2 + 67x - 35$
17. $9 - 47x + 10x^2$
18. $3x^2 + 6x + 9$
19. $12b^2 - 12b + 3$
20. $x^3 + 16x^2 + 64x$
21. $4x^2 + 12x + 9$
22. $x^2 - 2xy + y^2$
23. $2x^2 - 8x + 8$
24. $x^2 - 10xy + 25y^2$
25. $63x^2 - 28$
26. $100x^2 - 64$
27. $49a^2 - 144b^2$
28. $16x^2 - 25y^2$
29. $x^4 + 6x^2 + 9$
30. $p^4 - q^2$
31. $y^4 - 16x^4$
32. $x^6 - y^4$

0.5 Algebraic Fractions

Evaluating certain limits and graphing rational functions requires an understanding of algebraic fractions. The fraction 6/8 can be reduced to 3/4 by dividing both the numerator and denominator by 2. In the same manner, the algebraic fraction

$$\frac{(x + 2)(x + 1)}{(x + 1)(x + 3)}$$

can be reduced to

$$\frac{x + 2}{x + 3}$$

by dividing both the numerator and denominator by $x + 1$, if $x \neq -1$.

We *simplify* algebraic fractions by factoring the numerator and denominator and then dividing both the numerator and denominator by the common factors.

EXAMPLE 1   Simplify $\dfrac{3x^2 - 14x + 8}{x^2 - 16}$, $x^2 \neq 16$.

Solution

$$\frac{3x^2 - 14x + 8}{x^2 - 16} = \frac{(3x - 2)(x - 4)}{(x - 4)(x + 4)}$$

$$= \frac{(3x - 2)\overset{1}{\cancel{(x - 4)}}}{\underset{1}{\cancel{(x - 4)}}(x + 4)}$$

$$= \frac{3x - 2}{x + 4} \qquad\qquad \square$$

We can multiply fractions by writing the product as the product of the numerators divided by the product of the denominators. For example,

$$\frac{4}{5} \cdot \frac{10}{12} \cdot \frac{2}{5} = \frac{80}{300},$$

which reduces to 4/15.

We can also find the product by reducing the fractions before we indicate the multiplication in the numerator and denominator. For example, in

$$\frac{4}{5} \cdot \frac{10}{12} \cdot \frac{2}{5},$$

we can divide the numerator and denominator by 5 and then by 4, giving

$$\frac{1}{1} \cdot \frac{2}{3} \cdot \frac{2}{5} = \frac{4}{15}.$$

We *multiply* algebraic fractions by writing the product of the numerators divided by the product of the denominators, and then reduce to lowest terms. We may also reduce prior to finding the product.

EXAMPLE 2   Multiply: $\dfrac{4x^2}{5y} \cdot \dfrac{10x}{y^2} \cdot \dfrac{y}{8x^2}$

Solution

$$\frac{4x^2}{5y} \cdot \frac{10x}{y^2} \cdot \frac{y}{8x^2} = \frac{\overset{1}{\cancel{4x^2}}}{\underset{1\cdot1}{\cancel{5y}}} \cdot \frac{\overset{2}{\cancel{10x}}}{y^2} \cdot \frac{\overset{1}{\cancel{y}}}{\underset{2}{\cancel{8x^2}}}$$

$$= \frac{1}{1} \cdot \frac{\overset{1}{\cancel{2x}}}{y^2} \cdot \frac{1}{\underset{1}{\cancel{2}}} = \frac{x}{y^2} \qquad \square$$

We frequently have to factor the numerators and denominators of algebraic fractions to use this method of multiplication.

EXAMPLE 3   Multiply: $\dfrac{-4x + 8}{3x + 6} \cdot \dfrac{2x + 4}{4x + 12}$

Solution

$$\frac{-4x + 8}{3x + 6} \cdot \frac{2x + 4}{4x + 12} = \frac{-4(x - 2)}{3(x + 2)} \cdot \frac{2(x + 2)}{4(x + 3)}$$

$$= \frac{\overset{-1}{\cancel{-4}}(x - 2)}{\underset{1}{\cancel{3(x + 2)}}} \cdot \frac{2\overset{1}{\cancel{(x + 2)}}}{\underset{1}{\cancel{4}}(x + 3)}$$

$$= \frac{-2(x - 2)}{3(x + 3)} \qquad \square$$

In arithmetic we learned to divide one fraction by another by inverting the divisor and multiplying. The same rule applies to division of algebraic fractions.

EXAMPLE 4   Divide $\dfrac{a^2b}{c}$ by $\dfrac{ab}{c^2}$.

Solution

$$\frac{a^2b}{c} \div \frac{ab}{c^2} = \frac{a^2b}{c} \cdot \frac{c^2}{ab} = \frac{\overset{a\,\cdot\,1}{\cancel{a^2b}}}{\underset{1}{\cancel{c}}} \cdot \frac{\overset{c}{\cancel{c^2}}}{\underset{1\cdot1}{\cancel{ab}}} = \frac{ac}{1} = ac \qquad \square$$

EXAMPLE 5   Divide: $\dfrac{6x^2 - 6}{x^2 + 3x + 2} \div \dfrac{x - 1}{x^2 + 4x + 4}$

Solution

$$\frac{6x^2 - 6}{x^2 + 3x + 2} \div \frac{x - 1}{x^2 + 4x + 4} = \frac{6x^2 - 6}{x^2 + 3x + 2} \cdot \frac{x^2 + 4x + 4}{x - 1}$$

$$= \frac{6(x - 1)(x + 1)}{(x + 2)(x + 1)} \cdot \frac{(x + 2)(x + 2)}{x - 1}$$

$$= 6(x + 2) \qquad \square$$

If two fractions are to be added, it is convenient that each be expressed with the same denominator. If the denominators are not the same, we can write the equivalents of each of the fractions with a common denominator. We usually use the lowest common denominator (LCD) when we write the equivalent fractions. The **lowest common denominator** is the smallest number into which all denominators will divide. We can find the lowest common denominator as follows:

PROCEDURE	EXAMPLE
To find the lowest common denominator of a set of fractions:	Find the LCD of $\dfrac{1}{x^2 - x}$, $\dfrac{1}{x^2 - 1}$, $\dfrac{1}{x^2}$.
1. Completely factor each denominator.	1. The factored denominators are $x(x - 1)$, $(x + 1)(x - 1)$, $x \cdot x$.
2. Write the LCD as the product of each of these factors used the maximum number of times it occurs in any one denominator.	2. x occurs a maximum of 2 times in one denominator, $x - 1$ occurs once and $x + 1$ occurs once. Thus the LCD is $x \cdot x(x - 1)(x + 1) = x^2(x - 1)(x + 1)$.

The procedure for combining (adding or subtracting) two or more fractions is as follows.

PROCEDURE	EXAMPLE
To combine fractions:	Combine: $\dfrac{y - 3}{y - 5} + \dfrac{y - 23}{y^2 - y - 20}$.
1. Find the LCD of the fractions.	1. $y^2 - y - 20 = (y - 5)(y + 4)$, so the LCD is $(y - 5)(y + 4)$.
2. Write the equivalent of each fraction with the LCD as its denominator.	2. The sum is $\dfrac{(y - 3)(y + 4)}{(y - 5)(y + 4)} + \dfrac{y - 23}{(y - 5)(y + 4)}$.
3. Add or subtract as indicated.	3. $= \dfrac{y^2 + y - 12 + y - 23}{(y - 5)(y + 4)}$ $= \dfrac{y^2 + 2y - 35}{(y - 5)(y + 4)}$
4. Reduce the fraction, if possible.	4. $y - 5$ is a factor of the numerator, so the sum is $\dfrac{y + 7}{y + 4}$, if $y \neq 5$.

EXAMPLE 6 Add: $\dfrac{3x}{a^2} + \dfrac{4}{ax}$

Solution

1. The LCD is a^2x.

2. $\dfrac{3x}{a^2} = \dfrac{3x^2}{a^2x}, \qquad \dfrac{4}{ax} = \dfrac{4a}{a^2x}$

3. $\dfrac{3x^2}{a^2x} + \dfrac{4a}{a^2x} = \dfrac{3x^2 + 4a}{a^2x}$

4. The sum is in lowest terms. $\square$

EXAMPLE 7 Combine: $\dfrac{y-3}{(y-5)^2} + \dfrac{y-2}{y^2-y-20}$

Solution $y^2 - y - 20 = (y-5)(y+4)$, so the LCD is $(y-5)^2(y+4)$. Writing the equivalent fractions gives

$$\frac{y-3}{(y-5)^2} + \frac{y-2}{(y-5)(y+4)} = \frac{(y-3)(y+4)}{(y-5)^2(y+4)} + \frac{(y-2)(y-5)}{(y-5)(y-4)(y-5)}$$

$$= \frac{(y^2 + y - 12) + (y^2 - 7y + 10)}{(y-5)^2(y+4)}$$

$$= \frac{2y^2 - 6y - 2}{(y-5)^2(y+4)}. \qquad \square$$

Exercise 0.5

Simplify the following fractions.

1. $\dfrac{18x^3y^3}{9x^3z}$

2. $\dfrac{15a^4b^5}{30a^3b}$

3. $\dfrac{x - 3y}{3x - 9y}$

4. $\dfrac{x^2 - 6x + 8}{x^2 - 16}$

5. $\dfrac{x^2 - 2x + 1}{x^2 - 4x + 3}$

6. $\dfrac{x^2 - 5x + 6}{9 - x^2}$

Compute the following and simplify.

7. $\dfrac{6x^3}{8y^3} \cdot \dfrac{16x}{9y^2} \cdot \dfrac{15y^4}{x^3}$

8. $\dfrac{15ac^2}{7bd} \div \dfrac{4a}{14b^2d}$

9. $\dfrac{8x - 16}{x - 3} \cdot \dfrac{4x - 12}{3x - 6}$

10. $\dfrac{x^2 + 7x + 12}{3x^2 + 13x + 4} \cdot \dfrac{3x + 1}{x + 3}$

11. $\dfrac{16}{x - 2} \div \dfrac{4}{3x - 6}$

12. $\dfrac{y^2 - 2y + 1}{7y^2 - 7y} \div \dfrac{y^2 - 4y + 3}{35y^2}$

13. $\dfrac{4a}{3x + 6} + \dfrac{5a^2}{4x + 8}$

14. $\dfrac{b - 1}{b^2 + 2b} + \dfrac{b}{3b + 6}$

15. $\dfrac{x - 7}{x^2 - 9x + 20} + \dfrac{x + 2}{x^2 - 5x + 4}$

16. $\dfrac{x + 1}{x^2 + x - 6} - \dfrac{2x - 1}{2 - x}$

17. $\dfrac{3x - 1}{2x - 4} + \dfrac{4x}{3x - 6} - \dfrac{4}{5x - 10}$

18. $\dfrac{2x + 1}{4x - 2} + \dfrac{5}{2x} - \dfrac{x + 1}{2x^2 - x}$

In this chapter you will need to work problems like the following. If you have difficulty with any problem, return to the section where that type of problem was introduced and refresh your memory before starting the chapter.

Problem Type	Introduced in Section	Used in Sections	Answer
Evaluate: (a) $2(-1)^3 - 3(-1)^2 + 1$ (b) $3(-3) - 1$ (c) $14(10) - 0.02(10^2)$	0.1 Signed numbers	1.1, 1.2, 1.3, 1.4	(a) -4 (b) -10 (c) 138
Locate on a number line: (a) The integers from -1 to 3 inclusive (b) The integers from -3 to 2	0.1 Real number line	1.1, 1.2, 1.4	(a) number line from -2 to 4, points at $-1, 0, 1, 2, 3$ (b) number line from -4 to 3, points at $-3, -2, -1, 0, 1, 2$
(a) $\dfrac{1}{x}$ is *undefined* for which real numbers? (b) $\sqrt{x - 4}$ is a real number for which values of x?	0.2	1.2, 1.4	(a) Undefined for $x = 0$ (b) $x \geq 4$
Simplify: (a) $4(-c)^2 - 3(-c) + 1$ (b) $[3(x + h) - 1] - [3x - 1]$	0.3 Algebraic expressions	1.3	(a) $4c^2 + 3c + 1$ (b) $3h$

1

FUNCTIONS

A wide variety of problems from business, the social sciences, and the life sciences may be solved by using equations. Managers and economists use equations and their graphs to study costs, sales, national consumption, or supply and demand. Social scientists may plot demographic data or try to develop equations that predict population growth, voting behavior, or learning and retention rates. Life scientists use equations to model the flow of blood or the conduction of nerve impulses, and test theories or develop new ones by plotting experimental evidence.

In this chapter we will begin by investigating equations and their graphs. We will also define the concepts of relation and function, introduce functional notation, and then relate all of these back to equations and graphs.

Numerous applications of mathematics are given throughout the text, but all chapters contain special sections emphasizing business and economics applications. In particular, this chapter introduces three important applications that will be expanded and used throughout the text as increased mathematical skills permit: national consumption; supply and demand as functions of price (market analysis); and total cost, total revenue, and total profit as functions of the quantity produced or sold (theory of the firm).

1.1 Introduction to Equations and Graphs

Objectives
- To determine when an equation is an identity or a conditional equation
- To determine if equations are true for stated values of the variable
- To give a partial listing of solutions to certain equations in two variables
- To graph certain equations

A firm is said to break even if its total revenue *equals* its total costs. If we have an expression representing total revenue and an expression representing total cost for a product, these expressions are *equal* when the firm breaks even. An **equation** is a statement that two quantities or algebraic expressions are equal. The two quantities on either side of the equal sign are called **members** of an equation. For example, $2 + 2 = 4$ is an equation with members $2 + 2$ and 4; $3x - 2 = 7$ is an equation with $3x - 2$ as its left member and 7 as its right member. Note that the equation $7 = 3x - 2$ is the same statement as $3x - 2 = 7$. An equation with one literal number, such as $3x - 2 = 7$, is known as an equation in one variable. The literal number is called a variable because the value of the literal number determines whether the equation is true or not. For example, $3x - 2 = 7$ is true only for $x = 3$. Finding the value(s) of the variable that make the equation true is called *solving the equation*. The set containing the solutions to an equation is called a **solution set** of the equation. The variable in an equation is sometimes called the *unknown*.

Some equations involving variables are true only for certain values of the variables while others are true for all values of the variable(s). Equations that are true for all values of the variable(s) are called **identities.** The equation $2(x - 1) = 2x - 2$ is an example of an identity. Equations that are true only for certain values of the variable(s) are called **conditional equations** or simply **equations.** The values of the variable for which the equation is true are called the **solutions** of the equation.

EXAMPLE 1 Which of the following are identities and which are (conditional) equations?
(a) $2 + 2 = 4$ (b) $2 + x = 4$ (c) $2x + 1 = 3x + 1 - x$
(d) $2(1 + x) = 4$

Solution (a) Identity; both members represent 4.
(b) Conditional equation; only true when $x = 2$.
(c) Identity; right member can be reduced to $2x + 1$, so the equation is true for every value of x.
(d) Conditional equation; true only when $x = 1$.   □

Equations may have more than one variable. For example, the equation $y = 3x - 2$ has two variables. There are an infinite number of solutions to this equation, because any pair of values that satisfies the equation is a solution. For example, $x = 1$, $y = 1$ is a solution, as is $x = 4$, $y = 10$. We can find other solutions by substituting values for x and finding the value of y that satisfies the equation. For example, if we let $x = 5$, then letting $y = 3(5) - 2 = 13$ will satisfy the equation.

We denote an **ordered pair** of real numbers as (a, b), where a and b are real numbers. The number a is called the *first component* or *first coordinate* of the ordered pair, and b is called the *second component* or *second coordinate*. The ordered pairs (a, b) and (c, d) are said to be equal if and only if $a = c$ and $b = d$. We may write a **solution** to an equation in two variables x and y as an *ordered pair* of numbers (a, b), where the first number a is the x-value of the solution and the second number b is the y-value. Although it is impossible to list all the solutions to an equation in two variables, a partial listing of the solutions can be given. This listing is frequently given in the form of a table.

EXAMPLE 2   Use a table to give a partial listing of the solutions to the equation $y = (6 - x)/2$.

Solution   Substituting different values for x (integers from -1 to 7 in this case) and evaluating the equation for y gives the table of solutions at the left. Thus we have a partial list of solutions to $y = (6 - x)/2$: $(-1, \frac{7}{2})$, $(0, 3)$, $(1, \frac{5}{2})$, $(2, 2)$, $(3, \frac{3}{2})$, $(4, 1)$, $(5, \frac{1}{2})$, $(6, 0)$, $(7, -\frac{1}{2})$.

Note that $(4, 1)$ is a solution, but $(1, 4)$ is not; the first component of the pair represents the x-value of the solution.   □

x	y
-1	$\frac{7}{2}$
0	3
1	$\frac{5}{2}$
2	2
3	$\frac{3}{2}$
4	1
5	$\frac{1}{2}$
6	0
7	$-\frac{1}{2}$

Just as we can use a number line to graph the real numbers (see Section 0.1), we can use a rectangular (or Cartesian) coordinate plane to graph ordered pairs of real numbers. The coordinate plane is especially useful, since it permits us to represent geometrically solutions to equations in two variables.

We construct the coordinate system by drawing two real number lines perpendicular to each other so that they intersect at their origins. (See Figure 1.1.) The

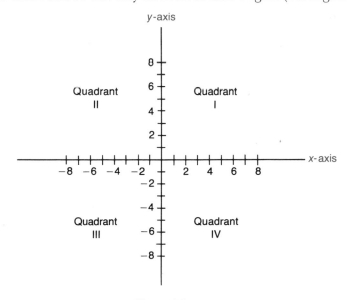

Figure 1.1

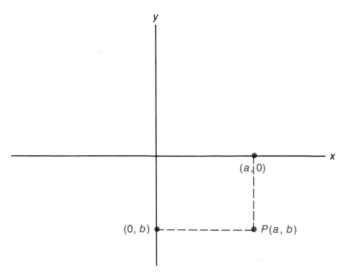

Figure 1.2

point of intersection is called the **origin** of the system, and the two lines are called the **coordinate axes.** We call the horizontal axis the x-axis (or the first coordinate axis), and the vertical axis the y-axis (or the second coordinate axis). The scales on the two axes are frequently (but not always) the same. The axes divide the plane into four parts, called **quadrants.**

Any point in the plane can be represented by an ordered pair of real numbers. The point on the x-axis representing the real number a is denoted by the ordered pair $(a, 0)$, and the point on the y-axis representing the real number b is denoted by the ordered pair $(0, b)$. Any point P that is a units from the y-axis and b units from the x-axis is denoted by the ordered pair (a, b). (See Figure 1.2.)

Note that the line drawn through the point denoted by (a, b) and perpendicular to the x-axis intersects the x-axis at $(a, 0)$ and that the line drawn through (a, b) and perpendicular to the y-axis intersects the y-axis at $(0, b)$. This correspondence between the points on the plane and all ordered pairs of real numbers is called a one-to-one correspondence. The values a and b in the ordered pair associated with the point P are called the **rectangular coordinates** of the point. The first coordinate of a point is called the x-*coordinate* (or *abscissa*), and the second coordinate is called the y-*coordinate* (or *ordinate*). To plot a point $P(a, b)$ means to locate the point with x-coordinate a and y-coordinate b.

EXAMPLE 3   Plot the points $A(5, 2)$, $B(-4, 1)$, $C(-4, -4)$, and $D(1, -5)$.

Solution   See Figure 1.3.   □

The **graph** of an equation is the picture that is drawn by plotting the points

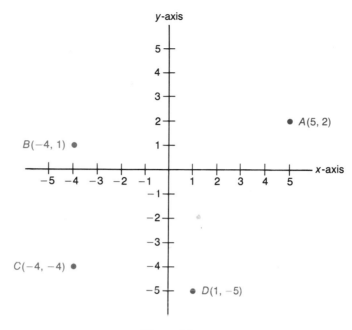

Figure 1.3

whose coordinates (x, y) satisfy the equation. Since there are an infinite number of such points, we cannot hope to plot them all. But we can plot enough points to determine the general outline of the graph. Then we connect the points with a smooth curve.

EXAMPLE 4   Graph the equation $y = 3x + 2$.

Solution   We choose some sample values of x and find the corresponding values of y. Placing these in a table, we have sample points to plot. When we have enough points to determine the shape of the graph, we connect them. The table and graph are shown in Figure 1.4 (page 32).

Notice that the graph of $y = 3x + 2$ (Figure 1.4) appears to be a straight line. This is indeed the case; all equations whose form is $y = mx + b$ have graphs that are straight lines. We will study these **linear equations** in Chapter 2.   □

EXAMPLE 5   Graph $y = x^3 + 1$.

Solution   Selecting values of x and finding the resulting values of y gives the table of values. Plotting a few points may lead us to conclude that this graph is also a straight line. However, if enough points are plotted, the graph of Figure 1.5 (page 32) results.   □

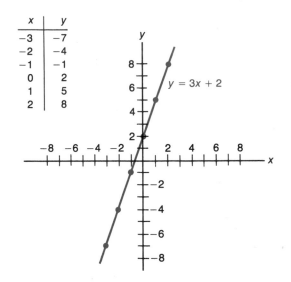

x	y
-3	-7
-2	-4
-1	-1
0	2
1	5
2	8

$y = 3x + 2$

Figure 1.4

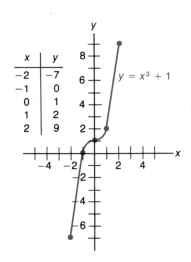

x	y
-2	-7
-1	0
0	1
1	2
2	9

$y = x^3 + 1$

Figure 1.5

Exercise 1.1

Which of the following are identities and which are conditional equations?

1. $x + 5 = 2$
2. $x - 4 = 3$
3. $x - 1 = 7$
4. $3 - x = 2$
5. $2x - 1 = 4$
6. $3x + 1 = 6$
7. $2x = x + x$
8. $4x = 5x - x$
9. $5x + 1 = 8x + 1 - 3x$
10. $6x - 2 = 6x - 2 + 2x$
11. $2x - 3 = 3x + 4$
12. $5x + 4 = 3x + 4 - 2x$
13. $2(x - 1) = 2x - 2$
14. $3(2x + 1) = 6x + 3$

Determine if the following equations are true for the given values of the variables.

15. $x + 4 = 6, x = 2$
16. $x - 5 = 7, x = 2$
17. $x - 5 = 12, x = 7$
18. $y + 7 = 8, y = 1$
19. $3y + 2 = -4, y = -2$
20. $2x - 3 = 5, x = 1$

Use a table to give a partial listing of the solutions to the following equations (for the given range of integer x values).

21. $y = 4x - 1$ ($x = -2$ to $x = 4$)
22. $y = 3x + 2$ ($x = -2$ to $x = 3$)
23. $y = 6 - x$ ($x = -1$ to $x = 8$)
24. $y = 7 - x$ ($x = -1$ to $x = 8$)
25. $y = 5x - 2$ ($x = -2$ to $x = 3$)
26. $y = 3x + 5$ ($x = -2$ to $x = 3$)
27. $3x - y = 6$ ($x = -2$ to $x = 4$)
28. $5x - y = 10$ ($x = -2$ to $x = 3$)
29. $2x - 3y = 12$ ($x = -3$ to $x = 3$)
30. $3x + 2y = 6$ ($x = -2$ to $x = 3$)

Graph the following equations.

31. $y = 4x$
32. $y = 5x$
33. $y = 6x + 1$
34. $y = 15 - 3x$
35. $y = x^2 + 1$
36. $y = x^3 - 1$
37. $y = x^3 + 1$
38. $y = 4 - x^2$

APPLICATIONS

39. The particulate readings for a city have been found to follow a certain pattern for a given month.

   7:00 A.M.–10:00 A.M.: an initial level of 100, with an increase of 15 units each hour
   10:00 A.M.– 3:00 P.M.: stable reading
   3:00 P.M.– 6:00 A.M.: increase of 15 units each hour
   6:00 P.M.– 4:00 A.M.: decrease of 9 units per hour
   4:00 A.M.– 7:00 A.M.: stable reading

   Make a graph that represents this situation for a 24-hour period beginning at 7:00 A.M. Use time as the horizontal axis.

40. In psychology, the study of threshold levels of stimulus are of interest. If s is the amount of stimulus, then Δs is the required change in s so that the subject notices a change. Research has shown that

$$\Delta s = ks \qquad (k = \text{constant})$$

Sketch graphs of this equation $(s > 0)$ for the values $k = \frac{1}{2}$, $k = 1$, and $k = 2$, putting s on the horizontal axis and Δs on the vertical axis.

1.2 Functions

Objectives
- To determine if a relation is a function
- To state the domain and range of certain functions

It is reasonable to assume that there exists a relation between the number of items a firm sells and its total revenue (the money brought into the firm by the sale of its product). It is frequently possible to express this relation by means of an equation. For example, if a firm sells its product for $35 per unit, then the total revenue for a period of time could be expressed by the equation

$$R = 35x,$$

where x represents the quantity sold by the firm during that period. If the firm sold 80 units of its product in a month, we can find the total revenue by substituting 80 for x in the equation. This gives a total revenue for the month of

$$R = 35(80) = \$2800.$$

If the quantity sold is 100, the total revenue is $3500.

An equation containing two variables expresses a **relation** between the two variables. For example, the equation

$$y = 4x - 3$$

expresses a relation between the variables x and y. We can find the value of y that

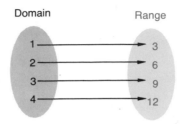

Figure 1.6

is associated with a given value of x by substituting the x-value into the equation and determining the resulting value of y. For example, if $x = 1$, then $y = 4(1) - 3 = 1$, and if $x = 5$, then $y = 4(5) - 3 = 17$.

Loosely speaking, we may think of a relation as a rule that determines how the elements of two sets are associated. Relations may be expressed by sets of ordered pairs. For example,

$$\{(1, 3), (2, 6), (3, 9), (4, 12)\}$$

expresses a relation between the set of first components, $\{1, 2, 3, 4\}$, and the set of second components, $\{3, 6, 9, 12\}$. The set of first components is called the **domain** of the relation, and the set of second components is called the **range** of the relation. Figure 1.6 uses arrows to indicate how the inputs from the domain (the first components) are associated with the outputs in the range (the second components).

An equation frequently expresses how the second component (the output) is obtained from the first component (the input). For example, the equation

$$y = 4x - 3$$

expresses how the output y results from the input x. This equation expresses a special relation between x and y, because each value of x that is substituted into the equation results in only one value for y. If each value of x put into the equation results in one value of y, we say that the equation expresses y as a **function** of x.

Definition of a   In general, a **function** is a relation between two sets such that to each
Function   element of the domain (input) there corresponds exactly one element
of the range (output).

When a function is defined by an equation, the variable that represents the numbers in the domain (input) is called the **independent variable** of the function, and the variable that represents the numbers in the range (output) is called the **dependent variable** (because its values depend on the values of the independent variable). When we say "the equation $y = 4x - 3$ defines y as a function of x," we are saying that the equation defines a function with independent variable x and dependent variable y.

The equation

$$y = 4x^2$$

defines y as a function of x, because only one value of y will result from each value of x that is substituted into the equation. Thus x is the independent variable and y is the dependent variable.

We will limit our discussion in this text to *real* functions, which are functions whose domains and ranges contain only real numbers. If the domain and range of a function are not specified, it is assumed that the domain consists of all real numbers that result in real numbers in the range, and the range is a subset of the real numbers. For example, for the function defined by $y = 4x^2$, there are no restrictions on the numbers substituted for x, so the domain consists of all real numbers. Because each value of x is squared, y cannot assume any negative values. Thus the range is the set of all nonnegative real numbers.

The equation $y = \sqrt{x - 4}$ also defines y as a function of x, because each value of x results in one value of y. Because we assume that both the range (y-values) and domain (x-values) must be real numbers, we note a restriction on x. In order that all y-values are real numbers, no value of x may be used that will make $x - 4$ negative. Thus the domain of the function contains only numbers greater than or equal to 4. Thus we may say the domain is $\{x: x \geq 4\}$. The range will contain only nonnegative numbers; that is, the range is $\{y: y \geq 0\}$.

EXAMPLE 1   Does $y^2 = 2x$ express y as a function of x?

Solution   No, because for some values of x there is more than one value for y. In fact, there are two y-values for each $x > 0$. For example, if $x = 8$, $y = \pm 4$. The equation $y^2 = 2x$ expresses a relation between x and y, but y is not a function of x.   □

EXAMPLE 2   What is the domain of the function $y = 1 + 1/x$?

Solution   The domain is the set of all real numbers except 0; $1/0$ is undefined, so $1 + 1/x$ is undefined at $x = 0$.   □

Equations may involve variables other than x and y. For example, the equation $s = 5C$ represents a relation between the cost of an item and its selling price, with C representing the cost and s representing the selling price. By inspecting the equation, we see that there is exactly one value of s (selling price) for each value of C (cost). Thus s is a function of C. Because the value of s *depends* on the value of C, we say that C is the independent variable and s is the dependent variable. The set of possible values for C (the domain) is the set of positive real numbers (because cost must be positive) and the range is the set of positive real numbers (all values of C will result in positive values for s).

Exercise 1.2

1. If $y = 3x^3$, is y a function of x?
2. If $y = 6x^2$, is y a function of x?
3. If $y^2 = 3x$, is y a function of x?
4. If $y^2 = 10x^2$, is y a function of x?
5. If $p = 2q$, is p a function of q?
6. If $y = \sqrt{4x}$, is y a function of x?
7. If $p = \pm\sqrt{2q}$, is p a function of q?
8. If $R = \sqrt[3]{x}$, is R a function of x?

State the domain of the following functions.

9. $y = x^2$

10. $y = x^3 - 1$

11. $y = \dfrac{1}{x}$

12. $c = \dfrac{4x - 1}{x}$

13. $c = \dfrac{1}{4 - x}$

14. $R = \dfrac{3}{x + 3}$

State the domain and range of the following functions.

15. $y = x^2 + 4$

16. $y = x^2 - 1$

17. $y = \sqrt{x - 1}$

18. $y = x + 2$

19. $y = \sqrt{x^2 + 1}$

20. $y = \sqrt{x^2 - 4}$

APPLICATIONS

21. The description of body-heat loss due to convection involves a coefficient of convection K_c, which depends on wind velocity v according to the equation

$$K_c = 4\sqrt{4v + 1}.$$

   (a) Is K_c a function of v?
   (b) What is the domain of the function defined by this equation?
   (c) What restrictions do nature and common sense put on v?

22. The efficiency E of a muscle performing a maximal contraction is related to the time t that the muscle is contracted according to

$$E = \frac{1 - 0.24t}{2 + t}.$$

   (a) Is E a function of t?
   (b) What is the domain?
   (c) What restrictions do nature and common sense put on the domain?

23. The pressure of P of a certain gas is related to volume V according to

$$P = \frac{100}{V}.$$

   (a) Is P a function of V?   (b) Is 0 in the domain of this function?

24. If a test having reliability r is lengthened by a factor n $(n > 1)$, the reliability of the new test R is given by

$$R = \frac{nr}{1 + (n - 1)r}, \qquad 0 < r \le 1.$$

If the reliability is $r = 0.6$, the equation becomes

$$R = \frac{0.6n}{0.4 + 0.6n}.$$

(a) Is R a function of n?   (b) Graph the equation.

1.3 Functional Notation

Objective   ■ To use functional notation

If we wish to state mathematically that the total cost C of producing a product is a function of quantity x, we may write $C = f(x)$. This is read "C is a function of x," or "C equals f of x." By the same token, to say that y is a function of x, we write $y = f(x)$. Letters other than f may also be used to indicate functions; for example, $y = g(x)$ or $y = h(x)$ may be used. If $y = 3x^2 + x + 1$, y is a function of x, so we may write $y = f(x) = 3x^2 + x + 1$, or $f(x) = 3x^2 + x + 1$. To express the value of y when $x = 2$, we may write $f(2)$; in the same manner, $f(-3)$ represents the value of y when $x = -3$ [not f times (-3)]. If $f(x) = 3x^2 + 2x + 1$, then $f(2) = 3(2)^2 + 2(2) + 1 = 17$, so $y = 17$ when $x = 2$.

EXAMPLE 1   If $y = f(x) = 2x^3 - 3x^2 + 1$, find
(a) $f(0)$ (b) $f(3)$ (c) $f(-1)$

Solution   (a) $f(0) = 2(0)^3 - 3(0)^2 + 1 = 1$, so $y = 1$ when $x = 0$.
(b) $f(3) = 2(3)^3 - 3(3)^2 + 1 = 2(27) - 3(9) + 1 = 28$, so $y = 28$ when $x = 3$.
(c) $f(-1) = 2(-1)^3 - 3(-1)^2 + 1 = 2(-1) - 3(1) + 1 = -4$,   so $y = -4$
when $x = -1$.   □

EXAMPLE 2   If $h(x) = 4x^2 - 3x + 1$, find
(a) $h(3)$ (b) $h(-c)$ (c) $h(a)$ (d) $h(a) - h(b)$

Solution   (a) $h(3) = 4(3)^2 - 3(3) + 1 = 28$
(b) $h(-c) = 4(-c)^2 - 3(-c) + 1 = 4c^2 + 3c + 1$
(c) $h(a) = 4(a)^2 - 3(a) + 1 = 4a^2 - 3a + 1$
(d) $h(a) - h(b) = [4(a)^2 - 3(a) + 1] - [4(b)^2 - 3(b) + 1] = 4a^2 - 3a - 4b^2 + 3b$
                                                                        □

EXAMPLE 3   Given $f(x) = 3x - 1$, find

(a) $f(4)$ (b) $f(-3)$ (c) $\dfrac{f(x + h) - f(x)}{h}$,   if $h \neq 0$.

Solution   (a) $f(4) = 3(4) - 1 = 11$
(b) $f(-3) = 3(-3) - 1 = -10$

(c) $\dfrac{f(x + h) - f(x)}{h} = \dfrac{[3(x + h) - 1] - [3x - 1]}{h}$

$$= \frac{3x + 3h - 1 - 3x + 1}{h} = \frac{3h}{h} = 3 \quad \square$$

EXAMPLE 4   If $R = R(x) = 14x - 0.02x^2$ is a revenue function for a good, find
(a) the revenue if 10 units are sold.
(b) the revenue if 100 units are sold.

Solution   (a) If 10 units are sold, $R(10) = 14(10) - 0.02(10)^2 = 138$.
(b) If 100 units are sold, $R(100) = 14(100) - 0.02(100)^2 = 1200$. $\square$

Exercise 1.3

1. If $R(x) = 8x - 10$, find
   (a) $R(0)$ (b) $R(2)$ (c) $R(-3)$ (d) $R(a)$
2. If $g(x) = 1 - 4x$, find
   (a) $g(1)$ (b) $g(3)$ (c) $g(-4)$ (d) $g(-b)$
3. If $C(x) = 4x^2 - 3$, find
   (a) $C(0)$ (b) $C(-1)$ (c) $C(-2)$ (d) $C(-x)$
4. If $h(x) = 3x^2 - 2x$, find
   (a) $h(3)$ (b) $h(-3)$ (c) $h(2)$ (d) $h(-x)$
5. If $g(x) = x^3 - 4x^2 + 3$, find
   (a) $g(-1)$ (b) $g(2)$ (c) $g(1)$
6. If $f(x) = x^3 - 8x - 1$, find
   (a) $f(0)$ (b) $f(2)$ (c) $f(-3)$ (d) $f(x + h)$
7. If $f(x) = x^2 - 3x$, find

   (a) $f(x + h)$ (b) $\dfrac{f(x + h) - f(x)}{h}$

8. The graph of a function is said to be **symmetric** with respect to the y-axis if the part on the left of the y-axis is a reflection (mirror image) of the part on the right side. The graph of $y = f(x)$ will be symmetric with respect to the y-axis if $f(-x) = f(x)$.
   (a) If $y = f(x) = 3x^2 + 4$, does $f(-x) = f(x)$?
   (b) Is the graph of $y = 3x^2 + 4$ symmetric with respect to the y-axis?
   (c) If $y = f(x) = 3x^2 - 2x$, does $f(-x) = f(x)$?
   (d) Is the graph of $y = 3x^2 - 2x$ symmetric with respect to the y-axis?

APPLICATIONS 9. The efficiency E of a muscle performing a maximal contraction can be described by

$$E = f(t) = \frac{1 - 0.24t}{2 + t},$$

where t represents time.
(a) What is $f(1)$?   (b) What is $f(3)$?

10. The population size y of a certain organism at time t is given by

$$y = f(t) = 4t^2 + 2t.$$

(a) What is $f(1)$?   (b) What is $f(2)$?   (c) What is $f(3)$?

11. The pressure of a certain gas is related to the volume according to

$$P = P(V) = \frac{100}{V}.$$

(a) What is $P(100)$?   (b) What is $P(50)$?   (c) What is $P(10)$?
(d) As volume decreases, what happens to pressure?
(e) As volume increases, what happens to pressure?

12. The reaction R to an injection of a drug is related to the dosage x according to

$$R(x) = x^2 \left(500 - \frac{x}{3}\right),$$

where 1000 mg is the maximum dosage. What is $R(100)$?

13. The number of action potentials produced by a nerve t seconds after a stimulus may be described by

$$N(t) = 25t + \frac{4}{t^2 + 2} - 2.$$

(a) What is $N(2)$?   (b) What is $N(10)$?

14. The total cost of producing a product is given by

$$C = 300x + 0.1x^2 + 1200,$$

where x represents the number of units produced.
(a) What is the total cost of producing 10 units?
(b) What is the average cost per unit when 10 units are produced?

1.4 Graphing Relations and Functions

Objectives   ■ To graph relations and functions
              ■ To determine if a graph represents a function

In addition to studying equations and inequalities that define functions and relations, we will be interested in their graphs. To appreciate the value of graphs in visualizing relations and functions, consider the *circle graph* in Figure 1.7. The graph tells at a glance what part of a sales dollar goes for operating expenses,

Distribution of a Sales Dollar

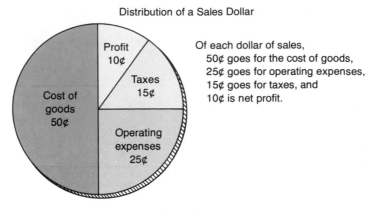

Of each dollar of sales,
   50¢ goes for the cost of goods,
   25¢ goes for operating expenses,
   15¢ goes for taxes, and
   10¢ is net profit.

Figure 1.7

taxes, and so on. Note that you can determine the way this money is distributed more quickly from the graph than by reading the verbal description of the distribution.

When a large amount of data is available regarding some relation, the data may be summarized pictorially by drawing a *bar graph*, such as the one in Figure 1.8. Businesses also use a *line graph* (such as Figure 1.9) to picture changes in sales, stocks, and so on. Line graphs also summarize interval data, with straight lines joining points that have been plotted at the midpoints of the intervals.

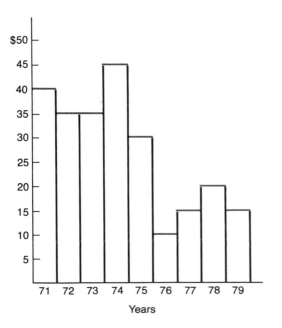

Figure 1.8

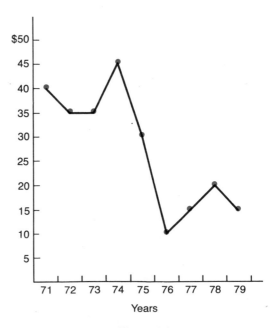

Figure 1.9

If we have the equation that describes a function or relation, we can plot values of the variables that satisfy the equation to obtain a "picture" of the relationship between the variables. If the domain is the set of real numbers, or any large set, we cannot plot all the ordered pairs that satisfy the function or relation. In this case we make a table that contains a number of values from the domain, with the corresponding values from the range. These ordered pairs are plotted. If the domain is the set of real numbers, we draw a smooth curve passing through the plotted points to represent the graph (see Figure 1.10). In later chapters we will develop methods that make graphing easier.

EXAMPLE 1   Graph the function $y = x^2 + 2x$, with the domain and range chosen from the real numbers.

Solution   The graph of $y = x^2 + 2x$ is shown in Figure 1.10.   □

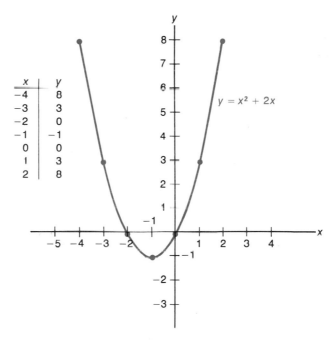

Figure 1.10

EXAMPLE 2   A firm uses the formula $C = \frac{6}{5}x + 2$ to determine the total cost of producing a product, where C is the cost and x is the quantity produced. Graph this function.

Solution   We construct a table of values, realizing that we would not have negative values for x (the quantity produced). Putting the values for x along the horizontal axis and the values for C on the vertical axis and connecting the points, we get the graph shown in Figure 1.11 (page 42). Note that the abscissa of a point is the x-value and the ordinate is the C-value. The graph lies along a straight line in the first quadrant.   □

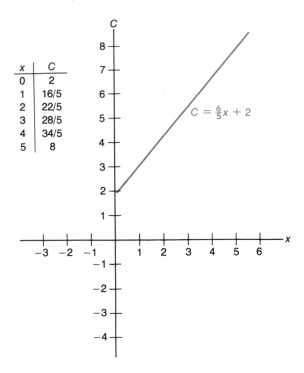

x	C
0	2
1	16/5
2	22/5
3	28/5
4	34/5
5	8

$C = \frac{6}{5}x + 2$

Figure 1.11

We can determine if a relation is a function by inspecting its graph. If the relation is a function, no two points will have the same first coordinate (component), so there can be no two points on a vertical line.

We can use the vertical-line "test" to determine if y is a function of x. The test consists of determining if any vertical line would intersect the graph of the relation in more than one point. If no such line can be drawn, the relation is a function. We can see that y is a function of x if $y = x^2 + 2x$ (see Figure 1.10), and C is a function of x if $C = \frac{6}{5}x + 2$ (see Figure 1.11), since a vertical line drawn anywhere on either of these graphs would not intersect the graph in more than one point.

EXAMPLE 3   Graph $y^2 = 2x$ and determine if y is a function of x.

Solution   Sample points of the relation are given in the table of values. Note that no negative values are in the domain of the relation. Choosing points that can be easily graphed and completing the curve gives the graph in Figure 1.12.

The vertical-line test indicates that y is not a function of x. For example, a vertical line at $x = 8$ would intersect the curve at $(8, 4)$ and $(8, -4)$. Note that the values in the table also show that y is not a function of x, because some values of x result in two values of y.   □

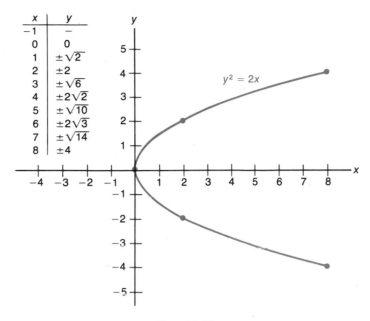

x	y
−1	−
0	0
1	$\pm\sqrt{2}$
2	± 2
3	$\pm\sqrt{6}$
4	$\pm 2\sqrt{2}$
5	$\pm\sqrt{10}$
6	$\pm 2\sqrt{3}$
7	$\pm\sqrt{14}$
8	± 4

$y^2 = 2x$

Figure 1.12

Exercise 1.4

1. Do the points in Figure 1.13 represent y as a function of x?

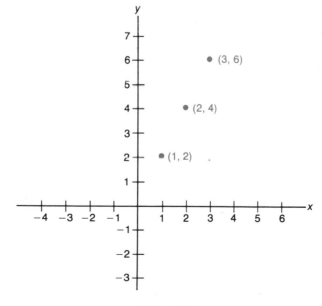

● (3, 6)

● (2, 4)

● (1, 2)

Figure 1.13

2. Do the points in Figure 1.14 represent y as a function of x?

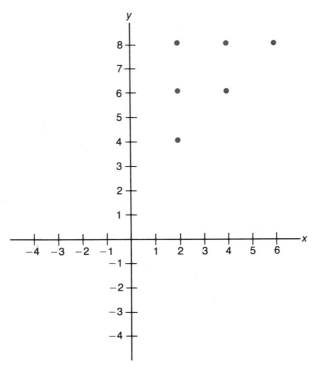

Figure 1.14

3. Does the graph of Figure 1.15 represent y as a function of x?

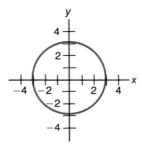

Figure 1.15

4. Does the graph of Figure 1.16 represent y as a function of x?

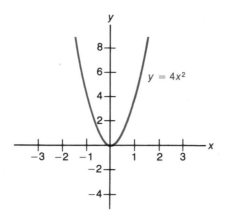

Figure 1.16

5. If $y = f(x)$ in Figure 1.13, what is $f(1)$?
6. If $y = f(x)$ in Figure 1.13, what is $f(2)$?
7. If $y - g(x)$ in Figure 1.16, what is $g(0)$?
8. Is there an x in the domain of the function represented by Figure 1.16 such that $g(x) = 0$?
9. The graph of $y = x^2 - 4x$ is shown in Figure 1.17.

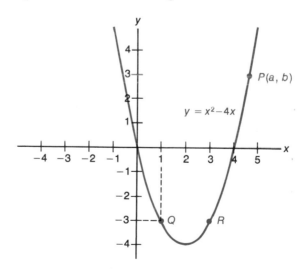

Figure 1.17

(a) If the coordinates of the point P on the graph are (a, b), how are a and b related?
(b) What are the coordinates of the point Q? Do they satisfy the equation?
(c) What are the coordinates of R? Do they satisfy the equation?
(d) What are the x-values of the points on the graph whose y-coordinates are 0? Are these x-values solutions to the equation $x^2 - 4x = 0$?

10. The graph of $y = 2x^2$ is shown in Figure 1.18.

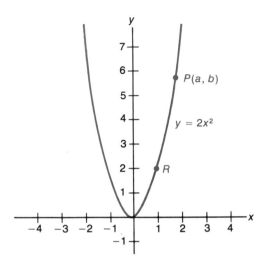

Figure 1.18

(a) If the point P, with coordinates (a, b), is on the graph, how are a and b related?

(b) Does the point $(1, 1)$ lie on the graph? Do the coordinates satisfy the equation?

(c) What are the coordinates of point R? Do they satisfy the equation?

(d) What is the x-value of the point whose y-coordinate is 0? Does this value of x satisfy the equation $0 = 2x^2$?

Graph the following relations and functions.

11. $y = 4x$

12. $y = 3x$

13. $y = 3x + 4$

14. $y = 2x + 1$

15. $P = Q - 1$

16. $P = 4 - q$

17. $y = \sqrt{x - 2}$

18. $y = \sqrt{x^2 - 1}$

19. $y = x^2 - 9$

20. $y = x^2$

21. $x^2 + y^2 = 4$

22. $x^2 - y^2 = 9,\ x, y \geq 0$

23. $3x^2 + y^2 = 3,\ x, y \geq 0$

24. $x^2 + 4y^2 = 16$

APPLICATIONS

25. The Shütz-Borisoff Law states that the amount of substrate y transformed by an enzyme in time t is given by

$$y = k\sqrt{cat},$$

where c is the concentration of the enzyme, a is the initial concentration of the substrate, and k is a constant that depends on the enzyme and the organism. Graph the equation when $a = 1$, $k = 1$, and $c = 4$.

26. Studies relating the magnitude of a sensation y to the magnitude of the stimulus x have shown the following,

$$y = (x - x_0)^n,$$

where x_0 is the threshold of effective stimulus and n is the power, which depends on the stimulus. For example, when the stimulus is brightness, the equation relating the magnitude of sensation to visual brightness is given by

$$y = \sqrt[3]{x - 1}.$$

Graph this equation.

1.5 Applications of Functions in Business and Economics

Objectives
- To formulate and evaluate consumption functions
- To evaluate and graph supply and demand functions
- To formulate and evaluate total cost, total revenue, and profit functions

We will discuss numerous applications of mathematics in this text, but in this section we will introduce three important business applications, which will be expanded and used in different circumstances throughout the text as increased mathematical skills permit. These applications are national consumption (Keynesian Analysis), supply and demand as functions of price (market analysis), and total cost, total revenue, and profit as functions of quantity sold (theory of the firm).

The Consumption Function

The consumption function is one of the basic ingredients in a larger discussion of how an economy can have persistent high unemployment or persistent high inflation. This study is often called Keynesian Analysis after its founder, John Maynard Keynes. During the Great Depression of the 1930s, the United States suffered through many years of high unemployment that threatened the collapse of capitalism in this country. The Keynesian theory was used by the Roosevelt administration (Keynes was a close friend of Roosevelt) in one of the most dramatic periods of our history.

A student versed in the language of functions could write a consumption function as

$$C = f(y) = 0.8y + 6,$$

where y is income (in billions of dollars) and C is consumption (in billions of dollars). This statement says that consumption is a function, and expresses exactly what the functional relationship is. In general, **consumption functions** are frequently assumed to be linear (their graphs are lines) over short periods of time. Over longer periods of time, consumption functions will be nonlinear. We will discuss linear and nonlinear consumption functions in more detail in later chapters.

EXAMPLE 1   If the consumption function is given by $C = f(y) = 20 + 0.6y$, where C is the consumption and y is the disposable income (in billions of dollars),
(a) what is the consumption when disposable income is 0?
(b) what is the consumption when disposable income is $5 billion?
(c) sketch the graph of the consumption function.

Solution   (a) $f(0) = 20$ (b) $f(5) = 20 + 3 = \$23$ billion   (c) See Figure 1.19.   □

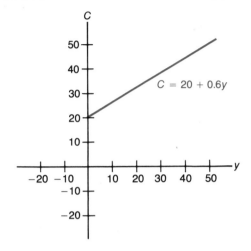

Figure 1.19

Supply and Demand Functions

It is a fact that consumers want more goods than they actually purchase. The goods that they actually buy are determined by (a) the price of the good desired, (b) the amount of money they have to spend on the item, (c) the strength of their tastes and preferences, (d) the prices of competing goods, and (e) their expectations of the future and its effect on this good.

If we concentrate on the relationship between the price of the good and the amount of the good a consumer is willing to purchase in a fixed period of time, the resulting function is called a **demand function.** Economists define demand for a commodity by using a schedule, or table, that shows the various amounts of the commodity that consumers are willing and able to purchase at specific prices in a set of possible prices during a specified period of time. The **law of demand** states that as price increases, the corresponding quantity demanded will fall or, as price decreases, the quantity demanded will increase.

Table 1.1 is a demand schedule that shows the relationship between the price of a particular brand of shirt and the number of shirts one person is willing and able to buy in a given period of time (the quantity demanded). This function (or schedule) is for only one person and for a fixed period (one month). Different people will have different demand schedules based on the other four factors

Table 1.1   ONE PERSON'S
DEMAND SCHEDULE
FOR ONE MONTH

q, Quantity Demanded	p, Price of One Shirt
0	24
1	21
2	18
3	15
4	12
5	9

mentioned. Usually we will be talking about the demand of a group of consumers. Note also that the demand schedule is for a specified period of time. The relationship from Table 1.1 is for a period of one month. Figure 1.20 shows its graph.

The relationship between the price of a commodity and the quantity demanded is functional; namely, quantity demanded is a function of price, which is denoted $q = f(p)$. However, economists traditionally have graphed the demand function on a two-dimensional graph with the quantity demanded on the horizontal axis and the price on the vertical axis, as we have done in Figure 1.20. Throughout the text, we will follow this tradition when graphing demand functions. Equations relating price and quantity demanded can be solved for either p or q, and we will have occasion to use the equations in both forms.

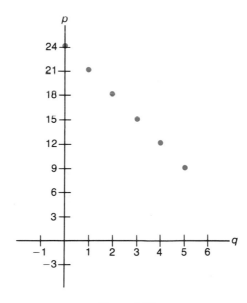

Figure 1.20

Although we only have a series of points as the graph of the demand function in Figure 1.20, it is common practice to draw a smooth curve joining the points and to call the curve the **demand curve.** In this case the smooth curve would be a straight line (see Figure 1.21) with the equation $p = 24 - 3q$. The graph implies that, for example, the consumer will buy 0.5 shirts per month if the cost is $22.50 per shirt. This can be interpreted as meaning he or she will buy 1 shirt every two months. Though some points on the graph, such as $(\sqrt{2}, 24 - 3\sqrt{2})$, will not have much meaning in a business sense, the advantage of dealing with continuous demand curves far outweighs any possible disadvantages. Thus we assume that demand functions will have continuous curves.

Except in very sophisticated economics models, negative price° and quantity have no meaning, so the graphs of demand curves will all be in the first quadrant. The demand curve will normally slope downward toward the right because the quantity demanded will be smaller as the price increases. The demand curve may be a vertical line, however, if price is not a factor in demand. For example, a diabetic person must continue to buy insulin regardless of its cost. The demand curve could also be a horizontal line if the price remains constant regardless of the demand.

Just as a consumer's willingness to buy is related to price, so is a manufacturer's willingness to supply goods. Economists define **supply** as a schedule that shows

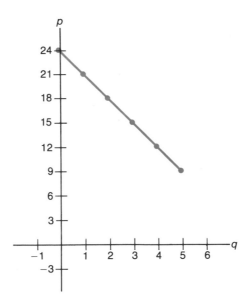

Figure 1.21

° Negative price values would result if buyers were paid to remove goods from the market.

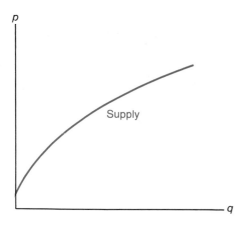

Figure 1.22

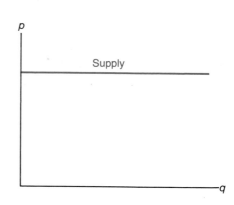

Figure 1.23

the various amounts of a commodity that a producer is willing and able to produce and make available for sale at specific prices during a specified time.

Economists usually interpret supply as showing the quantity producers will offer at various prices, so quantity supplied is a function of price. As with demand, price is placed on the vertical axis on the graph of the **supply curve.** The horizontal axis now represents quantity supplied rather than quantity demanded.

The **law of supply** states that as price rises, the corresponding quantity supplied for sale will also rise. Because the producer will supply more goods if the price increases, the supply curve will normally rise as it moves to the right (see Figure 1.22). Of course, certain special circumstances may result in horizontal lines representing supply curves. For example, a consumer may be supplied with the right to make an unlimited number of local phone calls per month for a fixed fee, resulting in a horizontal supply curve (see Figure 1.23). As with the demand curve, the supply curves will have meaning for us only in the first quadrant.

Total Cost, Total Revenue, and Profit Functions

Suppose you are the manager of a shoelace company, and it operates according to the following conditions:

1. It makes only shoelaces, and sells them for $.50 per pair.
2. Ten people are employed, and are paid $.10 for each pair of shoelaces they make. Note that they are paid *only* for what they produce.
3. Raw materials cost $.24 for each pair of shoelaces made.
4. Costs for equipment, plant, insurance, the manager's salary, and fringe benefits (these are called **fixed costs**) amount to $2000 per month.

If you were the manager of this shoelace factory, you would be interested in how many pairs of shoelaces you would have to make to break even. This means you would have to determine what your **total revenue** and your **total cost** would be at different levels of production. The information given is sufficient to formulate equations for the total revenue and the total cost, and from these equations we can formulate an equation that will determine the **profit** at different levels of production. From this equation you can determine when profit is 0; that is, when you break even. Let's discuss this problem in more detail.

The **total revenue function** states how much money is brought into the firm each month by the sale of its product. The total revenue for a month is the amount taken in before any expenses are paid. If x pairs of shoelaces are sold in a month, the total revenue for the shoelace factory is $0.50x$. Thus the total revenue function is

$$R = R(x) = 0.50x \qquad \text{(in dollars).}$$

Here x is the independent variable and R is the dependent variable. The graph of $R(x)$ for one month is shown in Figure 1.24. Note that the domain of the function is $\{x: x \geq 0\}$ because a negative quantity is meaningless.

We can also write the equation for the total cost function, which measures how many dollars the firm must pay to produce and sell its product. The total cost is comprised of two parts, fixed costs and variable costs. **Fixed costs** are those that remain constant regardless of the number of units produced. They include depreciation or rent on buildings, interest on investments, and so on. The fixed costs for the shoelace factory are given to be $2000 per month. Thus the cost for one month will always be at least $2000, even if no shoelaces are produced. The fixed cost is denoted by FC on the graph of Figure 1.25.

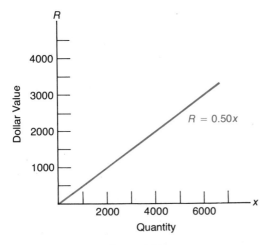

Figure 1.24

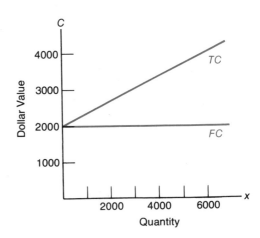

Figure 1.25

Variable costs are those directly related to the production of a commodity. The variable costs for producing x pairs of shoelaces are $0.10x$ for labor and $0.24x$ for raw materials, for a total of $0.34x$. The **total cost function** is the sum of the fixed and variable costs, or

$$C = C(x) = 2000 + 0.34x \qquad \text{(in dollars)}.$$

The total cost is denoted by TC on the graph of Figure 1.25. Note that the total cost equals the fixed cost when production is zero.

EXAMPLE 2   Find the total revenue and total cost if the shoelace factory produces and sells
(a) 10,000 pairs of shoelaces in a month.
(b) 15,000 pairs of shoelaces in a month.

Solution   (a) The total revenue is $R(10,000) = \$5000$.
The total cost is $C(10,000) = \$5400$.
(b) The total revenue is $R(15,000) = \$7500$.
The total cost is $C(15,000) = \$7100$.   □

We see that the profit or loss for a month can be found by subtracting the total cost from the total revenue. In the previous example, producing and selling 10,000 pairs of shoelaces results in a loss of \$400 (that is, \$5000 − 5400) while producing and selling 15,000 pairs results in a profit of \$7500 − 7100 = \$400. So the firm will break even at some point between 10,000 and 15,000 pairs of shoelaces.

If x units of a commodity are produced and sold, the profit is found by subtracting the total cost from the total revenue.[*]

$$\text{Profit (or loss)} = \text{total revenue} - \text{total cost}$$

We can define the **profit function** as follows:

$$P(x) = R(x) - C(x).$$

Thus for the total revenue function $R(x) = 0.50x$ and the total cost function $C(x) = 2000 + 0.34x$ in the shoelace example, the profit function is $P(x) = 0.50x - (2000 + 0.34x)$, or $P(x) = 0.16x - 2000$.

The graph of $P(x)$, for positive values of x, is shown in Figure 1.26. Note that the profit function is negative for some values of x (a loss is incurred) and positive for other values (a profit is made). For example, $P(10,000) = 1600 - 2000 = -400$, so a loss of \$400 will result from producing and selling 10,000 pairs of

---

[*] The symbols generally used in economics for total cost, total revenue, and profit are TC, TR, and π, respectively. We do not use these symbols to avoid confusion, especially with the use of π as a variable.

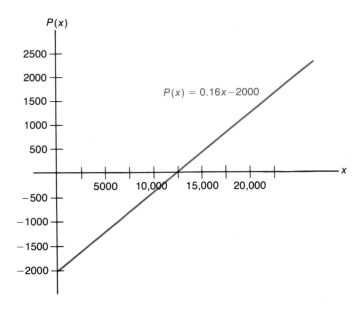

$P(x) = 0.16x - 2000$

Figure 1.26

shoelaces. Also, $P(15{,}000) = 400$, so a profit of \$400 will result from selling 15,000 pairs of shoelaces.

The point at which the profit function is zero is called the **break-even point.** By referring to the graph in Figure 1.26, it appears that the break-even point occurs when $x = 12{,}500$. We can check if this is correct. Letting $x = 12{,}500$, we have

$$P(12{,}500) = 0.16(12{,}500) - 2000 = 0,$$

so this is indeed the break-even point. This use of a graph is not always this reliable, however, and we will discuss break-even analysis more thoroughly in later chapters.

EXAMPLE 3   Suppose the price of a commodity is \$.40 each. If fixed costs are \$200 and the variable costs amount to \$.20 per item, find
(a) the total revenue function,   (b) the total cost function,   (c) the profit function.

Solution   (a) The total revenue function is $R(x) = 0.40x$.
(b) The total cost function is $C(x) = 200 + 0.20x$.
(c) The profit function is
$$P(x) = 0.40x - (200 + 0.20x)$$
or
$$P(x) = 0.20x - 200.$$ □

Exercise 1.5

NATIONAL CONSUMPTION

1. If $C = f(y) = 3 + 0.7y$ (in billions of dollars),
   (a) what is the consumption when disposable income is 0?
   (b) what is consumption when disposable income is $6 billion?
   (c) sketch the graph of the consumption function.
2. If $C = 4 + 0.65y$ (in billions of dollars),
   (a) what is the consumption when disposable income is 0?
   (b) what is consumption when disposable income is $18 billion?
   (c) sketch the graph of the consumption function.
3. If $C = 5.6 + 0.6y$ (in billions of dollars),
   (a) what is the consumption when disposable income is 0?
   (b) what is consumption when disposable income is $15 billion?
   (c) sketch the graph of the consumption function.
4. If $C = 9 + 0.5y$ (in billions of dollars), do parts (a)–(c) as in problem 3.

SUPPLY AND DEMAND FUNCTIONS

Price	Quantity
$52	0
48	1
44	3
40	6
36	12

5. Graph the demand function described in the table at the left.
6. As the price of a commodity increases, what happens to (a) demand?   (b) supply?
7. Given $p + 2q = 10$ and $5p - 4q = 20$.
   (a) Sketch these graphs on the same set of axes.
   (b) Which equation most likely represents a demand function, and which most likely represents a supply function?
   (c) If $p = 2$, compare the quantity supplied and the quantity demanded. Are there surplus goods or not enough to meet demand?
8. Given $3p + 5q = 40$ and $4p - 10q = 30$.
   (a) Sketch these graphs on the same set of axes.
   (b) Which equation represents supply and which represents demand?
   (c) If $p = 20$, compare the quantity supplied and the quantity demanded. Are there surplus goods or not enough to meet demand?

TOTAL COST, TOTAL REVENUE, AND PROFIT FUNCTIONS

9. A certain commodity has the following costs for a period: Fixed costs: $3400; variable cost: $17 for each item produced.
   (a) Write the equation that represents total cost.
   (b) What will it cost to produce 200 items during the given period?
10. A good has a fixed cost of $1650 and a variable cost of $35 for each item produced during a given month.
    (a) Write the equation that represents the total cost.
    (b) What will it cost to produce 215 items during the month?

11. The commodity of problem 9 is sold for $34 per item.
    (a) Write the total revenue function as an equation.
    (b) What will be the revenue from selling 300 items?
    (c) What is the profit function for the commodity?
    (d) What is the profit on 300 items?
    (e) How many items must be sold to ensure that no money will be lost during the period?

12. The good of problem 10 is sold for $85 per item.
    (a) Write the equation that represents the revenue function.
    (b) What will be the revenue from sales of 50 items?
    (c) What is the profit function for this good?
    (d) What is the profit on 50 items?
    (e) How many items must be sold in the month to avoid losing money?

Review Exercises

1. Is the equation $5x + 3 = x + 5$ true if $x = \frac{1}{2}$?
2. Graph the equation $y = 5x - 2$.
3. Graph the equation $p = q^3$.
4. If $p = 3q^3$, is p a function of q?
5. If $y^2 = 9x$, is y a function of x?
6. What is the domain of the function $y = \sqrt{9 - x^2}$?
7. If $f(x) = x^2 + 4x + 5$, find
    (a) $f(-3)$
    (b) $f(-x)$
8. If the point with coordinates (a, b) is on the graph of the equation $y = x^2 - 3x$, what is the relation between a and b?
9. Graph the equation $x^2 + 3y^2 = 3$, $x, y \geq 0$.

APPLICATIONS

10. Suppose the national consumption is described by $C = 0.8y + 2$, in billions of dollars.
    (a) What is consumption when disposable income is 0?
    (b) What is consumption when disposable income is $5 billion?
    (c) Sketch the graph of the consumption function.

11. If the demand function for a good is given by $p = 400 - q^2$, what is the quantity demanded if the price is $300?

12. If the supply function for a good is given by $p = q^2 + 4q - 5$, at what price will 20 units be supplied?

13. Suppose the price of a commodity is $4 per unit. If the fixed costs are $500 and the variable costs amount to $2 per unit, find
    (a) the total revenue function.
    (b) the total cost function.
    (c) the profit function.

14. In problem 13, what is the revenue if 100 units are sold?

15. In problem 13, what is the cost if 100 units are produced and sold?

PART TWO
Linear Models

Warmup In this chapter you will need to work problems like the following. If you have difficulty with any problem, return to the section where that type of problem was introduced and refresh your memory before starting the chapter.

Problem Type	Introduced in Section	Used in Sections	Answer
Simplify: (a) $\dfrac{3-1}{4-(-2)}$ (b) $\dfrac{-1-3}{2-(-2)}$ (c) $\dfrac{3(-8)}{4}$ (d) $2\left(\dfrac{23}{9}\right)-5\left(\dfrac{2}{9}\right)$	0.1 Signed numbers	2.1, 2.2, 2.3, 2.4, 2.5, 2.6	(a) $\dfrac{1}{3}$ (b) -1 (c) -6 (d) 4
Identify the coefficient of x and the constant term for (a) $y = -\frac{3}{2}x + 2$ (b) $R(x) = 9x$ (c) $P(x) = 7x - 300$	0.3 Algebraic expressions	2.1, 2.3, 2.4, 2.5, 2.6	*Coeff. of x* *Const. term* (a) $-\frac{3}{2}$ 2 (b) 9 0 (c) 7 -300
Simplify: (a) $12\left(\dfrac{3x}{4} + 3\right)$ (b) $9x - (300 + 2x)$ (c) $-\frac{1}{5}[x - (-1)]$ (d) $2(2y + 3) + 3y$	0.3 Algebraic expressions	2.1, 2.2, 2.3, 2.4, 2.5, 2.6	(a) $9x + 36$ (b) $7x - 300$ (c) $-\frac{1}{5}x - \frac{1}{5}$ (d) $7y + 6$
Plot the following points: (a) $(9, 0)$ and $(-6, 5)$ (b) $(-2, 1)$ and $(4, 3)$	1.1 Graphing	2.2, 2.3, 2.4, 2.5, 2.6	(a) (b)

2

LINEAR FUNCTIONS

Linear equations are used by most businesses to predict such things as future revenues and costs. Linear functions are used in economics, biology, and sociology to relate data, and are also used to a large extent in accounting courses. Even if the available data for a problem do not exactly fit a linear equation, a function can frequently be estimated by using a special technique, called linear regression, to develop the "best" linear equation that will satisfy the data. We will use this technique in a later chapter.

Keynes used the linear function as the model for national consumption. In this chapter we discuss several important features of Keynesian analysis. We also formulate linear supply and demand functions and then determine the price and quantity at which market equilibrium occurs. We use linear revenue and cost functions to obtain profit functions and to find break-even points, and we solve problems involving linear equations from the social and life sciences.

2.1 Solution of Linear Equations in One Variable

Objective ■ To solve linear equations in one variable

In Section 1.1 we noted that equations of the form $y = mx + b$ are called **linear equations** because they have graphs that are straight lines.

The variables in a linear equation have the exponent 1 only and do not appear in the denominator of any fraction. For this reason linear equations are also called **first-degree equations.**

Two equations are said to be *equivalent* if they have exactly the same solution set. For example,

$$4x - 12 = 16$$
$$4x = 28$$

and
$$x = 7$$

are equivalent equations because they all have the same solution, 7. We can often solve a complicated linear equation by finding an equivalent equation whose solution is easily found. We use the following properties of equality to reduce an equation to a simple equivalent equation.

PROPERTIES	EXAMPLES
Substitution Property	
The equation formed by substituting one expression for an equal expression is equivalent to the original equation.	$3(x - 3) - \frac{1}{2}(4x - 18) = 4$ is equivalent to $3x - 9 - 2x + 9 = 4$ and to $x = 4$. We say the solution set is $\{4\}$, or the solution is 4.
Addition Property	
The equation formed by adding the same quantity to both sides of an equation is equivalent to the original equation.	$x - 4 = 6$ is equivalent to $x = 10$. $x + 5 = 12$ is equivalent to $x = 7$. (Subtracting 5 from both sides is equivalent to adding -5 to both sides.)
Multiplication Property	
The equation formed by multiplying the same nonzero quantity times both sides of an equation is equivalent to the original equation.	$\frac{1}{3}x = 6$ is equivalent to $x = 18$. $5x = 20$ is equivalent to $x = 4$. (Dividing both sides by 5 is equivalent to multiplying both sides by $\frac{1}{5}$.)

These three properties permit us to reduce any linear equation in one unknown to an equivalent equation whose solution is obvious. We may solve linear equations in one unknown using the following procedure:

PROCEDURE	EXAMPLE
	Solve: $\dfrac{3x}{4} + 3 = \dfrac{2(x - 1)}{6}$
1. If the equation contains fractions, multiply both sides by the least common denominator (LCD) of the fractions.	1. LCD is 12. The equivalent equation is $$12\left(\frac{3x}{4} + 3\right) = 12\left[\frac{2(x - 1)}{6}\right]$$

2. Remove any parentheses in the equation.

3. Perform any additions or subtractions to get all terms containing the variable on one side and all other terms on the other side.

4. Divide both sides of the equation by the coefficient of the variable.

5. Check the solution by substitution in the original equation.

2. $9x + 36 = 4x - 4$

3. (Subtract $4x$ from both sides.)

$$5x + 36 = -4$$

(Subtract 36 from both sides.)

$$5x = -40$$

4. (Divide both sides by 5.)

$$x = \frac{-40}{5} = -8$$

5. $\dfrac{3(-8)}{4} + 3 = \dfrac{2(-8 - 1)}{6}$ since

$$-\frac{24}{4} + 3 = -\frac{18}{6};$$

that is, since $-3 = -3$.

EXAMPLE 1   Solve $2(3y - 1) = 4(y - 5)$ for y.

Solution
1. No fractions are involved.
2. $6y - 2 = 4y - 20$ (Removing parentheses.)
3. $2y - 2 = -20$ (Subtracting $4y$ from both sides.)
   $2y = -18$ (Adding 2 to both sides.)
4. $y = -9$ (Dividing both sides by 2.)   □

EXAMPLE 2   The relation between degrees Celsius and degrees Fahrenheit is given by

$$F = \tfrac{9}{5}C + 32.$$

What Celsius temperature is equivalent to 176°F?

Solution   If $F = 176$, the equation is $176 = \tfrac{9}{5}C + 32$. Solving for C gives

$$880 = 9C + 160$$
$$720 = 9C$$
$$80 = C$$

Thus 80°C is equivalent to 176°F.   □

EXAMPLE 3   Suppose a firm's profit function for a good product is given by

$$P = \tfrac{5}{4}x - 300.$$

(a) How many units must be produced to make a profit of $150?
(b) Producing how many units will result in a profit of 0?

Solution   (a) Setting $P = 150$ and solving for x gives

$$150 = \tfrac{5}{4}x - 300$$
$$600 = 5x - 1200$$
$$1800 = 5x$$
$$x = 360.$$

(b) Setting $P = 0$ and solving for x gives

$$0 = \tfrac{5}{4}x - 300$$
$$0 = 5x - 1200$$
$$1200 = 5x$$
$$x = 240.$$

We say the firm breaks even at 240 units.   □

EXAMPLE 4   A bicycle costs the wholesaler $28.00. What will the retailer sell it for if the wholesaler's markup is 20% of the wholesale selling price and the retailer's markup is 30% of the retail selling price?

Solution   The wholesaler's markup of 20% means his or her cost ($28.00) is 80% of the wholesale selling price. Thus $28.00 = 0.80\,S_w$. Dividing both sides of the equation by 0.80 gives $35.00 = S_w$. (See Figure 2.1.) The wholesaler's selling price is $35.00, so the retailer's cost is $35.00. The retailer's markup is 30%, so the retail cost ($35.00) is 70% of the retail selling price. Thus $35.00 = 0.70\,S_r$. Dividing both sides of this equation by 0.70 gives $50.00 = S_r$. The retailer will sell the bicycle for $50.00.   □

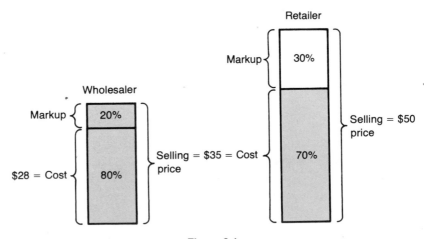

Figure 2.1

Exercise 2.1

Solve the following equations.

1. $x + 3 = 12$
2. $x + 8 = 7$
3. $y - 6 = 4$
4. $x - 4 = -2$
5. $2x - 3 = 5$
6. $4x + 2 = 5$
7. $2z + 5 = 3$
8. $3x + 2 = 2x + 4$
9. $2x - 4 = x + 1$
10. $5x - 12 = 12x$
11. $4x - 7 = 8x - 2$
12. $4x - 1 = 3(x - 1)$
13. $15 - x = 3(x - 1)$
14. $3(x - 2) = 4(3 - x)$

15. $3x + \dfrac{1}{2} = 8$
16. $\dfrac{x}{2} + 4 = \dfrac{1}{3}$

17. $\dfrac{5x}{2} - 4 = 2x - 7$
18. $\dfrac{2x}{3} - 1 = \dfrac{x - 2}{2}$

19. $\dfrac{5x - 1}{2} = 3(x - 1)$
20. $\dfrac{6x + 5}{2} = \dfrac{5(2 - x)}{3}$

21. $0.4x = 16$
22. $0.4x + 5 = 9$
23. $2x + 0.6 = 4$
24. $0.3x + 0.4 = 1$

APPLICATIONS

25. The manager of a hardware store marks all items so that the markup is 25% of the cost. How much would a saw sell for that costs the manager $25.50?

26. A toaster costs the Ace Department Store $22.74. If the store marks the toaster up by 40% of the selling price, what is the selling price?

27. A realtor sells a house and receives a 5% commission on its selling price. If the realtor's commission is $4250, what is the selling price of the house?

28. Joe bought a radio for $99.95. He paid $19.95 down and agreed to pay the balance plus a finance charge of $2.00 in three months. What rate of simple interest did he pay? (Use the formula interest = principal × rate × time.)

29. The equation $F = \frac{9}{5}C + 32$ describes the relation between temperature readings in Fahrenheit and Celsius. At what temperature will the two readings be the same?

30. A city had a population P at the beginning of a year. The birth rate during the year was 10 per thousand and the death rate was 12 per thousand (of the year's original population). During the year, 360 people moved into the city and 190 moved away. If the population at the end of the year is 30,110, what was the population at the beginning of the year?

31. In wildlife management, the capture-mark-recapture technique is used to estimate the populations of fish or birds in an area or to measure the infestation of insects such as Japanese beetles. Suppose 100 individuals of the species being studied are caught,

marked, and released, and one week later 100 more are caught. To estimate the total number of individuals, the following relationship is used:

$$\frac{\text{Total marked found in 2nd capture}}{\text{Total in 2nd capture}} = \frac{\text{Total number marked}}{\text{Total population}}.$$

(a) If in the second capture of 100, it is found that 3 are marked, what is the total population?
(b) Suppose that 1000 beetles are captured, marked, and released. Suppose further that in the second capture of 1000 it is found that 63 are marked. What is the population estimate?

32. It has been noted that for adults over 5 feet tall in the northeast United States, their weight is related to their height according to

$$3w + 110 = 11(h - 20)$$

where w is measured in pounds and h is measured in inches. Use the formula above to answer the following.
(a) Find the weight of an adult whose height is 5 feet, 6 inches.
(b) Find the height of adults weighing 160 pounds.

33. A room air conditioner costs the wholesaler $154.98. If the wholesaler's markup is 10% of the wholesale selling price and if the retailer's markup is 30% of the retail selling price, for what does the retailer sell the air conditioner?

34. An electric mixer retails for $48.54, which includes a markup of 40% for the retailer and a markup of 20% for the wholesaler. If these markups are based on selling price,
(a) what did the mixer cost the retailer?
(b) what did the mixer cost the wholesaler?

2.2 Graphing Linear Equations

Objectives   ■ To graph linear equations by plotting points
■ To graph linear equations using intercepts

One very special function is the **linear function.** In this type of function the rate of change of the dependent variable with respect to the independent variable is constant. A linear function is a function of the form $f(x) = ax + b$ or $y = ax + b$, where a and b are constants.

The graph of a linear function may be drawn by plotting the points whose coordinates (x, y) satisfy the equation $y = ax + b$. Because the graph of linear function is always a straight line, only two points are required to determine its graph (two points determine a straight line). A third point should be plotted as a check on the graph.

EXAMPLE 1   Graph the equation $3x + y = 9$.

Solution   1. Plot any two points that satisfy the equation.
            (a) If $x = 0$, $y = 9$, so $(0, 9)$ is one point.
            (b) If $x = 5$, $y = -6$, so $(5, -6)$ is another point.
          2. Draw a straight line through the points. (See Figure 2.2.)
          3. Plot a third point as a check: If $x = 2$, $y = 3$, so $(2, 3)$ should be on the line.

                                                                                    □

EXAMPLE 2   Graph $x = 2$.

Solution   We may think of this equation as $x + 0y = 2$, which indicates that $x = 2$ for all values of y. That is, y can have any value and x will still be 2. (See Figure 2.3.)

                                                                                    □

The two points where the graph of a linear equation crosses the x and y axes are called the **x-intercept** and the **y intercept,** respectively. These two points are usually easy to find, so they are frequently used to determine the graph of a linear equation.

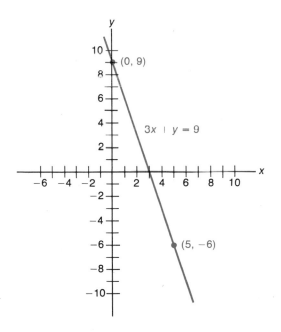

Figure 2.2

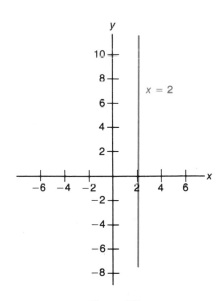

Figure 2.3

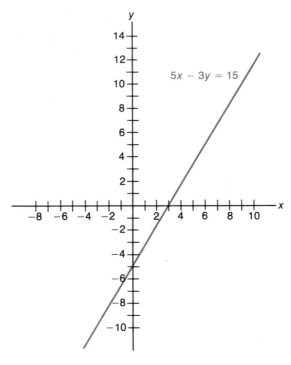

Figure 2.4

EXAMPLE 3   Find the x-intercept and y-intercept of the graph of $5x - 3y = 15$, and use them to sketch the graph of the equation.

Solution   Because the x-intercept is on the x-axis, the y-coordinate of the point is 0. Substituting 0 for y in $5x - 3y = 15$ and solving gives $x = 3$. Thus the graph meets the x-axis at $(3, 0)$. We say the x-intercept is 3.

Because the y-intercept is on the y-axis, the x-coordinate is 0. Substituting $x = 0$ into the equation gives $y = -5$. The line crosses the y-axis at $(0, -5)$. We say the y-intercept is -5.

A third point such as $(6, 5)$ can be used as a check. The graph is shown in Figure 2.4.   □

The intercept method may not always be the most convenient method to use when graphing a linear equation, especially if the intercepts are fractional values (for example, a y-intercept of $\frac{13}{25}$ would be difficult to plot). It should also be pointed out that the intercept method will not work if the line passes through the origin, because there would be an intersection at only one point, $(0, 0)$. If the intercepts are both very close to the origin, the resulting graph may be inaccurate.

Exercise 2.2

Graph the following linear equations.

1. $y = 6x - 2$ 2. $y = 2x + 8$
3. $y = 4x + 3$ 4. $y = 2x - 1$

5. $y = \dfrac{5 - x}{2}$ 6. $y = \dfrac{7 - x}{3}$

7. $3x - y = 6$ 8. $5x - y = 10$
9. $2x - 3y = 12$ 10. $3x + 2y = 0$
11. $6x + 5y = 9$ 12. $4x + 5y = 8$
13. $y = 3$ 14. $x = -5$

Use the intercept method to graph the following.

15. $3x - 2y = 12$ 16. $5x - 4y = -20$
17. $4x + 2y = 8$ 18. $5x - 3y = 15$
19. $6x - 3y = 12$ 20. $x - 3y = 9$
21. $2x - y = 4$ 22. $5x + 2y = 10$

APPLICATIONS

23. The fish population y in a certain river is related to the tons of pollutants x according to the following:

$$y = 100,000 - 1500x.$$

    (a) Sketch the graph of this equation.
    (b) Suppose that 17.5 tons of pollutants is deemed critical. How many fish would be in the stream at the critical level of pollution?

24. The activity of particles in a chemical reaction (such as digestion) or in the diffusion of a solution is related to the concentration of the particles according to the formula

$$A = KC,$$

where A is the activity, C is the concentration, and K is the fraction of the concentration that is effective in determining the diffusion or the chemical reaction.
    (a) Sketch the equation if $K = 1$.
    (b) Sketch the equation if $K = 0.7$.

25. Body heat loss due to convection depends on a number of factors. If H_c is body-heat loss due to convection, A_c is the exposed surface area of the body, $T_s - T_a$ is skin temperature — air temperature, and K_c is the convection coefficient (determined by air velocity and so on), then we have

$$H_c = K_c A_c (T_s - T_a).$$

When $K_c = 1$, $A_c = 1$, $T_s = 90$, the equation is

$$H_c = 90 - T_a.$$

Sketch the graph.

26. The rate of oxygen consumption of the blood x measures the cardiac output (blood flow through the lungs) y by

$$y = \frac{x}{A - V} = \left(\frac{1}{A - V}\right)x,$$

where A is the arterial concentration of oxygen and V is the venous concentration of oxygen. Sketch the graph for the above if $1/(A - V) = \frac{3}{4}$.

2.3 Slope of a Line

Objectives   ■ To find the slope of a line from its graph and from its equation
■ To find marginal cost, revenue, and profit, given linear total cost, total revenue, and profit functions

The cost of producing one additional unit at any level of production is called **marginal cost.** If the cost function is linear, the marginal cost will be the same at all levels of production. For example,

$$C = 2x + 10$$

is the cost function for a good whose fixed cost is $10 and whose variable cost is $2 per unit. Because producing one more unit adds $2 to the cost, the marginal cost is $2. Looking at the graph of this function (Figure 2.5), we see that the line

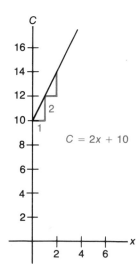

Figure 2.5

rises 2 units for each unit it moves to the right. This ratio of rise to run is called the **slope** of a line. The slope represents the rate of change in the total cost function. We could also use points on the graph to find the slope of this line. To do this, we divide the change in C by the change in x for any two points on the line. For example, the points $(1, 12)$ and $(3, 16)$ lie on the line that represents the graph of $C = 2x + 10$. The C-value changes $+4$ units (from 12 to 16) while the x-value changes $+2$ units (from 1 to 3). Thus the slope, symbolized by m, is

$$m = \frac{\text{change in } C}{\text{change in } x} = \frac{4}{2} = 2.$$

Slope of a Line   In general, if a line passes through the points $P_1(x_1, y_1)$ and $P_2(x_2, y_2)$ (see Figure 2.6), its **slope** is found by using the formula

$$m = \frac{y_2 - y_1}{x_2 - x_1}.$$

We may use this formula to find the slope of any line (that is not vertical) if we know the coordinates of two points on the line.

We will see that it does not matter which point we choose as $P_2(x_2, y_2)$ in using the formula.

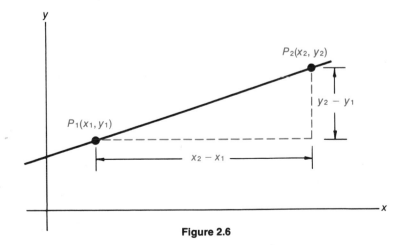

Figure 2.6

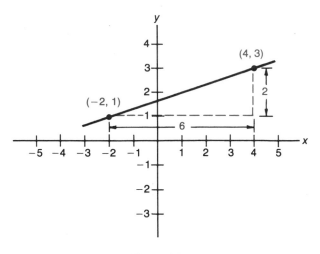

Figure 2.7

EXAMPLE 1   Find the slope of the line that passes through $(-2, 1)$ and $(4, 3)$.

Solution   The graph of this line is shown in Figure 2.7. The slope is

$$m = \frac{3 - 1}{4 - (-2)} = \frac{2}{6} = \frac{1}{3}.$$

This means that a point 3 units to the right and 1 unit up from any point on the line is also on the line. Thus if $(-2, 1)$ is on the line, $(-2 + 3, 1 + 1) = (1, 2)$ is also on the line.   □

EXAMPLE 2   Find the slope of the line passing through $(-2, 3)$ and $(2, -1)$.

Solution   The graph of this line is shown in Figure 2.8. The slope is

$$m = \frac{-1 - 3}{2 - (-2)} = -\frac{4}{4} = -1 \text{ or } -\frac{1}{1}.$$

This slope tells us that a point that is *down* 1 unit and 1 unit to the *right* of any point on the line is also on the line.   □

Note that if we interchange the points in the formula, we will get the same slope, *as long as* we find the change in y in the numerator and the *corresponding* change in x in the denominator. That is, we can also find the slope in Example 2 by $m = \dfrac{3 - (-1)}{-2 - 2} = -\dfrac{4}{4} = -1$.

From the previous examples we see that the slope describes the direction of a line, as follows:

1. The slope is positive if the line slopes upward toward the right.

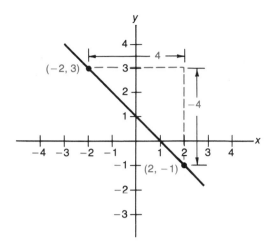

Figure 2.8

2. The slope is negative if the line slopes downward toward the right.

Two additional facts should be stated:

3. The slope of a horizontal line is 0 because the y values are the same for any two points on the line, making $y_2 - y_1 = 0$.
4. The slope of a vertical line is undefined, because $x_2 - x_1$ would equal 0, and division by 0 is undefined.

We can find the slope of a line from its equation if it is written in the proper form. The equation $y = mx + b$ is called the **slope-intercept form** of the equation of a line. The coefficient of x, namely m, is the slope of the line, and the constant b is the value of y where the graph crosses the y-axis (b is called the y-intercept).

If we reconsider the total cost function $C = 2x + 10$, we see that the equation is in slope-intercept form. We noted earlier that the slope of the graph of this function is 2. As Figure 2.5 shows, the graph crosses the C-axis at 10.

For a linear total cost function the **slope** represents the *rate of change in total cost* with respect to the number of units produced, or the **marginal cost.** If we are given a linear total revenue function, then the slope of the line represents the *rate of change in the total revenue function.* This rate of change is called the **marginal revenue.** The slope of a linear profit function is the **marginal profit.**

EXAMPLE 3   If a total revenue function is $R = 7x$, what is the marginal revenue?

Solution $R = 7x$ is in slope-intercept form with $m = 7$ and $b = 0$. The slope represents the marginal revenue, which is $7. That is, the sale of each additional unit will produce an additional $7 in revenue at all levels of production. Note that $b = 0$ indicates that if nothing is sold ($x = 0$), no revenue results.   □

EXAMPLE 4   If a total profit function is given by $P = 6x - 300$, find the marginal profit.

Solution   The profit function is in slope-intercept form, with $m = 6$ and $b = -300$. Thus the marginal profit is \$6. That is, the sale of each extra unit results in \$6 additional profit, at all levels of production. Also note that $b = -300$ indicates that when no items have been sold $(x = 0)$, the profit is $-\$300$; that is, there is a loss of \$300. □

EXAMPLE 5   If the total revenue function is given by $R(x) = 9x$ (dollars) and the total cost function is given by $C(x) = 300 + 2x$ (dollars), find the profit function and the marginal profit.

Solution   The profit function is $P(x) = 9x - (300 + 2x)$ or $P(x) = 7x - 300$. The profit function is linear, so the coefficient of x (the slope) is the marginal profit. Thus the marginal profit is \$7. □

These examples give us an idea of the importance of slope and the convenience of slope-intercept form. When a linear equation does not appear in this form, the equation can be solved for y, which gives it in the slope-intercept form.

EXAMPLE 6   Find the slope of the line whose equation is $3x + 2y = 4$.

Solution   We must solve the equation for y to put the equation in the slope-intercept form:

$$2y = -3x + 4, \quad \text{or} \quad y = -\tfrac{3}{2}x + 2.$$

Thus the slope is $-\tfrac{3}{2}$. The y-intercept is 2. □

Exercise 2.3

Find the slopes of the lines passing through the following points.

1. $(1, 2)$ and $(0, 0)$
2. $(0, 0)$ and $(3, 4)$
3. $(-1, 3)$ and $(0, 6)$
4. $(-1, 2)$ and $(2, -3)$
5. $(2, 1)$ and $(3, -4)$
6. $(-1, -2)$ and $(-2, -3)$
7. $(3, 2)$ and $(-1, -6)$
8. $(-4, 2)$ and $(2, 4)$
9. $(7, 3)$ and $(-6, 2)$
10. $(10, 2)$ and $(5, 7)$

Find the slopes and y-intercepts of the lines whose equations are given in problems 11–24.

11. $y = 4x - 6$
12. $y = 3x$
13. $x = 4y$
14. $x = 3y + 6$
15. $y = 3$
16. $y = -2$
17. $y = -\tfrac{1}{2}x - \tfrac{2}{3}$
18. $y = \tfrac{2}{3}x + \tfrac{1}{2}$
19. $x = -8$
20. $x = -\tfrac{1}{2}$
21. $2x - y = 3$
22. $2x + y = 2$
23. $2x + 3y = 6$
24. $4x - y = 3$

APPLICATIONS

25. If the total cost for producing a commodity is $C(x) = 6x + 3000$ (in dollars), what is the marginal cost?

26. If the total cost function for a commodity is $C(x) = 5x + 250$, what will be the cost of increasing production by one unit?

27. If a manufacturer receives $84 for each item produced,
    (a) what is the total revenue function?
    (b) what is the marginal revenue?

28. If the total revenue function for a product is $R(x) = 15x$ (in dollars), what is the marginal revenue?

29. If the total revenue function for a product is given by $R(x) = 10x$ (in dollars) and the total cost function is given by $C(x) = 400 + 5x$,
    (a) what is the profit function?
    (b) what is the marginal profit?

30. If the total revenue for a commodity is given by $R = 60x$ and the total cost is $C = 250 + 13x$,
    (a) what is the amount of profit that will be added by the production and sale of one additional unit?
    (b) what is the marginal profit?

31. Given a linear cost function $C(x) = 5x + 250$.
    (a) What is the slope and C-intercept?
    (b) What is the marginal cost, and what does it mean?
    (c) What are the fixed costs?
    (d) How are your answers to (a) and to (b) and (c) related?
    (e) What is the cost of producing *one more* item if 50 are currently being produced? What if 100 are currently being produced?

32. Given a linear cost function $C(x) = 21.75x + 4800$, answer parts (a) (e) of problem 31.

33. Given a linear revenue function $R = 27x$.
    (a) What is the slope?
    (b) What is the marginal revenue, and what does it mean?
    (c) What is the revenue received from selling *one more* item if 50 are currently being sold? If 100 are being sold?

34. Repeat problem 33 for $R = 38.95x$.

35. What is the R-intercept for the revenue functions in problems 33 and 34? Explain why these are the same. Is this always the case? Explain.

36. Given the linear profit function $P = 51x - 710$.
    (a) What is the slope and P-intercept of the profit function?
    (b) What is the marginal profit and what does it mean?
    (c) What is the significance of the P-intercept?
    (d) How much profit is expected if 20 items are produced and sold?
    (e) How much *additional* profit would be expected if production and sales increased from 20 to 21?

37. Let $C(x) = 5x + 250$ and $R(x) = 27x$.
    (a) Write the profit function $P(x)$.

(b) What is the slope of the profit function?

(c) What is the marginal profit?

(d) Interpret the marginal profit. What does this tell the manager of the firm with this profit function, if the objective is to make the most profit?

38. Given $C(x) = \$21.95x + 1400$ and $R(x) = 10x$. Find the profit function.

(a) What is marginal profit, and what does it mean?

(b) What should a firm with these cost, revenue, and profit functions do? (Hint: Graph the profit function and see where it goes.)

2.4 Using Slopes in Equation Writing and Graphing

Objectives
- To graph a line, given its slope and y-intercept or its slope and one point on the line
- To write the equation of a line, given information about its graph
- To write the equations of linear total cost, total revenue, and profit functions, using information given about the functions

If we are given the slope and y-intercept of a line, we can use the following procedure to sketch the graph of the line.

PROCEDURE	EXAMPLE
To graph a line using the slope-intercept method:	Sketch the graph of the line which has slope 3 and y-intercept -2.
1. Plot the intercept on the y-axis.	1. Plot the point $(0, -2)$. (See Figure 2.9.)
2. Write the slope as a fraction b/a. If the fraction is negative, place the minus sign in the numerator.	2. $m = 3 = \frac{3}{1}$
3. Plot a point that is a units to the right and b units above the y-intercept if b is positive or b units below the y-intercept if b is negative.	3. Plot the point that is 1 unit to the right and 3 units above the point $(0, -2)$. The point is $(1, 1)$. (See Figure 2.9.)
4. Draw the line through the points, using a third point as a check.	4. Figure 2.9 gives the graph.

EXAMPLE 1   Graph the line that has slope $-\frac{1}{2}$ and y-intercept 4.

Solution   We plot the y-intercept, $(0, 4)$, first. The point $(2, 3)$ is on the line, because it is 2 units to the right and 1 unit below $(0, 4)$. A third point (for a check) is plotted at $(4, 2)$. The graph is shown in Figure 2.10.   □

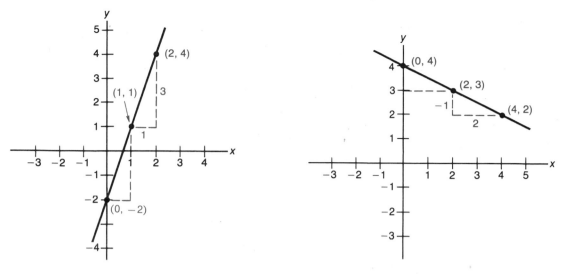

Figure 2.9   **Figure 2.10**

It is also possible to graph a straight line if we know its slope and a point that it passes through. We simply plot the point given and then use the slope to plot other points.

EXAMPLE 2   Graph the line that passes through $(-1, 2)$ with slope $\frac{2}{3}$.

Solution   We plot the point $(-1, 2)$ and then plot a second point, $(2, 4)$, by moving 3 units to the right and 2 units above $(-1, 2)$. Note that this procedure is the same as that used in Example 1 except we start at the given point rather than the y-intercept. We can also write the slope 2/3 as $-2/-3$, which implies that we can move 3 units to the left and 2 units down to plot the point $(-4, 0)$. The graph is shown in Figure 2.11.   □

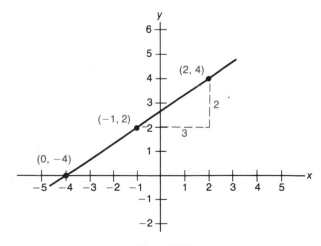

Figure 2.11

As the preceding examples show, the graph of a line is completely determined if its slope and intercept are known, or if its slope and a point on it are known. This same information can be used to determine the equation of the line. It is often more useful to have the equation than the graph because calculations are easily made with the equation.

> We use the **slope-intercept form,** $y = mx + b$, of the equation of a line to write the equation if we know the slope and the y-intercept.

EXAMPLE 3   Write the equation of the line with slope $\frac{1}{2}$ and y-intercept 3.

Solution   We are given $m = \frac{1}{2}$ and $b = 3$. Using these values in $y = mx + b$ gives $y = \frac{1}{2}x + 3$. The **general form** of the equation of a line is $ax + by + c = 0$, so the general form of this equation is $x - 2y + 6 = 0$.   □

> If we know the slope of a line and a point (x_1, y_1) on it, we can use the **point-slope form,** $y - y_1 = m(x - x_1)$ to write the equation of the line.

We note that this formula comes directly from the formula for slope, using the fact that the slope between a fixed point (x_1, y_1) and any point (x, y) on the line is

$$m = \frac{y - y_1}{x - x_1}.$$

EXAMPLE 4   Write the equation of the line passing through $(1, -2)$ with slope $\frac{2}{3}$.

Solution   Here $m = \frac{2}{3}$, $x_1 = 1$, and $y_1 = -2$. So the equation of the line is $y - (-2) = \frac{2}{3}(x - 1)$. Writing this equation in general form gives $2x - 3y - 8 = 0$.   □

EXAMPLE 5   Write the equation of the line passing through $(-1, 3)$ and $(4, 2)$.

Solution   Using the two points, we can find the slope of the line.

$$m = \frac{2 - 3}{4 - (-1)} = -\frac{1}{5}.$$

Using the slope of this line and *either* of the two points in the point-slope form of the equation, we can write the equation. Using $(-1, 3)$, we get $y - 3 = -\frac{1}{5}[x - (-1)]$, or $x + 5y - 14 = 0$. Note that using the point $(4, 2)$ would result in the same general equation of the line.   □

Table 2.1 summarizes the forms of equations of lines.

Table 2.1 FORMS OF LINEAR EQUATIONS

General form	$ax + by + c = 0$
Point-slope form	$y - y_1 = m(x - x_1)$
Slope-intercept form	$y = mx + b$
Vertical line	$x = a$
Horizontal line	$y = b$

We have seen that the slope of a linear total cost function is the marginal cost, and the C-intercept (where C lies along the vertical axis of the graph) represents the fixed cost. Thus, if we know that a linear cost function has a marginal cost of $30 and a fixed cost of $1000, we can write the equation that defines the function:

$$C = 30x + 1000.$$

Note that when total cost functions are linear, the marginal cost is the same as the variable cost. This is not the case, however, if the functions are not linear, as we shall see later.

EXAMPLE 6 Suppose the profit function for a good is linear, and the marginal profit is $5. If the profit is $200 when 125 units are sold, write the equation of the profit function.

Solution The marginal profit gives us the slope of the line representing the profit function. Using this slope and the point (125, 200), we have the equation

$$P - 200 = 5(x - 125),$$

or

$$P = 5x - 425.$$ ▫

Exercise 2.4

Write the equation and sketch the graph of each line with the given slope and y-intercept.

1. slope 3 and y-intercept -2
2. slope 2 and y-intercept 3
3. slope $\frac{1}{2}$ and y-intercept 3
4. slope $\frac{2}{3}$ and y-intercept -1
5. slope -2 and y-intercept $\frac{1}{2}$
6. slope -1 and y-intercept $\frac{3}{2}$
7. slope 0 and y-intercept -4
8. slope 0 and y-intercept 0

In problems 9–16, graph the line that passes through the given point and has the slope indicated.

9. $(2, 0)$ with slope $\frac{1}{2}$
10. $(0, 0)$ with slope 2
11. $(-1, 3)$ with slope -2
12. $(1, 1)$ with slope $-\frac{1}{3}$
13. $(2, 2)$ with slope -2
14. $(3, -1)$ with slope 1
15. $(1, 1)$ with 0 slope
16. $(-1, 1)$ with undefined slope
17. Graph the equation $y = 4x + 3$.
18. Graph the equation $y = -\frac{1}{2}x - 2$.

Write the equations of the lines passing through the following pairs of points.

19. $(3, 2)$ and $(-1, -6)$ 20. $(-4, 2)$ and $(2, 4)$
21. $(7, 3)$ and $(-6, 2)$ 22. $(10, 2)$ and $(5, 7)$
23. $(10, 2)$ and $(5, 2)$ 24. $(3, 6)$ and $(3, 8)$

APPLICATIONS

25. Suppose the total cost function for a good is linear, that the marginal cost is $27, and that the fixed costs amount to $3000. Write the equation of this cost function and graph it.

26. Suppose the total revenue function for a good is linear, with marginal revenue $30. Write the total revenue function, assuming the revenue from 0 units is $0.

27. Suppose that the production and sale of each additional unit of a good results in an increase of $10 in profit, regardless of the level of production. If the sale of 1000 units gives a profit $4000, write the equation of the profit function.

28. If the information regarding cost and revenue given in problems 25 and 26 refers to the same good, write the profit function for the good.

29. Suppose there is a linear relationship between the length (in centimeters) of a certain species of fish and the number of eggs laid. If it is known that a fish of 100 cm lays 20,000 eggs and a fish of 50 cm lays 6000 eggs, write an equation that gives the number of eggs as a function of the length of the fish.

30. Write the equation of linear relationship between temperature in Celsius (C) and Fahrenheit (F) if water freezes at 0°C and 32°F and boils at 100°C and 212°F.

31. Each day, a young person should sleep 8 hours plus $\frac{1}{4}$ hour for each year that the person is under 18 years of age. Assuming the relation is linear, write the equation relating hours of sleep y and age x.

2.5   Solution of Linear Equations in Two Variables

Objective   ■ To solve systems of linear equations in two unknowns

In the previous sections we graphed linear equations in two unknowns and observed that the graphs are straight lines. Each point on the graph represents a pair of values for x and y that satisfies the equation. We can see that there are an infinite number of values for x and y that will satisfy the equation. Now suppose we have two equations in two unknowns and we wish to find the solution(s) that satisfies both equations. We can find the solution by graphing the equations and noting their point(s) of intersection. If the graphs intersect at a point, both equations are satisfied by the same pair of values and they thus have a common solution. The equations are referred to as a **system of equations,** and values that satisfy both equations are the solutions to the system.

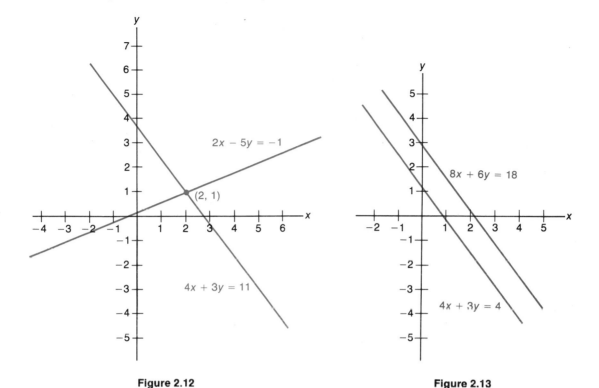

Figure 2.12

Figure 2.13

EXAMPLE 1   Use graphing to find the solution of $4x + 3y = 11$ and $2x - 5y = -1$.

Solution   The graphs of the two equations intersect (meet) at the point (2, 1). (See Figure 2.12.) The solution of the system is $x = 2$, $y = 1$. Note that these values satisfy both equations.   □

If the graphs of two equations are parallel lines, they have no point in common and thus no common solution. Such a system of equations is called **inconsistent.**

EXAMPLE 2   Find the solution, if it exists, for $4x + 3y = 4$ and $8x + 6y = 18$.

Solution   The graphs appear to be parallel (see Figure 2.13). We will show algebraically that they have no point in common, so there is no solution to the system. The system is inconsistent.   □

It is also possible to graph two equations and obtain only one line. When this happens the equations are equivalent, and represent a solution to the system.

While graphical methods for solving a system of equations illustrate what the solution represents, it is not very practical to solve systems with graphs. There are algebraic methods for solving the equations, including elimination of one of the variables by **substitution.** The procedure follows.

PROCEDURE	EXAMPLE
To solve a system of two equations in two unknowns by substitution:	Solve the system containing $2x + 3y = 4$ and $x - 2y = 3$.
1. Solve one of the equations for one of the variables in terms of the other.	1. $x = 2y + 3$
2. Substitute this expression in the other equation to give one equation in one unknown.	2. $2(2y + 3) + 3y = 4$
3. Solve this linear equation for the unknown.	3. $4y + 6 + 3y = 4$ $\quad 7y = -2$ $\quad y = -\dfrac{2}{7}$
4. Substitute this solution in the equation in step 1 or in one of the original equations to solve for the other unknown.	4. $x = 2\left(-\dfrac{2}{7}\right) + 3$, so $x = \dfrac{17}{7}$ or $x - 2\left(-\dfrac{2}{7}\right) = 3$, so $x = \dfrac{17}{7}$
5. Check the solution by substituting for x and y in both original equations.	5. $2\left(\dfrac{17}{7}\right) + 3\left(-\dfrac{2}{7}\right) = 4$ or $\dfrac{34}{7} - \dfrac{6}{7} = 4$ and $\dfrac{17}{7} - 2\left(-\dfrac{2}{7}\right) = 3$.

EXAMPLE 3   Solve the system

$$\begin{cases} 4x + 5y = 18 & (1) \\ x - 3y = -4 & (2) \end{cases}$$

Solution

1. $x = 3y - 4$ [Solving for x in equation (2)]
2. $4(3y - 4) + 5y = 18$ [Substituting for x in equation (1)]
3. $12y - 16 + 5y = 18$ (Solving for y)
                 $17y = 34$
                     $y = 2$
4. $x = 3(2) - 4$ [Substituting $y = 2$ in equation (2)
      $x = 2$ and solving for x]
5. $4(2) + 5(2) = 18$ and $(2) - 3(2) = -4$ (Checking)

Note that if we graphed the two equations, they would intersect at the point $(2, 2)$.   □

We can also eliminate one of the variables in a system by **addition** or **subtraction.**

We summarize this procedure as follows.

PROCEDURE	EXAMPLE

To solve a system of two equations in two unknowns by addition or subtraction:

Solve the system
$$\begin{cases} 2x - 5y = 4 \\ x + 2y = 3 \end{cases}$$

1. If necessary, multiply one or both equations by a nonzero number which will make the coefficients of one of the variables identical, except perhaps for signs.

1. $2x - 5y = 4$
   $-2x - 4y = -6$

2. Add or subtract the equations to eliminate one of the variables.

2. Adding gives
$$0x - 9y = -2$$

3. Solve for the variable in the resulting equation.

3. $y = \dfrac{2}{9}$

4. Substitute the solution into one of the original equations and solve for the remaining variable.

4. $2x - 5\left(\dfrac{2}{9}\right) = 4$

$$2x = 4 + \frac{10}{9} = \frac{36}{9} + \frac{10}{9}$$

$$x = \frac{23}{9}$$

5. Check the solutions in both original equations.

5. $\dfrac{23}{9} + 2\left(\dfrac{2}{9}\right) = 3$

$$2\left(\frac{23}{9}\right) - 5\left(\frac{2}{9}\right) = 4$$

EXAMPLE 4   Solve the system

$$\begin{cases} 2x - 7y = 4 & (1) \\ 3x + 2y = 3 & (2) \end{cases}$$

Solution

1. $6x - 21y = 12$
   $-6x - 4y = -6$ [Multiplying equation (1) by 3 and equation (2) by -2]

2. $-25y = 6$ (Adding the resulting equations to eliminate x)

3. $y = -\dfrac{6}{25}$ (or -0.24)   (Solving for y)

4. $2x - 7\left(-\dfrac{6}{25}\right) = 4$ [Substituting for y in equation (1) and solving for x]

$$2x = 4 - \frac{42}{25}$$

$$2x = \frac{58}{25}$$

$$x = \frac{29}{25} \text{ (or } 1.16\text{)}$$

5. Checking solutions in both equations:

$$3\left(\frac{29}{25}\right) + 2\left(-\frac{6}{25}\right) = 3 \text{ since } \frac{87}{25} - \frac{12}{25} = \frac{75}{25}$$

$$2\left(\frac{29}{25}\right) - 7\left(-\frac{6}{25}\right) = 4 \text{ since } \frac{58}{25} + \frac{42}{25} = \frac{100}{25} \qquad \square$$

EXAMPLE 5   Solve the system

$$\begin{cases} 4x + 3y = 4 \\ 8x + 6y = 18 \end{cases}$$

Solution   1. $-8x - 6y = -8$
                    $8x + 6y = 18$

2. $0x - 0y = 10$; that is, $0 = 10$. The system is solved when $0 = 10$.

This is impossible, so there are no solutions to the system. The equations are inconsistent. (Their graphs are parallel lines; see Figure 2.13.) $\qquad \square$

EXAMPLE 6   Solve the system

$$\begin{cases} 6x - 2y = 4 \\ 3x - y = 2 \end{cases}$$

Solution   1. $6x - 2y = 4$
                    $6x - 2y = 4$

2. $0x - 0y = 0$; that is, $0 = 0$. The equations have the same solutions when $0 = 0$.

This is an identity, so the two equations share infinitely many solutions. The equations are dependent (their graphs coincide, or are the same). $\qquad \square$

EXAMPLE 7   A person has $200,000 invested, part at 9% and part at 8%. If the total yearly income from the two investments is $17,200, how much is invested at 9%?

Solution   If x represents the amount invested at 9% and y represents the amount invested at 8%, then

$$x + y = 200,000$$

and

$$0.09x + 0.08y = 17,200.$$

We solve these equations as follows:

$$\begin{aligned}
-8x - 8y &= -1,600,000 \\
\underline{9x + 8y} &= \underline{\;\;1,720,000} \\
x\;\;\;\;\; &= \;\;\;\;120,000
\end{aligned}$$

Thus $120,000 is invested at 9%.   □

In many businesses, various departments may charge other departments a part of their total monthly costs because of services they perform. For example, suppose an engineering department's *total cost* for a month is made up of *direct costs* for running the department plus *indirect costs* it must pay the computer department for its services. If the engineering department in turn charges the computer department for services, the computer department's total costs will also consist of direct costs and indirect costs.

EXAMPLE 8   Suppose the engineering department of a firm charges 20% of its total monthly costs to the computer department, and that the computer department charges 25% of its total monthly costs to the engineering department. If during a given month the direct costs were $11,750 for the engineering department and $10,000 for the computer department, what are the total costs of each department?

Solution   Let x be the total costs of the engineering department and y the total costs of the computer department. Then the total costs of the engineering department will be the sum of its direct costs and the amount it was charged by the computer department:

$$x = 11,750 + 0.25y.$$

Similarly, the total costs for the computer department will be the sum of its direct costs and the amount it was charged by the engineering department:

$$y = 10,000 + 0.20x.$$

To find the total costs for each department we must solve the system

$$\begin{cases} x = 11,750 + 0.25y \\ y = 10,000 + 0.20x. \end{cases}$$

Substituting for x in $y = 10,000 + 0.20x$, we have

$$\begin{aligned}
y &= 10,000 + 0.20(11,750 + 0.25y) \\
y &= 10,000 + 2350 + 0.05y \\
0.95y &= 12,350 \\
y &= 13,000.
\end{aligned}$$

Then $x = 11,750 + 0.25(13,000) = 15,000.$

Therefore the total costs for the engineering department are $15,000 and the total costs for the computer department are $13,000.   □

Exercise 2.5

Solve the following systems of equations by using graphical methods.

1. $\begin{cases} 4x + y = 5 \\ 3x - 2y = 1 \end{cases}$
2. $\begin{cases} x - 2y = -1 \\ 2x + y = 8 \end{cases}$

3. $\begin{cases} 4x - 2y = 4 \\ x - 2y = -2 \end{cases}$
4. $\begin{cases} x - y = -2 \\ 2x + y = -1 \end{cases}$

5. $\begin{cases} 3x - y = 10 \\ 6x - 2y = 5 \end{cases}$
6. $\begin{cases} 2x - y = 3 \\ 4x - 2y = 6 \end{cases}$

Solve the following systems of equations by using substitution, addition, or subtraction.

7. $\begin{cases} 4x - y = 3 \\ 2x + 3y = 19 \end{cases}$
8. $\begin{cases} 5x - 3y = 9 \\ x + 2y = 7 \end{cases}$

9. $\begin{cases} 2x - y = 2 \\ 3x + 4y = 6 \end{cases}$
10. $\begin{cases} x - y = 4 \\ 3x - 2y = 5 \end{cases}$

11. $\begin{cases} 3x - 2y = 6 \\ 4y = 8 \end{cases}$
12. $\begin{cases} 5x - 2y = 4 \\ 2x - 3y = 5 \end{cases}$

13. $\begin{cases} x - 2y = 4 \\ 3x + 2y = 6 \end{cases}$
14. $\begin{cases} 3m + 2n = 2 \\ 3m - 3n = 1 \end{cases}$

15. $\begin{cases} 3u - 2v = 5 \\ u + 3v = 6 \end{cases}$
16. $\begin{cases} 6x - 3y = 6 \\ 2x - y = 3 \end{cases}$

17. $\begin{cases} 0.2x - 0.3y = 4 \\ 2.3x - y = 1.2 \end{cases}$
18. $\begin{cases} 0.5x + y = 3 \\ 0.3x + 0.2y = 6 \end{cases}$

19. $\begin{cases} 4x + 6y = 4 \\ 2x + 3y = 2 \end{cases}$
20. $\begin{cases} \dfrac{x}{4} + \dfrac{3y}{4} = 12 \\ \dfrac{y}{2} - \dfrac{x}{3} = -4 \end{cases}$

21. $\begin{cases} \dfrac{x + y}{4} = 2 \\ \dfrac{y - 1}{x} = 6 \end{cases}$

APPLICATIONS

22. A bank loaned $118,500 to a company for the development of two products. If the loan for product A was for $34,500 more than that for product B, how much was loaned for each product?

23. A woman has $23,500 invested in two rental properties. One earns 5% on the investment and the other yields 6%. Her total income from the two properties is $1275. How much is her income from each property?

24. Mr. Jackson borrowed money from his bank and on his life insurance to start a business. His interest rate on the bank loan is 5% and his rate on the insurance loan is 6%. If the total amount borrowed is $10,000 and his total yearly interest payment is $545, how much did he borrow from the bank?

25. Each ounce of substance A supplies 5% of the required nutrition a patient needs. Substance B supplies 12% of the required nutrition per ounce. If digestive restrictions require that the ratio of substance A to substance B be 3/5, how many ounces of each substance should be in the diet to provide 100% of the required nutrition?

26. A glass of skim milk supplies 0.1 mg of iron and 8.5 g of protein. A quarter pound of lean red meat provides 3.4 mg of iron and 22 g of protein. If a person on a special diet is to have 7.15 mg of iron and 73.75 g of protein, how many glasses of skim milk and how many quarter-pound servings of meat would provide this?

27. Bacteria of species A and species B are kept in a single test tube, where they are fed two nutrients. Each day the test tube is supplied with 10,600 units of the first nutrient and 19,650 units of the second nutrient. Each bacteria of species A requires 2 units of the first nutrient and 3 units of the second, and each bacteria of species B requires 1 unit of the first nutrient and 4 units of the second. What populations of each species can coexist in the test tube so that all the nutrients are consumed each day?

28. Suppose the shipping department of a firm charges 20% of its *total* monthly costs to the printing department, while the printing department charges 10% of its *total* monthly costs to the shipping department. If the direct costs of the shipping department are $12,000 and the direct costs of the printing department are $9,580 find the total costs for each department.

29. Suppose the development department of a firm charges 10% of its total monthly costs to the promotional department, and the promotional department charges 5% of its total monthly costs to the development department. If the direct costs of the development department are $19,895 and the direct costs of the promotional department are $10,000, find the total costs for each department.

2.6 Business Applications of Linear Equations in Two Variables

Objectives   ■ To solve problems involving consumption functions
             ■ To solve problems involving market equilibrium
             ■ To solve problems involving break-even analysis

National Consumption

The national consumption function is frequently considered to be linear over short periods of time. Thus we may write the general form of the consumption function as $C = my + b$.

The value of b will always be greater than zero, for there is always some amount of consumption necessary to maintain life, even though disposable income (money) is zero. Mathematically, we say $b > 0$. Consumption will increase whenever income increases, but at a slower rate. Thus the slope m of the line representing the consumption function is greater than 0 but less than 1; that is, $0 < m < 1$.

We call m the **marginal propensity to consume,** because it indicates the proportion of our income increases that we are willing to spend. The value of C for a given value of y is called the **aggregate consumption.**

EXAMPLE 1   Suppose that national consumption is $7 billion when national disposable income is zero, and that at each level of income above zero, consumption is 0.75 of disposable income.
(a) Write this consumption function as an equation.
(b) What is the marginal propensity to consume?
(c) If disposable income is $30 billion, what is the aggregate consumption?
(d) Graph the consumption function.

Solution   (a) The line representing the consumption function has $m = 0.75$ and $b = 7$, so the equation is $C = 0.75y + 7$ (in billions of dollars).
(b) The marginal propensity to consume is $m = 0.75$.
(c) $C = f(30) = 29.5$ (billions of dollars).
(d) See Figure 2.14.   □

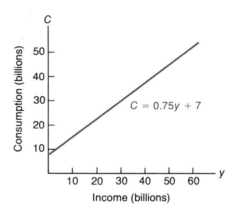

Figure 2.14

Market Equilibrium

We discussed demand functions and supply functions in Chapter 1. In many circumstances it is reasonable to assume that demand (and supply) functions are linear functions. Because demand will normally decrease as price increases, the slope of a demand curve (line) will be negative. On the other hand, a manufacturer will be willing to supply more goods as the price increases, so the supply curve will have a positive slope.

EXAMPLE 2   Suppose that the demand per month for a commodity is 24 if the price is $15 for each unit, 27 if the price is $13, 30 if the price is $11, and 33 if the price is $9.

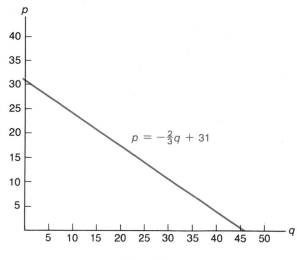

Figure 2.15

Assuming the demand curve is linear, write its equation. Graph the demand curve.

Solution   Using two of the points on the demand curve, say (24, 15) and (33, 9), we can find the slope of the line.

$$m = \frac{15 - 9}{24 - 33} = \frac{6}{-9} = -\frac{2}{3}$$

We can then use one of the points, say (24, 15), to write the equation $p - 15 = -\frac{2}{3}(q - 24)$ or $p = -\frac{2}{3}q + 31$. The graph of the demand function is shown in Figure 2.15.   □

EXAMPLE 3   A manufacturer will supply 200 electric motors per month when the price is $30 and 300 per month when the price is $40. Assuming the supply curve is linear, write its equation and sketch its graph.

Solution   The slope of the line connecting the points (200, 30) and (300, 40) is

$$m = \frac{40 - 30}{300 - 200} = \frac{10}{100} = \frac{1}{10}.$$

The equation is $p - 30 = \frac{1}{10}(q - 200)$ or $p = \frac{1}{10}q + 10$. The graph is shown in Figure 2.16. (page 90).   □

Producers of a commodity like high prices and consumers like low prices, but an agreement is made between these two opposing forces in something called a "market" (thus this area is called *market analysis*). The effects on prices of gasoline and natural gas shortages are painfully apparent to all consumers, and the effects of farm surpluses have led many small farmers to stop producing.

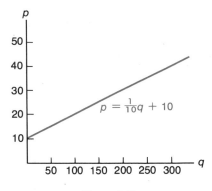

Figure 2.16

Consider the demand and supply schedules (Table 2.2) for a commodity over a period of one month. We can see from these schedules that when the price is $15, the producers are willing to supply many more units than consumers are willing to purchase. The $15 could not be the prevailing market price, for the producers would be producing many more than consumers are willing to buy at that price. This price would create a *surplus* of 36 units of this commodity each month. Eventually this surplus would force the price down below $15. If the price drops to $13, the demand is still less than the supply, so there will still be a surplus on the market, and this will force the price even lower. So the market prices of $15 and $13 will be unstable because they are too high. The price that will put the market in balance will have to be lower than $13.

On the other hand, if the price is $9, consumers will be willing to buy 33 units per month but producers will only supply 15 units. Thus the market will experience a *shortage*. Competition among consumers for the small number of items will force the price higher than the $9 price.

If the price is $11, consumers will be willing to purchase the same number of units (30) that the producers are willing to supply. So the market will be in balance if the price is $11.

When the quantity of a commodity demanded is equal to the amount supplied, **market equilibrium** is said to occur. If the demand and supply curves are graphed

Table 2.2

Demand Schedule		Supply Schedule	
Price per Unit	*Quantity Demanded*	*Price per Unit*	*Quantity Supplied*
$15	24	$15	60
13	27	13	45
11	30	11	30
9	33	9	15

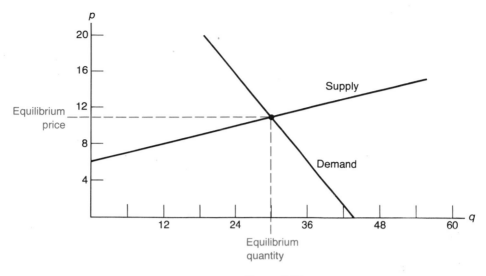

Figure 2.17

on the same coordinate system, with the same units, the point at which they intersect represents the **equilibrium point.** The price at that point is the **equilibrium price,** and the quantity at that point is the **equilibrium quantity.**

Graphing the curves associated with the schedules of Table 2.2 on the same graph, we see that the two lines intersect at (30, 11). This corresponds to the solution we have already found. (See Figure 2.17.)

In general, the equilibrium price and the equilibrium quantity must both be positive for the market equilibrium to have meaning.

We can find the market equilibrium by graphing the demand and supply functions on the same coordinate system, but solving the two equations simultaneously by algebraic methods will generally provide more accurate results.

EXAMPLE 4 Find the equilibrium point for the following supply and demand functions:

$$\text{Demand:} \quad p = -3q + 26$$
$$\text{Supply:} \quad p = 4q - 9$$

Solution Solving simultaneously by substitution gives

$$-3q + 26 = 4q - 9$$
$$35 = 7q$$

so
$$q = 5, \quad p = 11.$$

The equilibrium point is (5, 11).   □

EXAMPLE 5 A group of wholesalers will buy 50 dryers per month if the price is $200 and 30 per month if the price is $300. The manufacturer is willing to supply 20 if the

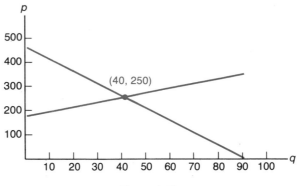

Figure 2.18

price is \$210 and 30 if the price is \$230. Assuming the resulting supply and demand functions are linear, find the equilibrium point for the market.

Solution

Demand function:
$$m = \frac{300 - 200}{30 - 50} = -5$$
$$p - 200 = -5(q - 50)$$
$$p = -5q + 450$$

Supply function:
$$m = \frac{230 - 210}{30 - 20} = 2$$
$$p - 230 = 2(q - 30)$$
$$p = 2q + 170$$

Solving simultaneously gives (by substitution)

$$-5q + 450 = 2q + 170$$
$$280 = 7q$$
$$q = 40$$
$$p = 250.$$

The equilibrium point is (40, 250). See Figure 2.18 for the graph of the functions.

□

Break-Even Analysis

As we stated in Chapter 1, the profit that a firm makes on its product is the difference between its total revenue (the total amount it receives from sales) and its total costs (both fixed and variable).

Profit (or loss) = total revenue − total cost

We can solve the equations for total revenue and total cost simultaneously to

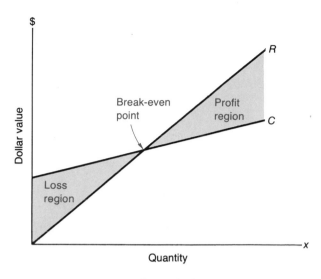

Figure 2.19

find the point where cost and revenue are equal. This point is called the **break-even point.** Figure 2.19 is called a break-even chart. The quantity produced is measured along the horizontal axis; the vertical axis represents the dollar value of the costs or revenue. We will use x to represent the quantity produced and y to represent the dollar value of revenue *and* cost. The line C represents the sum of the fixed and variable costs. The line R represents the total revenue. Note that the total revenue is zero when no units are produced, and it increases more rapidly than the total cost line. (If it didn't, the firm would never make a profit.) The point where the total revenue line crosses the total cost line is called the break-even point. To the left of this point the total revenue is less than the total cost (resulting in a loss), and to the right of this point the total revenue is greater than the total cost (resulting in a profit).

EXAMPLE 6   A manufacturer sells a product for $10 per unit. The manufacturer's fixed costs are $1200 per month, and the variable costs are $2.50 per unit. How many units must be produced each month to break even?

Solution   The total revenue for x units of the product is $10x$, so the equation for total revenue is $R = 10x$. The fixed costs are $1200, so the total cost for x units is $2.50x + 1200$. Thus the equation for total cost is $C = 2.50x + 1200$. We find the break-even point by solving the two equations simultaneously, noting that $R = C$ at the break-even point.

By substitution,

$$10x = 2.50x + 1200$$
$$7.5x = 1200$$
$$x = 160.$$

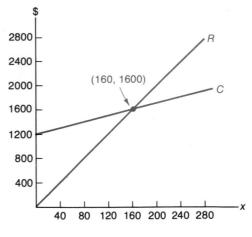

Figure 2.20

Thus the manufacturer will break even if 160 units are produced per month. The manufacturer will make a profit if more than 160 units are produced. (See Figure 2.20.) □

As we stated in Chapter 1, the profit function is found by subtracting the total cost function from the total revenue function.

$$\text{Profit} = \text{total revenue} - \text{total cost}$$

For the previous example, the profit function is given by

$$P(x) = 10x - (2.50x + 1200) \qquad \text{or} \qquad P(x) = 7.50x - 1200.$$

We can find the point where the profit is zero (the break-even point) by setting $P(x) = 0$ and solving for x.

$$0 = 7.50x - 1200$$
$$1200 = 7.50x$$
$$x = 160$$

Note that this is the same break-even point that was found by solving the total revenue and total cost equations simultaneously.

EXAMPLE 7 Suppose a firm requires a 15% return on its investment (fixed costs) to break even. (a) If the good sells for $1, the variable cost is $.50 per unit, and the fixed cost is $20,000, find the quantity the firm must produce to break even. (b) If the capacity of the firm's plant is 40,000 units, should it start production?

Solution The firm's minimum desired profit is 15% of its fixed costs, so the desired profit is $0.15(20,000) = 3000$. If this desired profit is added to fixed costs, the break-even quantity is the quantity that will provide the firm with its 15% return. Thus we seek the quantity that makes $R = C$, where

$$\begin{cases} C = 0.50x + 23{,}000 \\ R = \quad 1x \end{cases}$$

Solving $R = C$ gives

$$1x = 0.50x + 23{,}000$$
$$0.50x = 23{,}000$$
$$x = 46{,}000.$$

(a) The break-even quantity is 46,000.

(b) No, the plant does not have the capacity to produce enough units to reach the desired profit.   □

Exercise 2.6

NATIONAL CONSUMPTION

1. Suppose that national consumption is $8 billion when national disposable income is zero, and that at each level of income above zero, consumption is 0.6 of disposable income.
   (a) Write this consumption function as an equation.
   (b) What is the marginal propensity to consume?
   (c) If disposable income is $30 billion, what is the aggregate consumption?
2. If the national consumption function is given by the equation

$$C = 0.65y + 5 \qquad \text{(billions of dollars)},$$

   (a) what is the marginal propensity to consume?
   (b) graph the consumption function.
3. If the national consumption is $7 billion when national disposable income is zero, and if the marginal propensity to consume is 0.8, write the linear consumption function as an equation.

MARKET EQUILIBRIUM

4. Suppose the demand per month for a commodity is 24 if the price is $16, 20 if the price is $18, 16 if the price is $20, and 12 if the price is $22. Assuming the demand curve is linear, (a) graph the curve, (b) write its equation.
5. A manufacturer will supply the commodity of problem 4 as follows:

   8 if the price is $14
   14 if the price is $16
   20 if the price is $18
   26 if the price is $20

   Assuming the supply curve is linear, (a) graph the curve, (b) write its equation.
6. Find the equilibrium point for the demand and supply functions in problems 4 and 5.

7. Find the equilibrium point for the following supply and demand functions:

$$\text{Demand:} \quad p = -4q + 160$$
$$\text{Supply:} \quad p = 15q - 30$$

8. Find the equilibrium point for the following supply and demand functions:

$$\text{Demand:} \quad p = 480 - 3q$$
$$\text{Supply:} \quad p = 25q - 80$$

9. A group of retailers will buy 80 televisions from a wholesaler if the price is $350 and 120 if the price is $300. The wholesaler is willing to supply 60 if the price is $280 and 140 if the price is $370. Assuming the resulting supply and demand functions are linear, find the equilibrium point for the market.

BREAK-EVEN ANALYSIS

10. A manufacturer sells a product for $12 per unit. The fixed costs are $1600 per month, and the variable costs are $8 per unit. How many units must be produced each month to break even?

11. A manufacturer sells a product for $50 per unit. If the fixed costs related to this product amount to $10,000 per month, and the variable costs amount to $30 per unit, how many units must be produced and sold to break even each month?

12. Write the profit function for problem 10.

13. Write the profit function for problem 11.

14. Suppose a firm will not begin production of a good unless it returns a 20% return on its investment for fixed costs. If the fixed costs are $50,000, the variable cost is $2 per unit, and the good sells for $5 per unit, how many units must be produced to break even (that is, make the required return)?

15. Suppose a firm required a 10% return on its investment for fixed costs to break even. If the good sells for $2 per unit, the variable cost is $.50 per unit, and the fixed cost is $30,000, how many units must be produced to break even?

Review Exercises

Solve the equations in problems 1–6.

1. $x + 7 = 14$
2. $3x - 8 = 23$
3. $2x - 8 = 3x + 5$
4. $6x - 3 = 5x - 2$
5. $2x + \dfrac{1}{2} = \dfrac{x}{2} + \dfrac{1}{3}$
6. $0.6x + 4 = x - 0.02$
7. Graph $2x - 3y = 6$.
8. Graph $5x + 3y = 6$.
9. Graph $x = -2$.
10. What is the slope and y-intercept of the line with equation $2x + 5y = 10$?

11. Write the equation of the line passing through $(3, 2)$ with slope $\frac{1}{2}$.
12. Write the equation of the line passing through $(-1, 2)$ and $(2, -4)$.
13. Write the equation of the line passing through $(-1, 2)$ and $(3, -1)$.

Solve the following systems of equations.

14. $\begin{cases} 4x - 2y = 6 \\ 3x + 3y = 9 \end{cases}$

15. $\begin{cases} 3x + 2y = 5 \\ 2x - 3y = 12 \end{cases}$

APPLICATIONS

16. If the demand for a product is given by $p = 420 - 6q$ and the supply function is $p = 10q - 60$,
    (a) what is the equilibrium price?
    (b) what is the equilibrium quantity?

17. A national consumption function is given by $C = 4 + 0.6y$ (billions of dollars).
    (a) What is the consumption when disposable income is zero?
    (b) What is the consumption when disposable income is $8 million?
    (c) Graph the consumption function.

18. A certain commodity has the following costs for a period:

$$\text{Fixed costs: } \quad \$1500$$
$$\text{Variable costs: } \quad \$22 \text{ per unit}$$

If the commodity is sold for $52 per unit,
    (a) what is the total cost function?
    (b) what is the total revenue function?
    (c) what is the profit function?
    (d) what is the marginal cost?
    (e) what is the marginal revenue?
    (f) what is the marginal profit?
    (g) what is the break-even point?

19. If the supply function for a product is linear and determined by Table 2.3, and the demand function is linear and determined by Table 2.4, find the price that will give market equilibrium.

Table 2.3

Price	Quantity
100	200
200	400
300	600

Table 2.4

Price	Quantity
200	200
100	400
0	600

Warmup In this chapter you will need to work problems like the following. If you have difficulty with any problem, return to the section where that type of problem was introduced and refresh your memory before starting the chapter.

Problem Type	Introduced in Section	Used in Section	Answer
Evaluate: (a) $4 - (-2)$ (b) $-4(\frac{2}{3}) + 3$ (c) $(-5)(4) + (8)(1) + (2)(5)$ (d) Multiply each of the numbers 0, -3, -3, -2, 2 by $-\frac{1}{3}$	0.1 Signed numbers	3.1, 3.2, 3.3, 3.4, 3.5	(a) 6 (b) $\frac{1}{3}$ (c) -2 (d) $0, 1, 1, \frac{2}{3}, -\frac{2}{3}$

Write the coefficients of x, y, and z and the constant term in each equation:

Problem Type	Introduced in Section	Used in Section	Coefficients of			Constant term
	0.3 Algebraic expressions	3.3, 3.4, 3.5	x	y	z	
(a) $2x + 5y + 4z = 4$			(a) 2	5	4	4
(b) $x - 3y - 2z = 5$			(b) 1	-3	-2	5
(c) $3x + y = 4$			(c) 3	1	0	4

Problem Type	Introduced in Section	Used in Section	Answer
Solve (a) $x_1 - 2x_3 = 2$ for x_1 (b) $x_2 + x_3 = -3$ for x_2	2.1 Linear equations	3.3, 3.4, 3.5	(a) $x_1 = 2 + 2x_3$ (b) $x_2 = -3 - x_3$
Solve the system: $\begin{cases} x - 0.25y = 11{,}750 \\ -0.20x + y = 10{,}000 \end{cases}$	2.5 Linear equation in two variables	3.3, 3.4, 3.5	$x = 15{,}000$ $y = 13{,}000$

MATRICES

A business may collect and store or analyze various types of data as a regular part of its record-keeping procedures. The data may be presented in tabular form. For example, a building contractor who builds four different styles of houses may catalog the number of units of certain materials needed to build each style in a table like Table 3.1.

If we write the numbers from Table 3.1 in the rectangular array

$$A = \begin{bmatrix} 20 & 25 & 22 & 18 \\ 27 & 40 & 31 & 25 \\ 16 & 16 & 19 & 16 \end{bmatrix},$$

we say A is a **matrix** representing Table 3.1. In addition to storing data in a matrix, we can analyze data and make business decisions by defining the operations of addition, subtraction, and multiplication for matrices.

Table 3.1

	House Style			
Required Units	Ranch	Colonial	Split Level	Cape Cod
Wood	20	25	22	18
Siding	27	40	31	25
Roofing	16	16	19	16

Matrices are very useful in solving systems of linear equations in two or more variables. We will see how matrices can be used to solve two linear equations in two unknowns, and will extend the method to solve systems involving three and more variables.

3.1 Matrices

Objectives   ■ To organize and interpret data stored in matrices
■ To add and subtract matrices

As we noted in the introduction to this chapter, matrices can be used to store data and to perform operations with the data. We have noted that the matrix

$$A = \begin{bmatrix} 20 & 25 & 22 & 18 \\ 27 & 40 & 31 & 25 \\ 16 & 16 & 19 & 16 \end{bmatrix}$$

represents the data from Table 3.1. Matrix A contains the heart of the information from Table 3.1, without the labels. This rectangular array refers to very specific information, but the organizational format is useful in an assortment of problems. In general, any rectangular array of numbers is called a **matrix.**

The *rows* of the matrix A correspond to the types of building materials and the *columns* correspond to the types of houses. The rows of a matrix are numbered from the top to the bottom and the columns are numbered from the left to right.

	Column 1	Column 2	Column 3	Column 4
Row 1	20	25	22	18
Row 2	27	40	31	25
Row 3	16	16	19	16

Matrices are classified by the number of rows and columns they have. The matrix A has three rows and four columns, so we say this is a 3×4 (read "three by four") matrix.

The matrix

$$A = \begin{bmatrix} a_{11} & a_{12} & a_{13} & \cdots & a_{1n} \\ a_{21} & a_{22} & a_{23} & \cdots & a_{2n} \\ & \vdots & & & \vdots \\ a_{m1} & a_{m2} & a_{m3} & \cdots & a_{mn} \end{bmatrix}$$

has m rows and n columns, so it is an $m \times n$ matrix. When we designate A as an $m \times n$ matrix, we are indicating the size of the matrix. Two matrices are said to be the same size if they have the same number of rows and the same number of columns.

Some matrices take special names because of their size. If the number of rows equals the number of columns, we say the matrix is a **square matrix**. Matrix B is an example of a 3×3 square matrix.

$$B = \begin{bmatrix} 4 & 3 & 0 \\ 0 & 0 & 1 \\ -4 & 0 & 0 \end{bmatrix}$$

A matrix with one row, such as [9 5] or [3 2 1 6], is called a **row matrix**, and a matrix with one column, such as

$$\begin{bmatrix} 1 \\ 3 \\ 5 \end{bmatrix},$$

is called a **column matrix**. Row and column matrices are also called **vectors**.

The numbers in a matrix are called its **entries** or **elements**. Note that the subscripts on the entries in matrix A correspond respectively to the row and column in which the entry is located. Thus a_{23} represents the entry in the second row and the third column, and we refer to it as the "two-three entry." In matrix B, the entry denoted by b_{23} is 1.

We define two matrices to be *equal* if they are the same size and if each entry in one equals the corresponding entry in the other.

EXAMPLE 1   Are $A = \begin{bmatrix} 1 & 3 & 2 \\ 4 & 1 & 2 \end{bmatrix}$ and $B = \begin{bmatrix} 1 & 4 \\ 2 & 1 \\ 3 & 0 \end{bmatrix}$ the same size matrices?

Solution   No. A is a 2×3 matrix and B is a 3×2 matrix.   □

EXAMPLE 2   (a) Which element of

$$A = \begin{bmatrix} 1 & 2 & 3 \\ 4 & 5 & 6 \\ 7 & 8 & 9 \end{bmatrix}$$

is represented by a_{23}?
(b) Is A a square matrix?

Solution   (a) a_{23} represents the element in row 2 and column 3; that is, 6.
(b) Yes, it is a 3×3 (square) matrix.   □

If two matrices have the same number of rows and columns, we can add the matrices by adding their corresponding entries. More formally,

> **Sum of Two Matrices**   If matrix A and matrix B are the same size and have elements a_{ij} and b_{ij}, respectively, then their **sum** $A + B$ is a matrix C with elements $c_{ij} = a_{ij} + b_{ij}$ for all i and j.

That is,

$$\begin{bmatrix} a_{11} & a_{12} & \cdots & a_{1n} \\ a_{21} & a_{22} & \cdots & a_{2n} \\ \vdots & & & \vdots \\ a_{m1} & a_{m2} & \cdots & a_{mn} \end{bmatrix} + \begin{bmatrix} b_{11} & b_{12} & \cdots & b_{1n} \\ b_{21} & b_{22} & \cdots & b_{2n} \\ \vdots & & & \vdots \\ b_{m1} & b_{m2} & \cdots & b_{mn} \end{bmatrix}$$

$$= \begin{bmatrix} a_{11} + b_{11} & a_{12} + b_{12} & \cdots & a_{1n} + b_{1n} \\ a_{21} + b_{21} & a_{22} + b_{22} & \cdots & a_{2n} + b_{2n} \\ \vdots & & & \vdots \\ a_{m1} + b_{m1} & a_{m2} + b_{m2} & \cdots & a_{mn} + b_{mn} \end{bmatrix}.$$

EXAMPLE 3   Find the sum of A and B if

$$A = \begin{bmatrix} 1 & 2 & 3 \\ 4 & -1 & -2 \end{bmatrix} \quad \text{and} \quad B = \begin{bmatrix} -1 & 2 & -3 \\ -2 & 0 & 1 \end{bmatrix}.$$

Solution

$$A + B = \begin{bmatrix} 1 + (-1) & 2 + 2 & 3 + (-3) \\ 4 + (-2) & -1 + 0 & -2 + 1 \end{bmatrix} = \begin{bmatrix} 0 & 4 & 0 \\ 2 & -1 & -1 \end{bmatrix} \qquad \square$$

The matrix $-B$ is called the *negative* of the matrix B, and each element of $-B$ is the negative of the corresponding element of B. For example, if

$$B = \begin{bmatrix} -1 & 2 & -3 \\ -2 & 0 & 1 \end{bmatrix}, \quad \text{then} \quad -B = \begin{bmatrix} 1 & -2 & 3 \\ 2 & 0 & -1 \end{bmatrix}.$$

EXAMPLE 4   For matrices A and B of Example 3, find $A - B$.

Solution $A - B$ can be written as $A + (-B)$, so

$$A - B = \begin{bmatrix} 1 - (-1) & 2 - 2 & 3 - (-3) \\ 4 - (-2) & -1 - 0 & -2 - 1 \end{bmatrix} = \begin{bmatrix} 2 & 0 & 6 \\ 6 & -1 & -3 \end{bmatrix}. \qquad \square$$

EXAMPLE 5   Suppose the purchase prices and delivery costs (per unit) for wood, siding, and roofing used in construction are given by Table 3.2. If the supplier decides to

Table 3.2

	Wood	Siding	Roofing
Purchase	6	4	2
Delivery	1	1	0.5

raise the purchase prices by $.60 per unit, and the delivery costs by $.05 per unit, write the matrix that describes the unit costs.

Solution   The matrix representing the unit costs is

$$C = \begin{bmatrix} 6 & 4 & 2 \\ 1 & 1 & 0.5 \end{bmatrix},$$

and the matrix representing the increases is given by

$$H = \begin{bmatrix} 0.60 & 0.60 & 0.60 \\ 0.05 & 0.05 & 0.05 \end{bmatrix}.$$

The new unit cost for each item is its former cost plus the increase, so the new unit cost matrix is given by

$$C + H = \begin{bmatrix} 6 + 0.60 & 4 + 0.60 & 2 + 0.60 \\ 1 + 0.05 & 1 + 0.05 & 0.5 + 0.05 \end{bmatrix} = \begin{bmatrix} 6.60 & 4.60 & 2.60 \\ 1.05 & 1.05 & 0.55 \end{bmatrix}. \quad \square$$

Note that the sum of C and H in Example 5 could be found by adding the matrices in either order. That is, $C + H = H + C$. This is known as the Commutative Law of Addition for matrices. We will see in the next section that multiplication of matrices is not commutative.

Exercise 3.1

Use the following matrices in problems 1–8:

$$A = \begin{bmatrix} 1 & 0 & 2 \\ 3 & 2 & 1 \\ 4 & 0 & 3 \end{bmatrix} \quad B = \begin{bmatrix} 1 & 1 & 3 & 0 \\ 4 & 2 & 1 & 1 \\ 3 & 2 & 0 & 1 \end{bmatrix} \quad C = \begin{bmatrix} 5 & 3 \\ 1 & 2 \end{bmatrix}$$

$$D = \begin{bmatrix} 4 & 2 \\ 3 & 5 \end{bmatrix} \quad E = \begin{bmatrix} 1 & 0 & 4 \\ 5 & 1 & 0 \end{bmatrix} \quad F = \begin{bmatrix} 1 & 2 & 3 \\ -1 & 0 & 1 \\ 2 & -3 & -4 \end{bmatrix}$$

1. Which of the matrices A, B, C, D, E, and F are square?
2. Are any pairs of the matrices the same size?
3. Can matrices A and E be added?
4. Are any pairs of the matrices equal?
5. Compute $C + D$.
6. Compute $A + F$.
7. Compute $A - F$.
8. Compute $C - D$.

APPLICATIONS

The Book Equipment Company (BEC) produces bookcases and filing cabinets, operating from two plants. Matrix A summarizes its production for a week, with row 1 representing bookcases and row 2 representing filing cabinets.

$$A = \begin{bmatrix} 50 & 30 \\ 36 & 44 \end{bmatrix}$$

Matrix B gives the production for the second week, and matrix C that of the third and fourth weeks.

$$B = \begin{bmatrix} 30 & 45 \\ 22 & 62 \end{bmatrix} \quad C = \begin{bmatrix} 96 & 52 \\ 81 & 37 \end{bmatrix}$$

If column 1 in each matrix represents production from plant 1 and column 2 represents production from plant 2, answer the following questions.

9. How many bookcases were produced in the first week?

10. How many filing cabinets were produced in the first week?

11. How many units were produced by plant 1 in the first week?

12. How many units were produced by plant 2 in the first week?

13. If production during the second week is given by matrix B, write a matrix that describes production for the two weeks.

14. If production over the next two-week period is given by matrix C, describe production for the four-week period.

15. If BEC sells the bookcases and filing cabinets for the same price, was the week described by matrix A or the one described by matrix B better for the company?

16. Was total production better during the first two weeks or the last two described?

17. If matrix D

$$D = \begin{bmatrix} 40 & 26 \\ 29 & 42 \end{bmatrix}$$

describes the shipments made during the first week, write the matrix that describes the units added to the plants' inventories.

18. If D also describes the shipments during the second week, describe the change in inventory. What happened at plant 1?

In an experiment, three groups of baby laboratory animals were used. Group I had an enriched diet, group II (control) had the regular diet, and group III had a deficient diet. At the beginning of the experiment the animals were weighed and measured according to their group with group I averaging 140 g with a length of 5.5 cm. Group II and group III weighed 151 g and 141 g, with lengths of 5.7 cm and 5.5 cm, respectively.

19. Make a matrix that displays this information.

20. At the end of two weeks, the same measurements were made, with the following results: 12.5 cm, 250 g; 11.8 cm, 215 g; 9.8 cm, 190 g. Make a matrix that displays this information. Make sure the matrix is the same size as your answer in problem 19.

21. Calculate the changes in weight and length by using matrix subtraction.

3.2 Multiplication of Matrices

Objectives   ■ To multiply a matrix by a scalar (real number)
                 ■ To multiply two matrices

We have seen (in Section 3.1) how we can use matrices to store data, and how addition and subtraction of matrices can be used to gain new information from the data. In this section we will see how multiplication involving matrices can provide information about data. We will begin our discussion with scalar multiplication of a matrix.

Consider the matrix

$$A = \begin{bmatrix} 3 & 2 \\ 1 & 1 \\ 2 & 0 \end{bmatrix}.$$

Since $2A$ is $A + A$, we see that

$$2A = \begin{bmatrix} 3 & 2 \\ 1 & 1 \\ 2 & 0 \end{bmatrix} + \begin{bmatrix} 3 & 2 \\ 1 & 1 \\ 2 & 0 \end{bmatrix} = \begin{bmatrix} 6 & 4 \\ 2 & 2 \\ 4 & 0 \end{bmatrix}.$$

Note that $2A$ could have been found by multiplying each entry of A by 2. In the same manner,

$$3A = A + A + A = \begin{bmatrix} 3 & 2 \\ 1 & 1 \\ 2 & 0 \end{bmatrix} + \begin{bmatrix} 3 & 2 \\ 1 & 1 \\ 2 & 0 \end{bmatrix} + \begin{bmatrix} 3 & 2 \\ 1 & 1 \\ 2 & 0 \end{bmatrix}$$

$$= \begin{bmatrix} 9 & 6 \\ 3 & 3 \\ 6 & 0 \end{bmatrix} = \begin{bmatrix} 3(3) & 3(2) \\ 3(1) & 3(1) \\ 3(2) & 3(0) \end{bmatrix}.$$

We can define **scalar multiplication** as follows:

> Multiplying a matrix by a real number (called a *scalar*) results in a matrix in which each entry of the matrix is multiplied by the real number.

Thus, if

$$A = \begin{bmatrix} a_{11} & a_{12} \\ a_{21} & a_{22} \end{bmatrix}, \quad \text{then} \quad cA = \begin{bmatrix} ca_{11} & ca_{12} \\ ca_{21} & ca_{22} \end{bmatrix}.$$

EXAMPLE 1   If

$$A = \begin{bmatrix} 4 & 1 & 4 & 0 \\ 2 & -7 & 3 & 6 \\ 0 & 0 & 2 & 5 \end{bmatrix},$$

find $5A$ and $-2A$.

Solution

$$5A = \begin{bmatrix} 5 \cdot 4 & 5 \cdot 1 & 5 \cdot 4 & 5 \cdot 0 \\ 5 \cdot 2 & 5(-7) & 5 \cdot 3 & 5 \cdot 6 \\ 5 \cdot 0 & 5 \cdot 0 & 5 \cdot 2 & 5 \cdot 5 \end{bmatrix} = \begin{bmatrix} 20 & 5 & 20 & 0 \\ 10 & -35 & 15 & 30 \\ 0 & 0 & 10 & 25 \end{bmatrix}$$

$$-2A = \begin{bmatrix} -2 \cdot 4 & -2 \cdot 1 & -2 \cdot 4 & -2 \cdot 0 \\ -2 \cdot 2 & -2(-7) & -2 \cdot 3 & -2 \cdot 6 \\ -2 \cdot 0 & -2 \cdot 0 & -2 \cdot 2 & -2 \cdot 5 \end{bmatrix}$$

$$= \begin{bmatrix} -8 & -2 & -8 & 0 \\ -4 & 14 & -6 & -12 \\ 0 & 0 & -4 & -10 \end{bmatrix}$$

□

EXAMPLE 2   Suppose the purchase prices and delivery costs (per unit) for wood, siding, and roofing used in construction are given by Table 3.3.

Table 3.3

	Wood	Siding	Roofing
Purchase	6	4	2
Delivery	1	1	0.5

Then the table of unit costs may be represented by the matrix

$$C = \begin{bmatrix} 6 & 4 & 2 \\ 1 & 1 & 0.5 \end{bmatrix}.$$

If the supplier announces a 10% increase on both purchase and delivery of these items, find the new unit cost matrix.

Solution   A 10% increase means that the new unit costs are the former cost plus 0.10 times the former cost. That is, the new costs are 1.10 times the former, so the new unit cost matrix is given by

$$1.10C = 1.10 \begin{bmatrix} 6 & 4 & 2 \\ 1 & 1 & 0.5 \end{bmatrix}$$

$$= \begin{bmatrix} 6.60 & 4.40 & 2.20 \\ 1.10 & 1.10 & 0.55 \end{bmatrix}. \qquad\qquad \Box$$

Suppose one store of a firm has 30 washers, 20 dryers, and 10 dishwashers in its inventory. If the value of each washer is \$300, each dryer is \$250, and each dishwasher is \$350, then the value of this inventory is

$$30 \cdot 300 + 20 \cdot 250 + 10 \cdot 350 = \$17{,}500.$$

If we write the values of the appliances in the *row matrix*

$$A = [300 \qquad 250 \qquad 350]$$

and the numbers of each of the appliances in the *column matrix*

$$B = \begin{bmatrix} 30 \\ 20 \\ 10 \end{bmatrix},$$

then the value of the inventory may be represented by

$$AB = [300 \qquad 250 \qquad 350] \begin{bmatrix} 30 \\ 20 \\ 10 \end{bmatrix}$$

$$- 300 \cdot 30 + 250 \cdot 20 + 350 \cdot 10$$

$$= \$17{,}500.$$

This useful way of operating with a row matrix and a column matrix is called the product of A times B.

In general, we can multiply the row matrix

$$A = [a_1 \qquad a_2 \qquad a_3 \qquad \cdots \qquad a_n]$$

times the column matrix

$$B = \begin{bmatrix} b_1 \\ b_2 \\ b_3 \\ \vdots \\ b_n \end{bmatrix}$$

if A and B have the same number of elements. The product A times B is

$$AB = [a_1 \quad a_2 \quad a_3 \quad \cdots \quad a_n] \begin{bmatrix} b_1 \\ b_2 \\ b_3 \\ \vdots \\ b_n \end{bmatrix} = a_1 b_1 + a_2 b_2 + a_3 b_3 + \cdots + a_n b_n.$$

Suppose the firm has a second store, with 40 washers, 25 dryers, and 5 dishwashers. We can use matrix C to represent the inventories of the two stores.

$$\begin{array}{r} \text{Store I} \quad \text{Store II} \\ \begin{array}{r} \text{Washers} \\ C = \text{Dryers} \\ \text{Dishwashers} \end{array} \begin{bmatrix} 30 & 40 \\ 20 & 25 \\ 10 & 5 \end{bmatrix} \end{array}$$

Suppose the values of the appliances are \$300, \$250, and \$350, respectively. We have already seen that the value of the inventory of store I is \$17,500. The value of the inventory of store II is

$$300 \cdot 40 + 250 \cdot 25 + 350 \cdot 5 = \$20,000.$$

Because the value of the inventory of store I can be found by multiplying the row matrix A times the first column of the matrix C and the value of the inventory of store II can be found by multiplying matrix A times the second column of matrix C, we can write this result as

$$AC = [300 \quad 250 \quad 350] \begin{bmatrix} 30 & 40 \\ 20 & 25 \\ 10 & 5 \end{bmatrix} = [17,500 \quad 20,000].$$

The matrix we have represented as AC is called the product of the row matrix A and the 3×2 matrix C. We should note that matrix A is a 1×3 matrix, matrix C is a 3×2 matrix, and their product is a 1×2 matrix. In general, we can multiply an $m \times n$ matrix times an $n \times p$ matrix and the product will be an $m \times p$ matrix, as follows:

Product of Two Matrices   Given an $m \times n$ matrix A and an $n \times p$ matrix B, the **matrix product** AB is an $m \times p$ matrix C, with the ij entry of C given by the formula

$$c_{ij} = a_{i1} b_{1j} + a_{i2} b_{2j} + \cdots + a_{in} b_{nj},$$

which is illustrated in Figure 3.1.

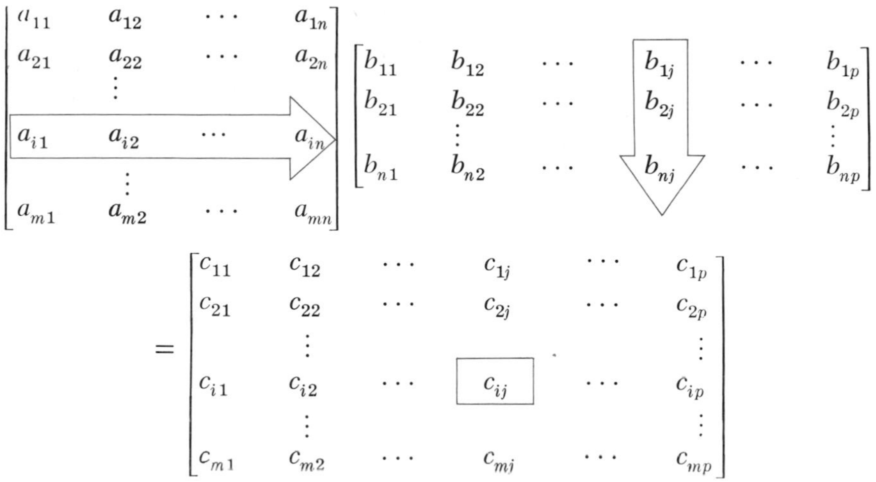

$$\begin{bmatrix} a_{11} & a_{12} & \cdots & a_{1n} \\ a_{21} & a_{22} & \cdots & a_{2n} \\ & \vdots & & \\ a_{i1} & a_{i2} & \cdots & a_{in} \\ & \vdots & & \\ a_{m1} & a_{m2} & \cdots & a_{mn} \end{bmatrix} \begin{bmatrix} b_{11} & b_{12} & \cdots & b_{1j} & \cdots & b_{1p} \\ b_{21} & b_{22} & \cdots & b_{2j} & \cdots & b_{2p} \\ & \vdots & & & & \vdots \\ b_{n1} & b_{n2} & \cdots & b_{nj} & \cdots & b_{np} \end{bmatrix}$$

$$= \begin{bmatrix} c_{11} & c_{12} & \cdots & c_{1j} & \cdots & c_{1p} \\ c_{21} & c_{22} & \cdots & c_{2j} & \cdots & c_{2p} \\ & \vdots & & & & \vdots \\ c_{i1} & c_{i2} & \cdots & \boxed{c_{ij}} & \cdots & c_{ip} \\ & \vdots & & & & \vdots \\ c_{m1} & c_{m2} & \cdots & c_{mj} & \cdots & c_{mp} \end{bmatrix}$$

Figure 3.1

EXAMPLE 3   Find AB if

$$A = \begin{bmatrix} 3 & 4 \\ 2 & 5 \\ 6 & 10 \end{bmatrix} \quad \text{and} \quad B = \begin{bmatrix} a & b & c & d \\ e & f & g & h \end{bmatrix}.$$

Solution A is a 3×2 matrix and B is a 2×4 matrix, so the number of columns of A equals the number of rows of B. Thus we can find the product AB, which is a 3×4 matrix. That is, $A_{32} \times B_{24} = C_{34}$.

$$AB = \begin{bmatrix} 3 & 4 \\ 2 & 5 \\ 6 & 10 \end{bmatrix} \begin{bmatrix} a & b & c & d \\ e & f & g & h \end{bmatrix} = \begin{bmatrix} 3a + 4e & 3b + 4f & 3c + 4g & 3d + 4h \\ 2a + 5e & 2b + 5f & 2c + 5g & 2d + 5h \\ 6a + 10e & 6b + 10f & 6c + 10g & 6d + 10h \end{bmatrix}$$

This example shows that if $AB = C$, element c_{32} is found by multiplying each entry of A's *third* row by the corresponding entry of B's *second* column, and then adding these products.   □

EXAMPLE 4   Given matrices

$$A = \begin{bmatrix} 3 & 2 \\ 1 & 0 \end{bmatrix} \quad \text{and} \quad B = \begin{bmatrix} 1 & 2 \\ 3 & 1 \end{bmatrix},$$

find AB and BA.

Solution   Both A and B are 2×2 matrices, so both AB and BA are defined.

$$AB = \begin{bmatrix} 3 & 2 \\ 1 & 0 \end{bmatrix} \begin{bmatrix} 1 & 2 \\ 3 & 1 \end{bmatrix} = \begin{bmatrix} 3 \cdot 1 + 2 \cdot 3 & 3 \cdot 2 + 2 \cdot 1 \\ 1 \cdot 1 + 0 \cdot 3 & 1 \cdot 2 + 0 \cdot 1 \end{bmatrix} = \begin{bmatrix} 9 & 8 \\ 1 & 2 \end{bmatrix}$$

$$BA = \begin{bmatrix} 1 & 2 \\ 3 & 1 \end{bmatrix} \begin{bmatrix} 3 & 2 \\ 1 & 0 \end{bmatrix} = \begin{bmatrix} 1 \cdot 3 + 2 \cdot 1 & 1 \cdot 2 + 2 \cdot 0 \\ 3 \cdot 3 + 1 \cdot 1 & 3 \cdot 2 + 1 \cdot 0 \end{bmatrix} = \begin{bmatrix} 5 & 2 \\ 10 & 6 \end{bmatrix}$$

Note that for these matrices the two products AB and BA are the same size matrices, but they are not equal. That is, $BA \neq AB$. Thus we say that *matrix multiplication is not commutative*. ☐

An $n \times n$ (square) matrix (where n is any natural number) that has 1's down its diagonal and 0's everywhere else is called an **identity matrix**. The matrix

$$I = \begin{bmatrix} 1 & 0 & 0 \\ 0 & 1 & 0 \\ 0 & 0 & 1 \end{bmatrix}$$

is a 3×3 identity matrix. The matrix I is called an identity matrix because $AI = IA = A$ for any 3×3 matrix A. That is, if I is multiplied times a 3×3 matrix A (or by a matrix A), the product matrix is A. Note that when one of the matrices being multiplied is an identity matrix, the product *is* commutative.

EXAMPLE 5   Suppose products A and B are made from plastic, steel, and glass, with the number units of each raw material required for each product given by Table 3.4.

Table 3.4   UNITS REQUIRED

	Plastic	Steel	Glass
Product A	3	1	0.50
Product B	4	0.50	2

Because of transportation costs to the firm's two plants, X and Y, the unit costs for some of the raw materials are different. Table 3.5 gives the unit costs for each of the raw materials at the two plants.

Table 3.5   UNIT COSTS

	Plant X	Plant Y
Plastic	10	9
Steel	22	26
Glass	14	14

Using the information just given, find the total cost of producing each of the products at each of the factories.

Solution   Table 3.4, which gives the units of raw material required for each of the products, may be represented by the *production matrix*

$$P = \begin{bmatrix} 3 & 1 & 0.50 \\ 4 & 0.50 & 2 \end{bmatrix},$$

and Table 3.5, which gives the unit costs of the raw materials at each of the sites, may be represented by the *unit cost matrix*

$$C = \begin{bmatrix} 10 & 9 \\ 22 & 26 \\ 14 & 14 \end{bmatrix}.$$

To find the total cost of product A at plant X, we must multiply the number of units of raw materials required for product A times the unit cost for the respective raw materials at plant X, and add these costs together. Note that the entry in the first row and the first column of the matrix product PC gives this cost.

The product PC is

$$PC = \begin{bmatrix} 3 & 1 & 0.50 \\ 4 & 0.50 & 2 \end{bmatrix} \begin{bmatrix} 10 & 9 \\ 22 & 26 \\ 14 & 14 \end{bmatrix} = \begin{bmatrix} 30 + 22 + 7 & 27 + 26 + 7 \\ 40 + 11 + 28 & 36 + 13 + 28 \end{bmatrix}$$

$$= \begin{bmatrix} 59 & 60 \\ 79 & 77 \end{bmatrix}.$$

We can see that the second entry of the first row gives the cost of product A at plant Y. The first entry of the second row is the cost of product B at plant X and the second entry in the second row is the cost of product B at plant Y. Thus matrix PC summarizes the costs for the products at each plant.

$$\begin{array}{cc} & X \quad\ Y \\ PC = & \begin{bmatrix} 59 & 60 \\ 79 & 77 \end{bmatrix} \begin{array}{l} A \\ B \end{array} \end{array}$$ □

Exercise 3.2

1. Is matrix multiplication commutative?
2. Is multiplication by the identity matrix commutative?

Use the following matrices in problems 3–18.

$$A = \begin{bmatrix} 1 & 0 & 2 \\ 3 & 2 & 1 \\ 4 & 0 & 3 \end{bmatrix} \quad B = \begin{bmatrix} 1 & 1 & 3 & 0 \\ 4 & 2 & 1 & 1 \\ 3 & 2 & 0 & 1 \end{bmatrix} \quad C = \begin{bmatrix} 5 & 3 \\ 1 & 2 \end{bmatrix}$$

$$D = \begin{bmatrix} 4 & 2 \\ 3 & 5 \end{bmatrix} \qquad E = \begin{bmatrix} 1 & 0 & 4 \\ 5 & 1 & 0 \end{bmatrix}$$

3. Compute $3A$.

4. Compute $4D$.

5. Compute $4C + 2D$.

6. Compute $5C - 3D$.

7. Compute AB, if possible.

8. Compute EC, if possible.

9. Compute BA, if possible.

10. Compute CE, if possible.

11. Compute CD, if possible.

12. Compute DC, if possible.

13. Does $CD = DC$ (see problems 11 and 12)?

14. Compute DE, if possible.

15. Compute EB, if possible.

16. Compute BE, if possible.

17. Compute EA, if possible.

18. Compute AE, if possible.

APPLICATIONS

19. Two departments of a firm, A and B, need differing amounts of the same products. The following table gives the amounts of the products needed by the departments.

	Steel	Plastic	Wood
Department A	30	20	10
Department B	20	10	20

These three products are supplied by two suppliers, Ace and Kink, with the unit prices given in the table.

	Ace	Kink
Steel	300	280
Plastic	150	100
Wood	150	200

(a) Use matrix multiplication to find how much these two orders will cost at the two suppliers.

(b) From which supplier should each department make its purchase?

20. A furniture manufacturer produces four styles of chairs, and has orders for 1000 of style A, 4000 of style B, 2000 of style C, and 1000 of style D. The table lists the number of units of raw material the manufacturer needs for each style.

	Wood	Nylon	Velvet	Spring
Style A	10	5	0	0
Style B	5	0	20	10
Style C	5	20	0	10
Style D	5	10	10	10

(a) Form a 1×4 matrix containing the number of units of each style ordered.

(b) Use matrix multiplication to determine the total number of units of each raw material needed.

21. Suppose, in problem 20, wood costs the manufacturer $5 per unit, nylon costs $3 per unit, velvet costs $4 per unit, and springs cost $4 per unit.
    (a) Write a 4×1 matrix representing the costs for the raw materials.
    (b) Use matrix multiplication to find the 1×1 matrix that represents the total investment to fill the orders.

22. Use matrix multiplication and the information given in problems 20 and 21 to determine the cost for materials for each style of chair.

23. In problem 20 of Exercise 3.1, we found the weights and measures of the laboratory animals to be given by matrix A, where

$$A = \begin{bmatrix} 12.5 & 250 \\ 11.8 & 215 \\ 9.8 & 190 \end{bmatrix}.$$

If the increase in both weight and length over the next two weeks is 20% for group I, 7% for group II, and 0% for group III, then the increases in the measures of the groups during the two weeks can be found by computing GA, where

$$G = \begin{bmatrix} 0.20 & 0 & 0 \\ 0 & 0.07 & 0 \\ 0 & 0 & 0 \end{bmatrix}.$$

(a) What are the increases in respective weights and measures at the end of these two weeks?
(b) Find the matrix that gives the new weights and measures at the end of this period by computing

$$(I + G)A,$$

where I is the 3×3 identity matrix.

3.3 Elementary Operations: Solving Systems of Equations

Objective   ■ To use matrices to solve systems of linear equations

There are many occasions in business when the simultaneous solution of linear equations is important. We have already seen examples of this in Chapter 2 when we found market equilibrium and solved an accounting problem by the simultaneous solution of two linear equations in two unknowns.

In this section we will concentrate on developing procedures for finding out whether a system of linear equations has a solution and for finding all such solutions.

In Section 2.5, we solved the system of equations

$$\begin{cases} 4x + 5y = 18 \\ x - 3y = -4 \end{cases}$$

by the substitution method. We could also reduce the system to a system whose solution is easily found by adding a multiple of one of the equations to the other and eliminating a variable. The operations that we can perform to change a system to an equivalent system (one having the same solution) are

1. Interchanging two of the equations
2. Adding a multiple of one equation to another equation
3. Multiplying both sides of an equation by a nonzero constant

Suppose we wish to reduce this system by eliminating the x variable from the equation $4x + 5y = 18$. Let us begin by interchanging the equations and solving the equivalent system

$$\begin{cases} x - 3y = -4 & (1) \\ 4x + 5y = 18. & (2) \end{cases}$$

The following shows how we can use these operations to solve this system.

OPERATION PERFORMED	RESULTING SYSTEM
1. Original system	1. $\begin{cases} x - 3y = -4 & (1) \\ 4x + 5y = 18 & (2) \end{cases}$
2. Add -4 times equation (1) to equation (2), to eliminate x from equation (2). Keep equation (1) in its original form.	2. $\begin{cases} x - 3y = -4 & (1) \\ 17y = 34 & (2) \end{cases}$
3. Multiply both sides of equation (2) by $\frac{1}{17}$ (divide both sides by 17) to solve equation (2) for y. Keep equation (1) in its original form.	3. $\begin{cases} x - 3y = -4 & (1) \\ y = 2 & (2) \end{cases}$
4. Add 3 times equation (2) to equation (1), to eliminate y from equation (1). The solutions for the system can be read from this form.	4. $\begin{cases} x = 2 & (1) \\ y = 2 & (2) \end{cases}$

In reducing this system of equations, we operate on the coefficients of x and y, and the constants. If we keep the x and y variables in distinctive columns, we do not need to write them. Thus we can save some needless writing by using matrices to represent the system.

The original system of equations can be written as the **matrix equation**

$$\begin{bmatrix} x - 3y \\ 4x + 5y \end{bmatrix} = \begin{bmatrix} -4 \\ 18 \end{bmatrix}.$$

Notice that both matrices are column matrices, since $x - 3y$ and $4x + 5y$ each represent a single number for a given value of x and y. This matrix equation can also be written in the form

$$\begin{bmatrix} 1 & -3 \\ 4 & 5 \end{bmatrix} \begin{bmatrix} x \\ y \end{bmatrix} = \begin{bmatrix} -4 \\ 18 \end{bmatrix}.$$

We can see that this second form of a matrix equation is equivalent to the first if we carry out the multiplication.

Now, if we denote the matrices as follows:

$$A = \begin{bmatrix} 1 & -3 \\ 4 & 5 \end{bmatrix}, \qquad X = \begin{bmatrix} x \\ y \end{bmatrix}, \qquad \text{and} \qquad C = \begin{bmatrix} -4 \\ 18 \end{bmatrix},$$

then the earlier equation can be written as $AX = C$, where each matrix represents one of the three essential ingredients of every system of linear equations. Matrix A is called the **coefficient matrix,** and each entry corresponds to an equation and to a variable to which that coefficient belongs. Matrix X is a column matrix listing the variables involved. Matrix C is the **matrix of constants** with the position of the entries corresponding to the equation in which they occurred.

As we noted earlier, the variables only served as labels or placeholders to ensure that we combined like terms. The actual calculations we performed involved only the coefficients and the constants. Thus the system can be described by a single matrix,

$$[A \mid C] = \begin{bmatrix} 1 & -3 & \bigm| & -4 \\ 4 & 5 & \bigm| & 18 \end{bmatrix},$$

called an **augmented matrix.** The solid line separates the coefficients from the constants much the same as the equal signs did in the original system. The entry on the right side of the line is called the **augment.** Furthermore, the operations used to reduce the system of equations can now be described as row operations on the augmented matrix.

When we solved the system, we first added -4 times equation (1) to equation (2), so we will begin by adding -4 times row 1 to row 2 in the augmented matrix to obtain

$$\begin{bmatrix} 1 & -3 & \bigm| & -4 \\ 4 + (-4)(1) & 5 + (-4)(-3) & \bigm| & 18 + (-4)(-4) \end{bmatrix}$$

$$= \begin{bmatrix} 1 & -3 & \bigm| & -4 \\ 0 & 17 & \bigm| & 34 \end{bmatrix}.$$

The entries in this matrix correspond to the augmented matrix for the system of equations given in step 2 above.

We next multiplied both sides of equation (2) by $\frac{1}{17}$, so we will multiply row 2 by $\frac{1}{17}$, which yields

$$\begin{bmatrix} 1 & -3 & \bigm| & -4 \\ \frac{1}{17}(0) & \frac{1}{17}(17) & \bigm| & \frac{1}{17}(34) \end{bmatrix} = \begin{bmatrix} 1 & -3 & \bigm| & -4 \\ 0 & 1 & \bigm| & 2 \end{bmatrix}.$$

This matrix is equivalent to the augmented matrix for the system in step 3.

Finally, we added 3 times equation (2) to equation (1). The equivalent matrix operation is to add 3 times row (2) to row (1). This gives us the matrix

$$\begin{bmatrix} 1 + (3)(0) & -3 + (3)(1) & \bigm| & -4 + (3)(2) \\ 0 & 1 & \bigm| & 2 \end{bmatrix} = \begin{bmatrix} 1 & 0 & \bigm| & 2 \\ 0 & 1 & \bigm| & 2 \end{bmatrix}.$$

This augmented matrix corresponds to the matrix equation

$$\begin{bmatrix} 1 & 0 \\ 0 & 1 \end{bmatrix} \begin{bmatrix} x \\ y \end{bmatrix} = \begin{bmatrix} 2 \\ 2 \end{bmatrix},$$

$$\begin{bmatrix} x \\ y \end{bmatrix} = \begin{bmatrix} 2 \\ 2 \end{bmatrix}.$$

Note that this matrix equation leads to the same reduced system of equations that we got algebraically, in step 4. That is, we can use matrices to solve systems of linear equations. Thus we see that we can perform the same operations on the rows of matrices to reduce them as we do on equations in a linear system to reduce it. The three different operations we used to reduce the matrix are called **elementary row operations.** These operations are
1. Interchange two rows
2. Add a multiple of one row to another row
3. Multiply a row by any nonzero constant

When a new matrix results from one or more of these elementary row operations being performed on a matrix, the new matrix is called *equivalent* to the original.

EXAMPLE 1   Use matrices to solve the system

$$\begin{cases} 2x + 5y + 4z = 4 \\ x + 4y + 3z = 1 \\ x - 3y - 2z = 5. \end{cases}$$

Solution   The matrix equation is

$$\begin{bmatrix} 2 & 5 & 4 \\ 1 & 4 & 3 \\ 1 & -3 & -2 \end{bmatrix} \begin{bmatrix} x \\ y \\ z \end{bmatrix} = \begin{bmatrix} 4 \\ 1 \\ 5 \end{bmatrix},$$

so the augmented matrix is

$$\begin{bmatrix} 2 & 5 & 4 & \bigm| & 4 \\ 1 & 4 & 3 & \bigm| & 1 \\ 1 & -3 & -2 & \bigm| & 5 \end{bmatrix}.$$

Note that this system has 3 equations in 3 unknowns, but the reduction procedure and row operations apply regardless of the size of the system.

The following display shows a series of step-by-step goals for reducing a matrix and shows a series of row operations that reduces this matrix.

GOAL (for each step)	ROW OPERATION	EQUIVALENT MATRIX
1. Get a 1 in row 1, col. 1.	Interchange row 1 and row 2.	$\begin{bmatrix} 1 & 4 & 3 & 1 \\ 2 & 5 & 4 & 4 \\ 1 & -3 & -2 & 5 \end{bmatrix}$
2. Use row 1 only to get other entries in col. 1 zeros.	Add -2 times row 1 to row 2, and add -1 times row 1 to row 3.	$\begin{bmatrix} 1 & 4 & 3 & 1 \\ 0 & -3 & -2 & 2 \\ 0 & -7 & -5 & 4 \end{bmatrix}$
3. Use rows below row 1 to get a 1 in row 2, col. 2.	Multiply row 2 by $-\frac{1}{3}$.	$\begin{bmatrix} 1 & 4 & 3 & 1 \\ 0 & 1 & \frac{2}{3} & -\frac{2}{3} \\ 0 & -7 & -5 & 4 \end{bmatrix}$
4. Use row 2 only to get other entries in col. 2 zeros.	Add -4 times row 2 to row 1, and add 7 times row 2 to row 3.	$\begin{bmatrix} 1 & 0 & \frac{1}{3} & \frac{11}{3} \\ 0 & 1 & \frac{2}{3} & -\frac{2}{3} \\ 0 & 0 & -\frac{1}{3} & -\frac{2}{3} \end{bmatrix}$
5. Use row below row 2 to get a 1 in row 3, col. 3.	Multiply row 3 by -3.	$\begin{bmatrix} 1 & 0 & \frac{1}{3} & \frac{11}{3} \\ 0 & 1 & \frac{2}{3} & -\frac{2}{3} \\ 0 & 0 & 1 & 2 \end{bmatrix}$
6. Use row 3 only to get other entries in col. 1 zeros.	Add $-\frac{1}{3}$ times row 3 to row 1, and add $-\frac{2}{3}$ times row 3 to row 2.	$\begin{bmatrix} 1 & 0 & 0 & 3 \\ 0 & 1 & 0 & -2 \\ 0 & 0 & 1 & 2 \end{bmatrix}$

This (equivalent) reduced matrix forms the equivalent matrix equation

$$\begin{bmatrix} 1 & 0 & 0 \\ 0 & 1 & 0 \\ 0 & 0 & 1 \end{bmatrix} \begin{bmatrix} x \\ y \\ z \end{bmatrix} = \begin{bmatrix} 3 \\ 2 \\ 2 \end{bmatrix},$$

or, by multiplying the matrices on the left side,

$$\begin{bmatrix} x \\ y \\ z \end{bmatrix} = \begin{bmatrix} 3 \\ -2 \\ 2 \end{bmatrix}.$$

Thus the solution to the system is $x = 3$, $y = -2$, and $z = 2$.   □

Note that the solution in Example 1 is unique, for no other values for x, y, and z will satisfy the system of equations. Note also that the matrix corresponding to the coefficients in Example 1 reduced to an identity matrix. Not all coefficients matrices will reduce to an identity matrix, so we need to define when a matrix is in a reduced form.

A matrix is said to be in **reduced form** when it is in the following form:

1. The first nonzero element in each row is a 1.
2. Every column containing a first nonzero element for some row has zeros everywhere else.
3. The first nonzero element of each row is to the right of the first nonzero element of every row above it.
4. All rows containing zeros are grouped together below the rows containing nonzero entries.

The following matrices are in reduced form because they satisfy these conditions:

$$\left[\begin{array}{cc|c} 1 & 0 & 4 \\ 0 & 1 & 2 \\ 0 & 0 & 0 \end{array}\right] \qquad \left[\begin{array}{ccc|c} 1 & 0 & 0 & 0 \\ 0 & 1 & 0 & 3 \\ 0 & 0 & 1 & 0 \\ 0 & 0 & 0 & 1 \end{array}\right] \qquad \left[\begin{array}{ccc|c} 1 & 4 & 0 & 1 \\ 0 & 0 & 1 & 2 \\ 0 & 0 & 0 & 0 \end{array}\right].$$

The following matrices are *not* in reduced form:

$$\left[\begin{array}{cc|c} 1 & ① & 0 \\ 0 & 1 & 3 \\ 0 & 0 & 0 \end{array}\right] \qquad \left[\begin{array}{cc|c} 1 & 0 & 1 \\ 0 & ② & 1 \\ 0 & 0 & 0 \end{array}\right] \qquad \left[\begin{array}{cc|c} 0 & 1 & 0 \\ 1 & 0 & 0 \\ 0 & 0 & 1 \end{array}\right].$$

In the first two matrices the circled element must be changed to obtain a reduced form. Can you see what row operations would transform each of these matrices into reduced form? The third matrix does not satisfy point 3 above.

We can solve a system of linear equations by using row operations on the augmented matrix until the coefficient matrix is transformed to an equivalent matrix in reduced form.

EXAMPLE 2   Solve the system

$$\begin{cases} x_1 + x_2 - x_3 + x_4 = 3 \\ x_2 + x_3 + x_4 = 1 \\ x_1 \quad\quad - 2x_3 + x_4 = 6 \\ 2x_1 - x_2 - 5x_3 - 3x_4 = -5. \end{cases}$$

Solution   First note that there are variables missing in the second and third equations. When we form the matrix equation we must enter zeros in these places so that each column represents the coefficients of one variable. The matrix equation is

$$\begin{bmatrix} 1 & 1 & -1 & 1 \\ 0 & 1 & 1 & 1 \\ 1 & 0 & -2 & 1 \\ 2 & -1 & -5 & -3 \end{bmatrix} \begin{bmatrix} x_1 \\ x_2 \\ x_3 \\ x_4 \end{bmatrix} = \begin{bmatrix} 3 \\ 1 \\ 6 \\ -5 \end{bmatrix}.$$

To solve this system we must reduce the augmented matrix

$$\begin{bmatrix} 1 & 1 & -1 & 1 & 3 \\ 0 & 1 & 1 & 1 & 1 \\ 1 & 0 & -2 & 1 & 6 \\ 2 & -1 & -5 & -3 & -5 \end{bmatrix}.$$

The reduction process follows. Entry in row 1, column 1 is a 1. To get 0's in the first column, add -1 times row 1 to row 3, and add -2 times row 1 to row 4.

$$\begin{bmatrix} 1 & 1 & -1 & 1 & 3 \\ 0 & 1 & 1 & 1 & 1 \\ 0 & -1 & -1 & 0 & 3 \\ 0 & -3 & -3 & -5 & -11 \end{bmatrix}$$

Entry in row 2, column 2 is a 1. To get 0's in the second column, add -1 times row 2 to row 1, add row 2 to row 3, and add 3 times row 2 to row 4.

$$\begin{bmatrix} 1 & 0 & -2 & 0 & 2 \\ 0 & 1 & 1 & 1 & 1 \\ 0 & 0 & 0 & 1 & 4 \\ 0 & 0 & 0 & -2 & -8 \end{bmatrix}$$

Entry in row 3, column 3 cannot be made 1 using rows *below* row 2. Move to column 4; entry in row 3, column 4 is a 1. To get 0's in the fourth column, add -1 times row 3 to row 2, and add 2 times row 3 to row 4.

$$\begin{bmatrix} 1 & 0 & -2 & 0 & 2 \\ 0 & 1 & 1 & 0 & -3 \\ 0 & 0 & 0 & 1 & 4 \\ 0 & 0 & 0 & 0 & 0 \end{bmatrix}$$

The augmented matrix is now reduced; this matrix corresponds to the matrix equation

$$\begin{bmatrix} 1 & 0 & -2 & 0 \\ 0 & 1 & 1 & 0 \\ 0 & 0 & 0 & 1 \\ 0 & 0 & 0 & 0 \end{bmatrix} \begin{bmatrix} x_1 \\ x_2 \\ x_3 \\ x_4 \end{bmatrix} = \begin{bmatrix} 2 \\ -3 \\ 4 \\ 0 \end{bmatrix},$$

or, by multiplying,

$$\begin{bmatrix} x_1 & -2x_3 \\ x_2 + & x_3 \\ & x_4 \\ & 0 \end{bmatrix} = \begin{bmatrix} 2 \\ -3 \\ 4 \\ 0 \end{bmatrix}.$$

Thus the equivalent system is

$$\begin{cases} x_1 - 2x_3 = 2 \\ x_2 + x_3 = -3 \\ x_4 = 4. \end{cases}$$

If we solve each of these equations for the leading variable (the variable corresponding to the first 1 in each row of the reduced form of the matrix), we obtain

$$\begin{aligned} x_1 &= 2 + 2x_3 \\ x_2 &= -3 - x_3 \\ x_4 &= 4. \end{aligned}$$

In this form we have the values of x_1 and x_2 dependent on the value of x_3, so we can get many different solutions to the system by specifying different values for x_3. For example, if $x_3 = 1$, then $x_1 = 4$, $x_2 = -4$, $x_3 = 1$, and $x_4 = 4$ is a solution to the system; if we let $x_3 = -2$, then $x_1 = -2$, $x_2 = -1$, $x_3 = -2$, and $x_4 = 4$ is a solution. The **general solution** to the system is given by

$$\begin{aligned} x_1 &= 2 + 2x_3 \\ x_2 &= -3 - x_3 \\ x_4 &= 4 \end{aligned}$$

or

$$\begin{aligned} x_1 &= 2 + 2x_3 \\ x_2 &= -3 - x_3 \\ x_3 &= x_3 \\ x_4 &= 4. \end{aligned} \qquad \square$$

In Examples 1 and 2 we have seen two different possibilities for solutions to systems of linear equations. In Example 1 there was only one solution, whereas in Example 2 we saw that there were many solutions. A third possibility exists, namely that the system will have no solution. Recall that these three possibilities also existed for two equations in two unknowns, as discussed in Chapter 2.

EXAMPLE 3   Solve the system

$$\begin{cases} x + 2y - z = 3 \\ 3x + y = 4 \\ 2x - y + z = 2. \end{cases}$$

Solution   The matrix equation is

$$\begin{bmatrix} 1 & 2 & -1 \\ 3 & 1 & 0 \\ 2 & -1 & 1 \end{bmatrix} \begin{bmatrix} x \\ y \\ z \end{bmatrix} = \begin{bmatrix} 3 \\ 4 \\ 2 \end{bmatrix},$$

and the augmented matrix is

$$\left[\begin{array}{ccc|c} 1 & 2 & -1 & 3 \\ 3 & 1 & 0 & 4 \\ 2 & -1 & 1 & 2 \end{array}\right],$$

This can be reduced as follows.

$$\left[\begin{array}{ccc|c} 1 & 2 & -1 & 3 \\ 3 & 1 & 0 & 4 \\ 2 & -1 & 1 & 2 \end{array}\right] \xrightarrow[\text{Add } (-2)R_1 \text{ to } R_3]{\text{Add } (-3)R_1 \text{ to } R_2} \left[\begin{array}{ccc|c} 1 & 2 & -1 & 3 \\ 0 & -5 & 3 & -5 \\ 0 & -5 & 3 & -4 \end{array}\right]$$

$$\xrightarrow{(-\frac{1}{5})R_2} \left[\begin{array}{ccc|c} 1 & 2 & -1 & 3 \\ 0 & 1 & -\frac{3}{5} & 1 \\ 0 & -5 & 3 & -4 \end{array}\right]$$

$$\xrightarrow[\text{Add } (5)R_2 \text{ to } R_3]{\text{Add } (-2)R_2 \text{ to } R_1} \left[\begin{array}{ccc|c} 1 & 0 & \frac{1}{5} & 1 \\ 0 & 1 & -\frac{3}{5} & 1 \\ 0 & 0 & 0 & 1 \end{array}\right].$$

The matrix equation corresponding to the reduced matrix is

$$\left[\begin{array}{ccc} 1 & 0 & \frac{1}{5} \\ 0 & 1 & -\frac{3}{5} \\ 0 & 0 & 0 \end{array}\right] \left[\begin{array}{c} x \\ y \\ z \end{array}\right] = \left[\begin{array}{c} 1 \\ 1 \\ 1 \end{array}\right],$$

or

$$\left[\begin{array}{c} x + \frac{1}{5}z \\ y - \frac{3}{5}z \\ 0 \end{array}\right] = \left[\begin{array}{c} 1 \\ 1 \\ 1 \end{array}\right],$$

so the equivalent system of equations is

$$\begin{cases} x + \frac{1}{5}z = 1 \\ y - \frac{3}{5}z = 1. \\ \quad\ 0 = 1 \end{cases}$$

Thus we see that this system has $0 = 1$ as an equation. This is clearly an impossibility, so there is no solution. □

Now that we have seen examples of each of the different solution possibilities, let us consider what we have learned. In all cases the solution procedure began by setting up and then reducing the augmented matrix. Once the matrix is reduced, we can write the corresponding reduced system of equations. The solutions, if they exist, are easily found from this reduced system.

EXAMPLE 4   Solve the system

$$\begin{cases} x_1 + 2x_2 + x_3 - x_4 = 4 \\ x_1 - x_2 + 2x_3 + x_4 = -1 \\ x_1 + 3x_2 - x_3 - x_4 = 5 \\ 2x_1 + x_2 - 3x_3 + x_4 = 2. \end{cases}$$

Solution   The augmented matrix for the system is

$$\left[\begin{array}{cccc|c} 1 & 2 & 1 & -1 & 4 \\ 1 & -1 & 2 & 1 & -1 \\ 1 & 3 & -1 & -1 & 5 \\ 2 & 1 & -3 & 1 & 2 \end{array}\right]$$

Reducing gives

$$\left[\begin{array}{cccc|c} 1 & 0 & 0 & 0 & 1 \\ 0 & 1 & 0 & 0 & 1 \\ 0 & 0 & 1 & 0 & 0 \\ 0 & 0 & 0 & 1 & -1 \end{array}\right]$$

so the solution to the system is $x_1 = 1$, $x_2 = 1$, $x_3 = 0$, $x_4 = -1$. □

EXAMPLE 5   The Walters Manufacturing Company makes three types of metal storage sheds. The company has three departments: stamping, painting, and packaging. The following table gives the number of hours each division requires for each shed.

Departments	Shed		
	Type I	Type II	Type III
Stamping	2	3	4
Painting	1	2	1
Packaging	1	1	2

Using the information in the table, determine how many of each type of shed can be produced if the stamping department has 3200 hours available, the painting department has 1700 hours, and the packaging department has 1300 hours.

Solution   If we let x_1 be the number of type I sheds, x_2 be the number of type II sheds, and x_3 be the number of type III sheds, the equation

$$2x_1 + 3x_2 + 4x_3 = 3200$$

represents the hours used by the stamping department. Similarly,

$$1x_1 + 2x_2 + 1x_3 = 1700$$

and

$$1x_1 + 1x_2 + 2x_3 = 1300$$

represent the hours used by the painting and packaging departments, respectively.

Writing this system of equations in matrix form, we have

$$\begin{bmatrix} 2 & 3 & 4 \\ 1 & 2 & 1 \\ 1 & 1 & 2 \end{bmatrix} \begin{bmatrix} x_1 \\ x_2 \\ x_3 \end{bmatrix} = \begin{bmatrix} 3200 \\ 1700 \\ 1300 \end{bmatrix}.$$

The augmented matrix for this matrix equation is

$$\left[\begin{array}{ccc|c} 2 & 3 & 4 & 3200 \\ 1 & 2 & 1 & 1700 \\ 1 & 1 & 2 & 1300 \end{array} \right].$$

Reducing this augmented matrix gives

$$\left[\begin{array}{ccc|c} 1 & 0 & 0 & 300 \\ 0 & 1 & 0 & 600 \\ 0 & 0 & 1 & 200 \end{array} \right].$$

Thus the reduced matrix equation is

$$\begin{bmatrix} 1 & 0 & 0 \\ 0 & 1 & 0 \\ 0 & 0 & 1 \end{bmatrix} \begin{bmatrix} x_1 \\ x_2 \\ x_3 \end{bmatrix} = \begin{bmatrix} 300 \\ 600 \\ 200 \end{bmatrix}.$$

The solution to the system is

$$x_1 = 300$$
$$x_2 = 600$$
$$x_3 = 200.$$

Thus the company should make 300 type I, 600 type II, and 200 type III sheds. □

Exercise 3.3 Write the augmented matrix associated with each of the following systems of linear equations.

1. $\begin{cases} 3x + 2y + 4z = 0 \\ 2x - y + 2z = 0 \\ x - 2y - 4z = 0 \end{cases}$

2. $\begin{cases} x - 3y + 4z = 0 \\ 2x + 2y + z = 1 \\ 3x - 4y + 2z = 9 \end{cases}$

3. $\begin{cases} x - 3y + 4z = 2 \\ 2x + 2z = 1 \\ x + 2y + z = 1 \end{cases}$

4. $\begin{cases} x + 2y - 2z = 3 \\ x - 2y = 4 \\ y - z = 1 \end{cases}$

Find the general solutions to the following systems of equations, if they exist.

5. $\begin{cases} x + y + z = 0 \\ 2x - y - z = 0 \\ -x + 2y + 2z = 0 \end{cases}$

6. $\begin{cases} 2x - y + 3z = 0 \\ x + 2y + 2z = 0 \\ x - 3y + z = 0 \end{cases}$

7. $\begin{cases} x - 3y + 3z = 7 \\ x + 2y - z = -2 \\ 3x + 2y + 4z = 5 \end{cases}$

8. $\begin{cases} 2x - 4y + 2z = 2 \\ x - 2y + z = 1 \\ x - 5y + 3z = 0 \end{cases}$

9. $\begin{cases} 2x + y - z = 2 \\ x - y + 2z = 3 \\ x + y - z = 1 \end{cases}$

10. $\begin{cases} 3x + 2y + z = 0 \\ x + y + 2z = 1 \\ 2x + y - z = -1 \end{cases}$

11. $\begin{cases} x + 3y + 2z = 2 \\ 2x - y - 2z = 1 \\ 3x + 2y = 3 \end{cases}$

12. $\begin{cases} 2x + 2y + z = 2 \\ x - 2y + 2z = 1 \\ -x + 2y - 2z = -1 \end{cases}$

13. $\begin{cases} 2x + 3y + 4z = 2 \\ x + 2y + 2z = 1 \\ x + y + 2z = 2 \end{cases}$

14. $\begin{cases} x + 2y + 3z = 1 \\ 2x - y = 3 \\ x + 2y + 3z = 2 \end{cases}$

15. $\begin{cases} x_1 + 3x_2 + 2x_3 + 2x_4 = 3 \\ x_1 + x_2 + 3x_3 = 4 \\ 2x_1 + 2x_3 - 3x_4 = 4 \\ x_1 - 3x_2 = 1 \end{cases}$

APPLICATIONS

16. A bank loaned $118,500 to a company for the development of two products. If the loan for product A was for $34,500 more than that for product B, how much was loaned for each product?

17. A person has $23,500 invested in two rental properties. One earns 5% on the investment and the other yields 6%. The total income from the two properties is $1275. How much is the income from each property?

18. Mr. Jackson borrowed money from his bank and on his life insurance to start a business. His interest rate on the bank loan is 5% and his rate on the insurance loan is 6%. If the total amount borrowed is $10,000 and his total yearly interest payment is $545, how much did he borrow from the bank?

19. The King Trucking Company has an order for three products to be delivered to a destination. The table gives the particulars for the products.

	Type I	Type II	Type III
Unit volume (cu ft)	10	8	20
Unit weight (lb)	10	20	40
Unit value ($)	100	20	200

If the carrier can carry 6000 cu ft, 11,000 lb, and is insured for $36,900, how many units of each type can be carried?

20. An airline company has three types of aircraft, which carry three types of cargo. The payload of each type is summarized in the table at the top of page 125. Suppose that on a given day the airline must move 1100 units of first class mail, 460 units of air freight, and 1200 passengers. How many aircraft of each type should be scheduled?

	Plane Type		
Units Carried	*Passenger*	*Transport*	*Jumbo*
First class mail	100	100	100
Passengers	150	20	350
Air freight	20	65	35

21. A brokerage house offers three stock portfolios. Portfolio I consists of 2 blocks of common stock and 1 municipal bond. Portfolio II consists of 4 blocks of common stock, 2 municipal bonds, and 3 blocks of preferred stock. Portfolio III consists of 7 blocks of common stock, 3 municipal bonds, and 3 blocks of preferred stock. A customer wants 21 blocks of common stock, 10 municipal bonds, and 9 blocks of preferred stock. How many of each portfolio should be offered?

22. Suppose, in problem 21, portfolios I and II are unchanged and portfolio III consists of 2 blocks of common stock, 1 municipal bond, and 3 blocks of preferred stock. A customer wants 16 blocks of common stock, 8 municipal bonds, and 6 blocks of preferred stock. How many of each portfolio should be offered?

23. Suppose the shipping department of a firm charges 20% of its *total* monthly costs to the printing department, while the printing department charges 10% of its *total* monthly costs to the shipping department. If the direct costs of the shipping department are $12,000 and the direct costs of the printing department are $9,580, find the total costs for each department.

24. Suppose the development department of a firm charges 10% of its total monthly costs to the promotional department, and the promotional department charges 5% of its total monthly costs to the development department. If the direct costs of the development department are $19,895 and the direct costs of the promotional department are $10,000, find the total costs for each department.

In the analysis of traffic flows, a certain city estimates the following situation for an area of its downtown district. Figure 3.2 indicates the traffic flow, with the arrows indicating

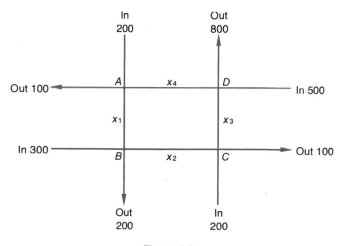

Figure 3.2

the flow of traffic. If x_1 represents the number of cars traveling between intersections A and B, x_2 represents the number of cars traveling between B and C, x_3 the number between C and D, and x_4 the number between D and A, we can formulate equations based on the principle that the number of vehicles entering an intersection equals the number leaving it. That is, for intersection A we obtain

$$200 + x_4 = 100 + x_1.$$

Use these data to answer problems 25–27.

25. Formulate equations for the traffic at B, C, and D.

26. Solve the system of these four equations.

27. It is obvious that all variables must be nonnegative. However, there are other restrictions; formulate restrictions on the maximum number each variable could assume.

3.4 Inverse of a Square Matrix (Optional)

Objectives
 ■ To find the inverse of a square matrix
 ■ To use inverse matrices to solve systems of linear equations

As we stated earlier, an $n \times n$ (square) matrix which has 1's down its diagonal and 0's everywhere else is called an **identity matrix**. The matrix

$$I = \begin{bmatrix} 1 & 0 & 0 \\ 0 & 1 & 0 \\ 0 & 0 & 1 \end{bmatrix}$$

is a 3×3 identity matrix.

Inverse Matrices   If the product of two square matrices is the identity matrix, each matrix is called the **inverse** of the other.

The multiplicative inverse of the square matrix A is denoted by A^{-1}. The inverse of A must satisfy

$$A^{-1}A = I \qquad \text{and} \qquad AA^{-1} = I.$$

EXAMPLE 1   Is B the inverse of A if $A = \begin{bmatrix} 1 & 2 \\ 1 & 1 \end{bmatrix}$ and $B = \begin{bmatrix} -1 & 2 \\ 1 & -1 \end{bmatrix}$?

Solution
$$A \cdot B = \begin{bmatrix} 1 & 2 \\ 1 & 1 \end{bmatrix} \cdot \begin{bmatrix} -1 & 2 \\ 1 & -1 \end{bmatrix} = \begin{bmatrix} 1 & 0 \\ 0 & 1 \end{bmatrix} = I.$$

Thus B is the inverse A. We also say A is the inverse of B.   □

We have seen how to use elementary row operations on augmented matrices to solve systems of linear equations. We can also find the inverse of a matrix using elementary row operations.

If the inverse A^{-1} exists for a square matrix A, we proceed as follows.

PROCEDURE	EXAMPLE
To find the inverse of the square matrix A:	Find the inverse of matrix $A = \begin{bmatrix} 1 & 2 \\ 1 & 1 \end{bmatrix}$.
1. Form the augmented matrix $[A\,|\,I]$ where A is the $n \times n$ matrix and I is the $n \times n$ identity matrix.	1. $\begin{bmatrix} 1 & 2 & | & 1 & 0 \\ 1 & 1 & | & 0 & 1 \end{bmatrix}$
2. Perform elementary operations on $[A\,|\,I]$ until we have an augmented matrix of the form $[I\,|\,B]$; that is, until the matrix A on the left is transformed into the identity matrix.	2. $\begin{bmatrix} 1 & 2 & | & 1 & 0 \\ 1 & 1 & | & 0 & 1 \end{bmatrix} \longrightarrow \begin{bmatrix} 1 & 2 & | & 1 & 0 \\ 0 & -1 & | & -1 & 1 \end{bmatrix}$ $\longrightarrow \begin{bmatrix} 1 & 0 & | & -1 & 2 \\ 0 & 1 & | & 1 & -1 \end{bmatrix}$
3. The matrix B (on the right) is the inverse of matrix A.	3. The inverse of A is $B = \begin{bmatrix} -1 & 2 \\ 1 & -1 \end{bmatrix}$. We have verified this in Example 1.

EXAMPLE 2   If $A = \begin{bmatrix} 1 & 0 & 3 \\ 1 & 2 & 0 \\ 1 & 1 & 1 \end{bmatrix}$, find the matrix A^{-1}.

Solution $\begin{bmatrix} 1 & 0 & 3 & | & 1 & 0 & 0 \\ 1 & 2 & 0 & | & 0 & 1 & 0 \\ 1 & 1 & 1 & | & 0 & 0 & 1 \end{bmatrix} \xrightarrow[-R_1+ \text{ to } R_3]{-R_1+ \text{ to } R_2} \begin{bmatrix} 1 & 0 & 3 & | & 1 & 0 & 0 \\ 0 & 2 & -3 & | & -1 & 1 & 0 \\ 0 & 1 & -2 & | & -1 & 0 & 1 \end{bmatrix}$

$\xrightarrow[-2R_2 \text{ (new)}+ \text{ to } R_3]{\text{Switch } R_2 \text{ and } R_3} \begin{bmatrix} 1 & 0 & 3 & | & 1 & 0 & 0 \\ 0 & 1 & -2 & | & -1 & 0 & 1 \\ 0 & 0 & 1 & | & 1 & 1 & -2 \end{bmatrix}$

$\xrightarrow[2R_3+ \text{ to } R_2]{-3R_3+ \text{ to } R_1} \begin{bmatrix} 1 & 0 & 0 & | & -2 & -3 & 6 \\ 0 & 1 & 0 & | & 1 & 2 & -3 \\ 0 & 0 & 1 & | & 1 & 1 & -2 \end{bmatrix}$

Thus

$$A^{-1} = \begin{bmatrix} -2 & -3 & 6 \\ 1 & 2 & -3 \\ 1 & 1 & -2 \end{bmatrix}.$$

Checking, we see $A \cdot A^{-1} = I$.   □

In Example 1 of Section 3.3, we solved the system

$$\begin{cases} 2x + 5y + 4z = 4 \\ x + 4y + 3z = 1 \\ x - 3y - 2z = 5 \end{cases}$$

by using the matrix equation

$$\begin{bmatrix} 2 & 5 & 4 \\ 1 & 4 & 3 \\ 1 & -3 & -2 \end{bmatrix} \begin{bmatrix} x \\ y \\ z \end{bmatrix} = \begin{bmatrix} 4 \\ 1 \\ 5 \end{bmatrix}.$$

We can also solve this matrix equation by multiplying both sides of the equation by the inverse of

$$\begin{bmatrix} 2 & 5 & 4 \\ 1 & 4 & 3 \\ 1 & -3 & -2 \end{bmatrix}.$$

Using the same elementary row operations as those used in Example 1 of Section 3.3, we can reduce

$$\left[\begin{array}{ccc|ccc} 2 & 5 & 4 & 1 & 0 & 0 \\ 1 & 4 & 3 & 0 & 1 & 0 \\ 1 & -3 & -2 & 0 & 0 & 1 \end{array}\right] \quad \text{to} \quad \left[\begin{array}{ccc|ccc} 1 & 0 & 0 & -1 & 2 & 1 \\ 0 & 1 & 0 & -5 & 8 & 2 \\ 0 & 0 & 1 & 7 & -11 & -3 \end{array}\right],$$

so the inverse we seek is

$$\begin{bmatrix} -1 & 2 & 1 \\ -5 & 8 & 2 \\ 7 & -11 & -3 \end{bmatrix}.$$

Now we can multiply both sides of the given equation by the inverse.

$$\begin{bmatrix} -1 & 2 & 1 \\ -5 & 8 & 2 \\ 7 & -11 & -3 \end{bmatrix} \cdot \begin{bmatrix} 2 & 5 & 4 \\ 1 & 4 & 3 \\ 1 & -3 & -2 \end{bmatrix} \begin{bmatrix} x \\ y \\ z \end{bmatrix} = \begin{bmatrix} -1 & 2 & 1 \\ -5 & 8 & 2 \\ 7 & -11 & -3 \end{bmatrix} \begin{bmatrix} 4 \\ 1 \\ 5 \end{bmatrix}$$

Notice that we must be careful to multiply both sides *from the left* since matrix multiplication is not commutative. If we carry out the multiplications, we obtain

$$\begin{bmatrix} 1 & 0 & 0 \\ 0 & 1 & 0 \\ 0 & 0 & 1 \end{bmatrix} \begin{bmatrix} x \\ y \\ z \end{bmatrix} = \begin{bmatrix} 3 \\ -2 \\ 2 \end{bmatrix},$$

which yields the same solution as that found in Example 1 of Section 3.3. Thus inverse matrices can be used to solve systems of equations. Unfortunately, this method will work only if the solution to the system is unique.

Exercise 3.4

1. If $A = \begin{bmatrix} 1 & 2 & 1 \\ 0 & 0 & 3 \\ 1 & 0 & 1 \end{bmatrix}$ and $B = \begin{bmatrix} 0 & -\frac{1}{3} & 1 \\ \frac{1}{2} & 0 & -\frac{1}{2} \\ 0 & \frac{1}{3} & 0 \end{bmatrix}$, does $B = A^{-1}$?

2. If $D = \begin{bmatrix} 0 & 2 & -6 \\ -3 & 0 & 3 \\ 0 & -2 & 0 \end{bmatrix}$ and $C = -\frac{1}{3}\begin{bmatrix} 2 & 4 & 2 \\ 0 & 0 & 6 \\ 2 & 0 & 2 \end{bmatrix}$, does $C = D^{-1}$?

3. What is the inverse of $A = \begin{bmatrix} 3 & 0 & 0 \\ 0 & 3 & 0 \\ 0 & 0 & 3 \end{bmatrix}$?

4. Find the inverse of $A = \begin{bmatrix} 1 & 2 \\ 3 & 0 \end{bmatrix}$, if it exists.

5. Find the inverse of $B = \begin{bmatrix} 0 & 1 & 0 \\ 1 & 1 & 0 \\ 0 & 1 & 1 \end{bmatrix}$, if it exists.

6. Find the inverse of $X = \begin{bmatrix} 0 & 2 & 1 \\ 3 & 0 & 1 \\ 1 & 1 & 1 \end{bmatrix}$, if it exists.

7. Find the inverse of $A = \begin{bmatrix} 3 & 1 & 2 \\ 1 & 2 & 3 \\ 1 & 1 & 1 \end{bmatrix}$, if it exists.

8. Find the inverse of $B = \begin{bmatrix} 1 & 2 & 3 \\ -1 & 5 & 6 \\ -1 & 3 & 3 \end{bmatrix}$, if it exists.

9. Use the inverse found in problem 5 to solve

$$\begin{bmatrix} 0 & 1 & 0 \\ 1 & 1 & 0 \\ 0 & 1 & 1 \end{bmatrix}\begin{bmatrix} x \\ y \\ z \end{bmatrix} = \begin{bmatrix} 1 \\ 2 \\ 3 \end{bmatrix}$$

10. Use the inverse found in problem 6 to solve

$$\begin{bmatrix} 0 & 2 & 1 \\ 3 & 0 & 1 \\ 1 & 1 & 1 \end{bmatrix}\begin{bmatrix} x \\ y \\ z \end{bmatrix} = \begin{bmatrix} 1 \\ 0 \\ 4 \end{bmatrix}$$

Use inverse matrices to solve the following systems of linear equations.

11. $\begin{cases} x + 2y = 4 \\ 3x + 4y = 10 \end{cases}$

12. $\begin{cases} 2x + y = 4 \\ 3x + y = 5 \end{cases}$

13. $\begin{cases} x + y + z = 3 \\ 2x + y + z = 4 \\ 2x + 2y + z = 5 \end{cases}$ 14. $\begin{cases} x + y + 2z = 8 \\ 2x + y + z = 7 \\ 2x + 2y + z = 10 \end{cases}$

3.5 Applications of Matrices: Leontief Input-Output Models

Objectives   ■ To interpret Leontief technology matrices
■ To use Leontief models to solve input-output problems

One interesting application of matrices is the Leontief Input-Output model, named for Wassily Leontief. Just as an airplane model approximates the real thing, a *mathematical model* attempts to approximate a real-world situation. Models that are carefully constructed from past information may often provide remarkably accurate forecasts. The model Leontief developed was useful in predicting the effects to the economy of price changes or shifts in government spending.°

Leontief's work divided the economy into 500 sectors, and in a subsequent article in *Scientific American* (October 1951), this was reduced to a more manageable 42 departments of production. We can examine the workings of input-output analysis with a very simplified view of the economy.

Suppose we consider a simple economy as being based on three commodities: agricultural products, manufactured goods, and fuels. Suppose further that production of 10 units of agricultural products requires 5 units of agricultural products, 2 units of manufactured goods, and 1 unit of fuels; production of 10 units of manufactured goods requires 1 unit of agricultural products, 5 units of manufactured products, and 3 units of fuels; and production of 10 units of fuels requires 1 unit of agricultural products, 3 units of manufactured goods, and 4 units of fuels.

Table 3.6 summarizes this information in terms of production of one unit. The first column represents the units of agricultural products, manufactured goods, and fuels, respectively, that are needed to produce one unit of agricultural products. Column 2 represents the units required to produce one unit of manufac-

Table 3.6

| | Outputs | | |
Inputs	Agricultural Products	Manufactured Goods	Fuels
Agricultural products	0.5	0.1	0.1
Manufactured goods	0.2	0.5	0.3
Fuels	0.1	0.3	0.4

° Leontief's work dealt with a massive analysis of the American economy. He was awarded a Nobel Prize in Economics in 1973 for his study.

tured goods, and column 3 represents the units required to produce one unit of fuels.

Note that the sum of the units of agricultural products, manufactured goods, and fuels required to produce 1 unit of fuels (column 3) does not add up to 1 unit. This is because not all commodities or industries are represented in the model. In particular, it is customary to omit labor from these models.

EXAMPLE 1   Use Table 3.6 to answer the following questions.
(a) How many units of fuels were required to produce 100 units of manufactured goods?
(b) Production of which commodity is least dependent on the other two?
(c) If fuel costs rise, which two industries will be most affected?

Solution   (a) Referring to column 2, manufactured goods, we see that one unit requires 0.1 unit of agricultural products and 0.3 unit of fuels. Thus 100 units of manufactured goods require 10 units of agricultural products and 30 units of fuels.
(b) Looking down the columns, we see that one unit of agricultural products requires 0.3 unit of the other two commodities; one unit of manufactured goods requires 0.4 unit of the other two; and one unit of fuels requires 0.4 unit of the other two. Thus production of agricultural products is less dependent on the others.
(c) A rise in the cost of fuels would most affect those industries using the larger amounts of fuels. One unit of agricultural products requires 0.1 unit of fuels, while a unit of manufactured goods requires 0.3 unit, and fuels requires 0.4 of its own units. Thus manufacturing and the fuel industry would be most affected by a cost increase in fuels.   □

From Table 3.6 we can form matrix A, called a **technology matrix** or a **Leontief matrix.**

$$A = \begin{bmatrix} 0.5 & 0.1 & 0.1 \\ 0.2 & 0.5 & 0.3 \\ 0.1 & 0.3 & 0.4 \end{bmatrix}$$

For this simplified model of the economy, not all information is contained within the technology matrix. In particular, each industry has a gross production. The **gross production matrix** for the economy can be represented by the column matrix

$$X = \begin{bmatrix} x_1 \\ x_2 \\ x_3 \end{bmatrix},$$

where x_1 is the gross production of agricultural products, x_2 is the gross production of manufactured goods, and x_3 is the gross production of fuels.

Those units of gross production not used by these industries are called **final demands** or **surpluses,** and may be considered as being available for consumers, the government, or export. If we place these surpluses in a column matrix D, then the surplus can be represented by the equation

$$X - AX = D, \quad \text{or} \quad (I - A)X = D,$$

where I is an identity matrix. This matrix equation is called the **technological equation.**

EXAMPLE 2   Use matrix A as the technology matrix. If we wish to have a surplus of 85 units of agricultural products, 65 units of manufactured goods, and 0 units of fuels, what should the gross outputs be?

Solution   Let X be the matrix as above. Then the technological equation is $(I - A)X = D$.

$$I - A = \begin{bmatrix} 1 & 0 & 0 \\ 0 & 1 & 0 \\ 0 & 0 & 1 \end{bmatrix} - \begin{bmatrix} 0.5 & 0.1 & 0.1 \\ 0.2 & 0.5 & 0.3 \\ 0.1 & 0.3 & 0.4 \end{bmatrix} = \begin{bmatrix} 0.5 & -0.1 & -0.1 \\ -0.2 & 0.5 & -0.3 \\ -0.1 & -0.3 & 0.6 \end{bmatrix}$$

Hence we must solve the system

$$\begin{bmatrix} 0.5 & -0.1 & -0.1 \\ -0.2 & 0.5 & -0.3 \\ -0.1 & -0.3 & 0.6 \end{bmatrix} \begin{bmatrix} x_1 \\ x_2 \\ x_3 \end{bmatrix} = \begin{bmatrix} 85 \\ 65 \\ 0 \end{bmatrix}.$$

The augmented matrix is

$$\begin{bmatrix} 0.5 & -0.1 & -0.1 & 85 \\ -0.2 & 0.5 & -0.3 & 65 \\ -0.1 & -0.3 & 0.6 & 0 \end{bmatrix}.$$

If we reduce this as in Section 3.3, we obtain

$$\begin{bmatrix} 1 & 0 & 0 & 300 \\ 0 & 1 & 0 & 400 \\ 0 & 0 & 1 & 250 \end{bmatrix},$$

so the gross outputs for the industries are

Agriculture: $x_1 = 300$
Manufacturing: $x_2 = 400$
Fuels: $x_3 = 250.$ □

A few comments are in order. First, the surplus matrix must contain positive or zero entries. If this is not the case, then the gross production of one or more industries is insufficient to supply the needs of the others. That is, the economy cannot use more of a certain good that it produces.

Second, the model we have considered is referred to as an **open Leontief model** because not all inputs and outputs were incorporated within the technology matrix. In particular, since labor was omitted, some (or all) of the surpluses must be used to support this labor.

If a model is developed in which all inputs and outputs are used within the system, then such a model is called a **closed Leontief model.** In such a model, labor (and perhaps other factors) must be included. Labor is included by considering a new industry, households, which produces labor. When such a closed model is developed, all outputs are used within the system and the sum of the entries in each column equals 1. In this case, there is no surplus matrix. Thus the technological equation is

$$AX = X. \quad \text{(closed Leontief model)}$$

EXAMPLE 3   The following closed Leontief model with technology matrix A might describe the economy of the entire country, with x_1 equal to government's budget, x_2 the value of industrial output (profit-making organizations), x_3 the budget of nonprofit organizations, and x_4 the household's budget.

$$A = \begin{array}{c} \\ \text{Govt.} \\ \text{Ind.} \\ \text{Nonprof.} \\ \text{Hshld.} \end{array} \begin{array}{cccc} G & I & N & H \\ \begin{bmatrix} 0.4 & 0.2 & 0 & 0.3 \\ 0.2 & 0.2 & 0.2 & 0.1 \\ 0.2 & 0 & 0.2 & 0.1 \\ 0.2 & 0.6 & 0.6 & 0.5 \end{bmatrix} \end{array}.$$

Find the total budgets (or outputs) x_1, x_2, x_3, and x_4.

Solution   Since this is a closed Leontief model, we must solve the system given by $AX = X$, that is,

$$\begin{array}{rll}
0.4x_1 + 0.2x_2 + 0x_3 + 0.3x_4 = x_1 & (1) \\
0.2x_1 + 0.2x_2 + 0.2x_3 + 0.1x_4 = x_2 & (2) \\
0.2x_1 + 0x_2 + 0.2x_3 + 0.1x_4 = x_3 & (3) \\
0.2x_1 + 0.6x_2 + 0.6x_3 + 0.5x_4 = x_4. & (4)
\end{array}$$

If we put this system in the form where the constants occur as the right members [by subtracting x_1 from both sides of equation (1), and so on], and then form the augmented matrix, we have

$$\begin{bmatrix} -0.6 & 0.2 & 0 & 0.3 & | & 0 \\ 0.2 & -0.8 & 0.2 & 0.1 & | & 0 \\ 0.2 & 0 & -0.8 & 0.1 & | & 0 \\ 0.2 & 0.6 & 0.6 & -0.5 & | & 0 \end{bmatrix}.$$

This matrix is easily converted to one in which all entries are whole numbers if we multiply each row by 10. Then, if we reduce the matrix by the methods of the previous section, we obtain

$$\begin{bmatrix} 1 & 0 & 0 & -\frac{53}{86} & | & 0 \\ 0 & 1 & 0 & -\frac{15}{43} & | & 0 \\ 0 & 0 & 1 & -\frac{12}{43} & | & 0 \\ 0 & 0 & 0 & 0 & | & 0 \end{bmatrix}.$$

The system of equations that corresponds to this augmented matrix is

$$x_1 \quad - \tfrac{53}{86}x_4 = 0 \qquad\qquad x_1 = \tfrac{53}{86}x_4$$
$$x_2 \quad - \tfrac{15}{43}x_4 = 0 \quad \text{or} \quad x_2 = \tfrac{15}{43}x_4.$$
$$x_3 - \tfrac{12}{43}x_4 = 0 \qquad\qquad x_3 = \tfrac{12}{43}x_4$$

Note that the economy satisfies the given equation if the government's budget is $\tfrac{53}{86}$ times the household's budget, if the value of industrial output is $\tfrac{15}{43}$ times the household's budget, and if the budget of nonprofit organizations is $\tfrac{12}{43}$ times the household's budget. The dependency here is expected. The fact that the system is closed suggests the dependency, but even more obvious is the fact that industrial output is limited by labor supply. □

We have examined two types of input-output models as they pertain to the economy as a whole. Since Leontief's original work with the economy, various other applications of input-output models have been developed. Consider the following parts-listing problem.

EXAMPLE 4   A storage shed consists of 4 walls and a roof. The walls and roof are made from stamped aluminum sheeting and are reinforced with 4 braces, each of which is held with 6 bolts. The final assembly joins the walls to each other and to the roof using a total of 20 more bolts. The parts listing for these sheds can be described by the matrix

	S	W	R	Sht	Br	Bo
Sheds	0	0	0	0	0	0
Walls	4	0	0	0	0	0
Roofs	1	0	0	0	0	0
Sheets	0	1	1	0	0	0
Braces	0	4	4	0	0	0
Bolts	20	24	24	0	0	0

$Q = $ (matrix above).

This matrix is a form of input-output matrix, with the rows representing inputs that are used directly to produce the items that head the columns. We note that the entries here are quantities used rather than proportions used.

Thus to produce a shed requires 4 walls, 1 roof, and 20 bolts, and to produce a roof requires 1 aluminum sheet, 4 braces, and 24 bolts.

Suppose that an order is received for 4 completed sheds and spare parts including 2 walls, 1 roof, 8 braces, and 24 bolts. How many of each of the assembly items is required to fill the order?

Solution   If matrix D represents the order and matrix X represents the gross production, we have

$$D = \begin{bmatrix} 4 \\ 2 \\ 1 \\ 0 \\ 8 \\ 24 \end{bmatrix} \begin{matrix} \text{Sheds} \\ \text{Walls} \\ \text{Roofs} \\ \text{Sheets} \\ \text{Braces} \\ \text{Bolts} \end{matrix} \quad X = \begin{bmatrix} x_1 \\ x_2 \\ x_3 \\ x_4 \\ x_5 \\ x_6 \end{bmatrix} = \begin{bmatrix} \text{total sheds required} \\ \text{total walls required} \\ \text{total roofs required} \\ \text{total sheets required} \\ \text{total braces required} \\ \text{total bolts required} \end{bmatrix}.$$

Then X must satisfy $X - QX = D$, which is the technological equation for an open Leontief model.

We can find X by solving the system $(I - Q)X = D$, which is represented by the augmented matrix

$$\begin{bmatrix} 1 & 0 & 0 & 0 & 0 & 0 & 4 \\ -4 & 1 & 0 & 0 & 0 & 0 & 2 \\ -1 & 0 & 1 & 0 & 0 & 0 & 1 \\ 0 & -1 & -1 & 1 & 0 & 0 & 0 \\ 0 & -4 & -4 & 0 & 1 & 0 & 8 \\ -20 & -24 & -24 & 0 & 0 & 1 & 24 \end{bmatrix}.$$

Although this matrix is quite large, it is easily reduced and yields the following:

$$\begin{bmatrix} 1 & 0 & 0 & 0 & 0 & 0 & 4 \\ 0 & 1 & 0 & 0 & 0 & 0 & 18 \\ 0 & 0 & 1 & 0 & 0 & 0 & 5 \\ 0 & 0 & 0 & 1 & 0 & 0 & 23 \\ 0 & 0 & 0 & 0 & 1 & 0 & 100 \\ 0 & 0 & 0 & 0 & 0 & 1 & 656 \end{bmatrix}.$$

Thus to fill the order, a total of 656 bolts, 100 braces, 23 stamped aluminum sheets, 5 roofs, 18 walls, and 4 complete sheds are required. □

Exercise 3.5

1. The following technology matrix describes the relationship of certain industries within the economy to each other.

	A&F	RM	M	F	U	SI
Agriculture and food	0.410	0.008	0	0.002	0	0.006
Raw materials	0.025	0.493	0.190	0.024	0.030	0.150
Manufacturing	0.015	0.006	0.082	0.009	0.001	0.116
Fuels industry	0.097	0.096	0.040	0.053	0.008	0.093
Utilities	0.028	0.129	0.039	0.058	0.138	0.409
Service industries	0.043	0.008	0.010	0.012	0.002	0.095

Use this matrix to answer the following questions.

(a) For each 1000 units of raw materials produced, how many units of agricultural and food products were required? How many units of service were required?

(b) How many units of fuels were required to produce 1000 units of manufactured goods? How many were required to produce 1000 units of power (utilities' goods)?

(c) Which industry is most dependent on its own goods for its operation? Which industry is least dependent on its own goods?

(d) Which industry is most dependent on the fuels industry?

(e) Which three industries would be most affected by a rise in the cost of raw materials?

2. Suppose that an economy has the same technological matrix as that given in Example 2. If surpluses of 180 units of agricultural goods, 90 units of manufactured goods, and 40 units of fuels are desired, find the gross production of each industry required to satisfy this.

3. Suppose a primitive economy consists of two industries, farm products and farm machinery. Suppose also that their technology matrix is

$$A = \begin{array}{c} \text{Products} \\ \text{Machinery} \end{array} \begin{array}{cc} \text{P} & \text{M} \\ \begin{bmatrix} 0.5 & 0.1 \\ 0.1 & 0.3 \end{bmatrix} \end{array}.$$

If the surpluses of 96 units of farm produce and 8 units of farm machinery are desired, find the gross production of each industry.

4. Suppose the economy of an underdeveloped country has an agricultural industry and an oil industry, with technology matrix

$$A = \begin{array}{c} \text{Agr. Prod.} \\ \text{Oil Prod.} \end{array} \begin{array}{cc} \text{A} & \text{O} \\ \begin{bmatrix} 0.3 & 0.1 \\ 0.2 & 0.1 \end{bmatrix} \end{array}.$$

If a surplus of 7.5 units of agricultural products and 1000 units of oil products are desired, find the gross production of each industry.

5. Suppose that for the primitive economy in problem 3 we form a closed model by including households. Suppose further that the resulting technology matrix is

$$A = \begin{array}{c} \text{Farm products} \\ \text{Farm machinery} \\ \text{Households} \end{array} \begin{array}{ccc} \text{P} & \text{M} & \text{H} \\ \begin{bmatrix} 0.5 & 0.1 & 0.2 \\ 0.1 & 0.3 & 0 \\ 0.4 & 0.6 & 0.8 \end{bmatrix} \end{array}.$$

Find the gross productions for these industries.

6. In Example 3 we gave a closed Leontief model for the economy. In the following matrix we combined the nonprofit organizations with industry (viewing nonprofit organizations as a service industry). Find the gross productions for the industries in this revised closed model.

$$A = \begin{array}{c} \text{Govt.} \\ \text{Ind.} \\ \text{House.} \end{array} \begin{array}{ccc} \text{G} & \text{I} & \text{H} \\ \begin{bmatrix} 0.4 & 0.1 & 0.3 \\ 0.4 & 0.3 & 0.2 \\ 0.2 & 0.6 & 0.5 \end{bmatrix} \end{array}$$

7. For the storage shed in Example 4, find the number of each type of part required to fill an order of 24 sheds, 12 braces, and 96 bolts.

8. Card tables are made by joining 4 legs and a top using 4 bolts. The legs are each made from a steel rod. The top has a frame made from 4 steel rods. A cover and four special clamps that brace the top and hold the legs are joined to the frame using a total of 8 bolts. The parts listing matrix for the card table assembly is given by

		CT	L	T	R	Co	Cl	B
	Card table	0	0	0	0	0	0	0
	Legs	4	0	0	0	0	0	0
	Top	1	0	0	0	0	0	0
$A =$	Rods	0	4	4	0	0	0	0
	Cover	0	0	1	0	0	0	0
	Clamps	0	0	4	0	0	0	0
	Bolts	4	0	8	0	0	0	0

If an order is received for 10 card tables, 4 legs, 1 top, 1 cover, 6 clamps, and 12 bolts, how many of each item are required to fill the order?

Review Exercises

Using the matrices

$$A = \begin{bmatrix} 4 & 4 & 2 & 5 \\ 6 & 3 & -1 & 0 \\ 0 & 0 & -3 & 5 \end{bmatrix}, \quad B = \begin{bmatrix} 2 & -5 & -11 & 8 \\ 4 & 0 & 0 & 4 \\ -2 & -2 & 1 & 9 \end{bmatrix},$$

$$C = \begin{bmatrix} 4 & -2 \\ 5 & 0 \\ 6 & 0 \\ 1 & 3 \end{bmatrix}, \quad D = \begin{bmatrix} 3 & 5 \\ 1 & 2 \end{bmatrix}, \quad E = \begin{bmatrix} 1 & 1 \\ 1 & 1 \\ 4 & 6 \\ 0 & 5 \end{bmatrix},$$

$$F = \begin{bmatrix} -1 & 6 \\ 4 & 11 \end{bmatrix}, \quad G = \begin{bmatrix} 2 & -5 \\ -1 & 3 \end{bmatrix}, \quad I = \begin{bmatrix} 1 & 0 \\ 0 & 1 \end{bmatrix},$$

in problems 1–18, determine the following.

1. $A + B$
2. $C - E$
3. $2A$
4. $3C$
5. $4I$
6. $-2F$
7. $D - I$
8. $F + 2D$
9. $3A - 5B$
10. AC
11. CD
12. DF
13. FD
14. FI
15. IF
16. DG
17. $(DG)F$
18. Are D and G inverse matrices?

19. Solve the following using matrices.

$$\begin{cases} -x + y + z = 3 \\ 3x \quad\quad - z = 1 \\ 2x - 3y - 4z = -2 \end{cases}$$

20. Solve the following matrix equation.

$$\begin{bmatrix} 1 & -1 & 0 \\ 1 & 1 & 4 \\ 2 & -3 & -2 \end{bmatrix} \begin{bmatrix} x_1 \\ x_2 \\ x_3 \end{bmatrix} = \begin{bmatrix} 3 \\ 1 \\ 7 \end{bmatrix}$$

21. Solve the following using matrices.

$$\begin{cases} x_1 + x_2 + x_3 + x_4 = 3 \\ x_1 - 2x_2 + x_3 - 4x_4 = -5 \\ x_1 \quad\quad - x_3 + x_4 = 0 \\ x_2 + x_3 + x_4 = 2 \end{cases}$$

Find the inverse of each of the following matrices

° 22. $\begin{bmatrix} 1 & 0 & 2 \\ 3 & 4 & -1 \\ 1 & 1 & 0 \end{bmatrix}$

° 23. $\begin{bmatrix} 3 & 3 & 2 \\ -1 & 4 & 2 \\ 2 & 5 & 3 \end{bmatrix}$

Solve the following systems of equations using inverses.

° 24.
$$\begin{cases} x \quad\quad + 2z = 5 \\ 3x + 4y - z = 2 \\ x + y \quad\quad = -3 \end{cases}$$
(See problem 22)

° 25.
$$\begin{cases} 3x + 3y + 2z = 1 \\ -x + 4y + 2z = -10 \\ 2x + 5y + 3z = -6 \end{cases}$$
(See problem 23)

APPLICATIONS

The Burr Cabinet Company manufactures bookcases and filing cabinets at two plants, A and B, respectively. Matrix M gives the production for the two plants during June and matrix N gives the production for July.

$$\begin{matrix} & A & B \\ N = & \begin{bmatrix} 100 & 60 \\ 200 & 400 \end{bmatrix} & \begin{matrix} \text{Bookcases} \\ \text{Files} \end{matrix} \end{matrix} \quad M = \begin{bmatrix} 150 & 80 \\ 280 & 300 \end{bmatrix}$$

$$S = \begin{bmatrix} 120 & 80 \\ 180 & 300 \end{bmatrix} \quad P = \begin{bmatrix} 1000 & 800 \\ 600 & 1200 \end{bmatrix}$$

26. Write the matrix that represents total production at the two plants for the two months.

27. If matrix P represents the inventories at the plants at the beginning of June and matrix S represents shipments from the plants during June, write the matrix that represents the inventories at the plants at the end of June.

° Problems 22–25 are from the optional Section 3.4.

28. If the company sells its bookcases to wholesalers for $100 and its filing cabinets for $120, for which month was the value of production higher at
(a) plant A?   (b) plant B?

29. A look at the industrial sector of an economy can be simplified to include three industries: the mining industry, the manufacturing industry, and the fuels industry. The technology matrix for this sector of the economy is given by

	Mi	Mf	F
Mining	0.1	0.2	0.1
A = Mfg.	0.2	0.3	0.2
Fuels	0.3	0.2	0.2

Find the gross production of each industry if a surplus of 55 units of mined goods, 260 units of manufactured goods, and 40 units of fuels is desired.

30. Suppose a closed Leontief model for a nation's economy has the following technology matrix.

	G	A	M	H
Govt.	0.4	0.2	0.2	0.2
Agr.	0.2	0.4	0.1	0.2
A = Mfg.	0.2	0.1	0.3	0.1
House.	0.2	0.3	0.4	0.5

Find the gross productions for this closed model.

In this chapter you will need to work problems like the following. If you have difficulty with any problem, return to the section where that type of problem was introduced and refresh your memory before starting the chapter.

Problem Type	Introduced in Section	Used in Section	Answer
(a) Solve $3x - 2 = 7$. (b) Solve $2(x - 4) = \dfrac{x - 3}{3}$.	2.1 Linear equations	4.1	(a) $x = 3$ (b) $x = \frac{21}{5}$
Graph the equation $y = \frac{3}{2}x - 2$.	2.4 Graphing linear equations	4.1	
Solve the systems: (a) $\begin{cases} x + 2y = 10 \\ 2x + y = 14 \end{cases}$ (b) $\begin{cases} x + 0.5y = 16 \\ x + y = 24 \end{cases}$	2.5 Linear equations in two variables	4.2, 4.3	(a) $x = 6, y = 2$ (b) $x = 8, y = 16$
Write the system in a matrix: $\begin{cases} x + 2y + w = 10 \\ 2x + y + z = 14 \\ 2x + 3y = f \end{cases}$	3.3 Matrices	4.4	$\begin{bmatrix} 1 & 2 & 1 & 0 & 10 \\ 2 & 1 & 0 & 1 & 14 \\ 2 & 3 & 0 & 0 & f \end{bmatrix}$
Write a matrix equivalent to matrix A with the entry in row 1, column 2 equal to 1 and with all other entries in column 2 equal to 0. First multiply row 1 by $\frac{1}{2}$. $A = \begin{bmatrix} 1 & 2 & 1 & 0 & 10 \\ 2 & 1 & 0 & 1 & 14 \\ 2 & 3 & 0 & 0 & f \end{bmatrix}$	3.3 Matrices	4.4	$\begin{bmatrix} \frac{1}{2} & 1 & \frac{1}{2} & 0 & 5 \\ \frac{3}{2} & 0 & -\frac{1}{2} & 1 & 9 \\ \frac{1}{2} & 0 & -\frac{3}{2} & 0 & f - 15 \end{bmatrix}$

INEQUALITIES AND LINEAR PROGRAMMING

A firm frequently requires several components for the manufacture of the items it produces, and there are usually several stages for each item's assembly and final shipment. The company's costs and profits depend on the availability of the components (for example, labor and raw materials), what the costs of these components are, what the unit profit for each product is, and how many products are required. If the relationships among the various resources, the production requirements, the costs, and the profits are all linear, then these activities may be planned (or programmed) in the best possible (optimal) way by means of linear programming.

Because linear programming is useful in solving the problem of allocating limited resources among various activities in the best possible way, its impact has been tremendous. Although it is a relatively recent development, it is a standard tool for companies of all sizes, and its application has been responsible for saving many thousands of dollars. Numerous textbooks have been written on the subject, and our intention here is to provide an introduction to the method.

Because the restrictions (constraints) on most business operations can often be expressed as linear inequalities, we begin this chapter by introducing methods for solving and graphing linear inequalities. We will show how graphs of the constraint inequalities can be used to solve linear programming problems. The simplex method provides a technique for converting a system of inequalities into a system of equations that can be used to solve linear programming problems.

4.1 Linear Inequalities in One Variable

Objective   ■ To graph and solve linear inequalities in one variable

An **inequality** is a statement that one quantity is greater than (or less than) another quantity. We have already encountered some very simple inequalities. For example, the number of items a firm produces and sells, x, must be a nonnegative quantity. Thus x is greater than or equal to zero, which is written $x \geq 0$. The inequality $3x - 2 > 2x + 1$ is a first-degree (linear) inequality that states that the left member is greater than the right member. Certain values of the variable will satisfy the inequality. These values form the solution set of the inequality. For example, 4 is in the solution set of $3x - 2 > 2x + 1$ because $3 \cdot 4 - 2 > 2 \cdot 4 + 1$. On the other hand, 2 is not in the solution set because $3 \cdot 2 - 2 \not> 2 \cdot 2 + 1$. *Solving* an inequality means finding its solution set, and two inequalities are *equivalent* if they have the same solution set. As with equations, we find the solutions to inequalities by finding equivalent inequalities from which the solutions can be easily seen. We use the following properties to reduce an inequality to a simple equivalent inequality.

PROPERTIES	EXAMPLES
Substitution Property	
The inequality formed by substituting one expression for an equal expression is equivalent to the original inequality.	$5x - 4x < 6$ is equivalent to $x < 6$. The solution set is $\{x: x < 6\}$.
Addition Property	
The inequality formed by adding the same quantity to both sides of an inequality is equivalent to the original inequality.	$x - 4 > 6$ is equivalent to $x > 10$. $x + 5 < 12$ is equivalent to $x < 7$. (Subtracting 5 from both sides is equivalent to adding -5 to both sides.)
Multiplication Property I	
The inequality formed by multiplying both sides of an inequality by the same *positive* quantity is equivalent to the original inequality.	$\frac{1}{2}x > 8$ is equivalent to $x > 16$. $3x < 6$ is equivalent to $x < 2$. (Dividing both sides by 3 is equivalent to multiplying both sides by $\frac{1}{3}$.)
Multiplication Property II	
The inequality formed by multiplying both sides of an inequality by a *negative* number and reversing the sense of the inequality is equivalent to the original inequality.	$-x < 6$ is equivalent to $x > -6$. $-3x > -27$ is equivalent to $x < 9$. (Dividing both sides by -3 is equivalent to multiplying both sides by $-\frac{1}{3}$.)

We may graph the solutions to inequalities in one unknown on the real number line. For example, the graph of $x < 2$ consists of all points to the left of 2 on the number line. The open circle on the graph indicates that all points up to but *not* including 2 are in the solution set.

EXAMPLE 1   Solve the inequality $s/(-2) < -4$ and graph the solution set.

Solution   Multiplying both sides of $s/(-2) < -4$ by -2 gives $s > 8$, which is equivalent to $s/(-2) < -4$. The solution set is $\{s : s > 8\}$. The graph of the solution set is

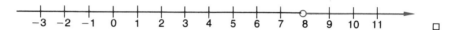

Some inequalities will require several operations to find their solution set. In this case, the order in which the operations are performed is the same as that used in solving linear equations.

EXAMPLE 2   Solve the inequality $2(x - 4) < \dfrac{x - 3}{3}$.

Solution   1. Remove fractions.

$$6(x - 4) < x - 3$$

2. Remove parentheses.

$$6x - 24 < x - 3$$

3. Perform additions and subtractions.

$$5x < 21$$

4. Multiply by $\frac{1}{5}$ to find the solution.

$$x < \frac{21}{5}$$

5. CHECK: $x = 4$ satisfies the inequality:

$$2(4 - 4) < \frac{4 - 1}{3}$$

$x = 5$ does not satisfy the inequality:

$$2(5 - 4) \not< \frac{5 - 3}{3}$$

Thus $x < \frac{21}{5}$ is a reasonable solution.   □

We may also solve inequalities of the form $a \leq b$. This means "a is less than b or $a = b$." The solution to $2x \leq 4$ is $x \leq 2$, since $x < 2$ is the solution of $2x < 4$ and $x = 2$ is the solution of $2x = 4$.

EXAMPLE 3   Solve the inequality $3x - 2 \leq 7$.

Solution   This inequality states that $3x - 2 = 7$ or that $3x - 2 < 7$. By solving in the usual manner, we get $3x \leq 9$, or $x \leq 3$.

Then $x = 3$ is the solution to $3x - 2 = 7$ and $x < 3$ is the solution to $3x - 2 < 7$, so the solution set for $3x - 2 \leq 7$ is $\{x : x \leq 3\}$.

The graph of the solution set includes the point $x = 3$ and all points $x < 3$.

We use the notation $-2 < x < 4$ to state that x satisfies the two conditions $-2 < x$ *and* $x < 4$. This *compound inequality* represents an *interval* on the number line. The graph of this compound inequality is called an **open interval** because neither *endpoint* $(-2$ or $4)$ is included in the graph. We may denote the interval $-2 < x < 4$ by $(-2, 4)$.

The graph of $-1 \leq x \leq 3$ is a **closed interval** because both endpoints are included. This closed interval may be denoted $[-1, 3]$.

In general, we denote the closed interval $a \leq x \leq b$ as $[a, b]$ and the open interval $a < x < b$ by (a, b).

Exercise 4.1

Solve the following inequalities.

1. $x + 2 < 4$
2. $x - 3 > 5$
3. $x - 3 \geq 2x + 1$
4. $2x - 1 \leq 3x + 4$
5. $3(x - 1) < 2x - 1$
6. $2(x + 1) > x - 1$
7. $2(x - 1) - 3 > 4x + 1$
8. $7x + 4 \leq 2(x - 1)$
9. $\frac{x}{3} > x - 1$
10. $\frac{x - 3}{4} \geq 2x$
11. $\frac{3(x - 1)}{2} \leq x - 2$
12. $\frac{x - 1}{2} + 1 > x + 1$

Graph the solutions to the following inequalities.

13. $2x + 1 < x - 3$ 14. $3x - 1 \geq 2x + 2$ 15. $3(x - 1) < 2x$

16. $3(x + 2) \geq 4x + 1$ 17. $2x + \dfrac{1}{2} \geq x - 3$ 18. $5x - 2 > 3(x + 3)$

Determine if the graphs of the following inequalities are open intervals or closed intervals.

19. $-3 \leq x \leq 5$ 20. $-5 < x < -3$
21. $-4 < x < 3$ 22. $-6 \leq x \leq -4$
23. $4 \leq x \leq 6$ 24. $-2 \leq x \leq -1$
25. $4 < x < 9$ 26. $5 < x < 8$

4.2 Linear Inequalities in Two Variables

Objectives   ■ To graph linear inequalities in two variables
                 ■ To solve systems of linear inequalities in two variables

We solved and graphed the solutions of linear inequalities in one variable in Section 4.1. We now consider linear inequalities in *two* variables. The inequality $y < x$ is a linear inequality in two variables. The solutions to this inequality are the ordered pairs (x, y) that satisfy the inequality. Thus $(1, 0)$, $(3, 2)$, $(0, -1)$, and $(-2, \ 5)$ are solutions to $y < x$ but $(3, 7)$, $(-4, -3)$, and $(2, 2)$ are not. The graph of $y < x$ consists of all points whose y-value is less than the x-value. Thus the graph consists of all points below the line $y = x$ (the shaded area in Figure 4.1).

Note that the points on the line $y = x$ do not satisfy the inequality, so they are not part of the graph. This is indicated by the dashed line in Figure 4.1.

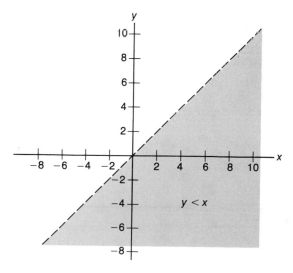

Figure 4.1

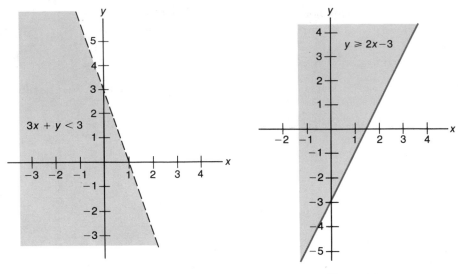

Figure 4.2   **Figure 4.3**

EXAMPLE 1   Graph the inequality $3x + y < 3$.

Solution   If we solve the inequality for y, we get $y < 3 - 3x$. Thus the graph of this inequality will consist of all points *below* the line $y = 3 - 3x$. The graph is shown in Figure 4.2.   □

EXAMPLE 2   Graph the inequality $4x - 2y \leq 6$.

Solution   Solving the inequality for y gives $y \geq 2x - 3$. Because y is greater than or equal to $2x - 3$, the graph consists of all points *on* or *above* the graph of $y = 2x - 3$. The line representing $y = 2x - 3$ is solid in Figure 4.3 to indicate that it is included in the solution.   □

If we have two inequalities in two variables, we can find the solutions that satisfy both inequalities. We call the inequalities a **system of inequalities,** and the solution to the system can be found by finding the intersection of the solution sets of the two inequalities.

The solution set of the system of inequalities can be found by graphing the inequalities on the same graph and noting their points of intersections.

EXAMPLE 3   Graph the solution to the system

$$\begin{cases} 3x - 2y \geq 4 \\ x + y - 3 > 0 \end{cases}$$

Solution   The inequalities can be written in the form

$$y \leq \tfrac{3}{2}x - 2$$
$$y > -x + 3$$

The graph of $y \leq \frac{3}{2}x - 2$ consists of all points on or below the line $y = \frac{3}{2}x - 2$. The graph of $y > -x + 3$ consists of all points above the line $y = -x + 3$. The points that satisfy both of these inequalities are shown in the heavily shaded region of Figure 4.4. This region is the graph of the solution to the system containing these two equations.   □

EXAMPLE 4   Graph the solution to the system

$$\begin{cases} x + 2y \leq 10 \\ 2x + y \leq 14 \\ x \geq 0 \\ y \geq 0 \end{cases}$$

Solution   We seek points in the first quadrant (above $y = 0$ and to the right of $x = 0$) that satisfy $x + 2y \leq 10$ *and* $2x + y \leq 14$. We can write these inequalities in their equivalent form $y \leq 5 - \frac{1}{2}x$ and $y \leq 14 - 2x$. The points that satisfy these inequalities (in the first quadrant) are shown by the heavily shaded area in Figure 4.5. The corners of the region that contains the solution are $(0, 0)$, $(7, 0)$, $(6, 2)$, and $(0, 5)$. The point $(6, 2)$ is found by solving the *equations* $y = 5 - \frac{1}{2}x$ and $y = 14 - 2x$ simultaneously. We will see that the corners of the region are important in solving linear programming problems.   □

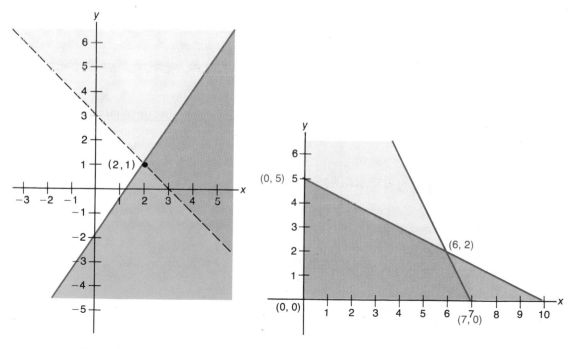

Figure 4.4   **Figure 4.5**

Exercise 4.2

Graph the following inequalities.

1. $y > x$
2. $y < 3x$
3. $y \leq 2x - 1$
4. $y \geq 4x - 5$
5. $2x + y < 4$
6. $y - 3x > 2$
7. $2x - y \leq 3$
8. $x - 2y \geq 4$

Graph the solution sets for each of the following systems of inequalities.

9. $\begin{cases} y < 2x \\ y > x - 1 \end{cases}$

10. $\begin{cases} y > 3x - 4 \\ y < 2x + 3 \end{cases}$

11. $\begin{cases} 2x + y < 3 \\ x - 2y \geq -1 \end{cases}$

12. $\begin{cases} 3x + y > 4 \\ x - 2y < -1 \end{cases}$

13. $\begin{cases} y \geq 3 - 2x \\ y \geq \frac{1}{2}x + \frac{1}{2} \\ y \geq 3 \end{cases}$

14. $\begin{cases} y \leq x + 1 \\ y \geq 2x - 1 \\ x \geq 0 \\ y \geq 0 \end{cases}$

4.3 Linear Programming: Graphical Solutions

Objective   ■ To use graphical methods to find the maximum value of a linear function subject to constraints

Many practical problems in business and economics involve complex relationships between capital, raw material, labor, and so forth. For example, we may want to find the maximum possible sales subject to fixed conditions (constraints) such as available raw material and labor. If the constraints can be expressed as linear inequalities, and if the function to be maximized (called the **objective function**) is a linear function, the problem fits a special mathematical model, and can be solved by a special technique called **linear programming.** Linear programming techniques can also be used with nonlinear systems if they can be approximated by linear systems, but we will consider only linear functions in our discussion.

When the linear programming problem is restricted to two variables, we can use graphical methods to solve the problem. The constraints form a system of linear inequalities in two variables, which we can solve by graphing. The solution of the system of inequalities of a linear programming problem will be the interior and boundary of a *convex polygon.* (A polygon is called convex when any line joining two points in the polygon lies entirely in the polygon. See Figure 4.6.)

Any point inside (or on) the convex polygon is a **feasible solution.** In a linear programming problem, we seek the feasible solution that will maximize (or minimize) the objective function. For example, suppose we wish to maximize the function $C = 2x + y$ subject to the constraints $x \geq 0$, $y \geq 0$, $x + 3y \leq 6$, and $x + y \leq 4$. The solution set for the system of constraints is the convex polygon

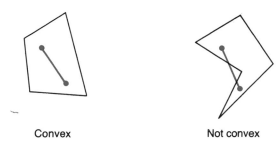

Convex   Not convex

Figure 4.6

shown in Figure 4.7. *Any* point inside this convex polygon (or on its boundary) is
a feasible solution to the problem. To determine which point will maximize the
objective function, we graph $C = 2x + y$, for different values of C, on the same
graph containing the region determined by the constraints. The different values
of C change the position, *but not the slope*, of the line. Letting $C = 0, 2, 3, 7$, and
8, we get the graphs shown in Figure 4.8. If any part of the line lies within the
convex polygon, we have feasible solutions.

Since we seek the value of x and y that will maximize $2x + y$, subject to the
constraints, we keep trying larger values of C while keeping some part of the line
intersecting with the polygon. It is clear from Figure 4.8 that any value of C
larger than 8 will cause the line $C = 2x + y$ to "miss" the polygon, and so the
maximum value for $2x + y$, subject to the constraints, is 8. The point where the
line $8 = 2x + y$ intersects the polygon is $(4, 0)$, so the function $2x + y$ is maximized when $x = 4$, $y = 0$. Note that the objective function was maximized at
one of the "corners" (or vertices) of the polygon determined by the constraints.
Of course, different constraints would lead to a different polygon, and thus the
maximum might occur at different values of x and y.

Not all linear programming problems have solutions, but *if a solution exists,*

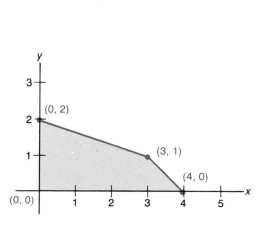

Figure 4.7

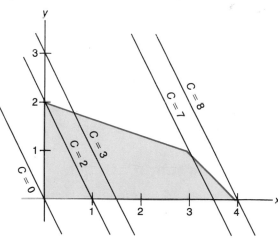

Figure 4.8

*the objective function will have its maximum value, subject to its constraints, at
one of the corners of the convex region determined by the inequalities.* Thus, to
find the maximum value of the objective function, we need only evaluate the
function at each of the corners of the region formed by the solution of the
constraint inequalities. If the objective function has its maximum value at two
corners, then it also has its maximum value at any point on the (boundary) line
connecting those two corners.

EXAMPLE 1   A young man decides to make pet food to sell. He decides to make two brands,
brand A and brand B. He uses 1 pound of meat for every 2 pounds of cereal in his
brand A pet food, and 2 pounds of meat for every 1 pound of cereal in his brand
B. If he has 10 pounds of meat and 14 pounds of cereal to begin his business, and
plans to charge $2 per 3-pound can for brand A and $3 per 3-pound can for
brand B, how many cans of each brand should he make to maximize his revenue?

Solution   Let x be the number of 3-pound cans of brand A sold at $2 per can and let y be
the number of 3-pound cans of brand B sold at $3 per can. Making x cans of brand
A will use x pounds of meat, and making y cans of brand B will use $2y$ pounds of
meat. He can use no more than 10 pounds of meat, so we know one constraint is
$x + 2y \leq 10$.
    Making x cans of brand A will use $2x$ pounds of cereal, and making y cans of
brand B will use y pounds of cereal. He can use no more than 14 pounds of cereal,
so a second constraint is $2x + y \leq 14$.
    Because we are not interested in negative quantities, two additional contraints
are needed: $x \geq 0$, $y \geq 0$. The function we want to maximize (the objective
function) is the function that determines revenue. Since the man is selling brand
A for $2 per can and brand B for $3 per can, his revenue function is $2x + 3y$.
    The region determined by constraint inequalities and some possible revenue
functions are shown in Figure 4.9. (Note that the region is identical to that found

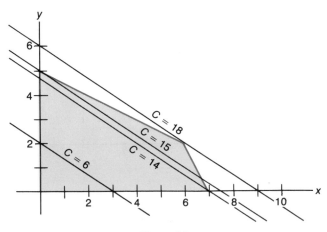

Figure 4.9

in Example 4 of Section 4.2—see Figure 4.5.) Since the solution of the constraint system is the interior of a convex polygon, we can find the maximum possible revenue by evaluating $2x + 3y$ at each of the corner points.

$$\text{At } (0, 0), \quad 2x + 3y = 0.$$
$$\text{At } (0, 5), \quad 2x + 3y = 15.$$
$$\text{At } (6, 2), \quad 2x + 3y = 18.$$
$$\text{At } (7, 0), \quad 2x + 3y = 14.$$

Since x and y represent the number of cans of brand A and brand B, respectively, that are to be produced, we see that the maximum revenue will result if 6 cans of brand A and 2 cans of brand B are produced.   □

We can also show that the function $2x + 3y$ has its maximum value at the point $(6, 2)$ in Example 1 by graphing the equation $2x + 3y = R$, for different values of R, on the same graph as the region determined by the constraints. Letting $R = 6, 14, 15$ and 18, we get the graphs shown in Figure 4.9.

From Figure 4.9, we see that the line with largest R-value that intersects the shaded region is $2x + 3y = 18$. Thus by using graphing we obtain the same result, namely that $18 will occur at $(6, 2)$, so 6 cans of brand A and 2 cans of brand B will result in the maximum revenue.

From Example 1, we can see that the steps involved in solving a linear programming problem are as follows.

PROCEDURE	EXAMPLE
To solve a linear programming problem:	Example 1 (again)
1. Write the objective function and constraint inequalities from the problem.	1. Objective function: $R = 2x + 3y$ Constraints: $x + 2y \le 10$ $2x + y \le 14$ $x \ge 0$ $y \ge 0$
2. Graph the solution to the constraint system.	2. See Figure 4.9.
3. Find the vertices of the resulting polygon. This may sometimes require simultaneous solution of two boundary equations.	3. Vertices are $(0, 0)$, $(0, 5)$, $(6, 2)$, $(7, 0)$.
4. Evaluate the objective function at each vertex of the polygon determined by the constraints.	4. At $(0, 0)$, $2x + 3y = 0$. At $(0, 5)$, $2x + 3y = 15$. At $(6, 2)$, $2x + 3y = 18$. At $(7, 0)$, $2x + 3y = 14$.
5. If two corners give the maximum value for the objective function, all points on that boundary also maximize the function.	5. The function is maximized at $x = 6, y = 2$. The maximum value is 18.

EXAMPLE 2   If our young man in Example 1 had decided to sell his brand A pet food for $1.00 per can and his brand B for $2.50 per can, how many cans of each brand should he have made to maximize his revenue?

Solution   The constraints are the same as in the previous example; only the revenue function has changed. It is $1.00x + 2.50y$.

Evaluating the function at the corners of the constraint region gives

$$\text{At } (0, 0), \quad 1.00x + 2.50y = 0.$$
$$\text{At } (0, 5), \quad 1.00x + 2.50y = 12.50.$$
$$\text{At } (6, 2), \quad 1.00x + 2.50y = 11.00.$$
$$\text{At } (7, 0), \quad 1.00x + 2.50y = 7.00.$$

Thus the maximum revenue will occur if he sells none of the brand A and 5 cans of brand B. He will have a surplus of cereal (9 pounds not used), but his highest revenue will result from selling 5 cans of brand B only.   □

EXAMPLE 3   A small firm manufactures two types of charms, a necklace and a bracelet. The combined number of necklaces and bracelets that it can handle per day is 24. The bracelet takes 1 hour of labor to make and the necklace takes $\frac{1}{2}$ hour. The total number of hours of labor available per day is 16. If the profit on the bracelet is $2 and the profit on the necklace is $1, how many of each product should be produced daily to maximize profit?

Solution   Let x be the number of bracelets produced per day and y be the number of necklaces produced per day. Then the daily profit function is given by the equation $2x + 1y$, or $2x + y$. This is the function that must be maximized, subject to the constraints.

The constraint on labor indicates that the total number of hours per day is 16, so if x bracelets and y necklaces are made, $1x + \frac{1}{2}y$ must be no more than 16. That is, $x + \frac{1}{2}y \leq 16$.

Since only 24 items can be handled each day, the second constraint is expressed as $x + y \leq 24$.

Since all quantities must be nonnegative, two additional constraints are $x \geq 0$ and $y \geq 0$.

The set that satisfies the constraints is shaded in Figure 4.10. The vertices of the polygon are $(0, 0)$, $(0, 24)$, $(16, 0)$, and $(8, 16)$. All of these are obvious except for $(8, 16)$. It can be found by solving $x + \frac{1}{2}y = 16$ and $x + y = 24$ simultaneously. Testing the objective function at the vertices gives

$$\text{At } (0, 0), \quad 2x + y = 0.$$
$$\text{At } (0, 24), \quad 2x + y = 24.$$
$$\text{At } (16, 0), \quad 2x + y = 32.$$
$$\text{At } (8, 16), \quad 2x + y = 32.$$

Thus the maximum value of the function occurs at *either* $x = 16$, $y = 0$ or $x = 8$, $y = 16$. Thus the profit will be maximized at any point on the line joining

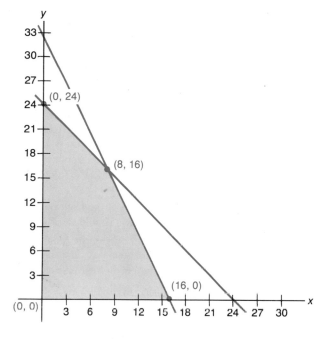

Figure 4.10

(8, 16) and (16, 0). For example, the point (12, 8) is on this line, and $2x + y = 32$ at $x = 12$, $y = 8$.   □

Exercise 4.3

1. Find the maximum value of the function $x + 3y$ subject to the constraints $x \geq 0$, $y \geq 0$, $x + 2y \leq 4$, and $2x + y \leq 4$.
2. Find the maximum value of the function $2x + y$ subject to the constraints $x \geq 0$, $y \geq 0$, $x + 2y \leq 4$, and $2x + y \leq 4$.
3. Find the maximum value of the function $x + 2y$ subject to the constraints $x + y \geq 4$, $y \leq 4$, and $2x + y \leq 8$.
4. Find the minimum value of the function $x + 2y$ subject to the constraints $x + y \geq 4$, $y \leq 4$, and $2x + y \leq 8$.

APPLICATIONS

5. A company manufactures two types of electric hedge trimmers, one of which is cordless. The cord-type trimmer requires 2 work hours to make, and the cordless model requires 4 work hours. The company has only 800 work hours to use in manufacturing each day, and the packing department can package only 300 trimmers per day. If the company sells the cord-type model for $30 and the cordless model for $40, how many of each type should it produce per day to maximize its revenue?

6. If, in problem 5, the profit on the cord-type trimmer is $10 and the profit on the cordless trimmer is $12, how many of each type should the company sell per day to maximize its profit?

7. If, in problem 5, the profit on each type is $10, how many of each type should the company produce per day to maximize its profit? Can its profit be maximized at more than one point in this case?

8. A firm manufactures bumper bolts and fender bolts for cars. One machine can produce 130 fender bolts and another machine can produce 120 bumper bolts per day. The combined number of fender bolts and bumper bolts the packaging department can handle is 230 per day. How many of each type of bolt should the firm produce daily to maximize its sales if fender bolts sell for $1 and bumper bolts sell for $2?

9. In problem 8, if the firm makes 50¢ profit on fender bolts and 40¢ profit on bumper bolts, how many of each type should it produce per day for maximum profit?

10. If the increased price of producing the fender bolts of problem 8 reduces the profit on fender bolts to 35¢, how many of each type should the firm produce per day for maximum profit (the bumper bolt profit remains at 40¢)?

11. If the prices on the bolts of problem 8 are changed so that the profit will be 50¢ each on both types of bolts, can profit be maximized at more than one point?

4.4 The Simplex Method: Maximization

Objective   ■ To use the simplex method to maximize functions subject to constraints

The graphical method for solving linear programming problems is suitable only when there are three or fewer variables. If there are more than three variables, we could still find the vertices of the convex region by simultaneously solving the equations of the boundaries. The objective function could then be evaluated at these vertices. However, as the number of variables and the number of constraints increases, it becomes increasingly difficult to discover the vertices and extremely time consuming to evaluate the function. Furthermore, some problems have no solution, and this cannot be determined by using the method of solving the equations simultaneously.

The method discussed in this section is called the **simplex method** for solving linear programming problems. Basically, this method gives a systematic way of moving from one feasible vertex of the convex region to another one in such a way that the value of the objective function increases until an optimum value is reached or it is discovered that no solution exists.

The simplex method was first developed by George Dantzig in the late 1940s. One of the earliest applications of the method was to the scheduling problem that arose in connection with the Berlin airlift, begun in 1948. There the objective was to maximize the amount of goods delivered, subject to such constraints as the number of personnel, the number and size of available aircraft, and the number of runways.

In discussing the simplex method, we initially restrict ourselves to linear programming problems satisfying the following conditions.

1. The objective function is to be maximized.
2. All variables are nonnegative.
3. The constraints are of the form

$$a_1x_1 + a_2x_2 + \cdots + a_nx_n \leq b,$$

where $b > 0$.

These may seem to restrict unduly the types of problems, but in applied situations where the objective function is to be maximized, the constraints generally satisfy conditions 2 and 3.

The simplex method depends on the use of matrices to solve systems of linear equations, and our constraints are in the form of inequalities. We can express each constraint inequality as a linear equation by introducing another variable. For example,

$$x_1 + 2x_2 \leq 10$$

can be written

$$x_1 + 2x_2 + x_3 = 10, \qquad (x_3 \geq 0),$$

where x_3 is called a **slack variable.** Since all our variables are assumed to be nonnegative, we will henceforth omit writing $x_3 \geq 0$.

Before using the simplex method to solve a linear programming problem, let us solve a problem by using algebraic methods.

EXAMPLE 1   Maximize $f = 2x + 3y$
Subject to $x + 2y \leq 10$
       and $2x + y \leq 14$

Since we assume $x \geq 0$ and $y \geq 0$ in these problems, we shall no longer state these conditions.

Solution   First we rewrite the constraints as equations, using a separate slack variable for each.

$$\begin{array}{lll} x + 2y \leq 10 & \text{becomes} & x + 2y + w = 10 \\ 2x + y \leq 14 & \text{becomes} & 2x + y + z = 14 \end{array}$$

Now the problem is to find values x, y, w, amd z that satisfy

$$\left.\begin{array}{r} x + 2y + w = 10 \\ 2x + y + z = 14, \\ \text{and maximize} \quad 2x + 3y = f. \end{array}\right\} \qquad \text{(I)}$$

To use this method, we substitute $x = 0$ and $y = 0$ into the equations (I) above, which yields

$$x = 0, \qquad y = 0, \qquad w = 10, \qquad \text{and} \qquad z = 14;$$

the value for f is zero.

Now we seek an improved value for f. We can improve f by changing either x or y, but not both, to a positive value in such a way that f is increased by the greatest amount. Since

$$f = 2x + 3y,$$

we see that increasing y will have a greater effect on f than increasing x. However, the amount by which y can be increased is limited by the constraining equations. If we solve the constraining equations for y, we obtain the following.

$$x + 2y + w = 10 \quad \text{becomes} \quad y = 5 - \tfrac{1}{2}x - \tfrac{1}{2}w \quad (1)$$
$$2x + y + z = 14 \quad \text{becomes} \quad y = 14 - 2x - z \quad (2)$$

Since all the original variables and the slack variables must be nonnegative, we see in equation (1) that y is restricted to values no larger than 5, and in equation (2) that y is restricted to values no larger than 14. To satisfy both of these restrictions, y can become no larger than 5. Note that we can find the largest amount by which y can be increased by dividing the coefficient of y into the constant term in each of the original equations and choosing the smaller quotient.

Using this largest possible value for y leads to a new vertex, $x = 0$, $y = 5$, and yields the following solution to the system:

$$x = 0, \qquad y = 5, \qquad w = 0, \qquad \text{and} \qquad z = 9;$$

the value of f is 15.

The problem we are solving is the same one we solved geometrically in Example 1 of Section 4.3. Note that we started this method using $x = 0$ and $y = 0$, which corresponds to the vertex $(0, 0)$ of the region in Figure 4.9. The values of x and y that we have just found, namely $x = 0$ and $y = 5$, correspond to a vertex adjoining $(0, 0)$ of the region. We will see that if we continue this method, then the next values for x and y will correspond to another vertex of the region.

To continue the solution, note that we used equation (1) to determine the largest value for y. We can "transform" the system of equations into an equivalent system by eliminating y from the remaining equations. If we also multiply the first equation by $\tfrac{1}{2}$, we obtain the following:

with
$$\left. \begin{array}{l} \tfrac{1}{2}x + y + \tfrac{1}{2}w \quad\;\; = 5 \\[4pt] \tfrac{3}{2}x \quad\quad - \tfrac{1}{2}w + z = 9, \\[12pt] \tfrac{1}{2}x \quad\quad - \tfrac{3}{2}w \quad\;\; = f - 15 \end{array} \right\} \quad \text{(II)}$$

to be maximized.

As we look at this transformed system, we note that the function $f - 15$ depends on both x and w. Also because the variables are nonnegative, we see that if the value of x is increased and the value of w remains equal to zero, then the value of $f - 15$ can be increased. Yet the amount of the increase for x is limited. We can discover the limitations on x by dividing the coefficient of x into the constant term in each of these equations and choosing the smaller quotient.

$$\tfrac{1}{2}x + y + \tfrac{1}{2}w \quad = 5 \qquad 5 \div \tfrac{1}{2} = (5)(2) = 10$$
$$\tfrac{3}{2}x \quad -\tfrac{1}{2}w + z = 9 \qquad 9 \div \tfrac{3}{2} = (9)(\tfrac{2}{3}) = 6$$

The smaller quotient is 6. We can verify that x can be no larger than 6 by solving these equations for x.

$$\tfrac{1}{2}x + y + \tfrac{1}{2}w \quad = 5 \quad \text{becomes} \quad x = 10 - 2y - w$$
$$\tfrac{3}{2}x \quad -\tfrac{1}{2}w + z = 9 \quad \text{becomes} \quad x = 6 \quad + \tfrac{1}{3}w - \tfrac{2}{3}z$$

Now if we keep $w = 0$ and increase x to $x = 6$ and use these values in the system of equations, we see that $y = 2$ and $z = 0$. Using these values for x and y in $f = 2x + 3y$ gives $f = 18$.

Let us again transform the system by eliminating x from all but the second equation in (II) and by multiplying the second equation in (II) by $\tfrac{2}{3}$. The new system is

with

$$\left. \begin{aligned} y + \tfrac{2}{3}w - \tfrac{1}{3}z &= 2 \\ x - \tfrac{1}{3}w + \tfrac{2}{3}z &= 0, \\ -\tfrac{4}{3}w - \tfrac{1}{3}z &= f - 18 \end{aligned} \right\} \quad \text{(III)}$$

to be maximized.

As we consider this transformed system, we see that the function $f - 18$ cannot be increased as long as w and z are nonnegative. Thus we have completed the solution to the problem, and we have (for the original variables) $x = 6$, $y = 2$, and (for the slack variables) $w = 0$, $z = 0$. The maximum value of the function $f = 2x + 3y$ is 18. ❑

Note that in Example 1 the solution $x = 6$, $y = 2$ corresponds to the vertex $(6, 2)$ of Figure 4.9, and the value $f = 18$, which was the maximum value we found in Example 1 of Section 4.3, was the value of f at that vertex.

Furthermore, if the system (I) had been represented by a matrix, then the systems (II) and (III) could have been obtained using row operations. The following summary shows how we can use matrices to solve the problem presented by Example 1.

Simplex Method for Linear Programming

PROCEDURE	EXAMPLE
To use the simplex method to solve linear programming problems:	Maximize $f = 2x + 3y$ Subject to $x + 2y \le 10$ $2x + y \le 14$
1. Write the constraints as constraining equalities using slack variables.	1. $x + 2y \le 10$ becomes $x + 2y + w = 10$ $2x + y \le 14$ becomes $2x + y + z = 14$, and maximize $2x + 3y = f$.

2. Represent the system of equations using a matrix, called the **simplex tableau** or **simplex matrix**.

2. $$\begin{bmatrix} 1 & \cdot 2 & 1 & 0 & | & 10 \\ 2 & 1 & 0 & 1 & | & 14 \\ 2 & 3 & 0 & 0 & | & f \end{bmatrix}$$

3. Determine the variable to be increased and the amount of that increase. This identifies an element in the matrix called the **pivot**, which is found as follows:
   (a) Identify the largest positive entry in the last row; this identifies the pivot column.

3.

   (a) $$\begin{bmatrix} 1 & 2 & 1 & 0 & | & 10 \\ 2 & 1 & 0 & 1 & | & 14 \\ 2 & 3 & 0 & 0 & | & f \end{bmatrix}$$

   └─Largest entry, so pivot column

   (b) For each row, divide the coefficient in the pivot column into the constant in the augment. The *smallest positive* quotient identifies the pivot row.

   (b) Row 1 quotient: $\dfrac{10}{2} = 5$

   Row 2 quotient: $\dfrac{14}{1} = 14$

   Therefore, pivot row is row 1.

   (c) The entry at the intersection of the pivot row and pivot column is the **pivot entry**.

   (c) $$\begin{bmatrix} 1 & ⊘2 & 1 & 0 & | & 10 \\ 2 & 1 & 0 & 1 & | & 14 \\ 2 & 3 & 0 & 0 & | & f \end{bmatrix}$$

   Pivot entry is circled.

4. Use row operations with the *pivot row only* to make the pivot entry a 1 and all other entries in the pivot column zeros.

4. Row operations:
   Multiply row 1 by $\frac{1}{2}$.
   Add -1 times new row 1 to row 2.
   Add -3 times new row 1 to row 3.

   Result: $$\begin{bmatrix} \frac{1}{2} & 1 & \frac{1}{2} & 0 & | & 5 \\ \frac{3}{2} & 0 & -\frac{1}{2} & 1 & | & 9 \\ \frac{1}{2} & 0 & -\frac{3}{2} & 0 & | & f-15 \end{bmatrix}$$

5. The numerical entries in the last row are the **indicators** of what to do next.
   (a) If there is a positive indicator, return to step 3.
   (b) If all indicators are negative or zero, the solution is complete.

5. $$\begin{bmatrix} \frac{1}{2} & 1 & \frac{1}{2} & 0 & | & 5 \\ \frac{3}{2} & 0 & -\frac{1}{2} & 1 & | & 9 \\ \frac{1}{2} & 0 & -\frac{3}{2} & 0 & | & f-15 \end{bmatrix}$$

   $\underbrace{\qquad\qquad\qquad}_{\text{Indicators}}$

   $\frac{1}{2}$ is positive, so we identify a new pivot and reduce again.

$$\begin{bmatrix} \frac{1}{2} & 1 & \frac{1}{2} & 0 & 5 \\ \textcircled{\frac{3}{2}} & 0 & -\frac{1}{2} & 1 & 9 \\ \hline \frac{1}{2} & 0 & -\frac{3}{2} & 0 & f-15 \end{bmatrix}$$

Pivot column

Row 1 quotient $= \dfrac{5}{\frac{1}{2}} = 10$

Row 2 quotient $= \dfrac{9}{\frac{3}{2}} = 6$ (smaller)

Hence the new pivot is $\frac{3}{2}$ (circled). Now reduce, using the new pivot row, to obtain:

$$\begin{bmatrix} 0 & 1 & \frac{2}{3} & -\frac{1}{3} & 2 \\ 1 & 0 & -\frac{1}{3} & \frac{2}{3} & 6 \\ \hline 0 & 0 & -\frac{4}{3} & -\frac{1}{3} & f-18 \end{bmatrix}$$

Indicators all 0 or negative, so the solution is complete.

6. To read the solution from the simplex matrix, examine the columns.

6.

$$\begin{array}{cccc} x & y & w & z \\ \begin{bmatrix} 0 & 1 & \frac{2}{3} & -\frac{1}{3} & 2 \\ 1 & 0 & -\frac{1}{3} & \frac{2}{3} & 6 \\ \hline 0 & 0 & -\frac{4}{3} & -\frac{1}{3} & f-18 \end{bmatrix} & \begin{array}{l} y = 2 \\ x = 6 \end{array} \end{array}$$

(a) If a column of the matrix contains all zeros except for an entry 1 in one row, the maximum value of f occurs when the variable corresponding to that column is set equal to the augment value in the row containing the 1.

(a) Column 2 has all zeros except a single entry of 1. Hence y has the value given in the augment of row 1. That is, $y = 2$. Similarly, $x = 6$.

(b) All other variables have value zero.

(b) $w = 0$, $z = 0$.

(c) The entry in the lower right corner will be of the form $f - m$. Hence $f - m = 0$, and $f = m$ is the maximum value for f.

(c) $f - 18 = 0$, so $f = 18$ is the maximum. Hence the solution is that $f = 18$ is the maximum, and it is attained when $x = 6$ and $y = 2$.

As we look back over our work, we can observe the following:
1. The matrices in steps 2, 4 and 6 correspond to the systems (I), (II), and (III).
2. The pivot selection and row operations were designed to move the system to a new vertex that achieved the greatest increase in the function, and at the same time was sensitive to the nonnegative limitations on the variables.

3. The use of matrices to implement the simplex method systematizes the steps of the algebraic method and streamlines the calculations.

EXAMPLE 2 A firm manufactures three different types of hand calculators and classifies them as small, medium, and large according to their calculating capabilities. The three types have production requirements given by the following table.

	Small	Medium	Large
Electronic circuit components	5	7	10
Assembly time (h)	1	3	4
Cases	1	1	1

The firm has a monthly limit of 90,000 circuit components, 30,000 hours of labor, and 9000 cases. If the profit is $6 for the small, $13 for the medium, and $20 for the large calculators, how many of each should be produced to yield maximum profit? What is the maximum profit?

Solution Let x_1 be the number of small calculators produced, x_2 the number of medium calculators produced, and x_3 the number of large calculators produced. Then the problem is to maximize the profit $= 6x_1 + 13x_2 + 20x_3 = f$ subject to

Inequalities	Equations with slack variables

$$5x_1 + 7x_2 + 10x_3 \leq 90{,}000 \qquad 5x_1 + 7x_2 + 10x_3 + s_1 \qquad\qquad = 90{,}000$$
$$x_1 + 3x_2 + 4x_3 \leq 30{,}000 \qquad x_1 + 3x_2 + 4x_3 \qquad + s_2 \qquad = 30{,}000$$
$$\text{and} \quad x_1 + x_2 + x_3 \leq 9{,}000 \qquad x_1 + x_2 + x_3 \qquad\qquad + s_3 = 9{,}000$$

The simplex matrix for this problem is

Slack variables

$$
\begin{array}{cccccc}
x_1 & x_2 & x_3 & s_1 & s_2 & s_3
\end{array}
$$

$$
\begin{bmatrix}
5 & 7 & 10 & 1 & 0 & 0 \\
1 & 3 & \textcircled{4} & 0 & 1 & 0 \\
1 & 1 & 1 & 0 & 0 & 1 \\
\hline
6 & 13 & 20 & 0 & 0 & 0
\end{bmatrix}
\begin{matrix}
90{,}000 \\
30{,}000 \\
9{,}000 \\
\\
f
\end{matrix}
\qquad
\begin{matrix}
90{,}000/10 = 9{,}000 \\
30{,}000/4\ \ = 7{,}500° \\
9{,}000/1\ \ = 9{,}000 \\
\\
°\,\text{Smallest positive quotient}
\end{matrix}
$$

Largest positive

and the pivot is circled.

We now use row operations to change the pivot entry to 1 and create zeros elsewhere in the pivot column. The row operations are

1. Multiply row 2 by $\frac{1}{4}$ to convert the pivot entry to 1.
2. Using the new row 2,
   (a) add -10 times new row 2 to row 1.
   (b) add -1 times new row 2 to row 3.
   (c) add -20 times new row 2 to row 4.

The result is the second simplex matrix:

$$
\begin{array}{cccccc}
x_1 & x_2 & x_3 & s_1 & s_2 & s_3
\end{array}
$$

$$
\left[
\begin{array}{cccccc|c}
\frac{5}{2} & -\frac{1}{2} & 0 & 1 & -\frac{5}{2} & 0 & 15{,}000 \\[4pt]
\frac{1}{4} & \frac{3}{4} & 1 & 0 & \frac{1}{4} & 0 & 7500 \\[4pt]
\frac{3}{4} & \frac{1}{4} & 0 & 0 & -\frac{1}{4} & 1 & 1500 \\[4pt]
\hline
1 & -2 & 0 & 0 & -5 & 0 & f - 150{,}000
\end{array}
\right]
$$

$$\dfrac{15{,}000}{\frac{5}{2}} = 6000$$

$$\dfrac{7500}{\frac{1}{4}} = 30{,}000$$

$$\dfrac{1500}{\frac{3}{4}} = 2000°$$

°Smallest positive quotient

Largest positive

For this new simplex matrix, we check the last row indicators. Since there is an entry that is positive, we repeat the simplex process. Again the pivot is circled and we apply row operations similar to the above. What are the row operations this time? The resulting matrix is

$$
\begin{array}{cccccc}
x_1 & x_2 & x_3 & s_1 & s_2 & s_3
\end{array}
$$

$$
\left[
\begin{array}{cccccc|c}
0 & -\frac{4}{3} & 0 & 1 & -\frac{5}{3} & -\frac{10}{3} & 10{,}000 \\[4pt]
0 & \frac{2}{3} & 1 & 0 & \frac{1}{3} & -\frac{1}{3} & 7000 \\[4pt]
1 & \frac{1}{3} & 0 & 0 & -\frac{1}{3} & \frac{4}{3} & 2000 \\[4pt]
\hline
0 & -\frac{7}{3} & 0 & 0 & -\frac{14}{3} & -\frac{4}{3} & f - 152{,}000
\end{array}
\right]
$$

Checking the last row, we see all the entries are 0 or negative, so the solution is complete. From the matrix we see that $x_1 = 2000$, $x_3 = 7000$, and $s_1 = 10{,}000$ are the variables that have nonzero value. Moreover, $f - 152{,}000 = 0$, so we obtain $f = 152{,}000$.

Thus the number of calculators that should be produced is

$$x_1 = 2000 \text{ small calculators,}$$
$$x_2 = 0 \text{ medium calculators,}$$
$$x_3 = 7000 \text{ large calculators,}$$

in order to obtain a maximum profit of $152,000 for the month. Note that s_1 being nonzero means that some circuit components are not used in this optimal situation.   □

In this section we have not covered all the possible complications that may arise in applying the simplex method. To cover every possible alternative would require an entire course in itself. However, we can answer a few of the questions.

1. If there is a tie for the largest positive entry in the last row, then either one may be selected as the pivot column.

2. In determining the pivot row, it is possible that there will be no positive quotients. When this is the case, we have one of the following possibilities.
   (a) There is a quotient of zero. Then no improvement can be made in the value of the objective function, and the solution is complete.
   (b) All the quotients are negative. Then the problem has no solution.

Exercise 4.4

In problems 1–4, a simplex matrix is given. In each case identify the pivot element.

1. $\begin{bmatrix} 2 & 4 & 1 & 0 & | & 24 \\ 1 & 1 & 0 & 1 & | & 5 \\ \hline 4 & 11 & 0 & 0 & | & f \end{bmatrix}$

2. $\begin{bmatrix} 3 & 1 & 1 & 1 & 0 & | & 100 \\ 4 & 3 & 6 & 0 & 1 & | & 250 \\ \hline 5 & 3 & 4 & 0 & 0 & | & f \end{bmatrix}$

3. $\begin{bmatrix} 10 & 27 & 1 & 0 & 0 & | & 200 \\ 4 & 51 & 0 & 1 & 0 & | & 400 \\ 15 & 27 & 0 & 0 & 1 & | & 350 \\ \hline 6 & 7 & 0 & 0 & 0 & | & f \end{bmatrix}$

4. $\begin{bmatrix} 5 & 5 & 7 & 1 & 0 & 0 & | & 12 \\ 4 & 0 & 6 & 0 & 1 & 0 & | & 48 \\ 0 & 1 & 1 & 0 & 0 & 1 & | & 8 \\ \hline 1 & 3 & 1 & 0 & 0 & 0 & | & f \end{bmatrix}$

In problems 5–10, a simplex matrix is given. Examine the indicators and determine if the solution is complete or not. If it is complete find it, and if not find the next pivot.

5. $\begin{bmatrix} 1 & 0 & \frac{3}{4} & -\frac{3}{4} & | & 11 \\ 0 & 1 & \frac{5}{12} & \frac{11}{12} & | & 9 \\ \hline 0 & 0 & -2 & -4 & | & f - 20 \end{bmatrix}$

6. $\begin{bmatrix} 0 & 4 & 1 & -\frac{1}{5} & | & 2 \\ 1 & 2 & 0 & 1 & | & 4 \\ \hline 0 & -2 & 0 & -2 & | & f - 12 \end{bmatrix}$

7. $\begin{bmatrix} 4 & 1 & 0 & 0 & \frac{3}{4} & 4 & | & 14 \\ -2 & 0 & 0 & 1 & -\frac{5}{8} & -2 & | & 6 \\ 3 & 0 & 1 & 0 & 2 & 6 & | & 11 \\ \hline -4 & 0 & 0 & 0 & -2 & -\frac{1}{2} & | & f - 525 \end{bmatrix}$

8. $\begin{bmatrix} 2 & 1 & 1 & 0 & 0 & | & 12 \\ -2 & 0 & -1 & 0 & 1 & | & 5 \\ 4 & 0 & 2 & 1 & 0 & | & 6 \\ \hline 2 & 0 & -5 & 0 & 0 & | & f - 30 \end{bmatrix}$

9. $\begin{bmatrix} 4 & 4 & 1 & 0 & 0 & 2 & | & 12 \\ 2 & 4 & 0 & 1 & 0 & -1 & | & 4 \\ -3 & -11 & 0 & 0 & 1 & -1 & | & 6 \\ \hline 3 & 3 & 0 & 0 & 0 & -4 & | & f - 150 \end{bmatrix}$

10. $\begin{bmatrix} 0 & 0 & -3 & 4 & -4 & | & 12 \\ 0 & 1 & -4 & 2 & 5 & | & 100 \\ 1 & 0 & -1 & -6 & -3 & | & 40 \\ \hline 0 & 0 & -6 & 1 & 3 & | & f - 380 \end{bmatrix}$

11. Maximize $4x + 9y$ subject to

$$x + 5y \le 200$$
$$2x + 3y \le 134$$

12. Maximize $2x + y$ subject to

$$-x + y \le 2$$
$$x + 2y \le 10$$
$$3x + y \le 15$$

13. Maximize $3x + 2y$ subject to

$$x + 2y \le 48$$
$$x + y \le 30$$
$$2x + y \le 50$$
$$x + 10y \le 200$$

14. Maximize $3x + 8y$ subject to the constraints in problem 13.

15. Maximize $7x + 10y + 4z$ subject to

$$3x + 5y + 3z \le 30$$
$$3x + 2y \le 4$$
$$x + 2y \le 8$$

16. Maximize $x + 3y + z$ subject to

$$x + 4y \le 12$$
$$3x + 6y + 4z \le 48$$
$$y + z \le 8$$

APPLICATIONS

17. A bicycle manufacturer makes a ten-speed and a regular bicycle. The ten-speed requires 2 units of steel and 6 units of aluminum in its frame and 12 special components for the hub, sprocket, and gear assembly. The regular bicycle requires 5 units each of steel and aluminum for its frame and 5 of the special components. Shipments are such that steel is limited to 100 units per day, aluminum is limited to 120 units per day, and the special components are limited to 180 units per day. If the profit is $30 on each ten-speed and $20 on each regular bike, how many of each should be produced to yield maximum profit? What is the maximum profit?

18. Suppose the bicycle manufacturer in problem 17 has a profit of $35 on each ten-speed and $30 on each regular bike. How many of each should be produced to yield maximum profit? What will that profit be?

19. A produce wholesaler has determined that it takes $\frac{1}{2}$ hour of labor to sort and pack a crate of tomatoes, and it takes $1\frac{1}{4}$ hours to sort and pack a crate of peaches. The crate of tomatoes weighs 60 pounds, and the crate of peaches weighs 50 pounds. The wholesaler has 2500 hours of labor available each week and can ship 120,000 pounds per week. If profits are $1 per crate of tomatoes and $2 per crate of peaches, how many crates of each should be sorted, packed, and shipped to maximize profits? What is the maximum profit?

20. A firm has decided to discontinue production of an unprofitable product. This will create excess capacity, and the firm is considering one or more of three possible new products, A, B, and C. The available weekly hours in the plant will be 477 hours in tool and die, 350 hours on the drill presses, and 150 hours on lathes. The hours of production required in each of these areas are as follows for each of the products.

	Tool and Die	Drill Press	Lathe
A	9	5	3
B	3	4	0
C	0.5	0	2

Furthermore, the sales department foresees no limitations on the sale of products A and C, but sees sales of only 20 or fewer per week for B. If the unit profits expected are $30 for A, $9 for B, and $15 for C, how many of each should be produced to maximize profits? What is maximum profit?

21. An experiment involves placing the male and female animals of a laboratory animal species in two separate controlled environments. There is a limited time available in these environments, and the experimenter wishes to maximize the number of animals subject to the constraints described.

	Males	Females	Time Available
Environment A	20 min	25 min	800 min
Environment B	20 min	15 min	600 min

How many male animals and how many female animals will be the maximum total?

4.5 The Simplex Method: Minimization

Objectives
- To formulate the dual for minimization problems
- To solve minimization problems using the simplex method on the dual

Up to this point all the linear programming problems we have considered have been what we could call maximization problems. That is, the objective function was to be maximized. Now let us turn our attention to problems in which the objective function is to be minimized. Such problems might arise when a company seeks to minimize its production costs yet still fill customer's orders or purchase items necessary for production.

As with maximization problems, we shall limit our discussion of minimization problems to only those in which the constraints satisfy the following conditions.

1. All variables are nonnegative.
2. The constraints are of the form

$$a_1y_1 + a_2y_2 + \cdots + a_ny_n \geq b,$$

where b is positive.

In this section we will show how minimization problems of this type can be solved using the methods we have already developed.

EXAMPLE 1   Minimize $g = 11y_1 + 7y_2$
Subject to $y_1 + 2y_2 \geq 10$
                    $3y_1 + y_2 \geq 15$

Solution   Matrix A has the form of the simplex matrix (without slack variables) for this problem.

$$A = \begin{bmatrix} 1 & 2 & | & 10 \\ 3 & 1 & | & 15 \\ \hline 11 & 7 & | & g \end{bmatrix}$$

Since the simplex method specifically seeks to increase the objective function, it does not apply to this minimization problem. So, rather than solve this problem, let us solve a different but related problem called the **dual problem.**

The simplex matrix for the dual problem is formed by interchanging the rows and columns of matrix A. Matrix B is the result of this procedure, and we say that B is the *transpose* of A.

$$B = \begin{bmatrix} 1 & 3 & | & 11 \\ 2 & 1 & | & 7 \\ \hline 10 & 15 & | & g \end{bmatrix}$$

Notice that row 1 of A became column 1 of B, row 2 of A became column 2 of B, and row 3 of A became column 3 of B.

We may think of matrix B as the simplex matrix (without slack variables) for the following maximization problem.

Maximize $f = 10x_1 + 15x_2$
Subject to $x_1 + 3x_2 \leq 11$
                  $2x_1 + x_2 \leq 7$

To emphasize the fact that this is a totally different problem from the original minimization problem, we use different letters to represent the variables and the function that is to be maximized.

The simplex method does apply to this maximization problem, so we solve it as follows. Successive matrices that occur using the simplex method are numbered accordingly, and the pivot is circled.

Beside the maximization problem is the solution to the original minimization problem, obtained using graphical methods.

MAXIMIZATION PROBLEM

1.
$$\left[\begin{array}{cccc|c} 1 & ③ & 1 & 0 & 11 \\ 2 & 1 & 0 & 1 & 7 \\ \hline 10 & 15 & 0 & 0 & f \end{array}\right]$$

MINIMIZATION PROBLEM

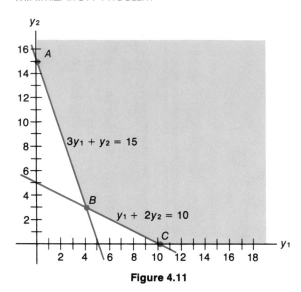

Figure 4.11

2.
$$\left[\begin{array}{cccc|c} \frac{1}{3} & 1 & \frac{1}{3} & 0 & \frac{11}{3} \\ ⑤⁄₃ & 0 & -\frac{1}{3} & 1 & \frac{10}{3} \\ \hline 5 & 0 & -5 & 0 & f-55 \end{array}\right]$$

Vertices:

$A = (0, 15)$
$B = (4, 3)$ obtained by solving
$C = (10, 0)$ simultaneously

3.
$$\left[\begin{array}{cccc|c} 0 & 1 & \frac{2}{5} & -\frac{1}{5} & 3 \\ 1 & 0 & -\frac{1}{5} & \frac{3}{5} & 2 \\ \hline 0 & 0 & -4 & -3 & f-65 \end{array}\right]$$

$g = 11y_1 + 7y_2;$
at $A, g = 105$
at $B, g = 65$
at $C, g = 110$

Maximum $f = 65$ occurs at $x_1 = 2, x_2 = 3$.

Minimum $g = 65$ occurs at $y_1 = 4, y_2 = 3$.

In comparing the solutions to the previous two problems the first thing to notice is that the maximum value for f in the maximization problem and the minimum value for g in the minimization problem are the same. Furthermore, looking at the final simplex matrix, we can also find the values of y_1 and y_2 that give the minimum value for g.

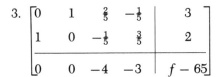

Negatives of these values give the values for y_1 and y_2
in the minimization problem   □

From this example we see that the given minimization problem and its dual maximization problem are very closely related. Furthermore, it appears that when problems enjoy this relationship, the simplex method might be used to solve them both. The question is whether the simplex method will always solve them both. The answer is yes. This fact was proved by John von Neuman, and it is summarized by the Principle of Duality.

Principle of   1. When a minimization problem and its dual have a solution, the
Duality   maximum value of the function to be maximized is the same
             value as the minimum value of the function to be minimized.
          2. When the simplex method is used to solve the maximization
             problem, the values for the variables that solve the correspond-
             ing minimization problem are the negatives of the last entries in
             the columns corresponding to the slack variables.

EXAMPLE 2   Given the problem

$$\text{Minimize} \quad g = 19y_1 + 15y_2$$
$$\text{Subject to} \quad 5y_1 + y_2 > 30$$
$$2y_1 + 6y_2 \geq 40$$

(a) State the dual of this minimization problem.
(b) Use the simplex method to solve the given problem.

Solution   (a) The dual of this minimization problem will be a maximization problem. To form the dual, write the simplex matrix (without slack variables) for the given problem, matrix A.

$$A = \begin{bmatrix} 5 & 1 & | & 30 \\ 2 & 6 & | & 40 \\ \hline 19 & 15 & | & g \end{bmatrix}$$

Transpose matrix A to yield matrix B.

$$B = \begin{bmatrix} 5 & 2 & | & 19 \\ 1 & 6 & | & 15 \\ \hline 30 & 40 & | & g \end{bmatrix}$$

Write the dual maximization problem, renaming the variables and the function.

Dual Problem

$$\text{Maximize} \quad f = 30x_1 + 40x_2$$
$$\text{Subject to} \quad 5x_1 + 2x_2 \leq 19$$
$$x_1 + 6x_2 \leq 15$$

(b) To solve the given minimization problem, we use the simplex method on its dual maximization problem. The complete simplex matrix for each step is given and each pivot is circled:

1.
$$\begin{bmatrix} 5 & 2 & 1 & 0 & \vline & 19 \\ 1 & ⑥ & 0 & 1 & \vline & 15 \\ \hline 30 & 40 & 0 & 0 & \vline & f \end{bmatrix}$$

2.
$$\begin{bmatrix} ⑭⁄₃ & 0 & 1 & -\frac{1}{3} & \vline & 14 \\ \frac{1}{6} & 1 & 0 & \frac{1}{6} & \vline & \frac{5}{2} \\ \hline \frac{70}{3} & 0 & 0 & -\frac{20}{3} & \vline & f - 100 \end{bmatrix}$$

3.
$$\begin{bmatrix} 1 & 0 & \frac{3}{14} & -\frac{1}{14} & \vline & 3 \\ 0 & 1 & -\frac{1}{28} & \frac{5}{28} & \vline & 2 \\ \hline 0 & 0 & -5 & -5 & \vline & f - 170 \end{bmatrix}$$

Thus $y_1 = 5$, $y_2 = 5$, and $g = 170$.   □

EXAMPLE 3   A beef producer is considering two different types of feed. Each feed contains some or all of the necessary ingredients for fattening beef. Brand 1 feed costs 2 cents per pound and brand 2 costs 3 cents per pound. The producer would like to determine how much of each brand to buy in order to satisfy the nutritional requirements at minimum cost. Table 4.1 contains all the relevant data about nutrition and cost of each brand and the minimum requirements per unit of beef.

Table 4.1

	Brand 1 (*lb*)	Brand 2 (*lb*)	Minimum Requirement (*lb*)
Ingredient A	3	5	40
Ingredient B	4	3	46
Cost per pound	2	3	

Solution   Let y_1 be the number of pounds of brand 1 and y_2 the number of pounds of brand 2. Then we can formulate the problem as follows:

$$\text{Minimize costs} \quad C = 2y_1 + 3y_2$$
$$\text{Subject to} \quad 3y_1 + 5y_2 \geq 40$$
$$4y_1 + 3y_2 \geq 46$$

The original linear programming problem is usually called the *primal problem*. If we write this in an augmented matrix, without the slack variables, then we can transpose to find the dual problem.

Primal

Dual
(with function renamed)

$$\begin{bmatrix} 3 & 5 & | & 40 \\ 4 & 3 & | & 46 \\ \hline 2 & 3 & | & C \end{bmatrix} \qquad \begin{bmatrix} 3 & 4 & | & 2 \\ 5 & 3 & | & 3 \\ \hline 40 & 46 & | & f \end{bmatrix}$$

Thus the dual maximum problem here is

$$\text{Maximize} \quad f = 40x_1 + 46x_2$$
$$\text{Subject to} \quad 3x_1 + 4x_2 \leq 2$$
$$5x_1 + 3x_2 \leq 3$$

The simplex matrix for this maximum problem, with slack variables *included*, is

1. $$\begin{bmatrix} 3 & \textcircled{4} & 1 & 0 & | & 2 \\ 5 & 3 & 0 & 1 & | & 3 \\ \hline 40 & 46 & 0 & 0 & | & f \end{bmatrix}$$

Solving the problem gives

2. $$\begin{bmatrix} \frac{3}{4} & 1 & \frac{1}{4} & 0 & | & \frac{1}{2} \\ \textcircled{\frac{11}{4}} & 0 & -\frac{3}{4} & 1 & | & \frac{3}{2} \\ \hline \frac{11}{2} & 0 & -\frac{23}{2} & 0 & | & f - 23 \end{bmatrix}$$ 3. $$\begin{bmatrix} 0 & 1 & \frac{5}{11} & -\frac{3}{11} & | & \frac{1}{11} \\ 1 & 0 & -\frac{3}{11} & \frac{4}{11} & | & \frac{6}{11} \\ \hline 0 & 0 & -10 & -2 & | & f - 26 \end{bmatrix}$$

The solution to this problem is

$$y_1 = 10 \text{ lb of brand 1}$$
$$y_2 = 2 \text{ lb of brand 2}$$
$$\text{Minimum cost} = 26 \text{ cents per unit of beef.} \qquad \square$$

In a more extensive study of linear programming the duality relationship that we have used in this section as a means to solve minimization problems could be shown to have many more properties than we have mentioned. For example, in applied problems where the objective is to minimize costs, it is possible to interpret the variables in the dual as "shadow prices" and interpret their values as marginal costs. Moreover, if the given problem is a profit maximization problem, then we can also form its dual, a minimization problem, by using matrix transposition, and we can think of the dual variables as representing "shadow prices" and interpret their values as marginal profits. Linear programming, the simplex method, and duality are topics of depth and beauty, and we have provided only a brief introduction to their terminology, areas of application, and power.

Exercise 4.5

In problems 1–6, form the matrix associated with each problem and find the transpose of the matrix.

1. Minimize $g = 3y_1 + y_2$ subject to

$$4y_1 + y_2 \geq 11$$
$$3y_1 + 2y_2 \geq 12$$

2. Minimize $g = 9y_1 + 10y_2$ subject to

$$y_1 + 2y_2 \geq 19$$
$$3y_1 + 2y_2 \geq 29$$

3. Minimize $g = 5y_1 + 2y_2$ subject to

$$4y_1 + y_2 \geq 12$$
$$y_1 + y_2 \geq 9$$
$$y_1 + 3y_2 \geq 15$$

4. Minimize $g = 2y_1 + 5y_2$ subject to the constraints in problem 3.
5. Minimize $g = 12y_1 + 48y_2 + 8y_3$ subject to

$$y_1 + 3y_2 \qquad \geq 1$$
$$4y_1 + 6y_2 + y_3 \geq 3$$
$$4y_2 + y_3 \qquad \geq 1$$

6. Minimize $g = 12y_1 + 8y_2 + 10y_3$ subject to

$$y_1 + 2y_3 \qquad \geq 10$$
$$y_1 + y_2 \qquad \geq 12$$
$$2y_1 + 2y_2 + y_3 \geq 8$$

7–12. Write the dual problem for problems 1–6. Be sure to rename the variables and the function.
13–18. Solve the linear programming problem given in problems 1–6. Use the simplex method.

APPLICATIONS

19. In a hospital ward, the patients can be grouped into two general categories depending on their condition and the amount of solid foods they require in their diet. A

combination of two diets is used for solid foods because they supply essential nutrients for recovery, but each diet has an amount of a substance deemed detrimental. The table summarizes the patient group, diet requirements, and the amount of the detrimental substance. How many servings from each diet should be given each day in order to minimize the intake of this detrimental substance?

	Diet A	Diet B	Daily Requirements
Patient group 1	4 oz per serving	1 oz per serving	26 oz
Patient group 2	2 oz per serving	1 oz per serving	18 oz
Detrimental substances (ounces per serving)	0.18 oz	0.07 oz	

20. Two factories produce three different types of kitchen appliances. The table summarizes the production capacity, the number of each type of appliance ordered, and the daily operating costs for the factories. How many days should each factory operate to fill the orders at minimum cost?

	Factory 1	Factory 2	Number Ordered
Appliance 1	80 per day	20 per day	1600
Appliance 2	10 per day	10 per day	500
Appliance 3	20 per day	70 per day	2000
Daily cost	$10,000	$20,000	

21. In a laboratory experiment, two separate foods are given to experimental animals. Each food contains essential ingredients, A and B, which have minimum requirements for the animals, and each food also has an ingredient C, which can be harmful to the animals. The table summarizes this information.

	Food 1	Food 2	Requirements
Ingredient A	10 units per g	3 units per g	49 units
Ingredient B	6 units per g	12 units per g	60 units
Ingredient C	3 units per g	1 unit per g	

How many grams of foods 1 and 2 should be given to the animals in order to satisfy the requirements for A and B, and in order to minimize the amount of ingredient C that is ingested?

22. A political candidate wishes to use a combination of radio and TV advertisements in her campaign. Research has shown that each 1-minute spot on TV reaches 0.9 million people and each 1 minute on radio reaches 0.6 million. The candidate feels she must reach 63 million people, and she must buy at least 90 minutes of advertisements. How many minutes of each medium should be used if TV costs $500 per minute and radio costs $100 per minute, and the candidate wishes to minimize costs?

Review Exercises

1. Solve $3x - 9 \leq 4(3 - x)$ and graph the solution.
2. Solve $\frac{2}{5}x \leq x + 4$ and graph the solution.
3. Solve $5x + 1 \geq \frac{2}{3}(x - 6)$ and graph the solution.
4. Determine if the following represent open or closed intervals:
   (a) $0 \leq x \leq 5$ (b) $3 \leq x \leq 7$ (c) $-3 < x < 2$

Graph the system of inequalities in problems 5 and 6.

5. $x + 2y \leq 20$
    $3x + 10y \leq 80$
    $x \geq 0$
    $y \geq 0$

6. $3x + y \geq 4$
    $x + y \geq 2$
    $-x + y \leq 4$
    $x \leq 5$

Solve the following linear programming problems using graphical methods. Restrict $x \geq 0$ and $y \geq 0$.

7. Maximize $f = 5x + 6y$
   Subject to $x + 3y \leq 24$
   $4x + 3y \leq 42$
   $2x + y \leq 20$

8. Maximize $f = 9x + 5y$ subject to the conditions in problem 7.

9. Maximize $f = x + 4y$
   Subject to $7x + 3y \leq 105$
   $2x + 5y \leq 59$
   $x + 7y \leq 70$

Use the simplex method to solve the following linear programming problems. Assume all variables are nonnegative.

10. Maximize $f = 7x + 12y$ subject to the conditions in problem 9.

11. Maximize $f = 3x + 4y$
    Subject to $x + 4y \leq 160$
    $x + 2y \leq 100$
    $4x + 3y \leq 300$

12. Maximize $f = 3x + 8y$ subject to the conditions in problem 11.

13. Maximize $f = 39x + 5y + 30z$
    Subject to $x + z \leq 7$
    $3x + 5y \leq 30$
    $3x + y \leq 18$

Form the dual and use the simplex method to solve the minimization problems 14–17.

14. Minimize $g = 7y_1 + 6y_2$
    Subject to $5y_1 + 2y_2 \geq 16$
    $3y_1 + 7y_2 \geq 27$

15. Minimize $g = 3y_1 + 4y_2$
    Subject to $3y_1 + y_2 \geq 8$
    $y_1 + y_2 \geq 6$
    $2y_1 + 5y_2 \geq 18$

16. Minimize $g = 2y_1 + y_2$ subject to the conditions of problem 15.

17. Minimize $g = 12y_1 + 48y_2 + 8y_3$
    Subject to $y_1 + 3y_2 \geq 1$
    $4y_1 + 6y_2 + y_3 \geq 3$
    $4y_2 + y_3 \geq 1$

APPLICATIONS

18. A manufacturer of blenders produces three different sizes: Regular, Special, and Kitchen Magic. The production of each type requires the materials and amounts given in the table.

	Regular	Special	Kitchen Magic
Electrical components	5	12	25
Units of aluminum	1	2	4
Blending containers	1	1	1

Suppose the manufacturer is opening a new plant, and anticipates weekly supplies of 90,000 electrical components, 15,000 units of aluminum, and 7000 containers. If the unit profit is $2 for the Regular, $4 for the Special, and $7.50 for the Kitchen Magic, how many of each should be produced to maximize profits? What is the maximum profit?

19. A company manufactures two different size backyard swing sets. The larger requires 5 hours of labor to complete, the smaller requires 2 hours, and there are 700 hours of labor each day. The packing department can pack at most 185 swing sets per day. If the profit is $4 on each larger set and $2 on each smaller set, how many of each should be produced to yield maximum profit? What is the maximum profit?

20. A company produces two different grades of steel, A and B, at two different factories, 1 and 2. The table summarizes the production capabilities of the factories, the cost per day, and the number of units of each grade of steel that are required to fill orders.

	Factory 1	Factory 2	Required
Grade A steel	1 unit	2 units	80 units
Grade B steel	3 units	2 units	140 units
Cost per day	$5000/day	$6000/day	

How many days should each factory operate in order to fill the orders at minimum cost? What is the minimum cost?

21. A laboratory wishes to purchase two different feeds, A and B, for their animals. The table summarizes the nutritional content of the feeds, the required amounts of each ingredient and the cost of each type of feed.

	Feed A	Feed B	Requirements
Carbohydrates	1 unit/lb	4 units/lb	40 units
Protein	2 units/lb	1 unit/lb	80 units
Cost	14¢/lb	16¢/lb	

How many pounds of each type of feed should the laboratory buy in order to satisfy their needs at minimum cost?

PART THREE
Nonlinear Models

Warmup In this chapter you will need to work problems like the following. If you have difficulty with any problem, return to the section where that type of problem was introduced and refresh your memory before starting the chapter.

Problem Type	Introduced in Section	Used in Section	Answer
Find $b^2 - 4ac$ if (a) $a = 1, b = 2, c = -2$ (b) $a = -2, b = 3, c = -1$ (c) $a = -3, b = -3, c = -2$	0.1 Signed numbers	5.1, 5.2	(a) 12 (b) 1 (c) -15
(a) Factor $6x^2 - x - 2$. (b) Factor $6x^2 - 9x$.	0.4 Factoring	5.1	(a) $(3x - 2)(2x + 1)$ (b) $3x(2x - 3)$
Is $\dfrac{1 + \sqrt{-3}}{2}$ a real number?	0.2 Radicals	5.1	No
(a) Find the y-intercept of $y = x^2 - 6x + 8$. (b) Find the x-intercept of $y = 3x(2x - 3)$.	2.2 x- and y-intercepts	5.2	(a) 8 (b) $0, \frac{3}{2}$

QUADRATIC FUNCTIONS

In previous chapters we studied linear equations and inequalities and their applications in detail, including their analysis using matrices and linear programming. Even though linear equations are relatively easy to formulate and to use, they are not sufficient to solve all problems that arise in business, the social sciences, or the life sciences. Thus we now direct our attention to equations of second degree, called quadratic equations.

We begin with the solution of quadratic equations of the form $ax^2 + bx + c = 0$. The knowledge of solution methods is then interpreted in a coordinate setting and extended when we carefully analyze the properties of quadratic functions of the form $y = ax^2 + bx + c$, whose graphs are called parabolas. As we develop these techniques and analyses, they are applied to the solution of problems that arise in the life sciences or the social sciences.

The use of these quadratic functions makes it possible to greatly expand our study of the special business functions we have been discussing in detail. In particular, we will see that the mathematical principles governing market equilibrium and break-even analysis still apply, but now the functions are quadratics. Furthermore, our analysis allows us to find maximum values for revenue and profit functions, which are parabolas of the form $f(x) = ax^2 + bx + c$.

5.1 Quadratic Equations

Objective   ■ To solve quadratic equations

It is important for us to know how to solve the equations that arise as we study different types of functions and consider their graphs and applications. This was true for linear equations and is again true for quadratic equations.

In general, a **quadratic equation** in one variable is an equation that can be put into the *general form*

$$ax^2 + bx + c = 0 \qquad (a \neq 0),$$

where a, b, and c represent constants. For example, the equations

$$3x^2 + 4x + 1 = 0 \qquad \text{and} \qquad 2x^2 + 1 = x^2 - x$$

are quadratic equations; the first of these is in general form, and the second may easily be put in general form.

When we solve quadratic equations we will only be interested in real solutions and will consider two methods of solution. One method of solving quadratic equations is by factoring. (For a review of factoring, see Section 0.4.)

Solution by factoring is based on the fact that, in our number system, when the product of two factors equals zero, then one of the factors (or both) must equal zero. Hence, to use factoring we *must* start with the quadratic equation in the general form.

EXAMPLE 1   Solve $6x^2 + 3x = 4x + 2$.

Solution
1. The proper form for factoring is $6x^2 - x - 2 = 0$.
2. Factoring gives $(3x - 2)(2x + 1) = 0$.
3. $3x - 2 = 0$, so $x = \frac{2}{3}$ is a solution. $2x + 1 = 0$, so $x = -\frac{1}{2}$ is a solution.
4. Check for $x = \frac{2}{3}$: Does $6(\frac{2}{3})^2 + 3(\frac{2}{3}) = 4(\frac{2}{3}) + 2$? Yes, because $6(\frac{4}{9}) + 2 = \frac{8}{3} + 2$.

   Check for $x = -\frac{1}{2}$: Does $6(-\frac{1}{2})^2 + 3(-\frac{1}{2}) = 4(-\frac{1}{2}) + 2$? Yes, because $6(\frac{1}{4}) - \frac{3}{2} = -2 + 2$.   □

EXAMPLE 2   Solve $6x^2 = 9x$.

Solution   As in Example 1, the proper form for solution by factoring is $6x^2 - 9x = 0$. Factoring yields $3x(2x - 3) = 0$. So

$$3x = 0 \qquad \text{or} \qquad 2x - 3 = 0,$$

and

$$x = 0 \qquad \text{or} \qquad x = \tfrac{3}{2}.$$

Check for $x = 0$: $6(0^2) = 9(0)$ or $0 = 0$, which checks.

Check for $x = \frac{3}{2}$: Does $6(\frac{3}{2})^2 = 9(\frac{3}{2})$? Yes, since $6(\frac{9}{4}) = 9(\frac{3}{2})$.

Note that in this example (and always) it is incorrect to divide both sides of the equation by x, since this results in the loss of the solution $x = 0$. □

EXAMPLE 3 Solve $(y - 3)(y + 2) = -4$ for y.

Solution The left side of the equation is factored, but the right member is not 0. Therefore we multiply the factors and put the equation in general form: $y^2 - y - 6 = -4$ or $y^2 - y - 2 = 0$. Factoring gives $(y - 2)(y + 1) = 0$. Thus $y - 2 = 0$ or $y = 2$ and $y + 1 = 0$ or $y = -1$. The solutions are $y = 2$, $y = -1$.

CHECK: If $y = 2$, $(2 - 3)(2 + 2) = -4$. If $y = -1$, $(-1 - 3)(-1 + 2) = -4$. □

For quadratic equations in which factorization is difficult or impossible to see, we may use the quadratic formula.

> *Quadratic Formula* If $ax^2 + bx + c = 0$, then $x = \dfrac{-b \pm \sqrt{b^2 - 4ac}}{2a}$.

Note once again that the equation *must* be in general form to begin the solution. Here the proper identification of values for a, b, and c to be substituted into the formula requires that the equation is in general form.

EXAMPLE 4 Use the quadratic formula to solve $2x^2 - 3x - 6 = 0$ for x.

Solution The equation is already in general form, with $a = 2$, $b = -3$, and $c = -6$. Hence for

$$x = \frac{-b \pm \sqrt{b^2 - 4ac}}{2a},$$

we have

$$x = \frac{-(-3) \pm \sqrt{(-3)^2 - 4(2)(-6)}}{2(2)} = \frac{3 \pm \sqrt{9 + 48}}{4}.$$

Thus

$$x = \frac{3 \pm \sqrt{57}}{4},$$

so the solutions are

$$x = \frac{3 + \sqrt{57}}{4} \quad \text{and} \quad x = \frac{3 - \sqrt{57}}{4}.$$

□

EXAMPLE 5   Find all real solutions to $x^2 = x - 1$, using the quadratic formula.

Solution   First put the equation in general form:

$$x^2 - x + 1 = 0.$$

Now, $a = 1$, $b = -1$, and $c = 1$, so using the quadratic formula we obtain the following:

$$x = \frac{-(-1) \pm \sqrt{(-1)^2 - 4(1)(1)}}{2(1)} = \frac{1 \pm \sqrt{1 - 4}}{2}.$$

Thus

$$x = \frac{1 \pm \sqrt{-3}}{2};$$

however these are not real solutions for x, since $\sqrt{-3}$ is not a real number. Hence there are no real solutions to the given equation.   □

In general, the part of the quadratic formula given by $b^2 - 4ac$ is called the *discriminant* because it tells us what types of solutions we will obtain.

If	$b^2 - 4ac > 0$,	we get	2 real solutions
	$b^2 - 4ac = 0$,		1 real solution
	$b^2 - 4ac < 0$,		no real solutions

In Example 5, $b^2 - 4ac = -3 < 0$, so there were no real solutions.

Exercise 5.1

Write the following equations in general form.

1. $x^2 + 5x = 3$
2. $y^2 + 4y = 2$
3. $x^2 = 6x - 2$
4. $z^2 = 4 - 3z$
5. $3x^2 = 4x$
6. $w^2 + 4 = 0$
7. $3y = y^2 - 2$
8. $2 = 4z - z^2$
9. $2x = 1 - x^2$
10. $3x^2 = 2x - 3$

Solve the following equations for x.

11. $3x^2 - 11x + 6 = 0$

12. $x^2 - 8x + 16 = 0$

13. $x^2 - x = x + 3$

14. $x^2 + 10x = 18x - 15$

15. $x^2 + 5x = 21 + x$

16. $x^2 + 17x = 8x - 14$

17. $1 - 2x + x^2 = 0$

18. $6x - 4 - 2x^2 = 0$

19. $3x + 10 - x^2 = 0$

20. $4x^2 + 12x + 8 = 0$

21. $5x^2 - 20x + 15 = 0$

22. $(x - 3)(x - 1) = -1$

23. $(x - 1)(x + 5) = 7$

24. $(x + 2)(x + 3) = 30$

25. $x^2 = 4$

26. $x^2 = 16$

Use the quadratic formula to find all real solutions, if any, for the following.

27. $x^2 + 7x + 10 = 0$

28. $3y^2 + 5y - 2 = 0$

29. $6x^2 = x + 1$

30. $x^2 = x + 2$

31. $x^2 - 9x - 3 = 0$

32. $w^2 - 4w - 2 = 0$

33. $y^2 + 4 = 0$

34. $z^2 + 2z + 4 = 0$

35. $2x^2 = 2x + 3$

36. $5x^2 + 1 = 10x$

37. $2w^2 + w + 1 = 0$

38. $x^2 - x - 1 = 0$

39. $x - \dfrac{3}{x} = 5$

40. $2 + \dfrac{1}{x} = 4r$

APPLICATIONS

41. The speed at which water travels in a pipe can be measured by directing the flow through an elbow and measuring the height it spurts out the top. If the elbow height is 10 cm, the equation relating the height of the water above the elbow (in centimeters) and its velocity v (in centimeters per second) is given by

$$v^2 = 1960(h + 10).$$

   (a) Find v if $h = 2$.

   (b) Find v if $h = 18$.

   (c) In these questions, the height has increased by a factor of 9. By what factor has the velocity increased?

42. Weather forecasters frequently report wind chill factors because a body exposed to wind loses heat due to convection. The amount of loss depends on many factors, but for a given situation there is a positive number called the coefficient of convection, K_c, which depends on the wind velocity v. The approximate relationship between K_c and v is given by

$$\frac{(K_c)^2}{64} - \frac{1}{4} = v.$$

   (a) Find the coefficient of convection when the wind velocity is 10 mph.

   (b) Find K_c when $v = 40$ mph.

   (c) What is the change in K_c for the change in v from 10 mph to 40 mph?

43. The velocity of a blood corpuscle in a vessel depends on how far the corpuscle is from the center of the vessel. Let R be the constant radius of the vessel, v_m the constant maximum velocity of the corpuscle, r the distance from the center to a particular blood corpuscle (variable), and v_r the velocity of that corpuscle. Then the velocity v_r is related to the distance r according to

$$v_r = v_m \left(1 - \frac{r^2}{R^2}\right).$$

(a) Find r when $v_r = \frac{1}{2}v_m$.

(b) Find r when $v_r = \frac{1}{4}v_m$.

(c) Find v_r when $r = R$.

5.2 Quadratic Functions: Parabolas

Objectives
- To find the zeros of quadratic functions
- To find the vertex of the graph of quadratic functions
- To graph quadratic functions

The polynomial equation $y = ax^2 + bx + c$, where a, b, and c are real numbers and $a \neq 0$, is the equation of a second-degree function, or **quadratic function.** The graph of a quadratic function is a **parabola.**

If $a > 0$, the parabola opens upward (see Figure 5.1). If $a < 0$, the parabola opens downward (see Figure 5.2).

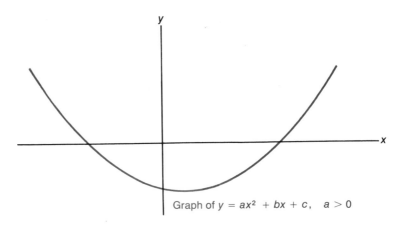

Graph of $y = ax^2 + bx + c$, $a > 0$

Figure 5.1

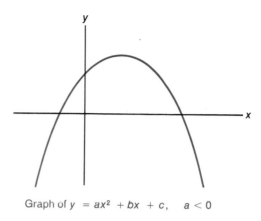

Graph of $y = ax^2 + bx + c$, $a < 0$

Figure 5.2

The following example will help us discover more properties of quadratic functions.

EXAMPLE 1 For the equation $y = x^2 - 4x + 3$,
(a) construct a table of values, using integer values of x from -1 to 5.
(b) graph the equation, using the points determined in (a) as a guide.

Solution   (a)

x	$y = x^2 - 4x + 3$
-1	$(-1)^2 - 4(-1) + 3 = 8$
0	$0^2 - 4(0) + 3 = 3$
1	$1^2 - 4(1) + 3 = 0$
2	$2^2 - 4(2) + 3 = -1$
3	$3^2 - 4(3) + 3 = 0$
4	$4^2 - 4(4) + 3 = 3$
5	$5^2 - 4(5) + 3 = 8$

(b) The graph is shown in Figure 5.3.

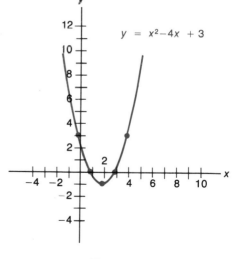

$y = x^2 - 4x + 3$

Figure 5.3   □

From the graph of the equation in Example 1, we can make the following observations:

1. The graph opens upward ($a = 1 > 0$).
2. One half of the parabola is a reflection (mirror image) of the other about some line. We say the parabola is *symmetric* about the line, called its *axis of symmetry*. In Example 1, the axis of symmetry is the vertical line with equation $x = 2$.
3. The parabola has a minimum (lowest) point where the axis of symmetry intersects the curve, at $(2, -1)$. Because the axis of symmetry lies midway between any two points with the same y-value, we can easily determine the x-value of the minimum point. A parabola that opens downward will have a maximum (highest) point.
4. The parabola crosses the x-axis where the y-value is zero. Thus the x-values of the points where the parabola crosses the x-axis are the solutions to the equation $0 = x^2 - 4x + 3$.

From the graph, the solutions to the equation $0 = x^2 - 4x + 3$ are $x = 1$ and $x = 3$. Solving the equation by factoring gives $0 = (x - 1)(x - 3)$, so $x = 1$ and $x = 3$ are the solutions. These values are called the *zeros* of the function.

EXAMPLE 2   Find the zeros of $y = x^2 - 6x + 8$, if they exist, and graph the equation.

Solution   Setting $y = 0$ and solving for x will tell us where the curve crosses the x-axis.

$$0 = x^2 - 6x + 8$$
or
$$0 = (x - 2)(x - 4)$$

so $x = 2$ or $x = 4$.

Thus the curve crosses the x-axis at $x = 2$ and at $x = 4$. Because the coefficient of x^2 is positive ($+1$) the parabola will open upward.

Making a table for x-values near the x-intercepts will help construct the graph shown in Figure 5.4.   □

x	$y = x^2 - 6x + 8$
0	$0^2 - 6(0) + 8 = 8$
1	$1^2 - 6(1) + 8 = 3$
2	0 (x-intercept, found above)
3	$3^2 - 6(3) + 8 = -1$
4	0 (x-intercept, found above)
5	$5^2 - 6(5) + 8 = 3$
6	$6^2 - 6(6) + 8 = 8$

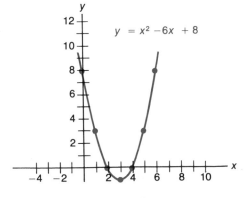

Figure 5.4

Again, the axis of symmetry is a vertical line, and it passes through the minimum point $(3, -1)$. Note that we can find the x-value of the minimum point, namely $x = 3$, by taking the value midway between the two x-values where the curve crosses the x-axis. This value, $x = 3$, represents the mean of the numbers 2 and 4; that is, $\frac{1}{2}(2 + 4) = 3$.

More generally, if we are given $y = ax^2 + bx + c$, then the zeros are solutions to $ax^2 + bx + c = 0$, and they are given by the quadratic formula as

$$x = \frac{-b + \sqrt{b^2 - 4ac}}{2a} \qquad \text{and} \qquad x = \frac{-b - \sqrt{b^2 - 4ac}}{2a}.$$

If we average these x-values (that is, take one-half their sum), then we obtain the x-coordinate of the vertex of the parabola, which is $-b/2a$.

We can summarize the information we have learned about quadratic functions as follows.

Graphs of Quadratic Functions   Form: $y = ax^2 + bx + c$

Graph: parabola $\begin{cases} \text{opening upward if } a > 0 \\ \text{opening downward if } a < 0 \end{cases}$

Zeros (if real): $x = \dfrac{-b + \sqrt{b^2 - 4ac}}{2a}, \qquad x = \dfrac{-b - \sqrt{b^2 - 4ac}}{2a}$

Vertex: $x = \dfrac{-b}{2a}$

EXAMPLE 3   Find the vertex and zeros, if they exist, for the parabola whose equation is $y = 4x - x^2$, and sketch the parabola.

Solution   The proper form is $y = -x^2 + 4x + 0$, so $a = -1$. Thus,

The parabola opens downward.
The vertex is the highest (maximum) point.

The vertex occurs at $x = \dfrac{-b}{2a} = \dfrac{-4}{2(-1)} = 2$.

The y-value of the vertex is $f(2) = (-2)^2 + 4(2) = 4$.
The zeros for the parabola are solutions to $0 = -x^2 + 4x$: $0 = x(-x + 4)$, so $x = 0$ or $0 = -x + 4$

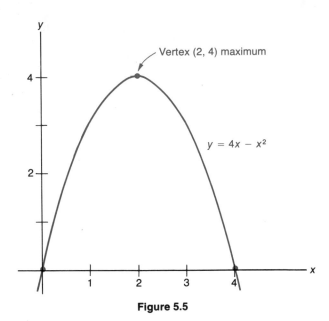

Figure 5.5

Thus the zeros are $x = 0$ and $x = 4$.

Plotting these three points (and others if necessary) gives the graph (see Figure 5.5). □

The vertex is the most important point on a parabola because it is the place where the graph changes direction. With the ability to locate the vertex, we need very few other points to make a good sketch.

EXAMPLE 4   Find the vertex and zeros, if any, for the parabola $f(x) = -2x^2 + 4x - 4$.

Solution   1. The vertex is at

$$x = \frac{-b}{2a} = \frac{-4}{2(-2)} = +1.$$

2. Zeros are solutions to $f(x) = 0$. Thus we must solve $0 = -2x^2 + 4x - 4$. If we use the quadratic formula, we obtain

$$x = \frac{-4 \pm \sqrt{(4)^2 - 4(-2)(-4)}}{2(-2)} = \frac{-4 \pm \sqrt{16 - 32}}{-4},$$

or

$$x = \frac{-4 \pm \sqrt{-16}}{-4}.$$

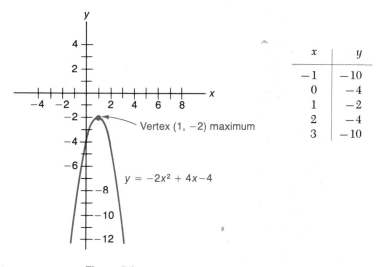

x	y
-1	-10
0	-4
1	-2
2	-4
3	-10

Vertex $(1, -2)$ maximum

$y = -2x^2 + 4x - 4$

Figure 5.6

These solutions are not real numbers, so the graph has no zeros and hence does not cross the x-axis.

The parabola opens downward, because the x^2 term has a negative coefficient. A table of values for x's on either side of the vertex $x = 1$ will allow us to accurately sketch the graph. (See Figure 5.6.)   □

The discussion applies to quadratic functions of the form $y = ax^2 + bx + c$. More generally, we define any equation that has at least one second-degree term and no term with degree higher than 2 as a **quadratic equation.**

The general form of a quadratic equation in two unknowns is

$$Ax^2 + Bxy + Cy^2 + Dx + Ey + F = 0,$$

with A, B, and C not all 0. The graphs of some of these equations will not be parabolas, but all equations that can be written in the form $y = ax^2 + bx + c$ will have parabolas as their graphs.

Techniques exist that make graphing the other forms of quadratic equations fairly easy, but we are primarily interested in parabolas, so we will not discuss those techniques. We can graph quadratic equations in two variables that are not of the form $y = ax^2 + bx + c$ by plotting a number of points or by using techniques we will learn in later chapters.

Perhaps a word should also be said about **polynomial functions,** such as $y = 3x^3 + 4x^2 + 5x + 2$ or $y = x^4 + 3x^2$. These functions can be graphed by plotting a (large) number of points and drawing a smooth curve through the points. Their graphs can be sketched easily using the techniques of calculus, so we will defer further discussion of their graphs until Chapter 12.

Exercise 5.2

Find the zeros, if any, and the vertex for the following quadratic functions, and sketch their graphs.

1. $y = x^2 - 4$
2. $y = x^2 + 5x + 4$
3. $y = -2x^2 + 18$
4. $y = 4 - x^2$
5. $y = x^2 + 4x + 4$
6. $y = x^2 + 6x - 9$
7. $y = x^2 + x + 2$
8. $y = -x^2 + 2x - 4$
9. $y = x^2 + 4$
10. $y = 1 + x - x^2$
11. $y = 25x - 6x^2$
12. $y = -4 + 7x - 4x^2$

APPLICATIONS

13. The amount of particulate pollution x depends on the wind velocity v, among other things. If the relationship between x and v can be approximated by

$$x = 20 - 0.01v^2,$$

sketch the graph relating these quantities.

14. In problem 43 of Exercise 5.1 we saw that the velocity of a blood corpuscle in a vessel, v_r, depends on the distance of the corpuscle from the center of the vessel, r, according to

$$v_r = v_m \left(1 - \frac{r^2}{R^2}\right),$$

where v_m is the maximum velocity and R the radius of the vessel.

   The blood pressure also affects the velocity of a corpuscle. If we make some simplifications in the formula, namely, let $v_m = 1$ and let $x^2 = r^2/R^2$, then we can observe the following.

Pressure	Equation
$p = 20$ mm	$v(x) = 8(1 - x^2)$
$p = 10$ mm	$v(x) = 3(1 - x^2)$
$p = 5$ mm	$v(x) = 1 - x^2$

Graph each of these equations on the same set of axes.

15. In problem 41 of Exercise 5.1 we saw that the speed of flowing water could be measured according to the equation

$$v^2 = 1960(h + 10).$$

Solve this equation for h and graph the result, using the velocity as the independent variable.

16. One of the early results in psychology relating the magnitude of a stimulus x to the magnitude of a response y is expressed by the equation

$$y = kx^2,$$

where k is an experimental constant. Sketch this graph for $k = 1$, $k = 2$, and $k = 4$.

5.3 Business Applications of Quadratic Functions

Objectives
- To graph quadratic supply and demand functions
- To find market equilibrium using quadratic supply and demand functions
- To find break-even points using quadratic cost and revenue functions
- To maximize quadratic revenue and profit functions

Supply, Demand, and Market Equilibrium

The first-quadrant parts of parabolas or other quadratic equations are frequently used to represent supply and demand functions. For example, the first-quadrant part of $p = q^2 + q + 2$ (Figure 5.7) may represent a supply curve, while the first-quadrant part of $q^2 + 2q + 6p - 23 = 0$ (Figure 5.8) may represent a demand curve.

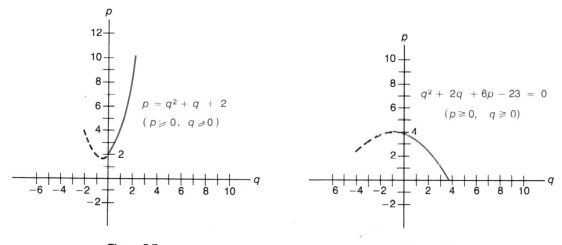

Figure 5.7   Figure 5.8

When quadratic equations are used to represent supply or demand curves, we can still solve their equations simultaneously to find the market equilibrium. To solve two equations simultaneously, we must eliminate one variable, as before, to obtain one equation in one unknown. When the functions are quadratic, the substitution method of solution is perhaps the best, and the resulting equation in one unknown will usually be quadratic.

EXAMPLE 1   If the supply function for a commodity is given by $p = q^2 + 100$ and the demand function is given by $p = -20q + 2500$, find the point of market equilibrium.

Solution   At market equilibrium, both equations will have the same p-value. So substituting $q^2 + 100$ for p in $p = -20q + 2500$, we get

$$q^2 + 100 = -20q + 2500$$
$$q^2 + 20q - 2400 = 0$$
$$(q - 40)(q + 60) = 0$$
$$q = 40 \quad \text{or} \quad q = -60.$$

Since a negative quantity has no meaning, the equilibrium point occurs when 40 units are sold, at $(40, 1700)$. The graphs of the functions are shown (in the first quadrant only) in Figure 5.9.   □

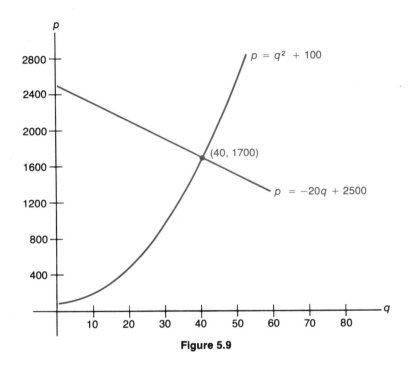

Figure 5.9

EXAMPLE 2   If the demand function for a commodity is given by $p(q + 4) = 400$ and the supply function is given by $2p - q - 38 = 0$, find the market equilibrium.

Solution   First note that the demand function is quadratic, but it is not a parabola. This causes no problems for us in trying to solve the equations simultaneously; we proceed as before. Solving $2p - q - 38 = 0$ for p gives $p = \frac{1}{2}q + 19$. Substituting for p in $p(q + 4) = 400$ gives

$$(\tfrac{1}{2}q + 19)(q + 4) = 400$$
$$\tfrac{1}{2}q^2 + 21q - 324 = 0.$$

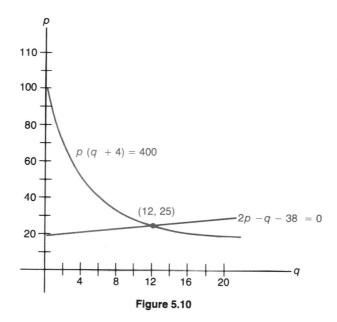

$p(q + 4) = 400$

$(12, 25)$

$2p - q - 38 = 0$

Figure 5.10

Multiplying both sides of the equation by 2 gives $q^2 + 42q - 648 = 0$. Factoring gives

$$(q - 12)(q + 54) = 0$$
$$q = 12 \quad \text{or} \quad q = -54.$$

Thus the market equilibrium occurs when 12 items are sold, at a price of $25 each. The graphs of the demand and supply functions are shown in Figure 5.10.

□

Break-Even Points and Profit Maximization

In Chapter 2, we discussed linear total cost and total revenue functions. Many total revenue functions may be linear, but costs tend to increase sharply after a certain level of production. Thus functions other than linear functions, including quadratic functions, are used to predict the total costs for a product.

For example, the monthly total cost curve for a commodity may be the parabola with equation $C(x) = 360 + 40x + 0.1x^2$. If the total revenue function is $R(x) = 60x$, we can find the break-even point by finding the quantity x that makes $C(x) = R(x)$.

Setting $C(x) = R(x)$, we have

$$360 + 40x + 0.1x^2 = 60x$$
$$0.1x^2 - 20x + 360 = 0$$
$$x^2 - 200x + 3600 = 0$$
$$(x - 20)(x - 180) = 0.$$

Thus $C(x) = R(x)$ at $x = 20$ and at $x = 180$. If 20 items are produced and sold, $C(x)$ and $R(x)$ are both \$1200; if 180 items are sold, $C(x)$ and $R(x)$ are both \$10,800.

EXAMPLE 3   The total cost per week of producing Ace electric shavers is $C(x) = 360 + 10x + 0.2x^2$. If the price per unit sold is $50 - 0.2x$, at what level(s) of production will the break-even point(s) occur?

Solution   The total cost function is $C(x) = 360 + 10x + 0.2x^2$, and the total revenue function is $R(x) = (50 - 0.2x)x = 50x - 0.2x^2$.
Setting $C(x) = R(x)$ and solving for x gives

$$360 + 10x + 0.2x^2 = 50x - 0.2x^2$$
$$0.4x^2 - 40x + 360 = 0$$
$$4x^2 - 400x + 3600 = 0$$
$$x^2 - 100x + 900 = 0$$
$$(x - 90)(x - 10) = 0.$$

Does this mean the firm will break even at 10 units and at 90 units? Yes. Figure 5.11 shows the graphs of $C(x)$ and $R(x)$. From the graph we can observe that the firm makes a profit after $x = 10$ *until* $x = 90$. At $x = 90$, the profit is 0, and the firm loses money if more than 90 units are produced per week.   □

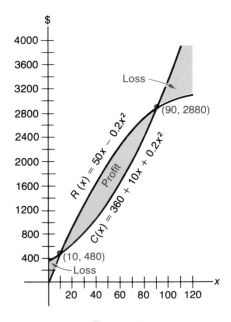

Figure 5.11

Notice that for Example 3, the revenue function

$$R(x) = 50x - 0.2x^2$$

is a parabola that opens downward. Thus the vertex is the point at which revenue is maximum. We can locate this vertex by using the methods discussed in the previous section.

$$\text{Vertex:} \quad x = \frac{-b}{2a} = \frac{-50}{2(-0.2)} = \frac{50}{0.4} = 125 \text{ items.}$$

It is interesting to note that when $x = 125$, the firm achieves its maximum revenues of

$$R(125) = 5(125) - 0.2(125)^2 = \$3125,$$

but the costs when $x = 125$ are

$$C(125) = 360 + 10(125) + 0.2(125)^2 = \$4735,$$

which results in a loss. This illustrates that maximizing revenue is not a good goal. We should seek to maximize profit.

EXAMPLE 4   Given total costs of $C(x) = 360 + 10x + 0.2x^2$ and total revenues of $R(x) = 50x - 0.2x^2$, form the profit function and find the maximum profit.

Solution   Note that these are the same cost and revenue functions that appear in the previous example.

$$\text{Profit} = \text{revenue} - \text{cost}$$

so we have

$$P(x) = (50x - 0.2x^2) - (360 + 10x + 0.2x^2),$$

or

$$P(x) = -360 + 40x - 0.4x^2.$$

Now, this profit function is a parabola that opens downward, so the vertex will be the maximum point.

$$\text{Vertex:} \quad x = \frac{-b}{2a} = \frac{-40}{2(-0.4)} = \frac{-40}{-0.8} = 50.$$

Furthermore, when $x = 50$, we have

$$P(50) = -360 + 40(50) - 0.4(50)^2 = \$640.$$

Thus, when 50 items are produced and sold, a maximum profit of \$640 results.

□

It is important to note that the procedures for finding maximum revenue and profit in these examples depend on the fact that these functions are parabolas. For more general functions, procedures for finding maximum or minimum values are discussed in Chapter 12.

Exercise 5.3

SUPPLY, DEMAND, AND MARKET EQUILIBRIUM

1. Sketch the first-quadrant portions of the following.
   (a) The supply function whose equation is $p = q^2 + 8q + 3$.
   (b) The demand function whose equation is $p = 4 - 4q - q^2$.
2. If the supply function for a commodity is $p = q^2 + 8q + 16$ and the demand function is $p = 216 - 2q$, find the equilibrium quantity and equilibrium price.
3. If the demand function for a commodity is given by the equation $p^2 + 4q = 1600$ and the supply function is given by the equation $300 - p^2 + 2q = 0$, find the equilibrium quantity and equilibrium price.
4. If the supply and demand functions for a commodity are $4p - q = 42$ and $(p + 2)q = 2100$, respectively, find the price that will result in market equilibrium.
5. If the supply and demand functions for a commodity are $q = p - 10$ and $q = 1200/p$, what is the equilibrium price and what is the corresponding number of units supplied and demanded?

BREAK-EVEN POINTS AND PROFIT MAXIMIZATION

6. If a firm has the following cost and revenue functions,

$$C(x) = 3600 + 25x + \tfrac{1}{2}x^2; \qquad R(x) = (175 - \tfrac{1}{2}x)x,$$

find the break-even points.
7. The total costs for a company are given by

$$C(x) = 2000 + 40x + x^2$$

and the total revenues are given by

$$R(x) = 130x.$$

Find the break-even points.
8. If total costs are $C(x) = 1344 + 1500x$ and total revenues are $R(x) = 1600x - x^2$, find the break-even points.
9. Suppose a company has fixed costs of 28,000 and variable costs of $(\tfrac{2}{5}x + 222)$ per unit. Suppose further that the selling price of its product is $1250 - \tfrac{3}{5}x$. Find the break-even points.
10. If the profit function for a firm is given by $P(x) = -1100 + 120x - x^2$ and limitations on space require that production is less than 100 units, find the break-even points.
11. Given $C(x) = 150 + x + 0.09x^2$ and $R(x) = 12.5x - 0.01x^2$, and given that production is restricted to fewer than 75 units, find the break-even points.
12. Find maximum revenue for $R(x) = (175 - \tfrac{1}{2}x)x$.
13. Form the profit function for the cost and revenue functions given in problem 6 and find maximum profit.
14. Form the profit function associated with problem 7 and find maximum profit.
15. For problem 11, find the x-values that yield maximum revenue and maximum profit. Do they agree? Why or why not?

Review Exercises

In problems 1–6, solve the equation.

1. $3x^2 + 10x = 5x$

2. $4x - 3x^2 = 0$

3. $x^2 + 5x + 6 = 0$

4. $11 - 10x - 2x^2 = 0$

5. $(x - 1)(x + 3) = -8$

6. $4x^2 = 3$

Find the vertex, the zeros, if any, and sketch the graph of each of the following.

7. $y = x^2 - 1$

8. $y = x^2 - 4x + 5$

9. $y = 3x - x^2$

10. $y = -10 + 7x - x^2$

11. $y = x^2 + .2x + 2$

12. $y = -(x^2 + 1)$

APPLICATIONS

13. The supply function for a good is given by $p = q^2 + 300$, and the demand is given by $p + q = 410$. Find the equilibrium quantity and price.

14. If the demand function for a commodity is given by the equation $p^2 + 5q = 200$, and the supply function is given by $40 - p^2 + 3q = 0$, find the equilibrium quantity and price.

15. If total costs for a good are given by $C(x) = 1760 + 8x + 0.6x^2$, and total revenues are given by $R(x) = 100x - 0.4x^2$, find the break-even points.

16. If total costs for a commodity are given by $C(x) = 900 + 25x$, and total revenues are given by $R(x) = 100x - x^2$, find the break-even points.

17. Find the maximum revenue and maximum profit for the functions described in problem 16.

18. Given total profit $P(x) = 1.3x - 0.01x^2 - 30$, find maximum profit and the break-even points and sketch the graph.

Warmup In this chapter you will need to work problems like the following. If you have difficulty with any problem, return to the section where that type of problem was introduced and refresh your memory before starting the chapter.

Problem Type	Introduced in Section	Used in Section	Answer
Write the following with positive exponents: (a) x^{-3} (b) $\dfrac{1}{x^{-2}}$ (c) $\sqrt{x}$	0.2 Exponents and radicals	6.1, 6.2, 6.3	(a) $\dfrac{1}{x^3}$ (b) x^2 (c) $x^{1/2}$
Simplify: (a) 2^0 (b) x^0 $(x \neq 0)$ (c) $49^{1/2}$ (d) 10^{-2}	0.2 Exponents	6.1, 6.2, 6.3	(a) 1 (b) 1 (c) 7 (d) $\frac{1}{100}$
Answer true or false. (a) $(\frac{1}{2})^x = 2^{-x}$ (b) $\sqrt{50} = 50^{1/2}$ (c) If $8 = 2^y$, then $y = 4$. (d) If $x^3 = 8$, then $x = 2$.	0.2 Exponents and radicals	6.1, 6.2	(a) True (b) True (c) False; $y = 3$ (d) True
(a) If $f(x) = 2^{-2x}$, what is $f(-2)$? (b) If $f(x) = 2^{-2x}$, what is $f(1)$? (c) If $f(t) = (1 + 0.02)^t$, what is $f(0)$? (d) If $f(t) = 100(0.03)^{0.02^t}$, what is $f(0)$?	1.3 Functional notation	6.1, 6.2, 6.3	(a) 16 (b) $\frac{1}{4}$ (c) 1 (d) 3

EXPONENTIAL AND LOGARITHMIC FUNCTIONS

In this chapter we study exponential and logarithmic functions, which provide models for many applications that at first seem remote and unrelated. For example, a business manager uses these functions to study the growth of money or corporations or the decay of new sales volume. A social scientist uses exponential and logarithmic functions to study the growth of organizations or populations or the dating of fossilized remains. And a biologist uses these functions to study the growth of microorganisms in a laboratory culture, the spread of disease, the measurement of pH, or the decay of radioactive material.

In our study of exponential and logarithmic functions we will examine their description, their properties, their graphs, and the special inverse relationship between these two functions. We will see how these functions are applied to some of the concerns of social scientists, business managers, and life scientists. In these applications, the inverse relationship of the exponential and logarithmic functions is used to solve some of the equations that arise. The work with these functions will be much easier if you have a calculator that computes powers of e and logarithms to the base e (denoted e^x and $\ln x$), but tables have been provided in case you do not have such a calculator.

6.1 Exponential Functions

Objective   ■ To graph exponential functions

If a microorganism is cultured in a laboratory, and if each minute it splits into two new organisms, then we can determine the number of organisms as a function of time. Some of the values for this function are given in Table 6.1.

Table 6.1

Minutes passed	0	1	2	3	4
Number	1	2	4	8	16

If y represents the number of organisms and x represents the number of minutes passed, then the equation that represents the number of organisms as a function of time is $y = 2^x$. This is an example of a special group of functions called **exponential functions.** In general, we define these functions as follows:

> If a is a positive real number, then the function
>
> $$f(x) = a^x$$
>
> is an *exponential function.*

The function $y = 2^x$ was restricted to $x \geq 0$ because of the physical setting, but we may graph $y = 2^x$ without this restriction on x. A table of values satisfying this equation and its graph are given in Figure 6.1.

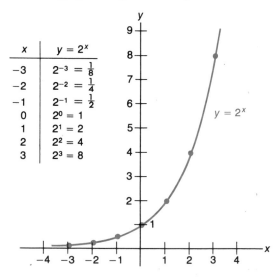

x	$y = 2^x$
-3	$2^{-3} = \frac{1}{8}$
-2	$2^{-2} = \frac{1}{4}$
-1	$2^{-1} = \frac{1}{2}$
0	$2^0 = 1$
1	$2^1 = 2$
2	$2^2 = 4$
3	$2^3 = 8$

Figure 6.1

Note that the section of the graph for $x \geq 0$ describes the growth of the organism discussed. Also note that the table of values contains only integer values of x, whereas the graph shows y-values for all values of x.

We have defined rational powers of x in terms of radicals in Chapter 0, so 2^x makes sense for any rational power of x. It can also be shown that the laws of exponents apply for irrational numbers. We will assume that if we graphed $y = 2^x$ for irrational values of x, those points would lie on the curve in Figure 6.1. Thus in general we can graph an exponential function by plotting easily calculated points, such as those in the table for Figure 6.1, and drawing a smooth curve through the points.

EXAMPLE 1   Graph $y = 10^x$.

Solution   A table of values and the graph are given in Figure 6.2.   □

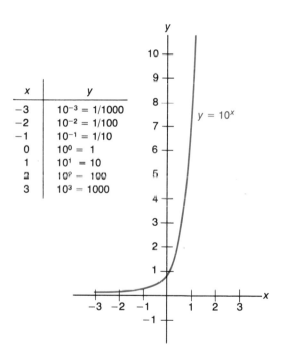

x	y
−3	$10^{-3} = 1/1000$
−2	$10^{-2} = 1/100$
−1	$10^{-1} = 1/10$
0	$10^0 = 1$
1	$10^1 = 10$
2	$10^2 = 100$
3	$10^3 = 1000$

Figure 6.2

Note that the graphs of $y = 2^x$ and $y = 10^x$ are very similar. In each case there is no x-value that makes 2^x or 10^x less than or equal to zero. Each graph approaches, but never touches, the x-axis on the left. The domain of each function contains all real numbers, and the range contains all positive real numbers. In fact, the only difference between the graphs of $y = 2^x$ and $y = 10^x$ is that $y = 10^x$ rises more rapidly than $y = 2^x$.

The shapes of the graphs of equations of the form $y = a^x$, with $a > 1$, are similar to those for $y = 2^x$ and $y = 10^x$. Exponentials of this type model growth in diverse applications, and their graphs have the following basic shape:

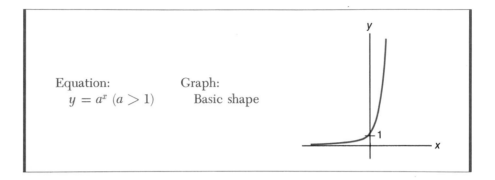

Equation: Graph:
$y = a^x \ (a > 1)$ Basic shape

A special function that occurs frequently in economics and biology is $y = e^x$, where e is a fixed irrational number (approximately $2.71828\ldots$). We will see how e arises in Section 7.2 when we discuss interest that is compounded continuously, and we will formally define e in Section 10.3.

Because $e > 1$, the graph of $y = e^x$ will have the same basic shape as other growth exponentials. We can plot points using a calculator or Table I in the Appendix (see Figure 6.3).

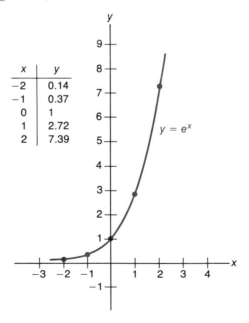

x	y
-2	0.14
-1	0.37
0	1
1	2.72
2	7.39

$y = e^x$

Figure 6.3

Exponential functions with base e often arise in natural ways. As we will see in Section 7.2, the growth of money that is compounded continuously is given by $A = P_0 e^{rt}$, where P_0 is the original principal, r the interest rate, and t the time in years. Certain populations (of insects, for example) grow exponentially, and the number of individuals can be closely approximated by the equation $y = P_0 e^{ht}$, where P_0 is the original population size, h is a constant that depends on the type of population, and y is the population size at any instant t. These are both examples of exponential growth with base e.

Exponentials whose base is between 0 and 1, such as $y = (\frac{1}{2})^x$, have graphs different from the exponentials just discussed. Using the properties of exponents, as in

$$y = (\tfrac{1}{2})^x = (2^{-1})^x = 2^{-x},$$

we can realize exponentials of this type as having the form $y = a^{-x}$, where $a > 1$.

EXAMPLE 2   Graph $y = 2^{-x}$.

Solution   A table of values and the graph are given in Figure 6.4.   □

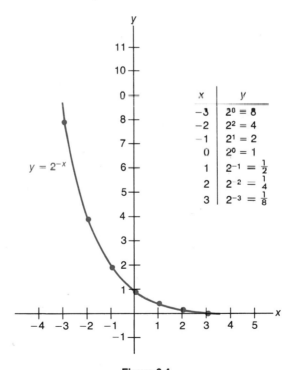

x	y
-3	$2^3 = 8$
-2	$2^2 = 4$
-1	$2^1 = 2$
0	$2^0 = 1$
1	$2^{-1} = \frac{1}{2}$
2	$2^{-2} = \frac{1}{4}$
3	$2^{-3} = \frac{1}{8}$

$y = 2^{-x}$

Figure 6.4

EXAMPLE 3   Graph $y = e^{-2x}$.

Solution   Using a calculator or Table I in the Appendix to find the values of powers of e, we get the graph shown in Figure 6.5.   □

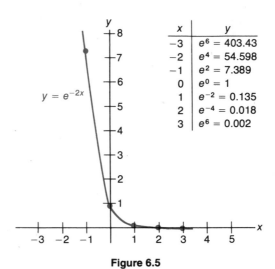

x	y
−3	$e^6 = 403.43$
−2	$e^4 = 54.598$
−1	$e^2 = 7.389$
0	$e^0 = 1$
1	$e^{-2} = 0.135$
2	$e^{-4} = 0.018$
3	$e^6 = 0.002$

$y = e^{-2x}$

Figure 6.5

Exponential functions of the form $y = a^{-x}$, where $a > 1$, all have a similar basic shape. They fall rapidly to the right, approaching but not touching the positive x-axis. Functions of this type model decay for various phenomena. For example, the number of atoms y of a radioactive element at an instant in time t is given by

$$y = w_0 e^{-h(t-t_0)},$$

where w_0 is the number of atoms at time t_0 and h is a constant that depends on the element.

There are some important exponential functions that use base e, but whose graphs are different from those we have discussed. For example, the standard normal probability curve, which will be studied in Section 9.6, is the graph of an exponential function with base e (see Figure 6.6).

Later in this chapter we will study other exponential functions that model growth, but whose graphs are also different from those discussed above.

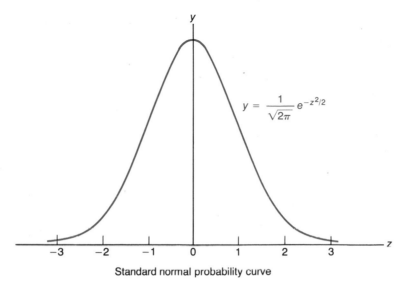

$$y = \frac{1}{\sqrt{2\pi}} e^{-z^2/2}$$

Standard normal probability curve

Figure 6.6

Exercise 6.1

1. Graph the function $y = 4^x$.
2. Graph the function $y = 8^x$.
3. Graph the function $y = 2(x^3)$.
4. Graph the function $y = 3(2^x)$.
5. Graph $y = 2^{x+1}$.
6. Graph $y = 3^{x-1}$.
7. Graph $y = e^x$.
8. Graph $y = 2e^x$.
9. Graph $y = 3^{-x}$.
10. Graph $y = 3^{-2x}$.
11. Graph $y = e^{-x}$.
12. Graph $y = \frac{1}{3}e^x$.

APPLICATIONS

World population can be considered as growing according to the equation

$$N = N_0(1 + r)^t$$

where N_0 is the number of individuals at time $t = 0$, r is the yearly rate of growth, and t is the number of years.

13. Sketch the graph for $t = 0$ to $t = 10$ when the growth rate is 2% and N_0 is 4.1 billion.

14. Sketch the graph for $t = 0$ to $t = 10$ when the growth rate is 3% and N_0 is 4.1 billion.

15. Repeat problem 13 when the growth rate is 5%.

16. Repeat problem 14 when the growth rate is 7%.

17. The number of molecules of a certain substance that have enough energy to activate a reaction is given by

$$y = 100{,}000 \, e^{-1/x},$$

where y is the number of molecules and x is the (absolute) temperature of the substance. Plot the graph of this equation for $x > 0$.

18. When a body is moved from one medium to another, its temperature T will change according to the equation

$$T = T_0 + ce^{kt},$$

where T_0 is the temperature of the new medium, c the temperature difference between the mediums (old − new), t the time in the new medium, and k a constant.

Take $T_0 = 70$, $c = 23$, and $k = -0.2$ and sketch the graph for $t \geq 0$. (Note that under certain circumstances this could be used to determine time of death in a homicide.)

6.2 Logarithmic Functions and their Properties

Objectives
- To find the inverse functions of certain functions
- To convert equations for logarithmic functions from logarithmic to exponential form and vice versa
- To evaluate some special logarithms
- To graph logarithmic functions
- To use properties of logarithmic functions to simplify expressions involving logarithms

Many applications in business and economics can be described by the equation $x = a^y$, $a > 0$, $a \neq 1$. To express this equation in the form $y = f(x)$, we write

$$y = \log_a x,$$

which is read "y equals the logarithm of x to the base a." The function described by $y = \log_a x$ is called a **logarithmic function.** The logarithmic function can be written in either the *logarithmic form*

$$y = \log_a x$$

or in the equivalent *exponential form*

$$x = a^y.$$

For example, the equation $y = \log_2 x$ can be written as $x = 2^y$, so y is the power to which we must raise 2 to get x.

Note that a is called the *base* in $y = \log_a x$ and $x = a^y$, and that y is the *logarithm* in $y = \log_a x$ and the *exponent* in $x = a^y$. That is, a logarithm is an exponent. Thus the properties of logarithms are closely related to the rules for exponents, as we will see shortly.

EXAMPLE 1   (a) Write $2 = \log_4 16$ in exponential form.
(b) Write $64 = 4^3$ in logarithmic form.

Solution   (a) $2 = \log_4 16$ is equivalent to $16 = 4^2$.
(b) $64 = 4^3$ is equivalent to $3 = \log_4 64$.   □

EXAMPLE 2   (a) Evaluate $\log_2 8$.
(b) Evaluate $\log_3 9$.

Solution   (a) If $y = \log_2 8$, then $8 = 2^y$. But $2^3 = 8$, so $\log_2 8 = 3$.
(b) If $y = \log_3 9$, then $9 = 3^y$. But $3^2 = 9$, so $\log_3 9 = 2$.   □

EXAMPLE 3   If $4 = \log_2 x$, what is x?

Solution   If $4 = \log_2 x$, then $2^4 = x$, so $x = 16$.   □

EXAMPLE 4   If $3 = \log_x 8$, what is x?

Solution   If $3 = \log_x 8$, then $x^3 = 8$, so $x = 2$.   □

EXAMPLE 5   Graph $y = \log_2 x$.

Solution   We may graph $y = \log_2 x$ by graphing $x = 2^y$. The table of values (found by substituting values in for y and calculating x) and the graph are shown in Figure 6.7.   □

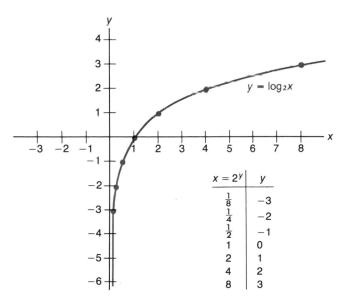

$x = 2^y$	y
$\frac{1}{8}$	-3
$\frac{1}{4}$	-2
$\frac{1}{2}$	-1
1	0
2	1
4	2
8	3

Figure 6.7

EXAMPLE 6   Graph $y = \log_e x$. (This is frequently written $y = \ln x$ and read "y equals the natural log of x.")

Solution   The values for $\log_e x$ are given in Table II of the Appendix. Using this table or a calculator, we can construct a table of values such as Table 6.2 and plot these points to get the graph in Figure 6.8. Note that we can also write $y = \log_e x$ in the form $x = e^y$. Table 6.3 gives some points that satisfy this equation. Note that the points that satisfy $y = \log_e x$ (see Table 6.2) and the points that satisfy $x = e^y$ (see Table 6.3) lie on the graph in Figure 6.8. This is because the two equations are equivalent forms of the same function.   □

Table 6.2

x	$y = \ln x$
0.05	-3
0.10	-2.303
0.50	-0.693
1	0
2	0.693
3	1.099
5	1.609
10	2.303

Table 6.3

y	$x = e^y$
-3	0.050
-2	0.135
-1	0.368
0	1
1	2.718
2	7.389
3	20.09

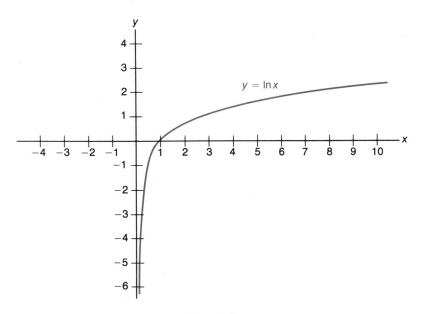

Figure 6.8

The definition of the logarithmic function and the previous examples suggest a special relationship between the logarithmic function $y = \log_a x$ and the exponential function $y = a^x$ $(a > 0, a \neq 1)$. Since we can write $y = \log_a x$ in exponential form as $x = a^y$, we see that the connection between

$$y = \log_a x \quad \text{and} \quad y = a^x$$

is that x and y have been interchanged from one function to the other. This is true for the functional description and hence for the pairs that satisfy these functions. This is illustrated in Table 6.4 for the functions $y = \log_2 x$ and $y = 2^x$.

Table 6.4

$y = \log_2 x$		$y = 2^x$	
Pair	Justification	Pair	Justification
$(8, 3)$	$3 = \log_2 8$	$(3, 8)$	$8 = 2^3$
$(4, 2)$	$2 = \log_2 4$	$(2, 4)$	$4 = 2^2$
$(\frac{1}{2}, -1)$	$-1 = \log_2 (\frac{1}{2})$	$(-1, \frac{1}{2})$	$\frac{1}{2} = 2^{-1}$

In general, we say $y = f(x)$ and $y = g(x)$ are **inverse functions** if, whenever the pair (a, b) satisfies $y = f(x)$, then the pair (b, a) satisfies $y = g(x)$. Furthermore, because the values of the x and y coordinates are interchanged for inverse functions, their graphs are reflections of each other in the line $y = x$.

Thus for $a > 0$ and $a \neq 1$, the logarithmic function $y = \log_a x$ (also written $x = a^y$) and the exponential function $y = a^x$ are inverse functions.

The logarithmic function $y = \log_{10} x$ (frequently written $y = \log x$) is the inverse of the exponential function $y = 10^x$. Thus the graphs $y = \log_{10} x$ and $y = 10^x$ are reflections of each other in the line $y = x$. The graphs of the two functions are given in Figure 6.9 (page 208).

As we stated previously, if $y = \log_a x$, then $x = a^y$. This means that the logarithm y is an exponent. For example, $\log_3 81 = 4$ because $3^4 = 81$. In this case the logarithm 4 was the exponent to which we had to raise the base to obtain 81. In general, if $y = \log_a x$, then y is the exponent to which the base a must be raised to obtain x.

Because logarithms are exponents, the properties of logarithms can be derived from the properties of exponents. (The properties of exponents are discussed in Chapter 0.) The following properties of logarithms are useful in simplifying expressions containing logarithms.

Logarithm If $a > 0$, $a \neq 1$, then $\log_a a^x = x$, for any real number x.
Property I

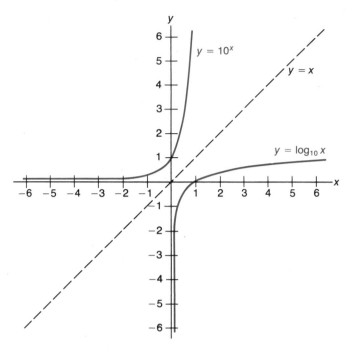

Figure 6.9

EXAMPLE 7   Use Property I to simplify:
(a) $\log_4 4^3$ (b) $\log_e e^x$

Solution   (a) $\log_4 4^3 = 3$
CHECK: The exponential form is $4^3 = 4^3$.
(b) $\log_e e^x = x$
CHECK: The exponential form is $e^x = e^x$.   □

    We note that two special cases for Property I are used frequently; these are when $x = 0$ and $x = 1$.

$$a^1 = a, \text{ so } \log_a a = 1.$$
$$a^0 = 1, \text{ so } \log_a 1 = 0.$$

Logarithm Property II   If $a > 0$, $a \neq 1$, then $a^{\log_a x} = x$, for any positive real number x.

EXAMPLE 8   Use Property II to simplify:
(a) $2^{\log_2 4}$ (b) $e^{\ln x}$

Solution   (a) $2^{\log_2 4} = 4$
CHECK: The logarithmic form is $\log_2 4 = \log_2 4$.
(b) $e^{\ln x} = x$
CHECK: The logarithmic form is $\log_e x = \ln x$.   □

Logarithm   If $a > 0$, $a \neq 1$, and M and N are positive real numbers, then
Property III $\log_a (MN) = \log_a M + \log_a N$.

EXAMPLE 9   (a) Find $\log_2 (4 \cdot 16)$, if $\log_2 4 = 2$ and $\log_2 16 = 4$.
(b) Find $\log_{10} (4 \cdot 5)$ if $\log_{10} 4 = 0.6021$ and $\log_{10} 5 = 0.6990$.

Solution   (a) $\log_2 (4 \cdot 16) = \log_2 4 + \log_2 16 = 2 + 4 = 6$
CHECK: $\log_2 (4 \cdot 16) = \log_2 (64) = 6$, because $2^6 = 64 = 4 \cdot 16$.
(b) $\log_{10} (4 \cdot 5) = \log_{10} 4 + \log_{10} 5 = 0.6021 + 0.6990 = 1.3011$
CHECK: Using a calculator, we can see that $10^{1.3011} = 20 = 4 \cdot 5$.   □

Logarithm   If $a > 0$, $a \neq 1$, and M and N are positive real numbers, then
Property IV $\log_a (M/N) = \log_a M - \log_a N$.

EXAMPLE 10   (a) Evaluate $\log_3 \left(\frac{9}{27}\right)$.
(b) Find $\log_{10} \left(\frac{16}{5}\right)$, if $\log_{10} 16 = 1.2041$ and $\log_{10} 5 = 0.6990$.

Solution   (a) $\log_3 \left(\frac{9}{27}\right) = \log_3 9 - \log_3 27 = 2 - 3 = -1$
CHECK: $\log_3 \left(\frac{1}{3}\right) = -1$ because $3^{-1} = \frac{1}{3}$.
(b) $\log_{10} \left(\frac{16}{5}\right) = \log_{10} 16 - \log_{10} 5 = 1.2041 - 0.6990 = 0.5051$
CHECK: Using a calculator, we can see that $10^{0.5051} = 3.2 = \frac{16}{5}$.   □

Logarithm   If $a > 0, a \neq 1$, M is a positive real number and N is any real number,
Property V   then $\log_a (M^N) = N \log_a M$.

EXAMPLE 11   (a) Simplify $\log_3 (9^2)$.
             (b) Simplify $\ln 8^{-4}$, if $\ln 8 = 2.079$.

Solution   (a) $\log_3 (9^2) = 2 \log_3 9 = 2 \cdot 2 = 4$
             CHECK: $\log_3 81 = 4$ because $3^4 = 81$.
             (b) $\ln 8^{-4} = -4 \ln 8 = -4(2.079) = -8.316$ □

Exercise 6.2

1. Write $4 = \log_2 16$ in exponential form.
2. Write $3 = \log_3 27$ in exponential form.
3. Write $\frac{1}{2} = \log_4 2$ in exponential form.
4. Write $-2 = \log_3 (\frac{1}{9})$ in exponential form.
5. Write $2^5 = 32$ in logarithmic form.
6. Write $5^3 = 125$ in logarithmic form.
7. Write $4^{-1} = \frac{1}{4}$ in logarithmic form.
8. Write $9^{1/2} = 3$ in logarithmic form.
9. Evaluate $\log_3 27$.
10. Evaluate $\log_4 16$.
11. Evaluate $\log_9 3$.
12. Evaluate $\log_5 (\frac{1}{5})$.
13. Graph $y = \log_3 x$.
14. Graph $y = \log_4 x$.
15. Graph $y = \log_e x = \ln x$.
16. Graph $y = \log_9 x$.
17. Graph $y = \log_2 (-x)$.
18. Graph $y = \log_e (-x) = \ln (-x)$.

Evaluate the following:

19. $\log_3 3^4$
20. $\log_5 5^{2/3}$
21. $\log_e e^x$
22. $\ln e^5$
23. $\log_{10} 10$
24. $\log_e e$
25. $\log 10$
26. $\ln e$
27. $3^{\log_3 x}$
28. $4^{\log_4 5}$
29. $10^{\log 2}$
30. $e^{\ln 3}$

31. Find $\log_{10} (3 \cdot 4)$, if $\log_{10} 3 = 0.4771$ and $\log_{10} 4 = 0.6021$.
32. Find $\log_{10} (12 \cdot 43)$, if $\log_{10} 12 = 1.0792$ and $\log_{10} 43 = 1.6335$.
33. Find $\log_{10} (\frac{13}{4})$, if $\log_{10} 13 = 1.1139$ and $\log_{10} 4 = 0.6021$.
34. Find $\log_3 (\frac{27}{9})$, if $\log_3 27 = 3$ and $\log_3 9 = 2$. Does the answer equal $\log_3 3$?
35. Find $\log_{10} (16^{-2})$, given that $\log_{10} 16 = 1.2041$.
36. Find $\log_{10} \sqrt{351}$, given $\log_{10} 351 = 2.5453$.
37. Find $\ln 16^3$, if $\ln 16 = 2.773$.
38. Find $\ln \sqrt{50}$ if $\ln 50 = 3.912$.
39. Prove Logarithm Property I. (Hint: Let $v = \log_a a^x$, and write the expression in exponential form.)
40. Prove Logarithm Property II. (Hint: Let $u = \log_a x$, and write the expression in exponential form.)
41. Prove Logarithm Property III. (Hint: Let $u = \log_a M$ and $v = \log_a N$, write them in exponential form, and find the product MN.)

APPLICATIONS

If $[H^+]$ represents the concentration of hydrogen ions, in gram atoms per liter, then the pH of the solution is defined by

$$pH = -\log [H^+].$$

42. Graph this equation. Use H^+ as the independent variable and pH as the dependent variable.

43. Sometimes pH is defined as the logarithm of the reciprocal of the concentration of hydrogen ions. Write an equation that represents this sentence, and explain how it and the given equation can both represent pH.

Let x and y represent sizes of two different body parts of a given species or group of species, for example x equals arm length and y equals leg length. As age varies, both x and y vary, but they are related according to

$$y = ax^b,$$

where a and b are constants. This is referred to as Huxley's law of simple allometry. Suppose that $a = 2$ and $b = 3$ in the formula for problems 44–47.

44. Graph $y = 2x^3$ by plotting points for $x = 1$ to $x = 4$.

45. Frequently relationships such as this are plotted by using $\log_{10} x$ vs $\log_{10} y$. Use the table of values in problem 44 to make a table for $\log_{10} x$ and $\log_{10} y$, then plot $\log_{10} x$ vs $\log_{10} y$.

46. Take $\log_{10}$ of both sides of $y = ax^b$ and simplify completely in the right member.

47. Refer to the equation in problem 46 that relates $\log_{10} x$ and $\log_{10} y$, decide what shape its graph should have, and compare this with your graph in problem 45.

6.3 Applications of Exponential and Logarithmic Functions

Objectives
- To solve exponential growth or decay equations when sufficient data are known
- To solve exponential and logarithmic equations representing demand or total cost when sufficient data are known

Growth and Decay

In business, economics, biology, and the social sciences, the growth of money, bacteria, or population is frequently of interest. If the growth takes place according to a function of the form

$$f(x) = ma^x,$$

with $a > 0$ and $m > 0$, then the growth is exponential. One example of exponential growth is the growth of money that is invested at compound interest.

As we mentioned in Section 6.1, the curve that models the growth of some populations is given by $y = P_0 e^{ht}$, where P_0 is the population size at a particular time t, h is a constant that depends on the population involved, and y is the total population at time t. This function may be used to model population growth for humans, insects, or bacteria.

EXAMPLE 1   The population of a certain city was 30,000 in 1970 and 40,500 in 1980. If the formula $y = P_0 e^{ht}$ applies to the growth of the city's population, what should the population be in 2000?

Solution   We can first use the data from 1970 and 1980 to find the value of h in the formula. Letting $P_0 = 30,000$ and $t = 10$, we get

$$40{,}500 = 30{,}000 e^{h(10)}$$
$$1.35 = e^{10h}.$$

Writing this in logarithmic form gives

$$\log_e 1.35 = 10h$$
$$0.3001 = 10h$$
$$h = 0.0300.$$

Thus the formula for this population is $y = P_0 e^{0.03t}$. To predict the population for 2000, we use $P_0 = 40,500$ (for 1980) and $t = 20$. This gives

$$y = 40{,}500 e^{0.03(20)}$$
$$= 40{,}500 e^{0.6}$$
$$= 40{,}500(1.822)$$
$$= 73{,}791. \qquad \square$$

One family of curves that has been used to describe human growth and development, the growth of organisms in a limited environment, and the growth of many types of organizations is the family of **Gompertz curves.** These curves are graphs of equations of the form

$$N = Ca^{R^t},$$

where t represents the time, R $(0 < R < 1)$ is a constant depending on the population, a represents the proportion of initial growth, C is the maximum possible number of individuals, and N is the number of individuals at a given time t.

For example, the equation $N = 100(0.03)^{0.2^t}$ could be used to predict the size of a deer herd introduced on a small island. Here the maximum number of deer C would be 100, the proportion of the initial growth a is 0.03, and R is 0.2. For this example, t represents time, measured in decades. The graph of this equation is given in Figure 6.10.

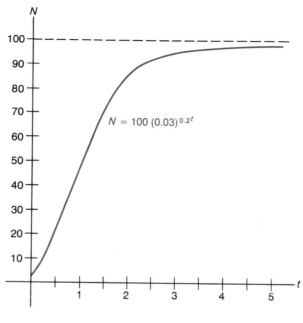

$$N = 100\,(0.03)^{0.2t}$$

Figure 6.10

EXAMPLE 2   A hospital administrator predicts that the growth in the number of hospital employees will follow the Gompertz equation

$$N = 2000(0.6)^{0.5^t},$$

where t represents the number of years after the opening of a new facility.
(a) What is the number of employees when the facility opens ($t = 0$)?
(b) How many employees are predicted after one year of operation ($t = 1$)?
(c) Graph the curve.
(d) What is the maximum value for N that the curve will approach?

Solution   (a) If $t = 0$, $N = 2000(0.6)^1 = 1200$.
(b) If $t = 1$, $N = 2000(0.6)^{0.5} = 2000\sqrt{0.6} = 2000(0.7746) = 1549.20 \cong 1549$.
(c) The graph is shown in Figure 6.11 (page 214).
(d) From the graph we can see that as larger values of t are substituted in the function, the values of N approach, but never reach, 2000. We say that the line $N = 2000$ (dashed) is an **asymptote** for this curve, and that 2000 is the maximum possible value.   □

   If the function modeling some situation is given by an equation of the form $f(x) = ma^{-x}$, with $a > 1$ and $m > 0$, we say the function represents *exponential decay*. We have already mentioned that radioactive decay has this form, as do the demand curves discussed later. Another example of exponential decay is the

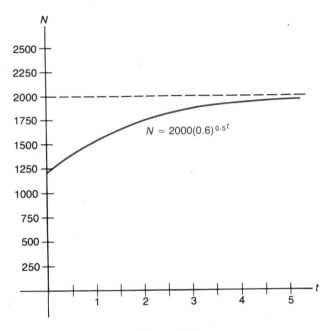

Figure 6.11

decline in the volume of new sales after the end of a sales campaign. This *sales decay* is illustrated by the following example.

EXAMPLE 3   A company finds that the number of its sales begin to fall after the end of an advertising campaign, and the rate of the decline is such that the number of sales x days after the end of the campaign is $S = 2000(2^{-0.1x})$.
(a) How many sales will be made 10 days after the end of the campaign?
(b) How many sales will be made 100 days after the end of the campaign?
(c) If they do not want sales to drop below 500 per day, when should they start a new campaign?

Solution   (a) If $x = 10$, sales are given by $S = 2000(2^{-1}) = 1000$.
(b) If $x = 100$, sales will be $S = 2000(2^{-10}) = 2000(0.0010) = 2$.
(c) Setting $S = 500$ and solving for x will give us the number of days after the end of the campaign when sales will reach 500.
$$500 = 2000(2^{-0.1x})$$
$$0.25 = 2^{-0.1x}$$

The question now is "What power of 2 equals 0.25?" Since $0.25 = \frac{1}{4} = 1/2^2 = 2^{-2}$, we see that $2^{-2} = 2^{-0.1x}$. Then -2 must equal $-0.1x$. Solving $-2 = -0.1x$ gives $x = 20$. Thus sales will be 500 on the twentieth day after the end of the campaign. If a new campaign isn't begun on or before the twenty-first day, sales will drop below 500. (See Figure 6.12.)   □

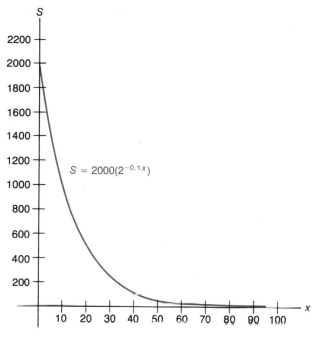

Figure 6.12

Example 3 is typical of many exponential decay models. In particular, once some action is completed, such as an advertising campaign, its effect on sales volume diminishes, or decays, with time. Another example of this phenomenon occurs in the life sciences when the valves to the aorta are closed, and blood flows into the heart. During this period of time, the blood pressure in the aorta falls exponentially. This is illustrated in the following example.

EXAMPLE 4   Medical research has shown that the pressure in the aorta of normal adults is a function of time and can be modeled by the equation

$$P = 95e^{-0.491t},$$

where t is in seconds.
(a) What is the aortic pressure when the valves are first closed $(t = 0)$?
(b) What is the aortic pressure after 0.1 seconds?
(c) How long before the pressure reaches 80?

Solution   (a) If $t = 0$, pressure is given by

$$P = 95e^0 = 95.$$

(b) If $t = 0.1$, pressure is given by

$$P = 95e^{-0.491(.01)}$$
$$= 95e^{-0.0491}$$
$$= 95(0.952)$$
$$= 90.44.$$

(c) Setting $P = 80$ and solving for t gives us the length of time before the pressure reaches 80.

$$80 = 95e^{-0.491t}$$
$$\tfrac{80}{95} = e^{-0.491t}$$

Rewriting this equation in logarithmic form gives

$$\ln\left(\tfrac{80}{95}\right) = -0.491t.$$

Using tables or a calculator, we have $-0.172 = -0.491t$, so $t = 0.35$ seconds.   □

Economic Applications

In Section 5.3, we discussed quadratic cost, revenue, demand, and supply functions. But cost, revenue, demand, and supply may also be represented by exponential or logarithmic equations. For example, suppose the demand for a product is given by $p = 30e^{-q/2}$, where q is the number of units demanded at a price of p dollars per unit. Then the graph of the demand curve is as given in Figure 6.13.

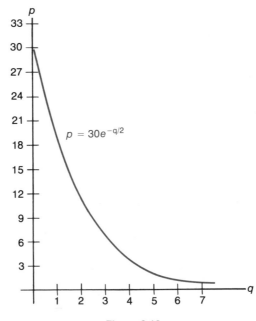

Figure 6.13

EXAMPLE 5   If the demand function for a certain commodity is given by $p = 50e^{-q/4}$,
(a) at what price per unit will the demand equal 4 units?
(b) how many units, to the nearest unit, will be demanded if the price is $25?

Solution   (a) If $q = 4$, $p = 50e^{-1}$. Using Table II or a calculator gives $p = 50(0.3679) = 18.40$, so the price is $18.40 when the demand is 4.
(b) Setting $p = 25$ gives $25 = 50e^{-q/4}$, or $\frac{1}{2} = e^{-q/4}$. Writing this in logarithmic form gives $-q/4 = \log_e (\frac{1}{2})$, or $q = -4 \ln (\frac{1}{2})$. Using Table III to find ln (0.5) gives $q = -4(-0.6931) = 2.7724$, so the number of units demanded would be 3, to the nearest unit.   □

EXAMPLE 6   Given that the total cost function for a product is $C(x) = 1000 + 300 \ln (x + 1)$, find the total cost of producing 8102 units.

Solution   The total cost is given by $C(8102) = 1000 + 300 \ln (8103)$,

$$1000 + 300(9.000) = 3700. \qquad □$$

EXAMPLE 7   If the demand function for a commodity is given by $p = 100e^{-x/10}$, where p is the price per unit when x units are sold,
(a) what is the total revenue function for the commodity?
(b) what would be the total revenue if 30 units are demanded and supplied?

Solution   (a) The total revenue can be computed by multiplying the quantity sold times the price per unit. Since the demand function gives the price per unit when x units are sold, the total revenue for x units is $x \cdot p = x(100e^{-x/10})$. Thus the total revenue function is $R(x) = 100xe^{-x/10}$.
(b) If 30 units are sold, the total revenue is $R(30) = 100(30)e^{-30/10} = 100(30)(0.0498) = \$149.40$.   □

Exercise 6.3

GROWTH AND DECAY

1. If the population of a certain county was 100,000 in 1970 and 110,517 in 1980, and if the formula $y = P_0 e^{ht}$ applies to the growth of the county's population, what should the population of the county be in 1995?
2. The population of a certain city grows according to the formula $y = P_0 e^{0.03t}$. If the population was 250,000 in 1980, what should the population be in the year 2100?
3. The president of a company predicts that sales will increase since she has assumed office, and that the number of monthly sales will follow the curve given by $N = 3000(0.2)^{0.6^t}$, where t represents the months since she assumed office.
   (a) What were sales when she assumed office?
   (b) What will be the sales after three months?
   (c) What will be the maximum sales she hopes to achieve?
   (d) Graph the curve.
4. Because of a new market opening, the number of employees of a firm is expected to

increase according to the equation $N = 1400(0.5)^{0.3t}$, where t represents the number of years after the new market opens.
(a) What is the level of employment when the new market opens?
(b) How many employees should be working at the end of two years?
(c) What is the expected upper limit on the number of employees?
(d) Graph the curve.
5. If the equation $N = 500(0.02)^{0.7t}$ represents the number of employees working each year after 1977, in what year will at least 100 employees be working?
6. A firm predicts that sales will increase during a promotional campaign, and that the number of daily sales will be given by $N = 200(0.01)^{0.8t}$, where t represents the number of days after the campaign begins. How many days after the beginning of the campaign would the firm expect to sell at least 60 units per day?

Gompertz curves describe situations in which growth is limited. There are other equations that describe this phenomenon under different assumptions. Two examples are

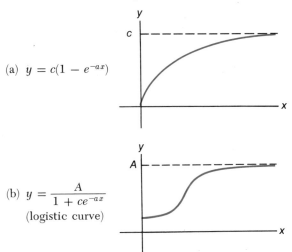

(a) $y = c(1 - e^{-ax})$

(b) $y = \dfrac{A}{1 + ce^{-ax}}$
(logistic curve)

These equations have many applications. In general both (a) and (b) can be used to describe learning or sales of new products, and (b) can be used to describe the spread of epidemics. Problems 7–9 illustrate applications.

7. The concentration y of a certain drug in the bloodstream at any time t is given by the equation

$$y = 100(1 - e^{-0.462t}).$$

(a) What is y after one hour ($t = 1$)?
(b) How long does it take for y to reach 50?
8. The number of people $N(t)$ in a community who are reached by a particular rumor at time t is given by the equation

$$N(t) = \frac{50{,}500}{1 + 100e^{-0.7t}}.$$

(a) Find $N(0)$.
(b) What is the upper limit on the number of people affected?
(c) How long before 75% of the upper limit is reached?

9. On a college campus of 10,000 students, a single student returned to campus infected by a disease. The spread of the disease through the student body is given by

$$y = \frac{10,000}{1 + 9999e^{-0.99t}},$$

where y is the total number infected at time t (in days).
(a) How many are infected after 4 days?
(b) If the school will shut down if 50% of the students are ill, during what day will it close?

10. The sales of a product decline after the end of an advertising campaign, with the sales decay given by $S = 100,000e^{-0.5x}$, where S represents the weekly sales and x represents the number of weeks since the end of the campaign.
(a) What will be the sales for the tenth week after the end of the campaign?
(b) During what week after the end of the campaign will sales drop below 400?

11. The sales decay for a product is given by $S = 50,000e^{-0.8x}$, where S is the monthly sales and x is the number of months that have passed since the end of a promotional campaign.
(a) What will be the sales 4 months after the end of the campaign?
(b) How many months after the end of the campaign will sales drop below 1000, if no new campaign is initiated?

12. A statistical study shows that the fraction of television sets of a certain brand that are still in service after x years is given by $f = e^{-0.15x}$.
(a) What fraction of the sets are still in service after 5 years?
(b) What fraction can be expected to be replaced in the sixth year?

13. Radioactive carbon-14 can be used to determine the age of fossils. Carbon-14 decays according to the equation

$$y = y_0 e^{-0.00012378t},$$

where y is the amount of carbon-14 at time t, in years, and y_0 is the original amount.
(a) How much of the original amount would be left after 3000 years?
(b) If a fossil is found to have $\frac{1}{100}$ the original amount of carbon-14, how old is the fossil?

14. A breeder reactor converts stable uranium-238 into the isotope plutonium-239. The decay of this isotope is given by

$$A(t) = A_0 e^{-0.00002876t},$$

where $A(t)$ is the amount of the isotope at time t, in years, and A_0 is the original amount.
(a) If $A_0 = 500$ lb, how much will be left after a human lifetime (use $t = 70$ years)?
(b) How long before half the original amount has disintegrated? This time is called the *half-life* of this isotope.

ECONOMIC APPLICATIONS

15. If the demand function for a certain commodity is given by $p = 100e^{-q/2}$,
(a) at what price per unit will the quantity demanded equal 6 units?
(b) if the price is $1.83 per unit, how many units will be demanded, to the nearest unit?

16. If the demand function for a product is given by $p = 3000e^{-q/3}$,

(a) at what price per unit will the quantity demanded equal 6 units?
(b) if the price is $149.40 per unit, how many units will be demanded, to the nearest unit?

17. If the supply function for a good is given by $p = 100e^q/(q + 1)$, where q represents the number of hundreds of units, what will be the price when the producers are willing to supply 300 units?

18. If the supply function for a product is given by $p = 200(2^q)$, where q represents the number of hundreds of units, what will be the price when the producers are willing to supply 500 units?

19. If the demand function for a product is $p = 1000/\ln{(q + 1)}$,
(a) what will be the price if 19 units are demanded?
(b) how many units, to the nearest unit, will be demanded if the price is $200?

20. If the supply function for a product is given by $p = 100 \ln{(q + 1)}$, then
(a) at what price will 9 items be supplied?
(b) how many units, to the nearest unit, will be supplied if the price is $346.57?

21. If the total cost function for a product is $C(x) = e^{0.1x} + 400$, where x is the number of items produced, what is the total cost of producing 30 units?

22. If the total cost for a product is given by $C(x) = 400 \ln{(x + 10)} + 100$, what is the total cost of producing 100 units?

23. If the demand function for a good is given by $p = 200e^{-0.02x}$, where p is the price per unit when x units are demanded, then what is the total revenue when 100 units are demanded and supplied?

24. If the demand function for a good is given by $p = 4000/\ln{(x + 10)}$, where p is the price per unit when x units are demanded, then what is total revenue when 40 units are demanded and supplied?

Review Exercises

Graph the following functions.

1. $y = e^x$
2. $y = \log_2{x}$
3. $y = 2^x$
4. $y = \ln{x}$
5. $y = 3^{-2x}$
6. $y = \log{(x + 2)}$

Evaluate the following.

7. $\ln{e}$
8. $\log_3{27}$

If $\log_{10}{16} = 1.2041$ and $\log_{10}{4} = 0.6021$, find each of the following using the properties of logarithms.

9. $\log_{10}{(16 \div 4)}$
10. $\log_{10}{\sqrt{16}}$
11. $\log_{10}{(16 \cdot 4)}$
12. $\log_{10}{4^3}$
13. Rewrite as sums and differences of several simpler logarithms.

$$\ln\left[\frac{x(2x+1)^2}{\sqrt{x-1}}\right]$$

APPLICATIONS

14. Because of a new advertising campaign, a company predicts that sales will increase, and that the yearly sales will be given by the equation

$$N = 10{,}000(0.3)^{0.5^t},$$

where t represents the number of years after the start of the campaign.
(a) What are the sales when the campaign begins?
(b) What are the predicted sales for the third year?
(c) What are the maximum predicted sales?

15. The sales decay for a product is given by $S = 50{,}000e^{-0.1x}$, where S is the weekly sales and x is the number of weeks that have passed since the end of an advertising campaign.
(a) What will sales be 6 weeks after the end of the campaign?
(b) How many weeks will pass before sales drop below $15,000?

16. The sales decay for a product is given by $S = 50{,}000e^{-0.6x}$, where S is the monthly sales and x is the number of months that have passed since the end of an advertising campaign. What will sales be 6 months after the end of a campaign?

Warmup In this chapter you will need to work problems like the following. If you have difficulty with any problem, return to the section where that type of problem was introduced and refresh your memory before starting the chapter.

Problem Type	Introduced in Section	Used in Section	Answer
What is $\dfrac{(-1)^n}{2n}$, if (a) $n = 1$ (b) $n = 2$ (c) $n = 3$	0.1 Signed numbers	7.2	(a) $-\frac{1}{2}$ (b) $\frac{1}{4}$ (c) $-\frac{1}{6}$
(a) What is $(-2)^6$? (b) What is $\dfrac{\frac{1}{2}[1 - (\frac{1}{2})^6]}{1 - \frac{1}{2}}$?	0.1 Signed numbers	7.3	(a) 64 (b) $\frac{63}{128}$
If $f(x) = \dfrac{1}{2x}$, what is (a) $f(2)$? (b) $f(4)$?	1.3 Functional notation	7.1	(a) $\frac{1}{4}$ (b) $\frac{1}{8}$

SEQUENCES AND MATHEMATICS OF FINANCE

Regardless of whether your career is in business or not, understanding how interest is computed on investments and loans is important to you as a consumer. The simple interest on an investment or loan can be calculated using the formula

$$I = Prt,$$

where P is the principal, r is the interest rate, and t is the time. Most investments (for example, savings accounts or bonds) pay compound interest, where the interest is calculated over short periods of time and added to the principal. Most loans are not simple interest loans, because they are repaid by making partial payments of both principal and interest during the period of the loan; one such method of repaying a loan is called *amortization*.

The goal of this chapter is to provide some understanding of the methods used to determine the interest and amount (principal plus interest) resulting from savings plans and the methods used in repayment of debts. We will begin by studying sequences and sigma notation, and by discussing some properties that will be used in this chapter and later chapters. Special attention will be paid to arithmetic and geometric sequences because of their applications in mathematics of finance. Sequences will be used to develop formulas for computing compound interest, the amount of annuities, amortization of debts, the amount paid into a sinking fund to discharge a debt, and the depreciation of business assets.

7.1 Sequences

Objectives
- To write a specified number of terms of a sequence
- To find specified terms of arithmetic sequences

If a sum of money (called the principal) P is invested for a time period t (frequently years) at an interest rate r per period, the simple interest is given by

$$I = Prt.$$

Simple interest is paid on investments involving time certificates issued by banks and on certain types of bonds, such as U.S. government series H bonds and municipal bonds. The interest for a given period is paid to the investor and the principal remains the same.

EXAMPLE 1   If $4000 is invested for 2 years at an annual interest rate of 9%, how much interest will be received at the end of the 2-year period?

Solution   The interest is

$$I = \$4000(0.09)(2) = \$720. \qquad \square$$

The *amount* of an investment at the end of an interest period is the sum of the principal and the interest:

$$S = P + I.$$

EXAMPLE 2   If $1000 is invested for 6 months at an annual rate of 10%, what is the amount of the investment at the end of the 6-month period?

Solution   The interest for the period is

$$I = \$1000(0.10)\left(\tfrac{6}{12}\right) = \$50.$$

Thus the amount of the investment is

$$S = \$1000 + \$50 = \$1050. \qquad \square$$

The second method of paying interest is the **compound interest** method, where the interest for each period is added to the principal before interest is calculated for the next period. With this method the principal grows as the interest is added to it. This method is used in investments such as savings accounts and U.S. government series E bonds.

An understanding of compound interest is important not only for people planning to work with financial institutions, but also for anyone planning to invest money. To see how compound interest is computed, we will first calculate the *amount* that will result if $1 is invested for three years at 5%, *compounded annually* (each year).

The principal for the first year is $1.
The interest at the end of the first year is $I = Prt = \$1 \cdot (0.05) \cdot 1 = \$.05$.
The amount at the end of the first year is $S = P + I = \$1 + 0.05 = \$1.05$.

Thus the principal for the second year is $1.05.

The interest at the end of the second year is $I = \$1.05 \cdot (.05) \cdot 1 = \$.0525$.
The amount at the end of the second year is $S = \$1.05 + .0525 = \$1.1025$.

Thus, the principal for the third year is $1.1025.

The interest at the end of the third year is $I = 1.1025 \cdot (.05) \cdot 1 = \$.055125$.
The amount at the end of the third year is $S = \$1.157625$.

We see that calculation of compound amount (and compound interest) is very tedious if we proceed in this manner. But notice that the compound amount for each year can be found by multiplying the amount from the preceding year by 1.05. That is, the compound amount at the end of the first year is $1 \cdot (1.05) = 1.05$, the compound amount at the end of the second year is $1 \cdot (1.05) \cdot (1.05) = 1 \cdot (1.05)^2 = 1.1025$, and the compound amount at the end of the third year is $1 \cdot (1.1025) \cdot (1.05) = 1 \cdot (1.05)^3 = 1.157625$. Thus we see that, in general, if P is invested at an interest rate of i per year, compounded at the end of each year, the *compound amount* at the end of each succeeding year is

$$P(1 + i), P(1 + i)^2, P(1 + i)^3, \ldots, P(1 + i)^n.$$

Compound   If P is invested at an interest rate of i per year, the compound
Amount   amount at the end of n years is given by

$$S = P(1 + i)^n$$

EXAMPLE 3   Find the amount if $2500 is invested for 6 years at 6%, compounded annually.

Solution   The amount is

$$\begin{aligned} S &= \$2500(1 + .06)^6 \\ &= \$2500(1.418519) \\ &= \$3546.2975 \\ &= \$3546.30, \text{ to the nearest cent.} \end{aligned} \qquad \square$$

The compound amounts for each of the succeeding years form a sequence. We define a sequence function as follows.

A **sequence function** is a function whose domain is the set of positive integers.

Because these functions are very special, it is customary to use the notation a_n to represent the function value $f(n)$. The n is used to remind us that the domain contains only positive integers. The set of functional values $a_1, a_2, a_3, \ldots$ of the sequence function is called a **sequence.** The values $a_1, a_2, a_3, \ldots$ are called **terms** of the sequence, with a_1 the first term, a_2 the second term, and so on.

EXAMPLE 4   Find the first four terms of the sequence defined by the formula $a_n = 1/(2n)$.

Solution   The first four terms of the sequence are

$$a_1 = \frac{1}{2(1)} = \frac{1}{2}, \qquad a_2 = \frac{1}{2(2)} = \frac{1}{4},$$

$$a_3 = \frac{1}{2(3)} = \frac{1}{6}, \qquad \text{and} \qquad a_4 = \frac{1}{2(4)} = \frac{1}{8}.$$

We usually write these terms in the form $\frac{1}{2}, \frac{1}{4}, \frac{1}{6}, \frac{1}{8}$.   □

EXAMPLE 5   Write the first four terms of the sequence whose nth term is $a_n = (-1)^n/n$.

Solution   The first four terms of the sequence are

$$a_1 = \frac{(-1)^1}{1}, \qquad a_2 = \frac{(-1)^2}{2}, \qquad a_3 = \frac{(-1)^3}{3},$$

$$a_4 = \frac{(-1)^4}{4}, \qquad \text{or} \qquad -1, \tfrac{1}{2}, -\tfrac{1}{3}, \tfrac{1}{4}.$$ □

EXAMPLE 6   If the nth term of sequence is

$$a_n = \frac{n-2}{n(n+1)},$$

write the first four terms and the eighth term of the sequence.

Solution   The first four terms of the sequence are

$$a_1 = \frac{1-2}{1(1+1)}, \qquad a_2 = \frac{2-2}{2(2+1)}, \qquad a_3 = \frac{3-2}{3(3+1)},$$

$$a_4 = \frac{4-2}{4(4+1)}, \qquad \text{or} \qquad -\tfrac{1}{2}, 0, \tfrac{1}{12}, \tfrac{1}{10}.$$

The eighth term is $\frac{1}{12}$.   □

If each term of a sequence after the first can be found by adding the same number to the preceding term, the sequence is called an arithmetic sequence, or arithmetic progression. That is, a sequence is called an **arithmetic sequence** if there exists a number d, called the **common difference,** such that $a_n = a_{n-1} + d$ for $n > 1$.

EXAMPLE 7   Write three additional terms of the following arithmetic sequences:
(a) $1, 3, 5, \ldots$ (b) $9, 6, 3, \ldots$ (c) $\frac{1}{2}, \frac{5}{6}, \frac{7}{6}, \ldots$

Solution   (a) The common difference is 2, so the next three terms are 7, 9, 11.
(b) The common difference is -3, so the next three terms are 0, -3, -6.
(c) The common difference is $\frac{1}{3}$, so the next three terms are $\frac{3}{2}, \frac{11}{6}, \frac{13}{6}$.   □

Because each term after the first in an arithmetic sequence is obtained by adding d, the second term is $a_1 + d$, the third is $a_1 + 2d, \ldots$ and the nth term is $a_1 + (n - 1)d$. Thus we have the following formula.

> The nth term of an arithmetic sequence (progression) is given by $a_n = a_1 + (n - 1)d$, where a_1 is the first term of the sequence, n is the number of the term, and d is the common difference between the terms.

EXAMPLE 8   Find the eleventh term of the arithmetic sequence with first term 3 and common difference -2.

Solution   The eleventh term is $a_{11} = 3 + (10)(-2) = -17$.   □

EXAMPLE 9   If the first term of an arithmetic sequence is 4 and the ninth term is 20, find the fifth term.

Solution   Substituting the values in $a_n = a_1 + (n - 1)d$ gives $20 = 4 + 8d$. Solving gives $d = 2$. The fifth term is $4 + 4(2) = 12$.   □

Exercise 7.1

1. Write the first 10 terms of the sequence defined by $a_n = 3n$.
2. Find the first six terms of the sequence defined by $a_n = 4n$.
3. Write the first eight terms of the sequence defined by $a_n = n/3$.
4. Write the first seven terms of the sequence defined by $a_n = 2/n$.
5. Write the first six terms of the sequence whose nth term is $(-1)^n/4$.
6. Write the first five terms of the sequence whose nth term is $(-1)^n/3$.
7. Write the first six terms of the sequence whose nth term is $(-1)^n/(2n)$.
8. Write the first five terms of the sequence whose nth term is

$$\frac{(-1)^n}{n + 1}.$$

9. If the nth term of a sequence is

$$a_n = \frac{n - 4}{n(n + 2)},$$

write the first four terms and the tenth term.

10. If the nth term of a sequence is

$$a_n = \frac{n(n-1)}{n+3},$$

write the sixth term.

11. Write three additional terms of the arithmetic sequence $2, 5, 8, \ldots$.

12. Write three additional terms of the arithmetic sequence $3, 9, 15, \ldots$.

13. Write four additional terms of the arithmetic sequence $3, \frac{9}{2}, 6, \ldots$.

14. Write four additional terms of the arithmetic sequence $2, 2.75, 3.5, \ldots$.

15. Find the eighth term of the arithmetic sequence with first term -3 and common difference 4.

16. Find the eleventh term of the arithmetic sequence with first term 7 and common difference 4.

17. Find the eighth term of the arithmetic sequence with first term 6 and common difference $-\frac{1}{2}$.

18. Find the sixth term of the arithmetic sequence with first term $\frac{1}{2}$ and common difference $-\frac{1}{3}$.

19. Find the sixth term of the arithmetic sequence with first term 5 and eighth term 19.

20. Find the sixth term of the arithmetic sequence with first term 20 and tenth term 47.

21. Find the fourth term of the arithmetic sequence with first term 16 and ninth term 0.

22. Find the sixth term of the arithmetic sequence with first term $\frac{1}{2}$ and eleventh term 3.

7.2 Geometric Sequences; Compound Interest

Objectives
- To find specified terms of geometric series
- To find the compound amount and compound interest of money invested where interest is compounded at regular intervals
- To find compound amount and interest of money where interest is compounded continuously
- To find the effective annual interest rate of money invested at compound interest

If each term of a sequence after the first can be found by multiplying the preceding term by the same number, the sequence is called a **geometric sequence,** or **geometric progression.** That is, a sequence is called a geometric sequence if there exists a number r, called the **common ratio,** such that $a_n = ra_{n-1}$ for $n > 1$.

EXAMPLE 1   Write three additional terms of the following geometric sequences:

(a) $1, 3, 9, \ldots$ (b) $4, 2, 1, \ldots$ (c) $3, -6, 12, \ldots$

Solution   (a) The common ratio is 3, so the next three terms are 27, 81, 243.

(b) The common ratio is $\frac{1}{2}$, so the next three terms are $\frac{1}{2}, \frac{1}{4}, \frac{1}{8}$.

(c) The common ratio is -2, so the next three terms are $-24, 48, -96$.   □

Because each term after the first in a geometric sequence is obtained by multiplying by r, the second term is $a_1 r$, the third is $a_1 r^2$, . . . and the nth term is $a_1 r^{n-1}$. Thus we have the following formula.

The nth term of a geometric sequence (progression) is given by $a_n = a_1 r^{n-1}$, where a_1 is the first term of the sequence, n is the number of the term, and r is the common ratio.

EXAMPLE 2   Find the seventh term of the geometric sequence with first term 5 and common ratio -2.

Solution   The seventh term is $a_7 = 5(-2)^6 = 5(64) = 320$.   □

EXAMPLE 3   A ball is dropped from a height of 125 feet. If it rebounds $\frac{3}{5}$ of the height from which it falls every time it hits the ground, how high will it bounce after it strikes the ground for the fifth time?

Solution   The first rebound is $\frac{3}{5}(125) = 75$ feet; the second rebound is $\frac{3}{5}(75) = 45$. The heights of the rebounds form a geometric sequence with first term 75 and common ratio $\frac{3}{5}$. Thus the fifth term is

$$a_5 = 75(\tfrac{3}{5})^4 = 75(\tfrac{81}{625}) = \tfrac{243}{25} = 9\tfrac{18}{25} \text{ feet.}$$ □

We have seen that the compound amounts for succeeding years form a sequence. This sequence of compound amounts,

$$P(1 + i), P(1 + i)^2, P(1 + i)^3, \ldots, P(1 + i)^n, \ldots,$$

is a *geometric sequence*. The first term of the sequence is $P(1 + i)$ and the common ratio is $(1 + i)$. Thus the nth term of the sequence is

$$P(1 + i)^n,$$

the compound amount at the end of n years.

EXAMPLE 4   If $3000 is invested for 4 years at 9%, compounded annually, how much interest is earned?

Solution   The compound amount is

$$\begin{aligned} S &= \$3000(1 + 0.09)^4 \\ &= \$3000(1.4115816) \\ &= \$4234.7448 \\ &= \$4234.74, \text{ to the nearest cent.} \end{aligned}$$

Since $3000 of this amount was originally invested, the interest earned is $4234.74 − $3000 = $1234.74.   □

Some accounts have the interest compounded semiannually, quarterly, monthly, or daily. Unless specifically stated otherwise, a stated interest rate is the rate per year, and is called the **nominal annual rate.** The interest rate *per period* is the nominal rate divided by the number of interest periods per year. The interest periods are also called *conversion periods*. Thus, if $100 is invested for five years at 6%, compounded semiannually (twice a year), it has been invested for 10 periods (5 · 2) at 3% per period (6 ÷ 2). The compound amount on this investment is

$$S = \$100(1 + 0.03)^{10}$$
$$= \$100(1.3439164)$$
$$= \$134.39164$$
$$= \$134.39, \text{ to the nearest cent.}$$

Compound If interest is compounded k times per year, we will have kn periods
Amount (k in n years and the interest rate per compounding period will be i/k,
periods per year) so the compound amount will be given by

$$S = P\left(1 + \frac{i}{k}\right)^{kn}.$$

EXAMPLE 5   If $500 is invested for 3 years at 8%, compounded quarterly, what interest is earned?

Solution   The $500 is compounded for 12 periods at 2% per period, so the amount is

$$S = \$500\left(1 + \frac{0.08}{4}\right)^{4(3)} = \$500(1 + 0.02)^{12}$$
$$= \$500(1.2682418)$$
$$= \$634.1209$$
$$= \$634.12.$$

Thus the interest is $634.12 − $500 = $134.12.   □

Note that we used sequences to find the formula that gives the compound amount of money invested at compound interest. Because compound interest is used so frequently in business, tables are available that give the compound amount of $1 invested for different periods and at different rates. Table 7.1 is a sample of such a table. The compound amount can also be calculated from the formula using a calculator.

EXAMPLE 6   If $8000 is invested for 6 years at 8%, compounded quarterly, find (a) the compound amount, (b) the compound interest.

Table 7.1   AMOUNT OF $1 AT COMPOUND INTEREST $\left(1 + \frac{i}{k}\right)^{kn}$

Periods	½%	¾%	1%	1½%	2%	3%	4%	5%	6%
1	1.005 000	1.007 500	1.010 000	1.015 000	1.020 00■	1.030 000	1.040 000	1.050 000	1.060 000
2	1.010 025	1.015 056	1.020 100	1.030 225	1.040 40■	1.060 900	1.081 600	1.102 500	1.123 600
3	1.015 075	1.022 669	1.030 301	1.045 678	1.061 208	1.092 727	1.124 864	1.157 625	1.191 016
4	1.020 151	1.030 339	1.040 604	1.061 364	1.082 432	1.125 509	1.169 859	1.215 506	1.262 477
5	1.025 251	1.038 067	1.051 010	1.077 284	1.104 081	1.159 274	1.216 653	1.276 282	1.338 226
6	1.030 378	1.045 852	1.061 520	1.093 443	1.126 162	1.194 052	1.265 319	1.340 096	1.418 519
7	1.035 529	1.053 696	1.072 135	1.110 845	1.148 686	1.229 874	1.315 932	1.407 100	1.503 630
8	1.040 707	1.061 599	1.082 857	1.126 493	1.171 659	1.266 770	1.368 569	1.477 455	1.593 848
9	1.045 911	1.069 561	1.093 685	1.143 390	1.195 093	1.304 773	1.423 312	1.551 328	1.689 479
10	1.051 140	1.077 583	1.104 622	1.160 541	1.218 994	1.343 916	1.480 244	1.628 895	1.790 848
11	1.056 396	1.085 664	1.115 668	1.177 949	1.243 374	1.384 234	1.539 454	1.710 339	1.898 299
12	1.061 678	1.093 807	1.126 825	1.195 618	1.268 242	1.425 761	1.601 032	1.795 856	2.012 196
13	1.066 986	1.102 010	1.138 093	1.213 552	1.293 607	1.468 534	1.665 074	1.885 649	2.132 928
14	1.072 321	1.110 276	1.149 474	1.231 756	1.319 479	1.512 590	1.731 676	1.979 932	2.260 904
15	1.077 683	1.118 603	1.160 969	1.250 232	1.345 868	1.557 967	1.800 944	2.078 928	2.396 558
16	1.083 071	1.126 992	1.172 579	1.268 986	1.372 786	1.604 706	1.872 981	2.182 875	2.540 352
17	1.088 487	1.135 445	1.184 304	1.288 020	1.400 241	1.652 848	1.947 901	2.292 018	2.692 773
18	1.093 929	1.143 960	1.196 147	1.307 341	1.428 246	1.702 433	2.025 817	2.406 619	2.854 339
19	1.099 399	1.152 540	1.208 109	1.326 951	1.456 811	1.753 506	2.106 849	2.526 950	3.025 600
20	1.104 896	1.161 184	1.220 190	1.346 355	1.485 947	1.806 111	2.191 123	2.653 298	3.207 135
21	1.110 420	1.169 893	1.232 392	1.367 058	1.515 666	1.860 295	2.278 768	2.785 963	3.399 564
22	1.115 972	1.178 667	1.244 716	1.387 564	1.545 980	1.916 103	2.369 919	2.925 261	3.603 537
23	1.121 552	1.187 507	1.257 163	1.408 377	1.576 899	1.973 587	2.464 716	3.071 524	3.819 750
24	1.127 160	1.196 414	1.269 735	1.429 503	1.608 437	2.032 794	2.563 304	3.225 100	4.048 935
25	1.132 796	1.205 387	1.282 432	1.450 945	1.640 606	2.093 778	2.665 836	3.386 355	4.291 871
26	1.138 460	1.214 427	1.295 256	1.472 710	1.673 418	2.156 591	2.772 470	3.555 673	4.549 383
27	1.144 152	1.223 535	1.308 209	1.494 500	1.706 886	2.221 289	2.883 369	3.733 456	4.822 346
28	1.149 873	1.232 712	1.321 291	1.517 222	1.741 024	2.287 928	2.998 703	3.920 129	5.111 687
29	1.155 622	1.241 957	1.334 504	1.539 981	1.775 845	2.356 566	3.118 651	4.116 136	5.418 388
30	1.161 400	1.251 272	1.347 849	1.563 080	1.811 362	2.427 262	3.243 398	4.321 942	5.743 491
31	1.167 207	1.260 656	1.361 327	1.586 526	1.847 589	2.500 080	3.373 133	4.538 039	6.088 101
32	1.173 043	1.270 111	1.374 941	1.610 324	1.884 541	2.575 083	3.508 059	4.764 941	6.453 387
33	1.178 908	1.279 637	1.388 690	1.634 479	1.922 231	2.652 335	3.648 381	5.003 189	6.840 590
34	1.184 803	1.289 234	1.402 577	1.658 696	1.960 676	2.731 905	3.794 316	5.253 348	7.251 025
35	1.190 727	1.298 904	1.416 603	1.683 081	1.999 890	2.813 862	3.946 089	5.516 015	7.686 087
36	1.196 681	1.308 645	1.430 769	1.709 140	2.039 887	2.898 278	4.103 933	5.791 816	8.147 252
37	1.202 664	1.318 460	1.445 076	1.734 477	2.080 685	2.985 227	4.268 090	6.081 407	8.636 087
38	1.208 677	1.328 349	1.459 527	1.760 798	2.122 299	3.074 783	4.438 813	6.385 477	9.154 252
39	1.214 721	1.338 311	1.474 123	1.787 510	2.164 745	3.167 027	4.616 366	6.704 751	9.703 507
40	1.220 794	1.348 349	1.488 864	1.814 018	2.208 040	3.262 038	4.801 021	7.039 989	10.285 718

Solution   (a) The compound amount is given by

$$S = P\left(1 + \frac{i}{k}\right)^{kn}$$

$$= \$8000\left(1 + \frac{0.08}{4}\right)^{4 \cdot 6} = \$8000(1 + 0.02)^{24}$$

$$= \$8000(1.608437) = \$12{,}867.50$$

(b) The compound interest is given by $\$12{,}867.50 - \$8000 = \$4867.50.$ □

If the conversion period for money invested at compound interest is less than one year, then the interest actually earned in a year is more than the nominal rate.

For example, $1 invested for one year at 8%, compounded semiannually, will amount to $1(1.04)^2 = \$1.0816$. Subtracting the $1 principal gives the interest for the year as $.0816, which represents an interest rate of 8.16%. Because the rate of 8% compounded semiannually gives interest at a rate that is equivalent to 8.16%, we say that the **effective annual rate** in this case is 8.16%. If we let r represent the effective annual rate, i/k the interest rate *per conversion period*, and k the number of conversion periods per year, then we can find r by using the formula

---

Effective Annual Rate (r) $r = \left(1 + \dfrac{i}{k}\right)^k - 1.$

To prove that this formula gives the true (effective) interest rate, consider the following: If I, S, and P represent interest, compound amount, and principal, respectively, for a 1-year period, then

$$I = S - P$$

$$I = P\left(1 + \frac{i}{k}\right)^k - P$$

$$\frac{I}{P} = \left(1 + \frac{i}{k}\right)^k - 1.$$

But if the time is 1 year, $I = Pr \cdot 1$, so the true yearly interest rate is

$$r = \frac{I}{P} = \left(1 + \frac{i}{k}\right)^k - 1.$$

EXAMPLE 7   Find the effective annual rate equivalent to the nominal rate of 6% compounded quarterly.

Solution   The rate *per period* is $i/k = 0.06/4 = 0.015$, and the number of periods is $k = 4$.

Thus

$$r = (1 + 0.015)^4 - 1 = 1.061364 - 1$$
$$= 0.061364$$
$$= 6.14\%. \qquad \square$$

It is reasonable to assume that the more frequently the interest is compounded, the larger the compound amount will become. In order to determine the interest that results from *continuous* compounding (compounding every instant), consider an investment of $1 for one year at a 100% interest rate. If the interest is compounded k times per year, the compound amount is given by

$$S = \left(1 + \frac{1}{k}\right)^k.$$

Table 7.2 shows the compound amount that results as the number of compounding periods increases.

Table 7.2

Compounded	Number of Periods per Year	Compound Amount
Annually	1	$(1 + \frac{1}{1})^1 = 2$
Monthly	12	$(1 + \frac{1}{12})^{12} = 2.6130 \cdots$
Daily	360 (business year)	$(1 + \frac{1}{360})^{360} = 2.7145 \cdots$
Hourly	8640	$(1 + \frac{1}{8640})^{8640} = 2.71812 \cdots$
Each minute	518,400	$(1 + \frac{1}{518,400})^{518,400} = 2.71827 \cdots$

It is clear that the compound amount increases as the number of periods per year increases, but not very rapidly. In fact, no matter how rapidly the interest is compounded, the compound amount will never exceed $2.72. We say that as the number of periods increases, the compound amount in this case approaches a **limit**, which is the number e:

$$e = 2.7182818\cdots.$$

We have discussed the number e and the function $y = e^x$ in Chapter 6. The discussion here shows one way the number we call e may be derived. We will define e more formally later.

Compound *Amount* (*continuous compounding*)	In general, if interest is compounded continuously for n years at a nominal rate i, the compound amount is given by the exponential function $$S = Pe^{in}.$$

EXAMPLE 8   Find the compound amount if $1000 is invested for 20 years at 8%, compounded continuously.

Solution   The amount is

$$S = \$1000e^{(0.08)(20)} = \$1000e^{1.6}$$
$$= \$1000(4.95303) \quad \text{(since } e^{1.6} = 4.95303\text{)}$$
$$= \$4953.03.$$

□

EXAMPLE 9   How much more will you earn if you invest $1000 for 5 years at 8% compounded continuously instead of 8% compounded quarterly?

Solution   If the interest is compounded continuously, the compound amount at the end of the 5 years is

$$S = \$1000e^{(0.08)(5)} = \$1000e^{0.4} = \$1000(1.49182)$$
$$= \$1491.82.$$

If the interest is compounded quarterly, the amount at the end of the 5 years is

$$S = \$1000(1.02)^{20} = \$1000(1.485947)$$
$$= \$1485.95, \text{ to the nearest cent.}$$

Thus the extra interest earned by compounding continuously is

$$\$1491.82 - \$1485.95 = \$5.87.$$

□

Exercise 7.2

1. Write four additional terms of the geometric sequence 3, 6, 12, ...
2. Write four additional terms of the geometric sequence 4, 12, 36, ...
3. Write three additional terms of the geometric sequence 81, 54, 36, ...
4. Write three additional terms of the geometric sequence 32, 40, 50, ...
5. Find the sixth term of the geometric sequence with first term 10 and common ratio 2.
6. Find the fifth term of the geometric sequence with first term 6 and common ratio 3.
7. Find the fifth term of the geometric sequence with first term 4 and common ratio $\frac{3}{2}$.
8. Find the fifth term of the geometric sequence with first term 3 and common ratio -2.

APPLICATIONS

9. A ball is dropped from a height of 128 feet. If it rebounds $\frac{3}{4}$ of the height from which it falls every time it hits the ground, how high will it bounce after it strikes the ground for the fourth time?
10. A pump removes $\frac{1}{3}$ of the water in a container with every stroke. What amount of water is still in an 81-cm^3 container after 5 strokes?

11. A machine is valued at $10,000. If the depreciation at the end of each year is 20% of its value at the beginning of the year, find its value at the end of 4 years.

12. Find the amount that will result if $3500 is invested for 6 years at 6%, compounded annually.

13. Find the amount that will accrue if $8000 is invested for 10 years at 6%, compounded annually.

14. Find the interest that will be earned if $5000 is invested for 3 years at 6%, compounded annually.

15. Find the interest that will be earned if $10,000 is invested for 8 years at 5%, compounded annually.

16. What amount will result if $8600 is invested for 8 years at 6%, compounded semiannually?

17. What amount will result if $3200 is invested for 5 years at 8%, compounded quarterly?

18. What interest will be earned if $6300 is invested for 3 years at 6%, compounded monthly?

19. Find the interest that will be earned if $8600 is invested for 6 years at 6%, compounded semiannually

20. Find the interest that will result if $8000 is invested at 7%, compounded continuously, for 8 years.

21. Find the amount that will result if $5100 is invested for 4 years at 6%, compounded continuously.

22. How much more interest will be earned if $5000 is invested for 6 years at 7%, compounded continuously, instead of 7%, compounded quarterly?

23. Which investment will earn more money, a $1000 investment for 5 years at 8%, compounded annually, or a $1000 investment for 5 years, compounded continuously at 7%?

24. If money is invested at 9%, compounded monthly, what is the equivalent effective annual rate?

25. What is the effective annual rate equivalent to a nominal rate of 8%, compounded quarterly?

26. What is the effective annual rate equivalent to a nominal rate of 10%, compounded continuously?

27. What is the compound interest if $410 is invested for 10 years at 8%, compounded continuously?

28. How long (in years) would $600 have to be invested at 8%, compounded continuously, to amount to $970?

29. How long (in years) would $700 have to be invested at 11.9%, compounded continuously, to earn $300 interest?

30. At what nominal rate, compounded annually, would $10,000 have to be invested to amount to $14,071 in 7 years?

31. At what nominal rate, compounded quarterly, would $20,000 have to be invested to amount to $26,425.82 in 7 years?

7.3 Sigma Notation

Objectives ■ To evaluate sums as indicated in sigma notation
■ To simplify expressions involving sigma notation
■ To find the sums of specified numbers of terms of special sequences

We can use the Greek letter Σ(sigma) to express the sum of numbers or expressions. For example, we may indicate the sum of the n numbers $a_1, a_2, a_3, a_4, \ldots,$ a_n by

$$\sum_{i=1}^{n} a_i = a_1 + a_2 + a_3 + \cdots + a_n.$$

This may be read as "The sum of a_i as i goes from 1 to n." The subscript i in a_i is replaced, first by 1, then by 2, then by 3, $\ldots$, until it reaches the value above sigma. The i is called the index of summation, and it starts with the lower limit, 1, and ends with the upper limit, n. For example, if $x_1 = 2$, $x_2 = 3$, $x_3 = -1$, and $x_4 = -2$, then

$$\sum_{i=1}^{4} x_i = x_1 + x_2 + x_3 + x_4 = 2 + 3 + (-1) + (-2) = 2.$$

We may use sigma notation to express the sum of functional expressions. For example,

$$\sum_{i=1}^{3} f(i) = f(1) + f(2) + f(3).$$

EXAMPLE 1   If $f(x) = x^2$, evaluate $\sum_{i=1}^{4} f(i)$.

Solution

$$\sum_{i=1}^{4} f(i) = f(1) + f(2) + f(3) + f(4)$$

$$= 1^2 + 2^2 + 3^2 + 4^2$$

$$= 30 \qquad \qquad \square$$

We could state the problem of Example 1 more simply as "Evaluate $\sum_{i=1}^{4} i^2$." The sum would then be evaluated as $\sum_{i=1}^{4} i^2 = 1^2 + 2^2 + 3^2 + 4^2 = 30$.
The lower limit need not be 1, as the following example illustrates.

EXAMPLE 2   (a) Evaluate $\displaystyle\sum_{i=2}^{5} \left(\frac{i-1}{i^2} \right)$.

(b) Evaluate $\displaystyle\sum_{i=-2}^{2}\left(\frac{1}{2i+5}\right)$.

Solution   (a) $\displaystyle\sum_{i=2}^{5}\left(\frac{i-1}{i^2}\right) = \frac{2-1}{2^2} + \frac{3-1}{3^2} + \frac{4-1}{4^2} + \frac{5-1}{5^2}$

$$= \frac{1}{4} + \frac{2}{9} + \frac{3}{16} + \frac{4}{25}$$

$$= \frac{2951}{3600}$$

(b) $\displaystyle\sum_{i=-2}^{2}\left(\frac{1}{2i+5}\right) = \frac{1}{-4+5} + \frac{1}{-2+5} + \frac{1}{0+5} + \frac{1}{2+5} + \frac{1}{4+5}$

$$= 1 + \frac{1}{3} + \frac{1}{5} + \frac{1}{7} + \frac{1}{9}$$

$$= \frac{563}{315} \qquad \square$$

The use of i as the index is arbitrary. It is a "dummy" symbol, since any letter may be used. The letters j and k are also frequently used as indices in sigma notation.

EXAMPLE 3   (a) Evaluate $\displaystyle\sum_{k=2}^{5}\frac{k-3}{k+1}$.   (b) Evaluate $\displaystyle\sum_{j=-2}^{2}\frac{j^2}{j+4}$.

Solution   (a) $\displaystyle\sum_{k=2}^{5}\frac{k-3}{k+1} = -\frac{1}{3} + \frac{0}{4} + \frac{1}{5} + \frac{2}{6} = \frac{1}{5}$

(b) $\displaystyle\sum_{j=-2}^{2}\frac{j^2}{j+4} = \frac{4}{2} + \frac{1}{3} + \frac{0}{4} + \frac{1}{5} + \frac{4}{6} = 3\frac{1}{5}$ $\square$

The following formulas are helpful in simplifying computations involving summations.

FORMULA 1 $$\sum_{i=1}^{n} 1 = n$$

We can verify this formula as follows:

$$\sum_{i=1}^{n} 1 = 1 + 1 + \cdots + 1 = n.$$

FORMULA II

$$\sum_{i=1}^{n} cx_i = c \sum_{i=1}^{n} x_i$$

We can verify this formula as follows:

$$\sum_{i=1}^{n} cx_i = cx_1 + cx_2 + \cdots + cx_n$$

$$= c(x_1 + x_2 + \cdots + x_n)$$

$$= c \sum_{i=1}^{n} x_i.$$

FORMULA III

$$\sum_{i=1}^{n} (x_i + y_i) = \sum_{i=1}^{n} x_i + \sum_{i=1}^{n} y_i$$

We can verify this formula as follows:

$$\sum_{i=1}^{n} (x_i + y_i) = x_1 + y_1 + x_2 + y_2 + \cdots + x_n + y_n$$

$$= x_1 + x_2 + \cdots + x_n + y_1 + y_2 + \cdots + y_n$$

$$= \sum_{i=1}^{n} x_i + \sum_{i=1}^{n} y_i.$$

In addition, we will find the following formulas for special sums useful.

FORMULA IV

$$\sum_{i=1}^{n} i = \frac{n(n + 1)}{2}$$

FORMULA V

$$\sum_{i=1}^{n} i^2 = \frac{n(n + 1)(2n + 1)}{6}$$

EXAMPLE 4   Evaluate:

(a) $\displaystyle\sum_{i=1}^{8} 5$ (b) $\displaystyle\sum_{i=1}^{5} 4i$ (c) $\displaystyle\sum_{i=1}^{6} i^2$

Solution   (a) $\displaystyle\sum_{i=1}^{8} 5 = 5 \sum_{i=1}^{8} 1 = 5 \cdot 8 = 40$

(b) $\displaystyle\sum_{i=1}^{5} 4i = 4 \sum_{i=1}^{5} i = 4 \cdot \frac{5(5 + 1)}{2} = 60$

(c) $\displaystyle\sum_{i=1}^{6} i^2 = \frac{6(7)(13)}{6} = 91$ □

EXAMPLE 5   Simplify $\displaystyle\sum_{i=1}^{n} \frac{i}{n^2}$.

Solution

$$\sum_{i=1}^{n} \frac{i}{n^2} = \sum_{i=1}^{n} \frac{1}{n^2} \cdot i$$

Now, $1/n^2$ is a constant relative to the index of summation, i, so

$$\sum_{i=1}^{n} \frac{1}{n^2} \cdot i = \frac{1}{n^2} \sum_{i=1}^{n} i$$

$$= \frac{1}{n^2} \cdot \frac{n(n+1)}{2}$$

$$= \frac{n+1}{2n}$$ □

Note that the formulas given above apply only if the index starts at 1. These formulas will be extremely useful when we study definite integrals in Chapter 14.

Consider the arithmetic sequence with first term a_1, common difference d, and nth term a_n. The first n terms of an arithmetic sequence can be written from a_1 to a_n as

$$a_1, a_1 + d, a_1 + 2d, a_1 + 3d, \ldots, a_1 + (n-1)d \qquad (1)$$

or backwards from a_n to a_1 as

$$a_n, a_n - d, a_n - 2d, a_n - 3d, \ldots, a_n - (n-1)d. \qquad (2)$$

We can find the sum of the n terms in two different forms as follows (letting s_n represent the sum).

The sum of sequence (1) gives

$$s_n = a_1 + (a_1 + d) + (a_1 + 2d) + \cdots + [a_1 + (n-1)d],$$

and the sum of sequence (2) gives

$$s_n = a_n + (a_n - d) + (a_n - 2d) + \cdots + [a_n - (n-1)d].$$

Adding (term by term) gives

$$2s_n = (a_1 + a_n) + (a_1 + a_n) + (a_1 + a_n) + \cdots + (a_1 + a_n) + (a_1 + a_n).$$

So $2s_n = n(a_1 + a_n)$ because there are n terms. Thus the sum

$$s_n = \frac{n}{2}(a_1 + a_n).$$

We may state this result as follows.

> The sum of the first n terms of an arithmetic sequence is given by the formula
>
> $$s_n = \frac{n}{2}(a_1 + a_n),$$
>
> where a_1 is the first term of the sequence and a_n is the nth term.

EXAMPLE 6   Find the sum of the first 10 terms of the arithmetic sequence with first term 2 and common difference 4.

Solution   First we find the tenth term: $a_{10} = 2 + 9 \cdot 4 = 38$. The sum is

$$s_{10} = \frac{10}{2}(2 + 38) = 200. \qquad \square$$

EXAMPLE 7   Find the sum of the first 7 terms of the arithmetic sequence $\frac{1}{4}, \frac{7}{12}, \frac{11}{12} \cdots$.

Solution   The first term is $\frac{1}{4}$ and the common difference is $\frac{1}{3}$. The seventh term is $a_7 = \frac{1}{4} + 6(\frac{1}{3}) = 2\frac{1}{4}$. The sum is $s_7 = \frac{7}{2}(\frac{1}{4} + \frac{9}{4}) = \frac{35}{4} = 8\frac{3}{4}.$ $\qquad \square$

The first n terms of a geometric sequence can be written as

$$a_1, a_1 r, a_1 r^2, \ldots, a_1 r^{n-1},$$

so the sum of the first n terms is

$$s_n = a_1 + a_1 r + a_1 r^2 + \cdots + a_1 r^{n-1}.$$

Then

$$r s_n = a_1 r + a_1 r^2 + a_1 r^3 + \cdots + a_1 r^n,$$

so

$$s_n - r s_n = a_1 + (a_1 r - a_1 r) + (a_1 r^2 - a_1 r^2) + \cdots + (a_1 r^{n-1} - a_1 r^{n-1}) - a_1 r^n.$$

Thus

$$s_n(1 - r) = a_1 - a_1 r^n, \qquad \text{so} \qquad s_n = \frac{a_1 - a_1 r^n}{1 - r}.$$

This gives the following.

> The sum of the first n terms of the geometric sequence with first term a_1 and common ratio r is
>
> $$s_n = \frac{a_1(1 - r^n)}{1 - r}.$$

EXAMPLE 8   Find the sum of the first 5 terms of the geometric progression with first term 4 and common ratio -3.

Solution
$$S_5 = \frac{4[1 - (-3)^5]}{1 - (-3)} = \frac{4[1 - (-243)]}{4} = 244 \qquad \square$$

EXAMPLE 9   Find the sum of the first six terms of the geometric sequence $\frac{1}{4}, \frac{1}{8}, \frac{1}{16}, \ldots$.

Solution $a_1 = \frac{1}{4}$ and $r = \frac{1}{2}$, so
$$S_6 = \frac{\frac{1}{4}[1 - (\frac{1}{2})^6]}{1 - \frac{1}{2}} = \frac{\frac{1}{4}(1 - \frac{1}{64})}{\frac{1}{2}} = \frac{1 - \frac{1}{64}}{2} = \frac{64 - 1}{128} = \frac{63}{128}. \qquad \square$$

Exercise 7.3

Find the sums in problems 1–20.

1. $\displaystyle\sum_{i=2}^{3} i$

2. $\displaystyle\sum_{j=4}^{5} j$

3. $\displaystyle\sum_{k=3}^{3} k$

4. $\displaystyle\sum_{i=-2}^{3} i$

5. $\displaystyle\sum_{i=1}^{4} a_i$

6. $\displaystyle\sum_{j=2}^{5} x_j$

7. $\displaystyle\sum_{k=1}^{3} x_k$, if $x_1 = 1, x_2 = 3, x_3 = -1, x_4 = 5$.

8. $\displaystyle\sum_{i=1}^{4} x_i$, if $x_1 - 3, x_2 = -1, x_3 = 3, x_4 = -2$.

9. $\displaystyle\sum_{i=3}^{5} (i^2 + 1)$

10. $\displaystyle\sum_{i=4}^{7} \left(\frac{i-3}{i^2}\right)$

11. $\displaystyle\sum_{j=2}^{5} (j^2 - 3)$

12. $\displaystyle\sum_{j=0}^{4} (j^2 - 4j + 1)$

13. $\displaystyle\sum_{k=1}^{50} 1$

14. $\displaystyle\sum_{j=1}^{60} 3$

15. $\displaystyle\sum_{i=1}^{40} i$

16. $\displaystyle\sum_{j=1}^{30} j$

17. $\displaystyle\sum_{k=1}^{50} 6k$

18. $\displaystyle\sum_{k=1}^{30} (k^2 + 4k)$

19. $\displaystyle\sum_{i=1}^{100} (4i^2 + 3i + 1)$ 20. $\displaystyle\sum_{i=1}^{25} (i^2 - 4i - 2)$

21. Find the sum of the first four terms of the sequence defined by $a_n = 3/n$.
22. Find the sum of the first five terms of the sequence defined by $a_n = n/4$.
23. Find the sum of the first eight terms of the arithmetic sequence with first term 2 and the common difference 3.
24. Find the sum of the first seven terms of the arithmetic sequence with first term 6 and the common difference 4.
25. Find the sum of the first six terms of the arithmetic sequence with first term 10 and common difference $\frac{1}{2}$.
26. Find the sum of the first eight terms of the arithmetic sequence with first term 12 and common difference -3.
27. Find the sum of the first five terms of the arithmetic sequence 2, 4, 6, ...
28. Find the sum of the first six terms of the arithmetic sequence 6, 9, 12, ...
29. Find the sum of the first eight terms of the arithmetic sequence 6, $\frac{9}{2}$, 3, ...
30. Find the sum of the first seven terms of the arithmetic sequence 12, 9, 6, ...
31. Find the sum of the first six terms of the geometric sequence with first term 6 and common ratio 3.
32. Find the sum of the first four terms of the geometric sequence with first term 3 and common ratio 4.
33. Find the sum of the first six terms of the geometric sequence with first term 4 and common ratio $-\frac{1}{2}$.
34. Find the sum of the first five terms of the geometric sequence with first term 9 and common ratio $\frac{1}{3}$.
35. Find the sum of the first five terms of the geometric sequence 1, 3, 9, ...
36. Find the sum of the first four terms of the geometric sequence 16, 64, 256, ...
37. Find the sum of the first five terms of the geometric sequence 6, 4, $\frac{8}{3}$, ...
38. Find the sum of the first five terms of the geometric sequence 9, -6, 4, ...

7.4 Annuities

Objectives
■ To compute the amount of an ordinary annuity
■ To compute the present value of an ordinary annuity

In Section 7.2 we learned how to compute the compound amount and interest if a fixed sum of money was deposited in an account that pays interest that is compounded periodically or continuously. But not many people are in a position to deposit a large sum of money at one time in an account. Most people save (or invest) money by depositing relatively small amounts at different times. If a depositor makes equal deposits at regular intervals, he or she is contributing to an **annuity.** The payments (deposits) may be made weekly, monthly, quarterly, yearly, or for any other period of time.

The time between successive payments of an annuity is its *payment interval,* and the time from the beginning of the first interval to the end of the last is its *term*.

Annuities may be classified into two types, *annuities certain* and *contingent annuities*. An annuity certain is one in which the payments begin and end on fixed dates. A contingent annuity has the payments related to events that cannot be paced regularly, so the payments are not regular. We will deal with annuities certain in this text, and we will deal only with annuities whose payment interval coincides with the compounding period of the interest.

Suppose you invested $100 at the end of each year for five years in an account that paid interest at 5%, compounded annually. How much money would you have in the account at the end of the five years?

Because you are making payments at the end of each period (year), this annuity is called an **ordinary annuity.**

To find the value of your annuity at the end of the five years, we compute the compound amount of each payment separately, and add the amounts. The $100 invested *at the end* of the first year will draw interest for 4 years, so it will amount to $100 $(1.05)^4$. The $100 invested at the end of the second year will draw interest for 3 years, so it will amount to $100 $(1.05)^3$. Similarly, the $100 invested at the end of the third year will amount to $100 $(1.05)^2$, and the $100 invested at the end of the fourth year will amount to $100 (1.05). The $100 invested at the end of the fifth year will draw no interest, so it will amount to $100.

Thus the amount of the annuity is given by

$$S = 100 + 100(1.05) + 100(1.05)^2 + 100(1.05)^3 + 100(1.05)^4.$$

But this sum forms a geometric progression with $a_1 = 100$, $r = 1.05$, and $n = 5$. Thus the sum is given by

$$S = \frac{100[1 - (1.05)^5]}{1 - 1.05} = \frac{100(-0.276282)}{-0.05}$$

$$= 552.56.$$

Thus the investment ($100 at the end of each year for 5 years, at 5% compounded annually) would return $552.56.

Because every such annuity will take the same form, we can state that if a periodic payment R is made for n periods at an interest rate i per period, the **amount of the annuity** will be given by

$$S = R \cdot \frac{1 - (1 + i)^n}{1 - (1 + i)}.$$

This simplifies to

$$S = R \cdot s_{\overline{n}|i} = R \cdot \frac{(1 + i)^n - 1}{i}.$$

The symbol $s_{\overline{n}|i}$ stands for $[(1 + i)^n - 1]/i$ and represents the amount of an ordinary annuity of $1 per period for n periods, with interest rate i per period.

Table 7.3   AMOUNT OF AN ORDINARY ANNUITY OF $1 $(s_{\overline{n}|i})$

Periods	1%	2%	3%	4%	5%	6%
1	1.000 000	1.000 000	1.000 000	1.000 000	1.000 000	1.000 000
2	2.010 000	2.020 000	2.030 000	2.040 000	2.050 000	2.060 000
3	3.030 100	3.060 400	3.090 900	3.121 600	3.152 500	3.183 600
4	4.060 401	4.121 608	4.183 627	4.246 464	4.310 125	4.374 616
5	5.101 005	5.204 040	5.309 136	5.416 323	5.525 631	5.637 093
6	6.152 015	6.308 121	6.468 410	6.632 975	6.801 913	6.975 319
7	7.213 535	7.434 283	7.662 462	7.898 294	8.142 009	8.393 838
8	8.285 671	8.582 969	8.892 336	9.214 226	9.549 108	9.897 468
9	9.368 527	9.754 628	10.159 106	10.582 795	11.026 564	11.491 316
10	10.462 213	10.949 721	11.463 879	12.006 107	12.577 893	13.180 795
11	11.566 835	12.168 715	12.807 796	13.486 351	14.206 787	14.971 643
12	12.682 503	13.412 090	14.192 030	15.025 805	15.917 127	16.869 941
13	13.809 328	14.680 332	15.617 790	16.626 838	17.712 983	18.882 138
14	14.947 421	15.973 938	17.086 324	18.291 911	19.598 632	21.015 066
15	16.096 896	17.293 417	18.598 914	20.023 588	21.578 564	23.275 970
16	17.257 864	18.639 285	20.156 881	21.824 531	23.657 492	25.672 528
17	18.430 443	20.012 071	21.761 588	23.697 512	25.840 366	28.212 880
18	19.614 748	21.412 312	23.414 435	25.645 413	28.132 385	30.905 653
19	20.810 895	22.840 559	25.116 868	27.671 229	30.539 004	33.759 992
20	22.019 004	24.297 370	26.870 374	29.778 079	33.065 954	36.785 591

The value of $s_{\overline{n}|i}$ can be computed directly, using a calculator or a table. Table 7.3 is such a table. It is read in a manner similar to Table 7.1.

EXAMPLE 1   Ruth Gearhart deposits $500 at the end of each year in a savings account that pays 6%, compounded annually. How much money will she have in the account at the end of 10 years?

Solution   Her savings forms an ordinary annuity with $n = 10$, $i = 6\%$, and $R = \$500$. Using Table 7.3, we see that the annuity will amount to

$$S = R \cdot s_{\overline{10}|6\%} = 500 \cdot \frac{(1 + 0.06)^{10} - 1}{0.06}$$

$$= \$6590.40. \qquad \square$$

EXAMPLE 2   Richard Floyd deposits $100 at the end of each month in an account that pays 12%, compounded monthly. How much money will he have in his account in a year and a half?

Solution   The number of periods is $n = 18$, and the rate *per period* is $i = 1\%$. At the end of

18 months the value of the annuity will be

$$S = 100 \cdot s_{\overline{18}|1\%} = 100(19.614748)$$
$$= \$1961.47.$$ $\square$

Many people who are retiring use their savings to purchase an annuity. This annuity pays them a fixed sum of money at regular intervals (usually each month). The single sum of money required to purchase an annuity that will provide these payments at regular intervals is called the **present value** of the annuity. For example, you could receive \$1000 at the end of each year for 16 years if you invested a lump sum of \$10,837.77 in an annuity that paid interest at 5%, compounded annually. This lump sum is called the present value of the annuity. But how do we determine that the present value of this annuity (of \$1000 per year) is \$10,837.77?

To answer this question, let us determine the final amount of an annuity that pays \$R per period for n periods, with money being worth a rate i per period. Using the formula for the amount of an annuity gives

$$S = R \cdot \frac{(1 + i)^n - 1}{i}.$$

The question now becomes "What amount must be invested now so that it will amount to S in n periods, with interest at i per period, compounded each period?" If we assume a lump-sum investment A_n is deposited, the compound amount after n periods will be

$$S = A_n(1 + i)^n.$$

Since both $R \cdot \dfrac{(1 + i)^n - 1}{i}$ and $A_n(1 + i)^n$ give us the amount S, we may set these quantities equal to each other. Solving for A_n will give us a formula for the **present value of an annuity**. Dividing both sides of

$$A_n(1 + i)^n = R \cdot \frac{(1 + i)^n - 1}{i}$$

by $(1 + i)^n$ gives

$$A_n = R \cdot \frac{(1 + i)^n - 1}{i(1 + i)^n}.$$

If the periodic return R is \$1, then the present value is given by

$$\frac{(1 + i)^n - 1}{i(1 + i)^n},$$

which we denote $a_{\overline{n}|i}$, and the present value of an annuity of \$R is given by

$$A_n = R \cdot a_{\overline{n}|i}.$$

Table 7.4   PRESENT VALUE OF AN ANNUITY OF $1 ($a_{\overline{n}|i}$)

Periods	1%	2%	3%	4%	5%	6%
1	0.990 099	0.980 392	0.970 874	0.961 538	0.952 381	0.943 396
2	1.970 395	1.941 561	1.913 470	1.886 095	1.859 410	1.833 393
3	2.940 985	2.883 883	2.828 611	2.775 091	2.723 248	2.673 012
4	3.901 966	3.807 729	3.717 098	3.629 895	3.545 951	3.456 106
5	4.853 431	4.713 460	4.579 707	4.451 822	4.329 477	4.212 364
6	5.795 476	5.601 431	5.417 191	5.242 137	5.075 692	4.917 324
7	6.728 195	6.471 991	6.230 283	6.002 055	5.786 373	5.582 381
8	7.651 678	7.325 481	7.019 692	6.732 745	6.463 213	6.209 294
9	8.566 018	8.162 237	7.786 109	7.435 332	7.107 822	6.801 692
10	9.471 305	8.982 585	8.530 203	8.110 896	7.721 735	7.360 087
11	10.367 628	9.786 848	9.252 624	8.760 477	8.306 414	7.886 875
12	11.255 078	10.575 341	9.954 004	9.385 074	8.863 252	8.383 844
13	12.133 740	11.348 374	10.634 955	9.985 648	9.393 570	8.852 683
14	13.003 703	12.106 249	11.296 073	10.563 123	9.898 649	9.294 984
15	13.865 053	12.849 264	11.937 935	11.118 387	10.379 658	9.712 249
16	14.717 874	13.577 709	12.561 102	11.652 296	10.837 770	10.105 895
17	15.562 251	14.291 872	13.166 118	12.165 669	11.274 066	10.477 260
18	16.398 269	14.992 031	13.753 513	12.659 297	11.689 587	10.827 604
19	17.226 009	15.678 462	14.323 799	13.133 939	12.085 321	11.158 116
20	18.045 553	16.351 433	14.877 475	13.590 326	12.462 210	11.469 921

The values of $a_{\overline{n}|i}$ may be found using a calculator or a table like Table 7.4. The present value of the annuity we discussed earlier (paying $1000 at the end of each year for 16 years) is

$$A_n = \$1000 \cdot a_{\overline{16}|0.05}$$

$$= \$1000 \cdot \frac{(1 + 0.05)^{16} - 1}{0.05(1 + 0.05)^{16}}$$

$$= \$1000 \cdot 10.83777$$

$$= \$10{,}837.77.$$

The formula for present value,

$$a_{\overline{n}|i} = \frac{(1 + i)^n - 1}{i(1 + i)^n},$$

is frequently given in finance books as

$$a_{\overline{n}|i} = \frac{1 - (1 + i)^{-n}}{i}.$$

Note the similarity of the second way of writing this formula and the formula for the final amount of an annuity of $1,

$$s_{\overline{n}|i} = \frac{(1 + i)^n - 1}{i}.$$

EXAMPLE 3 What lump sum would have to be invested at 6%, compounded annually, to provide an annuity of $1000 per year for 10 years?

Solution From Table 7.4 we find the present value of an annuity of $1 to be $7.360087. Thus the present value of a $1000 annuity is $7360.087 or $7360.09. □

EXAMPLE 4 What is the present value of an annuity of $1500 payable at the end of each 6-month period for 2 years if money is worth 4%, compounded semiannually?

Solution The number of periods is $n = 4$, the interest rate per period is $i = 2\%$. From Table 7.4, the present value of $1 is $a_{\overline{4}|2\%} = \$3.807729$. Thus the present value of the annuity is $A_n = Ra_{\overline{4}|2\%} = 1500 \times \$3.807729 = \$5711.59$, to the nearest cent. □

Exercise 7.4

1. Find the final amount of an annuity of $1 paid at the end of each year for 10 years, if it earns interest at 5%, compounded annually.

2. Find the amount of an ordinary annuity of $1 paid every 6 months for 3 years if the interest rate is 6%, compounded semiannually.

3. Find the amount of an annuity of $1300 paid at the end of each year for 5 years if interest is earned at a rate of 6%, compounded annually.

4. Find the amount of an annuity of $50 paid at the end of each year for 10 years, if it earns 4%, compounded annually.

5. Find the amount of an ordinary annuity of $80 paid quarterly for 3 years, if the interest rate is 8%, compounded quarterly.

6. Find the amount of an ordinary annuity of $300 paid quarterly for 5 years, if the interest rate is 4%, compounded quarterly.

7. Find the amount of an ordinary annuity of $40 paid at the end of each 6-month period for 10 years, if the interest rate is 6%, compounded semiannually.

8. Find the amount of an ordinary annuity of $75 paid every 6 months for 7 years, if the interest rate is 4%, compounded semiannually.

9. Mr. Gordon plans to invest $300 at the end of each year for 12 years in a savings account. If the account pays 5%, compounded annually, how much will he have at the end of the 12 years?

10. Sam saves $500 each 6 months and invests it at 4%, compounded semiannually. How much will he have at the end of 8 years?

11. Find the present value of an annuity of $100 paid at the end of each year for 17 years if the interest rate is 4%, compounded annually.

12. Find the present value of an annuity of $800 paid at the end of each year for 15 years if the interest rate is 3%, compounded annually.

13. Find the present value of an annuity of $100 paid at the end of each 6-month period for 8 years if the interest rate is 4%, compounded semiannually.

14. Find the present value of an annuity that pays $300 at the end of each 6-month period for 6 years if the interest rate is 6%, compounded semiannually.

15. What lump sum would have to be invested at 8%, compounded quarterly, to provide an annuity that pays $200 at the end of each quarter for 3 years?

16. A woman buying a home paid $10,000 down and agreed to make 18 quarterly payments of $500 beginning in 3 months. If money is worth 4%, compounded quarterly, how much should the house cost if she paid for it in cash?

17. Joe Burkhart inherited a sum of money. He wants to purchase an annuity that will give him $1000 at the end of each 6-month period for 9 years. If money is worth 4%, compounded semiannually, how much will he have to pay for the annuity?

18. Is it more profitable to buy an automobile for $3900 cash or to pay $800 down and $400 each quarter for 2 years, if money is worth 8%, compounded quarterly?

7.5 Loans; Debt Repayment

Objectives
- To find the regular payments required to amortize a debt
- To find the amount that must be invested periodically in a sinking fund to discharge a debt

Just as we invest money to earn interest, banks and lending institutions loan money and collect interest for its use. While your aunt may loan you money with the understanding that you will repay the full amount of the money plus simple interest at the end of a year, financial institutions generally expect you to make partial payments on a regular basis (frequently monthly).

Most consumer loans (for automobiles, appliances, televisions, and the like) are classed as *installment loans*. On one type of installment loan, interest is charged on the full principal of the loan for the full period of the loan, even though the principal is repaid in installments. This interest is then added to the principal to determine the amount that must be repaid. The size of each payment is determined by dividing the number of payments into the total amount. This method of computing interest is called the *add-on method*.

EXAMPLE 1   Mrs. Sentz obtained a loan from a finance company for $1200 plus add-on interest at 6% (per year) to be repaid in 12 monthly installments. What are her monthly payments?

Solution   The add-on interest for one year is

$$\$1200 \times 0.06 \times 1 = \$72,$$

so the amount of the loan is $1200 + $72 = $1272. Thus the monthly payments are $1272 ÷ 12 = $106.   □

Federal law requires that the full cost of the loan and the true annual percentage rate (APR) be disclosed with each loan. The APR is much higher than the stated rate for an add-on loan. For example, the APR for a 12-month add-on loan at 6% (like that in Example 1) is 11.08%.

Some installment loans are set up on a *discounted* basis. As with add-on loans, the interest is charged on the full amount for the full period of the loan, but the interest is deducted *before* the borrower receives the loan. The interest that is collected in advance is called *bank discount,* and the amount the borrower receives for his or her use is called the *proceeds of the loan.*

The true annual percentage rate (APR) for a discounted loan is even higher than that for an add-on loan. If the loan of Example 1 were given on a discounted basis, the APR would be 11.78% rather than 11.08%, and Mrs. Sentz would have to repay $1276.50 rather than $1272.

Amortization

Home mortgages and commercial loans for long periods of time are usually paid off by a series of partial payments with interest charged on the unpaid balance at the end of each payment period. In this case, the stated interest rate is the same as the APR.

A loan of this type can be repaid by applying an equal amount to the principal plus the interest on the unpaid balance for the payment period. In this case the payments will decrease as the interest on the unpaid balance decreases.

This type loan can also be repaid by making all payments (including principal and interest) in the same amount. The process of repaying this type loan is called **amortization.**

We may think of the loan as an annuity the bank purchases that pays a fixed return each payment period. Then the principal of the loan may be thought of as the present value of an annuity, and the payment the bank receives may be thought of as the payment from the annuity. The formula for present value (from Section 7.4) is $A_n = Ra_{\overline{n}|i}$, where R is the payment and $a_{\overline{n}|i}$ is the present value of an annuity of $1 for n periods at rate i. If we solve this formula for R, we have $R = A_n/a_{\overline{n}|i}$, which gives us the formula for finding the size of each payment.

EXAMPLE 2 A debt of $1000 with interest at 4%, compounded annually, is to be amortized by five annual payments (all the same size) over the next 5 years. What would be the size of these payments?

Solution The five equal payments of R form an annuity whose present value is $1000. Thus $1000 = R \cdot a_{\overline{5}|4\%}$ and $R = \$1000/a_{\overline{5}|4\%}$. From Table 7.4,

$$R = \frac{\$1000}{4.451822} = \$224.63.$$

Table 7.5 PERIODIC PAYMENT TO AMORTIZE $1 AT THE END OF n PERIODS $(1/a_{\overline{n}|\,i})$

Periods	1%	2%	3%	4%	5%	6%
1	1.010 000	1.020 000	1.030 000	1.040 000	1.050 000	1.060 000
2	0.507 512	0.515 050	0.522 611	0.530 196	0.537 805	0.545 437
3	0.340 022	0.346 755	0.353 530	0.360 349	0.367 209	0.374 110
4	0.256 281	0.262 624	0.269 027	0.275 490	0.282 012	0.288 591
5	0.206 040	0.212 158	0.218 355	0.224 627	0.230 975	0.237 396
6	0.172 548	0.178 526	0.184 598	0.190 762	0.197 017	0.203 363
7	0.148 628	0.154 512	0.160 506	0.166 610	0.172 820	0.179 135
8	0.130 690	0.136 510	0.142 456	0.148 528	0.154 722	0.161 036
9	0.116 740	0.122 515	0.128 434	0.134 493	0.140 690	0.147 022
10	0.105 582	0.111 327	0.117 231	0.123 291	0.129 505	0.135 868
11	0.096 454	0.102 178	0.108 077	0.114 149	0.120 389	0.126 793
12	0.088 849	0.094 560	0.100 462	0.106 552	0.112 825	0.119 277
13	0.082 415	0.088 118	0.094 030	0.100 144	0.106 456	0.112 960
14	0.076 901	0.082 602	0.088 526	0.094 669	0.101 024	0.107 585
15	0.072 124	0.077 825	0.083 767	0.089 941	0.096 342	0.102 963
16	0.067 945	0.073 650	0.079 611	0.085 820	0.092 270	0.098 952
17	0.064 258	0.069 970	0.075 953	0.082 199	0.088 699	0.095 445
18	0.060 982	0.066 702	0.072 709	0.078 993	0.085 546	0.092 357
19	0.058 052	0.063 782	0.069 814	0.076 139	0.082 745	0.089 621
20	0.055 415	0.061 157	0.067 216	0.073 582	0.080 243	0.087 185

To avoid division by $a_{\overline{n}|i}$, we may use Table 7.5 to find the value of $1/a_{\overline{n}|i}$. In the previous example,

$$R = \frac{\$1000}{a_{\overline{5}|4\%}} = \$1000 \cdot \frac{1}{a_{\overline{5}|4\%}}.$$

But from Table 7.5, $1/a_{\overline{5}|4\%} = 0.224627$. Thus $R = \$1000 \cdot 0.224627 = \$224.63$.

□

EXAMPLE 3   A man buys a house for $20,000. He makes a $5000 down payment and agrees to amortize the rest of the debt with quarterly payments over the next 5 years. If interest on the debt is 8%, compounded quarterly, what will be the size of the quarterly payments?

Solution
$$R = 15{,}000 \cdot \frac{1}{a_{\overline{20}|2\%}} = 15{,}000 \cdot 0.061157 = \$917.355$$

The quarterly payment is $917.36.

□

EXAMPLE 4   In the previous example, find the outstanding principal immediately after the fifteenth payment.

Solution The outstanding principal after the fifteenth payment is the present value of the annuity with $20 - 15 = 5$ payments to be made. So the principal is the payment times $a_{\overline{5}|2\%}$ (from Table 7.4):

$$A_n = 917.36 \cdot a_{\overline{5}|2\%} = 917.36 \cdot \$4.713460$$
$$A_n = \$4323.94 \text{ is the outstanding principal} \qquad \square$$

Sinking Funds

On some long-term debts for large amounts the borrower may establish a *sinking fund* into which periodic deposits are made so that a single sum may be paid on the date of maturity. For example, it may be necessary to provide a large amount of money by issuing bonds to cover the amount. Then a sinking fund is established that will produce an amount large enough to pay the face value of the bonds on their maturity date. The interest on the bonds is paid from other sources.

If each deposit is the same size and the deposits are made regularly, the deposits form an annuity whose amount is the value of the principal of the debt on the date of maturity. The size of each deposit can be found by solving the formula for the amount of an annuity $(S = Rs_{\overline{n}|i})$ for R.

Solving, we find $R = S/s_{\overline{n}|i}$, where R is the deposit, S is the principal of the debt, and $s_{\overline{n}|i}$ is the amount of an annuity of $1 for n periods at rate i per period (found in Table 7.3).

EXAMPLE 5 How much will have to be invested at the end of each year at 4%, compounded annually, to pay off a debt of $60,000 in 5 years?

Solution
$$R = \frac{S}{s_{\overline{n}|i}} = \frac{\$60,000}{s_{\overline{5}|4\%}} = \frac{\$60,000}{5.416323} \qquad \text{(From Table 7.3)}$$

thus the deposit is $R = \$11,077.62$.

Note that an annuity of $11,077.62 for 5 years at 4% will amount to $11,077.62 \cdot 5.416323 = 59,999.97$, or approximately $60,000. $\qquad \square$

As with the amortization, we can avoid the time-consuming division by making use of Table 7.6 (page 252) which gives the values of $1/s_{\overline{n}|i}$.

EXAMPLE 6 A company establishes a sinking fund to discharge a debt of $100,000 due in 5 years by making equal semiannual deposits, the first due in six months. If the deposits are placed in an account that pays 6% compounded semiannually, what is the size of the deposits?

Solution
$$R = 100,000 \cdot \frac{1}{s_{\overline{10}|3\%}} = 100,000 \cdot \$.087231 = \$8723.10$$

The semiannual deposit is $8723.10. $\qquad \square$

Table 7.6   PERIODIC PAYMENT FOR A SINKING FUND OF $1 AT END OF n PERIODS $(1/s_{\overline{n}|i})$

Periods	1%	2%	3%	4%	5%	6%
1	1.000 000	1.000 000	1.000 000	1.000 000	1.000 000	1.000 000
2	0.497 512	0.495 050	0.492 611	0.490 196	0.487 805	0.485 437
3	0.330 022	0.326 755	0.323 530	0.320 349	0.317 209	0.314 110
4	0.246 281	0.242 624	0.239 027	0.235 490	0.232 012	0.228 591
5	0.196 040	0.192 158	0.188 355	0.184 627	0.180 975	0.177 396
6	0.162 548	0.158 526	0.154 598	0.150 762	0.147 017	0.143 363
7	0.138 628	0.134 512	0.130 506	0.126 610	0.122 820	0.119 135
8	0.120 690	0.116 510	0.112 456	0.108 528	0.104 722	0.101 036
9	0.106 740	0.102 515	0.098 434	0.094 493	0.090 690	0.087 022
10	0.095 582	0.091 327	0.087 231	0.083 291	0.079 505	0.075 868
11	0.086 454	0.082 178	0.078 078	0.074 149	0.070 389	0.066 793
12	0.078 849	0.074 560	0.070 463	0.066 552	0.062 825	0.059 277
13	0.072 415	0.068 118	0.064 030	0.060 144	0.056 456	0.052 960
14	0.066 901	0.062 602	0.058 526	0.054 669	0.051 024	0.047 585
15	0.062 124	0.057 825	0.053 767	0.049 941	0.046 342	0.042 963
16	0.057 945	0.053 650	0.049 611	0.045 820	0.042 270	0.038 952
17	0.054 258	0.049 970	0.045 953	0.042 199	0.038 699	0.035 445
18	0.050 982	0.046 702	0.042 709	0.038 993	0.035 546	0.032 357
19	0.048 052	0.043 782	0.039 814	0.036 139	0.032 745	0.029 621
20	0.045 415	0.041 157	0.037 216	0.033 582	0.030 243	0.027 185

Exercise 7.5

AMORTIZATION

1. A debt of $10,000 is to be amortized by equal payments at the end of each year for 5 years. If the interest charged is 4%, compounded annually,
   (a) find the periodic payment.
   (b) find the outstanding principal immediately after the third payment.
2. A debt of $15,000 is to be amortized by equal payments at the end of each year for 10 years. If the interest charged is 6%, compounded annually,
   (a) find the periodic payment.
   (b) find the outstanding principal immediately after the eighth payment.
3. A debt of $8,000 is to be amortized with 8 equal semiannual payments. If the interest rate is 4%, compounded semiannually,
   (a) what is the size of each payment?
   (b) what is the outstanding principal immediately after the fifth payment?
4. A loan of $10,000 is to be amortized with 10 equal quarterly payments. If the interest rate is 8%, compounded quarterly,
   (a) what is the periodic payment?
   (b) what is the outstanding principal after the sixth payment?

5. A man buys a house for $25,000. He makes a $10,000 down payment and amortizes the rest of the debt with semiannual payments over the next 10 years. If the interest rate on the debt is 6%, compounded semiannually, what will be the size of the payments?

6. John Fare purchased $10,000 worth of equipment by making a $2000 down payment and promising to pay the remainder of the cost in semiannual payments over the next 4 years. If the interest rate on the debt is 4%, compounded semiannually, what will be the size of the payments?

SINKING FUNDS

7. What amount will have to be invested at the end of each year for 10 years to form a sinking fund of $100,000 if the interest rate is 5%, compounded annually?

8. What amount will have to be invested at the end of each year for 5 years to form a sinking fund of $25,000 if the interest rate is 6%, compounded annually?

9. How much will have to be invested at the end of each year at 5%, compounded annually, to pay off a debt of $50,000 in 8 years?

10. How much will have to be invested at the end of each year at 6%, compounded annually, to pay off a debt of $30,000 in 6 years?

11. A company establishes a sinking fund to discharge a debt of $75,000 due in 8 years by making equal semiannual deposits, the first due in 6 months. If their investment pays 6%, compounded semiannually, what is the size of the deposits?

12. A sinking fund is established to discharge a debt of $80,000 in 10 years. If deposits are made at the end of each 6-month period and interest is paid at the rate of 4%, compounded semiannually, what is the size of the deposits?

7.6 Depreciation (Optional)

Objectives
- To compute depreciation on business assets using the straight-line method
- To compute depreciation using the units-of-production method
- To compute depreciation using the declining-balance method
- To compute depreciation using the sum-of-years-digits method

Markups on a firm's merchandise must cover depreciation on the firm's assets as well as salaries and other expenses. Because certain business properties wear out and must be replaced, businesses are allowed tax credit for the depreciation of these assets. To be depreciable, the property must be for business use and it must have a limited useful lifespan. Land is not depreciable, but buildings, trucks, and equipment are. In order to determine the depreciation of business property, we must know its *useful life* (how long it is expected to be used) and its *basis* (original cost plus improvements). For most methods of computing depreciation we must also know the *resale* or *salvage value* of the property.

Straight-Line Methods

One method of computing depreciation is the straight-line method. One of the most frequently used methods, it is calculated by assuming equal depreciation over each year of the asset's useful life. We calculate the annual depreciation by the **straight-line method** as follows.

PROCEDURE	EXAMPLE
To calculate depreciation by the straight-line method:	Find the annual depreciation of a truck costing $10,500, with salvage value $1000, over a 5-year period.
1. Subtract the salvage value from the basis (cost) to get the total depreciation.	1. $10,500 − $1000 = $9500
2. Divide the total depreciation by the useful life (in years) to get the annual depreciation.	2. $9500 ÷ 5 = $1900 per year

The estimated life of a business asset is frequently converted to an *annual rate of depreciation*, which is stated as a percent. The rate of depreciation is usually based on the cost of the asset. Thus, in the previous example, we would divide the annual depreciation by the cost to get the annual rate of depreciation. This rate would be

$$\$1900 \div \$10{,}500 = 18.1\%.$$

EXAMPLE 1   Find the annual depreciation and annual rate of depreciation of a stamping machine which has a cost of $10,000, a useful life of 16 years, and a salvage value of $1200.

Solution   Total depreciation is $10,000 − $1200 = $8800.
Annual depreciation is $8800 ÷ 16 = $550.
Annual rate of depreciation is $550 ÷ $10,000 = 5.5%.   □

A second method of computing depreciation is the *units-of-production method*. This method relates depreciation to the estimated productive capacity of the property. An automobile or truck may be depreciated on the basis of the number of miles the company plans to run it, and a machine may be depreciated on the number of units it is estimated to produce or the number of hours it is expected to function.

EXAMPLE 2   A machine is expected to stamp 5,000,000 units during its life. If its cost was $53,000 and its resale value is $3000,
(a) what is the depreciation per unit of production?
(b) If the machine produces 339,500 units in a given year, what is the depreciation for that year?

Solution   (a) The total depreciation is $53,000 − $3000 = $50,000. The depreciation per unit is $50,000 ÷ 5,000,000 = $.01.

        (b) The depreciation for the specified year is 339,500 × $.01 = $3395.   □

Declining-Balance Method

Both methods of depreciation mentioned so far are *straight-line* methods, which assume that the relationship between the value of the asset and the number of years it is owned (or the number of units it has produced) is linear. But, in many cases, equipment (such as company trucks, etc.) depreciates very fast in the first few years, then more slowly in succeeding years. One method that will permit a larger charge for depreciation in the first years and less in later years is the **declining-balance method.** In this method, the depreciation at the end of each year is computed as a fixed percentage of its value at the beginning of the year. Because the value at the beginning of each year (called the *book value*) is multiplied by a fixed percentage, the book values and the yearly depreciations form geometric sequences.

The Internal Revenue Service permits businesses to use a maximum rate equal to *twice* the straight-line rate when computing depreciation by the declining-balance method. Thus the most common practice in using this method is to apply twice the straight-line depreciation rate to the book value for the year. The straight-line rate can be calculated (as a percentage) by dividing the number of years of useful life into 100%. Thus an asset with an estimated life of four years has a straight-line depreciation rate of 100% ÷ 4 = 25%, and the rate used in the declining-balance method for a four-year useful life would be twice 25%, or 50%. The procedure for this method is outlined as follows.

PROCEDURE	EXAMPLE
To calculate depreciation by the declining-balance method:	Use the declining-balance method to compute the depreciation on a $10,500 truck with an estimated useful life of 5 years and salvage value of $1000.
1. Divide the number of years of useful life into 100%.	1. 100% ÷ 5 = 20%
2. Double this rate (from step 1).	2. 20% · 2 = 40%
3. The first year's depreciation is the cost times this double rate.	3. The first year's depreciation is $10,500 · 0.40 = $4200.
4. Find the book value by subtracting the depreciation from the cost.	4. Book value is $10,500 − $4200 = $6300.
5. Take the double rate times the present book value to get the next year's depreciation, then subtract to find the book value at the end of that year.	5. $6300 · 0.40 = $2520 is the depreciation for the second year. $6300 − $2520 = $3780 is the book value at the end of the second year.

6. Repeat step 5 until the useful life is finished *or* until the book value is equal to the salvage value. (Frequently the depreciation for the final year will be the difference between the book value and the salvage value.)

6. $3780 · 0.40 = $1512 is the depreciation for the third year. $3780 − $1512 = $2268 is the book value at the end of the third year.

$2268 · 0.40 = $907.20 is the depreciation for the fourth year.

$2268 − $907.20 = $1360.80 is the book value at the end of the fourth year.

$1360.80 · $0.40 = $544.32 is the depreciation for the fifth year. $1360.80 − $544.32 = $816.48 is the book value at the end of the fifth year. *But* the salvage value is $1000, so the company can only claim depreciation down to a book value of $1000.

Thus the depreciation for the fifth year is limited to $1360.80 − $1000 = $360.80.

This example can be put in table form, which is easier to read (Table 7.7). Note that the salvage value is used only to put a lower limit on the book value. It is not used as it was in the straight-line depreciation.

We see that the book values at the end of each of the years form a geometric sequence with a common ratio of 60% = 0.60 (resulting from 100% minus the 40% depreciation rate), except for the last term, which is the salvage value. Similarly, the yearly depreciations (except for the last year) form a geometric sequence with ratio 0.60. This knowledge can be helpful in computing the depreciation.

Table 7.7   DECLINING-BALANCE DEPRECIATION TABLE

Year	Book Value at Beginning of Year	Rate	Depreciation for Year	Book Value at End of Year
1	$10,500 (cost)	40%	$4,200.00	$6,300.00
2	6,300.00	40	2,520.00	3,780.00
3	3,780.00	40	1,512.00	2,268.00
4	2,268.00	40	907.20	1,360.80
5	1,360.80	—	360.80	1,000.00 (salvage)
		Total depreciation	$9500.00	

EXAMPLE 3   A machine costing $156,250 has an estimated life of 10 years and an estimated salvage value of $18,000. Use the declining-balance method to find the book value and depreciation for each year.

Solution   The straight-line rate is 100% ÷ 10 = 10%, so the declining-balance rate is twice 10%, or 20%. Then the book values will form a geometric sequence with common

Table 7.8

Year	Book Value at Beginning of Year	End of Year	Depreciation
1	$156,250 (cost)	$125,000	$31,250
2	125,000	100,000	25,000
3	100,000	80,000	20,000
4	80,000	64,000	16,000
5	64,000	51,200	12,800
6	51,200	40,960	10,240
7	40,960	32,768	8,192
8	32,768	26,214.40	6,553.60
9	26,214.40	20,971.52	5,242.88
10	20,971.52	18,000 (salvage)	2,971.52

ratio 0.80. The book values and depreciation are given in Table 7.8.   □

Note that neither the book value nor the depreciation for the tenth year fit their respective sequences, because the book value cannot fall below the salvage value.

EXAMPLE 4   The Ace Tool Company purchased an automobile for $8300. If the car is depreciated over 4 years with a salvage value of $500, use the declining-balance method to find the depreciation for each year.

Solution   Table 7.9   DECLINING-BALANCE DEPRECIATION

Year	Book Value at Beginning of Year	Rate	Depreciation for Year	Book Value at End of Year
1	$8300.00	.50	$4150.00	$4150.00
2	4150.00	.50	2075.00	2075.00
3	2075.00	.50	1037.50	1037.50
4	1037.50	.50	518.75	518.75
		Total Depreciation	$7781.25	

□

Note that in this example the salvage value ($500) was not attained through the 4 years of depreciation. If the automobile was used beyond the estimated useful life (4 years), the company could claim additional depreciation until the book value reaches the salvage value ($518.75 − $500 = $18.75 in this case).

Sum-of-the-Years-Digits Method

Another method of computing depreciation, which assumes that depreciation is greatest during the first year, is the sum-of-the-years-digits method. As with the declining-balance method, the depreciation steadily decreases with each year of useful life. The procedure for computing depreciation by the **sum-of-the-years-digits method** follows.

PROCEDURE	EXAMPLE
To calculate depreciation by the sum-of-the-years-digits:	Use the sum-of-the-years-digits method to compute the depreciation on a $30,500 truck with an estimated useful life of 5 years and salvage value of $500.
1. Subtract the salvage value from the cost to determine the *total* depreciation.	1. The total depreciation is $30,500 − $500 = $30,000.
2. Add the digits representing each of the years of the useful life; this will be used as the denominator of a fraction which will be used in step 3.	2. The sum-of-digits is $1 + 2 + 3 + 4 + 5 = 15$.
3. To find the depreciation for the first year, multiply the *total depreciation* by a fraction that has the number of years of useful life as a numerator and the sum-of-digits (step 2) as the denominator.	3. The depreciation for the first year is $30,000 \cdot \frac{5}{15} = $10,000$.
4. Find the *book value* by subtracting the depreciation from the *cost*.	4. The book value at the end of the first year is $30,500 − 10,000 = $20,500.
5. To find the next year's depreciation, multiply the *total depreciation* by a fraction with the same denominator and a numerator that is one less than the numerator for the previous year. Subtract the depreciation from the old book value to find the new book value.	5. $30,000 \cdot \frac{4}{15} = $8,000$ is the depreciation for the second year. $20,500 − $8000 = $12,500 is the book value at the end of the second year.
6. Repeat step 5 until the useful life is finished.	6. $30,000 \cdot \frac{3}{15} = 6000 is the depreciation for the third year. $12,500 − $6000 = $6500 is the book value at the end of the third year.
	$30,000 \cdot \frac{2}{15} = 4000 is the depreciation for the fourth year. $6500 − $4000 = $2500 is the book value at the end of the fourth year.
	$30,000 \cdot \frac{1}{15} = 2000 is the depreciation for the fifth year. $2500 − $2000 = $500 is the book value at the end of the fifth year.

Table 7.10   SUM-OF-THE-YEARS DEPRECIATION

Year	Total Depreciation	Rate	Depreciation for Year	Book Value at End of Year
1	$30,000	$\frac{5}{15}$	$10,000	$20,500
2	30,000	$\frac{4}{15}$	8,000	12,500
3	30,000	$\frac{3}{15}$	6,000	6,500
4	30,000	$\frac{2}{15}$	4,000	2,500
5	30,000	$\frac{1}{15}$	2,000	500 (salvage)

This example can be put in table form (Table 7.10). Note that while the fraction is multiplied times the *total depreciation* (cost minus salvage value) to compute the depreciation, the book value for the first year is found by subtracting the depreciation from the *cost*.

EXAMPLE 5   Find the depreciation if machinery costing $64,000 is depreciated over a 6-year period and has a salvage value of $1,000.

Solution   The depreciation table is given in Table 7.11.   □

Table 7.11   SUM-OF-THE-YEARS DEPRECIATION

Year	Total Depreciation	Rate	Depreciation for Year	Book Value at End of Year
1	$63,000	$\frac{6}{21}$	$18,000	$46,000
2	63,000	$\frac{5}{21}$	15,000	31,000
3	63,000	$\frac{4}{21}$	12,000	19,000
4	63,000	$\frac{3}{21}$	9,000	10,000
5	63,000	$\frac{2}{21}$	6,000	4,000
6	63,000	$\frac{1}{21}$	3,000	1,000 (salvage)

The sum-of-the-years-digits method uses a different type of sequence from the declining-balance method to compute its accelerated depreciation. Instead of using a constant rate of depreciation, the yearly rates form an arithmetic sequence whose sum is 1. Looking at Table 7.10, we see that the rates form the sequence

$$\tfrac{5}{15}, \tfrac{4}{15}, \tfrac{3}{15}, \tfrac{2}{15}, \tfrac{1}{15},$$

which is an arithmetic sequence with common difference $-\frac{1}{15}$. The sum of this sequence is clearly 1, which we can verify by simply adding the terms or by using the formula $S = (n/2)(a_1 + a_n)$. Using the formula gives

$$S = \tfrac{5}{2}(\tfrac{5}{15} + \tfrac{1}{15}) = 1.$$

The reason this technique for finding the rates works so nicely is that we are seeking an arithmetic sequence of rates whose sum is 1 (so we get 100% of the depreciation) over n years, where the common difference decreases by one part each year. If we let the last term of this sequence be $1/p$, then solving the formula

$$1 = \frac{n}{2}\left(\frac{n}{p} + \frac{1}{p}\right)$$

(where n is the number of years) for p gives us

$$p = \frac{n(n+1)}{2}.$$

But we have seen that

$$\frac{n(n+1)}{2} = \sum_{i=1}^{n} i,$$

so we can find p by simply adding the years digits together! Thus the sum-of-the-years-digits method works for any number of years.

Exercise 7.6

STRAIGHT-LINE METHODS

1. Find the annual depreciation and the annual rate of depreciation of a machine that has a cost of $15,000, a useful life of 10 years, and a salvage value of $1000.
2. Find the annual depreciation and the annual rate of depreciation of a truck with a cost of $25,000, a useful life of 5 years, and a salvage value of $1000.
3. A machine is expected to produce 2,000,000 units during its lifetime. Its cost was $60,000 and its salvage value is $4000.
   (a) What is the depreciation per unit of production?
   (b) If the machine produces 250,000 units during a given year, what is the depreciation for that year?
4. A machine should produce 50,000,000 decals during its life. Its cost is $30,000 and its salvage value is $5000.
   (a) What is the depreciation per 1000 units of production?
   (b) If the machine produces 4,550,000 decals in a year, what is the depreciation for the year?

DECLINING-BALANCE METHOD

5. Use the declining-balance method to compute the depreciation for each year on an earth-moving machine with a cost of $36,500, a useful life of 4 years, and a salvage value of $2100.
6. Use the declining-balance method to compute the depreciation for each year on a machine with a cost of $9000, a useful life of 3 years, and a salvage value of $500.

SUM-OF-THE-YEARS-DIGITS METHOD

7. Use the sum-of-years-digits method to compute the depreciation for each year on a $3800 company car with a useful life of 3 years and a resale value of $800.
8. Use the sum-of-years-digits method to compute the depreciation for each year on a $16,500 machine with a useful life of 4 years and a salvage value of $3500.

Review Exercises

1. Find the first four terms of the sequence whose nth term is

$$a_n = \frac{1}{n^2}.$$

2. Find the tenth term of the arithmetic sequence with first term -2 and common difference 3.
3. Find the fourth term of the geometric sequence with first term 64 and eighth term $\frac{1}{2}$.

4. Evaluate $\displaystyle\sum_{i=1}^{4} \frac{i^2}{i+1}$.

5. Find the sum of the first six terms of the arithmetic sequence $\frac{1}{3}, \frac{1}{2}, \frac{2}{3}, \ldots.$
6. Find the sum of the first six terms of the geometric sequence $\frac{1}{9}, \frac{1}{3}, 1, \ldots.$

APPLICATIONS

7. If $1000 is invested for 4 years at 8% compounded quarterly, how much interest will be earned?
8. What is the compound amount if $1000 is invested for 6 years at 8% compounded semiannually?
9. What is the compound amount if $1000 is invested for 6 years at 8% compounded continuously?
10. Find the effective annual rate equivalent to the nominal rate of 8% compounded quarterly.
11. If $100 is deposited at the end of each quarterly period for 4 years in an account that pays 8% interest, compounded quarterly, how much money will accrue in the account?
12. What lump sum would have to be invested at 5%, compounded annually, to provide an annuity of $10,000 per year for 10 years?
13. A debt of $1000 with interest at 12%, compounded monthly, is amortized by 12 monthly payments (of equal size). What is the size of each payment?
14. How much would have to be invested at the end of each year at 6%, compounded annually, to pay off a debt of $80,000 in 10 years?

° 15. Use the straight-line method to find the annual depreciation of a machine that has a cost of $100,000, a useful life of 10 years, and a salvage value of $2000.

° 16. Use the declining-balance method to compute the depreciation for the first 4 years on the machine in problem 15.

° 17. Use the sum-of-the-years-digits to compute the depreciation for the first 4 years on the machine in problem 15.

PART FOUR
Probabilistic Models

Warmup In this chapter you will need to work problems like the following. If you have difficulty with any problem, return to the section where that type of problem was introduced and refresh your memory before starting the chapter.

Problem Type	Introduced in Section	Used in Section	Answer
(a) The sum of x, $\frac{1}{4}$, and $\frac{2}{3}$ is 1. What is x? (b) If the sum of x plus $\frac{1}{3}$ plus $\frac{1}{3}$ is 1, what is x?	2.1 Linear equations	8.1	(a) $x = \frac{1}{12}$ (b) $x = \frac{1}{3}$
If 12 numbers are weighted so that each of the 12 numbers has an equal weight and the sum of the weights is 1, what weight should be assigned to each number?	2.1 Linear equations	8.1	$\frac{1}{12}$
(a) List the set of integers that satisfy $2 \leq x < 6$. (b) List the set of integers that satisfy $4 \leq s \leq 12$.	4.1 Inequalities	8.1	(a) $\{2, 3, 4, 5\}$ (b) $\{4, 5, 6, 7, 8, 9, 10, 11, 12\}$

8

INTRODUCTION TO PROBABILITY

An economist cannot predict exactly how the gross national product will change, a sociologist cannot determine exactly how group behavior is affected by climatic conditions, and a psychologist cannot determine the exact effect of environment on behavior. Since the behavior of the economy and of people is subject to chance, their prediction involves probability. Answers to questions about the behavioral and life sciences, business, and economics are frequently found by conducting experiments with samples from the larger population and by using statistics (discussed in Chapter 9). The experiments are designed to compare what actually happens with what probability theory predicted would happen. For example, if a rat runs a T-maze, can it learn which way to turn to get food? If the food is on the right and the rat turns right many more times than probability indicates that it should, then we have evidence that it has learned. The conclusions drawn from experiments are usually given in terms of probability because they are extended to larger populations. For example, substances that cause cancer in experimental animals may not be proven to cause cancer in humans, but will be removed from the market because the probability is high that they will.

We will solve a number of problems involving games in this chapter because they lend themselves easily to probability. (In fact, probability theory really started as the result of gambling problems.) We will also see that the theory of probability can be useful in many applications in the management, social, and life sciences.

8.1 Probability

Objective   ■ To compute the probability of a single event's occurrence

Suppose an experiment can have a total of n equally likely outcomes, and that k of these outcomes would be considered a success. Then the probability of achieving a success in the experiment is k/n. That is, the probability of a success in an experiment is the number of ways the experiment can result in a success divided by the total number of possible outcomes. We may state the same idea a different way:

Probability of a   If an event E can happen in k ways out of a total of n equally likely
Single Event   possibilities, the probability of the occurrence of the event is
denoted by

$$\Pr(E) = \frac{k}{n} = \frac{\text{number of successes}}{\text{number of possible outcomes}}.$$

EXAMPLE 1   If we draw a ball from a bag containing 4 white balls and 6 black balls, what is the probability of
(a) getting a white ball? (b) getting a black ball? (c) not getting a white ball?

Solution   (a) A white ball can occur (be drawn) in 4 ways out of a total of 10 equally likely possibilities. Thus the probability of drawing a white ball is

$$\Pr(W) = \frac{4}{10} = \frac{2}{5}.$$

(b) We have 6 chances to succeed at drawing a black ball out of a total of 10 possible outcomes. Thus the probability of getting a black ball is

$$\Pr(B) = \frac{6}{10} = \frac{3}{5}.$$

(c) The probability of not getting a white ball is $\Pr(B)$, since not getting a white ball is the same as getting a black ball. Thus $\Pr(\text{not } W) = \Pr(B) = 3/5$.

□

The probability that event E will fail to occur is denoted by

$$\Pr(\text{not } E) = \frac{n - k}{n} = 1 - \frac{k}{n} = 1 - \Pr(E).$$

An event has probability 0 if and only if it cannot occur, and an event has probability 1 if and only if it is certain to occur. If E is any event,

$$0 \leq \Pr(E) \leq 1.$$

EXAMPLE 2   A dry cleaning firm has 12 employees: 7 women and 5 men. Three of the women and five of the men are 40 years old or older. The remainder are over 20 years of age and under 40. If a person is chosen at random from this firm,° what is the probability that the person is
(a) a woman?   (b) under 40 years of age?   (c) 20 years old?

Solution   (a) There are 7 women, so Pr(woman) = 7/12.
(b) Eight people are 40 or older, so

$$\text{Pr(under 40)} = 1 - \text{Pr(40+)} = 1 - \frac{8}{12} = \frac{4}{12} = \frac{1}{3}.$$

(c) All employees are over 20 years old, so Pr(20) = 0.   □

EXAMPLE 3   One ball is drawn from a box containing 4 white balls, 3 red balls, and 5 black balls. Find the probability that the ball is
(a) red.   (b) white.   (c) black.   (d) not red.

Solution   (a) $\text{Pr(red)} = \dfrac{3}{12} = \dfrac{1}{4}$

(b) $\text{Pr(white)} = \dfrac{4}{12} = \dfrac{1}{3}$

(c) $\text{Pr(black)} = \dfrac{5}{12}$

(d) $\text{Pr(not red)} = 1 - \dfrac{1}{4} = \dfrac{3}{4}$ □

EXAMPLE 4   If a number is to be selected at random from the integers 1 through 12, what is the probability that it is
(a) even?
(b) divisible by 3?
(c) even and divisible by 3?
(d) even or divisible by 3?

Solution   (a) Each number has an equal chance to be selected, and 6 of the 12 numbers are even. Thus

$$\text{Pr(even)} = \frac{6}{12} = \frac{1}{2}.$$

(b) The numbers 3, 6, 9, 12 are divisible by 3. Thus

$$\text{Pr(divisible by 3)} = \frac{4}{12} = \frac{1}{3}.$$

(c) The numbers 1 through 12 that are even *and* divisible by 3 are 6 and 12, so

---

° Selecting a person at random means every person has an equal chance of being selected.

$$\text{Pr(even and divisible by 3)} = \frac{2}{12} = \frac{1}{6}.$$

(d) The numbers that are even *or* divisible by 3 are 2, 3, 4, 6, 8, 9, 10, 12, so

$$\text{Pr(even or divisible by 3)} = \frac{8}{12} = \frac{2}{3}. \qquad \square$$

In the previous example, it was necessary (at least mentally) to list all the possible outcomes of the experiment (selecting a number at random). A set that contains all the possible outcomes of an experiment is called a **sample space.** In the previous example, a sample space is

$$S = \{1, 2, 3, 4, 5, 6, 7, 8, 9, 10, 11, 12\}.$$

Each element of the sample space is called a **sample point,** and an **event** is a subset of the sample space. Each sample point in the sample space is assigned a **probability measure** or **weight** such that the sum of the weights in the sample space is 1. The probability of an event is the sum of the weights of the sample points in the event's **subspace** (subset of S).

For example, the experiment "drawing a number at random from the numbers 1 through 12" has the sample space S given above. Because each element of S is equally likely to occur, we assign a probability weight of 1/12 to each element. The event "drawing an even number" in this experiment has the subspace

$$E = \{2, 4, 6, 8, 10, 12\}.$$

Because each of the 6 elements in the subspace has weight 1/12, the probability of event E is

$$\text{Pr(even)} = \text{Pr}(E) = \frac{6}{12} = \frac{1}{2}.$$

Note that using the sample space S for this experiment gives the same results as using the formula $\text{Pr}(E) = k/n$ [see Example 4(a)].

Some experiments can have an infinite number of outcomes, but we will concern ourselves only with experiments having finite sample spaces. We can usually construct more than one sample space for an experiment. The sample space in which each sample point is equally likely is called an **equiprobable sample space.**

EXAMPLE 5   Suppose a coin is tossed 3 times. Construct an equiprobable sample space for the experiment.

Solution   Perhaps the most obvious way to record the possibilities for this experiment is to list the number of heads that could result: {0, 1, 2, 3}. But the probability of obtaining 0 heads is different from the probability of obtaining 2 heads, so this sample space does not meet our needs. A sample space in which each outcome is equally likely is {HHH, HHT, HTH, THH, HTT, THT, TTH, TTT}, where HHT indicates the first two tosses were heads and the third was a tail. Because there are 8 equally likely possibilities, each has probability 1/8. Because only one of the eight gives 0 heads, Pr(0 heads) = 1/8; three of the eight result in 2 heads, so Pr(2 heads) = 3/8.   □

To find the probability of obtaining a given sum when a pair of dice is rolled, we need to determine how many outcomes are possible. If we distinguish between the two dice we are rolling, and we record all the possible outcomes for each die, we see that there are 36 possibilities, each of which is equally likely (see Table 8.1).

This list of possible outcomes for finding the sum of two dice is a sample space for the experiment. Because each *element* of this sample space has the same chance of occurring, this is an equiprobable sample space. Because the 36 elements in the sample space are equally likely, we can find the probability that a given sum results by determining the number of ways that sum can occur and dividing that number by 36. Thus the probability that a sum 6 will occur is 5/36, and the probability that a 9 will occur is 4/36 = 1/9. (See the 4 ways the sum 9 can occur in Table 8.1.)

Table 8.1

First Die \ Second Die	1	2	3	4	5	6
1	(1, 1)	(1, 2)	(1, 3)	(1, 4)	(1, 5)	(1, 6)
2	(2, 1)	(2, 2)	(2, 3)	(2, 4)	(2, 5)	(2, 6)
3	(3, 1)	(3, 2)	(3, 3)	(3, 4)	(3, 5)	(3, 6)
4	(4, 1)	(4, 2)	(4, 3)	(4, 4)	(4, 5)	(4, 6)
5	(5, 1)	(5, 2)	(5, 3)	(5, 4)	(5, 5)	(5, 6)
6	(6, 1)	(6, 2)	(6, 3)	(6, 4)	(6, 5)	(6, 6)

Note that we could have made a sample space for this experiment (finding the sum of a pair of dice) by listing the sums: (2, 3, 4, 5, 6, 7, 8, 9, 10, 11, 12). However, these outcomes are not equally likely; the probability of obtaining a 2 is different from the probability of obtaining a 6. We can see that the probabilities of events can be found more easily if an equiprobable sample space is used to determine the possibilities.

EXAMPLE 6   Use Table 8.1 to find the following probabilities if a distinguishable pair of dice is rolled:

(a) Pr (sum is 5)   (b) Pr (sum is 2)   (c) Pr (sum is 8)

Solution   (a) The sum 5 can occur in four ways: (4, 1), (3, 2), (2, 3), (1, 4). Thus Pr (sum is 5) = 4/36 = 1/9.

(b) The sum 2 results only from (1, 1). Thus Pr (sum is 2) = 1/36.

(c) The sample points that give a sum of 8 are in the subspace (6, 2), (5, 3), (4, 4), (3, 5), (2, 6). Thus Pr (sum is 8) = 5/36.   □

Exercise 8.1

1. A die is rolled. What is the probability that
   (a) a 4 will result?   (b) a 7 will result?   (c) an odd number will result?
2. If the probability that event E will occur is 3/5, what is the probability that E will not occur?
3. If you draw one card at random from a deck of 12 cards numbered 1 through 12 inclusive, what is the probability that the number you draw is divisible by 4?
4. A die is rolled. Find the probability of getting a number greater than 3.
5. From a deck of 52 ordinary playing cards, one card is drawn. Find the probability that it is
   (a) a queen.   (b) a red card.   (c) a spade.
6. One ball is drawn at random from a bag containing 4 red balls and 6 white balls. What is the probability that the ball is
   (a) red?   (b) not red?   (c) white?   (d) red or white?
7. An urn contains three red balls numbered 1, 2, 3, four white balls numbered 4, 5, 6, 7, and three black balls numbered 8, 9, 10. A ball is drawn from the urn. What is the probability that
   (a) it is red?   (b) it is odd-numbered?   (c) it is red and odd-numbered?   (d) it is red or odd-numbered?   (e) it is not black?
8. Using the urn described in problem 7, what is the probability that a ball drawn will be:
   (a) white?   (b) white and odd?   (c) white or even?   (d) black or white?
   (e) black and white?
9. Suppose a fair coin is tossed two times. Construct an equiprobable sample space for the experiment, and determine each of the following probabilities:
   (a) Pr (0 heads)   (b) Pr (1 head)   (c) Pr (2 heads)
10. Suppose a fair coin is tossed four times. Construct an equiprobable sample space for the experiment, and determine each of the following probabilities:
    (a) Pr (2 heads)   (b) Pr (3 heads)   (c) Pr (4 heads)
11. Use Table 8.1 to determine the following probabilities if a distinguishable pair of dice is rolled.
    (a) Pr (sum is 4)   (b) Pr (sum is 10)   (c) Pr (sum is 12)
12. (a) When a pair of distinguishable dice is rolled, what sum is most likely to occur?
    (b) When a pair of distinguishable dice is rolled, what is $Pr(4 \leq S \leq 8)$, where S represents the sum rolled?
13. If a pair of dice, one green and one red, is rolled, what is
    (a) $Pr(4 \leq S \leq 7)$, where S is the sum rolled?
    (b) $Pr(8 \leq S \leq 12)$, where S is the sum rolled?
14. If a green die and a red die are rolled, find
    (a) $Pr(2 \leq S \leq 6)$, where S is the sum rolled on the two dice.
    (b) $Pr(4 \leq S)$, where S is the sum rolled on the two dice.

APPLICATIONS

15. A class has 18 boys and 13 girls as students. A student is chosen at random to deliver a report. What is the probability that the person chosen is a girl?

16. A box contains 4 ten dollar bills, 10 five dollar bills, and 1 hundred dollar bill. If you are told you may keep whatever bill you draw randomly from the box, what is the probability that you will receive $100?

17. Three construction companies have bid for a job. Max knows that the two companies he is competing with have probabilities 1/3 and 1/6, respectively, of getting the job. What is the probability Max will get the job?

18. Because three airlines filed for the same air route on the same day, a lottery was held to determine who should get the route. If United Airlines is one of the airlines, what is the probability that
    (a) United is awarded the air route?   (b) United is not awarded the air route?

19. A car rental firm has 350 cars. Seventy of the cars have defective windshield wipers and 25 have defective tail lights. Two hundred of the cars have no defects; the remainder have other defects. What is the probability that a car chosen at random
    (a) has defective windshield wipers?
    (b) has defective tail lights?
    (c) does not have defective tail lights?
    (d) has at least one defect?

20. Forty percent of a company's total output consists of baseballs, 30% consists of softballs, and 10% consists of tennis balls. Its only remaining product is handballs. If they placed balls in a box in the same proportion as the company's output and selected a ball at random from the box, what is the probability that
    (a) the ball is a baseball?
    (b) the ball is a tennis ball?
    (c) the ball is not a softball?
    (d) the ball is a handball?

21. Because of a firm's growth, it is necessary to transfer one of its employees to one of its branch stores. Three of the nine employees are women and each of the nine employees is equally qualified for the transfer. If the person to be transferred is chosen at random, what is the probability that the transferred person is a woman?

22. A firm selling keypunches knows that four of its 100 keypunches will not duplicate properly and that five different ones have a defective key. If none of the other keypunches has a defect, what is the probability of a buyer selecting a defective keypunch from this group of 100?

23. A newly married couple plans to have three children. Assuming the probability of a girl being born equals that of a boy, what is the probability that exactly two of the three children born will be girls? (Hint: Construct the sample space.)

24. A frustrated store manager is asked to make four different yes-no decisions that have no relation to each other. Because he is impatient to leave work, he flips a coin for each decision. If the correct decision in each case was yes, what is the probability that
    (a) all of his decisions were correct?
    (b) none of his decisions was correct?
    (c) half of his decisions were correct?

8.2 Independent and Dependent Events

Objectives   ■ To compute the probability that two or more independent events will
occur
■ To compute the probability that two or more dependent events will occur

We may classify two events as independent or dependent. If the occurrence of
one event affects the occurrence of the other or others, the events are said to be
dependent. If the occurrence of one event does not affect the occurrence of the
other, the events are called **independent.**

For example, if a coin is tossed and a die is rolled, the result of the toss of the
coin does not affect the result of the roll of the die. Therefore the two events are
independent.

In addition, suppose that from a deck of 52 cards, two cards are drawn in
succession, without replacement. The result of the first draw will affect the result
of the second draw, so the second drawing is dependent on the first. We can see
this dependency as follows: Suppose we would like to draw a heart on both
draws; the number of hearts available in the deck for the second draw depends on
whether or not we got a heart on the first draw.

If we denote by $E_1 E_2$ the event "both E_1 and E_2 occur," then we can
write the formula for the probability that two events occur as

$$Pr(E_1 E_2) = Pr(E_1) \cdot Pr(E_2 | E_1),$$

where $Pr(E_2 | E_1)$ means "the probability of E_2, given that E_1 has oc-
curred." $Pr(E_2 | E_1)$ is **conditional probability.**

If E_1 and E_2 are independent events, the probability that E_2 occurs would not
be affected by whether E_1 occurred or did not occur. That is,

---

$Pr(E_2 | E_1) = Pr(E_2)$ *if* E_1 and E_2 are independent events. Thus we
may conclude that

$$Pr(E_1 E_2) = Pr(E_1) \cdot Pr(E_2)$$

if the events E_1 and E_2 are **independent.**

EXAMPLE 1   A die is rolled and a coin is tossed. Find the probability of getting a 4 on the die
and a head on the coin.

Solution   Let E_1 be "4 on the die" and E_2 be "head on the coin." The events are independent, because what occurs on the die does not affect what happens to the coin.

$$\Pr(E_1) = \Pr(4 \text{ on die}) = \frac{1}{6}, \quad \text{and} \quad \Pr(E_2) = \Pr(\text{head on coin}) = \frac{1}{2}.$$

Then

$$\Pr(E_1 E_2) = \Pr(E_1) \cdot \Pr(E_2) = \frac{1}{6} \cdot \frac{1}{2} = \frac{1}{12}. \qquad \square$$

EXAMPLE 2   A pair of dice is rolled, one after the other. What is the probability of getting an odd number on the first die and a 5 on the second?

Solution   What happens on the first die has no effect on what will happen on the second die, so the events are independent. If E_1 is "odd number on first die" and E_2 is "5 on second die," the probability that both will occur is

$$\Pr(E_1 E_2) = \Pr(E_1) \cdot \Pr(E_2) = \frac{3}{6} \cdot \frac{1}{6} = \frac{3}{36} = \frac{1}{12}.$$

Note that is the same probability we would get by using Table 8.1 to answer the question. Use of the appropriate formula will usually permit us to solve probability problems without listing the elements of the sample space. In this case, for example, we can answer the question with the formula and knowledge about the results of rolling one die rather than knowing the results of rolling a pair of dice.

$\square$

EXAMPLE 3   Suppose a card is drawn from a regular deck of 52 playing cards, is replaced, and a second card is drawn. What is the probability that the first card drawn is a spade and the second card is a king?

Solution   Since the first card drawn is replaced, the deck is the same for the second draw as it was originally. Therefore the events are independent. Let E_1 be "drawing a spade on the first draw." Since there are 13 spades in the 52 cards, $\Pr(E_1) = 13/52 = 1/4$.

Let E_2 be "drawing a king on the second draw." There are 4 kings in the 52 cards, so $\Pr(E_2) = 4/52 = 1/13$.

Since the events are independent

$$\Pr(E_1 E_2) = \Pr(E_1) \cdot \Pr(E_2) = \frac{1}{4} \cdot \frac{1}{13} = \frac{1}{52}. \qquad \square$$

EXAMPLE 4   A bag contains 3 red marbles, 4 white marbles, and 3 black marbles. Three marbles are drawn, one at a time, with replacement. Find the probability of getting a red marble on the first draw, a black marble on the second draw, and a white marble on the third draw.

Solution   The marbles are replaced after each draw, so the events are independent. Let E_1 be "red on first," E_2 be "black on second," and E_3 be "white on third." Then

$$\Pr(E_1 E_2 E_3) = \Pr(E_1) \cdot \Pr(E_2) \cdot \Pr(E_3) = \frac{3}{10} \cdot \frac{3}{10} \cdot \frac{4}{10} = \frac{36}{1000} = \frac{9}{250}. \qquad \square$$

EXAMPLE 5   A manager must make decisions about four independent problems. She can make one of three equally likely decisions for each problem, and she makes each decision by guessing. If each problem had only one correct solution, what is the probability she solved every problem correctly?

Solution   Her probability of solving each problem correctly by guessing is 1/3. Since the problems are independent, the probability all four decisions are correct is

$$\text{Pr(all correct)} = \frac{1}{3} \cdot \frac{1}{3} \cdot \frac{1}{3} \cdot \frac{1}{3} = \frac{1}{81}.$$ □

If one event (E_2) is **dependent** on another event (E_1), we use the formula

$$\text{Pr}(E_1 E_2) = \text{Pr}(E_1) \cdot \text{Pr}(E_2 | E_1),$$

where $\text{Pr}(E_2 | E_1)$ is the conditional probability that E_2 will occur given that E_1 occurs.

EXAMPLE 6   Find the probability that the second card drawn from a deck of 52 cards is a heart, given that the first card drawn was a heart and was not replaced.

Solution   If a heart was drawn from the deck, then there are only 12 hearts and 51 cards in the deck. Thus the conditional probability is Pr(heart on second draw | heart on first draw) = 12/51 = 4/17.   □

EXAMPLE 7   Suppose two cards are drawn, without replacement, from a deck of 52 playing cards. What is the probability that both cards are hearts?

Solution   As seen in the previous example, the two events are dependent. If we let E_1 be "heart on first card" and E_2 be "heart on second card," then the probability that both cards are hearts is

$$\text{Pr}(E_1 E_2) = \text{Pr}(E_1) \cdot \text{Pr}(E_2 | E_1) = \frac{13}{52} \cdot \frac{12}{51} = \frac{1}{4} \cdot \frac{4}{17} = \frac{1}{17}.$$ □

EXAMPLE 8   Suppose two cards are drawn, without replacement, from a deck of 52 cards. What is the probability that the first card is a spade and the second is a heart?

Solution   The events are dependent, because there are only 51 cards after the first card is drawn.

$$\text{Pr}(E_1) = \text{Pr(spade on first)} = \frac{13}{52} = \frac{1}{4}$$

$$\text{Pr}(E_2 | E_1) = \text{Pr(heart on second | spade on first)} = \frac{13}{51}$$

Thus

$$\Pr(E_1 E_2) = \Pr(E_1) \cdot \Pr(E_2 | E_1) = \frac{1}{4} \cdot \frac{13}{51} = \frac{13}{204}. \qquad \square$$

EXAMPLE 9 A box contains 3 black balls, 2 red balls, and 5 white balls. One ball is drawn, is *not* replaced, and a second ball is drawn. Find the probability that the first ball is red and the second is black.

Solution The events are dependent, since the total number and the number of one color of balls are changed by the first draw. Let E_1 be "red ball first" and E_2 be "black ball second." Then

$$\Pr(E_1 E_2) = \Pr(E_1) \cdot \Pr(E_2 | E_1) = \frac{2}{10} \cdot \frac{3}{9} = \frac{1}{15}.$$

Note that E_1 and E_2 would be independent events if the first ball were replaced before the second was drawn. $\qquad \square$

EXAMPLE 10 A bag contains 3 white, 4 blue, and 5 red balls. One ball is drawn from the bag, replaced, and a second ball is drawn.
(a) What is the probability that both balls are blue?
(b) What is the probability that neither ball is blue?

Solution (a) Since the first ball is replaced, the second draw is independent of the first. Thus the probability that both balls are blue is

$$\Pr(B_1 B_2) = \Pr(B_1) \cdot \Pr(B_2) = \frac{4}{12} \cdot \frac{4}{12} = \frac{1}{9}.$$

(b) The probability that neither ball is blue is $8/12 \cdot 8/12 = 4/9$. $\qquad \square$

EXAMPLE 11 Find the probabilities in Example 10 if the two balls are drawn simultaneously (that is, if the second ball is drawn without the first ball being replaced).

Solution (a) Because the first ball was not replaced before the second one was drawn, the events are dependent. The probability that both balls are blue is

$$\Pr(B_1 B_2) = \Pr(B_1) \cdot \Pr(B_2 | B_1)$$
$$= \frac{4}{12} \cdot \frac{3}{11} = \frac{1}{11}.$$

(b) The probability that neither ball is blue is $8/12 \cdot 7/11 = 14/33$. $\qquad \square$

EXAMPLE 12 All products on an assembly line must pass two inspections. It has been determined that the probability that the first inspector will miss a defective item is .09. If a defective item gets past the first inspector, the probability that the second inspector will not detect it is .01. What is the probability that a defective item will not be rejected by either inspector? (All good items pass both inspections.)

Solution   The two inspections are dependent, for the second inspector only inspects items passed by the first inspector. The probability a defective item will pass both inspections is

$$\text{Pr(pass both)} = \text{Pr(pass first)} \cdot \text{Pr(pass second} | \text{passed first)}$$
$$= .09 \cdot .01$$
$$= .0009. \qquad \square$$

Exercise 8.2

1. A die is thrown twice. What is the probability that a 3 will result the first time and a 6 will result the second time?

2. A coin is tossed three times. What is the probability of getting a head on all three tosses?

3. A box contains 3 red balls, 2 white balls, and 5 black balls. Two balls are drawn at random from the box (with replacement of the first before the second is drawn); what is the probability of getting a red ball on the first draw and a white ball on the second draw?

4. The probability that Sam will win in a certain game whenever he plays is 2/5. If he plays two games, what is the probability that he will win just the first game?

5. Two balls are drawn from a bag containing 3 white balls and 2 red balls. If the first ball is replaced before the second is drawn, what is the probability that
   (a) both balls are red?
   (b) both balls are white?
   (c) the first ball is red and the second is white?
   (d) one of the balls is black?

6. Two colored dice, one white and one red, are rolled. Find the probability that the white die is less than 2 and the red die is more than 2.

7. One card is drawn at random from a deck of 52 cards. The first card is replaced, and a second card is drawn. Find the probability that
   (a) both cards are hearts.
   (b) the first card is a heart and the second is a spade.

8. A red ball and 4 white balls are in a box. If two balls are drawn, without replacement, what is the probability
   (a) of getting a red ball on the first draw and a white ball on the second?
   (b) of getting 2 white balls?
   (c) of getting 2 red balls?

9. A bag contains 9 nickels, 4 dimes, and 5 quarters. If you draw 3 coins at random from the bag, without replacement, what is the probability that you will get a nickel, a quarter, a nickel, in that order?

10. A bag contains 6 red balls and 8 green balls. If two balls are drawn together, find the probability that
    (a) all are red.   (b) all are green.

11. From a deck of 52 playing cards two cards are drawn, one after the other without replacement. What is the probability that
    (a) the first will be a king and the second will be a jack?
    (b) the first will be a king and the second will be a jack of the same suit?

12. One card is drawn at random from a deck of 52 cards. The first card is not replaced,

and a second card is drawn. Find the probability that

(a) both cards are spades.

(b) the first card is a heart and the second is a club.

13. Two cards are drawn from a deck of 52 cards. What is the probability both are aces,

(a) if the first card was replaced before the second was drawn?

(b) if the cards were drawn without replacement?

APPLICATIONS

14. If 3% of all light bulbs a company manufactures are defective, the probability of any one bulb being defective is .03. What is the probability that three bulbs drawn independently from the company's stock will be defective?

15. To test its shotgun shells, a company fires 5 of them. What is the probability that all 5 of them will fire properly if 5% of its shells are actually defective?

16. One machine produces 30% of a product for a company. If 10% of the products from this machine are defective and the other machines produce no defective item, what is the probability that an article produced by this company is defective?

17. A company estimates that 30% of the country has seen its commercial and that if a person sees its commercial there is a 20% probability that the person will buy its product. What is the probability that a person chosen at random in the country will have seen the commercial and bought its product?

18. Ronald Lee has been told by a company that the probability that he will be offered a job in the quality control department is .6 and the probability that he will be asked to be foreman of the department, if he is offered the job, is .1. What is the probability that he will be offered the job and asked to be foreman?

19. In an actual case,° probability was used to convict a couple of mugging an elderly woman. Shortly after the mugging, a young white woman with blonde hair worn in a ponytail was seen running from the scene of the crime and entering a yellow car that was driven away by a black man with a beard. A couple matching this description were arrested for the crime. A prosecuting attorney argued that the couple arrested had to be the couple at the scene of the crime because the probability of a second couple matching the description was very small. He estimated the probabilities of six events as follows:

Probability of black-white couple: 1/1000
Probability of black man: 1/3
Probability of bearded man: 1/10
Probability of blonde woman: 1/4
Probability of hair in ponytail: 1/10
Probability of yellow car: 1/10

He multiplied these probabilities and concluded that the probability that another couple would have these characteristics is 1/12,000,000. Based on this circumstantial evidence, the couple were convicted and sent to prison. The conviction was overturned by the state supreme court because the prosecutor made an incorrect assumption. What error do you think he made?

° *Time*, January 8, 1965, p. 42, and April 26, 1968, p. 41.

8.3 Mutually Exclusive Events and Nonmutually Exclusive Events

Objectives   ■ To compute the probability that one or the other of two mutually exclusive events will occur
■ To compute the probability that one or the other of two nonmutually exclusive events will occur

If the occurrence of one event precludes the occurrence of another or others, the events are said to be **mutually exclusive.** This means that if two events are mutually exclusive, the success of one necessitates the failure of the other. If a die is rolled, the event E_1 "rolling a 6" and the event E_2 "rolling a 4" are mutually exclusive, because they cannot both result on a single roll of die. Thus if E_1 and E_2 are mutually exclusive events, $\Pr(E_1 E_2) = 0$.

> In general, the formula for the probability that one event *or* another will occur is
> $$\Pr(E_1 \text{ or } E_2) = \Pr(E_1) + \Pr(E_2) - \Pr(E_1 E_2).$$
> If E_1 and E_2 are **mutually exclusive,** $\Pr(E_1 E_2) = 0$; the formula is
> $$\Pr(E_1 \text{ or } E_2) = \Pr(E_1) + \Pr(E_2).$$

EXAMPLE 1   Find the probability of obtaining a 6 or a 4 in one roll of a die.

Solution   Rolling a 6 and rolling a 4 on one roll of a die are mutually exclusive events. Let E_1 be the event "rolling a 6" and E_2 be the event "rolling a 4."

$$\Pr(E_1) = \Pr(\text{rolling } 6) = \frac{1}{6} \quad \text{and} \quad \Pr(E_2) = \Pr(\text{rolling } 4) = \frac{1}{6}.$$

Then

$$\Pr(E_1 \text{ or } E_2) = \Pr(E_1) + \Pr(E_2) = \frac{1}{6} + \frac{1}{6} = \frac{1}{3}. \qquad \square$$

EXAMPLE 2   Find the probability of getting a head or a tail in one toss of a coin.

Solution   Let E_1 be "tossing a head" and E_2 be "tossing a tail." The events are mutually exclusive, so

$$\Pr(E_1 \text{ or } E_2) = \Pr(E_1) + \Pr(E_2) = \frac{1}{2} + \frac{1}{2} = 1.$$

The result is obvious, since the only possible results are heads or tails. $\square$

The same technique can be used to find the probability of the occurrence of one of three mutually exclusive events.

EXAMPLE 3   Find the probability of one toss of a die resulting in a 1, 3, or 5.

Solution   The events are mutually exclusive, so

$$\text{Pr}(1 \text{ or } 3 \text{ or } 5) = \text{Pr}(1) + \text{Pr}(3) = \text{Pr}(5) = \frac{1}{6} + \frac{1}{6} + \frac{1}{6} = \frac{1}{2}. \qquad \square$$

EXAMPLE 4   Sacco and Rosen are among 3 candidates running for a public office. The probability that Sacco will win is 1/3 and the probability that Rosen will win is 1/2. Only one candidate can win.
(a) What is the probability that Sacco or Rosen will win?
(b) What is the probability that neither Sacco nor Rosen will win?

Solution   (a) The two events are mutually exclusive, so

$$\text{Pr}(\text{Sacco or Rosen}) = \text{Pr}(\text{Sacco}) + \text{Pr}(\text{Rosen}) = \frac{1}{3} + \frac{1}{2} = \frac{5}{6}.$$

(b) The probability that neither will win is $1 - 5/6 = 1/6$. $\qquad \square$

If two events are **not mutually exclusive**, the general formula is used to find the probability that one or the other of the two events occur:

$$\text{Pr}(E_1 \text{ or } E_2) = \text{Pr}(E_1) + \text{Pr}(E_2) - \text{Pr}(E_1 E_2)$$

The events E_1 "rolling a number less than 5" and E_2 "rolling an even number" (in one roll of a die) are not mutually exclusive because if we get a 2 or a 4 we get numbers less than 5 *and* even numbers. Thus

$$\text{Pr}(E_1 E_2) = \text{Pr}(\text{number less than 5 } and \text{ even}) = \text{Pr}(2, 4) = \frac{2}{6} = \frac{1}{3}.$$

Then

$$\text{Pr}(\text{number less than 5 } or \text{ even}) = \text{Pr}(E_1 \text{ or } E_2) = \text{Pr}(E_1) + \text{Pr}(E_2) - \text{Pr}(E_1 E_2)$$

$$= \frac{4}{6} + \frac{3}{6} - \frac{2}{6} = \frac{5}{6}.$$

EXAMPLE 5   An integer between 1 and 6 inclusive is chosen at random. What is the probability that it is even or divisible by 3?

Solution   The events are not mutually exclusive, since 6 is even and divisible by 3. The probability of getting an even number is $\text{Pr}(\text{even}) = 3/6 = 1/2$, the probability of getting a number divisible by 3 is $\text{Pr}(\text{divisible by 3}) = 2/6 = 1/3$, and $\text{Pr}(\text{even } and \text{ divisible by 3}) = \text{Pr}(6) = 1/6$. Thus

$$\text{Pr}(\text{even or divisible by 3}) = \frac{1}{2} + \frac{1}{3} - \frac{1}{6} = \frac{5}{6} - \frac{1}{6} = \frac{4}{6} = \frac{2}{3}. \qquad \square$$

EXAMPLE 6   Find the probability of drawing a jack or a heart in one draw from a deck of 52 cards.

Solution   There is a jack of hearts, so the events are not mutually exclusive. Let E_1 be "heart" and E_2 be "jack." Then

$$\Pr(E_1 \text{ or } E_2) = \Pr(E_1) + \Pr(E_2) - \Pr(E_1 E_2) = \frac{13}{52} + \frac{4}{52} - \frac{1}{52} = \frac{16}{52} = \frac{4}{13}.$$

Note $\Pr(E_1 E_2) = \Pr(\text{jack of hearts}) = 1/52$.   □

Exercise 8.3

1. An ordinary die is tossed. What is the probability of getting a 3 or a 4?
2. A card is drawn from a deck of 52. What is the probability that it will be an ace, king, or jack?
3. A bag contains 4 white, 7 black, and 6 green balls. What is the probability that a ball drawn at random from the bag is white or green?
4. In a game where only one player can win, the probability that Jack will win is 1/5 and that Bill will win is 1/4. Find the probability that one of them will win.
5. A cube has 2 faces painted red, 2 painted white, and 2 painted blue. What is the probability of getting a red face or a white face?
6. A cube has 3 faces painted white, 2 faces painted red, and 1 face painted blue. What is the probability that a roll will result in a red or blue face?
7. If you draw one card from a deck of 12 cards, numbered 1 through 12 inclusive, what is the probability you will get an odd number or a number divisible by 4?
8. Suppose a die is biased (unfair) so that each odd-numbered face has probability 1/4 of resulting, and each even one has probability 1/12 of resulting. Find the probability of getting a number greater than 3.
9. If you draw one card from a deck of 12 cards numbered 1 through 12 inclusive, what is the probability that the card will be odd or divisible by 3?
10. A card is drawn at random from a deck of 52 playing cards. Find the probability that it is either a club or a king.
11. An urn contains 4 red, 5 white, and 6 black balls. One ball is drawn from the urn, replaced, and a second ball is drawn.
    (a) What is the probability that both balls are white?
    (b) What is the probability that one ball is white and one is red?
    (c) What is the probability that neither ball was black?
12. Answer the questions in problem 11 if the two balls were drawn simultaneously from the urn.
13. Suppose a fair coin is tossed 3 times.
    (a) What is the probability of obtaining 3 heads?
    (b) What is the probability of obtaining heads on the first two tosses and a tail on the third?
    (c) What is the probability of obtaining 2 heads and a tail?
    (d) What is the probability of obtaining a head and 2 tails?

APPLICATIONS

14. Of 100 students, 24 can speak French, 18 can speak German and 8 can speak both French and German. If a student is picked at random, what is the probability that he or she can speak French or German?
15. A company employs 65 people. Eight of the 30 men and 21 of the 35 women work in

the business office. What is the probability that an employee picked at random is a man or works in the business office?

16. In a group of 35 people, 15 play golf, 12 play tennis, and 6 play both golf and tennis. What is the probability that a person chosen at random can play golf or tennis?

17. A firm is considering three possible locations for a new factory. The probability that site A will be selected is 1/3 and the probability that site B will be selected is 1/5. If only one location will be chosen,
    (a) What is the probability that site A or site B will be chosen?
    (b) What is the probability that neither site A nor site B will be chosen?

18. Maria has ordered a washer and dryer from two different companies. Both the washer and the dryer are to be delivered Thursday. The probability that the washer will be delivered in the morning is .6 and the probability that the dryer will be delivered in the morning is .8. If the probability that either the washer or dryer is delivered in the morning is .9, what is the probability that both will be delivered in the morning?

19. Rob Lee knows his camera will take a good picture unless the flashbulb is defective or the batteries are dead. The probability of having a defective flashbulb is .05, the probability of the battery being dead is .3, and the probability that both these problems occur is .01. What is the probability that the picture will be good?

20. The cognitive complexity of a structure was studied by Scott[*] using a technique in which a person was asked to specify a number of objects and group them into as many groupings as he or she found meaningful. If a person groups 12 objects into three groups in such a way that

    7 objects are in group A
    7 objects are in group B
    8 objects are in group C
    3 objects are in both group A and group B
    5 objects are in both group B and group C
    4 objects are in both group A and group C
    2 objects are in all three groups

    (a) What is the probability an object chosen at random has been placed into group A or group B?
    (b) What is the probability an object chosen at random has been placed into group B or group C?

8.4 Conditional Probability; Bayes' Formula

Objectives   ■ To solve probability problems involving conditional probability
            ■ To use probability trees to solve problems
            ■ To use Bayes' formula to solve probability problems

We have seen that if one event E_2 is dependent on another event E_1, then the probability both events will occur is

---

[*] W. Scott, "Cognitive Complexity and Cognitive Flexibility," *Sociometry* 25 (1962), pp. 405–414.

$$\Pr(E_1 E_2) = \Pr(E_1) \cdot \Pr(E_2 \mid E_1),$$

where $\Pr(E_2 \mid E_1)$ denotes the **conditional probability** that E_2 will occur given that E_1 occurs. Solving the equation algebraically for $\Pr(E_2 \mid E_1)$ gives

Conditional Probability	$\Pr(E_2 \mid E_1) = \dfrac{\Pr(E_1 E_2)}{\Pr(E_1)}.$

This formula can be used directly to compute conditional probability.

EXAMPLE 1   A fair die is rolled. Find the probability the result is a 4, given that the result is even.

Solution   Using the conditional probability formula,

$$\Pr(4 \mid \text{even}) = \frac{\Pr(4 \text{ and even})}{\Pr(\text{even})}.$$

Since the result "4 and even" is satisfied when the result is a 4, we have

$$\Pr(4 \mid \text{even}) = \frac{\Pr(4 \text{ and even})}{\Pr(\text{even})} = \frac{\Pr(4)}{\Pr(\text{even})} = \frac{1/6}{3/6} = \frac{1}{3}.$$

Note that this is a reasonable result since the die can result in only 3 even numbers, one of which is a 4.   □

EXAMPLE 2   A red die and a green die are rolled. What is the probability the sum rolled on the dice is 6, given that the sum is less than 7.

Solution   Using the conditional probability formula and the sample space in Table 8.1, we have

$$\Pr(\text{sum is } 6 \mid \text{sum} < 7) = \frac{\Pr(\text{sum is } 6 \text{ and sum} < 7)}{\Pr(\text{sum} < 7)}.$$

Now

$$\Pr(\text{sum is } 6 \text{ and sum} < 7) = \Pr(\text{sum is } 6) = \frac{5}{36},$$

so

$$\Pr(\text{sum is } 6 \mid \text{sum} < 7) = \frac{5/36}{1/36 + 2/36 + 3/36 + 4/36 + 5/36}$$

$$= \frac{5/36}{15/36} = \frac{1}{3}.   \square$$

In dealing with probability problems that involve two or more stages, it is frequently useful to use a *probability tree*.

To illustrate how a tree is constructed, consider the following example.

EXAMPLE 3   A bag contains 5 red balls, 4 blue balls, and 3 white balls. Two balls are drawn, one after the other, without replacement. Draw a tree representing the experiment.

Solution   The first draw could result in a red ball (with probability 5/12), a blue ball (with probability 4/12) or a white ball (with probability 3/12). We can represent the results of the first draw by the tree shown in Figure 8.1.

The probabilities for red, blue, and white balls occurring on the second draw depend on the result of the first draw. We can represent all the possibilities by adding a second stage to the tree we have drawn, with the conditional probabilities noted (see Figure 8.2).   □

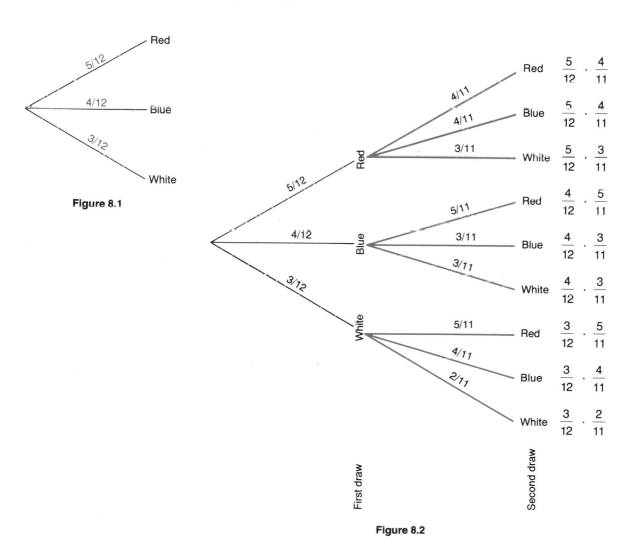

Figure 8.1

Figure 8.2

The first stage of this experiment has three possible outcomes, so the tree has three branches in the first stage. The second stage has three possible outcomes, so the tree has three branches in its second stage for each first outcome. The total number of possible outcomes in the compound experiment is the same as the total number of terminating branches, so each path through the tree represents a sample point for the experiment. For example, drawing a red ball and then drawing a blue ball is one possible outcome of this experiment, and it is represented by one path through the tree, namely the branch with red on the first draw and blue on the second draw.

The probability attached to *each branch* of the tree is the conditional probability that the specified event will occur, given that the events on the preceding branches have occurred. The probability of a *sample point* for the experiment described by a tree is the product of the probabilities associated with the branches along the path representing the sample point.

For example, the probability of drawing a red ball first and then a blue ball in the experiment described by Figure 8.2 is the product of 5/12 and 4/11, or 5/33.

EXAMPLE 4   In the experiment described by Example 3 (and Figure 8.2), find
(a) Pr (blue on first draw and white on second draw)
(b) Pr (white on both draws)
(c) Pr (drawing a blue ball and a white ball)
(d) Pr (second ball is red)

Solution   (a) By multiplying the probabilities along the path that represents blue on the first draw and white on the second draw, we obtain

$$\text{Pr (blue on first draw and white on second draw)} = \frac{4}{12} \cdot \frac{3}{11} = \frac{1}{11}.$$

(b) Multiplying the probabilities along the path that represents white on both draws gives

$$\text{Pr(white on both draws)} = \frac{3}{12} \cdot \frac{2}{11} = \frac{1}{22}.$$

(c) This result can occur by drawing a blue ball first, then a white ball *or* by drawing a white ball, then a blue ball. Thus either of two paths leads to this result. Because the results represented by these paths are mutually exclusive, the probability is found by *adding* the probabilities from the two paths. That is, letting B represent a blue ball and W represent a white ball,

$$\Pr(B \text{ and } W) = \Pr(B \text{ first, then } W) + \Pr(W \text{ first, then } B)$$

$$= \frac{4}{12} \cdot \frac{3}{11} + \frac{3}{12} \cdot \frac{4}{11} = \frac{2}{11}.$$

(d) $\Pr(\text{2nd ball is red}) = \Pr(R, \text{ then } R \text{ } or \text{ } B, \text{ then } R \text{ } or \text{ } W, \text{ then } R)$

$$= \Pr(R, \text{ then } R) + \Pr(B, \text{ then } R) + \Pr(W, \text{ then } R)$$

$$= \frac{5}{12} \cdot \frac{4}{11} + \frac{4}{12} \cdot \frac{5}{11} + \frac{3}{12} \cdot \frac{5}{11} = \frac{5}{12} \qquad \square$$

Using a probability tree permits us to answer more difficult questions regarding conditional probability. For example, in the experiment described by Figure 8.2, we can find the probability that the first ball is red, given that the second ball is blue. To find this probability we recall the formula for conditional probability, which is

$$\Pr(E_2 \mid E_1) = \frac{\Pr(E_1 E_2)}{\Pr(E_1)}.$$

So

$$\Pr(\text{1st is red} \mid \text{2nd is blue}) = \frac{\Pr(\text{1st is red and 2nd is blue})}{\Pr(\text{2nd is blue})}.$$

Now one path (red-blue) describes "1st is red and 2nd is blue" and three paths (red-blue, blue-blue, white-blue) describe "2nd is blue," so

$$\Pr(\text{1st is red} \mid \text{2nd is blue}) = \frac{\dfrac{5}{12} \cdot \dfrac{4}{11}}{\dfrac{5}{12} \cdot \dfrac{4}{11} + \dfrac{4}{12} \cdot \dfrac{3}{11} + \dfrac{3}{12} \cdot \dfrac{4}{11}}$$

$$= \frac{5/33}{5/33 + 1/11 + 1/11} = \frac{5}{11}$$

The preceding example illustrates a special type of problem, which we will call a Bayes problem. In this type of problem, we know the result of the second stage of a two-stage experiment and we wish to find the probability of a specified result in the first stage. In the preceding example we knew the second ball drawn was blue and we sought the probability that the first ball was red.

Suppose there are n possible outcomes in the first stage of the experiment, denoted $e_1, e_2, e_3, \ldots, e_n$ and m possible outcomes in the second stage, denoted $o_1, o_2, \ldots, o_m$ (see Figure 8.3). Then the probability event e_1 occurs in the first stage, given that o_1 occurred in the second stage is

$$\Pr(e_1 \mid o_1) = \frac{\Pr(e_1 \text{ and } o_1)}{\Pr(o_1)}. \qquad (1)$$

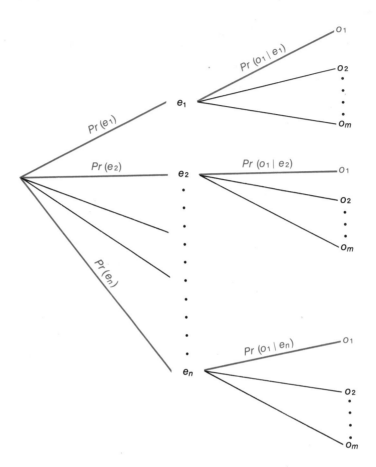

Figure 8.3

By looking at the probability tree in Figure 8.3 we see that

$$\Pr(e_1 \text{ and } o_1) = \Pr(e_1) \cdot \Pr(o_1|e_1)$$

and that

$$\Pr(o_1) = \Pr(e_1 \text{ and } o_1) + \Pr(e_2 \text{ and } o_1) + \cdots + \Pr(e_n \text{ and } o_1).$$

Thus using these facts, equation (1) becomes

$$\Pr(e_1|o_1) = \frac{\Pr(e_1) \cdot \Pr(o_1|e_1)}{\Pr(e_1 \text{ and } o_1) + \Pr(e_2 \text{ and } o_1) + \cdots + \Pr(e_n \text{ and } o_1)},$$

and since for any e_i, $\Pr(e_i \text{ and } o_1) = \Pr(e_i) \cdot \Pr(o_1|e_i)$, we have

$$\Pr(e_1|o_1) = \frac{\Pr(e_1) \cdot \Pr(o_1|e_1)}{\Pr(e_1) \cdot \Pr(o_1|e_1) + \Pr(e_2) \cdot \Pr(o_1|e_2) + \cdots + \Pr(e_n) \cdot \Pr(o_1|e_n)}.$$

Using sigma notation to indicate the sum in the denominator, we have the desired formula for problems of this type, known as **Bayes' Formula.**

$$\Pr(e_1|o_1) = \frac{\Pr(e_1) \cdot \Pr(o_1|e_1)}{\displaystyle\sum_{i=1}^{n} \Pr(e_i) \cdot \Pr(o_1|e_i)}$$

Note that Bayes problems can be solved either by this formula or by the use of a probability tree. Of the two methods, many students find using the tree easier because it is less abstract than the formula. The following example illustrates both methods.

EXAMPLE 5   Suppose a test for diagnosing a certain serious disease is successful in detecting the disease in 95% of all persons infected, but that it incorrectly diagnoses 4% of all healthy people as having the serious disease. Suppose also that it incorrectly diagnoses 12% of all people having another minor disease as having the serious disease. If it is known that 2% of the population has the serious disease, 90% of the population is healthy, and 8% has the minor disease, find the probability that a person selected at random has the serious disease if the test indicates that he or she does.

Solution   The tree that represents the health condition of a person chosen at random and the results of the test on that person is shown in Figure 8.4.

We seek $\Pr(D|\text{pos. test})$, where D denotes having the serious disease. Using the tree and the conditional probability formula gives

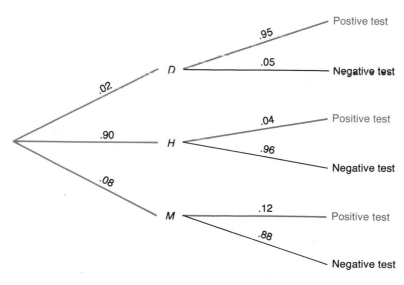

Figure 8.4

$$\Pr(D \,|\, \text{pos. test}) = \frac{\Pr(D \text{ and pos. test})}{\Pr(\text{pos. test})}$$

$$= \frac{(.02)(.95)}{(.90)(.04) + (.02)(.95) + (.08)(.12)}$$

$$= \frac{.0190}{.0360 + .0190 + .0096}$$

$$= .2941.$$

Using Bayes' formula directly gives the same result.

$$\Pr(D \,|\, \text{pos. test}) = \frac{\Pr(D) \cdot \Pr(\text{pos. test} \,|\, D)}{\Pr(H) \cdot \Pr(\text{pos. test} \,|\, H) + \Pr(D) \cdot \Pr(\text{pos. test} \,|\, D) + \Pr(M) \cdot \Pr(\text{pos. test} \,|\, M)}$$

$$= \frac{(.02)(.95)}{(.90)(.04) + (.02)(.95) + (.08)(.12)} = .2941 \qquad \square$$

Exercise 8.4

1. A card is drawn from a deck of 52 playing cards. Given that it is a red card, what is the probability that
   (a) it is a heart?   (b) it is a king?
2. A die has been "loaded" so that the probability of rolling any even number is 2/9. What is the probability of
   (a) rolling a 6, given that an even number is rolled?
   (b) rolling a 3, given that an odd number is rolled?
   (c) rolling a 5?
3. A bag contains 4 red balls and 6 white balls. Two balls are drawn without replacement.
   (a) What is the probability the second ball is white, given that the first ball is red?
   (b) What is the probability that the second ball is red, given that the first ball is white?
4. A fair coin is tossed 3 times. Find the probability of
   (a) throwing 3 heads, given that the first toss is a head.
   (b) throwing 3 heads, given that the first two tosses result in heads.
5. Two cards are drawn, without replacement, from a regular deck of 52 cards. What is the probability that
   (a) both cards are the same suit?
   (b) both cards are the same suit, given that the first card is the king of hearts?
6. Suppose the probability that a child is a male is 1/2. If a family has 3 children, what is the probability that
   (a) there are 3 girls, given that the first child is a girl?
   (b) there are 2 girls and 1 boy, given that at least 2 of the children are girls?
7. Three balls are drawn, without replacement, from a bag containing 4 red balls and 5 white balls. Find the probability that
   (a) three white balls are drawn.
   (b) two white balls and one red ball are drawn.
   (c) the third ball drawn is red.

8. A bag contains 5 coins, 4 of which are fair and 1 that has heads on both sides. If a coin is selected from the box and tossed twice, what is the probability of obtaining 2 heads?

9. A pair of dice, 1 red and 1 green, are rolled. What is the probability the red die is a 5, given that the sum of the dice is 10?

10. Two cards are drawn, without replacement, from a regular deck of 52 cards. What is the probability that both cards are aces, given that they are the same color?

11. There are 3 urns containing coins. Urn I contains 2 gold coins, Urn II contains 1 gold coin and 1 silver coin, and Urn III contains 2 silver coins. An urn is selected and a coin is drawn from the urn.
    (a) What is the probability the coin is gold?
    (b) If the selected coin is gold, what is the probability the urn selected was Urn I?

APPLICATIONS 12. The probability that an individual without a college education earns more than $20,000 is .2, whereas the probability that a person with a B.S. or higher degree will earn more than $20,000 is .6. The probability that a person chosen at random has a B.S. degree is .3. What is the probability a person has at least a B.S. degree if it is known that he or she earns more than $20,000?

13. A candidate for public office knows that whoever is nominated from her political party has a 60% chance of winning the election, and that she has a 25% chance of winning her party's nomination. What is the probability that she will win the election?

14. A small town has 8000 adult males and 6000 adult females. A sociologist conducted a survey and found that 40% of the males and 30% of the females drink heavily. An adult is selected at random from the town.
    (a) What is the probability the person is a male?
    (b) What is the probability the person drinks heavily?
    (c) What is the probability the person is a male or drinks heavily?
    (d) What is the probability the person is a male, if it is known that the person drinks heavily?

15. One hundred boys and one hundred girls were asked if they had ever been frightened by a television program. Thirty of the boys and sixty of the girls said they had been frightened. If one of these children is selected at random,
    (a) what is the probability that he or she has been frightened?
    (b) what is the probability the child is a girl, given that he or she has been frightened?

16. A candidate for public office knows that he has a 60% chance of being elected to the office if he is nominated by his political party, and that his party has a 50% chance of winning with another nominee. If the probability he will be nominated by his party is .25, and his party wins the election, what is the probability that he is the winning candidate?

17. A self-administered pregnancy test detects 85% of those who are pregnant, but does not detect pregnancy in 15%. It is 90% accurate in indicating women who are not pregnant, but indicates 10% of this group as being pregnant. Suppose it is known that 1% of the women in a city are pregnant. If a woman is chosen at random from those living in this city and if the test indicates she is pregnant, what is the probability she really is?

8.5 Counting; Permutations

Objectives   ■ To use the fundamental counting principle and permutations to solve
counting problems
■ To solve probability problems involving permutations

Suppose that you decide to dine at a restaurant that offers 3 appetizers, 8 entrees, and 6 desserts. How many different meals can you have? We can answer questions of this type using the **Fundamental Counting Principle.**

> *Fundamental*   If there are m ways in which an event can occur and if there are n
> *Counting*   ways in which a second event can occur after the first event has
> *Principle*   occurred, then the two events can occur in $m \cdot n$ ways.

The fundamental counting principle can be extended to any number of events as long as they are independent. Thus the total number of possible dinners is

$$3 \cdot 8 \cdot 6 = 144.$$

EXAMPLE 1   Suppose a person planning a banquet cannot decide how to seat 6 honored guests at the head table. In how many arrangements can they be seated in the six chairs on one side of a table?

Solution   If we think of the six chairs as spaces, we can determine how many ways each space can be filled. The planner could place any one of the 6 people in the first space (say the first chair on the left). One of the 5 remaining persons could then be placed in the second space, one of the 4 remaining persons in the third space, and so on, as follows:

$$\underline{6} \quad \underline{5} \quad \underline{4} \quad \underline{3} \quad \underline{2} \quad \underline{1}$$

By the fundamental counting principle, the total number of arrangements that can be made is the product of these numbers; that is, the total number of possible arrangements is

$$6 \cdot 5 \cdot 4 \cdot 3 \cdot 2 \cdot 1 = 720. \qquad \square$$

Because special products such as $6 \cdot 5 \cdot 4 \cdot 3 \cdot 2 \cdot 1$ frequently occur in counting theory, we use special notation to denote them. We write 6! (read "6 factorial") to denote $6 \cdot 5 \cdot 4 \cdot 3 \cdot 2 \cdot 1$. Likewise $4! = 4 \cdot 3 \cdot 2 \cdot 1$. For any positive integer n, we define

$$n! = n(n-1)(n-2) \cdots 3 \cdot 2 \cdot 1.$$

For reasons that will be apparent later, we define $0! = 1$.

EXAMPLE 2   Suppose the planner in Example 1 knows that 8 people feel they should be at the head table, but only 6 spaces are available. How many arrangements can be made that places 6 of the 8 people at the head table?

Solution   There are again 6 spaces to fill, but any of 8 people can be placed in the first space, any of 7 people in the second space, and so on. Thus the total number of possible arrangements is

$$\underline{8} \cdot \underline{7} \cdot \underline{6} \cdot \underline{5} \cdot \underline{4} \cdot \underline{3} = 20{,}160. \qquad \Box$$

The number of possible arrangements in Example 2 is called the number of permutations of 8 things taken 6 at a time, and is denoted $_8P_6$. Note that $_8P_6$ gives the first 6 factors of 8!, so we can use factorial notation to write the product.

$$_8P_6 = \frac{8!}{2!} = \frac{8!}{(8-6)!}.$$

In general,

Permutations   The number of possible distinct arrangements of r objects chosen from a set of n objects is called the number of **permutations** of n objects taken r at a time, and equals

$$_nP_r = \frac{n!}{(n-r)!}.$$

EXAMPLE 3   If a state wants each of its license plates to contain 7 different digits (numbers), how many different license plates could it make?

Solution   We seek the number of ways we can arrange 7 different digits from the 10 possible digits $(0, 1, 2, 3, \ldots, 9)$. The number is the number of permutations of 10 things taken 7 at a time, or

$$_{10}P_7 = \frac{10!}{(10-7)!} = \frac{10!}{3!} = 10 \cdot 9 \cdot 8 \cdot 7 \cdot 6 \cdot 5 \cdot 4 = 604{,}800. \qquad \Box$$

Note that we could have answered the question in Example 3 by using the fundamental counting principle or by using permutations. If, in Example 3, the state wanted each of its license plates to have *any* 7 digits rather than 7 *different* digits, the use of permutations would not apply. This is because permutations are used to determine the number of arrangements when each object in the set can be used only once.

We can use the fundamental counting principle to find the number of plates containing any 7 digits. Since any of the 10 digits could be used in each of the 7 places on the plate, the total number of possible plates is

$$10 \cdot 10 \cdot 10 \cdot 10 \cdot 10 \cdot 10 \cdot 10 = 10{,}000{,}000.$$

EXAMPLE 4   A psychologist claims she can teach four-year-old children to spell three-letter words very quickly. To test her, one of her students was given cards with the letters A, C, D, K, and T on them and told to spell CAT. What is the probability the child will spell CAT by chance?

Solution   The number of different three-letter "words" that can be formed using these 5 cards is $_5P_3 = 5!/(5 - 3)! = 60$. Since only one of those 60 arrangements will give CAT, the probability that the child will be successful by guessing is $1/60$.   □

Exercise 8.5

1. Compute $_6P_4$.
2. Compute $_8P_5$.
3. Compute $_{10}P_6$.
4. Compute $_7P_4$.

APPLICATIONS

5. The owner of a sailboat received 6 different signal flags when he purchased the sailboat. If the order in which the flags are arranged on the mast determines the signal being sent, how many 3-flag signals can be sent?

6. Eight horses are entered in a race. In how many ways can the horses finish?

7. Four candidates for manager of a department store are ranked according to the weighted average of several criteria. How many different rankings are possible if no two candidates receive the same rank?

8. An examination consists of 12 questions. If 10 questions must be answered, find the number of different orders a student can select the questions to answer.

9. The call letters for radio stations begin with K or W, followed by 3 additional letters. How many sets of call letters having 4 letters are possible?

10. Biologists have identified 4 kinds of small molecules, adenine, cytosine, quanine, and thymine, which link together to form larger molecules in genes. How many 3-molecule chains can be formed if the order of linking is important and each small molecule can occur more than once in a chain?

11. A member of a family of four is asked to rank all members of the family in the order of the power in the family. How many possible rankings are there?

12. A department store manager wants to display 6 brands of a product along one shelf of an aisle. In how many ways can he arrange the brands?

13. If a child is given cards with A, C, D, G, O, and T on them, what is the probability he or she could spell DOG by guessing the correct arrangement of the 3 cards?

14. Eight horses in a race wear numbers 1, 2, 3, 4, 5, 6, 7, and 8. What is the probability that the first three horses to finish the race are numbered 1, 2, 3, respectively?

15. Two men and a woman are lined up to have their picture taken. If they are arranged at random, what is the probability that
    (a) the woman will be on the left in the picture?
    (b) the woman will be in the middle in the picture?

16. If the first digit of a seven-digit telephone number cannot be a 0 or a 1, what is the probability that a number chosen at random will have all seven digits the same?

8.6 Combinations

Objectives
- To use combinations to solve counting problems
- To solve probability problems involving combinations

Suppose you are the president of a company and you want to pick 2 secretaries to work for you. If 5 people are qualified, how many different pairs of people can you select? If you select 2 people from the 5 in a specific order, the number of *arrangements* of the 5 people taken 2 at a time would be

$$_5P_2 = 20.$$

But $_5P_2$ gives the number of ways you can select *and* order the pairs, and we seek only the number of ways you can select them. If the names of the people are A, B, C, D, and E, then two of the arrangements, AB and BA, would represent only one pair. Because each of the pairs of people can be arranged in $2! = 2$ ways, the number of pairs that can be selected without regard to order is

$$\frac{_5P_2}{2!} = 10.$$

To find the number of ways you can select 3 people from the 5 without regard to order, we would first find $_5P_3$, then divide by the number of ways the 3 people could be ordered (3!).

Thus 3 people can be selected from 5 (without regard for order) in $_5P_3/3! = 10$ ways. We say that the number of combinations of 5 things taken 3 at a time is 10.

Combinations The number of ways r objects can be chosen from a set of n objects without regard to the order of selection is called the number of com-binations of n objects taken r at a time, and equals

$$_nC_r = \frac{_nP_r}{r!}.$$

Note that the fundamental difference between permutations and combinations is that permutations are used when order is a factor in the selection, and combi-nations are used when it is not. Because $_nP_r = n!/(n-r)!$, we have

$$_nC_r = \frac{\dfrac{n!}{(n-r)!}}{r!} = \frac{n!}{(n-r)!r!}.$$

The number of combinations of n objects taken r at a time is also frequently denoted by $\binom{n}{r}$; that is,

$$\binom{n}{r} = {_nC_r} = \frac{n!}{(n-r)!r!}.$$

EXAMPLE 1   An auto dealer is offering any of 6 special options at one price on a specially equipped car being sold. If the dealer will sell as many of these options as you want, and you decide to buy the car with 4 options, how many different choices of specially equipped cars do you have?

Solution   The order in which you choose the options is not relevant, so we seek the number of combinations of 6 things taken 4 at a time. Thus the number of possible choices is

$$_6C_4 = \frac{6!}{(6-4)!4!} = \frac{6!}{2!4!} = 15.$$ □

EXAMPLE 2   Suppose you are the junior class president, and you want to pick 4 people to serve on a committee. If 10 people are willing to serve, in how many different ways can you pick your committee?

Solution   Since the order in which the committee members are selected is not important, there are

$$_{10}C_4 = \frac{10!}{6!4!} = 210$$

ways in which the committee could be picked.   □

EXAMPLE 3   Six men and eight women have volunteered to serve on a committee. How many different committees can be formed containing three men and three women?

Solution   Three men can be selected from six in $\binom{6}{3}$ ways, and three women can be selected from eight in $\binom{8}{3}$ ways, so three men *and* three women can be selected in $\binom{6}{3} \cdot \binom{8}{3}$ = 1120 ways.   □

EXAMPLE 4   A box of 24 shotgun shells contains 4 shells that will not fire. If 8 shells are selected from the box, what is the probability
(a) that all 8 shells will be good?
(b) that 6 shells will be good and 2 will not fire?

Solution   (a) The 8 shells can be selected from 24 in $\binom{24}{8}$ ways, and 8 good shells can be selected from the 20 good ones in $\binom{20}{8}$ ways. Thus the probability that all 8 shells will be good is

$$Pr(8 \text{ good}) = \frac{\binom{20}{8}}{\binom{24}{8}} = \frac{\frac{20!}{12!8!}}{\frac{24!}{16!8!}} = .17.$$

(b) Six good shells *and* two defective shells can be selected in $\binom{20}{6} \cdot \binom{4}{2}$ ways, so

$$\Pr(6 \text{ good and } 2 \text{ defective}) = \frac{\binom{20}{6} \cdot \binom{4}{2}}{\binom{24}{8}} = \frac{\frac{20!}{14!6!} \cdot \frac{4!}{2!2!}}{\frac{24!}{16!8!}} = .316. \qquad \square$$

Exercise 8.6

1. Compute $\binom{6}{2}$.
2. Compute $\binom{8}{6}$.
3. Compute $_7C_5$.
4. Compute $_5C_2$.

APPLICATIONS

5. In how many ways can a committee of 5 be selected from 10 people willing to serve?

6. If 8 people are qualified for the next flight to a space station, how many different groups of 3 people can be chosen for the flight?

7. A traveling salesperson has 30 products to sell, but has room in her sample case for only 20 of the products. If all the products are the same size, in how many ways can she select 20 different products for her case?

8. A poker hand consists of 5 cards dealt from a deck of 52 cards. How many different poker hands are possible?

9. A psychological study of outstanding salespeople is to be made. If 5 salespeople are needed and 12 are qualified, in how many ways can the 5 be selected?

10. A company wishes to use the services of 3 different banks in the city. If 15 banks are available, in how many ways can it choose the 3 banks?

11. To determine voters' feelings regarding an issue, a candidate asked a sample of people to pick 4 words out of 10 which they felt best describe the issue. How many different groupings of 4 words are possible?

12. A sociologist wants to pick 3 fifth-grade students from each of four schools. If each of the schools has 50 fifth-grade students, how many different groups of 12 students can he select? (Set up in combination symbols; do not work out.)

13. What is the probability of being dealt a poker hand of 5 cards containing
    (a) 5 spades?   (b) 5 cards of the same suit?

14. A car dealer has 12 different cars he would like to display, but he only has room to display 5.
    (a) In how many ways can he pick 5 cars to display?
    (b) Suppose 8 of the cars are the same color, with the remaining 4 having distinct colors. If the dealer tells a salesperson to display any 5 cars, what is the probability that all 5 cars will be the same color?

15. A box of 12 transistors has 3 defective ones. If 2 transistors are drawn from the box together, what is the probability
    (a) that both transistors are defective?
    (b) that neither transistor is defective?
    (c) that one transistor is defective?

16. Four men and three women are semifinalists in a lottery. From this group, 3 finalists

are to be selected by a drawing. What is the probability that all three finalists will be men?

17. What is the probability that of 3 finalists in problem 16, 2 are men and 1 is a woman?

8.7 Expected Value

Objective   ■ To compute the expected value for an experiment

Many decisions in business and science are made on the basis of what the outcomes of specific decisions will be. One important property that can be developed using probability is expected value. Expected value is very useful in making decisions in business and the sciences. It was originally developed for, and is used frequently in, gambling, so we will introduce it in this context.

Suppose you toss a coin three times and you receive $1 for each head that results. How much would you expect to win each time you played if you played a large number of times?

The probabilities of 0, 1, 2, and 3 heads are 1/8, 3/8, 3/8, and 1/8, respectively. Thus you would expect to receive 0 dollars 1/8 of the time, 1 dollar 3/8 of the time, 2 dollars 3/8 of the time, and 3 dollars 1/8 of the time. Thus if you played this game a large number of times you would average

$$\$0 \cdot \frac{1}{8} + \$1 \cdot \frac{3}{8} + \$2 \cdot \frac{3}{8} + \$3 \cdot \frac{1}{8} = \$1.50$$

each time you played the game. Thus a fair price to pay to play this game is $1.50, and is called the expected value for this game. If a gambling casino offered to let people play this game for $2, the casino could expect to make an average of $.50 for every game that is played. It would have to pay $3 to some people, $2 to some, $1 to some, and $0 to others, but in the long run it could expect to average $.50 for each game that is played.

We define expected value as follows:

Expected Value   If an experiment has n possible numerical outcomes $x_1, x_2, x_3, \ldots, x_n$ with probabilities $\Pr(x_1)$, $\Pr(x_2)$, $\Pr(x_3)$, $\ldots$, $\Pr(x_n)$, respectively, then the **expected value** for the experiment is

$$E(x) = x_1 \cdot \Pr(x_1) + x_2 \cdot \Pr(x_2) + x_3 \cdot \Pr(x_3) + \cdots + x_n \cdot \Pr(x_n).$$

EXAMPLE 1   If a player rolls a die and receives $1 for each dot on the face he rolls, how much money should he expect to receive?

Solution   The following table gives the possible outcomes of the experiment and their probabilities.

x	1	2	3	4	5	6
Pr(x)	1/6	1/6	1/6	1/6	1/6	1/6

Then the expected value (in dollars) is

$$E(x) = 1\left(\frac{1}{6}\right) + 2\left(\frac{1}{6}\right) + 3\left(\frac{1}{6}\right) + 4\left(\frac{1}{6}\right) + 5\left(\frac{1}{6}\right) + 6\left(\frac{1}{6}\right) = \frac{21}{6} = 3.50.$$

He would expect to receive $3.50. □

EXAMPLE 2   A fire company sells chances to win a new car, with each ticket costing $5. If the car is worth $8000 and the company sells 3000 tickets, what is the expected value for a person buying one ticket?

Solution   For a person buying one ticket, there are two possible outcomes from the drawing—winning or losing. The probability of winning is 1/3000, and the amount won would be $8000 − 5 (the cost of the ticket). The probability of losing is 2999/3000, and the amount lost is written as a winning of −5. Thus the expected value is

$$7995\left(\frac{1}{3000}\right) + (-5)\left(\frac{2999}{3000}\right) = \frac{7995}{3000} - \frac{14,995}{3000} = -2.33.$$

Thus on the average a person can expect to lose $2.33 every time he or she buys a ticket. It is not possible to lose exactly $2.33 on one ticket—the person will either win an $8000 prize or lose $5; this means a person who buys large numbers of these tickets can expect to lose an average of $2.33 on each ticket he or she buys. That is, the fire company will make $2.33 on each ticket they sell if they sell 3000. □

EXAMPLE 3   The T. J. Cooper Insurance Company insures 100,000 cars. Their records indicate that during a year they will pay out the following for accidents:

$100,000 with probability .0001
$ 50,000 with probability .001
$ 25,000 with probability .002
$ 5000 with probability .008
$ 1000 with probability .02

What amount of money would the company expect to pay per car for accidents?

Solution   The expected value of the company's payments is

$100,000(.0001) + $50,000(.001) + $25,000(.002) + $5000(.008)
$$+ 1000(.02) = \$10 + \$50 + \$50 + \$40 + \$20 = \$170.$$

Thus the premium the company would charge each driver would be

$170 + operating costs + profit + reserve for bad years.   □

Exercise 8.7

The following tables give the possible numerical outcomes of experiments and the probabilities that they will occur. Find the expected value of each experiment.

1.

x	0	1	2	3
Pr(x)	1/8	1/4	1/4	3/8

2.

x	4	5	6	7
Pr(x)	1/3	1/3	1/3	0

3.

x	0	2	4
Pr(x)	1/6	2/6	3/6

4.

x	1	3	5
Pr(x)	2/3	1/6	1/6

APPLICATIONS

5. Suppose a youth has a part-time job in an ice cream shop. He receives $20 if he is called to work a full day, and $10 if he is called to work a half day. Over the past year he has been called to work a full day an average of 8 days per month and for a half day an average of 14 days per month. How much can he expect to earn per day during a 30-day month?

6. Suppose you are invited to play the following game: You toss 3 coins and receive $1 if one head results, $4 if two heads result, and $9 if three heads result. How much should you pay to play if the game is fair?

7. Suppose the coin used in problem 6 has been altered so that the probability of a head on any toss is 1/3. How much should you pay to play if the game is fair?

8. If the probability that a newborn child is a male is 1/2, what is the expected number of male children in a family having 4 children?

9. A student is completely unprepared for a 4-choice multiple choice test. If the test has 4 questions and all are guessed at, how many questions should he or she expect to get correct?

10. Suppose the instructor of the student in problem 9 tries to account for guessing on the test by counting the number of questions the student answers correctly and then subtracting from this number 1/4 of the number of questions a student answers. If the student guesses on all 4 problems on this test, for how many problems should he or she expect to get credit?

11. Suppose a student is offered a chance to draw a card from an ordinary deck of 52 playing cards and win $10 if he or she draws an ace, $2 for a king, and $1 for a queen. If $2 must be paid to play the game, what is the expected winnings every time the game is played by the student?

12. A charity sells raffle tickets for $1 each. First prize is $500, second prize is $100, and third prize is $10. If you bought one of the 1000 tickets sold, what are your expected winnings?

13. A young man plans to sell umbrellas at the city's Easter Parade. He knows that he can sell 180 umbrellas at $5 each if it rains hard, he can sell 50 if it rains lightly, and he can sell 10 if it doesn't rain at all. Past records show it rains hard 25% of the time on Easter, rains lightly 20% of the time, and does not rain at all 55% of the time. If he can buy 0, 100, or 200 umbrellas at $2 each and return the unsold ones for $1 each, how many should he buy?

14. If the young man in problem 13 learns from a highly reliable weather forecaster that the probability of a hard rain on Easter is 15%, of a light rain is 20%, and of no rain is 65%, should he still plan to sell umbrellas at the Easter Parade?

15. A car owner must decide if she should take out a $100 deductible collision policy in addition to her liability insurance policy. Records show that each year, in her area, 8% of the drivers have an accident that is their fault or for which no fault is assigned, and that the average cost of repairs for these types of accidents is $1000. If the $100 deductible collision policy costs $100 per year, would she save money in the long run by buying the insurance or "taking the chance?" (Hint: Find the expected value if she has the policy and if she doesn't have the policy and compare them.)

16. A candidate must decide if he should spend his time and money on TV commercials or making personal appearances. His staff determines that using TV he can reach 100,000 people with probability .01, 50,000 people with probability .47, and 25,000 with probability .52; and that by making personal appearances he can reach 80,000 people with probability .02, 50,000 people with probability .47, and 20,000 with probability .51. Which method will reach more people?

17. In studying endangered species, scientists have found that when animals are relocated it takes x years without offspring before the first young are born, where x and the probability of x are given below. What is the expected number of years before the first young are born?

x	0	1	2	3	4
$Pr(x)$	.04	.35	.38	.18	.05

Review Exercises

1. A bag contains 6 red and 3 blue balls. If 1 ball is drawn at random, what is the probability that it is blue?

2. From a deck of 52 cards, 1 card is to be drawn. What is the probability that it will be a queen?

3. If the probability of winning a game is 1/4 and there can be no ties, what is the probability of losing the game?

4. A card is drawn at random from an ordinary deck of 52 playing cards. What is the probability that it is a queen or a jack?

5. A deck of 52 cards is shuffled. A card is drawn, then replaced, the pack again

shuffled, and a second card drawn. What is the probability that both cards drawn are face cards (ace, king, queen, jack)?

6. A bag contains 4 red balls and 3 black balls. Two balls are drawn at random from the bag without replacement. Find the probability that both balls are red.

7. A card is drawn from a deck of 52 playing cards. What is the probability that it is an ace or a 10?

8. A card is drawn at random from a deck of playing cards. What is the probability that it is a king or a red card?

9. A box contains 2 red balls and 3 black balls. Two balls are drawn from the box without replacement. Find the probability that the second ball is red, given that the first ball is black.

10. What is the probability that a letter chosen at random from the word "wooden" is an o?

11. A bag contains 4 red balls numbered 1, 2, 3, 4 and 5 white balls numbered 5, 6, 7, 8, 9. A ball is drawn. What is the probability that the ball
    (a) is red and an even-numbered ball?
    (b) is red or an even number?
    (c) is white or an odd number?

12. How many 3-letter sets of initials are possible?

13. An urn contains 4 red and 6 white balls. One ball is drawn, is not replaced, and a second ball is drawn. What is the probability that one ball is white and one is red?

14. Compute $_6P_2$.

15. Urn I contains 3 red and 4 white balls and urn II contains 5 red and 2 white balls. An urn is selected and a ball drawn.
    (a) What is the probability that urn I is selected and a red ball is drawn?
    (b) What is the probability that a red ball is selected?
    (c) If a red ball is selected, what is the probability that urn I was selected?

16. For the following probability distribution, find the expected value $E(x)$.

x	1	2	3	4
$Pr(x)$	.2	.3	.4	.1

APPLICATIONS

17. In a certain city, 30,000 citizens out of 80,000 are over 50 years of age. What is the probability that a citizen selected at random will be 50 years old or younger?

18. Of 100 job applicants to the United Nations, 30 speak French, 40 speak German, and 12 speak both French and German. If an applicant is chosen at random, what is the probability the applicant speaks French or German?

19. A personnel director ranks 4 applicants for a job. How many rankings are possible?

20. An organization wants to select a president, vice-president, secretary, and treasurer. If 8 people are willing to serve and each of them is eligible for any of the offices, in how many different ways can the offices be filled?

21. Sixty men out of 1000 and 3 women out of 1000 are color blind. A person is picked at random from a group containing 10 men and 10 women.
    (a) What is the probability that the person is color blind?
    (b) What is the probability the person is a man if the person is color blind?

22. A utility company sends teams of 4 people each to perform repairs. If it has 12 qualified people, how many different teams can it form?

23. An organization wants to select a committee of 4 members from a group of 8 eligible members. How many different committees are possible?

24. A sample of 6 fuses is drawn from a lot containing 10 good fuses and 2 defective fuses. What is the probability that the sample will have
    (a) exactly 1 defective fuse?
    (b) at least 1 defective fuse?

25. A jury can be deadlocked if one person disagrees with the rest. There are 12 ways a jury can be deadlocked if one person disagrees, because any one of the 12 jurors could disagree.
    (a) In how many ways can a jury be deadlocked if 2 people disagree?
    (b) If 3 people disagree?

26. A state lottery pays $500 to anyone who selects the correct 3-digit number. If it costs $1 to play, what are the expected winnings of a person who plays?

In this chapter you will need to work problems like the following. If you have difficulty with any problem, return to the section where that type of problem was introduced and refresh your memory before starting the chapter.

Problem Type	Introduced in Section	Used in Section	Answer
Expand: (a) $(p + q)^2$ (b) $(p + q)^3$	0.3 Special products	9.5	(a) $p^2 + 2pq + q^2$ (b) $p^3 + 3p^2q + 3pq^2 + q^3$
Identify the graph of $y = -0.33x + 16.43$.	2.2 Graphs of first-degree equations	9.8	Straight line
Graph all real numbers satisfying (a) $100 \leq x \leq 115$ (b) $-1 \leq z \leq 2$	4.1 Linear inequalities	9.6	(a) (b)
If $x_1 = 2.1$, $x_2 = 6.3$, $x_3 = 7.1$, $x_4 = 4.8$, and $x_5 = 3.2$, find (a) $\sum\limits_{i=1}^{5} x_i$ (b) $\dfrac{\sum\limits_{i=1}^{5} x_i}{5}$ If $\begin{array}{c\|cccc} i & 1 & 2 & 3 & 4 \\ x_i & 50 & 25 & 10 & 5 \\ y_i & 2 & 4 & 10 & 20 \end{array}$, find (c) $\sum\limits_{i=1}^{4} x_i y_i$	7.2 Sigma notation	9.2, 9.3, 9.8	(a) 23.5 (b) 4.7 (c) 400
Evaluate: (a) $\binom{4}{3}$ (b) $\binom{5}{2}$ (c) $\binom{24}{0}$	8.6 Combinations	9.4, 9.5	(a) 4 (b) 10 (c) 1
(a) If 68% of the IQ scores of adults lie between 85 and 115, what is the probability that an adult chosen at random will have an IQ score between 85 and 115? (b) If a fair coin is tossed 3 times, find $\Pr[2 \text{ heads and 1 tail}]$	8.1 Probability	9.4, 9.5, 9.6, 9.7	(a) 0.68 (b) $\frac{3}{8}$
If a random variable x for an experiment has probabilities given by the table, $\begin{array}{c\|ccccccc} x & 0 & 1 & 2 & 3 & 4 & 5 & 6 \\ \hline \Pr[x] & \frac{1}{64} & \frac{6}{64} & \frac{15}{64} & \frac{20}{64} & \frac{15}{64} & \frac{6}{64} & \frac{1}{64} \end{array}$ find $E(x)$, the expected value for x.	8.7 Expected value	9.5	3

INTRODUCTION TO STATISTICS

In modern business, a vast amount of data is collected for use in making decisions about the production, distribution, and sale of merchandise. Businesses also collect and summarize data about advertising effectiveness, production costs, sales, wages, and profits. Behavioral scientists attempt to reach conclusions about general behavioral characteristics by studying the characteristics of a small sample of people. For example, election predictions are based on a careful sampling of the votes; correct predictions are frequently announced on television even though only 5% of the vote has been counted. Life scientists can use statistical methods with laboratory animals to detect substances that may be dangerous to humans.

A set of data taken from some source of data for the purpose of learning about the source is called a sample; the source of the data is called a population. The branch of statistics that deals with the collection, organization, summarization, and presentation of sample data is called descriptive statistics. The branch that deals with the methods of making estimates, predictions, or inferences about the population from collected sample data is called inferential statistics.

The descriptive statistics methods discussed in this chapter include graphical representation of data, measures of central tendency, and measures of dispersion. We will also discuss the binomial and normal probability distributions and use them to solve probability problems and make statistical inferences.

9.1 Frequency Histograms

Objective ■ To set up frequency tables and construct frequency histograms and frequency polygons for sets of data

The first step in statistical work is the collection of data. Data are regarded as statistics data if the numbers collected have some relationship. The heights of all female first-year students are statistical data because a definite relationship exists among the collected numbers.

A *graph* frequently is used to provide a picture of the statistical data that have been gathered and to show relationships among various quantities. The advantage of the graph for showing data is that a person can quickly get an idea of the relationships that exist. The disadvantage is that the data can be shown only approximately on a graph. One type of graph that is used frequently in statistical work is the **frequency histogram.** A histogram is really a bar graph. It is constructed by putting the scores (numbers collected) along the horizontal axis and the frequency with which they occur along the vertical axis. A frequency table is usually set up to prepare the data for the histogram.

EXAMPLE 1   Construct a frequency histogram for the following scores: 38, 37, 36, 40, 35, 40, 38, 37, 36, 37, 39, 38.

Solution   We first construct the frequency table, and then use the table to construct the histogram shown in Figure 9.1.   □

Score	Frequency
35	1
36	2
37	3
38	3
39	1
40	2

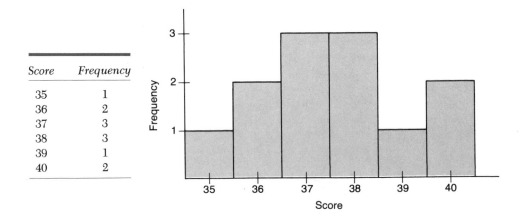

Figure 9.1

EXAMPLE 2   Construct a histogram from the following frequency table:

Interval	Frequency
0–5	0
6–10	2
11–15	5
16–20	1
21–25	3

Solution   The histogram is shown in Figure 9.2.   □

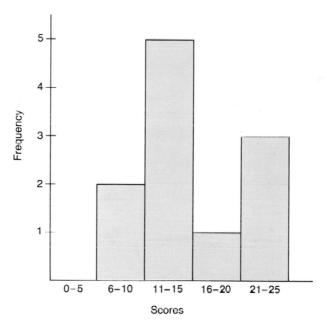

Figure 9.2

By drawing lines connecting the midpoints of the tops of the bars in a frequency histogram, we can construct a line graph called a **frequency polygon.**
Figure 9.3 (page 306) is a frequency polygon for the data in Example 2.

If the set of data contains a very large number of different scores, or if the data
are applied to variables such as length, weight, and temperature, which are
capable of assuming any value in an interval,° the data can be recorded in
classes. Class sizes are chosen that make the data easily handled. Consider the set

---

° Such a variable is called a *continuous variable.*

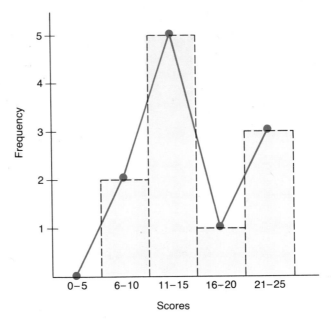

Figure 9.3

of heights of a sample of high school students in Table 9.1. Even though the heights are recorded as whole numbers of inches, it should be recognized that they could represent *any* number in a given interval, and they have been rounded off to the nearest inch.

Since the heights range from a low of 48 inches to a high of 77 inches, the data could be divided into 10 classes, each of which contains a 3-inch interval. The classes and the frequency of scores in each class are given in Table 9.2. Since the heights are measured to the nearest inch, the class containing heights that would round off to 48, 49, or 50 inches extends from 47.5 to 50.5 inches.

The frequency histogram for the data in Table 9.2 is shown in Figure 9.4.

Table 9.1 HEIGHTS OF 36 HIGH
SCHOOL STUDENTS

48	66	63	68	50	51
72	58	68	64	69	56
56	69	77	65	68	63
59	60	74	66	70	64
60	62	59	67	59	63
55	62	69	73	71	64

Table 9.2

Class Boundaries	Frequencies
47.5–50.5	2
50.5–53.5	1
53.5–56.5	3
56.5–59.5	4
59.5–62.5	4
62.5–65.5	7
65.5–68.5	6
68.5–71.5	5
71.5–74.5	3
74.5–77.5	1

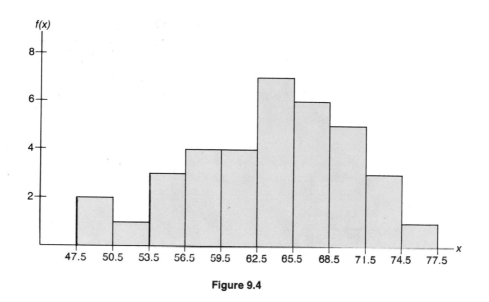

Figure 9.4

Exercise 9.1   Construct a frequency histogram for the data given in the following frequency tables.

1.

Score	Frequency
12	2
13	3
14	4
15	3
16	1

2.

Score	Frequency
22	1
23	4
24	3
25	2
26	3

3.

Score	Frequency
1	3
2	2
3	4
4	1
5	5
6	2

4.

Score	Frequency
16	2
17	4
18	3
19	3
20	2
21	4

5.

Interval	Frequency
0–4	1
5–8	0
9–12	2
13–16	3
17–20	1

6.

Interval	Frequency
10–14	2
15–19	4
20–24	3
25–29	2
30–34	3

Construct a frequency histogram for the data in problems 7–10.

7. 3, 2, 5, 6, 3, 2, 6, 5, 4, 2, 1, 6
8. 5, 4, 6, 5, 4, 6, 3, 6, 5, 4, 1, 7
9. 2, 1, 3, 7, 6, 4, 3, 2, 1, 6, 7
10. 14, 15, 14, 15, 15, 16, 18, 17, 16
11. Construct a frequency polygon for the data in problem 7.
12. Construct a frequency polygon for the data in problem 8.

APPLICATIONS 13. Suppose a department store manager has initiated a testing program to determine which employees would make good assistant managers. Make a frequency histogram for the classes of scores the employees made on the test, which follow.

x	$f(x)$
60–69	9
70–79	10
80–89	12
90–99	3

14. Given the data in Table 9.1, construct a frequency histogram for the heights using classes that contain 4 inches in each one.

15. The following table gives the hours per week worked by students at a given college. Draw a frequency histogram, assuming continuous time.

x	$f(x)$
$0. \le x < 6$	5
$6 \le x < 12$	10
$12 \le x < 18$	20
$18 \le x < 24$	10
$24 \le x < 30$	5
$30 \le x < 36$	3
$36 \le x < 42$	2

16. The following table gives the time required for rats to find food in a maze after two successful practice runs. Draw a frequency histogram.

t (min)	$f(t)$
$0 \le t \le 1$	1
$1 < t \le 2$	3
$2 < t \le 3$	2
$3 < t \le 4$	2
$4 < t \le 5$	1

9.2 Measures of Central Tendency

Objectives
- To find the mode of a set of scores (numbers)
- To find the median of a set of scores
- To find the mean of a set of scores

A set of data can be described by listing all the scores or by drawing a frequency histogram. But we often wish to describe a set of scores by giving the *average score* or the typical score in the set. There are three types of measures that are called "averages," or measures of central tendency. They are the **mode,** the **median,** and the **mean.**

To determine what value represents the most "typical" score in a set of scores, we use the mode of the scores.

> The **mode** of a set of scores is the score that occurs most frequently.

That is, the mode is the most popular score, the one that is most likely to occur. The mode can be readily determined from a frequency table or frequency histogram, because it is determined according to the frequency of the scores.

EXAMPLE 1 Find the mode of the following scores: 10, 4, 3, 6, 4, 2, 3, 4, 5, 6, 8, 10, 2, 1, 4, 3.

Solution The mode is 4, since it occurs more frequently than any other score. □

EXAMPLE 2 Determine the mode of the scores shown in the histogram in Figure 9.5.

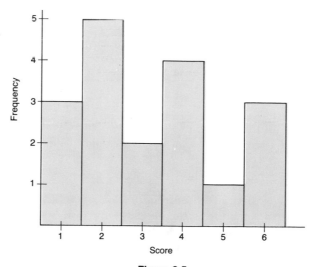

Figure 9.5

Solution   The most frequent score, as observed from the histogram, is 2.   □

EXAMPLE 3   Find the mode of the following scores: 4, 3, 2, 4, 6, 5, 5, 7, 6, 5, 7, 3, 1, 7, 2.

Solution   Both 5 and 7 occur three times. Thus they are both modes. This set of data is said to be *bimodal*, because it has two modes.   □

Although the mode of a set of scores tells us the most frequent score, it does not always represent the typical performance, or central tendency, of the set of scores. For example, the scores 2, 3, 3, 3, 5, 8, 9, 10, 13 have a mode of 3. But 3 is not a good measure of central tendency for this set of scores, for it is nowhere near the middle of the distribution.

One value that gives a better measure of central tendency is the **median.**

> The **median** is the score or point above and below which an equal number of the scores lie.

It is the middle of the distribution of scores. If there are an odd number of scores, we find the median by ranking the scores from smallest to largest and picking the middle score. That score will be the median.

EXAMPLE 4   Find the median of the following scores: 2, 3, 16, 5, 15, 38, 18, 17, 12.

Solution   We rank the scores from smallest to largest: 2, 3, 5, 12, 15, 16, 17, 18, 38. The median is the middle score, which is 15. Note that there are 4 scores above and 4 below 15.   □

EXAMPLE 5   Find the median of the following numbers: 3.1, 2.8, 6.1, 5.4, 2.7, 8.1, 3.2.

Solution   The ranking from smallest to largest is 2.7, 2.8, 3.1, 3.2, 5.4, 6.1, 8.1. The median is 3.2.   □

If the number of scores is even, there will be no middle score when the scores are ranked, so the *median* is the point that is the average of *the two middle scores.*

EXAMPLE 6   Find the median of the following scores: 3, 2, 6, 8, 12, 4, 3, 2, 1, 6.

Solution   We rank the scores from smallest to largest: 1, 2, 2, 3, 3, 4, 6, 6, 8, 12. The two scores that lie in the middle of the distribution are 3 and 4. Thus the median is a point that is midway between 3 and 4; that is, it is the arithmetic average of 3 and 4. The median is

$$\frac{3+4}{2} = \frac{7}{2} = 3.5.$$

In this case we say the median is a point, because there is no *score* which is 3.5.

□

It sometimes happens that when the number of scores is even, we find that the two middle scores (after ranking) are the same. When this happens, the median is the value of the two scores.

EXAMPLE 7 Find the median of the following numbers: 2, 3, 6, 7, 8, 7, 4, 6, 8, 3.

Solution The ranking is 2, 3, 3, 4, 6, 6, 7, 7, 8, 8. The two middle scores are both 6, so the median is 6.

□

The median is the most easily interpreted measure of central tendency, and it is the best indicator of central tendency when the set of scores contains a few extreme values. However, the most frequently used measure of central tendency is the mean.

The **mean** of a set of scores is the arithmetic average of the scores.

$$\text{Mean} = \frac{\text{sum of scores}}{\text{number of scores}}$$

The mean is used most often as a measure of central tendency because it is more useful in the general applications of statistics than the median.

The symbol $\bar{x}$ is used to represent the mean of a set of scores in a sample. We can use summation notation to write a formula for the mean. We write the formula as

$$\bar{x} = \frac{\sum\limits_{i=1}^{n} x_i}{n}.$$

When we are using summation notation to denote the sum of a set of scores, we frequently omit the index of summation and write Σx to denote the sum. The expression Σx means the sum of all x's, or in other words, the sum of all the scores.

Thus, if n is the number of scores, we can write the formula for the mean as

$$\bar{x} = \frac{\Sigma x}{n}.$$

EXAMPLE 8 Find the mean of the following numbers: 12, 8, 7, 10, 6, 14, 7, 6, 12, 9.

Solution $$\bar{x} = \frac{\Sigma x}{10} = \frac{12 + 8 + 7 + 10 + 6 + 14 + 7 + 6 + 12 + 9}{10}$$

So $\bar{x} = 91/10 = 9.1$.

Note that the mean need not be one of the numbers (scores) given.   □

EXAMPLE 9   Find the mean of the following numbers: 2.1, 6.3, 7.1, 4.8, 3.2.

Solution
$$\bar{x} = \frac{\Sigma x}{5} = \frac{2.1 + 6.3 + 7.1 + 4.8 + 3.2}{5}$$

So $\bar{x} = 23.5/5 = 4.7$.   □

Any of the three measures of central tendency (mode, median, mean) may be referred to as an average. The measure of central tendency that should be used with data depends on the purpose for which the data were collected. The mode is the number that occurs with the greatest frequency. It is used if we want the most popular value. For example, the mode salary for a company is the salary that is received by most of the employees of the company. The median salary for the company is the salary that falls in the middle of the distribution. The mean salary is the arithmetic average of the salaries. It is quite possible that the mode, median, and mean salaries for a company will be different. Figure 9.6 illustrates

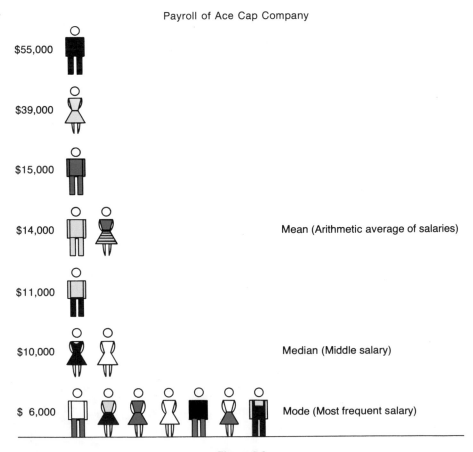

Payroll of Ace Cap Company

$55,000

$39,000

$15,000

$14,000   Mean (Arithmetic average of salaries)

$11,000

$10,000   Median (Middle salary)

$ 6,000   Mode (Most frequent salary)

Figure 9.6

how the mode, median and mean salaries might look for a company.

Which of the three measures represents the "average" salary? To say the average salary is $14,000 (the mean) helps conceal two things: the bosses' (or owners') very large salaries ($55,000 and $39,000), and the laborers' very small salaries ($6000). The mode tells us more: The most common salary in this company is $6000. The median gives us more information about these salaries than any other single figure. It tells us that if the salaries are ranked from lowest to highest, then the salary that lies in the middle is $10,000.

Because any of the three measures may be referred to as the average of a set of data, we must be careful to avoid being mislead. The owner of the Ace Cap Company will probably state that the average income for his company is $14,000, because it makes it appear that he pays high salaries. The local union president will likely claim that the mode ($6000) is the "average" salary. Advertising agencies may also make use of an "average" that will make their product appear in the best light. We run the danger of being mislead if we do not know which average is being cited.

One reason that we may be misled concerning these three measures is that they frequently fall very close to each other, as we shall see in more detail later. Also, since the mean is the most frequently used, we tend to associate it with the word average. In fact the mean can be extremely useful if we also have information about how the data vary about the mean. We will discuss measures of variation about the mean in Section 9.3.

Exercise 9.2

Find the modes of the following sets of scores.

1. 3, 4, 3, 2, 2, 3, 5, 7, 6, 2, 3
2. 5, 8, 10, 12, 5, 4, 6, 3, 5
3. 14, 17, 13, 16, 15, 12, 13, 12, 13
4. 38, 37, 36, 32, 34, 32, 33, 37, 31
5. 22, 23, 25, 26, 28, 32, 12

Find the modes of the scores shown in the following histograms.

6.

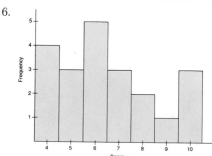

7.

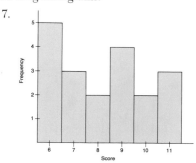

8.

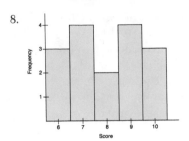

9.

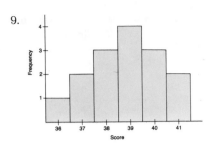

10.

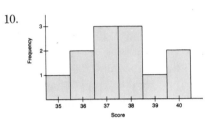

Find the medians of the following sets of scores.

11. 1, 3, 6, 7, 5
12. 2, 1, 3, 4, 2, 1, 2
13. 4, 7, 9, 18, 36, 14, 12
14. 1, 0, 2, 1, 1, 0, 2, 14, 37
15. 6, 7, 8, 4, 3, 6, 8, 2, 1
16. 2, 3, 4, 2, 8, 6, 2, 3
17. 2, 12, 17, 5, 8, 9, 10, 4
18. 1, 3, 2, 4, 4, 9, 10, 12
19. 2, 10, 6, 8, 13, 1, 4, 6
20. 1, 2, 4, 3, 6, 5, 10, 9, 13, 17, 46, 0

Find the mean of the following sets of numbers.

21. 3, 5, 7, 1, 2, 6, 8, 0
22. 9, 10, 8, 7, 5, 13, 11
23. 13, 14, 15, 16, 17, 12, 11

Find the mode, median, and mean of the following scores.

24. 5, 7, 7, 7, 9, 12, 4
25. 3, 2, 1, 6, 8, 12, 14, 2
26. 5, 8, 7, 6, 1, 1, 31
27. 14, 17, 20, 31, 17, 42
28. 3.2, 3.2, 3.5, 3.7, 3.4
29. 2.8, 6.4, 5.3, 5.3, 6.8
30. 1.14, 2.28, 7.58, 6.32, 5.17

APPLICATIONS   31. Suppose a company has 10 employees, 1 earning $80,000, 1 earning $60,000, 2 earning $30,000, 1 earning $20,000, and 5 earning $16,000.
(a) What is the mean salary for the company?

(b) What is the median salary?

(c) What is the mode of the salaries?

32. A taxi company tests a new brand of tires by putting a set of four on each of three taxis. The following table indicates the number of miles the tires lasted. What is the mean number of miles the tires lasted?

Number of Miles	Number of Tires
15,000	4
16,000	2
17,000	3
18,000	2
19,000	1

Suppose you live in a neighborhood with a few expensive homes and many modest homes.

33. If you wanted to impress people with the neighborhood where you lived, which measure would you give as the "average" property value?

34. Which "average" would you cite to the property tax committee if you wanted to convince them that property values aren't very high in your neighborhood?

35. What measure of central tendency would give the most representative "average" property value for your neighborhood?

9.3 Measures of Variation

Objectives   ■ To find the range of a set of data
               ■ To find the variance and standard deviation

Although the mean of a set of data is useful in locating the center of the distribution of the data, it doesn't tell us as much about the distribution as we might think at first. For example, a basketball coach will not be satisfied knowing the mean height of an opposing team. If the mean height of the opposing team is 6 ft, that could mean that every player is 6 ft tall or it could mean that one player is 6 ft tall, two players are 5 ft tall, and two players are 7 ft tall. These two possible teams are quite different. The difference in the distribution of the heights of these teams is not the mean height, but how the heights *vary* from the mean.

One measure of how a distribution varies is the range of the distribution.

> The **range** of a set of numbers is the difference between the largest and smallest numbers in the set.

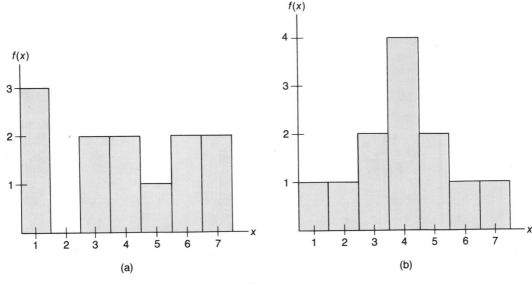

Figure 9.7

Consider the following set of heights of a basketball team, in inches: 69, 70, 75, 69, 73, 78, 74, 73, 78, 71. The range of this set of heights is 78 inches − 69 inches = 9 inches.

Note that the range of this set of heights is determined by only two numbers, and does not give any information about how the other heights vary.

We turn to another measure of variation, called standard deviation. The **standard deviation** is a measure of the concentration of the scores about their mean. The smaller the standard deviation, the closer the scores lie to the mean. For example, the histograms in Figure 9.7 describe two sets of data with the same means and the same ranges. From looking at the histograms we see that more of the data are concentrated about the mean $\bar{x} = 4$ in Figure 9.7(b) than in Figure 9.7(a). We will see that the standard deviation is smaller for the data in 9.7(b) than Figure 9.7(a).

The standard deviation for sample data is found using the following procedure.

PROCEDURE	EXAMPLE
To find the standard deviation of a set of scores:	Find the standard deviation of the scores 4, 6, 8, 9, 3.
1. Find the mean of the scores.	1. $\bar{x} = \dfrac{30}{5} = 6$
2. Calculate the deviation of the scores from the mean by subtracting the mean from each score.	2. $4 - 6 = -2$, $6 - 6 = 0$, $8 - 6 = 2$, $9 - 6 = 3$, $3 - 6 = -3$

3. Square each of these deviations, and add them.

3. $\Sigma(x - \bar{x})^2 = (-2)^2 + 0^2 + 2^2 + 3^2 + (-3)^2$
$= 4 + 0 + 4 + 9 + 9 = 26$

4. Divide $\Sigma(x - \bar{x})^2$ (from step 3) by $n - 1$, where n is the number of scores. This number is called the **variance** of the scores and is denoted by s^2.

4. $\dfrac{\Sigma(x - \bar{x})^2}{n - 1} = \dfrac{26}{4} = 6.5$, so $s^2 = 6.5$.

5. Take the square root of s^2 (from step 4). This is the **standard deviation**, denoted by s.

5. $s = \sqrt{6.5} = 2.55$.

EXAMPLE 1   Find the mean, variance, and standard deviation of the following: 13, 15, 18, 16, 14, 17, 19.

Solution

1. $\bar{x} = \dfrac{\Sigma x}{n} = \dfrac{112}{7} = 16$

2. $13 - 16 = -3$, $15 - 16 = -1$, $18 - 16 = 2$, $16 - 16 = 0$, $14 - 16 = -2$, $17 - 16 = 1$, $19 - 16 = 3$

3. $\Sigma(x - \bar{x})^2 = 9 + 1 + 4 + 4 + 1 + 9 = 28$

4. $s^2 = \dfrac{\Sigma(x - \bar{x})^2}{n - 1} = \dfrac{28}{6} = 4.67$

5. $s = \sqrt{\dfrac{\Sigma(x - \bar{x})^2}{n - 1}} = \sqrt{4.67} = 2.16$

Thus the mean is 16, the variance is 4.67, and the standard deviation is 2.16.

□

EXAMPLE 2   Figure 9.7(a) is the histogram for the set of data 1, 1, 1, 3, 3, 4, 4, 5, 6, 6, 7, 7. Figure 9.7(b) is the histogram for the data 1, 2, 3, 3, 4, 4, 4, 4, 5, 5, 6, 7. Both sets of data have a range of 6 and a mean of 4. Find their standard deviations.

Solution   For Figure 9.7(a),

$$\Sigma(x - \bar{x})^2 = (-3)^2 + (-3)^2 + (-3)^2 + (-1)^2 + (-1)^2$$
$$+ 0^2 + 0^2 + 1^2 + 2^2 + 2^2 + 3^2 + 3^2$$
$$= 9 + 9 + 9 + 1 + 1 + 0 + 0 + 1 + 4$$
$$+ 4 + 9 + 9 = 56$$
$$s^2 = \frac{\Sigma(x - \bar{x})^2}{n - 1} = \frac{56}{11} = 5.0909$$
$$s = \sqrt{s^2} = \sqrt{5.0909} = 2.26$$

For Figure 9.7(b),

$$\Sigma(x - \bar{x})^2 = (-3)^2 + (-2)^2 + (-1)^2 + (-1)^2$$
$$+ 0^2 + 0^2 + 0^2 + 0^2 + 1^2 + 1^2 + 2^2 + 3^2$$
$$= 9 + 4 + 1 + 1 + 0 + 0 + 0 + 0 + 1$$
$$+ 1 + 4 + 9 = 30$$

$$s^2 = \frac{30}{11} = 2.7273$$

$$s = \sqrt{\frac{30}{11}} = 1.65 \qquad \square$$

When a large number of scores is available, the data are usually presented in a frequency table rather than in a listing of the scores. We can also use the frequencies the scores occur to compute the mean and standard deviation, using the formulas

$$\bar{x} = \frac{\Sigma x_i \cdot f(x_i)}{n} \qquad \text{and} \qquad s = \sqrt{\frac{\Sigma(x_i - \bar{x})^2 \cdot f(x_i)}{n - 1}},$$

where $f(x_i)$ represents the frequency of the ith score.

EXAMPLE 3   Suppose the IQ scores of 20 people working for a company are measured and given by the following table. Find the mean and standard deviation of the IQ for this group.

x_i	$f(x_i)$
98	3
105	7
110	2
115	2
120	2
121	1
125	1
130	1
145	1

Solution

$$\bar{x} = \frac{98(3) + 105(7) + 110(2) + 115(2) + 120(2) + 121(1) + 125(1) + 130(1) + 145(1)}{20}$$

$$= 112$$

$$s^2 = \frac{(-14)^2(3) + (-7)^2(7) + (-2)^2(2) + (3)^2(2) + 8^2(2) + 9^2(1) + 13^2(1) + 18^2(1) + 33^2(1)}{19}$$

$$= 144.6316$$

$$s = \sqrt{144.6316} = 12.03 \qquad \square$$

Exercise 9.3

Find the mean, variance, and standard deviation of the following sets of data.
1. 5, 7, 1, 3, 0, 8, 6, 2
2. 7, 13, 5, 11, 8, 10, 9
3. 11, 12, 13, 14, 15, 16, 17
4. 4, 3, 6, 7, 8, 9, 12
5. 1, 2, 2, 3, 6, 8, 12, 14
6. 3.1, 3.2, 3.4, 3.6, 3.7
7. 8, 3, 5, 6, 8, 10, 13, 11
8. 2, 3, 5, 6, 8, 4, 2, 2

APPLICATIONS

9. A new car with a $9000 list price can be bought for different prices from different dealers. In one city the car can be bought for $8200 from 2 dealers, $8000 from 1 dealer, $7800 from 3 dealers, $7600 from 2 dealers, and $7500 from 2 dealers. What is the mean and standard deviation of the car prices?

10. The birth weights (in kilograms) of 160 children are given in the following table. Find the mean and standard deviation of the weights.

Weights (kg)	Frequency
2.0	4
2.3	12
2.6	20
2.9	26
3.2	20
3.5	26
3.8	20
4.1	16
4.4	10
4.7	6

11. The following table gives the number of games a baseball team had x hits in a baseball game. Find the mean number of hits they had per game, and the standard deviation.

x	$f(x)$
2	2
3	4
4	0
6	7
7	2
8	3
12	2

12. The fish commission recorded the weights (in pounds) of the fish caught in a lake. Find the mean and standard deviation of these weights, given in the table.

x	$f(x)$
1	3
2	3
3	5
4	2
5	2
6	3
10	2

9.4 Binomial Trials

Objective   ■ To solve probability problems related to binomial experiments

Suppose you have a coin that is biased so that when the coin is tossed the probability of getting a head is 2/3 and the probability of getting a tail is 1/3. What is the probability of tossing 2 heads in 3 tosses of this coin?

If the question were, What is the probability that the first two tosses will be heads and the third will be tails?, the answer would be

$$\mathrm{Pr(HHT)} = \frac{2}{3} \cdot \frac{2}{3} \cdot \frac{1}{3} = \frac{4}{27}.$$

However, the original question did not specify the order, so we must consider other orders that will give us 2 heads and 1 tail. We can use a tree to find all the possibilities (see Figure 9.8). We can see that there are 3 paths through the tree, which correspond to 2 heads and 1 tail in 3 tosses. Since the probability for each successful path is 4/27,

$$\mathrm{Pr(2\ H's\ and\ 1\ T)} = 3 \cdot \frac{4}{27} = \frac{4}{9}.$$

In this problem we can find the probability of 2 heads in 3 tosses by finding the probability for any one path of the tree (like HHT) and then multiplying that probability by the number of paths that result in 2 heads. We can also determine how many ways 2 heads and 1 tail can result by considering the 3 blanks below:

_____   _____   _____

The number of ways we can pick 2 blanks (for the 2 heads) from the 3 blanks will be equivalent to the number of paths that result in 2 heads. But the number of

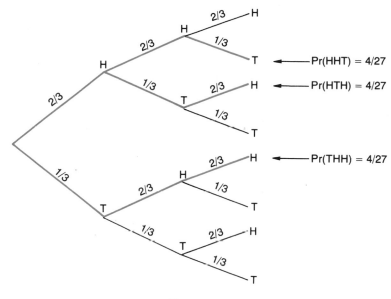

Figure 9.8

ways we can select 2 blanks from the 3 blanks is $_3C_2 = \binom{3}{2}$. Thus the probability of 2 heads resulting in 3 tosses is

$$\Pr(2\text{ H's and }1\text{ T}) = \binom{3}{2}\frac{2}{3}\cdot\frac{2}{3}\cdot\frac{1}{3} = \binom{3}{2}\left(\frac{2}{3}\right)^2\left(\frac{1}{3}\right)^1 = \frac{4}{9}.$$

The experiment discussed above (tossing a coin 3 times) is an example of a general class of experiments called **binomial probability experiments.**[°] A binomial probability experiment satisfies the following properties:

1. There are n repeated trials of the experiment.
2. Each trial results in one of two outcomes, with one denoted success (S) and the other failure (F).
3. The trials are independent, with the probability of success p the same for every trial. The probability of failure is $q = 1 - p$ for every trial.
4. The probability of x successes in n trials is $\Pr(x) = \binom{n}{x}p^x q^{n-x}$. $\Pr(x)$ is called a **binomial probability.**

EXAMPLE 1   If a die is rolled 4 times and the number of times a 6 results is recorded,
(a) is the experiment a binomial experiment?
(b) what is the probability that three 6's will result?

[°] These experiments are also called Bernoulli experiments, or Bernoulli trials, after the eighteenth-century mathematician Jacob Bernoulli.

Solution (a) Yes. There are 4 trials, resulting in success (a 6) or failure (to get a 6). The result of each roll is independent of previous rolls; the probability of success on each roll is 1/6.

(b) $\Pr(\text{three 6's}) = \binom{4}{3}\left(\frac{1}{6}\right)^3\left(\frac{5}{6}\right)^1 = \frac{4!}{1!3!}\left(\frac{1}{216}\right)\left(\frac{5}{6}\right) = \frac{5}{324}$ □

EXAMPLE 2 Suppose it has been determined that any child born in a specific area (near a chemical dump) will have a birth defect with probability .1. If 5 children are born during a given month,
(a) what is the probability that 2 of them will have a birth defect?
(b) what is the probability of that *at least* 2 of them will have a birth defect?

Solution (a) Note that we may consider a child having a birth defect as a success for this problem even though it is certainly not true in reality. Each of the 5 births is independent with probability of success $p = .1$ and probability of failure $q = .9$. Therefore the experiment is a binomial experiment, and

$$\Pr(2) = \binom{5}{2}(.1)^2(.9)^3$$

$$= \frac{5!}{3!2!}(.01)(.729)$$

$$= .0729.$$

(b) The probability of at least 2 of the children having a birth defect is

$$\Pr(2) + \Pr(3) + \Pr(4) + \Pr(5) = \binom{5}{2}(.1)^2(.9)^3 + \binom{5}{3}(.1)^3(.9)^2$$

$$+ \binom{5}{4}(.1)^4(.9)^1 + \binom{5}{5}(.1)^5(.9)^0$$

$$= .0729 + .0081 + .00045 + .00001$$

$$= .08146.$$ □

EXAMPLE 3 A manufacturer of motorcycle parts guarantees that a box of parts (24) will contain at most one defective part. If the records show that the manufacturer's machines produce 1% defective parts, what is the probability that a box of parts will satisfy the guarantee?

Solution The problem is a binomial experiment problem with $n = 24$ and (considering getting a defective part as a success) $p = .01$. Then the probability the manufacturer will have no more than 1 defective part is

$$\Pr(x \leq 1) = \Pr(0) + \Pr(1) = \binom{24}{0}(.01)^0(.99)^{24} + \binom{24}{1}(.01)^1(.99)^{23}$$

$$= 1(1)(.7857) + 24(.01)(.7936) = .9762.$$ □

Exercise 9.4

1. Suppose a fair coin is tossed 6 times. What is the probability that
   (a) 6 heads will occur?   (b) 3 heads will occur?   (c) 2 heads will occur?

2. If a fair die is rolled 3 times, what is the probability that
   (a) a 5 will result 2 times out of the 3 rolls?
   (b) an odd number will result 2 times?
   (c) a number divisible by 3 will occur 3 times?

3. A bag contains 6 red balls and 4 black balls. If we draw 5 balls, with each one replaced before the next is drawn, what is the probability that
   (a) 2 balls drawn are red?
   (b) at least 2 balls drawn are red?

4. Suppose a pair of dice is thrown 4 times. What is the probability that a sum of 9 occurs exactly 2 times?

APPLICATIONS

5. If the probability that a certain couple will have a blue-eyed child is 1/4 and they have 4 children, what is the probability that
   (a) 1 of their children has blue eyes?
   (b) 2 of their children have blue eyes?
   (c) none of their children has blue eyes?

6. Suppose that 10% of the patients having a certain disease die from it. If 5 patients have the disease, what is the probability that
   (a) exactly 2 patients will die from it?
   (b) no patients will die from it?
   (c) no more than 2 patients will die from it?

7. If the ratio of boys born to girls born is 105 to 100, and if 6 children are born in a certain hospital in a day, what is the probability that 4 of them are boys?

8. It has been determined empirically that the probability that a given cell will survive for a given period of time is .4. Find the probability that 3 out of 6 of these cells will survive for this period of time?

9. If records indicate that 4 houses out of 1000 are expected to be damaged by fire in any year, what is the probability that a woman owning 10 houses will have fire damage in 2 of them in a year?

10. Suppose 4 rats are placed in a T-maze in which they must turn right or left. If each rat makes a choice by chance, what is the probability that 2 of the rats will turn to the right?

9.5 The Binomial Distribution

Objectives
- To find the mean and standard deviation of a binomial distribution
- To graph a binomial distribution
- To expand a binomial to a power, using the binomial formula

If x is a variable that assumes the values $0, 1, 2, \ldots, r, \ldots, n$ with probabilities $\binom{n}{0}p^0q^n$, $\binom{n}{1}p^1q^{n-1}$, $\binom{n}{2}p^2q^{n-2}, \ldots, \binom{n}{r}p^rq^{n-r}, \ldots, \binom{n}{n}p^nq^0$, respectively, then x is called a **binomial variable.**

The values of x correspond to the number of successes in the binomial trials and the probabilities are calculated using the methods of the previous section.

> The values of x and their corresponding probabilities described above form the **binomial probability distribution.**

For example, suppose a fair coin is tossed 6 times and x represents the number of heads. Then Table 9.3 gives all possible outcomes and their probabilities; that is, Table 9.3 gives the theoretical binomial distribution for the experiment.

Table 9.3

x	0	1	2	3	4	5	6
$\Pr(x)$	$\binom{6}{0}\left(\frac{1}{2}\right)^0\left(\frac{1}{2}\right)^6$ $=\frac{1}{64}$	$\binom{6}{1}\left(\frac{1}{2}\right)^1\left(\frac{1}{2}\right)^5$ $=\frac{6}{64}$	$\binom{6}{2}\left(\frac{1}{2}\right)^2\left(\frac{1}{2}\right)^4$ $=\frac{15}{64}$	$\binom{6}{3}\left(\frac{1}{2}\right)^3\left(\frac{1}{2}\right)^3$ $=\frac{20}{64}$	$\binom{6}{4}\left(\frac{1}{2}\right)^4\left(\frac{1}{2}\right)^2$ $=\frac{15}{64}$	$\binom{6}{5}\left(\frac{1}{2}\right)^5\left(\frac{1}{2}\right)^1$ $=\frac{6}{64}$	$\binom{6}{6}\left(\frac{1}{2}\right)^6\left(\frac{1}{2}\right)^0$ $=\frac{1}{64}$

The expected value of the number of successes (expected value was discussed in Section 8.7) is given by

$$E(x) = 0 \cdot \frac{1}{64} + 1 \cdot \frac{6}{64} + 2 \cdot \frac{15}{64} + 3 \cdot \frac{20}{64} + 4 \cdot \frac{15}{64} + 5 \cdot \frac{6}{64} + 6 \cdot \frac{1}{64}$$

$$= \frac{192}{64} = 3.$$

This expected number of successes seems reasonable. If the probability of success is $1/2$, we would expect to succeed on half of the 6 trials. For any binomial distribution the expected number of successes is given by np, where n is the number of trials and p is the probability of success. Since the expected value of any probability distribution is defined as the mean of that distribution, we have the following.

> ***Mean of a Binomial Distribution***   The theoretical mean of any binomial distribution is
> $$\mu = np,$$
> where n is the number of trials in the corresponding binomial experiment and p is the probability of success on each trial.

The mean of a probability distribution is denoted by the Greek letter μ (mu) rather than $\bar{x}$, as it is for sample data.

A simple formula can also be developed for the standard deviation of a binomial distribution.

> *Standard* The standard deviation of a binomial distribution is
> *Deviation of a*
> *Binomial* $$\sigma = \sqrt{npq},$$
> *Distribution* where n is the number of trials, p is the probability of success on each trial, and $q = 1 - p$.

The Greek letter σ (sigma) is used to denote the standard deviation of a probability distribution. The standard deviation of the binomial distribution corresponding to the number of heads resulting when a coin is tossed 16 times is

$$\sigma = \sqrt{16 \cdot \frac{1}{2} \cdot \frac{1}{2}} = \sqrt{4} = 2.$$

EXAMPLE 1 A fair coin is tossed 4 times.
(a) Construct a table with each value of the binomial variable x, where x is the number of heads resulting, and the probability of each value of x
(b) Graph the distribution.
(c) Find the mean of this binomial distribution.
(d) Find the standard deviation of this distribution.

Solution (a)

x	$\Pr(x)$
0	$\binom{4}{0}\left(\frac{1}{2}\right)^{0}\left(\frac{1}{2}\right)^{4} = \frac{1}{16}$
1	$\binom{4}{1}\left(\frac{1}{2}\right)^{1}\left(\frac{1}{2}\right)^{3} = \frac{4}{16}$
2	$\binom{4}{2}\left(\frac{1}{2}\right)^{2}\left(\frac{1}{2}\right)^{2} = \frac{6}{16}$
3	$\binom{4}{3}\left(\frac{1}{2}\right)^{3}\left(\frac{1}{2}\right)^{1} = \frac{4}{16}$
4	$\binom{4}{4}\left(\frac{1}{2}\right)^{4}\left(\frac{1}{2}\right)^{0} = \frac{1}{16}$

(b)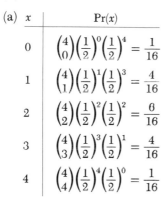

Figure 9.9

(c) The mean of this distribution is

$$\mu = np = 4 \cdot \frac{1}{2} = 2.$$

(d) The standard deviation of this binomial distribution is

$$\sigma = \sqrt{npq} = \sqrt{4 \cdot \frac{1}{2} \cdot \frac{1}{2}} = 1. \qquad \square$$

The binomial probability distribution is closely related to the powers of a binomial. For example, if a binomial experiment has 3 trials with probability of

Table 9.4

x	3	2	1	0
Pr(x)	$\binom{3}{3} p^3 q^0 = p^3$	$\binom{3}{2} p^2 q = 3p^2 q$	$\binom{3}{1} pq^2 = 3pq^2$	$\binom{3}{0} p^0 q^3 = q^3$

success p on each trial, then the probability distribution is given by Table 9.4. Now consider the expansion of $(p + q)^3$, which we used earlier.

$$(p + q)^3 = p^3 + 3p^2 q + 3pq^2 + q^3$$

The formula that we can use to expand a binomial $(a + b)$ to any power n is

Binomial Formula
$$(a + b)^n = \binom{n}{n} a^n + \binom{n}{n-1} a^{n-1}b + \binom{n}{n-2} a^{n-2}b^2 + \cdots$$
$$+ \binom{n}{2} a^2 b^{n-2} + \binom{n}{1} ab^{n-1} + \binom{n}{0} b^n$$

EXAMPLE 2   Expand $(x + y)^4$.

Solution
$$(x + y)^4 = \binom{4}{4} x^4 + \binom{4}{3} x^3 y + \binom{4}{2} x^2 y^2 + \binom{4}{1} xy^3 + \binom{4}{0} y^4$$
$$= x^4 + 4x^3 y + 6x^2 y^2 + 4xy^3 + y^4$$

Note that the coefficients in this expansion are related to the probabilities in Example 1.   □

EXAMPLE 3   (a) If a die is rolled 5 times, what is the probability that exactly 2 faces with 4 on them will result?
(b) What is the coefficient of $p^2 q^3$ in $(p + q)^5$?

Solution   (a) From Section 9.4,
$$\text{Pr(two 4's)} = \binom{5}{2}\left(\frac{1}{6}\right)^2\left(\frac{5}{6}\right)^3 = 10 \cdot \frac{1}{36} \cdot \frac{125}{216} = \frac{625}{3888}.$$

(b) By the binomial formula the coefficient of $p^2 q^3$ is $\binom{5}{2} = 10$.   □

Exercise 9.5

1. A die is rolled 3 times. If success is rolling a 5,
   (a) construct the binomial distribution for this experiment.
   (b) find the mean of this distribution.
   (c) find the standard deviation of this distribution.

2. A die is rolled 3 times. If success is rolling a number divisible by 3,
   (a) construct the binomial distribution for this experiment.
   (b) write the mean of this distribution.
   (c) write the standard deviation of this distribution.
3. Suppose a pair of dice is thrown 12 times. How many times would we expect a sum of 7 to occur?
4. Suppose the probability that a certain coin will result in heads is 2/3 when it is tossed. If it is tossed 6 times, how many heads would we expect?
5. What is the coefficient of the term containing a^4b^2 in $(a + b)^6$?
6. (a) What is the coefficient of the term containing a^2b^4 in $(a + b)^6$?
   (b) Does $\binom{6}{4} = \binom{6}{2}$?
7. Expand $(a + b)^6$.   8. Expand $(x + y)^5$.   9. Expand $(x + h)^4$.
10. Write the general expression for $(x + h)^n$.

APPLICATIONS

11. Suppose that 10% of the patients having a certain disease will die from it.
    (a) If 100 people have the disease, how many would we expect to die from it?
    (b) What is the standard deviation of the number of deaths that could occur?

12. Suppose it has been determined that the probability that a rat injected with cancerous cells will live is .6. If 35 rats are injected, how many would be expected to die?

13. A candidate claims 60% of the people in his district will vote for him.
    (a) If his district contains 100,000 voters, how many votes does he expect to get from his district?
    (b) What is the standard deviation of the number of his votes?

14. In a family with 2 children, the probability that both children will be boys is approximately 1/4.
    (a) If 1200 families with two children are selected at random, how many of the families would we expect to have 2 boys?
    (b) What is the standard deviation for the number of families with 2 boys?

15. If the number of votes the candidate in problem 13 gets is 2 standard deviations below what he expected, how many votes did he get (approximately)?

16. If the sample drawn in problem 14 had 315 families with two boys in it, how many standard deviations did the sample data lie above the mean?

9.6 The Normal Distribution

Objectives   ■ To convert normal distribution scores to z-scores
              ■ To find the probability that normally distributed scores lie in a certain interval

The binomial variables discussed in Section 9.5 could only assume the values 0, 1, 2, . . . , so a binomial probability distribution is called a *discrete probability distribution* and a binomial variable is called a *discrete random variable*. The binomial

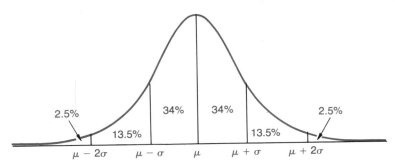

Figure 9.10

distribution is important, but it does not apply to many kinds of measurements. For example, the weights of people, the heights of trees, and the IQ scores of college students cannot be measured with whole numbers because each of them can assume any one of an infinite number of values on a measuring scale. These variables follow a distribution called the normal distribution, which is the most important probability distribution.

The **normal distribution** has the following properties:

1. Its graph is a bell-shaped curve like that of Figure 9.10. The graph is called the **normal curve.** It approaches the horizontal axis as it extends in both directions, but it never touches it.
2. The curve is symmetric about a vertical centerline. This centerline passes through the value that is the mean, the median, *and* the mode of the distribution. That is, the mean, median and mode are the same for a normal distribution. (That is why they are all called average.)
3. A normal distribution is completely determined when its mean μ and its standard deviation σ are known.
4. Sixty-eight percent of all scores lie within one standard deviation of the mean. Ninety-five percent of all scores lie within two standard deviations of the mean. Almost all scores will lie within three standard deviations of the mean.

EXAMPLE 1   If IQ scores follow a normal distribution with mean 100 and standard deviation 15, what percentage of the scores will be
(a) between 100 and 115?   (b) between 85 and 115?   (c) between 85 and 130?   (d) between 70 and 130?   (e) greater than 130?

Solution   Figure 9.11 is a graph of the distribution. We can find the percentages from this graph. (a) 34%, (b) 68%, (c) 81.5%, (d) 95%, (e) 2.5%.   □

The total area under the normal curve is 1. The area under the curve from value x_1 to value x_2 represents the percentage of the scores that lie between x_1 and x_2. Thus the *area* under the curve from x_1 to x_2 *represents* the *probability* that

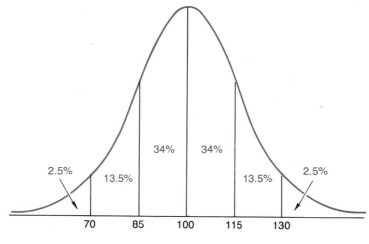

Figure 9.11

a score chosen at random will lie between x_1 and x_2. Thus, in Example 1, the probability that a score chosen at random would lie between 85 and 115 is .68, and the probability that it would lie between 70 and 130 is .95.

We have seen that 34% of the scores lie between 100 and 115 in the normal distribution graph in Figure 9.11. As we have mentioned, this also means that the area under the curve from $x = 100$ to $x = 115$ is .34, and that the probability that a score chosen at random from this normal population lies between 100 and 115 is .34. We can write this as

$$\Pr(100 \le x \le 115) = .34.$$

Because the probability of obtaining a score from a normal distribution is always related to how many standard deviations the score is away from the mean, it is desirable to convert all scores from a normal distribution to **standard scores**, or z-scores. The z-score for any score x is found by determining how many standard deviations x is from the mean μ. This is done using the formula

$$z = \frac{x - \mu}{\sigma}.$$

For example, the normal distribution of IQ scores (graphed in Figure 9.11) has mean $\mu = 100$ and standard deviation $\sigma = 15$. Thus the z-score for 115 is

$$z = \frac{115 - 100}{15} = 1.$$

A z-score of 1 indicates that 115 is 1 standard deviation above the mean.

If we convert all the scores from any normal distribution to z-scores, the distribution of z-scores will always be a normal distribution with mean 0 and standard deviation 1. This distribution is called the **standard normal distribution.**

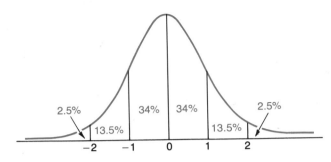

Figure 9.12

Figure 9.12 shows the graph of the standard normal distribution. The total area under the curve is 1, with .5 on either side of the mean 0.

By comparing Figure 9.12 with Figure 9.10, we see that each unit from 0 in the standard normal distribution corresponds to one standard deviation from the mean of the normal distribution.

We can use a table to more accurately determine the area under the standard normal curve between two z-scores. Table III in the Appendix gives the area under the standard normal curve from $z = 0$ to $z = z_0$, for values of z_0 from 0 to 3. As with the normal curve, the area under the curve from $z = 0$ to $z = z_0$ is the probability that a z-score lies between 0 and z_0.

EXAMPLE 2   (a) Find the area under the standard normal curve from $z = 0$ to $z = 1.50$.
(b) Find $\Pr(0 \leq z \leq 1.50)$.

Solution   (a) Looking in the column headed by z in Table III, we see 1.50. Across from the 1.50 in the column headed by A is .4332. Thus the area under the standard normal curve between $z = 0$ and $z = 1.50$ is .4332.
(b) Because the area under the curve from 0 to 1.50 equals the probability z lies between 0 and 1.50,

$$\Pr(0 \leq z \leq 1.50) = .4332. \qquad \square$$

EXAMPLE 3   (a) Find $\Pr(0 \leq z \leq 2)$.   (b) Find $\Pr(-1 \leq z \leq 0)$.

Solution   (a) $\Pr(0 \leq z \leq 2)$ is found in Table III by looking at the A corresponding to $z = 2$. $\Pr(0 \leq z \leq 2) = .4772$.
(b) As Figure 9.13 shows, the area we seek is to the left of the mean (because $z_0 = -1$). But because the normal curve is symmetric, the area between $z = -1$ and $z = 0$ is identical to the area between $z = 0$ and $z = 1$. Thus, using $z = 1$ in Table III, we get $\Pr(-1 \leq z \leq 0) = .3413$. Note that the area will always be positive, even if the z-score is negative. $\qquad \square$

EXAMPLE 4   (a) Find $\Pr(-1 \leq z \leq 2)$.   (b) Find $\Pr(1 \leq z \leq 2)$.

Solution   (a) The graph showing the area is in Figure 9.14. Table III only gives areas from 0 on, so we must do the problem in two parts. As we have seen in Example 3,

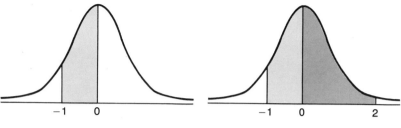

Figure 9.13   Figure 9.14

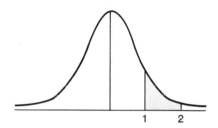

Figure 9.15

$$\Pr(-1 \leq z \leq 0) = .3413 \text{ and } \Pr(0 \leq z \leq 2) = .4772.$$

From the graph we see the area from $z = -1$ to $z = 2$ is the *sum* of the areas from -1 to 0 and from 0 to 2. Thus $\Pr(-1 \leq z \leq 2) = .3413 + .4772 = .8185$.

(b) The graph showing the area between $z = 1$ and $z = 2$ is in Figure 9.15. This area is the area from $z = 0$ to $z = 2$ minus the area from $z = 0$ to $z = 1$. Thus

$$\Pr(1 \leq z \leq 2) = \Pr(0 \leq z \leq 2) - \Pr(0 \leq z \leq 1)$$
$$= .4772 - .3413 = .1359. \qquad \square$$

In general, if we seek the area between two z-scores, we find the areas from 0 to each of the z-scores, and then
(a) add the areas if the two z-scores have opposite signs.
(b) subtract the areas if the two z-scores have the same signs.

EXAMPLE 5   If the mean height of a population of students is $\mu = 68$ in. with standard deviation $\sigma = 3$ in., what is the probability that a person chosen at random from the population
(a) will be between 68 in. and 74 in. tall?
(b) will be between 65 in. and 74 in. tall?

Solution   (a) To find $\Pr(68 \leq x \leq 74)$, we convert 68 and 74 to z-scores.

$$\text{For 68:} \quad z = \frac{68 - 68}{3} = 0. \qquad \text{For 74:} \quad z = \frac{74 - 68}{3} = 2.$$

Thus $\Pr(68 \le x \le 74) = \Pr(0 \le z \le 2) = .4772.$

(b) The z-score for 65 is

$$z = \frac{65 - 68}{3} = -1,$$

and the z-score for 74 is 2. Thus $\Pr(65 \le x \le 74) = \Pr(-1 \le z \le 2)$, and, as we have seen in Example 4(a), $\Pr(-1 \le z \le 2) = .8185.$ □

Exercise 9.6 If a population of scores is normally distributed with mean $\mu = 16$ and $\sigma = 3$, how many standard deviations from the mean is each of the following scores?

1. 22   2. 25
3. 13   4. 15

Use Table III in the Appendix to find the probability that a z-score from the standard normal distribution will lie within each of the following intervals.

5. 0 and 1.8   6. 0 and 2.4
7. −1.8 and 0   8. −3 and 0
9. −1.5 and 2.1   10. −1.25 and 3
11. −1.9 and −1.1   12. −2.45 and −1.45
13. 2.1 and 3.0   14. 1.85 and 2.85

If a population of scores is normally distributed with $\mu = 20$ and $\sigma = 5$, use the standard normal distribution to find the following.

15. $\Pr(20 \le x \le 22.5)$ 16. $\Pr(20 \le x \le 21.25)$
17. $\Pr(20 \le x \le 26.25)$ 18. $\Pr(20 \le x \le 27.75)$
19. $\Pr(13.75 \le x \le 20)$ 20. $\Pr(18.5 \le x \le 20)$
21. $\Pr(12.25 \le x \le 21.25)$ 22. $\Pr(18.5 \le x \le 27.75)$
23. $\Pr(13.75 \le x \le 18.75)$ 24. $\Pr(21.25 \le x \le 25)$

APPLICATIONS 25. If the fish commission states that the mean length of all fish in Spring Run is $\mu = 15$ cm, with a standard deviation of $\sigma = 4$ cm, what is the probability that a fish caught in Spring Run will
(a) be between 15 cm and 19 cm long?
(b) be between 11 cm and 15 cm long?
(c) be between 11 cm and 19 cm long?
(d) be between 7 cm and 23 cm long?

26. A quart of milk contains a mean of 39 grams of butterfat, with a standard deviation of 2 grams. What is the probability that a quart of milk will contain more than the following:
(a) 43 grams?
(b) 35 grams?

27. The heights of a certain species of plant are normally distributed with a mean $\mu = 20$ cm and $\sigma = 4$ cm. What is the probability that a plant chosen at random will lie between 10 cm and 30 cm?

28. The mean duration of the mating call of a population of tree toads is 189 msec with a standard deviation of 32 msec.

(a) What proportion of these calls would be expected to last between 157 msec and 221 msec?

(b) What proportion of these calls would be expected to last between 200 msec and 253 msec?

9.7 Samples from Normal Populations; Testing Hypotheses

Objectives
- To find the mean and standard deviation of the distribution of sample means where the samples are drawn from a normal population
- To test hypotheses involving samples drawn from normal populations

If all possible samples of size n are drawn from a normal population that has mean μ and standard deviation σ, then the distribution of the means of the samples $\bar{x}$ will also be normally distributed with mean μ and standard deviation $\sigma/\sqrt{n}$.

That is, the distribution of sample means will have the same mean but a smaller standard deviation. We denote the standard deviation of the sample means by $\sigma_{\bar{x}}$.

EXAMPLE 1   The height of a certain type of plant is normally distributed with mean $\mu = 30$ cm and standard deviation $\sigma = 5$ cm. If all possible samples of size $n = 100$ are drawn from this population of plants, what are the mean and standard deviation of the distribution of the means of these samples?

Solution   The mean is $\mu = 30$ cm. The standard deviation is $\sigma_{\bar{x}} = 5/\sqrt{100} = 0.5$ cm (see Figure 9.16).   □

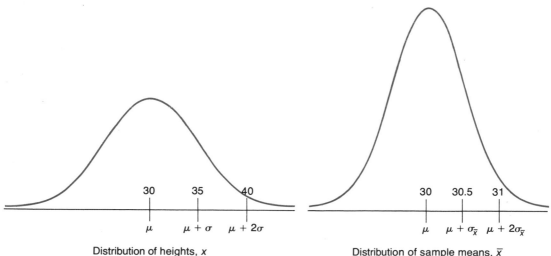

| 30 | 35 | 40 |
| μ | $\mu + \sigma$ | $\mu + 2\sigma$ |

Distribution of heights, x

| 30 | 30.5 | 31 |
| μ | $\mu + \sigma_{\bar{x}}$ | $\mu + 2\sigma_{\bar{x}}$ |

Distribution of sample means, $\bar{x}$

Figure 9.16

Since the distribution of sample means is normally distributed, it follows that 95% of all sample means will lie within 2 standard deviations of the mean. That is, 95% of all $\bar{x}$'s will lie between $\mu - 2\sigma_{\bar{x}}$ and $\mu + 2\sigma_{\bar{x}}$. Thus in Example 1, 95% of all sample means lie between 29 and 31 cm.

The standard deviation of the distribution of sample means is much smaller than that of the original population, because the sample means tend to average out the extreme scores in the population. Thus the sample means are more closely concentrated about the mean μ. (See Figure 9.16.)

EXAMPLE 2   In Example 1, what is the probability that a sample of 100 plants chosen at random will have an $\bar{x}$ that lies outside the interval from 29 cm to 31 cm?

Solution   Since 95% of all scores lie between 29 cm and 31 cm, the probability that $\bar{x}$ will lie outside the interval is $1 - .95 = .05$.

Thus if we had a sample of 100 plants whose mean height was greater than 31 cm, and we did not know if they were of the plant type discussed in Example 1 or not, we would be inclined to decide that they were not of that type.   □

Decisions about whether a random sample represents a desired population or not are a very important part of statistics, and are used every day in *quality control*. For example, suppose you buy a machine that converts tomatoes into tomato juice and squirts 20 oz of juice into cans. If the machine squirts more than 20 oz in each can, you will lose some of your profit; if the machine squirts less than 20 oz in each can, you may be accused of cheating your customers. How can you be reasonably sure your machine is working properly?

One way to test the machine would be to measure every can it produces. Another way would be to take a sample of, say, 100 cans. Suppose you do this and find a sample with $\bar{x} = 20.5$ oz. If you know that the amount squirted into the cans is normally distributed with a standard deviation of 2 oz, you can decide if obtaining a sample whose mean is $\bar{x} = 20.5$ is reasonable when the machine is working properly (that is, has a mean output of 20 oz).

If μ does equal 20 oz, then 95% of all sample means should lie within $\mu \pm 2\sigma_{\bar{x}}$; that is, between $20 - 2 \cdot 2/\sqrt{100}$ and $20 + 2 \cdot 2/\sqrt{100}$, or between 19.6 oz and 20.4 oz. Thus the probability that a sample mean $\bar{x}$ would be outside the interval from 19.6 to 20.4 is .05 *if* $\mu = 20$.

The mean of the sample is 20.5 oz, which lies outside the interval. The probability that this sample mean could occur from a population with a mean of 20 oz is so small that it is reasonable to conclude that the machine is not producing an average of 20 oz per can.

This is an example of a **statistical test,** which forms the basis for **inferential statistics.** An essential ingredient of a statistical test is the **null hypothesis,** which is the assumption or claim that is to be tested. The null hypothesis (denoted H_0) is *assumed* in a statistical test, so it cannot be proved; it can only be shown to be a reasonable or unreasonable assumption. An **alternative hypothesis** H_1 is stated in every statistical test; if the null hypothesis is *rejected* (that is, shown to be unreasonable), then the alternative hypothesis will be accepted as true.

In this example, the null hypothesis is that the machine is working properly, and the alternative hypothesis is that the machine is not working properly. Since the machine squirts 20 oz when it is working properly, the null hypothesis and its alternative may be stated as follows:

$$H_0: \mu = 20$$
$$H_1: \mu \neq 20$$

The test of the null hypothesis consists of deciding the conditions under which we will conclude that the null hypothesis is unreasonable and should be rejected in favor of the alternative hypothesis. In this example, we tested the data to see if the mean $\bar{x}$ of our sample was outside the region from $\mu - 2\sigma/\sqrt{n}$ to $\mu + 2\sigma/\sqrt{n}$ because the probability that this could happen when μ really equals 20 is .05 or less. We can summarize this statistical test as follows.

Statistical Test   The null hypothesis is $H_0: \mu = 20$. This is assumed and tested.
The alternative hypothesis is $H_1: \mu \neq 20$. This will be true if H_0 is rejected.

The test: Reject H_0 in favor of H_1 if the $\bar{x}$ from the sample lies outside the region from $\mu - 2\sigma/\sqrt{n}$ to $\mu + 2\sigma/\sqrt{n}$.
The data: $\bar{x} = 20.5$, $\sigma = 2$, $n = 100$

The work: $\mu - \dfrac{2\sigma}{\sqrt{n}} = 20 - 2 \cdot \dfrac{2}{\sqrt{100}} = 19.6$

$\mu + \dfrac{2\sigma}{\sqrt{n}} = 20 + 2 \cdot \dfrac{2}{\sqrt{100}} = 20.4$

The conclusion: $\bar{x} = 20.5$ lies outside the interval from 19.6 to 20.4, so we reject H_0 in favor of H_1 and conclude that μ is not 20 oz.

Note that it is possible for a machine averaging 20 oz per can to produce a sample of 100 cans with a sample mean of 20.5 oz, but the probability that it could happen is so small that we are willing to take the risk of being wrong. The test we used for this problem was designed so that the probability that we would reject the null hypothesis when it was true would be .05. In such a test we say the α-level is .05. Because we considered the possibility that the sample mean could lie outside 2 standard deviations on either side of the mean, we say this is a **two-tailed test.**

EXAMPLE 3   The fish commission claims that the average length of the fish in Spring Lake is $\mu = 15$ cm. The standard deviation of the lengths is $\sigma = 4$ cm and a sample of size 400 has a sample mean $\bar{x} = 14.7$ cm. Test the hypothesis $\mu = 15$ cm to see if their claim is accurate. Use a two-tailed test with an α-level of .05.

Solution H_0: $\mu = 15$ H_1: $\mu \neq 15$

Test: Reject H_0 in favor of H_1 if the $\bar{x}$ from the sample lies outside the region from $\mu - 2\sigma/\sqrt{n}$ to $\mu + 2\sigma/\sqrt{n}$.

Data: $\bar{x} = 14.7$, $\sigma = 4$, $n = 400$

Work: $\mu - \dfrac{2\sigma}{\sqrt{n}} = 15 - \dfrac{2(4)}{\sqrt{400}} = 14.6$ $\mu + \dfrac{2\sigma}{\sqrt{n}} = 15 + \dfrac{2(4)}{\sqrt{400}} = 15.4$

Conclusion: $\bar{x} = 14.7$ does not lie outside the interval from 14.6 to 15.4, so we cannot reject the claim. Thus we accept H_0.   □

It should be noted that the null and alternative hypotheses can have many different forms in inferential statistics, and the statistical tests differ for different forms of hypotheses. We leave the study of these tests to other courses.

Exercise 9.7

1. Samples of size 100 are drawn from a normal population with $\mu = 50$ and $\sigma = 10$.
   (a) Is the set of means of these samples normally distributed?
   (b) What is the mean of the distribution of sample means?
   (c) What is the standard deviation of the distribution of sample means?
2. Samples of size 49 are drawn from a normal population with $\mu = 80$ and $\sigma = 14$.
   (a) What is the mean of the distribution of sample means?
   (b) What is the standard deviation of the distribution of sample means?

APPLICATIONS

3. IQ scores are normally distributed with $\mu = 100$ and $\sigma = 15$. If samples of size 25 are drawn from the population at random,
   (a) what is the mean of the distribution of means of the samples?
   (b) what is the standard deviation of the distribution of means of the samples?
   (c) is it highly likely that a random sample would have a mean above 109?
4. If the mean height of a population of students is $\mu = 68$ in. with standard deviation $\sigma = 3$ in., what is the mean and standard deviation of the set of sample means of samples of size 100 that can be drawn from this population?
5. The Scholastic Aptitude Test (SAT) scores are normally distributed with a mean of 500 and a standard deviation of 100. What is the probability that a sample of 100 students
   (a) will have a mean score of between 480 and 520?
   (b) will have a mean score above 520?
   (c) will have a mean score outside the range from 480 to 520?

6. When a machine is working properly, it produces bolts that average $\mu = 20$ cm in length, with a standard deviation of $\sigma = 3$ cm. What is the probability that a sample of 9 bolts will have a mean between 18 cm and 22 cm?

7. Refer to problem 5. If a group of 100 students from a high school had a mean SAT score of 525, would you conclude these students were better than average?

8. If the machine in problem 6 is working properly, what is the probability that a sample of 9 bolts will be produced that has a sample mean less than 18 cm or greater than 22 cm?

9. Suppose a machine produces a large number of parts that must have a diameter very close to 3 cm, and that experience shows that the standard deviation is $\sigma = .5$ cm. If the mean varies too far from 3 cm, the machine will have to be repaired. To see if the machine is working properly, a sample of size 100 is measured and found to have mean $\bar{x} = 3.15$ cm. Test H_0: $\mu = 3$ cm against H_1: $\mu \neq 3$ cm, using $\alpha = .05$.

10. An automobile was designed to get 30 miles per gallon of gasoline. To test the production models, 36 cars were chosen at random and tested. The mean gasoline mileage was 27.5 miles per gallon, and the standard deviation was known to be $\sigma = 6$ miles per gallon. Use a two-tailed test with $\alpha = .05$ to determine if the cars are performing properly.

11. A firm decides to produce a new type of light bulb. It expects the bulbs to last $\mu = 1600$ hours. A sample of 100 bulbs is tested and found to have a mean $\bar{x} = 1580$. If the standard deviation is known to be $\sigma = 150$ hours, use a two-tailed test with $\alpha = .05$ to determine if 1600 hours is a reasonable estimate.

12. A packing machine is expected to pack $\mu = 25$ cartons per hour, with the number of cartons packed following the normal distribution. To check its efficiency, the number of cartons it packed per hour was recorded for 9 hours. The mean number of cartons packed per hour was $\bar{x} = 24$. Use $\sigma = 2$ and $\alpha = .05$ to determine if the machine is performing differently from its expectations. (Use a two-tailed test.)

9.8 Linear Regression and Correlation

Objectives
- To write the equation of the line that is the best fit for a set of data points
- To compute the correlation coefficient for a set of data points

We have seen in Section 2.4 that it is possible to write the equation of a straight line if we have two points on the line. Business firms frequently like to treat demand functions as though they are linear, even when they are not exactly linear. They do this because linear functions are much easier to handle than other functions. If a firm has more than two points describing the demand for its product, it is likely that the points will not all lie on the same straight line. However, by using a technique called **linear regression** the firm can determine the "best line" that fits these points.

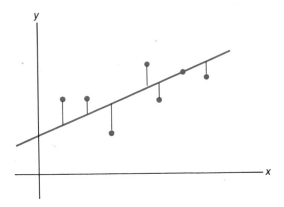

Figure 9.17

Suppose we have the points shown in Figure 9.17. We seek the line that is the "best fit" for the points. We can eyeball a line that appears to lie along the points.

Corresponding to each point (x_1, y_1) that we know, we can find a point $(x_1, \widehat{y}_1)$ on the line. If the line we have is a good fit for the points, the differences between the y values of the given points and the corresponding $\widehat{y}$ values on the line should be small. The line shown is the best line for the points only if the sum of the squares of these differences is a minimum.° In summation notation (sigma notation), we say the line is the best fit for the n points if

$$\sum_{i=1}^{n} (y_i - \widehat{y}_i)^2$$

is a minimum, where $\widehat{y}_i$ is the y-coordinate of the point $(x_i, \widehat{y}_i)$ *on* the line and y_i is the y-coordinate of the given data point (x_i, y_i).

Because we can write the equation of a line as $y = mx + b$, we can find the equation of the line that best fits n given points by assuming the points lie on or near a line with equation

$$\widehat{y} = Ax + B.$$

For each value of x, we get a value $\widehat{y}$, which lies on the line and is an estimate of y. We seek the numbers A and B such that

$$\Sigma (y - \widehat{y})^2$$

is a minimum. If we can find A and B, then we have the equation of the line that describes the data. Using this equation, we can estimate unknown y values for other values of x.

° Because linear regression involves minimizing the sum of squared numbers, it is also called the **least squares method.**

Linear Regression Using calculus, we can show that $\Sigma(y - \widehat{y})^2$ is a minimum, and thus
Equation $\widehat{y} = Ax + B$ is the equation of the line that is the best fit, if

$$A = \frac{\Sigma x \cdot \Sigma y - n\Sigma xy}{(\Sigma x)^2 - n\Sigma x^2}$$

and

$$B = \frac{\Sigma y - A\Sigma x}{n}.$$

EXAMPLE 1 Suppose the following four points are known. Write the equation of the line that is the best fit for the points.

x	50	25	10	5
y	2	4	10	20

Solution To find A, and then B, we first find

$$\Sigma x = 50 + 25 + 10 + 5 = 90$$
$$\Sigma x^2 = 2500 + 625 + 100 + 25 = 3250$$
$$\Sigma y = 2 + 4 + 10 + 20 = 36$$
$$\Sigma xy = 100 + 100 + 100 + 100 = 400$$

Then

$$A = \frac{90 \cdot 36 - 4 \cdot 400}{90^2 - 4 \cdot 3250} = \frac{1640}{-4900} = -.33,$$

and

$$B = \frac{36 - (-.33)(90)}{4} = \frac{65.7}{4} = 16.43.$$

Thus the line that gives the best fit to these points is

$$\widehat{y} = -.33x + 16.43.$$

Figure 9.18 (page 340) shows the points and the graph of the regression line. Although none of the given points lies on this line, it is the best line that fits the points. If these points represented a demand function, the equation would be written using p and q, as follows:

$$p = -.33q + 16.43.$$ □

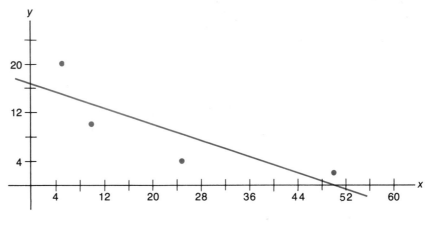

Figure 9.18

EXAMPLE 2   Accountants frequently use linear regression (least squares) to determine a linear equation for their marginal costs. If the following table gives the marginal cost for a product at different levels of production, find the best linear equation for the marginal cost.

x (units)	100	200	300	400
$\overline{MC}$ (Marginal Cost)	2400	4100	6000	8500

Solution   We seek the values A and B such that $\overline{MC} = Ax + B$ is the equation that best fits the points.

$$\Sigma x = 100 + 200 + 300 + 400 = 1000$$
$$\Sigma x^2 = 10{,}000 + 40{,}000 + 90{,}000 + 160{,}000 = 300{,}000$$
$$\Sigma y = 2400 + 4100 + 6000 + 8500 = 21{,}000$$
$$\Sigma xy = 240{,}000 + 820{,}000 + 1{,}800{,}000 + 3{,}400{,}000 = 6{,}260{,}000$$

$$A = \frac{1000(21{,}000) - 4(6{,}260{,}000)}{1000^2 - 4(300{,}000)} = \frac{21{,}000{,}000 - 25{,}040{,}000}{1{,}000{,}000 - 1{,}200{,}000} = 20.2$$

$$B = \frac{21{,}000 - (20.2)(1000)}{4} = \frac{800}{4} = 200$$

Thus the linear equation that best predicts marginal cost is

$$\overline{MC} = 20.2x + 200.$$

Figure 9.19 shows the points and the line.

This equation gives (approximate) values for marginal cost at different levels of production. For example, at $x = 500$, marginal cost should be approximately

$$\overline{MC} = 20.2(500) + 200 = 10{,}300,$$

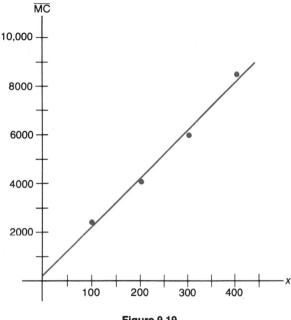

Figure 9.19

and at $x = 250$, it is approximately

$$\overline{MC} = 20.2(250) + 200 = 5250. \qquad \square$$

Linear regression gives us the equation of the line that is the best fit for our data, but it does not tell us how closely our data fit the line. One measure of goodness of fit is the **correlation coefficient,** denoted by r. The formula for r is

$$r = \frac{n(\Sigma\, xy) - (\Sigma\, x)(\Sigma\, y)}{\sqrt{n(\Sigma\, x^2) - (\Sigma\, x)^2}\,\sqrt{n(\Sigma\, y^2) - (\Sigma\, y)^2}}.$$

Although this formula looks very complicated, it is not difficult to use if we have already found the regression line. We have already calculated $\Sigma\, xy$, $\Sigma\, x$, $\Sigma\, y$, and $\Sigma\, x^2$ in finding the regression line for Example 1. Thus we need only compute $\Sigma\, y^2$ and substitute these values (with $n = 4$) into the formula for r. The values are $\Sigma\, xy = 400$, $\Sigma\, x = 90$, $\Sigma\, y = 36$, $\Sigma\, x^2 = 3250$, and $\Sigma\, y^2 = 520$. Thus

$$r = \frac{4(400) - (90)(36)}{\sqrt{4(3250) - (90)^2}\,\sqrt{4(520) - (36)^2}} = \frac{-1640}{1960} = -.84.$$

The formula for the correlation coefficient, developed by Karl Pearson, is designed so that $-1 \le r \le 1$, with a value of r close to 1 meaning the two variables will increase or decrease together, and there is a strong mathematical relationship between them. It does not necessarily mean that one of the variables has a direct effect on the other. For example, there is a high correlation between

Figure 9.20

the increase in the number of ministers in a certain area and the sale of liquor in that area. This does not mean the ministers are drinking the liquor; both increases reflect an increase in population in that area.

A correlation coefficient close to -1 indicates that there is a strong negative correlation; that is, one variable will tend to decrease as the other one increases. It is generally agreed that correlations between -0.2 and 0.2 indicate no significant relation between the variables. (See Figure 9.20.)

EXAMPLE 3   Find the correlation coefficient for the data given in Example 2.

Solution   From the data in Example 2, we have $\Sigma xy = 6{,}260{,}000$, $\Sigma x = 1000$, $\Sigma y = 21{,}000$, $\Sigma x^2 = 300{,}000$, and $\Sigma y^2 = 130{,}820{,}000$. Then

$$r = \frac{4(6{,}260{,}000) - (1000)(21{,}000)}{\sqrt{4(300{,}000) - (1000)^2}\sqrt{4(130{,}820{,}000) - (21{,}000)^2}}$$

$$= \frac{25{,}040{,}000 - 21{,}000{,}000}{\sqrt{1{,}200{,}000 - 1{,}000{,}000}\sqrt{523{,}280{,}000 - 441{,}000{,}000}}$$

$$= \frac{4{,}040{,}000}{\sqrt{200{,}000}\sqrt{82{,}280{,}000}} = \frac{4{,}040{,}000}{(447.21)(9070.83)}$$

$$= .9959.$$ □

Exercise 9.8

1. Find the least-squares line for the following data.

x	1	2	3	4
y	1	4	8	12

2. Find the least-squares line for the following data.

x	2	3	4	5
y	8	25	50	100

3. Write the linear equation (in the form $p = Aq + B$) that is the best fit for the following demand schedule.

q	10	20	30	40	50
p	300	250	220	200	180

4. Find the correlation coefficient for the data in problem 1.
5. Find the correlation coefficient for the data in problem 2.
6. Find the correlation coefficient for the data in problem 3.

APPLICATIONS

7. The following table compares the weekly wages for men and women. Write the linear equation (in the form $y = Ax + B$) that is the best fit for the data.

Year	x (Men)	y (Women)
1920	$31.69	17.71
1930	27.66	15.98
1940	30.64	17.43
1944	54.65	31.21

8. The table shows the temperature readings from two different thermometers placed in water as the temperature of the water changes.

x (thermometer 1)	12	30.5	50	76.5	90
y (thermometer 2)	60	88	110	165	203

(a) Write the linear equation that is the best fit for the data (in the form $y = Ax + B$).
(b) How are the thermometers different?

9. The table gives the high school and college grade point averages for six students,

where the highest possible grade point in both cases is 4.0. Write the equation of the least squares line for the data.

x (high school)	2.50	3.00	3.25	3.50	3.75	4.00
y (college)	1.80	2.80	2.50	3.00	3.20	3.50

10. Find the correlation coefficient for the data in problem 7.
11. Find the correlation coefficient for the data in problem 8.
12. Find the correlation coefficient for the data in problem 9.

Review Exercises

Consider the data in the following frequency table.

Score	Frequency
1	4
2	6
3	8
4	3
5	5

1. Construct a frequency histogram for the data.
2. What is the mode of the data?
3. What is the mean of the data?
4. What is the median of the data?

Consider the following scores: 4, 16, 35, 14, 17, 16, 32, 12, 3, 1.

5. What is the median of the scores?
6. What is the mode of the scores?
7. What is the mean of the scores?
8. Find the mean, variance, and standard deviation of the following data: 4, 3, 4, 6, 8, 0, 2.
9. Find the mean, variance, and standard deviation of the following data: 3, 2, 1, 5, 1, 4, 0, 2, 1, 1.
10. If a die is rolled 4 times, what is the probability that a number greater than 4 is rolled at least 2 times?
11. A coin has been altered so that the probability that a head will occur is 2/3. If the coin is tossed 6 times, give the mean and standard deviation of the distribution of the number of heads.
12. Expand $(x + y)^5$.
13. What is the area under the standard normal curve between $z = -1.6$ and $z = 1.9$?
14. If z is a standard normal score, find $Pr(-1 \leq z \leq -.5)$.

15. If a variable x is normally distributed with $\mu = 25$ and $\sigma = 5$, find
    (a) $\Pr(25 \leq x \leq 30)$ (b) $\Pr(20 \leq x \leq 30)$ (c) $\Pr(30 \leq x \leq 35)$

16. If a sample of size $n = 100$ is drawn from a normal population with mean $\mu = 25$ and standard deviation $\sigma = 5$, find
    (a) $\Pr(24 \leq \bar{x} \leq 26)$ (b) $\Pr(25 \leq \bar{x} \leq 26)$ (c) $\Pr(25.5 \leq \bar{x} \leq 26)$

APPLICATIONS

17. Suppose the probability that a certain couple will have a blond child is $1/4$. If they have 6 children, what is the probability that 2 of them will be blond?

18. Suppose 70% of a population opposes a proposal and a sample of size 5 is drawn from the population. What is the probability the majority of the sample will favor the proposal?

19. A machine produces a bolt whose mean length is 6 cm, with a standard deviation of 1 cm. To test the machine producing the bolt, a sample of 100 is drawn. Using a two-tailed test with $\alpha = .05$, determine if the machine is working properly if the mean length of the sample is $\bar{x} = 5.91$ cm.

20. Consider the following table of values, where x represents the annual income of a man (in thousands of dollars) and y represents his suit size. Use the least-squares method to find the linear equation that best describes suit size as a function of income.

x	20	25	30	35
y	38	40	44	48

21. Find the correlation between income and suit size for the data in problem 20. Does there appear to be a relation between income and suit size?

PART FIVE
Calculus

Warmup In this chapter you will need to work problems like the following. If you have difficulty with any problem, return to the section where that type of problem was introduced and refresh your memory before starting the chapter.

Problem Type	Introduced in Section	Used in Section	Answer
If $f(x) = \dfrac{x^2 - x - 6}{x + 2}$, then find (a) $f(-3)$ (b) $f(-2.5)$ (c) $f(-2.1)$ (d) $f(-2)$	1.3 Functional notation	10.1	(a) -6 (b) -5.5 (c) -5.1 (d) undefined
Factor: (a) $x^2 - x - 6$ (b) $x^2 - 4$ (c) $x^2 + 3x + 2$	0.3 Factoring	10.1	(a) $(x + 2)(x - 3)$ (b) $(x - 2)(x + 2)$ (c) $(x + 1)(x + 2)$
Simplify: (a) $\dfrac{x^2 - x - 6}{x + 2}$ if $x \neq -2$ (b) $\dfrac{x^2 - 4}{x - 2}$ if $x \neq 2$	0.5 Simplifying fractions	10.1	(a) $x - 3$ (b) $x + 2$
Represent graphically: (a) $x \geq 2$ (b) $x < 2$	4.1 Linear inequalities	10.2	(a) (b)

LIMITS AND CONTINUITY

Most of the functions that we have studied up to this point have been continuous functions. Intuitively, we may think of a function as continuous if its graph can be drawn without lifting the pencil from the paper. For example, the graph in Figure 10.1 represents a continuous function, while the graph in Figure 10.2 represents a function that is not continuous. Note that the graph of Figure 10.2 cannot be drawn without lifting your pencil, because of the "breaks" in the graph.

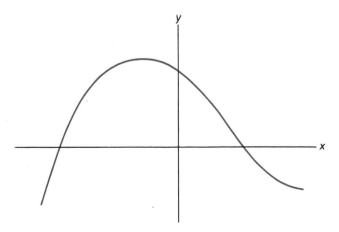

Figure 10.1

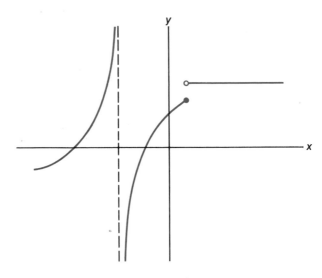

Figure 10.2

Whenever possible, we try to represent functions used in business, the social sciences, and life sciences by continuous functions, even if the functions do not fit the conditions exactly, because continuous functions are easier to work with than other functions. Suppose, for example, that a firm sells one type of shirt for $16. Then we say that the revenue function for this shirt is $R = 16x$. This revenue function really makes sense only for nonnegative integer values of x (the number of shirts sold), but if we assume that the revenue function is defined for all real numbers greater than or equal to 0, we can treat it as a continuous function.

But not all functions occurring in business and economics can be represented by continuous functions. For example, it is not possible to represent the post-office function, which gives the cost of first class postage as a function of the weight of the letter, by a smooth curve. Because the (1980) cost of a letter is 15¢ for the first ounce or part of an ounce, and 13¢ for each additional ounce or part of an ounce, the graph of this function will have "jumps" and cannot be represented by a continuous function.

This chapter introduces the concept of limit. This concept will help us determine when a function is continuous as well as determine where certain functions have horizontal and vertical asymptotes. Knowledge of asymptotes will help us understand and graph rational functions. Limits are also essential to the study of marginal cost, revenue, and profit for nonlinear functions, and to the study of various rates of change which are important in the social sciences and life sciences.

10.1 · Limits

Objective   ■ To find limits of functions, when they exist

Not all functions are as well behaved as the ones we have been discussing up to this point. Some functions have "jumps" or "breaks" in their graphs. For example, the function $f(x) = (x^2 - x - 6)/(x + 2)$ is undefined at $x = -2$. If we substitute -2 for x in the function, we get $0/0$, which is meaningless. Thus -2 is not in the domain of this function. To answer the question, What is $f(x)$ close to when x is close, but not equal, to -2?, we introduce the concept of **limit.**

By evaluating the function at values of x on either side of and close to -2, *but not at* -2, we can see what value the function approaches as x approaches -2.

Table 10.1 shows the values of y as x gets close to -2 from the left side and right side of -2.

Table 10.1

Left		Right	
x	y	x	y
-3	-6	-1	-4
-2.5	-5.5	-1.5	-4.5
-2.3	-5.3	-1.7	-4.7
-2.1	-5.1	-1.9	-4.9
-2.01	-5.01	-1.99	-4.99
-2.001	-5.001	-1.999	-4.999

It becomes apparent that *as x approaches* -2 *from either side, the function approaches* -5. We can write this using the notation

$$f(x) \to -5 \quad \text{as} \quad x \to -2 \quad \text{or} \quad \lim_{x \to -2} f(x) = -5.$$

In general, the notation

$$\lim_{x \to a} f(x) = L$$

means that as x gets "close" to a (but does not equal a), $f(x)$ gets "close" to L.

Two facts regarding limits must be kept in mind:

1. The limit of a function as x approaches a is independent of the value of the function at a. The value of the function at a may be undefined, may be the

same as the limit, or may be defined but different from the limit. For the function above we have seen that the limit as x approaches -2 exists even though the function is undefined *at* $x = -2$. That is, $f(-2)$ does not exist, but $\lim\limits_{x \to -2} f(x) = -5$.

2. The limit is said to **exist** only if the following conditions are satisfied:

(a) The limit L is a finite number.

(b) The limit as x approaches a from the left [written $\lim\limits_{x \to a^-} f(x)$] equals the limit as x approaches a from the right [written $\lim\limits_{x \to a^+} f(x)$]. That is, we must have

$$\lim_{x \to a^-} f(x) = \lim_{x \to a^+} f(x).$$

For many functions, the value of the limit as $x \to a$ will be the same as the value of the functions at $x = a$. But facts 1 and 2 tell us that this will not always be the case. For example, if $f(x) = 2x$, the limit of $f(x)$ as $x \to 2$ is 4, which is the same as $f(2)$. But if

$$f(x) = \frac{x^2 - x - 6}{x + 2},$$

we have seen that the limit as $x \to -2$ is -5, while $f(-2)$ is undefined. Those functions f for which the limit as $x \to a$ gives the same value as $f(a)$ for all values of a are special functions, called *continuous functions*. We will discuss continuous functions in the next section.

To evaluate limits we can use the definition, and form a table like that used to find

$$\lim_{x \to -2} \frac{x^2 - x - 6}{x + 2} = -5.$$

However, there are several properties of limits which we can use to facilitate our work. These properties follow, and each is illustrated with examples.

Properties of Limits

PROPERTY	EXAMPLE
I. $\lim\limits_{x \to a} c = c$, where c is constant	I. $\lim\limits_{x \to 2} 4 = 4;\ \lim\limits_{x \to -1} 5 = 5$
II. $\lim\limits_{x \to a} x = a$	II. $\lim\limits_{x \to 3} x = 3;\ \lim\limits_{x \to -5} x = -5$
III. If $\lim\limits_{x \to a} f(x) = L$ and $\lim\limits_{x \to a} g(x) = M$, then $\lim\limits_{x \to a} [\,f(x) \pm g(x)\,]$ $= \lim\limits_{x \to a} f(x) \pm \lim\limits_{x \to a} g(x) = L \pm M.$	III. (a) $\lim\limits_{x \to 2} (x + 4) = \left(\lim\limits_{x \to 2} x\right) + \left(\lim\limits_{x \to 2} 4\right)$ $= 2 + 4 = 6$ (b) $\lim\limits_{x \to -1} (x - 1) = \left(\lim\limits_{x \to -1} x\right) - \left(\lim\limits_{x \to -1} 1\right)$ $= -1 - 1 = -2$

IV. If $\lim\limits_{x\to a} f(x) = L$ and $\lim\limits_{x\to a} g(x) = M$,

then $\lim\limits_{x\to a} [\, f(x) \cdot g(x)]$

$= \left[\lim\limits_{x\to a} f(x)\right] \left[\lim\limits_{x\to a} g(x)\right] = LM.$

NOTE: $\lim\limits_{x\to a} cf(x) = c \cdot \lim\limits_{x\to a} f(x) = c \cdot L.$

V. If $\lim\limits_{x\to a} f(x) = L$ and $\lim\limits_{x\to a} g(x) = M$, *with*

$M \neq 0$ then $\lim\limits_{x\to a} \dfrac{f(x)}{g(x)} = \dfrac{\lim\limits_{x\to a} f(x)}{\lim\limits_{x\to a} g(x)} = \dfrac{M}{N}.$

IV. (a) $\lim\limits_{x\to 3} x^2 = \left(\lim\limits_{x\to 3} x\right)\left(\lim\limits_{x\to 3} x\right) = 3 \cdot 3 = 9$

(b) $\lim\limits_{x\to 2} 4x = 4\left[\lim\limits_{x\to 2} x\right] = 4 \cdot 2 = 8$

(c) $\lim\limits_{x\to -1} 2x^2 = 2\left(\lim\limits_{x\to -1} x\right)\left(\lim\limits_{x\to -1} x\right)$

$= 2(-1)(-1) = 2$

V. (a) $\lim\limits_{x\to 2} \dfrac{x^2 + 4}{x + 2} = \dfrac{\lim\limits_{x\to 2}(x^2 + 4)}{\lim\limits_{x\to 2}(x + 2)} = \dfrac{8}{4} = 2$

(b) $\lim\limits_{x\to 3} \dfrac{x^2 - 4x}{x - 2} = \dfrac{\lim\limits_{x\to 3}(x^2 - 4x)}{\lim\limits_{x\to 3}(x - 2)}$

$= \dfrac{-3}{1} = -3$

Note that Property V does not apply if the limit of the denominator is 0. This situation occurs frequently in calculus, so we will have to develop methods to deal with it. Before we develop those methods, however, we will consider more examples that use Properties I–V.

EXAMPLE 1   Evaluate $\lim\limits_{x\to 3} (2x^2 + 5)$, if it exists.

Solution

$\lim\limits_{x\to 3} (2x^2 + 5) = \lim\limits_{x\to 3} (2 \cdot x \cdot x + 5)$

$= \lim\limits_{x\to 3} 2 \cdot \lim\limits_{x\to 3} x \cdot \lim\limits_{x\to 3} x + \lim\limits_{x\to 3} 5$

$= 2 \cdot 3 \cdot 3 + 5 = 23$ □

EXAMPLE 2   Evaluate $\lim\limits_{x\to 2} \dfrac{4 + x^3}{2x + 1}$, if it exists.

Solution

$\lim\limits_{x\to -2} \dfrac{4 + x^3}{2x + 1} = \dfrac{\lim\limits_{x\to -2}(4 + x \cdot x \cdot x)}{\lim\limits_{x\to -2}(2 \cdot x + 1)}$

$= \dfrac{\lim\limits_{x\to -2} 4 + \left(\lim\limits_{x\to -2} x \cdot \lim\limits_{x\to -2} x \cdot \lim\limits_{x\to -2} x\right)}{\left(\lim\limits_{x\to -2} 2 \cdot \lim\limits_{x\to -2} x\right) + \lim\limits_{x\to -2} 1}$

$= \dfrac{4 + (-2)(-2)(-2)}{2(-2) + 1} = \dfrac{4 - 8}{-4 + 1} = \dfrac{-4}{-3} = \dfrac{4}{3}$ □

Note that if a function $f(x)$ is a polynomial (that is, of the form $f(x) = a_n x^n + a_{n-1} x^{n-1} + \cdots + a_1 x + a_0$), then Properties I through IV imply that $\lim_{x \to a} f(x)$ can be found simply by evaluating $f(a)$. Moreover, if $f(x)$ and $g(x)$ are both polynomials, then Property V implies

$$\lim_{x \to a} \frac{f(x)}{g(x)}$$

can be found by evaluating $f(a)/g(a)$, *as long as* $g(a) \neq 0$. With this realization the evaluation of some limits is greatly simplified.

EXAMPLE 3   Find $\lim_{x \to 4} \dfrac{x^2 - 4x}{x - 2}$, if it exists.

Solution   Note that this limit has the form

$$\lim_{x \to a} \frac{f(x)}{g(x)},$$

where $f(x)$ and $g(x)$ are polynomials and $g(a) \neq 0$. Therefore we have

$$\lim_{x \to 4} \frac{x^2 - 4x}{x - 2} = \frac{4^2 - 4(4)}{4 - 2} = \frac{0}{2} = 0. \qquad \square$$

In Example 3, the limit of the numerator was 0. Note that we cannot use Property V if the limit of the denominator is 0. To show how to evaluate the limit of a function of this type, let us return to the function

$$f(x) = \frac{x^2 - x - 6}{x + 2}.$$

We cannot use Property V to find

$$\lim_{x \to -2} \frac{x^2 - x - 6}{x + 2}$$

because $\lim_{x \to -2} (x + 2) = 0$. But because taking the limit as $x \to a$ means we are concerned with values close, *but not equal*, to a, we can find

$$\lim_{x \to -2} \frac{x^2 - x - 6}{x + 2}$$

without constructing a table of values. By factoring the numerator, we get

$$\lim_{x \to -2} \frac{x^2 - x - 6}{x + 2} = \lim_{x \to -2} \frac{(x + 2)(x - 3)}{x + 2}.$$

Since the limit is evaluated *near but not at* $x = -2$, $x + 2$ is not 0. Thus we can divide numerator and denominator by $x + 2$, giving $\lim_{x \to -2} (x - 3)$. We see that $x - 3$ will approach -5 as x approaches -2. Thus the limit is

$$\lim_{x \to -2} \frac{x^2 - x - 6}{x + 2} = \lim_{x \to -2} (x - 3) = -5.$$

EXAMPLE 4   Find $\lim\limits_{x \to 2} \dfrac{x^2 - 4}{x - 2}$, if it exists.

Solution   We cannot find the limit by using Property V, because the denominator is zero at $x = 2$. We can find the limit by factoring the numerator.

$$\lim_{x \to 2} \frac{x^2 - 4}{x - 2} = \lim_{x \to 2} \frac{(x - 2)(x + 2)}{x - 2}$$

$$= \lim_{x \to 2} (x + 2) \qquad \text{(We can divide by } x - 2 \text{ because } x$$
$$\text{is approaching 2 but cannot equal 2,}$$
$$= 4 \qquad\qquad\quad \text{by the definition of limit.)} \qquad \square$$

EXAMPLE 5   Find $\lim\limits_{h \to 0} \dfrac{(x + h)^2 - x^2}{h}$.

Solution   Substituting 0 for h results in $0/0$, so we must proceed as follows.

$$\lim_{h \to 0} \frac{(x + h)^2 - x^2}{h} = \lim_{h \to 0} \frac{x^2 + 2xh + h^2 - x^2}{h}$$

$$= \lim_{h \to 0} \frac{2xh + h^2}{h}$$

$$= \lim_{h \to 0} (2x + h) \qquad \text{(We can divide by } h \text{ because}$$
$$h \to 0, \text{ but does not equal 0.)}$$
$$= 2x \qquad\qquad\qquad\qquad\qquad\qquad\qquad \square$$

EXAMPLE 6   Find $\lim\limits_{x \to 1} \dfrac{x^2 + 3x + 2}{x - 1}$, if it exists.

Solution   Substituting 1 for x in the function results in $6/0$, so 1 is not in the domain of the function.

Factoring the numerator of the function gives

$$\lim_{x \to 1} \frac{(x + 1)(x + 2)}{x - 1}.$$

Since $x - 1$ is not a factor of the numerator, we cannot divide numerator and denominator by $x - 1$ as we did before. We see that as x approaches 1 from the right, the numerator will approach 6, and the denominator will approach 0, with each value being larger than 0. Thus as x approaches 1 on its right side, the ratio will become large without bound (see Table 10.2). We write this as

$$\lim_{x \to 1^+} \frac{x^2 + 3x + 2}{x - 1} = +\infty$$

and say the limit does not exist (because it is not a finite number). The symbol ∞ is used to indicate infinity, which is not a number, but which means that the function is increasing without bound.

Table 10.2

Left		Right	
x	$\dfrac{x^2 + 3x + 2}{x - 1}$	x	$\dfrac{x^2 + 3x + 2}{x - 1}$
0	-2	2	12
0.5	-7.5	1.5	17.5
0.7	-15.3	1.2	35.2
0.9	-55.1	1.1	65.1
0.99	-595.01	1.01	605.01
0.999	-5995.001	1.001	6005.001
0.9999	$-59{,}999.0001$	1.0001	60{,}005.0001

$$\lim_{x \to 1^-} \frac{x^2 + 3x + 2}{x - 1} = -\infty \qquad \lim_{x \to 1^+} \frac{x^2 + 3x + 2}{x - 1} = +\infty$$

As x approaches 1 from the left, we see that the numerator of the function will again approach 6, but the denominator will approach 0 through *negative* values. Thus the ratio will again become large without bound, *but* it will be negative (see Table 10.2). Thus we write

$$\lim_{x \to 1^-} \frac{x^2 + 3x + 2}{x - 1} = -\infty.$$

Even though the left-hand and right-hand limits are undefined, the knowledge that they are infinite is helpful in graphing the function. Its graph is shown in Figure 10.3.   □

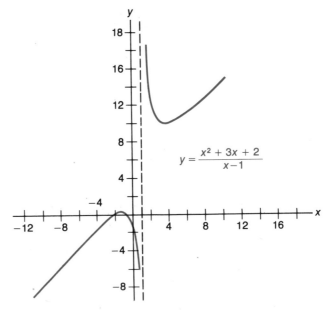

$$y = \frac{x^2 + 3x + 2}{x - 1}$$

Figure 10.3

We have discussed two types of limits that need special consideration. They both result when the denominator of a fraction approaches zero. We summarize as follows.

Evaluating Limits of the Form

$$\lim_{x \to a} \frac{f(x)}{g(x)},$$

where

$$\lim_{x \to a} g(x) = 0$$

Type I. If $\lim_{x \to a} f(x) = 0$ also, we can reduce the fraction $f(x)/g(x)$ by factoring (see Examples 4 and 5).

Type II. If

$$\lim_{x \to a} f(x) \neq 0 \text{ and } \lim_{x \to a} g(x) = 0,$$

then

$$\lim_{x \to a} \frac{f(x)}{g(x)} = \pm\infty.$$

We can test values on both sides of a to determine if the limit gives $+\infty$ or $-\infty$. In Example 6 the limit from the left was $-\infty$ and the limit from the right was $+\infty$.

We say that the limit does not exist (or is undefined) if it is not finite. But as we stated earlier, there is a second situation where the limit does not exist.

If $\lim_{x \to a^+} f(x) \neq \lim_{x \to a^-} f(x)$, then $\lim_{x \to a} f(x)$ does *not* exist.

First class postage is 15¢ for the first ounce or part of an ounce that a letter weighs, and each additional ounce or part of an ounce above one ounce costs an additional 13¢. Thus we can find the cost of mailing a first class letter that weighs 5 ounces or less by using Table 10.3. For example, the postage for a letter weigh-

Table 10.3

Weight x	Postage $f(x)$
$0 < x \leq 1$	15¢
$1 < x \leq 2$	28
$2 < x \leq 3$	41
$3 < x \leq 4$	54
$4 < x \leq 5$	67

ing 3.4 ounces is $f(3.4) = 54¢$ and the postage for a letter weighing 1.2 ounces is $f(1.2) = 28¢$. Notice that any letter weighing more than one ounce but not more than two ounces will cost 28¢ to mail, regardless of how close the weight is to one ounce.

To see if the limit of this post-office function exists as x approaches one ounce, we will examine the function's behavior on either side of $x = 1$ (see Table 10.4).

Table 10.4

Left of $x = 1$		Right of $x = 1$	
x	$f(x)$	x	$f(x)$
0.5	15	1.5	28
0.9	15	1.1	28
0.99	15	1.01	28
0.999	15	1.001	28

From Table 10.4 we see that the limit of this function as x approaches 1 from the left is 15. We write this

$$\lim_{x \to 1^-} f(x) = 15.$$

We also see that the limit as x approaches 1 from the right is 28. We write this as

$$\lim_{x \to 1^+} f(x) = 28.$$

Because the limit from the left does not equal the limit from the right, the limit does not exist. The graph of the post-office function is shown in Figure 10.4.

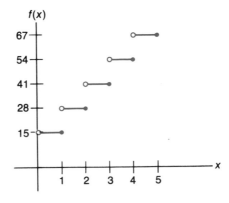

Figure 10.4

Exercise 10.1

Find the following limits, if they exist.

1. $\lim_{x\to 0} 4$

2. $\lim_{x\to 12} e$

3. $\lim_{x\to 3} x$

4. $\lim_{x\to -2} x$

5. $\lim_{x\to 3} 6x$

6. $\lim_{x\to -12} -4x$

7. $\lim_{x\to 2} (x - 3)$

8. $\lim_{x\to 2} (3x - 4)$

9. $\lim_{x\to -1} (4x^2 + 2)$

10. $\lim_{x\to 3} (2x^3 - 12x^2 + 5x + 3)$

11. $\lim_{x\to 2} \dfrac{x^3 - 4}{x - 3}$

12. $\lim_{x\to -1} \dfrac{x^3 - 3x + 1}{x - 1}$

13. $\lim_{x\to 4} \dfrac{4x^2 - 12x - 16}{x + 4}$

14. $\lim_{x\to 3} \dfrac{x^2 - 9}{x + 2}$

15. $\lim_{x\to 3} \dfrac{x^2 - 9}{x - 3}$

16. $\lim_{x\to -4} \dfrac{x^2 - 16}{x + 4}$

17. $\lim_{x\to -2} \dfrac{x^2 + 4x + 4}{x + 2}$

18. $\lim_{x\to 1} \dfrac{x^2 + x - 2}{x - 1}$

19. $\lim_{x\to 2} \dfrac{x^2 + 6x + 9}{x - 2}$

20. $\lim_{x\to 5} \dfrac{x^2 - 6x + 8}{x - 5}$

21. $\lim_{x\to -1} \dfrac{x^2 + 5x + 6}{x + 1}$

22. $\lim_{x\to 3} \dfrac{x^2 + 2x - 3}{x - 3}$

The function $f(x) = [\![x]\!]$ is called the *greatest integer function*. For each value of x, this function gives the greatest integer less than or equal to x. For example, $f(2.5) = 2$, $f(3) = 3$, and $f(-1.5) = -2$.

23. Graph the greatest integer function for $-2 \leq x \leq 4$.

24. Does $\lim_{x\to 3^+} f(x) = \lim_{x\to 3^-} f(x)$, if $f(x) = [\![x]\!]$?

Find the limits if they exist.

25. $\lim_{x\to 2} f(x)$, where $f(x) = [\![x]\!]$.

26. $\lim_{x\to 1.5} f(x)$, where $f(x) = [\![x]\!]$.

27. $\lim_{h\to 0} \dfrac{(x + h)^3 - x^3}{h}$

28. $\lim_{h\to 0} \dfrac{2(x + h)^2 - 2x^2}{h}$

APPLICATION

29. The Ace Parking Garage charges $2.00 for parking up to 2 hours, and 50¢ for each extra hour or part of an hour after the 2-hour minimum. The parking charges for the first 5 hours could be written as a function of the time. The following is a statement

of this function, with (a), (b), (c), and (d) to be determined.

$$f(t) = \begin{cases} \text{(a)} & \text{if} \quad 0 < t \le 2 \\ \$2.50 & \text{if} \quad 2 < t \le \text{(b)} \\ \text{(c)} & \text{if} \quad 3 < t \le 4 \\ \text{(d)} & \text{if} \quad 4 < t \le 5 \end{cases}$$

(e) Find $\lim_{t \to 1} f(t)$, if it exists.

(f) Find $\lim_{t \to 2} f(t)$, if it exists.

10.2 Continuous Functions

Objectives
- To determine if a function is continuous or discontinuous
- To determine what type of discontinuity exists at a point where a function is discontinuous

We have already mentioned that continuous curves can be thought of as those whose graphs can be drawn without lifting the pencil. We can now give a more formal definition of continuity.

A function f is said to be **continuous at the point** $x = a$ if the following conditions are satisfied:

1. $f(a)$ exists.

2. $\lim_{x \to a} f(x)$ exists.

3. $\lim_{x \to a} f(x) = f(a)$.

If one or more of these conditions are not satisfied, we say the function is discontinuous at $x = a$.

For example, the function $f(x) = 3x + 5$ is continuous at $x = 2$ because

1. $f(2) = 11$

2. $\lim_{x \to 2} f(x) = 11$

3. Thus $\lim_{x \to 2} f(x) = 11 = f(2)$.

Recall that in Section 10.1 we found that we can evaluate $\lim_{x \to a} f(x)$, when $f(x)$ is a polynomial, by evaluating $f(a)$. We can do this because every polynomial is continuous. If a function is not defined by a polynomial, it may have a point where it is not continuous. To determine if a function is continuous, we must investigate the point(s) where it may be discontinuous. A function that can be written as the ratio of two polynomials is called a **rational function.** A rational function may be discontinuous, for any value that makes the denominator 0 will be a point of discontinuity. The following examples illustrate methods of determining if a function has any points of discontinuity.

EXAMPLE 1   Is the function $f(x) = \dfrac{x^2 - 1}{x + 1}$ continuous at $x = 1$?

Solution
1. $f(1) = 0$
2. $\lim\limits_{x \to 1} f(x) = 0$
3. $\lim\limits_{x \to 1} f(x) = 0 = f(1)$

Thus $f(x)$ is continuous at $x = 1$.   □

EXAMPLE 2   Is the function of Example 1 continuous at $x = -1$?

Solution   The function is $f(x) = \dfrac{x^2 - 1}{x + 1}$.

$f(-1)$ is undefined. Thus the function is discontinuous at $x = -1$.
Note that $\lim_{x \to -1} f(x)$ does exist, since

$$\lim_{x \to -1} \frac{x^2 - 1}{x + 1} = \lim_{x \to -1} \frac{(x - 1)(x + 1)}{x + 1} = \lim_{x \to -1} (x - 1) = -2.$$ □

We see from Example 2 that there is at least one point where the function $f(x) = (x^2 - 1)/(x + 1)$ is discontinuous. The graph of the function of Example 2 is shown in Figure 10.5. Because there is no point corresponding to $x = -1$, this discontinuity is called a **missing point discontinuity**.

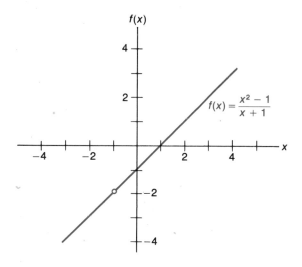

Figure 10.5

If there is *no point of discontinuity* for a function we say it is a **continuous function**; otherwise it is a *discontinuous function*. The function $y = x^2 - 3x + 1$ is a continuous function, because there is no point of discontinuity. The function $y = 5/(x - 3)$ is discontinuous because $f(3)$ is undefined.

EXAMPLE 3   Is the function $f(x) = 1/(x - 1)$ continuous?

Solution   The denominator of this function will be 0 if $x = 1$, so the trouble spot is at $x = 1$. We see that

1. the function is undefined at $x = 1$.
2. $\lim\limits_{x \to 1^-} f(x) = -\infty$ and $\lim\limits_{x \to 1^+} f(x) = +\infty$

We see that $f(x) = 1/(x - 1)$ is discontinuous at $x = 1$, but it is a different type of discontinuity than for the function in Example 2. The graph of $y = 1/(x - 1)$ (Figure 10.6) shows that the curve approaches $-\infty$ as x approaches 1 from the left and $+\infty$ as x approaches 1 from the right. A discontinuity of this type (where the curve approaches $+\infty$ or $-\infty$ at a given value of x) is called an **infinite discontinuity**.   □

The following information is useful in discussing continuity of functions.

1. A polynomial function is continuous everywhere. It has no points where it is undefined.

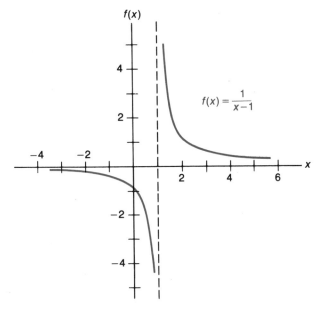

Figure 10.6

2. A rational function is a function of the form $\dfrac{f(x)}{g(x)}$, where $f(x)$ and $g(x)$ are polynomials.

   (a) It is defined and continuous everywhere except where $g(x) = 0$.

   (b) If $g(c) = 0$ and $f(c) \neq 0$, there is an infinite discontinuity at $x = c$.

   (c) If $g(d) = 0$ and $f(d) = 0$, $x - d$ can be factored from $g(x)$ and from $f(x)$.

   (d) If $g(d) = 0$ and $\lim\limits_{x \to d} \dfrac{f(x)}{g(x)} = L$ (a number), then there is a missing point discontinuity at $x = d$.

Sometimes functions cannot be defined by one equation. For example, a function may have a value 0 for all values of x less than 0, and a value equal to x for all values of $x \geq 0$. We can define this function by

$$f(x) = \begin{cases} 0 & \text{if } x < 0 \\ x & \text{if } x \geq 0 \end{cases}.$$

EXAMPLE 4 Is the function $f(x) = \begin{cases} 0 & \text{if } x < 0 \\ x & \text{if } x \geq 0 \end{cases}$ continuous?

Solution If the function has a point where it is discontinuous, the trouble spot will be at $x = 0$. So we will test this point, since the function is defined differently for $x < 0$ and $x \geq 0$.

1. $f(0) = 0$

2. $\lim\limits_{x \to 0^-} f(x) = 0$ and $\lim\limits_{x \to 0^+} f(x) = \lim\limits_{x \to 0^+} x = 0$, so $\lim\limits_{x \to 0} f(x) = 0$

3. $\lim\limits_{x \to 0} f(x) = f(0)$

Thus the function is continuous. □

EXAMPLE 5 Is the post office function $f(x)$ (see Section 10.1, Table 10.3) continuous or discontinuous?

Solution To show that the function is discontinuous, we only need to show it is discontinuous at one point. Consider the point where $x = 1$.

$$f(1) = 15$$
$$\lim\limits_{x \to 1^-} f(x) = 15 \qquad \text{and} \qquad \lim\limits_{x \to 1^+} f(x) = 28 \quad \text{(see Section 10.1, Table 10.4)}$$

Since the left and right limits as x approaches 1 disagree, we have $\lim\limits_{x \to 1} f(x)$ does not exist.

Therefore the post office function is discontinuous. See Figure 10.4 for the graph of this function. Note the jumps in the graph. This type of discontinuity is frequently called a **jump discontinuity**. □

EXAMPLE 6   Is the function $f(x) = \begin{cases} x & \text{if} \quad x \leq 0 \\ x^2 & \text{if} \quad 0 < x \leq 4 \\ 2x + 4 & \text{if} \quad x > 4 \end{cases}$ continuous?

Solution   There are two trouble spots for this function, one at $x = 0$ and one at $x = 4$. Checking $x = 0$ first, we see

1. $f(0) = 0$

2. $\lim\limits_{x \to 0^-} f(x) = 0 = \lim\limits_{x \to 0^+} f(x)$, so $\lim\limits_{x \to 0} f(x) = 0$

3. $\lim\limits_{x \to 0} f(x) = f(0)$

So $f(x)$ is continuous at $x = 0$.
   At $x = 4$, we have

1. $f(4) = 16$

2. $\lim\limits_{x \to 4^-} f(x) = \lim\limits_{x \to 4^-} x^2 = 16$ and $\lim\limits_{x \to 4^+} f(x) = \lim\limits_{x \to 4^+} 2x + 4 = 12$

Thus

$$\lim\limits_{x \to 4^-} f(x) \neq \lim\limits_{x \to 4^+} f(x),$$

so $\lim_{x \to 4} f(x)$ does not exist. Thus the function is discontinuous at $x = 4$.   □

Exercise 10.2

1. Is $f(x) = x^2 - 5x$ continuous at $x = 0$?

2. Is $y = 3x - 5x^3$ continuous at $x = 2$?

3. Is $f(x) = \dfrac{x^2 - 4}{x - 2}$ continuous at $x = -2$?

4. Is $y = \dfrac{x^2 - 9}{x + 3}$ continuous at $x = 3$?

5. Is $y = \dfrac{x^2 - 9}{x + 3}$ continuous at $x = -3$?

6. Is $f(x) = \dfrac{x^2 - 4}{x - 2}$ continuous at $x = 2$?

7. Is $f(x) = \dfrac{x^2 - 2x - 3}{x - 1}$ continuous at $x = 1$?

8. Is $f(x) = \dfrac{x^2 + 5x - 6}{x + 1}$ continuous at $x = 1$?

9. Is $y = \dfrac{x^2 + 5x - 6}{x + 1}$ continuous at $x = -1$?

10. Is $y = \dfrac{x^2 - 8x + 12}{x + 2}$ continuous at $x = -2$?

11. If $f(x) = \begin{cases} 2 & \text{if} \quad x \leq 0 \\ x + 2 & \text{if} \quad x > 0 \end{cases}$, is f continuous at $x = 0$?

12. If $f(x) = \begin{cases} x - 3 & \text{if} \quad x \leq 2 \\ 4x - 7 & \text{if} \quad x > 2 \end{cases}$, is f continuous at $x = 2$?

13. If $f(x) = \begin{cases} x^2 + 1 & \text{if} \quad x \leq 1 \\ 2x^2 - 1 & \text{if} \quad x > 1 \end{cases}$, is f continuous at $x = 1$?

14. If $f(x) = \begin{cases} x^2 - x & \text{if} \quad x \leq 2 \\ 8 - 3x & \text{if} \quad x > 2 \end{cases}$, is f continuous at $x = 2$?

15. Is $f(x) = [\![x]\!]$ continuous at $x = 1$?

16. Is $f(x) = [\![x]\!]$ continuous at $x = 1.5$?

Are each of the following functions continuous? If not, which type of discontinuity occurs?

17. $f(x) = 4x^2 - 1$

18. $y = 5x^2 - 2x$

19. $y = \dfrac{x^2 - 25}{x - 5}$

20. $f(x) = \dfrac{x^3 - 27}{x - 3}$

21. $g(x) = \dfrac{x^2 + 4x + 4}{x + 2}$

22. $y = \dfrac{x^2 - 5x + 4}{x - 4}$

23. $g(x) = \dfrac{4x^2 + 3x + 2}{x + 2}$

24. $y = \dfrac{4x^2 + 4x + 1}{x + \frac{1}{2}}$

25. $f(x) = \begin{cases} 3 & \text{if} \quad x \leq 1 \\ x^2 + 2 & \text{if} \quad x > 1 \end{cases}$

26. $f(x) = \begin{cases} x^3 + 1 & \text{if} \quad x \leq 1 \\ 2 & \text{if} \quad x > 1 \end{cases}$

27. $f(x) = \begin{cases} x - 4 & \text{if} \quad x \leq 3 \\ x^2 - 8 & \text{if} \quad x > 3 \end{cases}$

28. $f(x) = \begin{cases} x^2 + 4 & \text{if} \quad x \neq 1 \\ 5 & \text{if} \quad x = 1 \end{cases}$

APPLICATIONS

29. Is the function that describes the Ace Parking Garage's charges (problem 29 of Section 10.1)
    (a) continuous at $t = 1$?   (b) continuous at $t = 2$?   (c) continuous?

30. Is the demand function $p = 1/q$ continuous for $q > 0$?

31. Suppose the number of calories of heat required to raise 1 gram of water (or ice) from $-40°C$ to $x°C$ is given by

$$f(x) = \begin{cases} \frac{1}{2}x + 20, & -40 \leq x < 0 \\ x + 100, & 0 \leq x. \end{cases}$$

    (a) What can be said about the continuity of the function?
    (b) What accounts for the behavior of the function at $0°C$?

32. Experimental evidence suggests that the response y of the body to the concentration x of injected adrenaline is given by

$$y = \frac{x}{a + bx}$$

    where a and b are experimental constants.
    (a) Is this function continuous for all x?
    (b) Based on your conclusion to (a) and the fact that in reality $x \geq 0$ and $y \geq 0$, must a and b be both positive, both negative, or have opposite signs?

10.3 Limits at Infinity; Asymptotes

Objectives   ■ To evaluate limits as x increases without bound
■ To graph curves which contain vertical or horizontal asymptotes

In Example 6 of Section 10.1 we wrote

$$\lim_{x \to 1^+} \frac{x^2 + 3x + 2}{x - 1} = +\infty$$

to indicate that the function $(x^2 + 3x + 2)/(x - 1)$ increases without bound as x approaches 1 from values larger than 1.

It is often interesting and important to see what value(s) the function approaches as x gets large without bound. We can write $\lim_{x \to +\infty} f(x)$ to indicate the value the function approaches as the values of x get very large (or as x increases without bound), and $\lim_{x \to -\infty} f(x)$ to indicate the value the function approaches as x decreases without bound. For many functions, the functional values will become infinitely large as x does, but not all functions behave in this manner. For example, consider the function $f(x) = 1/x$. As x gets very large, the value of $1/x$ will get closer and closer to 0. We write this in limit form as

$$\lim_{x \to +\infty} \frac{1}{x} = 0.$$

The following examples illustrate other infinite limits.

EXAMPLE 1   Evaluate

$$\lim_{x \to +\infty} \frac{2x - 1}{x + 2},$$

if it exists.

Solution   If we let x approach $+\infty$, we see that both the numerator and denominator become very large. But we do not know what the ratio will equal. We can evaluate the limit if we first divide the numerator and denominator by x, giving

$$\lim_{x \to +\infty} \frac{2 - \dfrac{1}{x}}{1 + \dfrac{2}{x}}.$$

Now, the numerator approaches 2 and the denominator approaches 1, so

$$\lim_{x \to +\infty} \frac{2x - 1}{x + 2} = \lim_{x \to +\infty} \frac{2 - \dfrac{1}{x}}{1 + \dfrac{2}{x}} = \frac{2}{1} = 2. \qquad \square$$

In finding a limit like the one in Example 1, it is frequently helpful to divide the numerator and denominator by the highest power of x present. In Example 1 we divided both numerator and denominator by x because x^1 was the highest power present.

EXAMPLE 2   Evaluate

$$\lim_{x \to -\infty} \frac{x + 2}{x^2 - 1},$$

if it exists.

Solution   Both the numerator and denominator will become infinite as $x \to -\infty$. Dividing both the numerator and denominator by x^2 (the highest power present), we get

$$\lim_{x \to -\infty} \frac{\dfrac{1}{x} + \dfrac{2}{x^2}}{1 - \dfrac{1}{x^2}} = \frac{0 + 0}{1 - 0} = 0.$$

Thus

$$\lim_{x \to -\infty} \frac{x + 2}{x^2 - 1} = 0. \qquad \square$$

EXAMPLE 3   Find

$$\lim_{x \to +\infty} \frac{x^3 - 4x}{3x^2 - 1},$$

if it exists.

Solution   Both the numerator and denominator will become infinite as $x \to +\infty$. Dividing both numerator and denominator by x^3 gives

$$\lim_{x \to +\infty} \frac{x^3 - 4x}{3x^2 - 1} = \lim_{x \to +\infty} \frac{1 - \dfrac{4}{x^2}}{\dfrac{3}{x} - \dfrac{1}{x^3}} = +\infty.$$

The limit is $+\infty$ because the numerator approaches 1 and the denominator approaches 0 through positive values.

Thus

$$\lim_{x \to +\infty} \frac{x^3 - 4x}{3x^2 - 1}$$

does not exist. $\qquad \square$

An application that required an infinite limit was an investment problem studied in Section 7.2. It was shown that the compound amount of an investment of \$1 at an interest rate of 100%, compounded k times in one year, is

$$S = \left(1 + \frac{1}{k}\right)^k.$$

To find the amount when the interest was compounded continuously, we constructed a table of values for S using increasing values of k. As Table 7.2 (see Section 7.2) shows, as k increases in size, the value of S approaches the special number $e = 2.7182818. \ldots$. In fact, this *limit* defines the number e. That is,

$$e = \lim_{x \to \infty} \left(1 + \frac{1}{x}\right)^x \qquad \text{(by definition)}.$$

We also note that e is sometimes equivalently defined (see problem 24 in Exercise 10.3) as

$$e = \lim_{a \to 0} (1 + a)^{1/a}.$$

Recall from Chapter 6 that many growth and decay applications can be modeled using exponential functions of the form

$$y = ae^{bx}.$$

To see how these infinite limits can be useful in graphing functions, consider the function $y = 1/(x - 1)$. Looking at its graph will show us how infinite limits are related to **asymptotes**. In the graph of $y = 1/(x - 1)$ (Figure 10.7), the curve tends to approach the vertical line through $x = 1$; that is, the closer x gets to 1, the closer the curve comes to touching the line. When this occurs, the line $x = 1$ is called a vertical asymptote. In Example 3 of Section 10.2, we saw that this

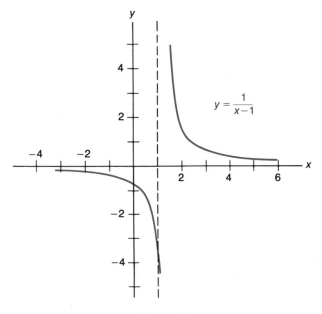

Figure 10.7

function has an infinite discontinuity at $x = 1$, with

$$\lim_{x \to 1^-} \frac{1}{x - 1} = -\infty \quad \text{and} \quad \lim_{x \to 1^+} \frac{1}{x - 1} = +\infty.$$

Note that knowledge of these limits is very useful in sketching the graph of the function near $x = 1$ (Figure 10.7).

> In general we define the line $x = x_0$ to be a **vertical asymptote** if the limit of the function is $+\infty$ or $-\infty$ as x approaches x_0 (from the left or right).

In other words, the curve will have a vertical asymptote at $x = x_0$ if the function has an infinite discontinuity at x_0. (This will happen if the denominator of the function approaches 0 but the numerator does not approach 0 as $x \to x_0$.)

We also see in Figure 10.7 that the curve approaches the x-axis ($y = 0$) as values of x get large (both positive and negative). We say the x-axis is a horizontal asymptote for this curve.

Since the horizontal asymptotes determine behavior at the extremes of the graph, we can find horizontal asymptotes, if they exist, by evaluating the limits $\lim_{x \to +\infty} f(x)$ and $\lim_{x \to -\infty} f(x)$.

> If $\lim_{x \to +\infty} f(x)$ or $\lim_{x \to -\infty} f(x)$ exists and equals a number b, then there is a **horizontal asymptote** at $y = b$.

We see that

$$\lim_{x \to +\infty} \frac{1}{x - 1} = 0 \quad \text{and} \quad \lim_{x \to -\infty} \frac{1}{x - 1} = 0,$$

so the graph of $y = 1/(x - 1)$ has a horizontal asymptote at $y = 0$, as Figure 10.7 shows.

EXAMPLE 4   Find the horizontal and vertical asymptotes of the graph of $y = (2x - 4)/(3x + 6)$.

Solution   The denominator is 0 at $x = -2$. Because the numerator is *not also zero*, we know the limit will be undefined, giving us a vertical asymptote. To determine how the curve approaches the asymptote, we will evaluate the limit as $x \to -2$ from the left and right. As $x \to -2$ from values less than -2, we get very large positive numbers,

$$\lim_{x \to -2^-} \frac{2x - 4}{3x + 6} = +\infty,$$

so the curve increases rapidly to the left of the vertical asymptote. As $x \to -2$

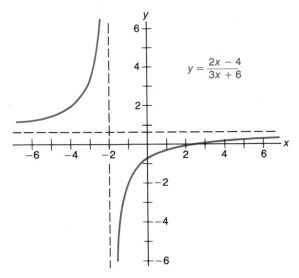

Figure 10.8

from values greater than -2, we get very large negative numbers,

$$\lim_{x \to -2^+} \frac{2x - 4}{3x + 6} = -\infty,$$

so the graph is very low to the right of the vertical asymptote (see Figure 10.8). To find horizontal asymptotes, if any exist, we evaluate

$$\lim_{x \to +\infty} \frac{2x - 4}{3x + 6} \quad \text{and} \quad \lim_{x \to -\infty} \frac{2x - 4}{3x + 6}:$$

1. $\displaystyle\lim_{x \to +\infty} \frac{2x - 4}{3x + 6} = \lim_{x \to +\infty} \frac{2 - 4/x}{3 + 6/x} = \frac{2}{3}$

2. $\displaystyle\lim_{x \to -\infty} \frac{2x - 4}{3x + 6} = \lim_{x \to -\infty} \frac{2 - 4/x}{3 + 6/x} = \frac{2}{3}$

Thus there is a horizontal asymptote at $y = 2/3$.

Plotting a few points (especially the intercepts) and using the information we know about the asymptotes gives the graph, shown in Figure 10.8.   □

The following facts are useful in graphing polynomials and rational functions.

---

1. A polynomial function has no asymptotes.
2. If, in a rational function of the form $\dfrac{f(x)}{g(x)}$, $g(c) = 0$ and $f(c) \neq 0$, there is a vertical asymptote in its graph at $x = c$.
3. If $\lim_{x \to +\infty} h(x) = L$ or $\lim_{x \to -\infty} h(x) = L$, where L is a number, then $y = L$ is a horizontal asymptote for the graph of $h(x)$.

Exercise 10.3

Evaluate the following limits.

1. $\lim\limits_{x \to +\infty} \dfrac{3}{x+1}$

2. $\lim\limits_{x \to -\infty} \dfrac{4}{x^2 - 2x}$

3. $\lim\limits_{x \to +\infty} \dfrac{x^3 - 1}{x^3 + 4}$

4. $\lim\limits_{x \to -\infty} \dfrac{3x^2 + 2}{x^2 - 4}$

5. $\lim\limits_{x \to -\infty} \dfrac{5x^3 - 4x}{3x^3 - 2}$

6. $\lim\limits_{x \to +\infty} \dfrac{4x^2 + 5x}{x^2 - 4x}$

7. $\lim\limits_{x \to +\infty} \dfrac{4x + 3}{x^2 - 1}$

8. $\lim\limits_{x \to -\infty} \dfrac{5x^2 + 4x}{2x^3 - 1}$

9. $\lim\limits_{x \to +\infty} \dfrac{3x^2 + 5x}{6x + 1}$

10. $\lim\limits_{x \to -\infty} \dfrac{5x^3 - 8}{4x^2 + 5x}$

Use the graph of $y = f(x)$ in Figure 10.9 to complete the following.

11. $\lim\limits_{x \to -2} f(x) =$

12. $\lim\limits_{x \to -1^+} f(x) -$

13. $\lim\limits_{x \to 2^-} f(x) =$

14. $\lim\limits_{x \to 2^+} f(x) =$

15. $f(-2) =$

16. $f(1) =$

17. $\lim\limits_{x \to +\infty} f(x) =$

18. $\lim\limits_{x \to 1} f(x) -$

For each of the following functions or relations, find the vertical and horizontal asymptotes when they exist, and sketch the graph.

19. $y = \dfrac{1}{x}$

20. $y = \dfrac{4}{x^2 - 9}$

21. $y = \dfrac{x - 5}{x}$

22. $y = \dfrac{x^2 - 9}{x}$

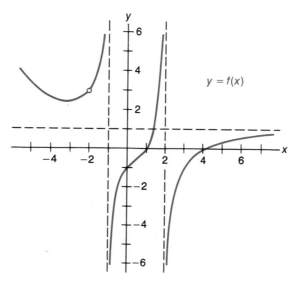

Figure 10.9

23. How does the function $f(x) = \dfrac{x^2 - 1}{x - 1}$ differ from the function $g(x) = x + 1$?

24. Use values 0.1, 0.01, 0.001, 0.0001, and 0.00001 with your calculator to show that

$$(1 + a)^{1/a}$$

approaches e as a approaches 0.

APPLICATIONS

25. The pressure P of a gas at constant temperature is related to the volume V according to

$$P = \frac{K}{V},$$

where K is a constant. Sketch the graph of this function when $K = 1$.

26. Experimental evidence suggests that the response y of the body to the concentration x of injected adrenaline is given by

$$y = \frac{x}{a + bx},$$

where a and b are experimental constants. Suppose $a = 1$ and $b = 10$; sketch the graph of

$$y = \frac{x}{1 + 10x}.$$

27. The force/velocity relationships of weight lifting can be described in a certain case by the equation

$$V = \frac{200 - 2F}{F + 1},$$

where F is the force of the weight and V is the velocity of the lift. Sketch the graph of this relationship.

28. What is the limit of the parking garage charges as t approaches 1 hour in problem 29 of Exercise 10.1?

29. Does the limit of the parking garage charges exist as t approaches 2 hours in problem 29 of Exercise 10.1?

Review Exercises

1. $\lim\limits_{x \to 4} (3x^2 + x + 3)$

2. $\lim\limits_{x \to 4} \dfrac{x^2 - 16}{x + 4}$

3. $\lim\limits_{x \to -1} \dfrac{x^2 - 1}{x + 1}$

4. $\lim\limits_{x \to 3} \dfrac{x^2 - 9}{x - 3}$

5. $\lim\limits_{x \to 3} \dfrac{x^2 - 16}{x - 3}$

6. $\lim\limits_{x \to +\infty} \dfrac{3 - x^2}{2x^2 - 1}$

7. $\lim\limits_{x\to-\infty} \dfrac{x^2 - 2x}{3x^3 - 4}$

Are each of the functions in problems 8–12 continuous? If not, which type of discontinuity occurs?

8. $y = \dfrac{x^2 + 25}{x - 5}$

9. $y = \dfrac{x^2 - 3x + 2}{x - 2}$

10. $f(x) = \begin{cases} x + 2 & \text{if } x \le 2 \\ 5x - 6 & \text{if } x > 2 \end{cases}$

11. $y = \begin{cases} x^4 - 3 & \text{if } x \le 1 \\ 2x - 3 & \text{if } x > 1 \end{cases}$

12. $f(x) = [\![x]\!]$

13. Graph $y = \dfrac{2x - 1}{x}$.

14. Graph $y = \dfrac{x}{x - 3}$.

Warmup In this chapter you will need to be able to work problems like the following. If you have difficulty with any problem, return to the section where that type of problem was introduced and refresh your memory before starting the chapter.

Problem Type	Introduced in Section	Used in Section	Answer
Write as a power: (a) $\sqrt{t}$ (b) $\dfrac{1}{x}$ (c) $\dfrac{1}{\sqrt[3]{x^2 + 1}}$	0.2 Exponents	11.3, 11.4, 11.5, 11.6	(a) $t^{1/2}$ (b) x^{-1} (c) $(x^2 + 1)^{-1/3}$
Simplify: (a) $\dfrac{4(x + h)^2 - 4x^2}{h}$ (b) $(2x^3 + 3x + 1)(2x) + (x^2 + 4)(6x^2 + 3)$ (c) $\dfrac{x(3x^2) - x^3(1)}{x^2}$	0.3 Simplifying algebraic expressions	11.1, 11.2, 11.4, 11.6	(a) $8x + 4h$ (b) $10x^4 + 33x^2 + 2x + 12$ (c) $2x$
Simplify by factoring: (a) $(x^2 + 1)^5(3x^2 + 1) +$ $\qquad 10x(x^2 + 1)^4(x^3 + x + 1)$ (b) $\dfrac{2(x^2 + 1)^3(x - 1) - 6x(x - 1)^2(x^2 + 1)^2}{(x^2 + 1)^6}$	0.4 Factoring	11.6	(a) $(x^2 + 1)^4(13x^4 + 14x^2 +$ $\qquad 10x + 1)$ (b) $\dfrac{2(x - 1)(-2x^2 + 3x + 1)}{(x^2 + 1)^4}$
If $f(x) = 3x^2 + 2x$, find $\dfrac{f(x + h) - f(x)}{h}$.	1.3 Functional notation	11.1, 11.2	$6x + 3h + 2$
Find the slope of the line passing through $(1, 2)$ and $(2, 4)$.	2.3 Slopes	11.2	2
Write the equation of the line passing through $(1, 5)$ with slope 8.	2.4 Point-slope equation of a line	11.2, 11.3, 11.5	$y = 8x - 3$
Evaluate the limit: (a) $\displaystyle\lim_{h \to 0} \dfrac{40h - h^2}{h}$ (b) $\displaystyle\lim_{h \to 0} \dfrac{6xh + 3h^2 + 2h}{h}$	10.1 Limits	11.1, 11.2	(a) 40 (b) $6x + 2$

DERIVATIVES

If a firm receives $30,000 in revenue during a 30-day month, its average revenue per day is $30,000/30 = $1000. This does not necessarily mean that the actual revenue was $1000 on any one day, just that the average is $1000 per day. Similarly, if a person drives a car 50 miles in an hour's time, the car's average velocity is 50 miles per hour, but the driver could have gotten a speeding ticket for traveling 70 miles per hour on this trip. When we say a car is moving at a velocity of 50 miles per hour, we are talking about the velocity of the car at an instant in time (the instantaneous velocity). We can use the average velocity to find the instantaneous velocity, as follows.

If a car travels in a straight line from the spot y_1 at time x_1 and arrives at spot y_2 at time x_2, then it has traveled the distance $y_2 - y_1$ in the elapsed time $x_2 - x_1$. If we represent the distance traveled by Δy and the elapsed time by Δx, the average velocity is given by

$$V_{av} = \frac{\Delta y}{\Delta x}.$$

The smaller the time interval, the more nearly the average velocity will be to the instantaneous velocity. For example, knowing that a car traveled 50 miles in an hour does not tell us much about its instantaneous velocity at any time during that period of time. But knowing that it traveled 1 mile in 1 minute, or 50 feet in one second, tells us much more about the velocity at a given time. Continuing to decrease the length of the time interval (Δx) will get us closer and closer to the instantaneous velocity.

Some police departments have equipment that measures how fast a car is traveling by measuring how much time elapses while the car travels between two sensors placed 60 inches apart on the road. This is not the instantaneous velocity of the car, but it is an excellent approximation.

We define the *instantaneous velocity* to be the limit of $\Delta y / \Delta x$ as Δx approaches 0. We write this as

$$V = \lim_{\Delta x \to 0} \frac{\Delta y}{\Delta x}.$$

Thus we may think of velocity as the instantaneous rate of change of distance with respect to time.

This chapter is concerned with *rates of change*. We will see that the *derivative* of a function can be used to determine the rate of change of the dependent variable with respect to the independent variable. In this chapter the derivative will be used to find the marginal profit, marginal cost, and marginal revenue, given the respective profit, total cost, and total revenue functions, and we will find other rates of change, such as rates of change of populations and velocity. We will also use the derivative to determine the slope of a tangent to a curve at a point on the curve. In Chapter 12, more applications of the derivative will be discussed. For example, we will use differentiation to minimize average cost, maximize total revenue, maximize profit, and find the maximum dosage for certain medications.

11.1 The Derivative: Rates of Change

Objectives   ■ To define the derivative as a rate of change
■ To use the definition of derivative to find derivatives of functions

Suppose a firm's revenue is given by the equation

$$f(x) = 100x - x^2, \qquad x \geq 0,$$

where x is the number of units of oil produced per day. (See Figure 11.1.) If the firm produces and sells 10 units per day, the revenue is

$$f(10) = \$900$$

and if it produces 20 units, its revenue is $f(20) = \$1600$. But if it produces 40 units, its revenue is $f(40) = \$2400$. Thus the revenue the firm receives is different at different levels of production. We can also see that the rate at which the revenue changes is different at different levels of production. For example, if production is increased from 20 units to 40 units, revenue increases from $1600 to $2400, so the average rate of change of revenue per unit is

$$\frac{f(40) - f(20)}{40 - 20} = \frac{2400 - 1600}{40 - 20} = \frac{800}{20} = 40.$$

However, if production is increased from 20 units to 30 units, the average rate of change of revenue per unit is

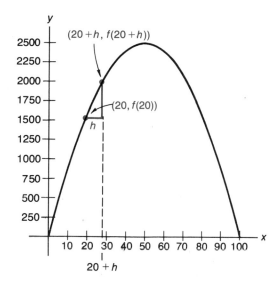

Figure 11.1

$$\frac{f(30) - f(20)}{30 - 20} = \frac{2100 - 1600}{10} = 50.$$

If production increases from 20 units to 21 units, the average rate of change of revenue per unit is

$$\frac{f(21) - f(20)}{21 - 20} = \frac{1659 - 1600}{1} = 59.$$

In considering the rate of change of the revenue function from some fixed point, as above with $x = 20$, we see that the rate of change is different for different increases. Thus the rate of change depends on the size of the increase as well as the level of production. Economists define the rate of change of revenue (the *marginal revenue*) as the **instantaneous rate of change.**

To find the instantaneous rate of change of revenue at $x = 20$, let us first compute the average rate of change as x increases by the small amount h. If we have $20 + h$ units, the revenue is $f(20 + h) = 100(20 + h) - (20 + h)^2$, so the increase in revenue is $f(20 + h) - f(20)$. (See Figure 11.1.) Since the increase in units is h, the average rate of change is

$$\frac{f(20 + h) - f(20)}{h} = \frac{[100(20 + h) - (20 + h)^2] - [100(20) - 20^2]}{h}$$

$$= \frac{2000 + 100h - (400 + 40h + h^2) - 2000 + 400}{h}$$

$$= \frac{60h - h^2}{h}$$

$$= 60 - h.$$

Now, as h gets smaller and smaller, this average rate of change becomes the instantaneous rate

$$\lim_{h \to 0} (60 - h) = 60.$$

Thus if the revenue function is $f(x) = 100x - x^2$, $x \geq 0$, the marginal revenue at 20 units is 60. This means the revenue is increasing at a rate of $60 per unit if production is at 20 units.

To find the instantaneous rate of change of this revenue function at $x = 30$ units of production, we could evaluate

$$\lim_{h \to 0} \frac{f(30 + h) - f(30)}{h} = \lim_{h \to 0} \frac{[100(30 + h) - (30 + h)^2] - [100(30) - 30^2]}{h}$$

$$= \lim_{h \to 0} \frac{40h - h^2}{h}$$

$$= \lim_{h \to 0} 40 - h$$

$$= 40.$$

Rather than evaluate the rates of change at different levels this way, we can develop a means of evaluating the rate of change at *any* point. If the production increases from any value x to $x + h$, revenue will increase from $f(x)$ to $f(x + h)$. Thus the average rate of change in revenue is given by

$$\frac{f(x + h) - f(x)}{h},$$

and the instantaneous rate of change is given by

$$\lim_{h \to 0} \frac{f(x + h) - f(x)}{h}.$$

Thus, for the revenue function $f(x) = 100x - x^2$, the instantaneous rate of change at any point is

$$\lim_{h \to 0} \frac{f(x + h) - f(x)}{h} = \lim_{h \to 0} \frac{[100(x + h) - (x + h)^2] - [100x - x^2]}{h}$$

$$= \lim_{h \to 0} \frac{[100x + 100h - (x^2 + 2xh + h^2)] - [100x - x^2]}{h}$$

$$= \lim_{h \to 0} \frac{100h - 2xh - h^2}{h}$$

$$= \lim_{h \to 0} 100 - 2x - h$$

$$= 100 - 2x.$$

This new function gives a formula for the *instantaneous rate of change of revenue* (the *marginal revenue*) at any level of production. For example, this function gives the instantaneous rate of change at $x = 20$ as $100 - 2(20) = 60$

and at $x = 30$ as $100 - 2(30) = 40$. The function that we have developed to find the instantaneous rate of change of revenue from the revenue function is called the **derivative** of the function $f(x) = 100x - x^2$, and is denoted $f'(x) = 100 - 2x$.

The Derivative   If f is a function defined by $y = f(x)$, then the limit

$$f'(x) = \lim_{h \to 0} \frac{f(x + h) - f(x)}{h},$$

if it exists, defines f', the **derivative** of f. If $f'(x_0)$ exists, we say f is *differentiable* at x_0. The process of finding the derivative is called *differentiation*.

EXAMPLE 1   If $f(x) = 4x^2$,
(a) find $f'(x)$.
(b) evaluate $f'(x)$ at $x = 3$.

Solution   (a) $f'(x) = \lim\limits_{h \to 0} \dfrac{f(x + h) - f(x)}{h}$

$$= \lim_{h \to 0} \frac{4(x + h)^2 - 4x^2}{h}$$

$$= \lim_{h \to 0} \frac{4(x^2 + 2xh + h^2) - 4x^2}{h}$$

$$= \lim_{h \to 0} \frac{4x^2 + 8xh + 4h^2 - 4x^2}{h}$$

$$= \lim_{h \to 0} \frac{8xh + 4h^2}{h}$$

$$= \lim_{h \to 0} 8x + 4h$$

$$= 8x$$

(b) $f'(x)$ at $x = 3$ is $f'(3) = 8(3) = 24$.   □

As was mentioned in the introduction to this chapter, the velocity of a moving object is the instantaneous rate of change of the distance traveled with respect to the elapsed time. Thus, if the distance traveled is given as a function of the time, the derivative of the function will give the velocity at any time. Note that we mentioned that the velocity could be found by evaluating

$$\lim_{\Delta x \to 0} \frac{\Delta y}{\Delta x}.$$

If we represent the change in x values by Δx rather than h, and if we use Δy to denote $f(x + h) - f(x)$, then we can write the definition of derivative in the (shorter) form

$$\lim_{\Delta x \to 0} \frac{\Delta y}{\Delta x}.$$

For this reason the derivative of the function defined by $y = f(x)$ is also denoted by

$$\frac{dy}{dx}.$$

In addition to $\dfrac{dy}{dx}$ and $f'(x)$, the derivative at any point x may be denoted by y',

$\dfrac{d}{dx}f(x)$, $D_x y$, or $D_x f(x)$.

We can, of course, use variables other than x and y to represent functions and their derivatives. For example, we can represent the derivative of the function defined by $p = 2q^2 - 1$ by dp/dq or by $f'(q)$.

EXAMPLE 2   If $p = 2q^2 - 1$, find dp/dq.

Solution   Letting $p = f(q)$, we get

$$\begin{aligned}
\frac{dp}{dq} &= \lim_{h \to 0} \frac{f(q + h) - f(q)}{h} \\
&= \lim_{h \to 0} \frac{[2(q + h)^2 - 1] - [2q^2 - 1]}{h} \\
&= \lim_{h \to 0} \frac{[2(q^2 + 2qh + h^2) - 1] - 2q^2 + 1}{h} \\
&= \lim_{h \to 0} \frac{4qh + 2h^2}{h} \\
&= \lim_{h \to 0} 4q + 2h \\
&= 4q.
\end{aligned}$$

$\square$

Just as we may use different variables in functions, we may use different letters to represent functions. For example, the derivative of $P = P(x)$ is

$$P'(x) = \lim_{h \to 0} \frac{P(x + h) - P(x)}{h}.$$

EXAMPLE 3   If the profit on a commodity is given by $P(x) = 400x - x^2$, where x is the number of units produced, what is the marginal profit, $P'(x)$,
(a) at $x = 20$ units?
(b) at $x = 100$ units?

(c) at $x = 300$ units?

(d) what is happening to profit when 300 units are sold?

Solution   To find the marginal profit at different levels, we will first find the derivative.

$$P'(x) = \lim_{h \to 0} \frac{P(x + h) - P(x)}{h}$$

$$= \lim_{h \to 0} \frac{[400(x + h) - (x + h)^2] - [400x - x^2]}{h}$$

$$= \lim_{h \to 0} \frac{400x + 400h - x^2 - 2xh - h^2 - 400x + x^2}{h}$$

$$= \lim_{h \to 0} \frac{400h - 2xh - h^2}{h}$$

$$= \lim_{h \to 0} 400 - 2x - h$$

$$= 400 - 2x$$

Thus the marginal profit function is $P'(x) = 400 - 2x$. (We may also denote marginal profit by $\overline{MP}$, so $\overline{MP} = 400 - 2x$.)

(a) The marginal profit at 20 units is

$$P'(20) = 400 - 2(20) = 360.$$

(b) The marginal profit at 100 units is

$$P'(100) = 400 - 2(100) = 200.$$

(c) The marginal profit at 300 units is

$$P'(300) = 400 - 2(300) = -200.$$

(d) A marginal profit of -200 indicates that the profit is decreasing at the rate of $200 per unit. Thus the profit is decreasing rapidly when production is at 300 units. Any increase in production will result in loss of profit. □

Exercise 11.1

1. If $f(x) = 5x^2$, find $f'(x)$.
2. If $f(x) = 6x^2$, find $f'(x)$.
3. If $f(x) = x^2 + 1$, find $f'(x)$.
4. If $f(x) = x^2 - 4$, find $f'(x)$.
5. If $y = x^3$, find dy/dx.
6. If $y = 4x^3$, find dy/dx.
7. If $p = 3q - 2$, find dp/dq.
8. If $C = 300 + 4x^2$, find C'.
9. If $y = 4x^2 - 2x + 1$, find y'.
10. If $y = 16x^2 - 4x + 2$, find dy/dx.
11. If $R(x) = 34x - 3$, find $R'(x)$.
12. If $C(x) = 16x + 3x^2$, find $C'(x)$.

13. If $p = q^2 + 4q + 1$, what is the instantaneous rate of change of p with respect to q at $q = 5$?

14. If $p = q^3 - 4q + 5$, what is the instantaneous rate of change of p with respect to q at $q = 2$, $p = 5$?

15. If $C = 14x^2 + 5x + 60$, what is the rate of change of C with respect to x when $x = 4$?

16. If $C = 500 + 40x + 0.5x^2$, what is the rate of change of C with respect to x when $x = 5$?

APPLICATIONS

17. If the revenue function for a good is

$$R(x) = 300x - x^2,$$

where x denotes the number of units produced,
   (a) what is the marginal revenue if 50 units are produced?
   (b) what is the marginal revenue if 100 units are produced?
   (c) what is the marginal revenue if 150 units are produced?
   (d) what is happening to revenue when 150 units are produced?

18. If the profit function for a good is

$$P(x) = 500x - x^2 - 100,$$

   (a) what is the marginal profit if 200 units are sold?
   (b) what is the marginal profit when 300 units are sold?
   (c) what is happening to profit when 300 units are sold?

19. If 0.05 second elapses while a car travels over two sensors on the road which are 5 feet apart, what is the average velocity (*in miles per hour*) of the car as it travels between the sensors (88 feet per second is equivalent to 60 miles per hour)?

11.2 The Slope of the Tangent to a Curve

Objective   ■ To use derivatives to find slopes of tangents to curves

In Chapter 2 we learned that the rate of change of profit (the marginal profit) for a linear profit function is given by the slope of the line. But will the slope of the profit curve give us the marginal profit if the profit function is not linear? Before we can answer this question, we must define the slope of a curve at a point on the curve. We will define the slope of a curve at a point as the slope of the line tangent to the curve at the point.

In geometry, we defined a tangent to a circle as a line that had one point in common with the circle. This definition does not apply to all curves, as Figure 11.2(b) shows. Many lines can be drawn through the point A. One of the lines, line l, looks like it is tangent to the curve, but it intersects the curve at two points.

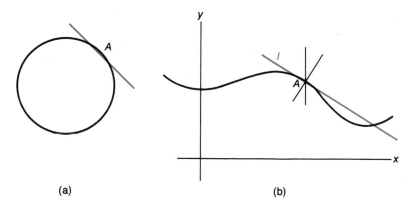

(a)   (b)

Figure 11.2

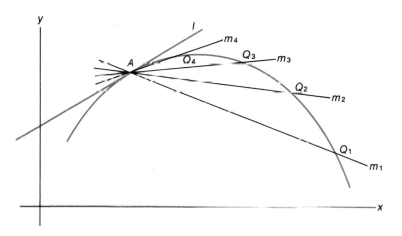

Figure 11.3

We can use *secant lines* (lines intersecting the curve in two points) to determine the tangent to a curve at a point A. In Figure 11.3, we have a set of secant
lines passing through point A, with the line l representing the tangent to the
curve at point A. Note that the secant lines m_1, m_2, m_3, m_4 have their second
points (Q_1, Q_2, Q_3, Q_4) approaching A, and that as these points approach A, the
secant lines get closer to the tangent line l. We can get a secant line as close as
we wish to the tangent line by choosing a "second point" Q sufficiently close to
point A.

Because the limiting position of secant lines that pass through point A and
points to the left of A will also be the same line (line l), we may say that the
common limiting position of the secant lines passing through A is the **tangent
line** to the curve at the point A.

We can find the slope of the tangent to the curve at a point A by finding the
slope of a secant line passing through A and taking the limit of this slope as the

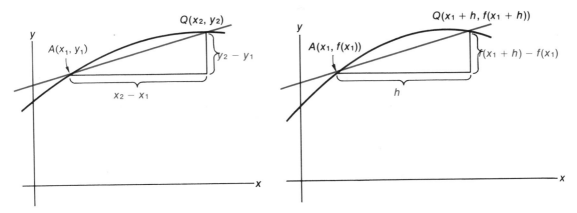

Figure 11.4   **Figure 11.5**

"second point" Q approaches the point A. Consider the function $y = f(x)$, which passes through the point $A(x_1, y_1)$. To find the slope of the tangent to $y = f(x)$ at A, we first draw a secant line from point A to a second point $Q(x_2, y_2)$ on the curve (see Figure 11.4).

The slope of this secant line is

$$m_{AQ} = \frac{y_2 - y_1}{x_2 - x_1}.$$

But because we want to find the limit of this slope as Q approaches A, we will write the slope in a different form. Because $y = f(x)$, we can write the coordinates of A as $(x_1, f(x_1))$. If we represent the difference $x_2 - x_1$ by the letter h, then we can write the coordinates of the point Q as $(x_1 + h, f(x_1 + h))$. The graph is shown with these new coordinates in Figure 11.5.

This notation is somewhat awkward, but it will make finding the slope of the tangent line possible. The slope of the secant line (in the new notation) is

$$m_{AQ} = \frac{f(x_1 + h) - f(x_1)}{h}.$$

Now, as the point Q approaches the point A on the curve, the secant line will approach the tangent to $y = f(x)$ at point A. But how will the slope of the line change as Q approaches A? We see that the difference between their x-values will decrease, so h will approach 0. But we cannot set $h = 0$ to find the slope of the tangent, for the *difference quotient*

$$\frac{f(x_1 + h) - f(x_1)}{h}$$

will be undefined if $h = 0$. Thus the slope of the tangent is the limit of this difference quotient as $h \to 0$.

> The **slope of the tangent** to $y = f(x)$ at point $A(x_1, f(x_1))$ is
>
> $$m = \lim_{h \to 0} \frac{f(x_1 + h) - f(x_1)}{h}.$$ (1)

We can use the formula (1) to find the slope of a tangent to a curve at a point without consideration of the secant lines involved.

EXAMPLE 1   Find the slope of $y = f(x) = x^2$ at the point $A(2, 4)$.

Solution   The formula for the slope of the tangent to $y = f(x)$ at $(2, 4)$ is

$$m = \lim_{h \to 0} \frac{f(2 + h) - f(2)}{h}.$$

So

$$m = \lim_{h \to 0} \frac{(2 + h)^2 - 2^2}{h}.$$

Taking the limit immediately would result in both the numerator and the denominator approaching 0. To avoid this, we simplify the fraction before taking the limit.

$$m = \lim_{h \to 0} \frac{4 + 4h + h^2 - 4}{h} = \lim_{h \to 0} \frac{4h + h^2}{h} = \lim_{h \to 0} (4 + h) = 4$$

Thus the slope of the tangent to $y = x^2$ at $(2, 4)$ is 4 (see Figure 11.6).   □

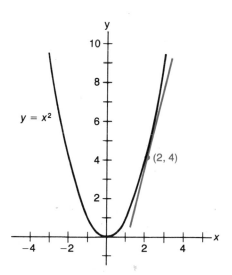

Figure 11.6

The statement that "the slope of the tangent to the curve at $(2, 4)$ is 4" is frequently simplified to the statement "the slope of the curve at $(2, 4)$ is 4." Knowledge that the slope is a positive number on an interval tells us that the function is increasing on that interval, which means the graph of the function is rising as it moves to the right on that interval. If the derivative (and thus the slope) is negative on an interval, the curve is decreasing on the interval; that is, the graph is falling as it moves to the right.

In order to avoid taking the limit of the difference quotient every time we desire the slope of the tangent to a curve at a particular point, we can evaluate the limit at *any* point, denoted $(x, f(x))$. But the resulting limit is

$$\lim_{h \to 0} \frac{f(x + h) - f(x)}{h},$$

which is the *derivative* as we defined it in Section 11.1. Thus we see that *the slope of the graph of a revenue function and the marginal revenue are identical, even when the graph is not a line.*

EXAMPLE 2   Given $y = f(x) = x^2$, find
(a) the derivative of f at any point $(x, f(x))$.
(b) the slope of the curve at $(2, 4)$.
(c) the slope of the curve at $(1, 1)$.

Solution   (a) The derivative of f at any point x is denoted by $f'(x)$, and is

$$f'(x) = \lim_{h \to 0} \frac{f(x + h) - f(x)}{h}$$

$$= \lim_{h \to 0} \frac{(x + h)^2 - x^2}{h}$$

$$= \lim_{h \to 0} \frac{x^2 + 2xh + h^2 - x^2}{h}$$

$$= \lim_{h \to 0} \frac{2xh + h^2}{h}$$

$$= \lim_{h \to 0} 2x + h$$

$$= 2x.$$

That is, the derivative of $y = f(x) = x^2$ is $y' = f'(x) = 2x$.
(b) $f'(x) = 2x$ represents the slope of the tangent to the curve at any point, so the slope at $(2, 4)$ is $f'(2) = 2(2) = 4$.
(c) The slope of $y = x^2$ at $x = 1$ is $f'(1) = 2(1) = 2$.   □

Note that part (b) of Example 2 gave us the same result as the (longer) method used in Example 1.

EXAMPLE 3   Find the equation of the line tangent to $y = 3x^2 + 2x$ at $(1, 5)$.

Solution   We can write the equation of the tangent line by using the point and the slope at that point. We will find the derivative to determine the slope:

$$y' = f'(x) = \lim_{h \to 0} \frac{f(x + h) - f(x)}{h}$$

$$= \lim_{h \to 0} \frac{[3(x + h)^2 + 2(x + h)] - (3x^2 + 2x)}{h}$$

$$= \lim_{h \to 0} \frac{3(x^2 + 2xh + h^2) + 2x + 2h - 3x^2 - 2x}{h}$$

$$= \lim_{h \to 0} \frac{6xh + 3h^2 + 2h}{h}$$

$$= \lim_{h \to 0} 6x + 3h + 2$$

$$= 6x + 2$$

The derivative is $f'(x) = 6x + 2$, so the slope of the tangent at $(1, 5)$ is $f'(1) = 6(1) + 2 = 8$. Then the equation of the tangent line is

$$y - 5 = 8(x - 1),$$

or

$$y = 8x - 3.$$

The curve and tangent line are shown in Figure 11.7.   □

Note that we can denote the value of the derivative of $y = f(x)$ at $x = 1$ by either $f'(1)$ or $y'|_{x=1}$.

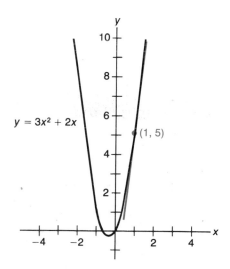

Figure 11.7

Exercise 11.2

1. (a) Find the derivative of $f(x) = x$ at any point on the line.
   (b) What is the slope of the tangent to $f(x) = x$ at $(3, 3)$?
2. (a) Find the derivative of $f(x) = x^2 + 1$.
   (b) What is the slope of the tangent to $f(x) = x^2 + 1$ at $(2, 5)$?
   (c) What is the slope of the curve $f(x) = x^2 + 1$ at $(3, 10)$?
3. (a) If $f(x) = x^2 + x$, find $f'(x)$.
   (b) What is the slope of the curve at $(2, 6)$?
4. (a) If $y = f(x) = x^2 + 3x$, find $f'(x)$.
   (b) What is the slope of the tangent to the curve at $(-1, -2)$?
5. Find the slope of the tangent to $f(x) = x^2$ at the point $(3, 9)$.
6. Find the slope of the tangent to $f(x) = x^3$ at the point $(2, 8)$.
7. Find the equation of the line tangent to $y = x^2$ at $(3, 9)$. (See problem 5.)
8. Find the equation of the line tangent to $y = x^3$ at $(2, 8)$. (See problem 6.)
9. Find the equation of the line tangent to $y = 3x^2 + 1$ at $(1, 4)$.
10. Find the equation of the line tangent to $y = x^2 - 5x$ at $(2, -6)$.

11.3 Derivative Formulas

Objectives
- To find derivatives of constant functions
- To find derivatives of powers of x
- To find derivatives of functions involving constant coefficients
- To find the derivatives of sums and differences of functions

We have already used the definition of derivative to find the following derivatives:

$$\text{If } f(x) = x^2, \text{ then } f'(x) = 2x. \qquad \text{(Example 2, Section 11.2)}$$
$$\text{If } f(x) = x^3, \text{ then } f'(x) = 3x^2. \qquad \text{(Problem 6, Exercise 11.2)}$$

In addition, it can be shown that

$$\text{If } f(x) = x^4, \quad f'(x) = 4x^3.$$
$$\text{If } f(x) = x^5, \quad f'(x) = 5x^4.$$

Do you recognize a pattern that could be used to find the derivative of $f(x) = x^6$? What is the derivative of $f(x) = x^n$? If you guessed that the derivative of $f(x) = x^6$ is $f'(x) = 6x^5$ and the derivative of $f(x) = x^n$ is nx^{n-1}, you're right. We can use the definition of derivative to show this. If n is a positive integer, then

$$f'(x) = \lim_{h \to 0} \frac{f(x + h) - f(x)}{h}$$

$$= \lim_{h \to 0} \frac{(x + h)^n - f(x)}{h}.$$

Because we are assuming n is a positive integer, we can use the binomial formula (see Chapter 9) to expand $(x + h)^n$.

$$f'(x) = \lim_{h \to 0} \frac{\left[x^n + \frac{n}{1} x^{n-1} h + \frac{n(n-1)}{1 \cdot 2} x^{n-2} h^2 + \cdots + h^n \right] - x^n}{h}$$

$$= \lim_{h \to 0} \left[n x^{n-1} + \frac{n(n-1)}{1 \cdot 2} x^{n-2} h + \cdots + h^{n-1} \right]$$

Now, each term after $n x^{n-1}$ contains h as a factor, so all terms except $n x^{n-1}$ will approach 0 as $h \to 0$. Thus

$$f'(x) = n x^{n-1}.$$

We state this derivative rule formally as follows.

Powers of x Rule   If $f(x) = x^n$, where n is a real number, then $f'(x) = n x^{n-1}$. (The derivative of x to a power n is n times x to the $n - 1$ power.)

Note that the rule applies for any real number n even though we proved it only for the case when n is a positive integer.

EXAMPLE 1   Find the derivatives of the following functions.

(a) $f(x) = x^2$ (b) $g(x) = x^6$ (c) $y - x^{1/3}$ (d) $y = \dfrac{1}{x}$

Solution   (a) If $f(x) = x^2$, then $f'(x) = 2x^{2-1} = 2x$.
(b) If $g(x) = x^6$, then $g'(x) = 6x^{6-1} = 6x^5$.
(c) The rule was proved only for positive integers, but it applies for all real values of n. Thus

$$y' = \frac{1}{3} x^{1/3-1} = \frac{1}{3} x^{-2/3} = \frac{1}{3x^{2/3}}$$

(d) The function must be expressed in the form $y = x^n$, so we will rewrite the equation.

$$y = \frac{1}{x} = x^{-1}$$

Then

$$\frac{dy}{dx} = -1x^{-1-1} = -x^{-2}.$$

We can rewrite this derivative in a form similar to that of the original function, as follows.

$$\frac{dy}{dx} = -\frac{1}{x^2}.$$ □

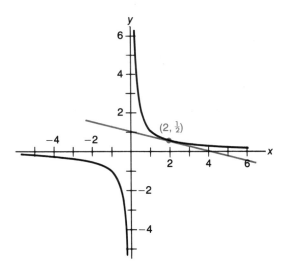

Figure 11.8

Because the derivative of $y = 1/x$ is $dy/dx = -1/x^2$, the slope of the tangent to $y = 1/x$ at $(2, \frac{1}{2})$ is

$$\frac{dy}{dx}\bigg|_{x=2} = -\frac{1}{2^2} = -\frac{1}{4}.$$

The graph and tangent line are shown in Figure 11.8. Note that neither the function nor its derivative exists when $x = 0$.

The differentiation rules are stated and proved for the independent variable x, but they also apply to other independent variables. The following examples illustrate differentiation with variables other than x.

EXAMPLE 2   Find the derivatives of the following functions.

    (a) $u(s) = s^3$ (b) $p = q^{2/3}$ (c) $C(t) = \sqrt{t}$ (d) $s = \dfrac{1}{\sqrt{t}}$

Solution   (a) If $u(s) = s^3$, then $u'(s) = 3s^{3-1} = 3s^2$.
    (b) If $p = q^{2/3}$, then $dp/dq = \frac{2}{3}q^{2/3-1} = \frac{2}{3}q^{-1/3}$.
    (c) Writing $\sqrt{t}$ in its equivalent form, $t^{1/2}$, permits us to use the derivative formula:

$$C'(t) = \frac{1}{2}t^{1/2-1} = \frac{1}{2}t^{-1/2}.$$

Writing the derivative in radical form gives

$$C'(t) = \frac{1}{2}\cdot\frac{1}{t^{1/2}} = \frac{1}{2\sqrt{t}}.$$

(d) Writing $1/\sqrt{t}$ as a power of t gives

$$s = \frac{1}{t^{1/2}} = t^{-1/2}, \qquad \text{so} \qquad \frac{ds}{dt} = -\frac{1}{2}t^{-1/2-1} = -\frac{1}{2}t^{-3/2}.$$

Writing the derivative in a form similar to that of the original function gives

$$\frac{ds}{dt} = -\frac{1}{2} \cdot \frac{1}{t^{3/2}} = -\frac{1}{2\sqrt{t^3}}. \qquad\qquad \square$$

EXAMPLE 3   Find the slope of the tangent to the curve $y = x^3$ at $x = 1$.

Solution   The derivative of $y = x^3$ is $y' = f'(x) = 3x^2$. The slope of the tangent to $y = x^3$ at $x = 1$ is $y'|_{x=1} = f'(1) = 3(1)^2 = 3$. The graph and the tangent line are shown in Figure 11.9. $\qquad \square$

A function of the form $y = f(x) = c$, where c is a constant, is called a constant function. We can easily show that the derivative of a constant function is 0, as follows.

$$f'(x) = \lim_{h \to 0} \frac{f(x + h) - f(x)}{h} = \lim_{h \to 0} \frac{c - c}{h} = \lim_{h \to 0} 0 = 0$$

We can state this rule formally as shown on page 392.

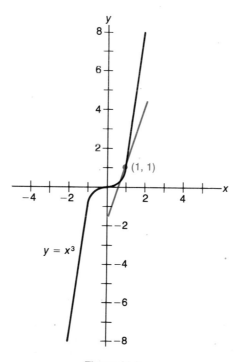

Figure 11.9

> *Constant-*   If $f(x) = c$, where c is a constant, then $f'(x) = 0$.
> *Function Rule*

EXAMPLE 4   Find the derivative of the function defined by $y = 4$.

Solution

$$\frac{dy}{dx} = 0$$

Recall that the function defined by $y = 4$ has as its graph a horizontal line. Thus the slope of the line (and the derivative of the function) is 0.   □

We now can take derivatives of constant functions and powers of x. But we do not yet have a rule to take derivatives of functions of the form $f(x) = 4x^5$ or $g(t) = \frac{1}{2}t^2$. The following rule provides a method for handling functions of this type.

> *Coefficient Rule*   If $f(x) = c \cdot u(x)$, where c is a constant, then $f'(x) = c \cdot u'(x)$. (The derivative of a constant times a function is the constant times the derivative of the function.)

We can use the fact that

$$\lim_{h \to 0} c \cdot g(h) = c \cdot \lim_{h \to 0} g(h),$$

which was discussed in Chapter 10, to verify the coefficient rule. If $f(x) = c \cdot u(x)$, then

$$f'(x) = \lim_{h \to 0} \frac{f(x + h) - f(x)}{h}$$

$$= \lim_{h \to 0} \frac{c \cdot u(x + h) - c \cdot u(x)}{h}$$

$$= \lim_{h \to 0} c \cdot \left[\frac{u(x + h) - u(x)}{h} \right]$$

$$= c \cdot \lim_{h \to 0} \frac{u(x + h) - u(x)}{h}.$$

So $f'(x) = c \cdot u'(x)$.

EXAMPLE 5   Find the derivatives of the following functions.

(a) $f(x) = 4x^5$ (b) $g(t) = \frac{1}{2}t^2$ (c) $p = \dfrac{5}{\sqrt{q}}$

Solution (a) $f'(x) = 4(5x^4) = 20x^4$
(b) $g'(t) = \frac{1}{2}(2t) = t$

(c) $p = \dfrac{5}{\sqrt{q}} = 5q^{-1/2}$, so

$$\frac{dp}{dq} = 5\left(-\frac{1}{2}q^{-3/2}\right) = -\frac{5}{2\sqrt{q^3}} \qquad \square$$

Note that while the derivative of a constant function is 0, the derivative of a constant times a function is the constant times the derivative of the function. For example, the derivative of $y = 4$ is $y' = 0$, but the derivative of $y = 4x^2$ is $y' = 4(2x) = 8x$.

In Example 2 of Section 11.1, we found the derivative of $p = 2q^2 - 1$ to be $dp/dq = 4q - 0 = 4q$, and in problem 3 of Exercise 11.2 we found the derivative of $f(x) = x^2 + x$ to be $f'(x) = 2x + 1$. In Exercise 11.1, we found that the derivative of $p = 3q - 2$ was $dp/dq = 3 - 0 = 3$ (in problem 7) and that the derivative of $C = 300 + 4x^2$ is $C' = 0 + 8x = 8x$. These results suggest that we can find the derivative of a polynomial by finding the derivatives of its terms and combining them. The following rules, which are easily proved, state this formally.

Sums Rule If $f(x) = u(x) + v(x)$, where u and v are functions of x, then $f'(x) = u'(x) + v'(x)$. (The derivative of a sum of two functions is the sum of their derivatives.)

Difference Rule If $f(x) = u(x) - v(x)$, where u and v are functions of x, then $f'(x) = u'(x) - v'(x)$.

EXAMPLE 6 Find the following derivatives.

(a) $y = x^2 + 3$ (b) $p = q^2 - 4q$ (c) $y = 3x + 5$

Solution (a) $y' = 2 \cdot x + 0 = 2x$
(b) $dp/dq = 2 \cdot q - 4 \cdot 1 = 2q - 4$
(c) $y' = 3 \cdot 1 + 0 = 3$ $\square$

In Example 6(c) we saw that the derivative of $y = 3x + 5$ is 3. Because the slope of a line is the same at all points on the line, it is reasonable that the derivative of a linear equation is a constant. In particular, the slope of the graph of the equation $y = mx + b$ is m at all points on its graph, because the derivative of $y = mx + b$ is $y' = f'(x) = m$.

The rules regarding the derivatives of sums and differences of two functions will apply if more than two functions are involved. For example, if $f(x) = 4x^3 - 2x^2 + 5x - 3$, then $f'(x) = 12x^2 - 4x + 5$. We may think of the functions that are added and subtracted as terms of the function f. Then it would be correct to say that we may take the derivative of a function term by term.

EXAMPLE 7   Find the derivative of
(a) $y = 3x^3 - 4x^2$ (b) $p = \frac{1}{3}q^3 + 2q^2 - 3$ (c) $u(x) = 5x^4 + x^{1/3}$

Solution   (a) $y' = 3(3x^2) - 4(2x) = 9x^2 - 8x$

(b) $\dfrac{dp}{dq} = \frac{1}{3}(3q^2) + 2(2q) - 0 = q^2 + 4q$

(c) $u'(x) = 5(4x^3) + \frac{1}{3}x^{-2/3} = 20x^3 + \dfrac{1}{3x^{2/3}}$ □

EXAMPLE 8   Find the derivative of

(a) $y = 4x^3 + \sqrt{x}$ (b) $s = 5t^6 - \dfrac{1}{t^2}$

Solution   (a) We may write the equation as

$$y = 4x^3 + x^{1/2},$$

so

$$y' = 4(3x^2) + \frac{1}{2}x^{-1/2} = 12x^2 + \dfrac{1}{2x^{1/2}},$$

or

$$y' = 12x^2 + \dfrac{1}{2\sqrt{x}}.$$

(b) We may write $s = 5t^6 - 1/t^2$ as

$$s = 5t^6 - t^{-2},$$

so

$$\dfrac{ds}{dt} = 5(6t^5) - (-2t^{-3}) = 30t^5 + 2t^{-3},$$

or

$$\dfrac{ds}{dt} = 30t^5 + \dfrac{2}{t^3}.$$ □

EXAMPLE 9   Find the slope of the tangent to $y = \frac{1}{2}x^2 + 5x$ at

(a) $x = 2$ (b) $x = -5$

Solution   The derivative of $y = \frac{1}{2}x^2 + 5x$ is $f'(x) = x + 5$.

(a) At $x = 2$, the slope is $f'(2) = 2 + 5 = 7$.
(b) At $x = -5$, the slope is $f'(-5) = -5 + 5 = 0$. Thus the tangent to the curve is horizontal at $x = -5$.   □

EXAMPLE 10   Suppose a business person wants to ship instruments in a shock-proof package. To test the packaging material, a package is dropped off the top of a 144-foot building. If the distance (in feet) that the package falls from the top of the building in x seconds is given by

$$y = f(x) = 16x^2,$$

what will be the velocity of the package when it hits the ground?

Solution   We can answer this question by finding the derivative

$$f'(x) = 32x.$$

Since it will take 3 seconds to fall the 144 feet $[16(3)^2 = 144]$, the velocity of the package will be

$$f'(3) = 32(3) = 96$$

feet per second when the package hits the ground.   □

Exercise 11.3

Find the derivatives of the following functions.

1. $y = 4$
2. $f(s) = 6$
3. $y = x$
4. $s = t^2$
5. $c(x) = x^3$
6. $u(x) = x^5$
7. $y = 4x^3$
8. $y = 8x^5$
9. $p = 5q^8$
10. $f(q) = 8q^3$
11. $f(x) = 3x + 8$
12. $y = 5x^3 - 3x^2$
13. $y = 3x^6 - 12x^2$
14. $f(s) = s^2 + 4s + 1$
15. $p = 5q^3 + 4q^2 + 2$
16. $c(x) = x^3 - 5x^2 + 4x$
17. $y = x^{2/3}$
18. $f(q) = q^{11/5}$
19. $f(x) = x^{-4/5}$
20. $y = x^{-8/3}$
21. $v(x) = \sqrt{x}$
22. $u(x) = \sqrt[3]{x}$
23. $p = \sqrt[3]{q^2}$
24. $f(q) = \sqrt[5]{q^3}$

25. $y = \dfrac{1}{x^2}$
26. $y = \dfrac{1}{x^5}$

27. $f(x) = \dfrac{1}{x^3}$
28. $g(x) = \dfrac{1}{x^4}$

29. $u = u(x) = \dfrac{1}{x^{1/3}}$
30. $v = v(x) = \dfrac{1}{x^{3/2}}$

31. $y = 3\sqrt{x} + 3x^3$
32. $y = 5x^3 - \dfrac{1}{\sqrt{x}}$

33. $y = \frac{1}{2}x^2 - 6x^{-1/3}$
34. $y = \sqrt[3]{x^2} + \sqrt{x^3}$

Find the slopes of the tangents to the following curves at the indicated points.

35. $y = 4x^2 + 3x$, $x = 2$
36. $C(x) = 3x^2 - 5$, $(3, 22)$
37. $P(x) = x^2 - 4x$, $(2, -4)$
38. $R(x) = 16x + x^2$, $x = 1$

Write the equations of the tangents to the curves in problems 39–42 at the indicated points.

39. $y = 3x^2 + 2x$, $(1, 5)$
40. $y = 4x - x^2$, $(5, -5)$
41. $y = x^3 - 4x^2 + 1$,   at $x = 2$

42. $y = \dfrac{1}{x} + 3x^2$,   at $x = 2$

43. At what point(s) will the slope of the tangent to $y = x^2 - 4x + 3$ be 0?
44. At what point(s) will the slope of the tangent to $y = x^3 - 5x^2 - 8x + 5$ be 0?

APPLICATIONS

45. A ball is thrown up in the air according to the equation $s = 112t - 16t^2$, t in seconds, s in feet.
    (a) What equation describes the velocity of the ball?
    (b) What is the velocity when $t = 2$? Is the ball going up or going down?

46. A projectile is shot vertically into the air, with its motion described by $s = 960t - 16t^2 + 100$, where s is in feet and t is in seconds.
    (a) What equation describes the velocity of the projectile?
    (b) What is the velocity when $t = 20$?

47. The population size y of a certain organism at time t is given by

$$y = 4t^2 + 2t.$$

Find the rate of change of population.

48. The number of organisms of a certain bacteria at time t can be modeled according to the equation

$$N(t) = 2500(1 + 2t^2).$$

Find the rate of change of the number.

49. A swimming pool is filled by an inlet pipe. The number of gallons N in the pool at time t is

$$N = 2t^2 + 30t,$$

where t is in minutes. At what rate is the pool filling when t is 10?

50. Pressure P of a gas is related to volume V according to Boyle's law, and this relationship is expressed by the equation

$$P = \frac{C}{V},$$

where C is constant. Find the rate of change of pressure with respect to volume.

51. The total revenue for a commodity is described by the function

$$R = 300x - 0.02x^2.$$

What is the marginal revenue when 40 units are sold?

52. If the profit function for a product is

$$P = 400x - 0.1x^2 + 0.01x^3 - 3000,$$

what is the marginal profit when 100 units are sold?

11.4 Product and Quotient Rules

Objectives
- To use the Product Rule to find the derivative of certain functions
- To use the Quotient Rule to find the derivative of certain functions
- To find the differential of a function

We have formulas that permit us to find the derivatives of the sums and differences of functions easily. But we are not so lucky with products. The derivative of a product is *not* the product of the derivatives. To see this, consider the function $f(x) = x \cdot x$. Since this function is $f(x) = x^2$, its derivative is $f'(x) = 2x$. But the product of the derivatives of x and x would give $1 \cdot 1 = 1 \neq 2x$. Thus we need a different formula to find the derivative of a product. This formula is given by the **Product Rule**.

Product Rule If $f(x) = u(x) \cdot v(x)$, where u and v are differentiable functions of x, then

$$f'(x) = u(x) \cdot v'(x) + v(x) \cdot u'(x).$$

(The derivative of a product of two functions is the first function times the derivative of the second plus the second function times the derivative of the first.)

EXAMPLE 1 Use the Product Rule to find the derivative of $f(x) = x^2 \cdot x$.

Solution Using the formula with $u(x) = x^2$, $v(x) = x$, we have
$$\begin{aligned}
f'(x) &= u(x) \cdot v'(x) + v(x) \cdot u'(x) \\
&= x^2 \cdot 1 + x(2x) \\
&= x^2 + 2x^2 \\
&= 3x^2.
\end{aligned}$$ □

Note that we could have found the same result by multiplying the factors and finding the derivative of $f(x) = x^3$. But we will soon see how valuable the Product Rule is.

EXAMPLE 2 Find dy/dx if $y = (2x^3 + 3x + 1)(x^2 + 4)$.

Solution Using the Product Rule with $u(x) = 2x^3 + 3x + 1$ and $v(x) = x^2 + 4$, we have
$$\begin{aligned}
\frac{dy}{dx} &= (2x^3 + 3x + 1)(2x) + (x^2 + 4)(6x^2 + 3) \\
&= 4x^4 + 6x^2 + 2x + 6x^4 + 3x^2 + 24x^2 + 12 \\
&= 10x^4 + 33x^2 + 2x + 12.
\end{aligned}$$ □

We could, of course, avoid using the Product Rule by multiplying the two factors before taking the derivative. But multiplying the factors first may involve more work than using the Product Rule.

EXAMPLE 3   Find the slope of the tangent to $f(x) = (4x^3 + 5x^2 - 6x + 5)(x^3 - 4x^2 + 1)$ at $x = 1$.

Solution $f'(x) = (4x^3 + 5x^2 - 6x + 5)(3x^2 - 8x) + (x^3 - 4x^2 + 1)(12x^2 + 10x - 6)$

The slope of the curve at $x = 1$ is

$$f'(1) = 8(-5) + (-2)(16) = -72.$$ □

The rule for finding the derivative of a function which is the quotient of two polynomials requires a new formula.

Quotient Rule   If $f(x) = u(x)/v(x)$, where u and v are differentiable functions of x, with $v(x) \neq 0$, then

$$f'(x) = \frac{v(x) \cdot u'(x) - u(x) \cdot v'(x)}{[v(x)]^2}.$$

(The derivative of a quotient is the denominator times the derivative of the numerator minus the numerator times the derivative of the denominator, all divided by the square of the denominator.)

To see that this rule is reasonable, consider the function $f(x) = x^3/x$, $x \neq 0$. Using the Quotient Rule, with $u(x) = x^3$ and $v(x) = x$, we get

$$f'(x) = \frac{x(3x^2) - x^3(1)}{x^2} = \frac{3x^3 - x^3}{x^2} = \frac{2x^3}{x^2} = 2x.$$

Because $f(x) = x^3/x = x^2$ if $x \neq 0$, we see that $f'(x) = 2x$ is the correct derivative.

EXAMPLE 4   If $f(x) = \dfrac{x^2 - 4x}{x + 5}$, find $f'(x)$.

Solution   Using the Quotient Rule with $u(x) = x^2 - 4x$ and $v(x) = x + 5$, we get

$$f'(x) = \frac{(x + 5)(2x - 4) - (x^2 - 4x)(1)}{(x + 5)^2}$$

$$= \frac{2x^2 + 6x - 20 - x^2 + 4x}{(x + 5)^2}$$

$$= \frac{x^2 + 10x - 20}{(x + 5)^2}.$$ □

EXAMPLE 5   If $f(x) = \dfrac{x^3 - 3x^2 + 2}{x^2 - 4}$, find $f'(x)$.

Solution   Using the Quotient Rule, with $u(x) = x^3 - 3x^2 + 2$ and $v(x) = x^2 - 4$, we get

$$f'(x) = \frac{(x^2 - 4)(3x^2 - 6x) - (x^3 - 3x^2 + 2)(2x)}{(x^2 - 4)^2}$$

$$= \frac{(3x^4 - 6x^3 - 12x^2 + 24x) - (2x^4 - 6x^3 + 4x)}{(x^2 - 4)^2}$$

$$= \frac{x^4 - 12x^2 + 20x}{(x^2 - 4)^2}. \qquad\qquad \square$$

EXAMPLE 6   Use the Quotient Rule to find the derivative of $y = 1/x^3$.

Solution   Letting $u(x) = 1$ and $v(x) = x^3$, we get

$$y' = \frac{x^3(0) - 1(3x^2)}{(x^3)^2}$$

$$= -\frac{3x^2}{x^6}$$

$$= -\frac{3}{x^4}.$$

Note that we could have found the derivative more easily by writing

$$y = 1/x^3 = x^{-3},$$

so

$$y' = -3x^{-1} = -\frac{3}{x^4}. \qquad\qquad \square$$

It is not necessary to use the Quotient Rule when the numerator or denominator of the function in question contains only a constant. For example, the function $y = (x^3 - 3x)/3$ can be written as $y = \frac{1}{3}(x^3 - 3x)$, so the derivative is $y' = \frac{1}{3}(3x^2 - 3) = x^2 - 1$.

We have used the symbol dy/dx as one of the symbols to denote the derivative of $y = f(x)$ with respect to x, but there are advantages to using the symbols dy and dx separately. We can define the **differential** dy as follows:

The Differential   If $f'(x)$ is the derivative of $y = f(x)$, then the **differential** of y is
$$dy = f'(x)\,dx.$$

EXAMPLE 7   If $y = x^3 - 4x^2 + 5$, find dy.

Solution $$dy = f'(x) \cdot dx = (3x^2 - 8x)\,dx \qquad\qquad \square$$

EXAMPLE 8   If $y = \dfrac{x-2}{x^2}$, find

(a) $\dfrac{dy}{dx}$ (b) dy

Solution   Using the Quotient Rule gives

(a) $\dfrac{dy}{dx} = \dfrac{x^2(1) - (x-2)2x}{(x^2)^2}$

$= \dfrac{x^2 - 2x^2 + 4x}{x^4}$

$= \dfrac{-x^2 + 4x}{x^4} = \dfrac{-x+4}{x^3}$

(b) $dy = \dfrac{-x+4}{x^3}\,dx$

Exercise 11.4

1. Find y' if $y = (x+3)(x^2 - 2x)$.
2. Find $f'(x)$ if $f(x) = (3x - 1)(x^3 + 1)$.

3. Find $\dfrac{dp}{dq}$ if $p = (3q - 1)(q^2 + 2)$.

4. Find $\dfrac{ds}{dt}$ if $s = (t^4 + 1)(t^3 - 1)$.

5. If $f(x) = (x^2 + 3x + 4)(x^3 - 1)$, find $f'(x)$.

6. If $y = (3x^2 + 4)(x^3 - 6x^2 + 1)$, find $\dfrac{dy}{dx}$.

7. If $R(x) = (3x - 1)(100 + 2x^2)$, find $R'(x)$.
8. If $C(x) = (34x + 300)(25 + x^2)$, find $C'(x)$.
9. If $y = (x + 1)\sqrt{x}$, find y'.

10. If $y = \sqrt[3]{x}(x^2 + 1)$, find $\dfrac{dy}{dx}$.

11. What is the slope of the tangent to $y = (x^2 + 1)(x^3 - 4x)$ at $(1, -6)$?
12. What is the slope of the tangent to $y = (x^3 - 3)(x^2 - 4x + 1)$ at $(2, -15)$?

13. Find y' if $y = \dfrac{x}{x^2 - 1}$.

14. Find $f'(x)$ if $f(x) = \dfrac{x^2}{x - 3}$.

15. Find $\dfrac{dp}{dq}$ if $p = \dfrac{q^2 + 1}{q - 2}$.

16. Find $C'(x)$ if $C(x) = \dfrac{x^2 + 1}{x^2 - 1}$.

17. Find $\dfrac{dy}{dx}$ if $y = \dfrac{x^2 - 1}{x - 1}$.

18. Find y' if $y = \dfrac{x^3 - 4x}{x + 2}$.

19. If $p = \dfrac{q^2 + 2q + 3}{q^2 + 4q}$, find $\dfrac{dp}{dq}$.

20. If $p = \dfrac{q^2 + 4q}{q^2 + 5q}$, find p'.

21. Find y' if $y = \dfrac{x(x^2 + 4)}{x - 2}$.

22. Find $f'(x)$ if $f(x) = \dfrac{(x + 1)(x - 2)}{x^2 + 1}$.

23. Find the derivative of $y = \dfrac{x - 2}{x + 1}$ at $\left(1, -\dfrac{1}{2}\right)$.

24. Find the derivative of $y = \dfrac{x^2 + 1}{x - 2}$ at $(1, -2)$.

25. Find the slope of the tangent to $y = \dfrac{x^2 + 1}{x + 3}$ at $(2, 1)$.

26. Find the slope of the tangent to $y = \dfrac{x^2 - 4x}{x^2 + 2x}$ at $\left(2, -\dfrac{1}{2}\right)$.

27. At what point(s) will the slope of the tangent to $y = (x^2 + 1)(x - 2)$ be 0?

28. At what point(s) will the slope of the tangent to $y = \dfrac{x^2}{x - 2}$ be 0?

29. If $y = x^3 + 4x^2 + 5x + 5$, find dy.
30. If $p = q^4 - 5q^2$, find dp.
31. If $s = x^2(x + 1)$, find ds.
32. If $y = \dfrac{x + 1}{x - 1}$, find dy.

33. If $C = (x^2 - 1)(x + 1)$, find dC.

34. If $R = \dfrac{x^2 - 1}{x}$, find dR.

APPLICATIONS

35. If a test having reliability r is lengthened by a factor n, the reliability of the new test is given by

$$R = \frac{nr}{1 + (n - 1)r}, \qquad 0 < r \leq 1.$$

Find the rate at which R changes with respect to n.

36. The number of action potentials produced by a nerve, t seconds after a stimulus, is given by

$$N(t) = 25t + \frac{4}{t^2 + 2} - 2.$$

Find the rate at which the action potentials are produced.

37. The reaction R to an injection of a drug is related to the dosage x according to

$$R(x) = x^2 \left(500 - \frac{x}{3}\right),$$

where 1000 mg is the maximum dosage. If the rate of reaction with respect to the dosage defines the sensitivity to the drug, find the sensitivity.

38. Experimental evidence has shown that the concentration of injected adrenaline, x, is related to the response, y, of a muscle according to the equation

$$y = \frac{x}{a + bx},$$

where a and b are constants. Find the rate of change of response with respect to the concentration.

39. Suppose

$$P = \frac{1000t}{t + 10}$$

represents the size of a population of bacteria, where t represents time. What is the rate of growth of the population?

40. It is determined that a wildlife refuge can support a group of up to 100 of a certain endangered species. If 75 are introduced on the refuge and their population after t years is given by

$$p(t) = 75 \left(1 + \frac{4t}{t^2 + 16}\right),$$

find the rate of population growth after t years. Find the rate after each of the first seven years.

11.5 The Chain Rule and Power Rule

Objectives
- To form the composite of two functions
- To use the chain rule to differentiate functions
- To use the power rule to differentiate functions

Up to this point, we have found derivatives of sums of functions, differences of functions, products of functions, and quotients of functions. We will now consider a new way to combine two functions and a method of finding the derivative of the new function that is formed. This new function is called a composite function. Just as we can substitute a number for the independent variable in a function, we can substitute a second function for the variable. This creates a new function, called a **composite function.**

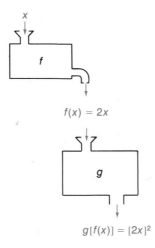

$f(x) = 2x$

$g[f(x)] = [2x]^2$

Figure 11.10

Composite	The **composite function** g of f is the function $g \circ f$ defined by
Functions	$$(g \circ f)(x) = g[f(x)].$$
	The domain of $g \circ f$ is the subset of the domain of f for which $g \circ f$ is defined.

Figure 11.10 illustrates how the composite function $g \circ f$ is created from f and g, where $f(x) = 2x$ and $g(x) = x^2$.

EXAMPLE 1 If $f(x) = 2x$ and $g(x) = x^2$, find $g[f(x)]$.

Solution Substituting $f(x) = 2x$ for x in $g(x)$ gives

$$g[f(x)] = g[2x] = [2x]^2 = 4x^2. \qquad \square$$

EXAMPLE 2 If $f(x) = 3x^2$ and $g(x) = 2x - 1$, then find $F(x) = f[g(x)]$.

Solution Substituting $g(x) = 2x - 1$ for x in $f(x)$ gives

$$f[g(x)] = f(2x - 1) = 3(2x - 1)^2.$$

Thus $F(x) = 3(2x - 1)^2$. $\qquad \square$

We could find the derivative of the function $F(x) = 3(2x - 1)^2$ by multiplying out the expression $3(2x - 1)^2$. Then

$$F(x) = 3(4x^2 - 4x + 1) = 12x^2 - 12x + 3,$$

so $F'(x) = 24x - 12$. But we can also use a very powerful rule, called the Chain

Rule, to find derivatives of functions of this type. If we write the composite function $y = f[g(x)]$ in the form $y = f(u)$, where $u = g(x)$, we can state the **Chain Rule** as follows.

Chain Rule   If f and g are differentiable functions and $y = f(u)$, where $u = g(x)$, then y is a differentiable function of x, and

$$\frac{dy}{dx} = \frac{d}{du} f(u) \cdot \frac{d}{dx} g(x)$$

or, written another way,

$$\frac{dy}{dx} = \frac{dy}{du} \cdot \frac{du}{dx}.$$

Note that dy/du represents the derivative of $y = f(u)$ *with respect to u* and du/dx represents the derivative of $u = g(x)$ *with respect to x*. For example, if $y = 3(2x - 1)^2$, we may write $y = f(u) = 3u^2$, where $u = 2x - 1$. Then the derivative is

$$\frac{dy}{dx} = \frac{dy}{du} \cdot \frac{du}{dx} = 6u \cdot 2 = 12u.$$

To write the derivative in terms of x, we can substitute $2x - 1$ for u. Thus

$$\frac{dy}{dx} = 12(2x - 1) = 24x - 12.$$

Note that we get the same result using the Chain Rule as we did by multiplying out $F(x) = 3(2x - 1)^2$. The Chain Rule is important because it is not always possible to rewrite the function as a polynomial. Consider the following example.

EXAMPLE 3   If $y = \sqrt{x^2 - 1}$, find $\dfrac{dy}{dx}$.

Solution   If we write this function as $y = f(u) = \sqrt{u}$, where $u = x^2 - 1$, we can find the derivative.

$$\frac{dy}{dx} = \frac{dy}{du}\frac{du}{dx} = \frac{1}{2} \cdot u^{-1/2} \cdot 2x$$

$$= u^{-1/2} \cdot x = \frac{1}{\sqrt{u}} \cdot x$$

$$= \frac{x}{\sqrt{u}}$$

To write the derivative in terms of x alone, we substitute $x^2 - 1$ for u. Then

$$\frac{dy}{dx} = \frac{x}{\sqrt{x^2 - 1}}. \qquad \Box$$

Note that we could not find the derivative of a function like that of Example 3 by the methods learned previously.

EXAMPLE 4   If $y = \dfrac{1}{(x^2 + 3x + 1)^2}$, find $\dfrac{dy}{dx}$.

Solution   If we let $u = x^2 + 3x + 1$, we can write $y = f(u) = \dfrac{1}{u^2}$, or $y = u^{-2}$. Then

$$\frac{dy}{dx} = \frac{dy}{du} \cdot \frac{du}{dx} = -2u^{-3}(2x + 3) = \frac{-4x - 6}{u^3}.$$

Substituting for u gives

$$\frac{dy}{dx} = \frac{-4x - 6}{(x^2 + 3x + 1)^3}. \qquad \Box$$

A direct result of the Chain Rule is a very useful rule, called the **Power Rule.**

Power Rule   If $y = u^n$, where u is a differentiable function of x, then

$$\frac{dy}{dx} = nu^{n-1} \cdot \frac{du}{dx}.$$

EXAMPLE 5   If $y = (x^2 - 4x)^6$, find $\dfrac{dy}{dx}$.

Solution   The right side of the equation is in the form u^n, with $u = x^2 - 4x$. Thus by the Power Rule,

$$\frac{dy}{dx} = nu^{n-1} \cdot \frac{dy}{dx}$$

$$= 6u^5(2x - 4).$$

Substituting for u gives

$$\frac{dy}{dx} = 6(x^2 - 4x)^5(2x - 4)$$

$$= (12x - 24)(x^2 - 4x)^5. \qquad \Box$$

EXAMPLE 6   If $y = \sqrt[3]{x^2 - 3x + 1}$, find y'.

Solution   Since $y = (x^2 - 3x + 1)^{1/3}$, we can use the Power Rule with $u = x^2 - 3x + 1$.

$$y' = nu^{n-1}\frac{du}{dx}$$

$$= \frac{1}{3}u^{-2/3}(2x - 3)$$

$$= \frac{1}{3}(x^2 - 3x + 1)^{-2/3}(2x - 3)$$

$$= \frac{2x - 3}{3(x^2 - 3x + 1)^{2/3}} \qquad \square$$

EXAMPLE 7   If $p = \dfrac{1}{3q^2 + 1}$, find $\dfrac{dp}{dq}$.

Solution   We can use the Power Rule to find dp/dq if we write the equation in the form

$$p = (3q^2 + 1)^{-1}.$$

Then

$$\frac{dp}{dq} = -1(3q^2 + 1)^{-2}(6q)$$

$$= \frac{-6q}{(3q^2 + 1)^2}. \qquad \square$$

The derivative of the function in Example 7 can also be found using the Quotient Rule, but the Power Rule provides a more efficient method.

EXAMPLE 8   Find the derivative of $g(x) = \dfrac{1}{\sqrt{(x^2 + 1)^3}}$.

Solution   Writing $g(x)$ as a power gives

$$g(x) = (x^2 + 1)^{-3/2}$$

Then

$$g'(x) = -\frac{3}{2}(x^2 + 1)^{-5/2}(2x)$$

$$= -3x \cdot \frac{1}{(x^2 + 1)^{5/2}}$$

$$= \frac{-3x}{\sqrt{(x^2 + 1)^5}}. \qquad \square$$

Exercise 11.5

Differentiate the functions in problems 1–20.

1. $y = (x^2 + 1)^3$
2. $p = (q^2 + 4q)^4$
3. $y = (4x^2 - 4x + 1)^4$
4. $r = (s^2 + 5s)^{10}$

5. $f(x) = \dfrac{1}{(x^2 + 2)^3}$

6. $g(x) = \dfrac{1}{4x^3 + 1}$

7. $g(x) = (x^2 + 4x)^{-2}$

8. $p = (q^3 + 1)^{-5}$

9. $c(x) = (x^2 + 3x + 4)^{-3}$

10. $y = (x^2 - 8x)^{2/3}$

11. $g(x) = \dfrac{1}{(2x^3 + 3x + 5)^{3/4}}$

12. $y = (3x^3 + 4x + 1)^{-3/2}$

13. $y = \sqrt{x^2 + 4x + 5}$

14. $y = \dfrac{1}{\sqrt{x^2 + 3x}}$

15. $s = \sqrt{3x - x^2}$

16. $y = \sqrt[3]{(x - 1)^2}$

17. $y = 8(x^2 - 3)^5$

18. $y = 5\sqrt{1 - x^3}$

19. $y = \dfrac{6}{(4x^2 + 5)^2}$

20. $y = \dfrac{14}{\sqrt{3x^2 + 5}}$

21. Find the slope of the tangent to $y = (x^3 + 2x)^4$ at $x = 2$.
22. Find the slope of the tangent to $y = \sqrt{5x^2 + 2x}$ at $x = 1$.
23. Find the slope of the tangent to $y = \sqrt{x^3 + 1}$ at $(2, 3)$.
24. Find the slope of the tangent to $y = (4x^3 - 5x + 1)^3$ at $(1, 0)$.
25. Write the equation of the tangent to $y = (x^2 - 3x + 3)^3$ at $(1, 1)$.
26. Write the equation of the tangent to $y = \sqrt{3x^2 - 2}$ at $(3, 5)$.
27. Write the equation of the tangent to $y = (x^2 + 1)^3$ at $(2, 125)$.
28. Write the equation of the tangent to $y = \left(\dfrac{1}{x^3 - x}\right)^3$ at $(2, \frac{1}{216})$.

29. At what values of x will the slope of the tangent to $y = (x^2 - 4)^3$ be 0?
30. At what value(s) of x will the slope of the tangent to $y = \sqrt{4 - x^2}$ be 0?

APPLICATIONS

31. Suppose the number of grams of bacteria in a population is given by $y = (t^2 + 1)^2$, where t is the number of hours of growth. Find the rate of growth of the bacteria (a) at time t.   (b) at $t = 10$.

32. The description of body heat loss due to convection involves a coefficient of convection, K_c, which depends on wind velocity according to the equation
$$K_c = 4\sqrt{4v + 1}.$$
Find the rate of change of the coefficient with respect to the wind velocity.

33. The Schütz-Borisoff law relates the amount of substrate, y, transformed by an enzyme as a function of time, t, according to the equation
$$y = k\sqrt{cat},$$
where k, a, and c are constants. Find the rate at which the substrate is transformed.

The relation between the magnitude of a sensation y and the magnitude of the stimulus, x, is given by
$$y = k(x - x_0)^n,$$
where k is a constant and x_0 is the threshold of effective stimulus, and n depends on the

type of stimulus. Find the rate of change of sensation with respect to the amount of stimulus for each of problems 34–36.

34. For the stimulus of visual brightness $y = k(x - x_0)^{1/3}$.

35. For the stimulus of warmth $y = k(x - x_0)^{8/5}$.

36. For the stimulus of electrical stimulation $y = k(x - x_0)^{7/2}$.

37. The concentration C of a substance in the body depends on the quantity of the substance, Q, and the volume, V, through which it is distributed. For a static substance this is given by

$$C = \frac{Q}{V}.$$

For a situation like that in the kidneys, where the fluids are moving, the concentration is the ratio of the rate of change of quantity with respect to time and the rate of change of volume with respect to time.

(a) Formulate the equation for concentration of a moving substance.

(b) Show this is equal to the rate of change of quantity with respect to volume.

11.6 Using Derivative Formulas (Optional)

Objective   ■ To use derivative formulas separately and in combination with each other

We have used the Power Rule to find the derivative of functions like

$$y = (x^3 - 3x^2 + x + 1)^5,$$

but we have not found the derivative of functions like

$$y = [(x^2 + 1)(x^3 + x + 1)]^5.$$

This function is different because the function u (which is raised to the fifth power) is the product of two functions ($x^2 + 1$ and $x^3 + x + 1$). The equation is of the form $y = u^5$, where $u = (x^2 + 1)(x^3 + x + 1)$. This means that the Product Rule should be used to find du/dx. Then

$$\frac{dy}{dx} = 5u^4 \cdot \frac{du}{dx}$$

$$= 5[(x^2 + 1)(x^3 + x + 1)]^4[(x^2 + 1)(3x^2 + 1) + (x^3 + x + 1)(2x)]$$

$$= 5[(x^2 + 1)(x^3 + x + 1)]^4(5x^4 + 6x^2 + 2x + 1)$$

$$= (25x^4 + 30x^2 + 10x + 5)[(x^2 + 1)(x^3 + x + 1)]^4.$$

A different type of problem involving the Power Rule and the Product Rule is finding the derivative of

$$y = (x^2 + 1)^5(x^3 + x + 1).$$

We may think of y as the *product* of two functions, one of which is a power. Thus the fundamental formula to be used is the Product Rule. The two functions are

$u(x) = (x^2 + 1)^5$ and $v(x) = x^3 + x + 1$. The Product Rule is

$$\frac{dy}{dx} = u(x) \cdot v'(x) + v(x) \cdot u'(x)$$

$$= (x^2 + 1)^5(3x^2 + 1) + (x^3 + x + 1) \cdot 5(x^2 + 1)^4 2x.$$

Note that the Power Rule was used to find $u'(x)$, since $u(x) = (x^2 + 1)^5$. We can simplify dy/dx by factoring out $(x^2 + 1)^4$:

$$\frac{dy}{dx} = (x^2 + 1)^4[(x^2 + 1)(3x^2 + 1) + (x^3 + x + 1) \cdot 5 \cdot 2x]$$

$$= (x^2 + 1)^4(13x^4 + 14x^2 + 10x + 1)$$

EXAMPLE 1   If $y = \left(\dfrac{x^2}{x - 1}\right)^2$, find y'.

Solution   We again have an equation of the form $y = u^n$, but this time the u is a quotient. Thus we will need the Quotient Rule to find du/dx.

$$y' - nu^{n-1} \cdot \frac{du}{dx}$$

$$= 2u^1 \frac{(x - 1) \cdot 2x - x^2 \cdot 1}{(x - 1)^2}$$

Substituting for u and simplifying gives

$$y' = 2 \cdot \frac{x^2}{x - 1} \cdot \frac{2x^2 - 2x - x^2}{(x - 1)^2}$$

$$= \frac{2x^2(x^2 - 2x)}{(x - 1)^3}$$

$$= \frac{2x^4 - 4x^3}{(x - 1)^3}. \qquad\qquad \square$$

EXAMPLE 2   Find $f'(x)$ if $f(x) = \dfrac{(x - 1)^2}{(x^2 + 1)^3}$.

Solution   The function is the quotient of two functions, $(x - 1)^2$ and $(x^2 + 1)^3$, so we must use the Quotient Rule to find the derivative of $f(x)$. *But* taking the derivative of $(x - 1)^2$ and $(x^2 + 1)^3$ will require the Power Rule.

$$f'(x) = [v(x) \cdot u'(x) - u(x) \cdot v'(x)]/[v(x)]^2$$

$$= \frac{(x^2 + 1)^3[2(x - 1)^1] - (x - 1)^2[3(x^2 + 1)^2 2x]}{[(x^2 + 1)^3]^2}$$

$$= \frac{2(x^2 + 1)^3(x - 1) - 6x(x - 1)^2(x^2 + 1)^2}{(x^2 + 1)^6}$$

We see that 2, $(x^2 + 1)^2$, and $(x - 1)$ are all factors in both terms of the numerator, so we can factor them out.

$$f'(x) = \frac{2(x^2 + 1)^2(x - 1)[(x^2 + 1) - 3x(x - 1)]}{(x^2 + 1)^6}$$

$$= \frac{2(x - 1)(-2x^2 + 3x + 1)}{(x^2 + 1)^4} \qquad \square$$

EXAMPLE 3   Find $f'(x)$ if $f(x) = (x^2 - 1)\sqrt{3 - x^2}$.

Solution   The function is the product of two functions, $x^2 - 1$ and $\sqrt{3 - x^2}$, so we will use the Product Rule to find the derivative of $f(x)$. *But* the derivative of $\sqrt{3 - x^2} = (3 - x^2)^{1/2}$ will require the Power Rule.

$$f'(x) = u(x) \cdot v'(x) + v(x) \cdot u'(x)$$
$$= (x^2 - 1)[\tfrac{1}{2}(3 - x^2)^{-1/2}(-2x)] + (3 - x^2)^{1/2}(2x)$$
$$= (x^2 - 1)[-x(3 - x^2)^{-1/2}] + (3 - x^2)^{1/2}(2x)$$
$$= \frac{-x^3 + x}{(3 - x^2)^{1/2}} + 2x(3 - x^2)^{1/2}$$

We can combine these terms over the common denominator $(3 - x^2)^{1/2}$ as follows.

$$f'(x) = \frac{-x^3 + x}{(3 - x^2)^{1/2}} + \frac{2x(3 - x^2)^1}{(3 - x^2)^{1/2}}$$

$$= \frac{-x^3 + x + 6x - 2x^3}{(3 - x^2)^{1/2}}$$

$$= \frac{-3x^3 + 7x}{(3 - x^2)^{1/2}} \qquad \square$$

We should note that in Example 3 we could have written $f'(x)$ in the form

$$f'(x) = (-x^3 + x)(3 - x^2)^{-1/2} + 2x(3 - x^2)^{1/2}.$$

Now, the factor $(3 - x^2)$, to different powers, is contained in both terms of the expression. Thus we can factor $(3 - x^2)^{-1/2}$ from both terms. (We choose the $-1/2$ power because it is the smaller of the two powers.) Dividing $(3 - x^2)^{-1/2}$ into the first term gives $(-x^3 + x)$ and dividing it into the second term gives $2x(3 - x^2)^1$. Why? Thus we have

$$f'(x) = (3 - x^2)^{-1/2}[(-x^3 + x) + 2x(3 - x^2)]$$

$$= \frac{-3x^2 + 7x}{(3 - x^2)^{1/2}},$$

which agrees with our previous answer.

It may be helpful to review the formulas needed to find the derivatives of various types of functions. Table 11.1 has examples of different types of functions and the formulas needed to find their derivatives.

Table 11.1

Example	Formula
$f(x) = 14$	If $f(x) = c, f'(x) = 0$
$y = x^4$	If $f(x) = x^n, f'(x) = nx^{n-1}$
$g(x) = 5x^3$	If $g(x) = cf(x), g'(x) = cf'(x)$
$y = 3x^2 + 4x$	If $f(x) = u(x) + v(x), f'(x) = u'(x) + v'(x)$
$y = (x^2 - 2)(x + 4)$	If $f(x) = u(x) \cdot v(x), f'(x) = u(x) \cdot v'(x) + v(x) \cdot u'(x)$
$f(x) = \dfrac{x^3 + 1}{x^2}$	If $f(x) = \dfrac{u(x)}{v(x)}, f'(x) = \dfrac{v(x) \cdot u'(x) - u(x) \cdot v'(x)}{[v(x)]^2}$
$y = (x^3 - 4x)^{10}$	If $y = u^n, u = g(x), \dfrac{dy}{dx} = nu^{n-1} \cdot \dfrac{du}{dx}$
$y = \left(\dfrac{x - 1}{x^2 + 3}\right)^3$	Power Rule, then Quotient Rule to find $\dfrac{du}{dx}$, $u = \dfrac{x - 1}{x^2 + 3}$
$y = (x + 1)\sqrt{x^3 + 1}$	Product Rule, then Power Rule to find $v'(x)$, $v(x) = \sqrt{x^3 + 1}$
$y = \dfrac{(x^2 - 3)^4}{x}$	Quotient Rule, then Power Rule to find the derivative of the numerator

Exercise 11.6

Find the derivatives of the following functions.

1. $f(x) = 14$

2. $y = x^4$

3. $g(x) = 5x^3$

4. $y = 3x^2 + 4x$

5. $y = (x^2 - 2)(x + 4)$

6. $f(x) = \dfrac{x^3 + 1}{x^2}$

7. $y = (x^3 - 4x)^{10}$

8. $y = \left(\dfrac{x - 1}{x^2 + 3}\right)^3$

9. $y = (x + 1)\sqrt{x^3 + 1}$

10. $y = \dfrac{(x^2 - 3)^4}{x}$

11. $p = [(q + 1)(q^3 - 3)]^3$

12. $y = [(4 - x^2)(x^2 + 5x)]^4$

13. $R(x) = [x^2(x^2 + 3x)]^4$

14. $c(x) = [x^3(x^2 + 1)]^{-3}$

15. $y = \left(\dfrac{2x - 1}{x^2 + x}\right)^4$

16. $y = \left(\dfrac{5 - x^2}{x^4}\right)^3$

17. $f(x) = \dfrac{\sqrt[3]{x^2 + 5}}{4 - x^2}$

18. $g(x) = \dfrac{\sqrt[3]{2x - 1}}{2x + 1}$

19. $y = (x - 1)^2(x^2 + 1)$

20. $y = x^3(4x^5 - 5)^3$

21. $y = (x^2 + 4)^2(x^3 - 4x^2)$

22. $y = (x^3 - 5x^2 + 1)(x^3 - 3)$

23. $c(x) = x\sqrt{x^3 + 1}$

24. $R(x) = x\sqrt[3]{3x^3 + 2}$

25. $y = (x^2 + 4x)(x^5 + 1)^3$

26. $f(x) = (5x^3 + 1)(x^4 + 5x)^2$

27. $g(x) = (8x^4 + 3)^2(x^3 - 4x)^3$

28. $y = (3x^3 - 4x)^3(4x^2 - 8)^2$

29. $y = \dfrac{(x^2 - 4)^3}{x^2 + 1}$

30. $y = \dfrac{(2x - 4)^4}{(x^2 + 3)^3}$

11.7 Applications of Derivatives in Business and Economics

Objectives
- To find the marginal cost and marginal revenue at different levels of production
- To find the marginal profit function, given information about total cost and total revenue

In Chapter 2, we defined marginal cost as the rate of change of the total cost function. For a linear total cost function, the marginal cost was defined as the slope of the function's graph. For any total cost function defined by an equation, we can find the instantaneous rate of change of cost (the marginal cost) at any level of production by finding the derivative of the function.

> If $C = C(x)$ is a total cost function for a commodity, then its derivative, $\overline{MC} = C'(x)$ is the **marginal cost function**.

The linear cost function with equation

$$C(x) = 300 + 6x \quad \text{(in dollars)}$$

has marginal cost \$6 because its slope is 6. Taking the derivative of $C(x)$ gives

$$\overline{MC} = C'(x) = 6,$$

which verifies that the marginal cost is \$6 at all levels of production.
The cost function

$$C(x) = 1000 + 6x + x^2$$

has derivative

$$C'(x) = 6 + 2x.$$

Then the marginal cost at $x = 10$ (when 10 units are produced) is

$$C'(10) = 6 + 20 = 26,$$

and the marginal cost at 40 units is

$$C'(40) = 6 + 80 = 86.$$

Thus the marginal cost is \$26 at 10 units and \$86 at 40 units of production.
As noted previously, when the derivative of a function is positive (and thus the slope of the tangent to the curve is positive), the function is increasing, and the value of the derivative gives us a measure of how fast it is increasing. Since marginal cost is the derivative of total cost, we can use marginal cost to measure increases in the total cost function. For example, the marginal cost for

$$C(x) = 1000 + 6x + x^2$$

is 86 at $x = 40$ and 26 at $x = 10$. This tells us the cost is increasing faster at $x = 40$ than it is at $x = 10$.

Because producing more units can never reduce the total cost of production, the following properties are valid:

1. The total cost can never be negative. If there are fixed costs, the cost of producing 0 units is positive; otherwise, the cost of producing 0 units is 0.
2. The total cost function is always increasing; the more units produced, the higher the total cost. Thus the marginal cost is always positive.
3. There may be limitations on the units produced, by factors such as plant space.

The graphs of many marginal cost functions tend to be U-shaped; they eventually will rise, even though there may be an initial interval where they decrease.

EXAMPLE 1   If the total cost function for a commodity is given by $C(x) = x^3 - 9x^2 + 33x + 30$, find the marginal cost and sketch its graph.

Solution   The marginal cost is

$$\overline{MC} = C'(x) = 3x^2 - 18x + 33.$$

The graph of the total cost function is shown in Figure 11.11, and the graph of the marginal cost function is shown in Figure 11.12.   □

As we have seen in Section 11.1, the instantaneous rate of change (the derivative) of the revenue function is the marginal revenue.

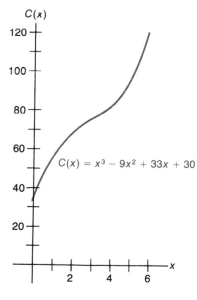

Figure 11.11

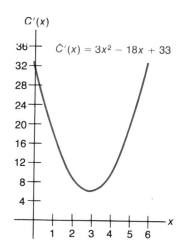

Figure 11.12

> If $R = R(x)$ is the total revenue function for a commodity, then the
> **marginal revenue function** is $\overline{MR} = R'(x)$.

EXAMPLE 2   (a) Find the marginal revenue function for the total revenue function

$$R(x) = 16x - 0.02x^2.$$

(b) Find the marginal revenue for this good at $x = 40$.

Solution   (a) The marginal revenue function is

$$\overline{MR} = R'(x) = 16 - 0.04x.$$

(b) At $x = 40$, $R'(40) = 16 - 1.6 = 14.40$. Thus the forty-first item sold will
increase the total revenue by \$14.40.   □

EXAMPLE 3   Graph the total revenue and marginal revenue functions of Example 2.

Solution   The graphs are shown in Figures 11.13 and 11.14, respectively. Note that the
total revenue function has a maximum value at $x = 400$. After that, the total
revenue function decreases. This means that, because of the discount, the total
revenue will be reduced each time a unit is sold, if more than 400 are produced
and sold. The graph of the marginal revenue function (Figure 11.14) shows the
marginal revenue is positive to the left of 400. This indicates that the rate at
which the total revenue is changing is positive until 400 units are sold. Thus the
total revenue is increasing. Then, at 400 units, the rate of change is 0. After 400
units are sold, the marginal revenue is negative, which indicates that the total
revenue is now decreasing. It is clear from looking at either graph that no more

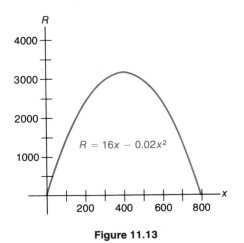

Figure 11.13

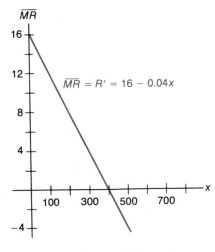

Figure 11.14

than 400 units should be produced and sold if the total revenue function is $R(x) = 16 - 0.02x^2$. That is, the *total revenue* function has its maximum at $x = 400$.   □

As with marginal cost and marginal revenue, the derivative of a profit function for a commodity gives us the marginal profit function for the commodity.

> If $P = P(x)$ is the profit function for a commodity, then the **marginal profit function** is $\overline{MP} = P'(x)$.

EXAMPLE 4   If the total profit for a good is given by $P(x) = 20\sqrt{x + 1} - 2x$, what is the marginal profit at a production level of 15 units?

Solution   The marginal profit function is

$$P'(x) = 20 \cdot \frac{1}{2}(x + 1)^{-1/2} - 2 = \frac{10}{\sqrt{x + 1}} - 2.$$

If 15 units are produced, the marginal profit is

$$P'(15) = \frac{10}{\sqrt{15 + 1}} - 2 = \frac{1}{2}.$$ □

EXAMPLE 5   If the total revenue function is $R(x) = 47x$ and the total cost function is $C(x) = 100 + x + x^2$, $0 \le x \le 25$, find the marginal profit function.

Solution   The total profit function is

$$P(x) = 47x - (100 + x + x^2)$$

or

$$P(x) = 46x - 100 - x^2.$$

The marginal profit function is

$$P'(x) = 46 - 2x.$$ □

The marginal profit in Example 5 is not always positive, so producing and selling a certain number of items will maximize profit. Note that the marginal profit will be negative (that is, profit will decrease) if more than 23 items are produced. We will discuss methods of maximizing total revenue and profit, and for minimizing average cost, in Chapter 12.

Exercise 11.7

Find the marginal cost functions related to the cost functions in problems 1–8.

1. $C(x) = 40 + 8x$
2. $C(x) = 200 + 16x$
3. $C(x) = 500 + 13x + x^2$
4. $C(x) = 300 + 10x + \frac{1}{100}x^2$

5. $C = x^3 - 6x^2 + 24x + 10$

6. $C = x^3 - 12x^2 + 63x + 15$

7. $C = 400 + 27x + x^3$

8. $C(x) = 50 + 48x + x^3$

9. If the cost function for a commodity is $C(x) = 40 + x^2$, find the marginal cost at $x = 5$.

10. If the cost function for a commodity is $C(x) = 300 + 6x + \frac{1}{10}x^2$, find the marginal cost at $x = 8$.

11. If the cost function for a commodity is $C(x) = x^3 - 4x^2 + 30x + 20$, find the marginal cost at $x = 4$.

12. If the cost function for a commodity is $C(x) = \frac{1}{90}x^3 + 4x^2 + 4x + 10$, find the marginal cost at $x = 3$.

13. If the cost function for a commodity is $C(x) = 300 + 4x + x^2$, graph the marginal cost function.

14. If the cost function for a commodity is $C(x) = x^3 - 12x^2 + 63x + 15$, graph the marginal cost function.

15. (a) If the total revenue function for a good is $R(x) = 4x$, what is the marginal revenue function?

   (b) What does this marginal revenue function tell us?

16. If the total revenue function for a product is $R(x) = 32x$, what is the marginal revenue for the product?

17. If the total revenue function for a commodity is $R = 36x - 0.01x^2$,

   (a) find the marginal revenue function.

   (b) find the marginal revenue at $x = 100$.

18. If the total revenue function for a commodity is $R(x) = 25x - 0.05x^2$,

   (a) find the marginal revenue function.

   (b) find the marginal revenue at $x = 50$.

19. (a) Graph the marginal revenue function from problem 17.

   (b) At what value of x will total revenue be maximized?

20. (a) Graph the marginal revenue function from problem 18.

   (b) Sale of how many units will maximize total revenue?

21. If the total profit function is $P(x) = 5x - 25$, find the marginal profit.

22. If the total profit function is $P(x) = 16x - 32$, find the marginal profit.

23. If the total revenue function is $R(x) = 32x$ and the total cost function is $C(x) = 200 + 2x + x^2$, find the marginal profit function.

24. If the total revenue function is $R(x) = 46x$ and the total cost function is $C(x) = 100 + 30x + \frac{1}{10}x^2$, find the marginal profit function.

25. (a) Graph the marginal profit function of problem 23.

   (b) What level of production will give a 0 marginal profit?

26. (a) Graph the marginal profit function of problem 24.

   (b) What level of production will give a 0 marginal profit?

Review Exercises

1. If $c = 4x^5 - 6x^3$, find c'.

2. If $f(x) = 4x^2 - 1$, find $f'(x)$.

3. If $p = 3q + \sqrt{7}$, find dp/dq.

4. If $y = \sqrt{x}$, find y'.

5. If $f(z) = \sqrt[3]{2^4}$, find $f'(z)$.

6. If $v(x) = 4/\sqrt[3]{x}$, find $v'(x)$.

7. If $y = \dfrac{1}{x} - \dfrac{1}{\sqrt{x}}$ find y'.

8. If $g(x) = (3x - 1)(x^2 - 4x)$, find $g'(x)$.

9. Find y' if $y = (x^2 + 1)(3x^3 + 1)$.

10. If $p = \dfrac{2q - 1}{q^2}$, find $\dfrac{dp}{dq}$.

11. Find ds/dt if $s = \sqrt{t}/(3t + 1)$.

12. If $y = (x^3 - 4x^2)^3$, find y'.

13. If $y = (5x^6 + 6x^4 + 5)^6$, find y'.

14. If $y = (x^3 - 4x^2)^3$, find dy/dx.

15. Find $g'(x)$ if $g(x) = 1/\sqrt{x^3 - 4x}$.

° 16. Find y' if $y = x\sqrt{x^2 - 4}$.

° 17. Find y' if $y = \left(\dfrac{x + 1}{1 - x^2}\right)^3$.

18. Find y' if $y = \dfrac{1}{(x^2 - 3x + 1)^2}$.

° 19. Find S' if $S = \dfrac{(3x + 1)^2}{x^2 - 4}$.

° 20. Find z' if $z = \left(\dfrac{x}{x - 1}\right)^3$.

21. Write the equation of the tangent to $y = 3x^5 - 6$ at $x = 1$.

22. Write the equation of the line tangent to the curve $y = 3x^3 - 2x$ at the point $(2, 20)$.

APPLICATIONS

23. If the cost function for a good is $C(x) = 3x^2 + 6x + 600$,
    (a) what is the marginal cost function?
    (b) what is the marginal cost if 30 units are produced?

24. If the total cost function for a commodity is $C(x) = 400 + 5x + x^3$, what is the marginal cost when 4 units are produced?

25. If the total revenue function for a commodity is $R = 40x - 0.02x^2$, with x representing the number of units,
    (a) find the marginal revenue function.
    (b) at what level of production will marginal revenue be 0?

26. If the total revenue function is $R(x) = 60x$ and the total cost function is $C = 200 + 10x + 0.1x^2$, what is the marginal profit at $x = 10$?

27. If the total revenue function for a commodity is given by $R = 80x - 0.04x^2$,
    (a) find the marginal revenue function.
    (b) what is the marginal revenue at $x = 100$?

In this chapter you will need to work problems like the following. If you have difficulty with any problem, return to the section where that type of problem was introduced and refresh your memory before starting the chapter.

Problem Type	Introduced in Section	Used in Section	Answer
Write $\frac{1}{3}(x^2 - 1)^{-2/3}(2x)$ with positive exponents.	0.2 Exponents	12.2	$\dfrac{2x}{3(x^2 - 1)^{2/3}}$
Factor: (a) $x^3 - x^2 - 6x$ (b) $8000 - 80x - 3x^2$	0.4 Factoring	12.1, 12.3	(a) $x(x - 3)(x + 2)$ (b) $(40 - x)(200 + 3x)$
(a) For what values of x is $\dfrac{2}{3\sqrt[3]{x + 2}}$ undefined? (b) For what values of x is $\frac{1}{3}(x^2 - 1)^{-2/3}(2x)$ undefined?	1.2 Domains of functions	12.2	(a) $x = -2$ (b) $x = -1, x = 1$
If $f(x) = \frac{1}{3}x^3 - x^2 - 3x + 2$, and $f'(x) = x^2 - 2x - 3$, (a) find $f(-1)$. (b) find $f'(-2)$.	1.3 Functional notation	12.1	(a) $\frac{11}{3}$ (b) 5
(a) Solve $0 = x^2 - 2x - 3$ (b) If $f'(x) = 3x^2 - 3$, what values of x make $f'(x) = 0$?	5.1 Solving quadratic equations	12.1	(a) $x = -1, x = 3$ (b) $x = -1, x = 1$
(a) Is the function $y = x^{1/3}$ continuous at $x = 0$? (b) Is the function $y = \dfrac{1}{x^2}$ continuous at $x = 0$?	10.2 Continuity	12.2	(a) Yes (b) No
Find the derivatives: (a) $y = \frac{1}{3}x^3 - x^2 - 3x + 2$ (b) $f(x) = x^{1/3}$ (c) $f = x + 2\left(\dfrac{80,000}{x}\right)$ (d) $p(t) = 1 + \dfrac{4t}{t^2 + 16}$ (e) $y = (x + 2)^{2/3}$ (f) $y = \sqrt[3]{x^2 - 1}$	11.3, 11.4, 11.5 Derivatives	12.1, 12.2, 12.3	(a) $y' = x^2 - 2x - 3$ (b) $f'(x) = \frac{1}{3}x^{-2/3}$ (c) $f' = 1 - \dfrac{160,000}{x^2}$ (d) $p'(t) = \dfrac{64 - 4t^2}{(t^2 + 16)^2}$ (e) $\dfrac{2}{3(x + 2)^{1/3}}$ (f) $\dfrac{2x}{3(x^2 - 1)^{2/3}}$

APPLICATIONS OF DERIVATIVES

In Chapter 11 we learned that the derivative could be used to determine rates of change, including velocity, marginal cost, marginal revenue, marginal profit, and rates of growth. We also used the derivative to determine the slope of the tangent to the curve at a given point.

In this chapter we will consider methods of determining when functions are maximized and minimized. We will see that the derivative can be used to determine the "turning points" of the graph of a function, so we can determine when a curve reaches its highest (or lowest) point. Knowledge of where a curve has a relative maximum and/or relative minimum will be very helpful in sketching its graph.

The relative maximum of a function can be useful in determining the levels of production that will maximize profit functions and revenue functions, the maximum dosage for certain medications, and maximum sizes of some changing populations. The relative minimum of an average cost function can be used to find the level of production that will minimize the average cost per unit.

12.1 Relative Maxima and Minima; Curve Sketching

Objectives
- To find relative maxima and minima and horizontal points of inflection of functions
- To sketch graphs of functions using information about maxima, minima, and horizontal points of inflection

Except for very simple graphs (straight lines and parabolas, for example), plotting points will not give a very accurate graph of a function. In addition to intercepts and asymptotes, we can use the first derivative as an aid in graphing. The first derivative identifies the "turning points" of a curve, which will help determine the general shape of the curve.

In Figure 12.1 we see that the graph of $y = \frac{1}{3}x^3 - x^2 - 3x + 2$ has two "turning points", at $(-1, \frac{11}{3})$ and $(3, -7)$. The curve has a relative maximum at $(-1, \frac{11}{3})$, because this point is higher than any other point "near" it on the curve; the curve has a relative minimum at $(3, -7)$, because this point is lower than any other point "near" it on the curve. A formal definition follows.

> A function f has a **relative maximum** at $x = x_1$ if there is an interval around x_1 on which $f(x_1) \geq f(x)$ for all x on the interval.
> A function f has a **relative minimum** at $x = x_2$ if there is an interval around x_2 on which $f(x_2) \leq f(x)$ for all x on the interval.

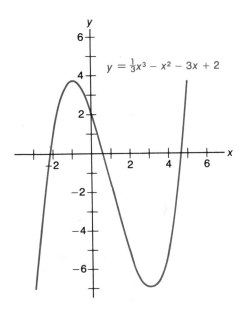

$$y = \tfrac{1}{3}x^3 - x^2 - 3x + 2$$

Figure 12.1

A function f is said to be *increasing* over an interval in its domain if for every x_1 and x_2 in the interval $f(x_2) > f(x_1)$, if $x_2 > x_1$. A function f is *decreasing* over an interval if for every x_1 and x_2 in the interval, $f(x_2) < f(x_1)$ if $x_2 > x_1$.

If a function f is increasing, the slope of the tangent to the curve is positive, and if f is decreasing, the slope of the tangent to the curve is negative. This leads us to conclude the following.

> If f is a function that is differentiable on an interval (a, b), then
> If $f'(x) > 0$ for all x in (a, b), f is increasing on (a, b).
> If $f'(x) < 0$ for all x in (a, b), f is decreasing on (a, b).

The derivative $f'(x)$ can change signs only at values of x where $f'(x) = 0$ or $f'(x)$ is undefined. We call these values of x **critical values.** The point corresponding to a critical value for x is a **critical point.** Because a curve changes from increasing to decreasing at a relative maximum (see Figure 12.1), we have the following fact.

> If f has a relative maximum at $x = x_0$, then $f'(x_0) = 0$ or $f'(x_0)$ is undefined.

Figure 12.2 shows the graph of a function with two relative maxima, one at $x = x_1$ and the second at $x = x_3$. At $x = x_1$ the derivative is 0, and at $x = x_3$ the derivative does not exist.

As Figure 12.2 shows, the function changes from decreasing to increasing at a relative minimum. Thus we have the following fact.

> If f has a relative minimum at $x = x_0$, then $f'(x_0) = 0$ or $f'(x_0)$ is undefined.

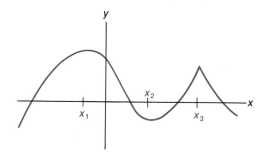

Figure 12.2

Thus we can find relative maxima and minima for a curve by finding values of x for which the first derivative* is 0 or undefined. The behavior of the derivative to the left and right (and near) these values will tell us if they are relative maxima or relative minima, or, occasionally, neither one.

Suppose the point (x_1, y_1) is a critical point. If $f'(x)$ is positive to the left of, and near, this critical point, and if $f'(x)$ is negative to the right of, and near, this critical point, then the curve is increasing to the left of the point and decreasing to the right. This means that a relative maximum occurs at the point. If we draw tangent lines to the curve to the left of and to the right of the critical point, they would be as follows:

To the left, $f'(x) > 0$:   ╱

To the right, $f'(x) < 0$:   ╲

If $f'(x_1) = 0$, the tangent line is horizontal there, so these tangent lines form the pattern

which shows us the curve has the shape

so the curve has a relative maximum at (x_1, y_1).

This can be *illustrated* as follows†:

Left of critical point, $f'(x) > 0$:
At critical point, $f'(x_1) = 0$: $\Rightarrow$
Right of critical point, $f'(x) < 0$:

Similarly, suppose the point (x_2, y_2) is a critical point, $f'(x)$ is negative to the left of, and near, (x_2, y_2), and $f'(x)$ is positive to the right of, and near, this critical point. Then the curve is decreasing to the left of the point and increasing to the right, and a relative minimum occurs at the point. If we draw tangent lines to the curve to the left of and to the right of this critical point, they would be as follows:

To the left, $f'(x) < 0$:   ╲

To the right, $f'(x) > 0$:   ╱

If $f'(x_2) = 0$, the tangent line is horizontal there, so these tangent lines form the pattern

╲＿╱

---

* The derivatives we have been discussing thus far are called *first* derivatives. We will discuss higher-order derivatives in Chapter 13.
† The word "implies" is symbolized by "$\Rightarrow$."

which shows us the curve has the shape

so the curve has a relative minimum at (x_2, y_2).
   This can be illustrated as follows:

Left of critical point, $f'(x) < 0$:
At critical point, $f'(x_2) = 0$: $\Rightarrow$
Right of critical point, $f'(x) > 0$:

rel. min.

If $f'(x)$ does not change signs as x passes from one side of a critical point (x_3, y_3) to the other, the critical point is neither a maximum nor a minimum. If $f'(x_3) = 0$, we can illustrate the two possible cases as follows:

Left of critical point, $f'(x) > 0$:
At critical point, $f'(x_3) = 0$: $\Rightarrow$
Right of critical point, $f'(x) > 0$:

or

Left of critical point, $f'(x) < 0$:
At critical point, $f'(x_3) = 0$: $\Rightarrow$
Right of critical point, $f'(x) < 0$:

The preceding discussion suggests the following procedure for finding relative maxima and minima of a function.

First-Derivative Test

PROCEDURE	EXAMPLE
To find relative maxima and minima of a function:	Find the relative maxima and minima of $f(x) = \frac{1}{3}x^3 - x^2 - 3x + 2$.
1. Find the first derivative of the function.	1. $f'(x) = x^2 - 2x - 3$
2. Set the derivative equal to 0, and solve for values of x that satisfy $f'(x) = 0$. These are called *critical values*. Values that make f' undefined are also critical values.	2. $0 = x^2 - 2x - 3$ has solutions $x = -1$, $x = 3$. No values of x make $x^2 - 2x - 3$ undefined.
3. Substitute the critical values into the *original function* to find the *critical points*.	3. $f(-1) = \frac{11}{3}$ $f(3) = -7$ The critical points are $(-1, \frac{11}{3})$ and $(3, -7)$

4. Evaluate $f'(x)$ at some value of x to the left and right of each critical value:

(a) If $f'(x) > 0$ to the left and $f'(x) < 0$ to the right of the critical value, the critical point is a relative maximum.

(b) If $f'(x) < 0$ to the left and $f'(x) > 0$ to the right of the critical value, the critical point is a relative minimum.

4. $f'(-2) = 5 > 0$ and $f'(0) = -3 < 0$; thus $(-1, 11/3)$ is a relative maximum.

$f'(2) = -3 < 0$ and $f'(4) = 5 > 0$; thus $(3, -7)$ is a relative minimum.

The graph of this function is shown in Figure 12.3.

We can test to the left and right of each critical value by testing to the left of the smallest critical value, then testing a value *between* each critical value, then testing to the right of the largest critical value. The following example illustrates this procedure.

EXAMPLE 1 Find the relative maxima and minima of $y = x^3 - 3x + 6$.

Solution 1. The first derivative of $y = f(x)$ is $y' = f'(x) = 3x^2 - 3$.
2. Setting $f'(x) = 0$ gives $0 = 3x^2 - 3$.
   Solving for x gives

$$0 = 3(x - 1)(x + 1)$$
$$x = -1, \qquad x = 1.$$

3. Substituting the critical values ($x = -1$ and $x = 1$) into the original function gives the critical points: $f(-1) = 8$, so $(-1, 8)$ is a critical point.

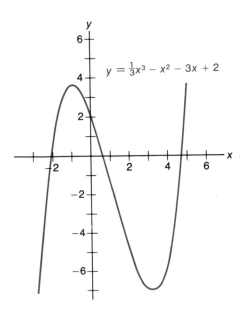

$$y = \tfrac{1}{3}x^3 - x^2 - 3x + 2$$

Figure 12.3

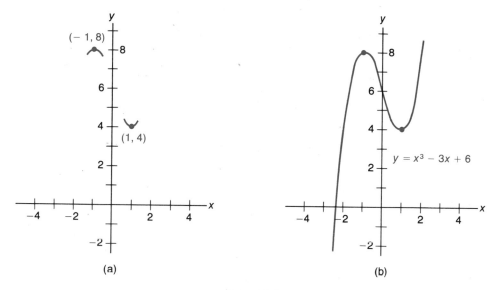

Figure 12.4

$f(1) = 4$, so $(1, 4)$ is a critical point.

4. Testing $f'(x)$ to the left of the smaller critical value, then between the two critical values, then to the right of the larger critical value gives

$$f'(-2) = 3(-2)^2 - 3 = 9 > 0$$

Critical value $f'(-1) = 0$

$$f'(0) = 3(0)^2 - 3 = -3 < 0$$

Critical value $f'(1) = 0$

$$f'(2) = 3(2)^2 - 3 = 9 > 0$$

rel. max.   at $(-1, 8)$.

rel. min.   at $(1, 4)$.

Thus $(-1, 8)$ is a relative maximum and $(1, 4)$ is a relative minimum. The relative maximum and relative minimum are shown in Figure 12.4(a) and the graph of the curve is given in Figure 12.4(b). Notice how easy it is to graph the equation once the relative maxima and minima are graphed.

Note that we substitute the critical values into the *original function $f(x)$* to find the y values of the critical points, but we test for relative maxima and minima by substituting values near the critical values into the *derivative of the function, $f'(x)$*.   □

EXAMPLE 2   Find the relative maxima and minima of $f(x) = \frac{1}{4}x^4 - \frac{1}{3}x^3 - 3x^2 + 8$.

Solution   1. $f'(x) = x^3 - x^2 - 6x$
2. $0 = x^3 - x^2 - 6x$, or $0 = x(x - 3)(x + 2)$ has solutions $x = 0$, $x = 3$, $x = -2$
3. $f(-2) = \frac{8}{3}$, so $(-2, \frac{8}{3})$ is a critical point.
    $f(0) = 8$, so $(0, 8)$ is a critical point.
    $f(3) = -\frac{31}{4}$, so $(3, -\frac{31}{4})$ is a critical point.

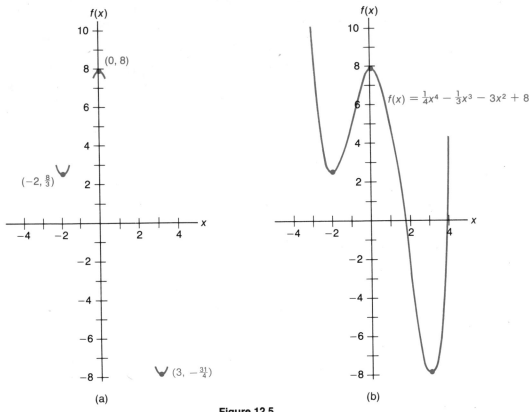

Figure 12.5

4. $f'(-3) = -18 < 0$
$f'(-2) = 0$ $\Bigg\} \Rightarrow$ ⌣ $(-2, \frac{8}{3})$ is a relative minimum.
$f'(-1) = 4 > 0$
$f'(0) = 0$ $\Bigg\} \Rightarrow$ ⌢ $(0, 8)$ is a relative maximum.
$f'(1) = -6 < 0$
$f'(3) = 0$ $\Bigg\} \Rightarrow$ ⌣ $(3, -\frac{31}{4})$ is a relative minimum.
$f'(4) = 24 > 0$

The graph of the function is given in Figure 12.5.   □

NOTE: Only four values were needed to test three critical points in Example 2. This method will work *only if* the critical values are tested in order from smallest to largest.

   Not all critical points will result in relative maxima or minima. If the first derivative of f is 0 at x_0, but does not change from positive to negative or negative to positive as x passes through x_0, then we say f has a **horizontal point of inflection** at x_0.

EXAMPLE 3   Find the relative maxima and minima and horizontal points of inflection of $h(x) = \frac{1}{4}x^4 - \frac{2}{3}x^3 - 2x^2 + 8x + 4$.

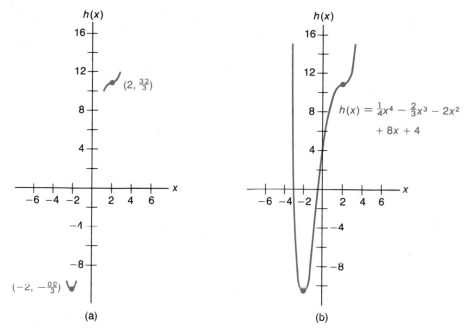

Figure 12.6

Solution

1. $h'(x) = x^3 - 2x^2 - 4x + 8$
2. $0 = x^3 - 2x^2 - 4x + 8$ or $0 = x^2(x - 2) - 4(x - 2)$,   so $0 = (x - 2)(x^2 - 4)$. Thus $x = -2$ and $x = 2$ are solutions.
3. The critical points are $(-2, -\frac{32}{3})$ and $(2, \frac{32}{3})$.
4. $h'(-3) = -25 < 0$
   $h'(-2) = 0$
   $h'(0) = 8 > 0$ $\Rightarrow (-2, -\frac{32}{3})$ is a relative minimum.
   $h'(2) = 0$
   $h'(3) = 5 > 0$ $\Rightarrow (2, \frac{32}{3})$ is a horizontal point of
                               inflection.

The graph of $y = h(x)$ is shown in Figure 12.6.   □

Exercise 12.1

Find the relative maxima, relative minima, and horizontal points of inflection, and sketch the graphs of the following functions.

1. $y = x^3 - 3x^2$
2. $y = x^4 - 2x^2$
3. $y = \frac{1}{3}x^3 - x^2 + x + 1$
4. $y = \frac{1}{4}x^4 - \frac{2}{3}x^3 + \frac{1}{2}x^2 - 2$
5. $y = x^4 - 4x^3$
6. $y = x^3(x - 1)$
7. $y = (x - 2)^2$
8. $y = x(x - 1)^2$
9. $y = x(x - 2)^3$
10. $y = (x^2 - 4)^2$
11. $p = q^2 - 4q + 4$
12. $p = \frac{1}{3}q^3 - 2q^2 - 12q$
13. $p = q^3 + q^2 - 8q + 3$
14. $C(x) = x^3 - \frac{3}{2}x^2 - 6x + 4$

12.2 More Maxima and Minima; Undefined Derivatives

Objectives
■ To use information from derivatives to sketch graphs
■ To find absolute maxima and minima of functions

As we mentioned in the First Derivative Test in Section 12.1, values of x that make the first derivative undefined are also critical values for a function. The first derivative may be undefined at the point $x = x_0$ because

1. The function is undefined at x_0 (see Figure 12.7).
2. The point $x = x_0$ is not in the domain of the derivative even though it is in the domain of the function (see Figure 12.8).
3. The limit of the difference quotient

$$\frac{f(x + h) - f(x)}{h}$$

is different from the left than it is from the right; thus

$$f'(x) = \lim_{h \to 0} \frac{f(x + h) - f(x)}{h}$$

does not exist (see Figure 12.9).

Figure 12.7 is the graph of $y = f(x) = 1/x^2$.

$$f'(x) = -\frac{2}{x^3}$$

Both $f(x)$ and $f'(x)$ are undefined at $x = 0$.

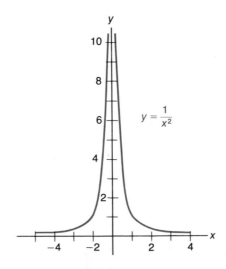

Figure 12.7

Figure 12.8 is the graph of $y = f(x) = x^{1/3}$.

$$f'(x) = \frac{1}{3x^{2/3}}$$

The function $f(x)$ is defined at $x = 0$, but $f'(x)$ is not defined at $x = 0$.

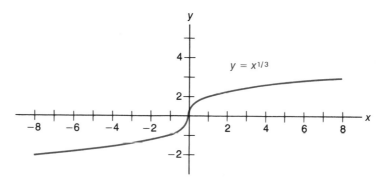

Figure 12.8

Figure 12.9 is the graph of $y = f(x) = |x|$. The function $f(x)$ is defined at $x = 0$, but $f'(x)$ does not exist at $x = 0$. Slopes (derivatives) for $x < 0$ are all -1, and slopes for $x > 0$ are all $+1$.

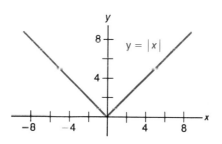

Figure 12.9

Several observations can be made using these figures.

First note that in Figures 12.8 and 12.9, the functions are continuous at $x = 0$, but do not have derivatives at $x = 0$. What is the relationship between differentiability and continuity? The answer is as follows.

If a function f is differentiable at $x = a$, then f is continuous at $x = a$.

Also note that the equations graphed in Figures 12.8 and 12.9 show that the converse of this statement is false.

Finally note that, in Figure 12.8, the value at $x = 0$ is neither maximum nor minimum, and in Figure 12.9, the value $x = 0$ yields a minimum. How do we classify these cases? The answer is to use the First Derivative Test just as we did in Section 12.1. Some further examples will be helpful.

EXAMPLE 1   Find the relative maxima and minima (if any) of the graph of $y = (x + 2)^{2/3}$.

Solution   1. $y' = f'(x) = \frac{2}{3}(x + 2)^{-1/3} = \dfrac{2}{3\sqrt[3]{x + 2}}$

2. $0 = \dfrac{2}{3\sqrt[3]{x + 2}}$ has no solutions; $f'(x)$ is undefined at $x = -2$.

3. $f(-2) = 0$, so the critical point is $(-2, 0)$.

4. $\left.\begin{array}{l} f'(-3) = -\frac{2}{3} \\ f'(-1) = \frac{2}{3} \end{array}\right\} \Rightarrow$ a relative minimum occurs at $(-2, 0)$.

The graph is shown in Figure 12.10.   □

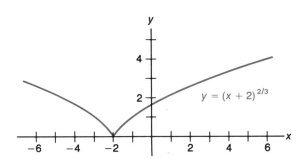

Figure 12.10

EXAMPLE 2   Find the relative maxima and minima of the function $g(x) = \sqrt[3]{x^2 - 1}$.

Solution   1. $g'(x) = \frac{1}{3}(x^2 - 1)^{-2/3}(2x) = \dfrac{2x}{3(x^2 - 1)^{2/3}}$

2. $0 = \dfrac{2x}{3(x^2 - 1)^{2/3}}$ has solution $x = 0$. But $g'(x)$ is undefined at $x = -1$ and $x = 1$. Thus critical values are -1, 0, and 1.

3. The critical points are $(-1, 0)$, $(0, -1)$, and $(1, 0)$.

4. $\left.\begin{array}{l} g'(-2) < 0 \\ g'(-\frac{1}{2}) < 0 \\ g'(\frac{1}{2}) > 0 \\ g'(2) > 0 \end{array}\right\}$ $\Rightarrow$ no maximum or minimum at $(-1, 0)$.
$\Rightarrow (0, -1)$ is a relative minimum.
$\Rightarrow$ no maximum or minimum at $(1, 0)$.

The graph of g is shown in Figure 12.11.   □

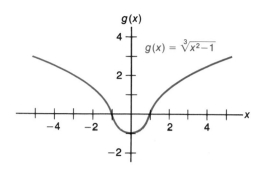

Figure 12.11

Notice that in Figure 12.11 the relative minimum is the lowest point on the graph. In this case we call the point an **absolute minimum** for the function. Similarly, when there is a point that is the highest point on the graph over the domain of the function, then we call the point an **absolute maximum** for the function.

In Figure 12.11, we see that there is no relative maximum. However, if the domain of the function is restricted to the interval $[-\frac{1}{2}, 1]$, then there is an absolute maximum at the point $(1, 0)$, and the absolute minimum is still at $(0, -1)$. If we consider the function in Figure 12.11 with the domain restricted to the interval $[1, 3]$, then its absolute minimum would occur at the point $(1, 0)$, and its absolute maximum at $(3, 2)$.

As the above discussion indicates, if the domain of a function is limited, an absolute maximum or minimum may occur at the endpoints of the domain. In testing functions with limited domains for absolute maxima and minima, we must compare the endpoints of the domain with the relative maxima and minima found by taking derivatives. In applications to the management, life, and social sciences, a limited domain occurs very often, since many quantities are required to be positive, or at least nonnegative.

EXAMPLE 3   Find the absolute maximum and absolute minimum of the function

$$y = x^2 - 1. \qquad (-1 \le x \le 2)$$

Solution   We first find points where the derivative is 0.

1. $y' = f'(x) = 2x$
2. $0 = 2x$ has solution $x = 0$.
3. The critical point is $(0, -1)$.
4. $\left. \begin{array}{l} f'(-1) = -2 < 0 \\ f'(1) = 2 > 0 \end{array} \right\} \Rightarrow (0, 0)$ is a relative minimum.

We now compare the values of the function at the endpoints of the domain with this relative minimum.

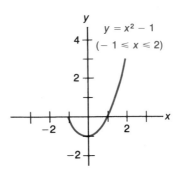

Figure 12.12

$$f(-1) = 0; \; f(2) = 3$$

Thus we see that $(0, -1)$ is the absolute minimum and $(2, 3)$ is the absolute maximum. The graph of the function is shown in Figure 12.12.   □

Exercise 12.2

Use information about their derivatives to sketch the graphs of the functions in problems 1–12.

1. $y = 1/x^2$

2. $y = 4/(x - 4)^2$

3. $y = 1/(x - 1)^2$

4. $y = 1/x^3$

5. $y = \sqrt[3]{x^2 - 4}$

6. $y = \sqrt{x + 3}$

7. $y = \dfrac{x^2 + 4}{x}$

8. $y = \dfrac{4}{(x + 4)^2}$

9. $c(x) = \sqrt{x}(x - 1)^2$

10. $R(x) = x^{2/3}(x - 1)^2$

11. $f(x) = \begin{cases} x + 2 & \text{if } x \le 2 \\ 4 & \text{if } x > 2 \end{cases}$

12. $f(x) = \begin{cases} 3 & \text{if } x \le 0 \\ x + 1 & \text{if } x > 0 \end{cases}$

Find the absolute maxima and minima, if they occur, for the functions in problems 13–17.

13. $f(x) = 16 - x^2$

14. $f(x) = x^2 - 2x$

15. $g(x) = 2x^2 - x \quad (0 \le x \le 3)$

16. $h(x) = 2x^2 - x \quad (1 \le x \le 4)$

17. $f(x) = 16 - x^2 \quad (0 \le x \le 3)$

18. Does the function

$$f(x) = \begin{cases} 3 & \text{if } x \le 0 \\ x + 3 & \text{if } x > 0 \end{cases}$$

have a derivative existing at $x = 0$?

19. Will every function that is differentiable at $x = a$ also be continuous at that point?

20. Will every function that is continuous at $x = a$ also be differentiable at that point?

12.3 Applications of Maxima and Minima

Objective
■ To apply the procedures for finding maxima and minima to solve problems from the management, life, and social sciences

One of the most important applications of calculus in applied situations is in finding maxima and minima. As individuals, workers, or consumers, we may be interested in such things as maximum population, maximum area, maximum revenue, minimum cost, minimum competency, or maximum dosage. If we have a function that models population, area, or revenue, we can apply the methods of this chapter to find maxima or minima for that function.

EXAMPLE 1 Population of an endangered species at a wildlife refuge is a function of time, given by

$$p(t) = 80 \left(1 + \frac{4t}{t^2 + 16} \right).$$

If the species is introduced to the refuge when $t = 0$, find the maximum number of individuals that will populate the refuge.

Solution This function will have its maximum when $p'(t) = 0$.

$$p'(t) = 80 \left[\frac{(t^2 + 16)(4) - (4t)(2t)}{(t^2 + 16)^2} \right]$$

$$p'(t) = 80 \left[\frac{4t^2 + 64 - 8t^2}{(t^2 + 16)^2} \right]$$

$$p'(t) = 80 \left[\frac{64 - 4t^2}{(t^2 + 16)^2} \right]$$

Now, $p'(t) = 0$ when its numerator is 0 (note the denominator is never 0), so we must solve

$$64 - 4t^2 = 0$$
$$4(4 + t)(4 - t) = 0$$

so $$t = -4 \text{ or } t = 4$$

We are only interested in positive t-values so we test $t = 4$.

$$\left. \begin{array}{l} p'(0) = 80 \left(\dfrac{64}{256} \right) > 0 \\[2mm] p'(10) = 80 \left[-\dfrac{336}{(116)^2} \right] < 0 \end{array} \right\} \Rightarrow \text{relative maximum}$$

For $t \geq 0$ we have $t = 4$ yields an absolute maximum of

$$p(4) = 80 \left(1 + \frac{16}{32} \right) = 120 \text{ individuals} \qquad \square$$

EXAMPLE 2   The rate of change of photosynthesis depends on the intensity of light x according to the equation

$$R(x) = 270x - 90x^2.$$

Find the intensity that maximizes this rate.

Solution $R'(x) = 270 - 180x$, so we must solve $270 - 180x = 0$ for x. Hence

$$x = \tfrac{270}{180} = \tfrac{3}{2}.$$

Now we verify that $x = \tfrac{3}{2}$ yields the maximum rate.

$$\left.\begin{array}{l} R'(0) = 270 > 0 \\ R'(2) = -90 < 0 \end{array}\right\} \implies \text{relative maximum}$$

In fact, we could also note that $R(x) = 270x - 90x^2$ is a parabola that opens downward, so $x = \tfrac{3}{2}$ must yield the maximum value for R. The maximum rate is

$$R(\tfrac{3}{2}) = 270(\tfrac{3}{2}) - 90(\tfrac{3}{2})^2 = 202\tfrac{1}{2}.$$ □

Sometimes we must develop the function we need from the statement of the problem. In this case it is important to understand what is to be maximized or minimized, and to express that quantity as a function of *one* variable.

EXAMPLE 3   A farmer wants to make a rectangular pasture with 80,000 square feet. If the pasture lies along a river and he fences the remaining three sides, what dimensions should he use to minimize the amount of fence needed?

Solution   If x represents the length of the pasture (parallel to the river), and y represents the width, then the amount of fence needed is

$$f = y + x + y = x + 2y.$$

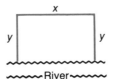

Since the fence is to be minimized, this is the desired function, but we must express the fence as a function of either x or y only.

Returning to the problem we see that the area is given by $xy = 80,000$. Solving for y and substituting gives

$$f = x + 2\left(\frac{80,000}{x}\right) = x + \frac{160,000}{x}$$

The derivative of f is

$$\frac{df}{dx} = 1 - \frac{160,000}{x^2},$$

so

$$0 = 1 - \frac{160,000}{x^2}$$

$$x^2 = 160,000$$

$$x = \pm 400.$$

Of course, only $x = 400$ applies to this problem. Testing, we see that

$$\left.\begin{array}{l} f'(200) = 1 - 4 < 0 \\ f'(400) = 0 \\ f'(800) = 1 - \frac{1}{4} > 0 \end{array}\right\} \Rightarrow \text{ relative minimum at } x = 400$$

Since $x = 400$ and $y = 200$, the minimum amount of fence needed is $f = 800$ feet.   □

Because the marginal revenue is the first derivative of the total revenue, it should be obvious that the total revenue function will have a critical point at the point where the marginal revenue is 0. With the total revenue function $R(x) = 16x - 0.02x^2$, the point where $R'(x) = 0$ is clearly a maximum since $R(x)$ is a parabola that opens downward as in Example 2. But the critical point may not always be a maximum, so it is wise to verify that the maximum value occurs at the critical point.

EXAMPLE 4   If total revenue for a firm is given by

$$R(x) = 8000x - 40x^2 - x^3,$$

where x is the number of units sold, find the number of units that must be sold to maximize revenue.

Solution $R'(x) = 8000 - 80x - 3x^2$ so we must solve $8000 - 80x - 3x^2 = 0$ for x.

$$(40 - x)(200 + 3x) = 0$$

$$40 - x = 0 \qquad 200 + 3x = 0$$

so

$$x = 40 \text{ or } x = -\frac{200}{3}$$

Now, we reject the negative value for x, but we must verify that $x = 40$ will yield maximum revenue.

$$\left.\begin{array}{l} R'(0) = 8000 > 0 \\ R'(100) = 8000 - 8000 - 30,000 < 0 \end{array}\right\} \Rightarrow \text{ relative maximum}$$

This test shows that $x = 40$ yields the maximum revenue when $x \geq 0$. The maximum revenue is

$$R(40) = 8000(40) - 40(40)^2 - (40)^3 = \$192,000.$$ □

EXAMPLE 5   A travel agency will plan a group tour for groups of size 25 or larger. If the group contains exactly 25 people, the cost is $300 per person. However, each person's cost is reduced by $10 for each additional person above the 25. What size group will produce the largest revenue for the agency?

Solution   The total revenue is

$$R = \text{(number of people)(cost per person)}.$$

If 25 people go, the total revenue will be

$$R = 25 \cdot \$300 = \$7500.$$

But if x additional people go, the number of people will be $25 + x$, and the cost per person will be $(300 - 10x)$ dollars. Then the total revenue will be a function of x,

$$R = R(x) = (25 + x)(300 - 10x),$$

or

$$R(x) = 7500 + 50x - 10x^2.$$

This function will have its maximum where $\overline{MR} = R'(x) = 0$; $R'(x) = 50 - 20x$, and the solution to $0 = 50 - 20x$ is $x = 2.5$. Thus adding 2.5 people to the group should maximize the total revenue. But we cannot add half a person. So we will test the total revenue function for 27 people and 28 people. This will determine the most profitable number.

For $x = 2$ (giving 27 people) we get $R(2) = 7500 + 50(2) - 10(2)^2 = 7560$. For $x = 3$ (giving 28 people) we get $R(3) = 7500 + 50(3) - 10(3)^2 = 7560$. Note that both 27 and 28 people give the same total revenue, and that this revenue is greater than the revenue for 25 people. Thus the revenue is maximized at either 27 or 28 people in the group.   □

Exercise 12.3

1. The velocity v of an autocatalytic reaction can be represented by the equation

$$v = x(a - x),$$

where a is the amount of material originally present and x is the amount that has been decomposed at any given time. Find the maximum velocity of the reaction.

2. According to B. F. Visser, the velocity v of air in the trachea during a cough is related to the radius r of the trachea according to

$$v = ar^2(r_0 - r),$$

where a is constant and r_0 is the radius of the trachea in a relaxed state. Find the maximum velocity of air in the trachea during a cough.

3. The efficiency E of a muscle performing a maximal contraction is a function of the time of the contraction t, and has been found to satisfy the following equation:

$$E = \frac{1 - 0.24t}{2 + t}.$$

Find the maximum efficiency.

4. The amount of photosynthesis that takes place in a certain plant depends on the intensity of light x according to the equation

$$f(x) = 145x^2 - 30x^3.$$

Find the intensity of light for which photosynthesis is greatest.

5. If the product of the concentrations of hydrogen ions $[H^+]$ and hydroxyl ions $[OH^-]$ in a certain solution is known to be 10^{-12}, what is the hydrogen ion concentration at which the sum of the hydrogen and hydroxyl ion concentrations is a minimum?

6. The running yard for a dog kennel must contain at least 900 square feet. If a 20-foot side of the kennel is used as part of one side of a rectangular yard with 900 square feet, what dimensions will use the least amount of fencing?

7. A rectangular box with a square base is to be formed from a square piece of metal with 12-inch sides. If a square piece with side x is cut from the corners of the metal and the sides are folded up to form an open box, the volume of the box is $V = (12 - 2x)^2 x$. What value of x will maximize the volume of the box?

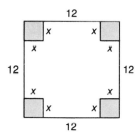

8. A square piece of cardboard 32 cm on a side is to be formed into a rectangular box by cutting squares with length x from each corner and folding up the sides. What is the maximum volume possible for the box?

9. The owner of an orange grove must decide when to pick one variety of oranges. She can sell them for $8 a bushel if she sells them now, with each tree yielding an average of 5 bushels. The yield increases by one half bushel per week for the next 5 weeks, but the price per bushel decreases by $.50 per bushel. When should the oranges be picked for maximum return?

10. The yield from a grove of orange trees is given by $x(800 - x)$, where x is the number of orange trees per acre. How many trees per acre will maximize the yield?

11. Sensitivity to a drug depends on the dosage size x according to the equation

$$S = 1000x - x^2.$$

Find the dosage that maximizes sensitivity.

12. If the total revenue function for a commodity is $R = 36x - 0.01x^2$, sale of how many units will maximize the total revenue?

13. If the total revenue function for a commodity is $R(x) = 25x - 0.05x^2$, sale of how many units will provide the maximum total revenue?

14. If the total revenue function for a commodity is $R(x) = 2000x - 20x^2 - x^3$, find the level of sales that maximizes revenue and find the maximum revenue.

15. A firm has total revenues given by

$$R(x) = 2800x - 8x^2 - x^3$$

for a product. Find the maximum revenue from sales of that product.

16. A company handles an apartment building with 50 units. Experience has shown that if the rent for each of the units is $160 per month, all of the units will be filled, but one unit will become vacant for each $5 increase in the monthly rate. What rent should be charged to maximize the total revenue from the building?

17. An agency charges $10 for a trip to a concert if 30 people travel in a group. But for each person above the 30, the charge will be reduced by $.20. How many people will maximize the total revenue for the agency?

18. A company has determined that its monthly sales revenue S is related to the number of dollars x spent on advertising, with

$$S = 5000 + 8000x - 0.2x^2.$$

Spending how much money on advertising will maximize their revenue?

19. A printer has a contract to print 100,000 posters for a political candidate. He can run the posters off by using any number of plates from one to 30 on his press. If he uses x metal plates, they will produce x copies of the poster with each impression of the press. The metal plates cost $2.00 to prepare, and it costs $12.50 per hour to run the press. If the press can make 1000 impressions per hour, how many metal plates should he make to minimize his costs?

12.4 Applications of Maxima and Minima to Business and Economics

Objectives   ■ To minimize the average cost, given the total cost function
■ To find the maximum profit from total cost and total revenue functions, or from a profit function

Minimizing Average Cost

Because the total cost function is always increasing, we cannot find the number of units that will make the total cost a minimum (except for producing 0 units, which is an absolute minimum). However, we usually can find the number of units that will make the average cost per unit a minimum.

If the total cost is represented by

$$C = C(x),$$

then the **average cost per unit** is

$$\bar{C} = \frac{C(x)}{x}.$$

For example, if $C = 3x^2 + 4x + 2$ is the total cost function for a commodity, the *average cost function* is

$$\overline{C} = \frac{3x^2 + 4x + 2}{x} = 3x + 4 + \frac{2}{x}.$$

Note that the average cost per unit is undefined if no units are produced.

We can use the first-derivative test to find the minimum of the average cost function, as the following example shows.

EXAMPLE 1   If the total cost function for a commodity is given by $C = \frac{1}{4}x^2 + 4x + 100$, where x represents the number of units produced, producing how many units will result in a minimum *average cost* per unit?

Solution   The *average cost* function is given by

$$\overline{C} = \frac{\frac{1}{4}x^2 + 4x + 100}{x} = \frac{x}{4} + 4 + \frac{100}{x}.$$

Then

$$\overline{C}' = \overline{C}'(x) = \frac{1}{4} - \frac{100}{x^2}.$$

Setting $\overline{C}' = 0$ gives

$$0 = \frac{1}{4} - \frac{100}{x^2},$$

so $0 = x^2 - 400$, or $x = \pm 20$.

Because the quantity produced must be positive, 20 units should minimize the average cost per unit. We show it is a minimum by testing derivatives to the right and left of $x = 20$.

$$\left.\begin{array}{l} \overline{C}'(10) = -\frac{3}{4} < 0 \\ \overline{C}'(30) = \frac{5}{36} > 0 \end{array}\right\} \rightarrow \text{relative minimum}$$

Thus the minimum average cost per unit occurs if 20 units are produced. The graph of the average cost per unit is shown in Figure 12.13. The minimum cost per unit is $\overline{C}(20) = \$14$.   □

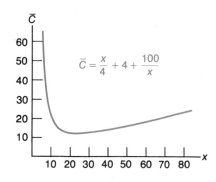

Figure 12.13

Maximizing Profits

In Chapter 11, we defined the marginal profit function as the derivative of the profit function. That is,

$$\overline{MP} = P'(x).$$

In this chapter we have seen how to use the derivative to find maxima and minima for various functions. Now we can apply those same techniques, in the context of marginal profit, in order to maximize profit functions.

EXAMPLE 2   If the total cost function for a certain period for a commodity is $C(x) = 100 + 2x + x^2$ and the total revenue function is $R(x) = 36x$, how many items will produce a maximum profit?

Solution   The profit function is

$$P(x) = R(x) - C(x) = 36x - (100 + 2x + x^2),$$

or $$P(x) = 34x - 100 - x^2.$$

Then the marginal profit is

$$\overline{MP} = P'(x) = 34 - 2x.$$

Setting marginal profit equal to 0 and solving gives

$$0 = 34 - 2x$$
$$x = 17.$$

The profit function has a parabola as its graph, so the relative maximum at $x = 17$ is the maximum. Thus the maximum profit occurs if 17 items are produced and sold per period.   □

If there is a physical limitation on the number of units that can be produced in a given period of time, then the endpoints of the interval caused by these limitations should also be checked.

EXAMPLE 3   The total profit function for a commodity is

$$P(x) = 4x^3 - 210x^2 + 3600x - 200 \qquad (0 \le x \le 30),$$

where x is the number of units sold. Find the number of items that will maximize profit.

Solution   The marginal profit function is

$$P'(x) = 12x^2 - 420x + 3600.$$

Setting it equal to 0, we get

$$0 = 12(x - 15)(x - 20),$$

so $P'(x) = 0$ at $x = 15$ and $x = 20$. Testing to the right and left of these values (as

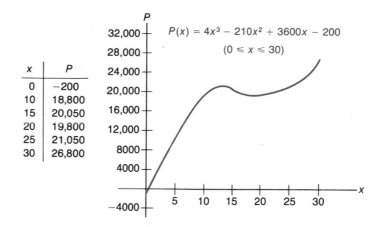

Figure 12.14

in the first-derivative test) we get

$$P'(0) = 3600 > 0$$
$$P'(18) = -72 < 0$$
$$P'(25) = 600 > 0$$

$\Rightarrow$ relative maximum at $x = 15$
$\Rightarrow$ relative minimum at $x = 20$

Thus the total profit function has a *relative* maximum at $(15, 20050)$ but we must check the endpoints (0 and 30) before deciding it is the absolute maximum.

$$P(0) = -200 \quad \text{and} \quad P(30) = \$26,800$$

Thus the absolute maximum occurs at the endpoint, $x = 30$. Figure 12.14 shows the graph of the profit function. □

Recall that in Chapter 11 we showed that if

$$h(x) = f(x) \pm g(x)$$

then

$$h'(x) = f'(x) \pm g'(x).$$

In particular, if

$$P(x) = R(x) - C(x)$$

then

$$P'(x) = R'(x) - C'(x).$$

But since these derivatives represent marginal profit, marginal revenue and marginal cost, respectively, we may write $\overline{MP} = \overline{MR} - \overline{MC}$.

Now, we know that marginal profit is 0 when profit is maximized, so we may write

$$0 = \overline{MR} - \overline{MC}$$

or

$$\overline{MR} = \overline{MC}.$$

That is, *marginal profit will be 0 when marginal revenue equals marginal cost.*
   The statement that "profit will be maximized when marginal revenue equals marginal cost" is found frequently in economics texts, and is true in *many* cases.[°] But we should always check the point where $\overline{MR} = \overline{MC}$ to make sure this critical point is the absolute maximum on the interval determined by the physical limitations.

EXAMPLE 4   The total cost per day to produce Ace electric shavers is

$$C(x) = 360 + 10x + \tfrac{1}{5}x^2.$$

Physical limitations permit only 80 shavers to be produced each day. If the total revenue function for the shavers is

$$R(x) = 45x - \tfrac{1}{2}x^2,$$

at what level of production will profit be maximized?

Solution   To maximize the profit, we will find $\overline{MR}$ and $\overline{MC}$ and find the value of x that makes them equal.

$$\overline{MR} = 45 - x$$
$$\overline{MC} = 10 + \tfrac{2}{5}x$$

Solving $\overline{MR} = \overline{MC}$ gives

$$45 - x = 10 + \tfrac{2}{5}x$$
$$35 = \tfrac{7}{5}x$$
$$x = 25.$$

Thus the maximum profit appears to occur when 25 shavers are produced. Because the profit function,

$$P(x) = R(x) - C(x) = 35x - \tfrac{7}{10}x^2 - 360$$

has as its graph a parabola opening downward, and because 25 is within the firm's physical limitations, the maximum profit will occur when 25 shavers are produced.   □

Exercise 12.4

MINIMIZING AVERAGE COST

1. If the total cost function for a product is $C(x) = 25 + 13x + x^2$, producing how many units will result in a minimum average cost per unit?
2. If the total cost function for a product is $C(x) = 300 + 10x + 0.03x^2$, producing how many units will result in a minimum average cost per unit?

[°] Most profit curves developed by companies for their products will not be as complex as the one in Example 3, so the points where $\overline{MR} = \overline{MC}$ are the points of maximum profit *for them.*

3. If the total cost function for a product is $C(x) = 100 + x^2$, producing how many units will result in a minimum average cost per unit?

4. If the total cost function for a product is $C(x) = 250 + 6x + 0.1x^2$, producing how many units will minimize the average cost?

5. If the total cost function for a good is $C(x) = (x + 4)^3$, where x represents the number of hundreds of units produced, producing how many units will minimize average cost?

6. If the total cost function for a good is $C(x) = (x + 5)^3$, where x represents the number of hundreds of units produced, producing how many units will minimize average cost?

MAXIMIZING PROFIT

7. If the profit function is $P(x) = 5x^2 - 250$, find the number of units (x) that will maximize the profit.

8. If the profit function is $P(x) = 16x - 320$, find the number of units that will maximize the profit.

9. If the total revenue function is $R(x) = 32x$ and the total cost function is $C(x) = 200 + 2x + x^2$, selling how many units will maximize profit?

10. If the total revenue function is $R(x) = 16x$ and the total cost function is $C(x) = 100 + 30x + \frac{1}{10}x^2$, find the number of units that should be produced and sold to maximize profit.

11. If the profit function for a good is $P(x) = 5600x + 85x^2 - x^3 - 200,000$, selling how many items will produce a maximum profit?

12. If the profit function for a commodity is $P = 6400x - 18x^2 - \frac{1}{3}x^3 - 40,000$, selling how many units will result in a maximum profit?

13. A firm estimates that x units of its product can be produced at a total cost of $C(x) = 45,000 + 100x + x^3$. If the firm's total revenue from the sale of x units is $R(x) = 4000x$, determine the level of production x that will maximize the profit.

14. A product can be produced at a total cost $C(x) = 800 + 100x^2 + x^3$, where x is the number produced. If the total revenue is given by $R(x) = 60,000x - 50x^2$, determine the level of production that will maximize the profit.

15. A firm can produce only 1000 units per month. The monthly total cost is given by $C(x) = 300 + 200x$, where x is the number produced. If the total revenue is given by $R(x) = 250x - \frac{1}{100}x^2$, how many items should they produce for maximum profit?

16. A firm can produce only 100 units per week. If its total cost function is $C = 500 + 1500x$ and its total revenue function is $R = 1600x - x^2$, how many units should it produce to maximize its profit?

17. A company handles an apartment building with 50 units. Experience has shown that if the rent of each of the units is $160 per month, all of the units are filled, but one unit will become vacant for each $5 increase in this monthly rate. If the monthly cost of maintaining the apartment building is $30 per unit, what rent should be charged per month to maximize the profit?

18. A travel agency will plan a group tour for groups of size 25 or larger. If the group contains exactly 25 people, the cost is $500 per person. However, each person's cost is reduced by $10 for each additional person above the 25. If the travel agency incurs a cost of $125 per person for the tour, what size group will give the agency the maximum profit?

Review Exercises

In problems 1–5,
(a) find the relative maxima and minima if any exist.
(b) find the horizontal points of inflection if any exist.
(c) sketch the graph.

1. $p = q^2 - 4q - 5$
2. $y = x^3 + x^2 - x - 1$
3. $f(x) = 4x^3 - x^4$
4. $f(x) = x^3 - \frac{15}{2}x^2 - 18x + \frac{3}{2}$
5. $y = \sqrt[3]{x} - 4$
6. Given $y = 6400x - 18x^2 - \frac{1}{3}x^3$,
   (a) find the absolute maximum and minimum for y, if $0 \le x \le 50$.
   (b) find the absolute maximum and minimum for y if $0 \le x \le 100$.

APPLICATIONS

7. If the total cost function for a product is
$$C(x) = 3x^2 + 15x + 75,$$
how many units will minimize the average cost?

8. If the total revenue function for a product is given by
$$R(x) = 32x - 0.01x^2,$$
how many units will maximize the total revenue?

9. The reaction R to an injection of a drug is related to the dosage x according to
$$R(x) = x^2 \left(500 - \frac{x}{3}\right).$$
Find the dosage that yields maximum reaction.

10. The total cost function for a good is $C = 2x^2 + 54x + 98$. Producing how many units will minimize average cost?

11. McRobert's TV Shop sells 200 sets per month at a price of $400 per unit. Market research indicates that they can sell one additional set for each $1 they reduce the price. At what selling price will they maximize revenue?

12. The number of parts produced per hour by a worker is given by
$$N = 4 + 3t^2 - t^3,$$
where t is the number of hours on the job without a break. If the worker starts at 8 A.M., when will she be at maximum production during the morning?

13. Population estimates show that the equation $P = 300 + 10t - t^2$ represents the size of the graduating class of a high school, with t representing the number of years after 1980, $0 \le t \le 10$. What will be the largest graduating class in the decade?

14. If $R(x) = 46x - x^2$ and $C(x) = 5x^2 + 10x + 3$, how many units (x) maximize profit?

15. If, in problem 11, the sets cost the shop $250 each, when will profit be maximized?

16. A product can be produced at a total cost $C(x) = 800 + 4x$, where x is the number produced. If the total revenue is given by $R(x) = 80x - \frac{1}{4}x^2$, determine the level of production that will maximize the profit.

Warmup In this chapter you will need to work problems like the following. If you have difficulty with any problem, return to the section where that type of problem was introduced and refresh your memory before starting the chapter.

Problem Type	Introduced in Section	Used in Section	Answer
(a) Simplify: $\dfrac{1}{(3x)^{1/2}} \cdot \dfrac{1}{2}(3x)^{-1/2} \cdot 3$ (b) Write with positive exponents: $\sqrt{x^2 - 1}$	0.2 Exponents	13.4	(a) $\dfrac{1}{2x}$ (b) $(x^2 - 1)^{1/2}$
If $f''(x) = 36x^2 + 36 - 6$, what is $f''(1)$?	1.3 Functional notation	13.1, 13.2	66
(a) Vertical lines have _____ slopes. (b) Horizontal lines have _____ slopes.	2.3 Slopes	13.3	(a) Undefined (b) 0
Write the equation of the line passing through $(-2, -2)$ with slope 5.	2.4 Equations of lines	13.3	$y = 5x + 8$
Solve: (a) $0 = 12x^3 - 12x^2$ (b) $x^2 + y^2 - 9 = 0$, for y.	5.1 Quadratic equations	13.2, 13.3	(a) $x = 1, x = 0$ (b) $y = \pm\sqrt{9 - x^2}$
(a) Write $\log_a (x + h) - \log_a x$ as an expression involving one log function. (b) Does $\ln x^4 = 4 \ln x$? (c) Does $\dfrac{x}{h} \log_a \left(\dfrac{x+h}{x}\right) = \log_a \left(1 + \dfrac{h}{x}\right)^{x/h}$? (d) Expand $\ln (xy)$ to separate x and y. (e) If $y = a^x$, then $x = $ _____. (f) Simplify $e^{\ln x^2}$	6.2 Logarithms	13.4	(a) $\log_a \left(\dfrac{x + h}{x}\right)$ (b) Yes (c) Yes (d) $\ln x + \ln y$ (e) $\log_a y$ (f) x^2
Evaluate the limits. (a) $\lim\limits_{a \to 0} (1 + a)^{1/a}$ (b) $\lim\limits_{h \to 0} \left(1 + \dfrac{h}{x}\right)^{x/h}$	10.3 Limits	13.4	(a) e (b) e
Find the derivative of (a) $y = x^4 - 3x^2 + x^{-2}$ (b) $y = (2x - 1)^{1/2}$ (c) $y = \sqrt{9 - x^2}$	11.3, 11.5 Derivatives	13.1, 13.2, 13.3	(a) $4x^3 - 6x - 2x^{-3}$ (b) $(2x - 1)^{-1/2}$ (c) $-x(9 - x^2)^{-1/2}$

13

DERIVATIVES CONTINUED

In Chapter 11 we developed formulas to find the (first) derivative of certain functions, and in Chapter 12 we used (first) derivatives to sketch curves and to find the relative maxima and minima of functions. In this chapter we will see that the derivative formulas can be used to find derivatives of first derivatives, which we call second derivatives. In a similar manner we can also find higher derivatives.

The second derivative can be used to determine where the graph of an equation will be concave up, where it will be concave down, and where the graph will change from concave up to concave down, or vice versa. (Points where this occurs are called points of inflection.) The second-derivative test uses concavity to determine where the graph of an equation has a relative maximum or minimum.

In this chapter we will also develop derivative formulas for logarithmic and exponential functions, and apply them to problems in the management, life, and social sciences. We will also develop methods for finding derivatives of one variable with respect to another variable even though the relationship between them may not be functional. This method is called implicit differentiation.

The special business and economics applications include profit maximization in competitive and monopoly markets, elasticity of demand, and maximization of taxation revenue.

13.1 Higher-Order Derivatives

Objective   ■ To find second derivatives and higher derivatives of certain functions

In Chapter 11 we introduced the first derivative of a function. Because the derivative of a function is itself a function, we can take a derivative of the derivative. The derivative of a first derivative is called a **second derivative.** We can find the second derivative of a function f by differentiating it twice. If f' represents the first derivative of a function, then f'' represents the second derivative of that function.

EXAMPLE 1   If $f(x) = 3x^3 - 4x^2 + 5$, find $f''(x)$.

Solution   The first derivative is $f'(x) = 9x^2 - 8x$.
The second derivative is $f''(x) = 18x - 8$.   □

EXAMPLE 2   Find the second derivative of $y = x^4 - 3x^2 + x^{-2}$.

Solution   The first derivative is $y' = 4x^3 - 6x - 2x^{-3}$.
The second derivative, which we may denote by y'', is $y'' = 12x^2 - 6 + 6x^{-4}$.   □

We may also use $\dfrac{d^2y}{dx^2}$ and $\dfrac{d^2}{dx^2} f(x)$ to denote the second derivative of a function.

EXAMPLE 3   If $y = \sqrt{2x - 1}$, find d^2y/dx^2.

Solution   The first derivative is

$$\frac{dy}{dx} = \frac{1}{2}(2x - 1)^{-1/2}(2) = (2x - 1)^{-1/2}.$$

The second derivative is

$$\frac{d^2y}{dx^2} = -\frac{1}{2}(2x - 1)^{-3/2}(2)$$

$$= -(2x - 1)^{-3/2}$$

$$= \frac{-1}{(2x - 1)^{3/2}} = \frac{-1}{\sqrt{(2x - 1)^3}}.$$ □

We can also find third, fourth, fifth, and so on, derivatives, continuing indefinitely. The third, fourth, and fifth derivatives of a function f are denoted by f''', $f^{(4)}$, and $f^{(5)}$, respectively. Other notations for the third and fourth derivatives include:

$$y''' \qquad y^{(4)}$$

$$\frac{d^3y}{dx^3} \qquad \frac{d^4y}{dx^4}$$

$$\frac{d^3f(x)}{dx^3} \qquad \frac{d^4f(x)}{dx^4}$$

EXAMPLE 4   Find the first four derivatives of $f(x) = 4x^3 + 5x^2 + 3$.

Solution
$$f'(x) = 12x^2 + 10x$$
$$f''(x) = 24x + 10$$
$$f'''(x) = 24$$
$$f^{(4)}(x) = 0 \qquad \square$$

Just as the first derivative, $f'(x)$, can be used to determine the rate of change of a function $f(x)$, the second derivative $f''(x)$ can be used to determine the rate of change of $f'(x)$.

EXAMPLE 5   If $f(x) = 3x^4 + 6x^3 - 3x^2 + 4$,
(a) how fast is $f(x)$ changing at $(1, 10)$?
(b) how fast is $f'(x)$ changing at $(1, 10)$?
(c) is $f'(x)$ increasing or decreasing at $(1, 10)$?

Solution   (a) $f'(x) = 12x^3 + 18x^2 - 6x$, so $f'(1) = 12 + 18 - 6 = 24$. Thus the rate of change of $f(x)$ is 24.
(b) $f''(x) = 36x^2 + 36x - 6$, so $f''(1) = 66$. Thus the rate of change of $f'(x)$ is 66.
(c) Since $f''(1) = 66 > 0$, $f'(x)$ is increasing at $(1, 10)$. $\qquad \square$

EXAMPLE 6   Suppose a particle travels according to the equation $s = 100t - 16t^2 + 200$, where s is the distance and t is the time. Then ds/dt is the velocity, and $d^2s/dt^2 = dv/dt$ is the acceleration of the particle. Find the acceleration.

Solution   The velocity is $v = ds/dt = 100 - 32t$, and the acceleration is

$$\frac{dv}{dt} = \frac{d^2s}{dt^2} = -32. \qquad \square$$

Exercise 13.1

In problems 1–8, find the second derivative.

1. $f(x) = 4x^3 - 15x^2 + 3x + 2$

2. $f(x) = 2x^{10} - 18x^5 - 12x^3 + 4$

3. $y = 10x^3 - x^2 + 14x + 3$

4. $y = 6x^5 - 3x^4 + 12x^2$

5. $g(x) = x^3 - \dfrac{1}{x}$

6. $h(x) = x^2 - \dfrac{1}{x^2}$

7. $y = x^3 - \sqrt{x}$

8. $y = 3x^2 - \sqrt[3]{x^2}$

9. If $y = x^5 - x^{1/2}$, find $\dfrac{d^2y}{dx^2}$.

10. If $y = x^4 + x^{1/3}$, find $\dfrac{d^2y}{dx^2}$.

11. If $f(x) = \sqrt{x - 1}$, find $\dfrac{d^2}{dx^2} f(x)$.

12. If $f(x) = \sqrt[3]{x + 2}$, find $\dfrac{d^2}{dx^2} f(x)$.

° 13. If $y = \sqrt{x^2 + 4}$, find y''.

° 14. If $f(x) = \sqrt{4x^2 - 2}$, find $f''(x)$.

In problems 15–24, find the third derivative.

15. $y = x^5 - 16x^3 + 12$

16. $y = 6x^3 - 12x^2 + 6x$

17. $f(x) = 2x^9 - 6x^6$

18. $f(x) = 3x^5 - x^6$

19. $y = 1/x$

20. $y = 1/x^2$

21. $y = \sqrt{x}$

22. $y = \sqrt[3]{x}$

23. $f(x) = \sqrt{x + 1}$

24. $f(x) = \sqrt{x - 5}$

25. Find $\dfrac{d^4y}{dx^4}$ if $y = 4x^3 - 16x$.

26. Find $y^{(4)}$ if $y = x^6 - 15x^3$.

27. Find $f^{(4)}(x)$ if $f(x) = \sqrt{x}$.

28. Find $f^{(4)}(x)$ if $f(x) = 1/x$.

29. If $f(x) = 16x^2 - x^3$, what is the rate of change of $f'(x)$ at $(1, 15)$?

30. If $y = 36x^2 - 6x^3 + x$, what is the rate of change of y' at $(1, 31)$?

APPLICATIONS

31. The amount of photosynthesis that takes place in a certain plant depends on the intensity of light x according to the equation

$$f(x) = 145x^2 - 30x^3.$$

   (a) Find the rate of change of photosynthesis with respect to the intensity.
   (b) What is the rate of change when $x = 1$? when $x = 3$?
   (c) How fast is the rate changing when $x = 1$? when $x = 3$?

32. The reaction R to an injection of a drug is related to the dosage x according to

$$R(x) = x^2 \left(500 - \frac{x}{3}\right).$$

   (a) If the sensitivity is defined to be dR/dx, what is the sensitivity when $x = 350$? when $x = 700$?
   (b) What is the rate of change of sensitivity when $x = 350$? when $x = 700$?

33. If a particle travels according to the formula $s = 100 + 80t - t^2$, find the acceleration of the particle.

34. If the formula describing the distance an object travels is

$$s = 100 + 160t - 16t^2,$$

   (a) what is the acceleration of the object when $t = 4$?
   (b) is the velocity of the object increasing or decreasing at $t = 4$?

35. If the revenue from sales of a good can be described by $R(x) = 100x - 0.01x^2$, is the marginal revenue for the good increasing or decreasing?

° Finding the second derivative for these problems requires methods discussed in Section 11.6, an optional section.

36. If the total cost of producing the good of problem 35 is given by $C(x) = 100 + 30x + 0.02x^2$, does the marginal cost increase or decrease?

37. Does the marginal profit for the good mentioned in problems 35 and 36 increase or decrease?

38. The reaction R to an injection of a drug is related to the dosage x according to

$$R(x) = x^2\left(500 - \frac{x}{3}\right).$$

The sensitivity to the drug is defined by dR/dx, and was found in problem 32. Find the dosage that maximizes sensitivity.

39. The amount of photosynthesis that takes place in a certain plant depends on the intensity of light x according to the equation

$$f(x) = 145x^2 - 30x^3.$$

The rate of change of the amount of photosynthesis with respect to the intensity was found in problem 31. Find the intensity that maximizes this rate of change.

13.2 Concavity; Points of Inflection

Objectives
- To find points of inflection of graphs of functions
- To use the second-derivative test to graph functions

Just as we used the first derivative to determine if a curve was increasing or decreasing on a given interval, we can use the second derivative to determine if the curve is concave up or concave down on an interval.

A curve is said to be **concave up** on an interval $[a, b]$ if at each point on the interval the curve is above its tangent at that point (Figure 13.1). If the curve is below all its tangents on a given interval, it is **concave down** on the interval (Figure 13.2).

The second derivative can be used to determine the concavity of a curve.

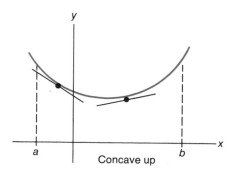

Concave up

Figure 13.1

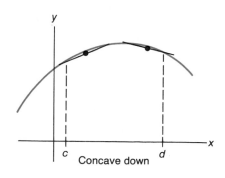

Concave down

Figure 13.2

Assume the first and second derivatives of function f exist. Then if $f''(x) > 0$ on an interval I, the graph of f is **concave up** on the interval. If $f''(x) < 0$ on an interval I, then the graph of f is **concave down** on I.

EXAMPLE 1   Is the graph of $f(x) = x^3 - 4x^2 + 3$
(a) concave up or down at $(1, 0)$?
(b) concave up or down at $(2, -5)$?

Solution   We must find $f''(x)$ before we can answer the questions.
$$f'(x) = 3x^2 - 8x$$
$$f''(x) = 6x - 8$$

(a) Then $f''(1) = 6(1) - 8 = -2$, so the graph is concave down at $(1, 0)$.
(b) $f''(2) = 6(2) - 8 = 4$, so the graph is concave up at $(2, -5)$. The graph of $f(x) = x^3 - 4x^2 + 3$ is shown in Figure 13.3.   □

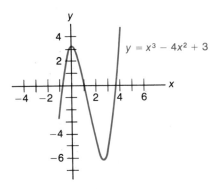

$y = x^3 - 4x^2 + 3$

Figure 13.3

Looking at the graph of $y = x^3 - 4x^2 + 3$ (Figure 13.3) we see that the curve is concave down on the left and concave up on the right. Thus it has changed from concave down to concave up at some point. But at what point? According to the discussion earlier, it is the point where the second derivative changes from negative to positive. This point is called a **point of inflection**.

A point (x_0, y_0) on the graph of a function f is called a **point of inflection** if $f''(x_0) = 0$ *and* if the curve is concave up on one side of the point and concave down on the other side.

In general, we can find points of inflection as follows.

PROCEDURE	EXAMPLE
To find the point(s) of inflection of a curve:	Find the points of inflection of the graph of $y = \dfrac{x^4}{2} - x^3 + 5.$
1. Find the second derivative of the function.	1. $y' = f'(x) = 2x^3 - 3x^2$ $y'' = f''(x) = 6x^2 - 6x$
2. Set the second derivative equal to 0, and solve for x. Potential points of inflection occur at these values of x.	2. $0 = 6x^2 - 6x$ has solutions $x = 0$, $x = 1$.

3. If the second derivative has opposite signs on either side of one of these values of x, a point of inflection occurs.	3. $f''(-1) = 12 > 0$
	   $f''(\tfrac{1}{2}) = -\tfrac{3}{2} < 0$ $\Bigr\}$ $\Rightarrow$ $(0, 5)$ is a point of inflection
	   $f''(2) = 12 > 0$ $\Bigr]$ $\rightarrow$ $(1, \tfrac{9}{2})$ is a point of inflection

	See the graph in Figure 13.4.

The graph of $y = \frac{1}{2}x^4 - x^3 + 5$ is shown in Figure 13.4. Note the points of inflection at $(0, 5)$ and $(1, \frac{9}{2})$. The point of inflection at $(0, 5)$ is a horizontal point of inflection because $f'(x)$ is also 0 at $x = 0$.

We can use information about points of inflection and concavity to help sketch graphs. For example, if we know the curve is concave up at a critical point, then the point must be a relative minimum, because the tangent to the curve is horizontal at the critical point and only a point at the bottom of a "concave up" curve could have a horizontal tangent (see Figure 13.5).

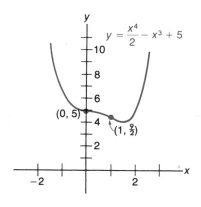

Figure 13.4

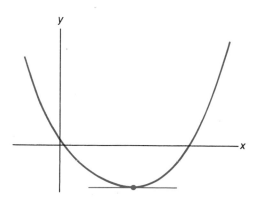

Figure 13.5

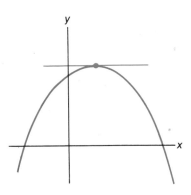

Figure 13.6

On the other hand, if the curve is concave down at a critical point, then the point is a relative maximum (see Figure 13.6).

Thus we can use the **second-derivative test** to determine if a critical point is a relative maximum or minimum.

Second-Derivative Test

PROCEDURE	EXAMPLE
To find relative maxima and minima of a function:	Find the relative maxima and minima of $y = f(x) = \frac{1}{3}x^3 - x^2 - 3x + 2$.
1. Find the critical values of the function.	1. $f'(x) = x^2 - 2x - 3$ $0 = x^2 - 2x - 3$ has solutions $x = -1$ and $x = 3$. No values of x make $x^2 - 2x - 3$ undefined.
2. Substitute the critical values into $f(x)$ to find the critical points.	2. $f(-1) = \frac{11}{3}$ $f(3) = -7$ The critical points are $(-1, \frac{11}{3})$ and $(3, -7)$.
3. Evaluate $f''(x)$ at each critical value.	3. $f''(x) = 2x - 2$ $f''(-1) = -4 < 0$, so $(-1, \frac{11}{3})$ is a relative maximum.
(a) If $f''(x_0) < 0$, a relative maximum occurs at x_0.	
(b) If $f''(x_0) > 0$, a relative minimum occurs at x_0.	$f''(3) = 4 > 0$, so $(3, -7)$ is a relative minimum.
(c) If $f''(x_0) = 0$, or if $f''(x_0)$ is undefined, the second-derivative test fails; use the first-derivative test.	(The graph is shown in Figure 13.7.)

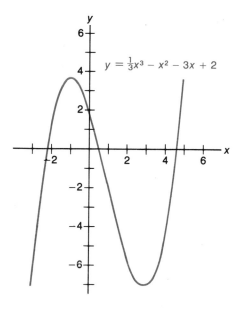

$$y = \tfrac{1}{3}x^3 - x^2 - 3x + 2$$

Figure 13.7

EXAMPLE 2   Find the relative maxima and minima and points of inflection of the graph of
$y = 3x^4 - 4x^3$.

Solution
$$y' = f'(x) = 12x^3 - 12x^2$$

Solving $0 = 12x^3 - 12x^2$ gives $x = 1$, $x = 0$. Thus the critical points are $(1, -1)$ and $(0, 0)$.

$$y'' = f''(x) = 36x^2 - 24x$$

$$f''(1) = 12 > 0 \implies (1, -1) \text{ is a relative minimum}$$

$$f''(0) = 0 \implies \text{The Second-Derivative Test fails}$$

Since the Second-Derivative Test fails, we must use the First-Derivative Test to test the critical point $(0, 0)$.

$$\left.\begin{array}{l} f'(-1) = -24 \\ f'(\tfrac{1}{2}) = -\tfrac{3}{2} \end{array}\right\} \implies (0, 0) \text{ is a horizontal point of inflection}$$

We look for points of inflection by setting $f''(x) = 0$ and solving for x. $0 = 36x^2 - 24x$ has solutions $x = 0$ and $x = \tfrac{2}{3}$.

Testing for concavity at $x = 0$ gives

$$\left.\begin{array}{l} f''(-1) = 60 > 0 \\ f''(\tfrac{1}{2}) = -3 < 0 \end{array}\right\} \implies (0, 0) \text{ is a point of inflection}$$

Thus we see again that $(0, 0)$ is a horizontal point of inflection. This is a special

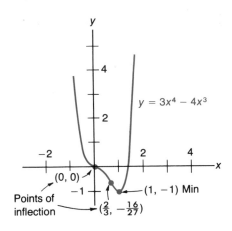

Figure 13.8

point, where the curve changes concavity *and* has a horizontal tangent (see Figure 13.8). Testing for concavity at $x = \frac{2}{3}$ gives

$$\left. \begin{array}{l} f''(\frac{1}{2}) = -3 < 0 \\ f''(1) = 12 > 0 \end{array} \right\} \Rightarrow (\frac{2}{3}, -\frac{16}{27}) \text{ is a point of inflection.} \qquad \square$$

Exercise 13.2

Find the points of inflection of the graphs of the following functions, if they exist.

1. $y = x^3 - 3x^2$
2. $y = x^3 + 6x$
3. $y = 2x^3 + 4x$
4. $y = 4x^3 - 3x^2$
5. $y = x^2 - 4x + 3$
6. $y = 4x^2 + 5x + 6$
7. $f(x) = x^3 - 6x^2 + 5x + 6$
8. $f(x) = 2x^3 - 4x^2 + 5x - 2$
9. $y = \frac{1}{4}x^4 + \frac{1}{2}x^3 - 3x^2 + 3$
10. $f(x) = \dfrac{x^4}{3} + 2x^3 - 48x^2 + 8x + 4$
11. $p = q^3 - 9q^2$
12. $p = 2q^4 - 6q^2 + 4$

Find the relative maxima, relative minima, and points of inflection, and graph the following equations.

13. $y = x^2 - 4x + 2$
14. $y = x^3 - x^2$
15. $y = 4x^3 - x^2$
16. $y = x^4 - 8x^3 + 16x^2$
17. $y = x^4 - 16x^2$
18. $y = x^3 + 1$
19. $y = x^4 - 4$
20. $y = \frac{1}{3}x^3 - 2x^2 + 3x + 2$
21. $f(y) = 3y^4 - 4y^3 + 1$
22. $y = \dfrac{x^2}{4} - \dfrac{1}{x}$
23. $w = \dfrac{z^2}{8} - \dfrac{1}{z}$
24. $f(w) = 4w^3 - 6w^2 - 24w$
25. $p = 2q^2 + 4q$
26. $p = 8q - 2q^2 + 5$

13.3 Implicit Differentiation

Objectives
- To find derivatives using implicit differentiation
- To find slopes of tangents using implicit differentiation

Up to this point, we have taken derivatives of functions of the form $y = f(x)$. Some functions are given in equations of the form $F(x, y) = 0$. For example, the equation $xy - 4x + 1 = 0$ is in the form $F(x, y) = 0$, but we can solve for y to write the equation in the form $y = (4x - 1)/x$. We can say that $xy - 4x + 1 = 0$ defines y **implicitly** as a function of x, while $y = (4x - 1)/x$ defines the function explicitly.

The equation $x^2 + y^2 - 9 = 0$ has a circle as its graph. If we solve the equation for y, we get $y = \pm\sqrt{9 - x^2}$, which indicates that y is not a function of x. We can, however, consider the equation as defining *two* functions, $y = \sqrt{9 - x^2}$, and $y = -\sqrt{9 - x^2}$ (see Figure 13.9).

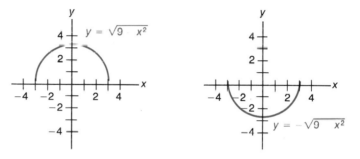

Figure 13.9

We can consider the equation $x^2 + y^2 - 9 = 0$ as defining the two functions implicitly.

Even though an equation (like $\ln xy + xe^y + x - 3 = 0$) may be difficult or even impossible to solve for y, and even though the equation does not represent y as a single function of x, we can use a technique called **implicit differentiation** to find the derivative of y with respect to x. The word *implicit* means that we are implying that y is a function of x without verifying it. We simply take the derivative of both sides of $f(x, y) = 0$ and then solve algebraically for dy/dx.

For example, we can find the derivative dy/dx from $x^2 + y^2 - 9 = 0$ by taking the derivative of both sides of the equation:

$$\frac{d}{dx}(x^2 + y^2 - 9) = \frac{d}{dx}(0)$$

$$\frac{d}{dx}(x^2) + \frac{d}{dx}(y^2) + \frac{d}{dx}(-9) = \frac{d}{dx}(0)$$

We have assumed y is a function of x; the derivative of y^2 is treated like the derivative of u^n, where u is a function of x. Thus the derivative is

$$2x + 2y^1 \cdot \frac{dy}{dx} + 0 = 0$$

Solving for dy/dx gives

$$\frac{dy}{dx} = -\frac{2x}{2y} = -\frac{x}{y}.$$

Let us compare this derivative with the derivatives of the two functions $y = \sqrt{9 - x^2}$ and $y = -\sqrt{9 - x^2}$. The derivative of $y = \sqrt{9 - x^2}$ is

$$\frac{dy}{dx} = \frac{1}{2}(9 - x^2)^{-1/2}(-2x) = \frac{-x}{\sqrt{9 - x^2}}$$

and the derivative of $y = -\sqrt{9 - x^2}$ is

$$\frac{dy}{dx} = -\frac{1}{2}(9 - x^2)^{-1/2}(-2x) = \frac{x}{\sqrt{9 - x^2}}.$$

Note that if we substitute $\pm\sqrt{9 - x^2}$ for y in our "implicit" derivative, we would get the two derivatives that were derived from the "explicit" functions.

EXAMPLE 1   Find the slope of the tangent to the graph of $x^2 + y^2 - 9 = 0$ at $(\sqrt{5}, 2)$.

Solution   The slope of the tangent to the curve is the derivative of the equation, evaluated at the given point. Taking the derivative implicitly gives us $dy/dx = -x/y$. Evaluating the derivative at $(\sqrt{5}, 2)$ gives the slope of the tangent as $-\sqrt{5}/2$.

We also found the derivative of $x^2 + y^2 - 9 = 0$ by solving for y explicitly. The function whose graph contains $(\sqrt{5}, 2)$ is $y = \sqrt{9 - x^2}$, and its derivative is

$$\frac{dy}{dx} = \frac{-x}{\sqrt{9 - x^2}}.$$

Evaluating the derivative at $(\sqrt{5}, 2)$, we get the slope of the tangent is $-\sqrt{5}/2$.

Thus we see that both methods give us the same slope for the tangent, but that the implicit method is easier to use.   □

EXAMPLE 2   Find dy/dx if $x^2 + 4x - 3y^2 + 4y = 0$.

Solution   Taking the derivative implicitly gives

$$\frac{d}{dx}(x^2) + \frac{d}{dx}(4x) + \frac{d}{dx}(-3y^2) + \frac{d}{dx}(4y) = \frac{d}{dx}(0).$$

Now, $$\frac{d}{dx}(x^2) = 2x$$

$$\frac{d}{dx}(4x) = 4$$

$$\frac{d}{dx}(-3y^2) = -3(2y)\frac{dy}{dx} = -6y\frac{dy}{dx}$$

$$\frac{d}{dx}(4y) = 4(1)\frac{dy}{dx} = 4\frac{dy}{dx}$$

and

$$\frac{d}{dx}(0) = 0.$$

So

$$2x + 4 - 6y\frac{dy}{dx} + 4\frac{dy}{dx} = 0$$

or

$$(-6y + 4)\frac{dy}{dx} = -2x - 4,$$

which gives

$$\frac{dy}{dx} = \frac{-2x - 4}{-6y + 4}$$

or

$$\frac{dy}{dx} = \frac{x + 2}{3y - 2}.$$ □

EXAMPLE 3   Write the equation of the tangent to the graph of $x^3 + xy + 4 = 0$ at the point $(-2, -2)$.

Solution   Taking the derivative implicitly gives

$$\frac{d}{dx}(x^3) + \frac{d}{dx}(xy) + \frac{d}{dx}(4) = \frac{d}{dx}(0).$$

The $\frac{d}{dx}(xy)$ indicates that we should take the derivative of the *product* of x and y. Since we are assuming y is a function of x and since x is a function of x, we must use the **Product Rule** to find $\frac{d}{dx}(xy)$.

$$\frac{d}{dx}(xy) = x \cdot 1\frac{dy}{dx} + y \cdot 1 = x\frac{dy}{dx} + y.$$

Thus we have

$$3x^2 + \left(x\frac{dy}{dx} + y\right) + 0 = 0.$$

Solving for dy/dx gives

$$\frac{dy}{dx} = \frac{-3x^2 - y}{x}.$$

The slope of the tangent to the curve at $x = -2$, $y = -2$ is

$$m = \frac{-3(-2)^2 - (-2)}{-2} = 5.$$

The equation of the tangent line is

$$y - (-2) = 5[x - (-2)], \qquad \text{or} \qquad y = 5x + 8. \qquad \square$$

EXAMPLE 4   At what point(s) does $x^2 + 4y^2 - 2x + 4y - 2 = 0$ have a horizontal tangent? At what point(s) does it have a vertical tangent?

Solution   First we find the derivative implicitly:

$$2x + 8y \cdot y' - 2 + 4y' - 0 = 0$$

$$y' = \frac{2 - 2x}{8y + 4} = \frac{1 - x}{4y + 2}$$

Horizontal tangents will occur where $y' = 0$; that is, where $x = 1$. We find the corresponding y value(s) by substituting 1 for x in the original equation and solving.

$$1 + 4y^2 - 2 + 4y - 2 = 0$$
$$4y^2 + 4y - 3 = 0$$
$$(2y - 1)(2y + 3) = 0$$
$$y = \tfrac{1}{2}, \qquad y = -\tfrac{3}{2}$$

Thus horizontal tangents occur at $(1, \tfrac{1}{2})$ and $(1, -\tfrac{3}{2})$ (see Figure 13.10).

Vertical tangents will occur where the derivative is undefined; that is, where $y = -\tfrac{1}{2}$. To find the corresponding x value(s), we substitute $-\tfrac{1}{2}$ in the equation for y and solve for x.

$$x^2 + 4(-\tfrac{1}{2})^2 - 2x + 4(-\tfrac{1}{2}) - 2 = 0$$
$$x^2 - 2x - 3 = 0$$
$$(x - 3)(x + 1) = 0$$
$$x = 3, \qquad x = -1$$

Thus vertical tangents occur at $(3, -\tfrac{1}{2})$ and $(-1, -\tfrac{1}{2})$ (see Figure 13.10). $\square$

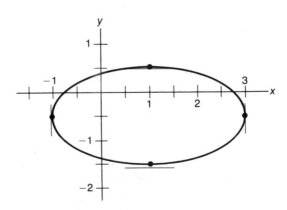

Figure 13.10

Exercise 13.3

Find dy/dx for the functions in problems 1–4.

1. $x^2 + 2y^2 - 4 = 0$
2. $x + y^2 - 4y + 6 = 0$
3. $x^2 + 4x + y^2 - 3y + 1 = 0$
4. $x^2 - 5x + y^3 - 3y - 3 = 0$
5. If $p^2 + q^2 = 4$, find dp/dq.
6. If $p^2 + 4p - q = 4$, find dp/dq.
7. If $x^2 + 3xy = 4$, find y'.
8. If $xy^2 - y^2 = 1$, find y'.
9. If $pq = 4$, find dp/dq.
10. If $pq = 4p - 2$, find dp/dq.
11. If $\sqrt{x^2 + y^2} = 4$, find $\dfrac{dy}{dx}$.
12. If $p\sqrt{q} = 5$, find dp/dq.
13. If $\dfrac{\sqrt{p}}{q} - 4 = 0$, find dp/dq.
14. If $\dfrac{x - y}{y} = 9$, find y'.
15. If $\dfrac{x + y}{y} = 5$, find y'.
16. Find the slope of the tangent to the curve $x^2 + 4x + y^2 + 2y - 4 = 0$ at $(1, -1)$.
17. Find the slope of the tangent to the curve $x^2 - 4x + 2y^2 - 4 = 0$ at $(2, 2)$.
18. Find the slope of the tangent to the curve $x^2 + 2xy + 3 = 0$ at $(-1, 2)$.
19. Find the slope of the tangent to the curve $y + x^2 = 4$ at $(0, 4)$.
20. Write the equation of the tangent to the curve $x^2 - 2y^2 + 1 = 0$ at $(2, 2)$.
21. Write the equation of the tangent to the curve $x^2 + y^2 + 2x - 3 = 0$ at $(-1, 2)$.
22. Write the equation of the tangent to the curve $4x^2 + 3y^2 - 4y - 3 = 0$ at $(-1, 1)$.
23. Write the equation of the tangent to the curve $xy + y = 0$ at $(3, 0)$.
24. At what points does the curve defined by $x^2 + 4y^2 - 4x - 4 = 0$ have
    (a) horizontal tangents? (b) vertical tangents?
25. At what points does the curve defined by $x^2 + 4y^2 - 4 = 0$ have
    (a) horizontal tangents? (b) vertical tangents?

13.4 Derivatives of Logarithmic Functions

Objective   ■ To find derivatives of logarithmic functions

In Chapter 6, we discussed the exponential function $y = a^u$ and the logarithmic function $y = \log_a u$. We have seen the importance of functions of the form $y = e^u$. In this section we will develop the derivative of the function $y = \log_a x$, which will again show the importance of the number e.

Derivative of a   If $y = \log_a x$, $\dfrac{dy}{dx} = \dfrac{1}{x} \log_a e$.   ***Logarithmic***   ***Function***

The proof of this statement follows.

If $y = f(x) = \log_a x,$

$$\frac{dy}{dx} = \lim_{h \to 0} \frac{f(x + h) - f(x)}{h}$$

$$= \lim_{h \to 0} \frac{\log_a (x + h) - \log_a x}{h}$$

$$= \lim_{h \to 0} \frac{\log_a \left(\dfrac{x + h}{x}\right)}{h}$$

because

$$\log_a M - \log_a N = \log_a \frac{M}{N}.$$

Now, introducing the factor x/x, we have

$$\frac{dy}{dx} = \lim_{h \to 0} \frac{x}{x} \cdot \frac{1}{h} \log_a \left(\frac{x + h}{x}\right)$$

$$= \lim_{h \to 0} \frac{1}{x} \cdot \frac{x}{h} \log_a \left(1 + \frac{h}{x}\right)$$

$$= \lim_{h \to 0} \frac{1}{x} \log_a \left(1 + \frac{h}{x}\right)^{x/h},$$

because

$$N \log_a M = \log_a M^N.$$

So

$$\frac{dy}{dx} = \frac{1}{x} \lim_{h \to 0} \log_a \left(1 + \frac{h}{x}\right)^{x/h}.$$

The logarithmic function is continuous where it is defined, so

$$\frac{dy}{dx} = \frac{1}{x} \log_a \left[\lim_{h \to 0} \left(1 + \frac{h}{x}\right)^{x/h}\right].$$

Now

$$\lim_{h \to 0} \left(1 + \frac{h}{x}\right)^{x/h}$$

is of the same form as

$$\lim_{a \to 0} (1 + a)^{1/a} = e,$$

so

$$\frac{dy}{dx} = \frac{1}{x} \log_a e.$$

Thus we have

$$\frac{d}{dx} \log_a x = \frac{1}{x} \log_a e.$$

That means that if the logarithm were to the base e, the derivative would be $1/x$. That is,

$$\frac{d}{dx}(\log_e x) = \frac{d}{dx}(\ln x) = \frac{1}{x}.$$

If $y = \log_e x$, then $\dfrac{dy}{dx} = \dfrac{1}{x}$.

We see the derivatives of logarithmic functions have a simpler form if the base of the logarithm is e.

EXAMPLE 1   If $y = x^3 + 3\ln x$, find dy/dx.

Solution
$$\frac{dy}{dx} = 3x^2 + 3\left(\frac{1}{x}\right) = 3x^2 + \frac{3}{x} \qquad \square$$

EXAMPLE 2   If $y = x^2 \ln x$, find y'.

Solution   By the Product Rule,
$$y' = x^2 \cdot \frac{1}{x} + \ln x\,(2x) = x + 2x \ln x. \qquad \square$$

We can use the Chain Rule to determine the formula for the derivatives of $y = \log_a u$ and $y = \ln u$, where $u = f(x)$.

Derivatives of   If $y = \log_a u$, where $u = f(x)$, then
Logarithmic
Functions
$$\frac{dy}{dx} = \frac{1}{u}(\log_a e)\frac{du}{dx}.$$

If $y = \ln u$, where $u = f(x)$, then
$$\frac{dy}{dx} = \frac{1}{u} \cdot \frac{du}{dx}.$$

EXAMPLE 3   If $y = \log_4(x^3 + 1)$, find dy/dx.

Solution   The function is of the form $y = \log_4 u$, where $u = x^3 + 1$. Thus
$$\frac{dy}{dx} = \frac{1}{x^3 + 1}(\log_4 e)\,3x^2$$
$$= \frac{3x^2}{x^3 + 1}\log_4 e. \qquad \square$$

EXAMPLE 4   If $f(x) = \ln x^4$, find $f'(x)$.

Solution   The function is of the form $f(x) = \ln u$, where $u = x^4$. Then

$$f'(x) = \frac{1}{x^4} \cdot 4x^3 = \frac{4}{x}.$$ □

Note that we could also have found the derivative by first writing $f(x) = \ln x^4 = 4 \ln x$. Then,

$$f'(x) = 4 \cdot \frac{1}{x} = \frac{4}{x}.$$

EXAMPLE 5   If $y = \ln \sqrt{3x}$, find y'.

Solution   Letting $u = \sqrt{3x} = (3x)^{1/2}$, we have

$$y' = \frac{1}{(3x)^{1/2}} \cdot \frac{1}{2}(3x)^{-1/2} \cdot 3 = \frac{3}{2(3x)} = \frac{1}{2x}.$$

Or, writing $y = \frac{1}{2} \ln 3x$ gives

$$y' = \frac{1}{2} \cdot \frac{1}{3x} \cdot 3 = \frac{1}{2x}.$$ □

EXAMPLE 6   If $\ln xy = 6$, find dy/dx.

Solution   Using the properties of logarithms, we have

$$\ln x + \ln y = 6,$$

which gives

$$\frac{1}{x} + \frac{1}{y}\frac{dy}{dx} = 0.$$

Solving gives

$$\frac{dy}{dx} = -\frac{y}{x}.$$ □

Exercise 13.4

Find the derivatives of the functions in problems 1–14.

1. $y = \log_4 x$
2. $y = \log_5 x$
3. $y = \ln x$
4. $y = \ln(2x)$
5. $y = \ln(x^3 - 4x)$
6. $y = \log_e(x^5 - x^4)$
7. $y = \ln\left(\frac{4x - 1}{x}\right)$
8. $y = \ln\left(\frac{x^3}{x + 1}\right)$
9. $y = \ln(x^3\sqrt{x + 1})$
10. $y = \ln[x^2(x^4 - x + 1)]$

11. $y = \ln \sqrt{2}$ 12. $y = \ln \sqrt{e}$

13. $p = \ln (q^2 + 1)$ 14. $p = \ln \left(\dfrac{q^2 - 1}{q}\right)$

15. If $x \ln y = 4$, find dy/dx.
16. If $\ln xy = 2$, find dy/dx.
17. Find the slope of the tangent to the curve $x^2 + \ln y = 4$ at the point $(2, 1)$.
18. Write the equation of the tangent to the curve $x \ln y + 2xy = 2$ at the point $(1, 1)$.

APPLICATIONS

19. If the pH of a solution is given by

$$pH = -\log [H^+],$$

where $[H^+]$ is the concentration of hydrogen ions (in gram atoms per liter), what is the rate of change of pH with respect to $[H^+]$?

20. Suppose the proportion of people affected by a certain disease is described by

$$\ln \left(\frac{P}{1 - P}\right) = 0.5t,$$

where t is the time in months. Use implicit differentiation to find dP/dt, which represents the rate at which P grows.

21. If the Reynolds number relating to the flow of blood exceeds

$$R = A \ln r - Br,$$

where r is the radius of the aorta and A and B are positive constants, the blood flow becomes turbulent. What is the radius r that makes R a maximum?

13.5 Derivatives of Exponential Functions

Objective   ■ To find derivatives of exponential functions

In the previous section we found derivatives of logarithmic functions. In this section we turn our attention to exponential functions. The formula for the derivative of $y = a^x$ follows:

$$\text{If } y = a^x, \text{ then } \frac{dy}{dx} = \frac{a^x}{\log_a e}.$$

We can verify that the derivative of $y = a^x$ is $dy/dx = a^x/\log_a e$ as follows: We can write the function $y = a^x$ in the logarithmic form

$$\log_a y = x.$$

Taking the derivatives with respect to x of both sides of this equation, we get

$$\frac{1}{y} \cdot \frac{dy}{dx} \cdot \log_a e = 1.$$

Solving this equation for dy/dx gives $dy/dx = y/\log_a e$. But $y = a^x$, so

$$\frac{dy}{dx} = \frac{a^x}{\log_a e}.$$

EXAMPLE 1   If $y = 4^x$, find dy/dx.

Solution

$$\frac{dy}{dx} = \frac{4^x}{\log_4 e}$$ □

Using the derivative formula with $y = e^x$ gives

$$\frac{dy}{dx} = \frac{e^x}{\log_e e} = e^x,$$

since $\log_e e = 1$.

If $y = e^x$, then $dy/dx = e^x$.

EXAMPLE 2   If $p = e^q$, find dp/dq.

Solution

$$dp/dq = e^q$$ □

As with the logarithmic functions, the Chain Rule will permit us to expand our derivative formulas.

Derivatives of   If $y = a^u$, where u is a function of x, then
Exponential
Functions

$$\frac{dy}{dx} = \frac{a^u}{\log_a e} \cdot \frac{du}{dx}.$$

If $y = e^u$, where u is a function of x, then

$$\frac{dy}{dx} = e^u \cdot \frac{du}{dx}$$

EXAMPLE 3   If $y = 10^{x^2}$, find dy/dx.

Solution

$$\frac{dy}{dx} = 10^{x^2} \cdot 2x \cdot \frac{1}{\log e} = \frac{2x \cdot 10^{x^2}}{\log e}$$ □

EXAMPLE 4 If $f(x) = e^{4x^3}$, find $f'(x)$.

Solution
$$f'(x) = e^{4x^3} \cdot 12x^2 = 12x^2 e^{4x^3} \qquad \square$$

EXAMPLE 5 If $p = qe^{5q}$, find dp/dq.

Solution
$$\frac{dp}{dq} = (q \cdot e^{5q} \cdot 5) + (e^{5q} \cdot 1)$$
$$= 5qe^{5q} + e^{5q} \qquad \square$$

EXAMPLE 6 If $s = 3te^{3t^2+5t}$, find ds/dt.

Solution
$$\frac{ds}{dt} = 3t \cdot e^{3t^2+5t}(6t + 5) + e^{3t^2+5t} \cdot 3$$
$$= (18t^2 + 15t)e^{3t^2+5t} + 3e^{3t^2+5t} \qquad \square$$

EXAMPLE 7 If $y = e^{\ln x^2}$, find y'.

Solution
$$y' = e^{\ln x^2} \cdot \frac{1}{x^2} \cdot 2x = \frac{2}{x} e^{\ln x^2}$$

But by Property II of logarithms (Section 6.2) $e^{\ln u} - u$, so we can simplify the derivative to

$$y' = \frac{2}{x} \cdot x^2 = 2x.$$

Note that if we had used this property *before* taking the derivative, we would have

$$y = e^{\ln x^2} = x^2. \text{ Then the derivative is } y' = 2x. \qquad \square$$

EXAMPLE 8 If $u = w/e^{3w}$, find u'.

Solution The function is a quotient, with the denominator equal to e^{3w}. Using the Quotient Rule gives

$$u' = \frac{e^{3w} \cdot 1 - w \cdot e^{3w} \cdot 3}{(e^{3w})^2}$$
$$= \frac{e^{3w} - 3we^{3w}}{e^{6w}}$$
$$= \frac{1 - 3w}{e^{3w}} \qquad \square$$

EXAMPLE 9 If $q = e^{-p}$ describes the demand for a product, find dq/dp.

Solution
$$\frac{dq}{dp} = e^{-p}(-1) = -e^{-p} \qquad \square$$

Exercise 13.5

Find the derivatives of the functions in problems 1–20.

1. $y = 4^x$ 2. $y = 5^x$
3. $y = e^x$ 4. $y = e^{2x}$
5. $y = e^{3x}$ 6. $y = e^{x^2}$
7. $y = e^{x^2+3x}$ 8. $y = e^{4x^2-x}$
9. $m = e^3 + e^{\ln x}$ 10. $s = e^{t^2}$
11. $y = 2^{x^2}$ 12. $y = 3^{4x-1}$
13. $y = xe^x$ 14. $y = xe^{2x}$
15. $c = x^2 e^x$ 16. $p = 3xe^{5x}$
17. $p = 4qe^{q^3}$ 18. $c = x^3 e^{x^3}$
19. $y = \ln e^x$ 20. $y = \ln e^{7x}$
21. If $xe^y = 6$, find dy/dx.   22. If $x + e^{xy} = 10$, find dy/dx.
23. If $e^{xy} = 4$, find dy/dx.   24. If $x - xe^y = 3$, find dy/dx.
25. If $ye^x - y = 3$, find dy/dx.
26. Find the slope of the tangent to the curve $ye^x = 4$ at $(0, 4)$.
27. Write the equation of the tangent to the curve $xe^y = 3$ at $(3, 0)$.
28. The equation for the standard normal probability distribution is

$$y = \frac{1}{\sqrt{2\pi}} e^{-z^2/2}.$$

At what value of z will the curve be at its highest point?
29. (a) Find the mode of the normal distribution° given by

$$y = \frac{1}{\sqrt{2\pi}} e^{-(x-10)^2/4}.$$

(b) What is the mean of this normal distribution?

APPLICATIONS

30. The amount of the radioactive iostope thorium-234 is given by $Q(t) = 100e^{-0.02828t}$. Find the rate of radioactive decay of the isotope.

31. The compound amount that accrues when \$100 is invested at 8%, compounded continuously, is

$$S(t) = 100e^{0.08t},$$

where t is the number of years.
(a) At what rate is the money in this account growing when $t = 1$?
(b) At what rate is it growing when $t = 10$?

32. Suppose world population can be considered as growing according to the equation $N = N_0(1 + r)^t$, where N_0 and r are constants. Find the rate of change of N with respect to t.

33. The number of molecules of a certain substance which have enough energy to activate a reaction is given by $y = 100{,}000e^{-1/x}$, where y is the number of molecules

---

° The mode occurs at the highest point on the normal curves.

and x is the (absolute) temperature of the substance. What is the rate of change of y with respect to temperature?

34. When a body is moved from one medium to another, its temperature T will change according to the equation

$$T = T_0 + Ce^{kt},$$

where T_0 is the temperature of the new medium, C the temperature difference between the mediums (old - new), t the time in the new medium, and k a constant.

If T_0, C, and k are held constant, what is the rate of change of T with respect to time?

13.6   Applications in Business and Economics

Objectives   ■ To find the maximum profit, given the average cost and price in a competitive market
■ To find the maximum profit, given the demand function and average cost function in a monopoly
■ To find the tax per unit that will maximize tax revenue
■ To find the elasticity of demand

Profit Maximization in a Competitive Market

We have discussed total cost, total revenue, and profit functions in previous chapters, and we have also discussed demand functions. But we have not discussed how the demand for a product affects the total revenue of a firm and thus the firm's profit. In a *competitive market*, each firm is so small in the market that its actions cannot affect the price of the good. The price of the good is determined in the market by the intersection of the market demand curve (from all consumers) and market supply curve (from all firms that supply this good). The firm can sell as little or as much as it desires at the given market price, which it cannot change.

Thus a firm in a competitive market has a total revenue function given by $R(x) = px$, where p is the price that is the market equilibrium price for the product and x is the quantity it sells.

EXAMPLE 1   A firm in a competitive market must sell its product for $200 per unit. The average cost per unit (per month) is $\overline{C} = 80 + x$, where x represents the number of units sold per month. How many units should be sold to maximize profit?

Solution   If the average cost per unit is $\overline{C} = 80 + x$, then the total cost of x units is given by $C = (80 + x)x = 80x + x^2$. The revenue per unit is $200, so the total revenue is given by $R = 200x$. Thus the profit function is $P = R - C = 200x - (80x + x^2)$, or $P = 120x - x^2$. Then $P' = 120 - 2x$. Setting $P' = 0$ and solving for x gives $x = 60$. Since $P'' = -2$, the profit is maximized when the firm sells 60 units per month.   □

Profit Maximization in a Monopolistic Market

We have seen that a seller in a competitive market cannot change the market price. But a seller who has a monopoly can control the price by regulating the supply of the product. Since the seller controls the supply, he or she can force the price higher by limiting supply. If the seller increases the supply, prices will fall. Figure 13.11 shows the graph of the demand function $p = 3300/x$.

For a price of $33 per unit for a good whose demand curve is given in Figure 13.11, the monopolist will only supply 100 units. To sell 300 units, the monopolist will have to settle for $11 per unit. That is, if the monopolist wants to sell all that he or she produces, the price charged will have to be the price consistent with that level of output on the demand curve.

If the demand function for the product is $p = f(x)$, the total revenue for the sale of x units is $R = px = f(x) \cdot x$. Note that the price p is fixed by the market in a competitive market, but varies with output for the monopolist.

If $\bar{C} = \bar{C}(x)$ represents the average cost per unit sold, then the total cost for the x units sold is $C = \bar{C}x$. Since we have both total cost and total revenue as a function of the quantity, x, we can maximize the profit function, $P(x) = px - \bar{C}x$, where p represents the demand function $p = f(x)$ and $\bar{C}$ represents the average cost function $\bar{C} = \bar{C}(x)$.

EXAMPLE 2   The daily demand function for a product is $p = 168 - 0.2x$. If a monopolist finds the average cost is $\bar{C} = 120 + x$,
(a) how many units must be sold to maximize profit?
(b) what is the selling price at this "optimal" level of production?
(c) what is the maximum possible profit?

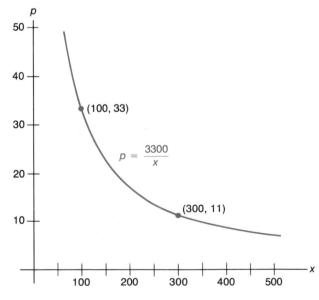

Figure 13.11

Solution   (a) The total revenue function for the product is

$$R(x) = px = (168 - 0.2x)\,x = 168x - 0.2x^2,$$

and the total cost function is

$$C(x) = \bar{C}x = (120 + x)x = 120x + x^2.$$

Thus the profit function is

$$P(x) = R(x) - C(x) = 168x - 0.2x^2 - (120x + x^2),$$

or $P(x) = 48x - 1.2x^2$. Then $P'(x) = 48 - 2.4x$, so $P'(x) = 0$ when $x = 20$. We see that $P''(x) = -2.4$, so by the second-derivative test, $P(x)$ is a maximum at $x = 20$. That is, selling 20 units will maximize profit.

(b) The selling price is determined by $p = 168 - 0.2x$, so the price that will result from supplying 20 units per day is $p = 168 - 0.2(20) = 164$. That is, the "optimal" selling price is $164 per unit.

(c) The profit at $x = 20$ is $P(20) = 48(20) - 1.2(20)^2 = 960 - 480 = 480$. Thus the maximum possible profit is $480 per day.   □

Taxation in a Competitive Market

Many taxes imposed by governments are "hidden." That is, the tax is levied on goods produced, and the producers must pay the tax. Of course, the tax becomes a cost to the producers, and they pass the tax on to the consumer in the form of higher prices for goods. But it isn't quite that simple, as the following discussion shows.

Suppose the government imposes a tax of t dollars on each unit produced and sold by producers. If we are in pure competition in which the consumers' demand depends only on price, the *demand function* will not change. The tax will change the supply function, of course, because at each level of output q, the firm will want to charge a price higher by the amount of the tax. This will shift the entire supply curve upward by the amount of the tax t, and market equilibrium will occur at a point where quantity demanded is lower.

The graph of the market demand function, the original market supply function, and the market supply function after taxes is shown in Figure 13.12. Because the tax added to each item is constant, the supply function is parallel to the original supply function and t units above it.

Note in this case that after the taxes are imposed, *no* items are supplied at the price that was the equilibrium price before taxation. After the taxes are imposed, the consumers will simply have to pay more for the product. Because taxation does not change the demand curve, the quantity purchased at market equilibrium will be less than it was before taxation. Thus governments planning taxes should recognize that they will not collect taxes on the original equilibrium quantity. They will collect on the *new* equilibrium quantity, a quantity reduced by their taxation. Thus a large tax on each item may reduce the quantity de-

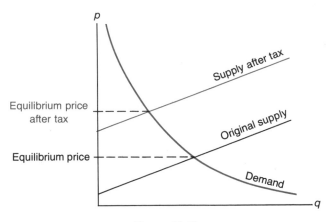

Figure 13.12

manded at the new market equilibrium so much that very little revenue would result from the tax.

If the tax revenue is represented by $T = tq$, where t is the tax per unit and q is the equilibrium quantity of the supply and demand functions after taxation, we can use the following procedure for maximizing the total tax revenue.

PROCEDURE	EXAMPLE
To find the tax per item (under pure competition) that will maximize total tax revenue:	If the demand and supply functions are $p = 600 - q$ and $p = 200 + \frac{1}{3}q$, respectively, find the tax rate t that will maximize the total tax revenue T.
1. Write the supply function after taxation.	1. $p = 200 + \frac{1}{3}q + t$
2. Set the demand and (new) supply functions equal, and solve for t.	2. $600 - q = 200 + \frac{1}{3}q + t$ $400 - \frac{4}{3}q = t$
3. Form the total tax revenue function, $T = tq$, and take its derivative with respect to q.	3. $T = tq = 400q - \frac{4}{3}q^2$ $T'(q) = \dfrac{dT}{dq} = 400 - \dfrac{8}{3}q$
4. Set $T' = 0$, solve for q. This is the q that should maximize T. Use the second-derivative test to verify it.	4. $0 = 400 - \frac{8}{3}q$ $q = 150$ $T''(q) = -\frac{8}{3}$. Thus T is maximized at $q = 150$.
5. Substitute the value of q into the equation for t (in step 2). This is the value of t that will maximize T.	5. $t = 400 - \frac{4}{3}(150) = 200$ A tax of \$200 per item will maximize the total tax revenue. The total tax revenue for the period would be $\$200 \cdot (150) = \$30,000$.

Note that in the example just given, if a tax of $300 were imposed, the total tax revenue the government would receive would be

$$(\$300)\,(75) = \$22{,}500.$$

This means that consumers would spend $100 more for each item, suppliers would sell 75 fewer items, and the government would lose $7500 in tax revenue, so everyone suffers if the tax rate is raised above $200.

Elasticity of Demand

We know from the law of demand that consumers will respond to changes in prices; if prices increase, the quantity demanded will decrease. But the degree of responsiveness of the consumers to price changes will vary widely for different products. For example, a price increase in insulin will not decrease greatly the demand for it by diabetics, but a price increase in clothes may cause consumers to buy considerably less and wear their old clothes longer. When the response to price changes is considerable, we say the demand is *elastic*. When price changes cause relatively small changes in demand for a product, the demand is called *inelastic* for that product.

The *elasticity of demand* is measured by economists by dividing the rate of change in demand by the rate of change in price. We may write this as

$$E_d = -\,\frac{\text{change in quantity demanded}}{\text{original quantity demanded}} \div \frac{\text{change in price}}{\text{original price}}$$

or

$$E_d = -\,\frac{\Delta q}{q} \div \frac{\Delta p}{p}$$

The demand curve usually has a negative slope, so we have introduced a negative sign into the formula to give us a positive elasticity.

We can write the equation for elasticity as

$$E_d = -\frac{p}{q} \cdot \frac{\Delta q}{\Delta p},$$

and define the **point elasticity of demand** as

$$\eta = \lim_{\Delta p \to 0} \left(-\frac{p}{q} \cdot \frac{\Delta q}{\Delta p}\right) = -\frac{p}{q} \cdot \frac{dq}{dp}.$$

The **point elasticity of demand** at the point (q_A, p_A) is

$$\eta = -\frac{p}{q} \cdot \frac{dq}{dp} \bigg|_{(q_A,\, p_A)}.$$

EXAMPLE 3   If a commodity has a demand curve given by $p + 5q = 100$, find the point elasticity of demand at $q = 8$, $p = 60$.

Solution   We can find dq/dp by using implicit differentiation with respect to p.

$$1 + 5\frac{dq}{dp} = 0, \quad \text{or} \quad \frac{dq}{dp} = -\frac{1}{5}.$$

Thus

$$\eta = -\frac{p}{q}\left(-\frac{1}{5}\right)\Bigg|_{(8,\,60)} = -\frac{60}{8}\left(-\frac{1}{5}\right) = \frac{3}{2}. \qquad \square$$

In the next example, we will see that the derivative dq/dp for $p + 5q = 100$ is also $-\frac{1}{5}$ when it is found by first solving for q.

EXAMPLE 4   Find the point elasticity of the demand function $p + 5q = 100$ at $(10, 50)$.

Solution   Solving the demand function for q gives $q = 20 - p/5$. Then $dq/dp = -\frac{1}{5}$, so

$$\eta = -\frac{p}{q}\left(-\frac{1}{5}\right)\Bigg|_{(10,\,50)} = -\frac{50}{10}\left(-\frac{1}{5}\right) = 1 \qquad \square$$

Note that in the Examples 3 and 4 the demand equation was $p + 5q = 100$, so the demand "curve" is a straight line, with slope $m = -5$. But the elasticity was $\eta = 3/2$ at $(8, 60)$ and $\eta = 1$ at $(10, 50)$. The elasticity for this same demand curve is $\eta = 2/3$ at $(12, 40)$. This illustrates that the elasticity of demand may be different at different points on the demand curve, even though the slope of the demand "curve" is constant. (See Figure 13.13.)

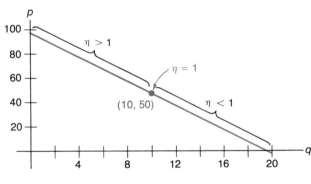

Figure 13.13

These examples show that the elasticity of demand is more than just the slope of the demand curve, which is the rate at which the demand is changing. Recall that the elasticity measures the consumers' degree of responsiveness to a price change. We can look at the relation between elasticity and a firm's total revenue as follows:

1. If $\eta > 1$, the demand is **elastic,** and an increase in price will result in decrease in total revenue. On the other hand, a decrease in price will increase total revenue.

2. If $\eta < 1$, the demand is **inelastic,** and an increase in price will result in an increase in total revenue. A decrease in price will lead to a decrease in revenue.

3. If $\eta = 1$, the demand is **unitary elastic,** and neither an increase nor decrease in price will change total revenue.

Exercise 13.6

PROFIT MAXIMIZATION IN A COMPETITIVE MARKET

1. The price of a good in a competitive market is $300. If the average cost of producing the good is $\bar{C} = 160 + x$, where x is the number of units produced per month, how many units should the firm produce and sell to maximize its profit?

2. The average cost of producing a product is $\bar{C} = 00 + 2x$, where x represents the number of units produced per week. If the equilibrium determined by a competitive market is $220, how many units should the firm produce and sell each week to maximize its profit?

3. If the daily average cost of producing a good by the Ace Company is $\bar{C} = 10 + 2x$, and if the price on the competitive market is $50, what is the maximum daily profit the Ace Company can expect on this good?

4. The Mary Ellen Candy Company produces chocolate Easter bunnies at an average cost of $\bar{C} = 0.10 + 0.01x$, where x is the number produced. If the price on the competitive market for this size bunny is $2.50, how many should it produce to maximize its profit?

PROFIT MAXIMIZATION IN A MONOPOLISTIC MARKET

5. The weekly demand function for a good sold by only one firm is $p = 600 - \frac{1}{2}x$ and the average cost of production and sale is $\bar{C} = 300 + 2x$.
   (a) Find the quantity that will maximize profit.
   (b) Find the selling price at this optimal level of production.
   (c) What is the maximum profit?

6. The monthly demand function for a good sold by a monopoly is $p = 8000 - x$, and its average cost is $\bar{C} = 4000 + 5x$. Determine
   (a) the quantity that will maximize profit.
   (b) the selling price at the optimal quantity.
   (c) the maximum profit.

7. If the monthly demand function for a good sold by a monopoly is $p = 1960 - \frac{1}{3}x^2$, and the average cost is $\bar{C} = 1000 + 2x + x^2$, find
   (a) the quantity that will give maximum profit.
   (b) the maximum profit.

8. The monthly demand function for a good sold by a monopoly is $p = 5900 - \frac{1}{2}x^2$, and its average cost is $\bar{C} = 3020 + 2x$. Will the firm make a profit or loss?

TAXATION IN A COMPETITIVE MARKET

9. If the weekly demand function is $p = 30 - q$ and the supply function before taxation is $p = 6 + 2q$, what tax per item will maximize the total tax revenue?

10. If the demand function for a fixed period of time is $p = 38 - 2q$ and the supply function before taxation is $p = 8 + 3q$, what tax per item will maximize the total tax revenue?

11. If the weekly demand function is $p = 200 - 2q^2$ and the supply function before taxation is $p = 20 + 3q$, what tax per item will maximize the total tax revenue?

12. If the monthly demand function is $p = 7230 - 5q^2$ and the supply function before taxation is $p = 30 + 30q^2$, what tax per item will maximize the total tax revenue?

ELASTICITY OF DEMAND

13. (a) Find the point elasticity of the demand function $p + 4q = 80$ at $(10, 40)$.
    (b) How will a price increase affect total revenue?

14. (a) Find the point elasticity of the demand function $2p + 3q = 150$ at the price $p = 15$.
    (b) How will a price increase affect total revenue?

15. (a) Find the point elasticity of the demand function $p^2 + 2p + q = 49$ at $p = 6$.
    (b) How will a price increase affect total revenue?

16. (a) Find the point elasticity of the demand function $pq = 81$ at $p = 3$.
    (b) How will a price increase affect total revenue?

17. Find the point elasticity of the demand curve defined by $q = 100e^{-2p}$ when $p = 4$.

18. Find the point elasticity of the demand function $q = 80e^{-p/2}$ if the price is \$4.

19. If the demand function for a good is $q = 12 - \ln p$, find the point elasticity of demand when the price is \$405 and the quantity is 6.

20. If the demand function for a good is $q = 15 - \frac{1}{3}\ln p$, find the point elasticity of demand when price is \$20, quantity is 14.

21. We have stated that when

$$\eta = -\frac{p}{q} \cdot \frac{dq}{dp} = 1$$

the total revenue is unchanged as price increases. Given the total revenue function

$$R = p \cdot q, \qquad \text{with } q = f(p),$$

use implicit differentiation with respect to p to show that R is unchanged $(dR/dp = 0)$ when $\eta = 1$.

22. We have stated that when

$$\eta = -\frac{p}{q} \cdot \frac{dq}{dp} > 1$$

the total revenue is decreasing as price increases. Given the total revenue function

$$R = p \cdot q, \qquad \text{with } q = f(p),$$

use implicit differentiation with respect to p to show that R is decreasing $(dR/dp < 0)$ when $\eta > 1$.

23. Show that $R = p \cdot q$ is increasing $(dR/dp > 0)$ when $\eta < 1$.

Review Exercises

Find the second derivative of the functions in problems 1 and 2.

1. $y = x^4 - \dfrac{1}{x}$

2. $f(x) = \sqrt{x^2 - 4}$

3. Find the third derivative of $y = 4x^4 - 3x^2$.

4. Find the relative maxima, relative minima, points of inflection, and graph the equation $y = x^3 - 12x$.

5. Graph $p = q^3 - q^2 + 1$.

6. If $y = x^2 e^x$, find dy/dx.

7. If $y = \ln e^{x^2}$, find y'.

8. If $p = \ln \left(\dfrac{q}{q^2 - 1} \right)$, find $\dfrac{dp}{dq}$.

9. Find the slope of the tangent to the curve $x^2 + 4x - 3y^2 + 6 = 0$ at $(3, 3)$.

10. If $y \ln x = 5$, find dy/dx.

APPLICATIONS

11. The price of a good in a competitive market is $250. If the average cost of producing the good is $\overline{C} = 70 + 3x$, where x is the number of units produced per week, how many will maximize profit?

12. The monthly demand function for a good sold by a monopoly is $p = 800 - x$, and its average cost is $\overline{C} = 200 + x$. Determine
    (a) the quantity that will maximize profit.
    (b) the selling price at the optimal quantity.

13. Can increasing the tax per unit sold actually lead to a decrease in tax revenues?

14. (a) Find the point elasticity of the demand function $pq = 27$ at $(9, 3)$.
    (b) How will a price increase affect total revenue?

Warmup In this chapter you will need to work problems like the following. If you have difficulty with any problem, return to the section where that type of problem was introduced and refresh your memory before starting the chapter.

Problem Type	Introduced in Section	Used in Section	Answer
Write as a power: (a) $\sqrt{x}$ (b) $\sqrt{x^2-9}$	0.2 Radicals	14.1–14.9	(a) $x^{1/2}$ (b) $(x^2-9)^{1/2}$
Expand $(x^2+4)^2$.	0.3 Special powers	14.2	$x^4 + 8x^2 + 16$
Divide $x^4 - 2x^3 + 4x^2 - 7x - 1$ by $x^2 - 2x$.	0.4 Division	14.3	$x^2 + 4 + \dfrac{x-1}{x^2-2x}$
Simplify: $\dfrac{1}{n^3}\left[\dfrac{n(n+1)(2n+1)}{6} - \dfrac{2n(n+1)}{2} + n\right]$	0.5 Fractions	14.5	$\dfrac{2n^2 - 3n + 1}{6n^2}$
(a) If $F(x) = \dfrac{x^4}{4} + 4x + C$, what is $F(4) - F(2)$? (b) If $F(x) = -\dfrac{1}{9}\ln\dfrac{9 + \sqrt{81 - 9x^2}}{3x}$, what is $F(3) - F(2)$?	1.3 Functional notation	14.6, 14.8	(a) 68 (b) $\dfrac{1}{9}\ln\left(\dfrac{3 + \sqrt{5}}{2}\right)$
(a) Does $\displaystyle\sum_{i=1}^{n} \dfrac{i}{n}\cdot\dfrac{1}{n} = \dfrac{1}{n^2}\sum_{i=1}^{n} i$? (b) $\displaystyle\sum_{i=1}^{n} i = \underline{\quad}$. (c) $\displaystyle\sum_{i=1}^{n} i^2 = \underline{\quad}$.	7.3 Sigma notation	14.5	(a) Yes (b) $\dfrac{n(n+1)}{2}$ (c) $\dfrac{n(n+1)(2n+1)}{6}$
Find the limit: (a) $\displaystyle\lim_{n\to+\infty} \dfrac{n^2 + n}{2n^2}$ (b) $\displaystyle\lim_{n\to+\infty} \dfrac{2n^2 - 3n + 1}{6n^2}$	10.3 Limits	14.5	(a) $\frac{1}{2}$ (b) $\frac{1}{3}$
Find the derivative of (a) $f(x) = 2x^{1/2}$ (b) $u = x^3 - 3x$	11.3 Derivatives	14.1, 14.2, 14.3, 14.6, 14.8	(a) $f'(x) = x^{-1/2}$ (b) $u' = 3x^2 - 3$
If $y = \dfrac{(x^2+4)^6}{6}$, what is y'?	11.5 Derivatives	14.2	$(x^2+4)^5\, 2x$
(a) If $y = \ln u$, what is y'? (b) If $y = e^u$, what is y'?	13.4 Derivatives	14.3	(a) $y' = \dfrac{1}{u}\cdot u'$ (b) $y' = e^u \cdot u'$
(a) If $u = x^2 + 4$, what is du?	11.4 Differentials	14.2, 14.8, 14.9	(a) $2x\,dx$

INTEGRATION

If the marginal cost for a product is $36 at all levels of production, we know that the total cost function is a linear function. In particular, $C(x) = 36x + FC$, where FC is the fixed cost. But if the marginal cost changes at different levels of production, the total cost function cannot be linear. In this chapter we will use integration to find total cost functions, given information about marginal costs and fixed costs.

Accountants can use linear regression to translate information about marginal cost into a linear equation defining (approximately) the marginal cost function. By integrating this marginal cost function, it is possible to find an (approximate) function that defines the total cost.

We can also use integration to find total revenue functions from marginal revenue functions, to optimize profit using information about marginal cost and marginal revenue, to find national consumption functions from information about marginal propensity to consume, and to find the consumer's surplus and the producer's surplus.

Integration can be used in the social and life sciences to predict growth or decay from expressions giving rates of change. For example, we can determine equations for population size from the rate of growth; we can write equations for the number of radioactive atoms remaining in a substance if we know the rate of disintegration of the substance; and we can determine the volume of blood flow from information about the rate of flow.

14.1 The Indefinite Integral

Objective   ■ To find certain indefinite integrals using $\int x^n \, dx \, (n \neq -1)$

We have discussed methods of finding derivatives of functions in the previous chapters. We will now turn our attention to reversing this operation. Given the derivative of a function, we can find the function whose derivative we know. This process is called **antidifferentiation.** For example, if the derivative of a function is $2x$, we know the function could be $f(x) = x^2$, because $\frac{d}{dx}(x^2) = 2x$. But the function could also be $f(x) = x^2 + 4$, because $\frac{d}{dx}(x^2 + 4) = 2x$. It is clear that any function of the form $f(x) = x^2 + C$, where C is a constant, will have $f'(x) = 2x$ as its derivative. Thus we say the **antiderivative** of $f'(x) = 2x$ is the function $f(x) = x^2 + C$.

EXAMPLE 1   If $f'(x) = 3x^2$, what is $f(x)$?

Solution   The derivative of the function $f(x) = x^3$ is $f'(x) = 3x^2$. But other functions also have this derivative. They will all be of the form $f(x) = x^3 + C$, where C is a constant. Thus we say $f(x) = x^3 + C$ is the antiderivative of $f'(x) = 3x^2$.   □

EXAMPLE 2   If $f'(x) = x^3$, what is $f(x)$?

Solution   We know that the derivative of $f(x) = x^4$ is $4x^3$, so the derivative of $f(x) = x^4/4$ is $f'(x) = x^3$. Thus any function of the form $f(x) = x^4/4 + C$ will have the derivative $f'(x) = x^3$.   □

It is easily seen that

$$\text{If } f'(x) = x^4, \qquad \text{then } f(x) = \frac{x^5}{5} + C;$$

$$\text{If } \frac{dy}{dx} = x^5, \qquad \text{then } y = \frac{x^6}{6} + C.$$

In general,

$$\text{If } f'(x) = x^n, \text{ then } f(x) = \frac{x^{n+1}}{n+1} + C, \text{ for } n \neq -1.$$

We can see that this general formula applies for any $n \neq -1$ by noting that the derivative of

$$f(x) = \frac{x^{n+1}}{n+1} + C \quad \text{is} \quad f'(x) = \frac{(n+1)\,x^n}{n+1} + 0 = x^n.$$

We will discuss the case when $n = -1$ later.

EXAMPLE 3   What is the antiderivative of $f'(x) = x^{-1/2}$?

Solution   Using the formula, we get

$$f(x) = \frac{x^{1/2}}{1/2} + C = 2x^{1/2} + C.$$

We can check by noting that the derivative of $2x^{1/2} + C$ is $x^{-1/2}$.   □

The process of finding an antiderivative is called **integration.** The function that results when integration takes place is called an **indefinite integral,** or more simply, an **integral.** We can denote the indefinite integral (that is, the antiderivative) of a function $f(x)$ by $\int f(x)\,dx$. Thus we can write $\int x^2\,dx$ to indicate the antiderivative of the function $f(x) = x^2$. The expression is read as "the integral of x^2 with respect to x." The $\int$ indicates the integration, and the dx indicates that the integral is to be taken with respect to x. Because the antiderivative of x^2 is $x^3/3 + C$, we can write

$$\int x^2\,dx = \frac{x^3}{3} + C.$$

Note that integration results in a function (actually a number of functions, one for each value of C). This is reasonable, since the derivative of a function is a function.

We can now use the integral sign and rewrite the formula for integrating powers of x.

> *Powers of x* $\int x^n\,dx = \dfrac{x^{n+1}}{n+1} + C$ (for $n \neq -1$)
> *Formula*

EXAMPLE 4   Find $\int \sqrt[3]{x}\,dx$.

Solution

$$\int \sqrt[3]{x}\,dx = \int x^{1/3}\,dx = \frac{x^{4/3}}{\frac{4}{3}} + C$$

$$= \frac{3}{4}x^{4/3} + C = \frac{3x}{4}\sqrt[3]{x} + C.$$ □

Other formulas will be useful in evaluating integrals. For example, the derivative of $y = x$ is $dy/dx = 1$, so

$$\int 1\ dx = \int dx = x + C$$

We know that if $y = c \cdot u(x)$, $dy/dx = c \cdot u'(x)$, so

$$\int cu(x)\ dx = c \int u(x)\ dx.$$

EXAMPLE 5   Evaluate $\int 4\ dx$.

Solution

$$\int 4\ dx = 4 \int dx = 4(x + C_1) = 4x + C$$

(Since C_1 is an unknown constant, we can write $4C_1$ as the unknown constant C.)   □

EXAMPLE 6   Evaluate $\int 8x^5\ dx$.

Solution

$$\int 8x^5\ dx = 8 \int x^5\ dx = 8(\frac{x^6}{6} + C_1) = \frac{4x^6}{3} + C$$ □

Just as we were able to take derivatives term-by-term, we can integrate sums of functions separately and add the integrals:

$$\int [u(x) + v(x)]\ dx = \int u(x)\ dx + \int v(x)\ dx.$$

EXAMPLE 7   Evaluate $\int (x^3 + 4x)\ dx$.

Solution

$$\int (x^3 + 4x)\ dx = \int x^3\ dx + \int 4x\ dx$$

$$= (\frac{x^4}{4} + C_1) + (4 \cdot \frac{x^2}{2} + C_2)$$

$$= \frac{x^4}{4} + 2x^2 + C_1 + C_2$$

$$= \frac{x^4}{4} + 2x^2 + C$$

Note that we need only one constant because the sum of C_1 and C_2 is just a new constant.   □

EXAMPLE 8   Evaluate $\int (x - 4)^2\ dx$.

Solution   We can multiply out the square before we integrate.

$$\int (x - 4)^2\ dx = \int (x^2 - 8x + 16)\ dx = \frac{x^3}{3} - 4x^2 + 16x + C$$ □

EXAMPLE 9   Sales records show that the rate of change of the revenue (that is, the marginal revenue) for a product is $\overline{MR} = 300 - 0.2x$, where x represents the quantity sold. Use this marginal revenue and the fact that revenue is 0 when $x = 0$ to find the total revenue function for the product.

Solution   We know that the marginal revenue can be found by differentiating the total revenue function. That is,

$$R'(x) = 300 - 0.2x.$$

Thus integrating the marginal revenue function will give the total revenue function.

$$R = \int (300 - 0.2x)\, dx = 300x - 0.1x^2 + K°$$

Since $R = 0$ when $x = 0$, we can evaluate K: setting $x = 0$ and $R = 0$ gives $0 = 300(0) - 0.1(0)^2 + K$, so $K = 0$. Thus the total revenue function is

$$R = 300x - 0.1x^2.$$

□

Exercise 14.1

1. If $f'(x) = 4x^3$, what is $f(x)$?
2. If $f'(x) = 5x^4$, what is $f(x)$?
3. If $f'(x) = x^6$, what is $f(x)$?
4. If $g'(x) = x^4$, what is $g(x)$?

Evaluate the following integrals.

5. $\int x^7\, dx$

6. $\int x^5\, dx$

7. $\int x^{3/2}\, dx$

8. $\int x^{2/3}\, dx$

9. $\int \sqrt{x}\, dx$

10. $\int \sqrt{x^3}\, dx$

11. $\int 5\, dx$

12. $\int 6\, dx$

13. $\int 5x^3\, dx$

14. $\int 4x^5\, dx$

15. $\int 6\sqrt{x}\, dx$

16. $\int 3\sqrt[3]{x^2}\, dx$

17. $\int (x^4 - 3x^2)\, dx$

18. $\int (3x^2 - 4x)\, dx$

19. $\int (x^3 - 3x^2 + 4)\, dx$

20. $\int (x^3 - 4x + 3)\, dx$

21. $\int (x^4 - 2x + \sqrt{x})\, dx$

22. $\int (3x^3 - x^2 - \sqrt[3]{x})\, dx$

23. $\int (x + 5)^2\, dx$

24. $\int (2x + 1)^2\, dx$

25. $\int (4x^2 - 1)^2\, dx$

26. $\int (x^3 + 1)^2\, dx$

27. $\int (x^2 + 1)^3\, dx$

28. $\int (x - 1)^3\, dx$

APPLICATIONS

29. If the marginal revenue for a month for a commodity is $\overline{MR} = 3$, what is the total revenue function?

° We are using K rather than C here to represent the constant of integration to avoid confusion between the constant C and the cost function $C = C(x)$.

30. If the marginal revenue for a month for a good is $\overline{MR} = 5$, what is the total revenue function?

31. If the marginal revenue for a month for a commodity is $\overline{MR} = 4x - 3$, find the total revenue function.

32. If the marginal revenue for a month for a commodity is $\overline{MR} = 5x - 2$, find the total revenue function.

33. If the marginal revenue for a month is given by $\overline{MR} = 3x - 1$, what is the total revenue from the production and sale of 50 units?

34. If the marginal revenue for a month is given by $\overline{MR} = 5x - 3$, find the total revenue from the sale of 75 units.

35. Suppose that when a sense organ receives a stimulus at time t, the total number of action potentials is $P(t)$. If the rate at which action potentials are produced is given by $t^3 + 4t^2 + 6$, and if there are 0 action potentials when $t = 0$, find the formula for $P(t)$.

36. Suppose a particle has been shot into the air in such a way that the rate at which its height is changing is $v = 320 - 32t$, in feet per second, and suppose that it is 1600 feet high when $t = 10$. Write the equation that describes the height of the particle at any time t.

37. A factory is dumping pollutants into a river at a rate given by $dx/dt = t^{3/4}/600$ tons per week, where t is the time in weeks since they began dumping and x is the numbers of tons of pollutants.
    (a) Find the equation for total tons of pollutants dumped.
    (b) How many tons were dumped during the first year?

38. The rate at which the radius of an oil slick is spreading from an offshore oil well is 4 feet per hour. If the radius is 100 feet when $t = 25$, write the radius of the oil slick as a function of time.

14.2 The Power Rule

Objective   ■ To evaluate integrals of the form $\int u^n \cdot u' \, dx$ if $n \neq -1$

In problem 24 of Exercise 14.1, we evaluated

$$\int (2x + 1)^2 \, dx$$

by squaring $2x + 1$ and integrating the resulting polynomial term-by-term. In this section we will attempt to integrate powers of some functions without multiplying out the powers.

Recall that if $y = [u(x)]^n$, the derivative of y is

$$\frac{dy}{dx} = n[u(x)]^{n-1} \cdot u'(x).$$

Using this formula for derivatives, we can see that

$$\int n[u(x)]^{n-1} \cdot u'(x) = [u(x)]^n + C.$$

It is easy to see that this formula is equivalent to the following formula, called the **Power Rule**.

Power Rule $\quad \int [u(x)]^n \cdot u'(x)\, dx = \dfrac{[u(x)]^{n+1}}{n+1} + C, \quad$ if $n \neq -1$.

Note that the Power Rule is similar to the formula

$$\int x^n\, dx = \frac{x^{n+1}}{n+1} + C,$$

except that the Power Rule requires that $u'(x)$ be present in the integral. However, if $u(x) = x$, then $u'(x) = 1$, so the Power Rule is actually an extension of the powers of x rule.

Recalling that the differential

$$du = u'(x)\, dx,$$

we can write the Power Rule in the form

$$\int u^n\, du = \frac{u^{n+1}}{n+1} + C, \quad \text{if } n \neq 1.$$

EXAMPLE 1   Evaluate $\int (x^2 + 4)^5 \cdot 2x\, dx$.

Solution   To use the Power Rule, we must be sure we have the function $u(x)$, its derivative $u'(x)$, and n.

$$u = x^2 + 4, \quad n = 5$$
$$u' = 2x$$

All required parts are present, so the integral is of the form

$$\int u^5 \cdot u'\, dx = \int u^5\, du.$$

Thus the integral is

$$\frac{u^6}{6} + C = \frac{(x^2 + 4)^6}{6} + C.$$

We can check the integration by noting that the derivative of

$$\frac{(x^2 + 4)^6}{6} + C \quad \text{is} \quad (x^2 + 4)^5 \cdot 2x.$$

$\square$

EXAMPLE 2   Evaluate $\int \sqrt{2x + 3} \cdot 2 \, dx$.

Solution   If we let $u = 2x + 3$, then $u' = 2$ and this integral has the form $\int \sqrt{u} \, u' \, dx = \int u^{1/2} \cdot u' \, dx$. This integral will be

$$\frac{u^{3/2}}{3/2} + C.$$

Since $u = 2x + 3$, we have

$$\int \sqrt{2x + 3} \cdot 2 \, dx = \frac{2}{3} (2x + 3)^{3/2} + C.$$

CHECK: The derivative of $\frac{2}{3}(2x + 3)^{3/2} + C$ is $(2x + 3)^{1/2} \cdot 2$.   □

EXAMPLE 3   Evaluate $\int (x^2 + 4)^4 \cdot x \, dx$.

Solution   If we let $u = x^2 + 4$, then $u' = 2x$. Thus we do not have an integral of the form $u^n \cdot u' \, dx$, as we did in Example 1. But since we are missing *only the constant factor* 2 to make it the correct form, we can multiply by 2 and divide it out as follows:

$$\int (x^2 + 4)^4 \cdot x \, dx = \int (x^2 + 4)^4 \cdot \frac{1}{2} (2x) \, dx.$$

We can factor the $\frac{1}{2}$ outside the integral sign since it is a constant, getting $\frac{1}{2} \int (x^2 + 4)^4 \cdot 2x \, dx$.
Now the integral is in the form $\frac{1}{2} \int u^4 \cdot u' \, dx$. Thus

$$\int (x^2 + 4)^4 \cdot x \, dx = \frac{1}{2} \int (x^2 + 4)^4 \cdot 2x \, dx$$

$$= \frac{1}{2} \frac{(x^2 + 4)^5}{5} + C$$

$$= \frac{1}{10} (x^2 - 4)^5 + C.$$ □

EXAMPLE 4   Evaluate $\int \sqrt{x^3 - 4} \cdot x^2 \, dx$.

Solution   If we let $u = x^3 - 4$, then $u' = 3x^2$. Thus if we multiply by the constant factor 3 (and divide it out) we have

$$\int \sqrt{x^3 - 4} \cdot x^2 \, dx = \int \sqrt{x^3 - 4} \cdot \frac{1}{3} (3x^2) \, dx$$

$$= \frac{1}{3} \int (x^3 - 4)^{1/2} \cdot 3x^2 \, dx.$$

This integral is of the form $\frac{1}{3} \int u^{1/2} \cdot u' \, dx$, resulting in

$$\frac{1}{3} \cdot \frac{u^{3/2}}{\frac{3}{2}} + C = \frac{1}{3} \cdot \frac{(x^3 - 4)^{3/2}}{\frac{3}{2}} + C$$

$$= \frac{2}{9} (x^3 - 4)^{3/2} + C.$$ □

Note that we can introduce *only a constant factor* to get the integral into the proper form. If the integral requires the introduction of a *variable* to get it into the form $u^n \cdot u' \, dx$, we *cannot* use the form, and must try something else.

EXAMPLE 5   Evaluate $\int (x^2 + 4)^2 \, dx$.

Solution   If we let $u = x^2 + 4$, then $u' = 2x$. Since we would have to introduce a variable to get u' in the integral, we cannot treat this problem as a u^n problem. We must find another method. We can evaluate this integral by squaring the factor and then integrating term-by-term.

$$\int (x^2 + 4)^2 \, dx = \int (x^4 + 8x^2 + 16) \, dx$$

$$= \frac{x^5}{5} + \frac{8x^3}{3} + 16x + C \qquad \square$$

Note that if we had tried to introduce the factor $2x$ into the integral, we would get

$$\int (x^2 + 4)^2 \, dx = \int (x^2 + 4)^2 \cdot \frac{1}{2x} (2x) \, dx$$

$$= \frac{1}{2} \int (x^2 + 4)^2 \cdot \frac{1}{x} (2x) \, dx$$

But we cannot factor the $1/x$ outside the integral, so we do not have the proper form. Again, we can only introduce *a constant factor* to get an integral in the proper form.

EXAMPLE 6   Evaluate $\int (2x^2 - 4x)^2 (x - 1) \, dx$.

Solution   If we want to treat this as an integral of the form $\int u^n u' \, dx$, we will have to let $u = 2x^2 - 4x$. Then u' will be $4x - 4$. Multiplying and dividing by 4 will give us this form, as follows:

$$\int (2x^2 - 4x)^2 (x - 1) \, dx = \int (2x^2 - 4x)^2 \cdot \frac{1}{4} \cdot 4(x - 1) \, dx$$

$$= \frac{1}{4} \int (2x^2 - 4x)^2 (4x - 4) \, dx$$

$$= \frac{1}{4} \frac{(2x^2 - 4x)^3}{3} + C$$

$$= \frac{1}{12} (2x^2 - 4x)^3 + C \qquad \square$$

EXAMPLE 7   Evaluate $\int \frac{x^2 - 1}{(x^3 - 3x)^3} \, dx$.

Solution   This integral can be treated as $\int u^{-3} u' \, dx$ if we let $u = x^3 - 3x$. Then we can multiply (and divide) by 3 to get $u' = 3(x^2 - 1)$:

$$\int \frac{x^2 - 1}{(x^3 - 3x)^3} \, dx = \int (x^3 - 3x)^{-3} \cdot \frac{1}{3} \cdot 3(x^2 - 1) \, dx$$

$$= \frac{1}{3} \int (x^3 - 3x)^{-3} (3x^2 - 3) \, dx$$

$$= \frac{1}{3} \left[\frac{(x^3 - 3x)^{-2}}{-2} \right] + C$$

$$= \frac{-1}{6(x^3 - 3x)^2} + C \qquad \square$$

Exercise 14.2

Evaluate the following integrals.

1. $\int (x^2 + 3)^3 \, 2x \, dx$

2. $\int (3x^3 + 1)^4 \, 9x^2 \, dx$

3. $\int (3x - x^3)^2 (3 - 3x^2) \, dx$

4. $\int (4x^2 - 3x)^4 (8x - 3) \, dx$

5. $\int (x^2 + 5)^3 x \, dx$

6. $\int (3x^2 - 4)^6 x \, dx$

7. $\int \sqrt{x^4 + 6} \, x^3 \, dx$

8. $\int \sqrt{5 - x^2} \, x \, dx$

9. $\int (3 - x^2)^2 \, dx$

10. $\int (5 - x)^3 \, dx$

11. $\int (x^2 + 1)^3 x \, dx$

12. $\int (x^2 - 3)^3 \, dx$

13. $\int (x^2 - 2x)^4 (x - 1) \, dx$

14. $\int \sqrt{x^3 - 3x} (x^2 - 1) \, dx$

15. $\int (x + 1) \sqrt[3]{x^2 + 2x} \, dx$

16. $\int (x^4 - x^2)^6 (2x^3 - x) \, dx$

17. $\int \frac{x^2}{(x^3 - 1)^2} \, dx$

18. $\int \frac{x}{(x^2 - 1)^3} \, dx$

19. $\int \frac{x^2}{(x^3 - 5)^4} \, dx$

20. $\int \frac{x^3}{\sqrt[3]{x^4 + 5}} \, dx$

21. $\int \frac{3x^5 - 2x^3}{(x^6 - x^4)^5} \, dx$

22. $\int \frac{x^2 - 4x}{\sqrt{x^3 - 6x^2}} \, dx$

23. $\int \frac{8x^2}{(x^3 - 4)^2} \, dx$

24. $\int \frac{x^3}{(x^4 - 8)^3} \, dx$

25. $\int \frac{x^3 - 1}{(x^4 - 4x)^3} \, dx$

26. $\int \frac{x^2 + 1}{\sqrt{x^3 + 3x}} \, dx$

APPLICATIONS

27. The total physical output of a number of machines or workers is called *physical productivity*, and is a function of the number of machines or workers. If $P = f(x)$ is the productivity, dP/dx is the marginal physical productivity. If the marginal physical productivity for bricklayers is

$$\frac{dP}{dx} = 90(x + 1)^2,$$

where P is the number of bricks laid per day, find the physical productivity of 4 bricklayers.

28. Suppose the marginal revenue for a product is given by

$$\overline{MR} = \frac{-30}{(2x + 1)^2} + 30.$$

Find the total revenue.

29. The marginal revenue for a new calculator is given by

$$\overline{MR} = 60,000 - \frac{40,000}{(10 + x)^2},$$

where x represents hundreds of calculators. Find the total revenue function for these calculators.

30. The rate of production of a new line of products is given by

$$\frac{dx}{dt} = 200\left[1 + \frac{400}{(t + 40)^2}\right],$$

where x is the number of items and t is the number of weeks the product has been in production.
   (a) Assuming $x - 0$ when $t = 0$, find the equation that represents the total number of items produced as a function of time t.
   (b) How many items were produced in the fifth week?

14.3 Integrals Involving Logarithmic and Exponential Functions

Objectives
- To evaluate integrals of the form $\int \frac{u'}{u} \, dx$
- To evaluate integrals of the form $\int e^u \, u' \, dx$

Recall that the Power Rule for integrals applies only if $n \neq -1$. That is,

$$\int u^n u' \, dx = \frac{u^{n+1}}{n+1} + C \qquad \text{if } n \neq -1.$$

The following formula applies when $n = -1$.

$$\int u^{-1} u' \, dx = \int \frac{u'}{u} \, dx = \ln |u| + C$$

This formula is a direct result of the fact that

$$\frac{d}{dx}(\ln u) = \frac{1}{u} \cdot u'.$$

The absolute value is used with the natural logarithm because u may be positive or negative, but the logarithm is defined only when the quantity is positive.

EXAMPLE 1   Evaluate $\int \dfrac{4}{4x+1}\,dx$.

Solution   This integral is of the form

$$\int \frac{u'}{u}\,dx,$$

with $u = 4x + 1$ and $u' = 4$. Thus

$$\int \frac{4}{4x+1}\,dx = \ln|4x+1| + C. \qquad \square$$

EXAMPLE 2   Evaluate $\int \dfrac{x-3}{x^2-6x+1}\,dx$.

Solution   This integral is of the form $u'/u\,dx$, *almost*. If we let $u = x^2 - 6x + 1$, then $u' = 2x - 6$. If we multiply (and divide) the numerator by 2, we get

$$\int \frac{x-3}{x^2-6x+1}\,dx = \frac{1}{2}\int \frac{2(x-3)}{x^2-6x+1}\,dx$$

$$= \frac{1}{2}\int \frac{2x-6}{x^2-6x+1}\,dx$$

$$= \frac{1}{2}\ln|x^2-6x+1| + C. \qquad \square$$

If an integral contains a fraction in which the degree of the numerator is equal to or greater than that of the denominator, we should divide the denominator into the numerator as a first step.

EXAMPLE 3   Evaluate $\int \dfrac{x^4 - 2x^3 + 4x^2 - 7x - 1}{x^2 - 2x}\,dx$.

Solution   Because the numerator is of higher degree than the denominator, we begin by dividing $x^2 - 2x$ into the numerator, which gives the integral in the form

$$\int \left(x^2 + 4 + \frac{x-1}{x^2-2x} \right)dx.$$

Integrating gives

$$\frac{x^3}{3} + 4x + \frac{1}{2}\ln|x^2-2x| + C. \qquad \square$$

We know that

$$\frac{d}{dx}(e^u) = e^u \cdot u'.$$

The corresponding integral is given by the following.

> If u is a function of x, $\int e^u \cdot u' \, dx = e^u + C$.

EXAMPLE 4   Evaluate $\int 2xe^{x^2} \, dx$.

Solution   This is of the form $\int e^u \cdot u' \, dx$. Letting $u = x^2$ implies $u' = 2x$. Thus

$$\int 2xe^{x^2} \, dx = \int e^{x^2}(2x) \, dx$$
$$= e^{x^2} + C. \qquad \square$$

EXAMPLE 5   Evaluate $\int x^2 e^{x^3} \, dx$.

Solution   This is *almost* of the form $\int e^u \cdot u' \, dx$. Letting $u = x^3$ implies $u' = 3x^2$. Thus

$$\int x^2 e^{x^3} \, dx = \frac{1}{3} \int e^{x^3} 3x^2 \, dx = \frac{1}{3} e^{x^3} + C. \qquad \square$$

We can also integrate functions of variables other than x. For example,

$$\int 2e^{2y} \, dy = e^{2y} + C.$$

EXAMPLE 6   Evaluate $\int \frac{z}{z^2 + 1} \, dz$.

Solution   This integral is almost of the form $\int \frac{du}{u}$. Letting $u = z^2 + 1$, we see that du must be $2z \, dz$.
So

$$\int \frac{z}{z^2 + 1} \, dz = \frac{1}{2} \int \frac{2z}{z^2 + 1} \, dz = \frac{1}{2} \ln|z^2 + 1| + C. \qquad \square$$

Exercise 14.3

Evaluate the following integrals.

1. $\int \dfrac{3x^2}{x^3 + 4} \, dx$

2. $\int \dfrac{8x^7}{x^8 - 1} \, dx$

3. $\int \dfrac{3x^2 - 2}{x^3 - 2x} \, dx$

4. $\int \dfrac{4x^3 + 2x}{x^4 + x^2} \, dx$

5. $\int \dfrac{x^3}{x^4 + 1} \, dx$

6. $\int \dfrac{x^2}{x^3 - 9} \, dx$

7. $\int \dfrac{4x}{x^2 - 4} \, dx$

8. $\int \dfrac{5x^2}{x^3 - 1} \, dx$

9. $\int \dfrac{dz}{4z + 1}$

10. $\int \dfrac{y}{y^2 + 1} \, dy$

11. $\int \dfrac{z^2 + 1}{z^3 + 3z} \, dz$

12. $\int \dfrac{x + 2}{x^2 + 4x} \, dx$

13. $\int \dfrac{x^3 - x^2 + 1}{x - 1} \, dx$

14. $\int \dfrac{2x^3 + x^2 + 2x + 3}{2x + 1} \, dx$

15. $\int \dfrac{x^2 + x + 3}{x^2 + 3} \, dx$

16. $\int \dfrac{x^4 - 2x^2 + x}{x^2 - 2} \, dx$

17. $\int 3e^{3x} \, dx$

18. $\int 4e^{4x} \, dx$

19. $\int e^{-x} \, dx$

20. $\int xe^{2x^2} \, dx$

21. $\int x^3 e^{x^4} \, dx$

22. $\int (e^x + e^{-x}) \, dx$

23. $\int y e^{y^2} \, dy$

24. $\int 6e^{3y} \, dy$

APPLICATIONS

25. Suppose the marginal revenue from the sale of a product is

$$\overline{MR} = R'(x) = 6e^{0.01x}.$$

What is the revenue on the sale of 100 units of the product?

26. Suppose the rate at which the concentration of a drug in the blood changes with respect to time t is given by

$$C'(t) = \frac{c}{b - a}(be^{-bt} - ae^{-at}), \qquad t \geq 0,$$

where a, b, and c are constants depending on the drug administered, with $b > a$. Assuming $C(t) = 0$ when $t = 0$, find the formula for the concentration of the drug in the blood at any time t.

27. The rate of disintegration of a radioactive substance can be described by

$$\frac{dn}{dt} = n_0(-K)e^{-Kt},$$

where n_0 is the number of radioactive atoms present when time t is 0, and K is a positive constant that depends on the substance involved. Using the fact that the constant of integration is 0, integrate dn/dt to find the number of atoms n that are still radioactive after time t.

28. Because the world contains only about 10 billion acres of arable land, world population is limited. Suppose the world population is limited to 40 billion people and that the rate of population growth is proportional to how close the world is to this upper limit. Then the rate of growth would be

$$\frac{dP}{dt} = K(40 - P),$$

where K is a positive constant. This means

$$t = \frac{1}{K} \int \frac{1}{40 - P} \, dP.$$

(a) Evaluate this integral to find an expression relating P and t.
(b) Use the properties relating logarithms and exponential functions to write P as a function of t.

14.4 Applications of the Indefinite Integral in Business and Economics

Objectives
- To use integration to find total cost functions from information involving marginal cost
- To optimize profit, given information regarding marginal cost and marginal revenue
- To use integration to find national consumption functions from information about marginal propensity to consume and marginal propensity to save

We again turn our attention to applications involving cost, profit, and consumption. We have been continually returning to these and other basic applications because a thorough understanding of these concepts is imperative for success in any study of economics and business.

Total Cost and Profit

We can use integration to derive total cost and profit functions from the marginal cost and marginal revenue functions. One of the reasons for the marginal approach in economics is that firms can observe marginal changes in real life. If they know the marginal cost and the total cost when a given quantity is sold, they can develop their total cost function.

We know that the marginal cost for a commodity is $\overline{MC} = C'(x)$, where $C(x)$ is the total cost function. Thus if we have the marginal cost function, we can integrate to find the total cost. That is, $C(x) = \int \overline{MC}\, dx$.

If, for example, the marginal cost is $\overline{MC} = 4x + 3$, the total cost is given by

$$C(x) = \int \overline{MC}\, dx$$

$$= \int (4x + 3)\, dx$$

$$= 2x^2 + 3x + K,$$

where K represents the constant of integration. Now, we know that the total revenue is 0 if no goods are produced, but the total cost may not be 0 if nothing is produced. The fixed costs accrue whether goods are produced or not. Thus the constant of integration that results corresponds to the fixed costs FC of production.

Thus we cannot determine the total cost function from the marginal cost unless additional information is available to help us determine the fixed costs.

EXAMPLE 1   If the marginal cost function for a month for a certain product is $\overline{MC} = 3x + 50$, and if the fixed costs related to the product amount to $100 per month, find the total cost function for the month.

Solution   The total cost function is

$$C(x) = \int (3x + 50)\, dx$$

$$= \frac{3x^2}{2} + 50x + FC$$

But the constant of integration FC represents the fixed costs for the month. Thus, the total cost for the month is given by

$$C(x) = \frac{3x^2}{2} + 50x + 100.$$

□

EXAMPLE 2   If the monthly records show that the rate of change of the cost (that is, the marginal cost) for a product is $\overline{MC} = 10x + 40$, and that the total cost of producing 100 items in the month is $60,000, what would be the total cost of producing 400 items per month?

Solution   We can integrate the marginal cost to find the total cost function.

$$C(x) = \int \overline{MC}\, dx = \int (10x + 40)\, dx$$

$$= 5x^2 + 40x + FC$$

We can find the fixed costs FC using the fact that the cost for 100 items is $60,000.

$$C(100) = 60{,}000 = 5(100)^2 + 40(100) + FC,$$

so

$$FC = 6000$$

Thus the total cost function is $C(x) = 5x^2 + 40x + 6000$, so the cost of producing 400 items is

$$C(400) = 800{,}000 + 16{,}000 + 6000$$
$$= \$822{,}000.$$

□

We stated in an earlier chapter that the profit is usually maximized when $\overline{MR} = \overline{MC}$. To see that this does not always give us a maximum positive profit, consider the following facts concerning the manufacture of widgets over the period of a month:

(a) The marginal revenue is $\overline{MR} = 40 - 3x$.
(b) The marginal cost is $\overline{MC} = 2x + 5$.
(c) When 5 widgets are produced and sold, the total cost is $175.

The profit *should* be maximized when $\overline{MR} = \overline{MC}$; that is, when $40 - 3x = 2x + 5$. Solving for x gives $x = 7$. To see if our profit is maximized when 7 units are produced and sold, let us examine the profit function.

The profit function is given by $P(x) = R(x) - C(x)$, where

$$R(x) = \int \overline{MR} \, dx \qquad \text{and} \qquad C(x) = \int \overline{MC} \, dx.$$

Integrating, we get

$$R(x) = \int (40 - 3x) \, dx = 40x - \frac{3x^2}{2} + K;$$

but $K = 0$ for this total revenue function, so

$$R(x) = 40x - \frac{3x^2}{2}.$$

The total cost function is

$$C(x) = \int (2x + 5) \, dx = x^2 + 5x + FC.$$

The value of fixed cost can be determined by using the fact that 5 widgets cost $175. This tells us $C(5) = 175 = 25 + 25 + FC$, so $FC = 125$.

Thus the total cost is $C(x) = x^2 + 5x + 125$. Now, the profit is

$$P(x) = R(x) - C(x),$$

or

$$P(x) = \left(40x - \frac{3x^2}{2}\right) - (x^2 + 5x + 125).$$

Simplifying gives

$$P(x) = 35x - \frac{5x^2}{2} - 125.$$

We have found that $\overline{MR} = \overline{MC}$ if $x = 7$. But if $x = 7$, profit is

$$P(7) = 35(7) - \frac{5(49)}{2} - 125 = -2.50.$$

That is, the production and sale of 7 items results in a loss of $2.50.

The discussion above indicates that, although setting MR = MC may optimize profit, it does not indicate the level of profit or loss, as forming the profit function does.

If a firm is in a competitive market, and its optimal level of production results in a loss, it has two options. It can continue to produce at the optimal level in the short run until it can lower or eliminate its fixed costs, even though it is losing money; or it can take a larger loss (its fixed cost) by stopping production. If this firm and many others like it cease production, the supply will be reduced, causing an eventual increase in price. The firm can resume production if the price increase indicates it can now make a profit.

EXAMPLE 3   Given the following information, at what level should the Wagbat firm hold production for the short run?
(a) $\overline{MR} = 200 - 4x$
(b) $\overline{MC} = 50 + 2x$
(c) The total cost of producing 10 Wagbats is $700.

Solution   Setting $\overline{MR} = \overline{MC}$, we can solve for the maximum production level.

$$200 - 4x = 50 + 2x$$
$$150 = 6x$$
$$25 = x$$

The level of production that should optimize profit is 25 units. To see whether 25 units maximizes profits or minimizes the losses (in the short run), we must find the total revenue and total cost functions.

$$R(x) = \int (200 - 4x)\, dx = 200x - 2x^2 + K$$
$$= 200x - 2x^2, \quad \text{since } K = 0$$
$$C(x) = \int (50 + 2x)\, dx = 50x + x^2 + FC$$

We find FC by noting $C = 700$ when $x = 10$.

$$700 = 50(10) + (10)^2 + FC,$$

so FC $= 100$.

Since the fixed costs are $100, the cost is given by

$$C = C(x) = 50x + x^2 + 100.$$

At $x = 25$,

$$R = 200(25) - 2(25)^2 = \$3750$$

and

$$C = 50(25) + (25)^2 + 100 = \$1975.$$

We see that the total revenue is greater than the total cost, so production should be held at 25 units, which results in a maximum profit.   □

National Consumption and Savings

In Chapters 1 and 2 we discussed the **national consumption function,** $C = f(y)$, where y is the disposable national income. The **marginal propensity to consume** is the derivative of the consumption function with respect to y, $dC/dy = f'(y)$.

If we know the marginal propensity to consume, we can integrate with respect to y to find the national consumption function.

$$C = \int f'(y) = f(y) + K$$

We can find the unique consumption function if we have additional information to help us determine the value of K, the constant of integration.

EXAMPLE 4   If consumption is $6 billion when disposable income is 0, and if the marginal propensity to consume is $dC/dy = 0.3 + 0.4/\sqrt{y}$ (in billions of dollars), then find the national consumption function.

Solution   If

$$\frac{dC}{dy} = 0.3 + \frac{0.4}{\sqrt{y}},$$

then

$$C = \int \left(0.3 + \frac{0.4}{\sqrt{y}} \right) dy = 0.3y + 0.8y^{1/2} + K.$$

Now, if $y = 0$, $C = 6$, so $6 = 0.3(0) + 0.8\sqrt{0} + K$. Thus the constant of integration is $K = 6$, so the consumption function is $C = 0.3y + 0.8\sqrt{y} + 6$ (billions of dollars).   □

If S represents national savings, we can assume $y = C + S$, or $S = y - C$. Then the **marginal propensity to save** is $dS/dy = 1 - dC/dy$.

EXAMPLE 5   If the consumption is $9 billion when income is 0, and if the marginal propensity to save is 0.25, find the consumption function.

Solution   If $dS/dy = 0.25$, then $0.25 = 1 - dC/dy$, or $dC/dy = 0.75$. Thus,

$$C = \int 0.75 \, dy = 0.75y + K.$$

If $y = 0$, $C = 9$, so $9 = 0.75(0) + K$, or $K = 9$. Then the consumption function is $C = 0.75y + 9$ (billions of dollars).   □

Exercise 14.4

TOTAL COST AND PROFIT

1. If the monthly marginal cost for a good is $\overline{MC} = 2x + 100$, with fixed costs amounting to $200, find the total cost function for the month.
2. If the monthly marginal cost for a good is $\overline{MC} = x + 30$, and the related fixed costs are $50, find the total cost function for the month.
3. If the marginal cost for a product is $\overline{MC} = 4x + 2$, and the production of 10 units results in a total cost of $300, find the total cost function.
4. If the marginal cost for a product is $\overline{MC} = 3x + 50$, and the total cost of producing 20 units is $2000, what will be the total cost function?
5. If the marginal cost for a product is $\overline{MC} = 4x + 40$, and the total cost of producing 25 units is $3000, what will be the cost of producing 30 units?

6. If the marginal cost for producing a good is $\overline{MC} = 5x + 10$, with a fixed cost of $800, what will be the cost of producing 20 units?

7. A firm knows that its marginal cost for a product is $\overline{MC} = 3x + 20$, that its marginal revenue is $\overline{MR} = 44 - 5x$, and that the cost of production and sale of 80 units is $11,400. Given this information, find
   (a) the optimal level of production.
   (b) the profit function.
   (c) the profit or loss at the optimal level.

8. A firm's marginal cost for a product is $\overline{MC} = 6x + 60$, its marginal revenue is $\overline{MR} = 180 - 2x$, and its total cost of production of 10 items is $1000. Given this information,
   (a) find the optimal level of production.
   (b) find the profit function.
   (c) find the profit or loss at the optimal level of production.
   (d) should production be continued for the short run?
   (e) should production be continued for the long run?

NATIONAL CONSUMPTION AND SAVINGS

9. If consumption is $5 billion when disposable income is 0, and if the marginal propensity to consume is

$$\frac{dC}{dy} = 0.4 + \frac{0.3}{\sqrt{y}} \qquad \text{(in billions of dollars)},$$

then find the national consumption function.

10. If consumption is $7 billion when disposable income is 0, and if the marginal propensity to consume is 0.80, find the national consumption function (in billions of dollars).

11. If consumption is $8 billion when income is 0, and if the marginal propensity to save is

$$\frac{dS}{dy} = 0.7 - \frac{0.2}{\sqrt{y}} \qquad \text{(in billions of dollars)},$$

find the national consumption function.

12. If national consumption is $9 billion when income is 0, and if the marginal propensity to consume is 0.30, what is consumption when disposable income is $20 billion?

14.5 Area Under a Curve

Objective   ■ To use the sum of areas of rectangles to approximate the area under a curve

One way to find the accumulated production (such as the production of ore from a mine) over a period of time is to graph production as a function of time, and find the area under the resulting curve over a specified time interval. For

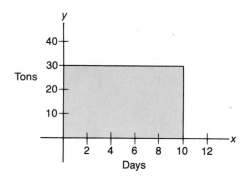

Figure 14.1

example, if a coal mine produced 30 tons per day, the production over 10 days
$(30 \cdot 10 = 300)$ could be represented by the area under the line $y = 30$ between
$x = 0$ and $x = 10$ (see Figure 14.1).

Although we did not need area to find the total production in this case, using
area to determine the accumulated production is very useful when the
production function varies at different points in time. For example, if production
is represented by

$$y = 100e^{-0.1x}, \qquad 0 \le x \le 20,$$

where x represents the number of days, then the area under the curve (and above
the x-axis) from $x = 0$ to $x = 10$ represents the total production over the 10 day
period (see Figure 14.2).

In order to determine the accumulated production and solve other types of
problems, we need a method for finding areas under curves. For example,
suppose we wish to find the area between the curve $y = x$ and the x-axis from

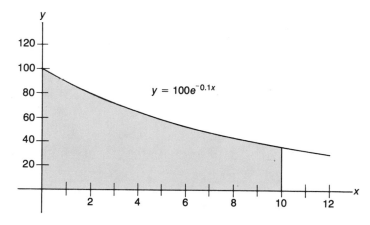

Figure 14.2

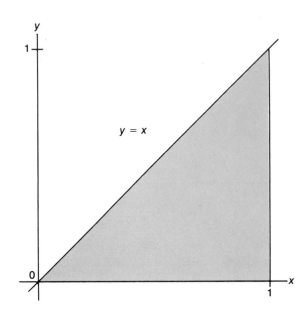

Figure 14.3

$x = 0$ to $x = 1$ (see Figure 14.3). One way to approximate this area is to draw rectangles that fit between the curve and the x-axis. We can divide the interval $[0, 1]$ into n equal subintervals and use them as the bases of n rectangles whose heights are determined by the curve (see Figure 14.4). The width of each of these rectangles is $1/n$. Using the functional value at the right endpoint of each subinterval as the height of the rectangle, we get n rectangles that fit between the curve and the x-axis in the interval. Because part of each rectangle lies above the curve, the sum of the areas of the rectangles will overestimate the area (see Figure 14.4).

Then, with $y = f(x) = x$ and subinterval width $1/n$, we have

$$x_1 = \frac{1}{n}, \qquad f(x_1) = \frac{1}{n}, \quad \text{so the area of the 1st rectangle is } \frac{1}{n} \cdot \frac{1}{n} = \frac{1}{n^2}$$

$$x_2 = \frac{2}{n}, \qquad f(x_2) = \frac{2}{n}, \quad \text{so the area of the 2nd rectangle is } \frac{2}{n} \cdot \frac{1}{n} = \frac{2}{n^2}$$

$$\vdots$$

$$x_i = \frac{i}{n}, \qquad f(x_i) = \frac{i}{n}, \quad \text{so the area of the } i\text{th rectangle is } \frac{i}{n} \cdot \frac{1}{n} = \frac{i}{n^2}$$

$$\vdots$$

$$x_n = \frac{n}{n} = 1, \quad f(x_n) = 1, \quad \text{so the area of the } n\text{th rectangle is } 1 \cdot \frac{1}{n} = \frac{1}{n} = \frac{n}{n^2}$$

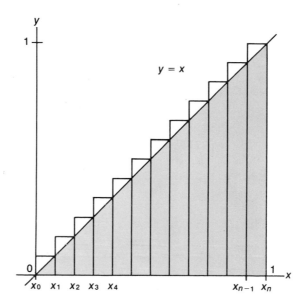

Figure 14.4

Note that i/n^2 gives the area of the ith rectangle for *any* value of i. Thus the area can be approximated by

$$S = \sum_{i=1}^{n} f(x_i) \cdot \frac{1}{n} = \sum_{i=1}^{n} \frac{i}{n} \cdot \frac{1}{n} = \frac{1}{n^2} \sum_{i=1}^{n} i = \frac{1}{n^2} \cdot \frac{n(n+1)}{2} = \frac{n^2+n}{2n^2}.$$

If $n = 10$, $S = \dfrac{100 + 10}{200} = 0.55.$

If $n = 100$, $S = \dfrac{10{,}000 + 100}{20{,}000} = 0.505.$

Thus, if n is very large, there will be a large number of smaller rectangles, and the approximation will be good. To get the best approximation possible, we will let n increase without bound. This gives

$$A = \lim_{n \to +\infty} \frac{n^2 + n}{2n^2} = \lim_{n \to +\infty} \frac{1 + 1/n}{2} = \frac{1}{2}.$$

We can see that this area is correct, for we are computing the area of a triangle with base 1 and height 1. The formula for the area of a triangle gives

$$A = \tfrac{1}{2} bh = \tfrac{1}{2} \cdot 1 \cdot 1 = \tfrac{1}{2}.$$

The following example shows we can find the area by evaluating the function at the left-hand endpoints of the subintervals.

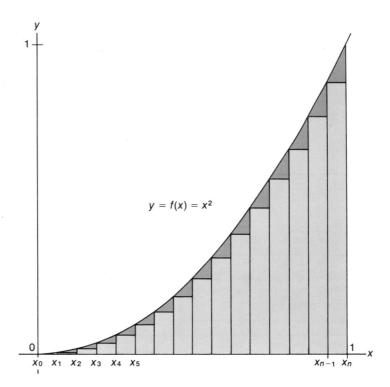

Figure 14.5

EXAMPLE 1   Use rectangles to find the area under $y = x^2$ (and above the x-axis) from $x = 0$ to $x = 1$.

Solution   We again divide the interval $[0, 1]$ into n equal subintervals of length $1/n$. If we evaluate the function at the left-hand endpoints of these subintervals to determine the heights of the rectangles, the sum of the areas of the rectangles will underestimate the area (see Figure 14.5).

Then

$$x_0 = \frac{0}{n} = 0, f(x_0) = 0, \qquad \text{so area of 1st rectangle is } 0 \cdot 0 = 0$$

$$x_1 = \frac{1}{n}, \qquad f(x_1) = \left(\frac{1}{n}\right)^2 = \frac{1}{n^2}, \qquad \text{so area of 2nd rectangle is } \frac{1}{n^2} \cdot \frac{1}{n} = \frac{1}{n^3}$$

$$x_2 = \frac{2}{n}, \qquad f(x_2) = \left(\frac{2}{n}\right)^2, \qquad \text{so area of 3rd rectangle is } \frac{4}{n^2} \cdot \frac{1}{n} = \frac{4}{n^3}$$

$$x_3 = \frac{3}{n}, \qquad f(x_3) = \left(\frac{3}{n}\right)^2, \qquad \text{so area of 4th rectangle is } \frac{9}{n^2} \cdot \frac{1}{n} = \frac{9}{n^3}$$

$$x_{i-1} = \frac{i-1}{n}, \qquad f(x_{i-1}) = \left(\frac{i-1}{n}\right)^2,$$

so the area of the ith rectangle is $\dfrac{(i-1)^2}{n^2} \cdot \dfrac{1}{n} = \dfrac{i^2 - 2i + 1}{n^3}$

$$\vdots$$

$$x_{n-1} = \frac{n-1}{n}, \qquad f(x_{n-1}) = \left(\frac{n-1}{n}\right)^2,$$

so the area of the nth rectangle is $\dfrac{(n-1)^2}{n^2} \cdot \dfrac{1}{n} = \dfrac{(n-1)^2}{n^3}$.

Note that $(i^2 - 2i + 1)/n^3$ gives the area of the ith rectangle for *any* value of i.

The sum of these areas may be written as

$$S = \sum_{i=1}^{n} \frac{i^2 - 2i + 1}{n^3} = \frac{1}{n^3}\left(\sum_{i=1}^{n} i^2 - 2\sum_{i=1}^{n} i + \sum_{i=1}^{n} 1\right)$$

$$= \frac{1}{n^3}\left[\frac{n(n+1)(2n+1)}{6} - \frac{2n(n+1)}{2} + n\right]$$

$$= \frac{2n^3 + 3n^2 + n}{6n^3} - \frac{n^2 + n}{n^3} + \frac{n}{n^3}$$

$$= \frac{2n^2 - 3n + 1}{6n^2}.$$

If n is large, there will be a large number of smaller rectangles and the approximation of the area under the curve will be good; the larger n, the better the approximation. For example, if $n = 10$, the area approximation is

$$S(10) = \frac{200 - 30 + 1}{600} = 0.285,$$

while if $n = 100$,

$$S(100) = \frac{20{,}000 - 300 + 1}{60{,}000} = 0.328.$$

To get the best approximation possible, we let n increase without bound. This gives

$$A = \lim_{n\to\infty}\left(\frac{2n^2 - 3n + 1}{6n^2}\right)$$

$$= \lim_{n\to\infty}\left(\frac{2 - \dfrac{3}{n} + \dfrac{1}{n^2}}{6}\right) = \frac{1}{3}.$$

Note that the approximations with $n = 10$ and $n = 100$ were less than $\frac{1}{3}$. This is because all the rectangles were *under* the curve (see Figure 14.5).   □

Thus we see that we can determine the area under a curve $y = f(x)$ from $x = a$ to $x = b$ by dividing the interval $[a, b]$ into n equal subintervals and evaluating

$$A = \lim_{n \to \infty} \sum_{i=1}^{n} f(x_i)(x_i - x_{i-1}) \qquad \text{(using right endpoints)}$$

or

$$A = \lim_{n \to \infty} \sum_{i=1}^{n} f(x_{i-1}')(x_i - x_{i-1}). \qquad \text{(using left endpoints)}$$

Exercise 14.5

1. Approximate the area between $y = x$ and the x-axis from $x = 0$ to $x = 1$ by dividing the interval into n equal subintervals (as in Example 1), and evaluating the function at the *left-hand* endpoints of the subintervals to find the areas of the rectangles.
   (a) If $n = 10$, what is the approximate area?
   (b) If $n = 100$, what is the approximate area?
   (c) Take the limit of the sum of the areas of the rectangles as $n \to +\infty$ to find the area.
   (d) How do your answers to (a) – (c) differ from the corresponding calculations in the discussion of the area under $y = x$ using *right-hand* endpoints?

2. Use rectangles to approximate the area between the x-axis and $y = x^2$ from $x = 0$ to $x = 1$, finding heights of the rectangles at the *right-hand* endpoints of the equal subintervals (see Example 1).
   (a) If $n = 10$, what is the approximate area?
   (b) If $n = 100$, what is the approximate area?
   (c) Find the area by taking the limit of the sum of the areas as $n \to +\infty$.
   (d) How do your answers to (a) – (c) differ from the corresponding calculations in Example 1?

3, Use rectangles to find the area between $y = x^2 - 6x + 8$ and the x-axis from $x = 0$ to $x = 2$. Divide the interval $[0, 2]$ into n equal subintervals, so each subinterval has length $2/n$.

4. Use rectangles to find the area between $y = 4x - x^2$ and the x-axis from $x = 0$ to $x = 4$. Divide the interval $[0, 4]$ into n equal subintervals, so each subinterval has length $4/n$.

14.6 The Definite Integral

Objective   ■ To evaluate definite integrals using the Fundamental Theorem of Calculus

In the previous section we saw that we could determine the area under a curve using equal subintervals and the functional values at either the left-hand end-points or the right-hand endpoints of the subintervals. In fact, we can use subintervals that are not of equal length, and we can use any point within each subinterval to determine the height of each rectangle. Suppose we wish to find the area under the curve $y = f(x)$ over a closed interval $[a, b]$. We can divide the interval into n subintervals (not necessarily equal), with the endpoints of these intervals at $x_0 = a, x_1, x_2, \ldots, x_n = b$. We now choose a point (*any* point) in each subinterval, and denote the points $x_1{}^*, x_2{}^*, \ldots, x_i{}^*, \ldots, x_n{}^*$. Then the ith rectangle (for any i) has height $f(x_i{}^*)$ and width $x_i - x_{i-1}$, so its area is $f(x_i{}^*)$ $(x_i - x_{i-1})$. Then the sum of the areas of the n rectangles is

$$S = \sum_{i=1}^{n} f(x_i{}^*) \, (x_i - x_{i-1})$$

$$= \sum_{i=1}^{n} f(x_i{}^*) \, \Delta x_i, \qquad \text{where } \Delta x_i = x_i - x_{i-1}.$$

Because the points in the subinterval may be chosen anywhere in the subinterval, we cannot be sure if the rectangles will underestimate the area under the curve. But increasing the number of subintervals (increasing n) and making sure that every interval becomes smaller (just increasing n will not guarantee this if the subintervals are unequal) will improve the estimation. Thus for any subdivision of $[a, b]$ and any $x_i{}^*$ the area is given by

$$A = \lim_{\substack{n \to \infty \\ \max \Delta x_i \to 0}} \sum_{i=1}^{n} f(x_i{}^*) \, \Delta x_i, \qquad \text{provided this limit exists.}$$

Because of the special importance of this limit and its applications beyond area determination, we give it a special definition.

Definite Integral If f is a function on the interval $[a, b]$, then the *definite integral* of f from a to b is

$$\int_a^b f(x) \, dx = \lim_{\substack{n \to \infty \\ \max \Delta x \to 0}} \sum_{i=1}^{n} f(x_i{}^*) \, \Delta x_i$$

if the limit exists. If the definite integral exists, we say f is integrable on $[a, b]$.

The obvious question is, How is this definite integral related to the indefinite integral (antiderivative) we have been studying? The answer to this question is given by the **Fundamental Theorem of Calculus.**

Fundamental Theorem of Calculus Let f be a continuous function on the closed interval $[a, b]$; then $\int_a^b f(x) \, dx = F(b) - F(a)$, where F is any function such that $F'(x) = f(x)$ for all x in $[a, b]$.

Stated differently, the theorem says that if the function F is an indefinite integral of a function f that is continuous on the interval $[a, b]$, then

$$\int_a^b f(x)\, dx = F(x)\, \Big|_a^b = F(b) - F(a).$$

EXAMPLE 1   Evaluate $\int_2^4 (x^3 + 4)\, dx.$

Solution
$$\int_2^4 (x^3 + 4)\, dx = \frac{x^4}{4} + 4x + C\, \Big|_2^4$$

Then

$$F(x) = \frac{x^4}{4} + 4x + C$$

$$F(4) = 64 + 16 + C = 80 + C$$
$$F(2) = 4 + 8 + C = 12 + C$$

So
$$F(4) - F(2) = (80 + C) - (12 + C) = 68. \qquad \square$$

Note that the Fundamental Theorem states that F can be *any* indefinite integral of f, so we need not add the constant of integration to the integral. (See Example 1.)

EXAMPLE 2   Evaluate $\int_1^3 (3x^2 + 6x)\, dx.$

Solution
$$\int_1^3 (3x^2 + 6x)\, dx = x^3 + 3x^2\, \Big|_1^3$$

$$= (3^3 + 3 \cdot 3^2) - (1^3 + 3 \cdot 1^2)$$
$$= 54 - 4 = 50 \qquad \square$$

EXAMPLE 3   Evaluate $\int_3^5 x\sqrt{x^2 - 9}\, dx$

Solution
$$\int_3^5 x\sqrt{x^2 - 9}\, dx = \frac{1}{2} \int_3^5 (x^2 - 9)^{1/2}(2x)\, dx$$

$$= \frac{1}{2} \left[\frac{2}{3}(x^2 - 9)^{3/2} \right] \Big|_3^5$$

$$= \frac{1}{2} \left[\frac{2}{3} \cdot 16^{3/2} - \frac{2}{3} \cdot 0 \right]$$

$$= \frac{1}{3} \cdot 64 = \frac{64}{3} \qquad \square$$

In the integral $\int_a^b f(x)\, dx$, we call a the *lower limit* and b the *upper limit* of integration. Although we developed the definite integral with the assumption that the lower limit was less than the upper limit, the following properties permit us to evaluate the definite integral even when that is not the case.

1. $\displaystyle\int_a^a f(x)\, dx = 0$

2. If f is integrable on $[a, b]$, then

$$\int_b^a f(x)\, dx = -\int_a^b f(x)\, dx.$$

The following examples illustrate these definitions.

EXAMPLE 4 Evaluate $\displaystyle\int_4^4 x^2\, dx$.

Solution

$$\int_4^4 x^2\, dx = \left.\frac{x^3}{3}\right|_4^4 = \frac{4^3}{3} - \frac{4^3}{3} - 0$$

□

EXAMPLE 5 Compare $\displaystyle\int_2^4 3x^2\, dx$ and $\displaystyle\int_4^2 3x^2\, dx$.

Solution

$$\int_2^4 3x^2\, dx = \left. x^3\right|_2^4 = 4^3 - 2^3 = 56$$

$$\int_4^2 3x^2\, dx = \left. x^3\right|_4^2 = 2^3 - 4^3 = -56$$

Then

$$\int_4^2 3x^2\, dx = -\int_2^4 3x^2\, dx.$$

□

Another property of definite integrals is called the additive property:

If f is continuous on some interval containing a, b, and c, then

$$\int_a^b f(x)\, dx = \int_a^c f(x)\, dx + \int_c^b f(x)\, dx.$$

EXAMPLE 6 Show $\displaystyle\int_2^3 4x\, dx + \int_3^5 4x\, dx = \int_2^5 4x\, dx$.

Solution

$$\int_2^3 4x\, dx = \left. 2x^2\right|_2^3 = 18 - 8 = 10$$

$$\int_3^5 4x\, dx = \left. 2x^2\right|_3^5 = 50 - 18 = 32$$

$$\int_2^5 4x\, dx = \left. 2x^2\right|_2^5 = 50 - 8 = 42$$

Then

$$\int_2^3 4x \, dx + \int_3^5 4x \, dx = \int_2^5 4x \, dx.$$

□

Let us now return to the area problems, to see if the definite integral gives us the area under a curve. By the formula for the area of a triangle and by summing areas of rectangles, we found the area under the curve (line) $y = x$ from $x = 0$ to $x = 1$ to be $\frac{1}{2}$. Using the definite integral to find the area gives

$$A = \int_0^1 x \, dx = \frac{x^2}{2} \Big|_0^1 = \frac{1}{2} - 0 = \frac{1}{2}.$$

In Example 1 of Section 14.5 we used rectangles to find that the area under $y = x^2$ from $x = 0$ to $x = 1$ was $\frac{1}{3}$. Using the definite integral, we get

$$A = \int_0^1 x^2 \, dx = \frac{x^3}{3} \Big|_0^1 = \frac{1}{3} - 0 = \frac{1}{3},$$

which agrees.

However, not every definite integral represents the area between the curve and the x-axis over an interval. For example,

$$\int_0^2 (x - 2) \, dx = \frac{x^2}{2} - 2x \Big|_0^2 = (2 - 4) - (0) = -2.$$

This would indicate that the area between the curve and the x-axis is negative, but area must be positive. A look at the graph of $y = x - 2$ (see Figure 14.6) shows us what is happening. The region bounded by $y = x - 2$ and the x-axis between $x = 0$ and $x = 2$ is a triangle whose base is 2 and height is 2, so its area is

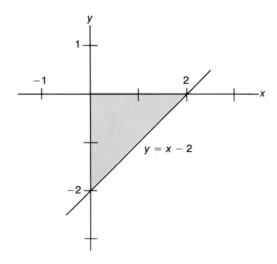

Figure 14.6

$\frac{1}{2} bh = \frac{1}{2} (2) (2) = 2$. The reason the integral has value -2 is because $y = x - 2$ lies below the x-axis from $x = 0$ to $x = 2$, so the functional values over the interval $[0, 2]$ are negative.

Thus the value of the definite integral over this interval does not represent the area between the curve and the x-axis. The definite integral will give the area under the curve and above the x-axis only when $f(x) \geq 0$ for all x in $[a, b]$.

Exercise 14.6

Evaluate the following definite integrals.

1. $\int_{2}^{4} x^3 \, dx$

2. $\int_{0}^{5} x^2 \, dx$

3. $\int_{-1}^{2} 5x^4 \, dx$

4. $\int_{-2}^{4} 4x^3 \, dx$

5. $\int_{-2}^{3} 5 \, dx$

6. $\int_{8}^{-5} 7 \, dx$

7. $\int_{0}^{5} 4 \sqrt[3]{x^2} \, dx$

8. $\int_{2}^{4} 3 \sqrt{x} \, dx$

9. $\int_{2}^{4} (4x^3 - 6x^2 - 5x) \, dx$

10. $\int_{0}^{2} (x^4 - 5x^3 + 2x) \, dx$

11. $\int_{2}^{3} (x - 4)^2 \, dx$

12. $\int_{1}^{3} (x + 2)^3 \, dx$

13. $\int_{2}^{4} (x^2 + 2)^3 x \, dx$

14. $\int_{0}^{3} (2x - x^2)^4 (1 - x) \, dx$

15. $\int_{1}^{2} (x^3 - 3x^2)^3 (x^2 - 2x) \, dx$

16. $\int_{0}^{4} (3x^2 - 2)^4 x \, dx$

17. $\int_{2}^{3} x \sqrt{x^2 + 3} \, dx$

18. $\int_{-1}^{2} x \sqrt[3]{x^2 \quad 5} \, dx$

19. $\int_{4}^{4} \sqrt{x^2 - 2} \, dx$

20. $\int_{2}^{2} (x^3 - 4x) \, dx$

21. $\int_{3}^{6} \frac{x}{3x^2 + 4} \, dx$

22. $\int_{0}^{2} \frac{x}{x^2 + 4} \, dx$

23. Find the area between the curve $y = -x^2 + 3x - 2$ and the x-axis from $x = 1$ to $x = 2$.

24. Find the area between the curve $y = x^2 + 3x + 2$ and the x-axis from $x = -1$ to $x = 3$.

25. Find the area between the curve $y = xe^{x^2}$ and the x-axis from $x = 1$ to $x = 3$.

26. Find the area between the curve $y = e^{-x}$ and the x-axis from $x = -1$ to $x = 1$.

27. How does $\int_{-1}^{-3} x \sqrt{x^2 + 1} \, dx$ compare with $\int_{-3}^{-1} x \sqrt{x^2 + 1} \, dx$?

28. If $\int_{-1}^{0} x^3 \, dx = -\frac{1}{4}$ and $\int_{0}^{1} x^3 \, dx = \frac{1}{4}$, what does $\int_{-1}^{1} x^3 \, dx$ equal?

29. If $\int_{1}^{2} (2x - x^2) \, dx = \frac{2}{3}$ and $\int_{2}^{4} (2x - x^2) \, dx = -\frac{20}{3}$, what does $\int_{1}^{4} (x^2 - 2x) \, dx$ equal?

APPLICATIONS The velocity of blood through a vessel is given by $v = K(R^2 - r^2)$ where K is the (constant) maximum velocity of the blood, R the (constant) radius of the vessel, and r the distance of the particular corpuscle from the center of the vessel. The rate of flow can be found by measuring the volume of blood that flows past a point in a given time period. This volume, V, is given by

$$V = \int_0^R v(2\pi r\, dr).$$

30. Find the volume if $R = 0.30$ cm and $v = (0.30 - 3.33r^2)$ cm/sec.

31. Develop a general formula by evaluating

$$V = \int_0^R v(2\pi r\, dr)$$

using $v = K(R^2 - r^2)$.

The rate of production of a new line of products is given by

$$\frac{dx}{dt} = 200\left[1 + \frac{400}{(t + 40)^2}\right],$$

where x is the number of items produced and t is the number of weeks the products have been in production.

32. How many units were produced in the first five weeks?

33. How many units were produced in the sixth week?

34. Figure 14.7 shows how an inventory of a product is depleted each quarter of a given year.

If the average value of a continuous function f over the interval $[a, b]$ is

$$\frac{1}{b - a} \int_a^b f(x)\, dx,$$

what is the average inventory per month for the first three months for this product? [Assume the graph is a line joining $(0, 1300)$ and $(3, 100)$.]

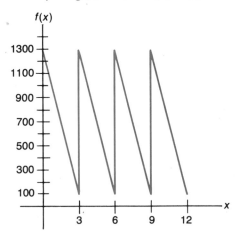

Figure 14.7

14.7 Applications of Definite Integrals in Business and Economics

Objectives   ■ To use definite integrals to find consumer's surplus
■ To use definite integrals to find producer's surplus

The definite integral can be used in a number of applications in business and economics, including price discrimination, revenue versus cost, consumer's surplus and producer's surplus. In this section we will concentrate on two applications, **consumer's surplus** and **producer's surplus**.

Consumer's Surplus

Suppose the demand for a product is given by $p = f(x)$, while supply of the product is described by $p = g(x)$. The price p_1 where the graphs of these functions intersect is the **equilibrium price** (see Figure 14.8). As the demand curve shows, some consumers (but not all) would be willing to pay more than $\$p_1$ for the product. For example, some consumers would be willing to buy x_3 units if the price is $\$p_3$. Those consumers willing to pay more than $\$p_1$ are benefiting from the lower price. The total gain for all those consumers willing to pay more than $\$p_1$ is called the **consumer's surplus**, and under proper assumptions the area of the shaded region in Figure 14.8 represents this consumer's surplus.

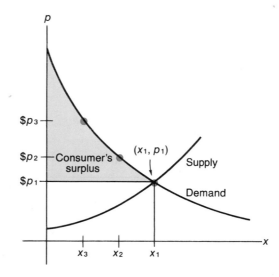

Figure 14.8

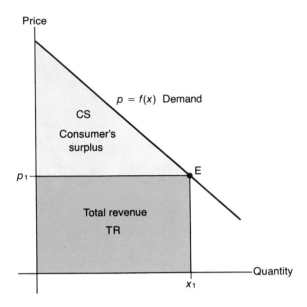

Price

$p = f(x)$ Demand

CS

Consumer's
surplus

p_1

E

Total revenue

TR

x_1

Quantity

Figure 14.9

Looking at Figure 14.9, we see that if the demand curve has equation $p = f(x)$, the consumer's surplus is given by the area between $f(x)$ and the x-axis from 0 to x_1, *minus* the area of the rectangle denoted TR:

$$\text{CS} = \int_0^{x_1} f(x) \, dx - p_1 x_1.$$

Note that $p_1 x_1$ is the area of the rectangle that represents the total revenue (see Figure 14.9).

EXAMPLE 1   The demand function for a product is $p = 100/(x + 1)$. If the equilibrium price is \$20, what is the consumer's surplus?

Solution   We must first find the quantity that will be purchased at this price. Letting $p = 20$, and solving for x gives

$$20 = \frac{100}{x + 1}$$
$$20 (x + 1) = 100$$
$$x + 1 = 5$$
$$x = 4.$$

Thus the equilibrium point is (4, 20). The consumer's surplus is given by the formula

$$CS = \int_0^4 f(x)\, dx - 20 \cdot 4$$

$$= \int_0^4 \frac{100}{x+1}\, dx - 80$$

$$= 100 \ln |x+1| \Big|_0^4 - 80$$

$$= 100\,(\ln 5 - \ln 1) - 80$$
$$= 100\,(1.6094 - 0) - 80$$
$$= 160.94 - 80$$
$$= 80.94.$$

The consumer's surplus is \$80.94.   □

EXAMPLE 2   The demand function for a product is $p = \sqrt{49 - 6x}$ and the supply function is $p = x + 1$. Find the equilibrium point and the consumer's surplus there.

Solution   The graphs of the supply and demand functions are shown in Figure 14.10. We can find the equilibrium point by solving the two equations simultaneously.

$$\sqrt{49 - 6x} = x + 1$$
$$49 - 6x = (x + 1)^2$$
$$0 = x^2 + 8x - 48$$
$$0 = (x + 12)(x - 4)$$
$$x = 4 \text{ or } x = -12$$

Thus the equilibrium quantity is 4 and the equilibrium price is \$5.

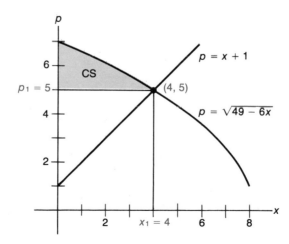

Figure 14.10

The consumer's surplus is given by

$$CS = \int_0^4 f(x)\,dx - p_1 x_1$$

$$= \int_0^4 \sqrt{49 - 6x}\,dx - 5 \cdot 4$$

$$= -\frac{1}{6} \int_0^4 \sqrt{49 - 6x}\,(-6\,dx) - 20$$

$$= -\frac{1}{9}(49 - 6x)^{3/2} \Big|_0^4 - 20$$

$$= -\frac{1}{9}[(25)^{3/2} - (49)^{3/2}] - 20$$

$$= -\frac{1}{9}(125 - 343) - 20$$

$$= 24.22 - 20 = 4.22$$

The consumer's surplus is $4.22.   □

EXAMPLE 3   If a monopoly has a total cost function $C = 60 + 2x^2$ for a product whose demand is given by $p = 30 - x$, find the consumer's surplus at the point where the monopoly has maximum profit.

Solution   We must first find the point where the profit function is maximized. If the demand for x units is given by $p = 30 - x$, then the total revenue is given by $R(x) = (30 - x)x = 30x - x^2$. Thus the profit function is

$$P(x) = R(x) - C(x)$$
$$P(x) = 30x - x^2 - (60 + 2x^2)$$
$$P(x) = 30x - 60 - 3x^2.$$

Then $P'(x) = 30 - 6x.$
So $0 = 30 - 6x$ has solution $x = 5$.

The profit for the monopolist is maximized when $x = 5$ units are sold at price $p = 25$.

The consumer's surplus at $x = 5$, $p = 25$ is given by

$$CS = \int_0^5 f(x)\,dx - 5 \cdot 25,$$

when $f(x)$ is the demand function.

$$= \int_0^5 (30 - x)\,dx - 125$$

$$= 30x - \frac{x^2}{2} \Big|_0^5 - 125$$

$$= \left(150 - \frac{25}{2}\right) - 125$$

$$= \frac{25}{2} = 12.50$$

The consumer's surplus is $12.50.   □

Producer's Surplus

When a product is sold at the equilibrium price, some producers will also benefit, for they would have sold the product at a lower price. The area between the line $p = p_1$ and the supply curve (from $x = 0$ to $x = x_1$) gives the producer's surplus (see Figure 14.11).

If the supply function is $p = g(x)$, the **producer's surplus** is given by the area between $g(x)$ and the x-axis from 0 to x, *subtracted from* the area of the rectangle $0x_1 E p_1$.

$$PS = p_1 x_1 - \int_0^{x_1} g(x)\, dx$$

Note that $p_1 x_1$ represents the total revenue at the equilibrium point.

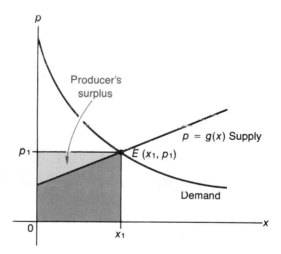

Figure 14.11

EXAMPLE 4   Suppose the supply function for a product is $p = x^2 + x$. If the equilibrium price is $20, what is the producer's surplus?

Solution   If $p = 20$, we can find x as follows:

$$20 = x^2 + x$$
$$0 = x^2 + x - 20$$
$$0 = (x + 5)(x - 4)$$
$$x = -5, \; x = 4$$

The equilibrium point is $x = 4$, $p = 20$. The producer's surplus is given by

$$PS = 20 \cdot 4 - \int_0^4 (x^2 + x)\, dx$$

$$= 80 - \left(\frac{x^3}{3} + \frac{x^2}{2}\right)\Big|_0^4$$

$$= 80 - \left(\frac{64}{3} + 8\right)$$

$$= 50.67.$$

The producer's surplus is $50.67. See Figure 14.12.   □

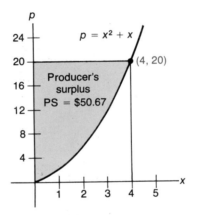

Figure 14.12

EXAMPLE 5   The demand function for a product is $p = \sqrt{49 - 6x}$ and the supply function is $p = x + 1$. Find the producer's surplus.

Solution   We found the equilibrium point for these functions to be $(4, 5)$ in Example 2 (see Figure 14.10). The producer's surplus is

$$PS = 5 \cdot 4 - \int_0^4 (x + 1)\, dx$$

$$= 20 - \left(\frac{x^2}{2} + x\right)\Big|_0^4$$

$$= 20 - (8 + 4) = 8.$$ □

Exercise 14.7

CONSUMER'S SURPLUS

1. The demand function for a product is $p = 34 - x^2$. If the equilibrium price is $9, what is the consumer's surplus?

2. The demand function for a product is $p = 100 - 4x$. If the equilibrium price is $40, what is the consumer's surplus?

3. The demand function for a product is $p = 200/(x + 2)$. If the equilibrium quantity is 8 units, what is the consumer's surplus?

4. The demand function for a product is $p = 100/(1 + 2x)$. If the equilibrium quantity is 12 units, what is the consumer's surplus?

5. The demand function for a product is $p = 81 - x^2$ and the supply function is $p = x^2 + 4x + 11$. Find the equilibrium point and the consumer's surplus there.

6. The demand function for a product is $p = 49 - x^2$ and the supply function is $p = 4x + 4$. Find the equilibrium point and the consumer's surplus there.

7. If the demand function for a product is $p = 12/(x + 1)$ and the supply function for it is $p = 1 + 0.2x$, find the consumer's surplus under pure competition.

8. If the demand function for a good is $p = 110 - x^2$ and the supply function for it is $p = 2 - \frac{9}{5}x + \frac{1}{5}x^2$, find the consumer's surplus under pure competition.

9. A monopoly has a total cost function $C = 1000 + 120x + 6x^2$ for its product, which has demand function $p = 360 - 3x - 2x^2$. Find the consumer's surplus at the point where the monopoly has maximum profit.

10. A monopoly has a total cost function $C = 500 + 2x^2 + 10x$ for its product, which has demand function $p = -\frac{1}{3}x^2 - 2x + 30$. Find the consumer's surplus at the point where the monopoly has a maximum profit.

PRODUCER'S SURPLUS

11. Suppose the supply function for a good is $p = 4x^2 + 2x + 2$. If the equilibrium price is $422, what is the producer's surplus there?

12. Suppose the supply function for a good is $p = 0.1x^2 + 3x + 20$. If the equilibrium price is $36, what is the producer's surplus there?

13. If the supply function for a commodity is $p = 10e^{x/3}$, what is the producer's surplus when 15 units are sold?

14. If the supply function for a commodity is $p = 40 + 100(x + 1)^2$, what is the producer's surplus at $x = 20$?

15. Find the producer's surplus for the product in problem 5 (at market equilibrium).

16. Find the producer's surplus for the product in problem 6 (at the market equilibrium).

17. Find the producer's surplus for the product in problem 7.

18. Find the producer's surplus for the good in problem 8.

19. The demand function for a product is $p = 144 - 2x^2$ and the supply function is $p = x^2 + 33x + 48$. Find the producer's surplus at the equilibrium point.

20. The demand function for a product is $p = 280 - 4x - x^2$ and the supply function for it is $p = 160 + 4x + x^2$. Find the producer's surplus at the equilibrium point.

14.8 Using Tables of Integrals

Objective   ■ To use tables of integrals to evaluate certain integrals

We have used some special integration formulas to evaluate integrals, but many integration problems exist that require additional formulas or methods. In this section we will learn how to use a table of integration formulas already developed for us. Table 14.1 contains a selected number of integration formulas (many more exist). Using the formulas is not quite as easy as it may sound, for finding the correct formula and using it properly may present some problems. The following examples illustrate how these formulas are used.

EXAMPLE 1   Evaluate $\displaystyle\int \frac{dx}{\sqrt{x^2 + 4}}$.

Solution   We must find a formula in the table that is of the same form as this integral. We see that formula 8 has the desired form, *if* we let $u = x$ and $a = 2$. Thus

$$\int \frac{dx}{\sqrt{x^2 + 4}} = \ln |x + \sqrt{x^2 + 4}| + C.$$ □

EXAMPLE 2   Evaluate $\displaystyle\int_1^2 \frac{dx}{x^2 + 2x}$.

Solution   There does not appear to be any formula having exactly the same form as our integral. But if we rewrite our integral as

$$\int_1^2 \frac{dx}{x(x + 2)},$$

we see that formula 13 will work. Letting $u = x$, $a = 1$, and $b = 2$, we get

$$\int_1^2 \frac{dx}{x(x + 2)} = \frac{1}{2} \ln \left| \frac{x}{x + 2} \right| \Big|_1^2$$

$$= \frac{1}{2} \ln \left| \frac{2}{4} \right| - \frac{1}{2} \ln \left| \frac{1}{3} \right|$$

$$= \frac{1}{2} \left(\ln \frac{1}{2} - \ln \frac{1}{3} \right)$$

$$= \frac{1}{2} \ln \frac{3}{2}$$

$$= \frac{1}{2} \ln 1.5$$ □

Although the formulas are given in terms of the variable u, they may be used with any variable.

Table 14.1 INTEGRATION FORMULAS

1. $\int u^n \, du = \dfrac{u^{n+1}}{n+1} + C, \qquad \text{for } n \neq -1$

2. $\int \dfrac{du}{u} = \int u^{-1} \, du = \ln |u| + C$

3. $\int a^u \, du = a^u \log_a e + C$

4. $\int e^u \, du = e^u + C$

5. $\int \dfrac{du}{a^2 - u^2} = \dfrac{1}{2a} \ln \left| \dfrac{a+u}{a-u} \right| + C$

6. $\int \sqrt{u^2 + a^2} \, du = \dfrac{1}{2} \left(u \sqrt{u^2 + a^2} + a^2 \ln |u + \sqrt{u^2 + a^2}| \right) + C$

7. $\int \sqrt{u^2 - a^2} \, du = \dfrac{1}{2} \left(u \sqrt{u^2 - a^2} - a^2 \ln |u + \sqrt{u^2 - a^2}| \right) + C$

8. $\int \dfrac{du}{\sqrt{u^2 + a^2}} = \ln |u + \sqrt{u^2 + a^2}| + C$

9. $\int \dfrac{du}{u\sqrt{a^2 - u^2}} = \dfrac{1}{a} \ln \left| \dfrac{a + \sqrt{a^2 - u^2}}{u} \right| + C$

10. $\int \dfrac{du}{\sqrt{u^2 - a^2}} = \ln |u + \sqrt{u^2 - a^2}| + C$

11. $\int \dfrac{du}{u\sqrt{a^2 + u^2}} = -\dfrac{1}{a} \ln \left| \dfrac{a + \sqrt{a^2 + u^2}}{u} \right| + C$

12. $\int \dfrac{u \, du}{au + b} = \dfrac{u}{a} - \dfrac{b}{a^2} \ln |au + b| + C$

13. $\int \dfrac{du}{u(au + b)} = \dfrac{1}{b} \ln \left| \dfrac{u}{au + b} \right| + C$

14. $\int \ln u \, du = u(\ln u - 1) + C$

15. $\int \dfrac{u \, du}{(au + b)^2} = \dfrac{1}{a^2} \left(\ln |au + b| + \dfrac{b}{au + b} \right) + C$

16. $\int u \sqrt{au + b} \, du = \dfrac{2(3au - 2b)(au + b)^{3/2}}{15a^2} + C$

17. $\int u \, dv = uv - \int v \, du$

EXAMPLE 3   Evaluate $\int \dfrac{dq}{9 - q^2}$.

Solution   The formula that applies in this case is formula 5, with $a = 3$ and $u = q$. Then

$$\int \frac{dq}{9 - q^2} = \frac{1}{2 \cdot 3} \ln \left| \frac{3+q}{3-q} \right| + C = \frac{1}{6} \ln \left| \frac{3+q}{3-q} \right| + C \qquad \square$$

EXAMPLE 4   Evaluate $\int \ln (2x + 1)\, dx.$

Solution   This integral has the form of formula 14, with $u = 2x + 1$. But if $u = 2x + 1$, du must be represented by the differential of $2x + 1$ (that is, $2\, dx$). Thus

$$\int \ln (2x + 1)\, dx = \frac{1}{2} \int \ln (2x + 1)(2\, dx)$$

$$= \frac{1}{2} (2x + 1)[\ln (2x + 1) - 1] + C. \qquad \square$$

EXAMPLE 5   Evaluate $\displaystyle\int_2^3 \frac{dx}{x\sqrt{81 - 9x^2}}.$

Solution   This integral is similar to that of formula 9 in Table 14.1. Letting $a = 9$ and $u = 3x$, and multiplying the numerator and denominator by 3 gives the proper form.

$$\int_2^3 \frac{dx}{x\sqrt{81 - 9x^2}} = \int_2^3 \frac{3\, dx}{3x\sqrt{81 - 9x^2}}$$

$$= -\frac{1}{9} \ln \left| \frac{9 + \sqrt{81 - 9x^2}}{3x} \right| \Big\|_2^3$$

$$= -\frac{1}{9} \ln \left(\frac{9 + \sqrt{0}}{9} \right) - \left[-\frac{1}{9} \ln \left(\frac{9 + \sqrt{45}}{6} \right) \right]$$

$$= \frac{1}{9} \left[\ln \left(\frac{9 + \sqrt{45}}{6} \right) - \ln (1) \right] = \frac{1}{9} \ln \left(\frac{3 + \sqrt{5}}{2} \right) \qquad \square$$

It should be pointed out again that the formulas given in Table 14.1 represent a very small sample of the integration formulas. Additional formulas may be found in books of mathematical tables.

Exercise 14.8

Evaluate the following integrals.

1. $\displaystyle\int \frac{dx}{16 - x^2}$

2. $\displaystyle\int \frac{dx}{x(3x + 5)}$

3. $\displaystyle\int_1^4 \frac{dx}{x\sqrt{9 + x^2}}$

4. $\displaystyle\int \frac{dx}{x\sqrt{9 - x^2}}$

5. $\displaystyle\int \ln w\, dw$

6. $\displaystyle\int \frac{dv}{v(3v + 8)}$

7. $\displaystyle\int_0^2 \frac{q\, dq}{6q + 9}$

8. $\displaystyle\int_1^5 \frac{dq}{q\sqrt{25 + q^2}}$

9. $\displaystyle\int \frac{dx}{\sqrt{(3x + 1)^2 + 1}}$

10. $\displaystyle\int \frac{dx}{9 - (2x + 3)^2}$

11. $\displaystyle\int_0^3 x\sqrt{(x^2 + 1)^2 + 9}\, dx$

12. $\displaystyle\int_1^e x \ln x^2\, dx$

13. $\displaystyle\int \frac{dx}{\sqrt{9x^2 - 4}}$

14. $\displaystyle\int \frac{dx}{16 - 4x^2}$

15. $\displaystyle\int_5^6 \frac{dx}{x^2 - 16}$

16. $\displaystyle\int_0^1 \frac{x\,dx}{6 - 5x}$

17. $\displaystyle\int \frac{x\,dx}{7 - 3x^2}$

18. $\displaystyle\int_0^1 \frac{e^x}{1 + e^x}\,dx$

19. $\displaystyle\int \frac{x^3\,dx}{(4x^2 + 5)^2}$

20. $\displaystyle\int e^{2x}\sqrt{3e^x + 1}\,dx$

APPLICATIONS

21. If the supply function for a commodity is $p = 40 + 100 \ln (x + 1)^2$, what is the producer's surplus at $x = 20$?

22. If the demand function for a good is $p - 5000e^{-x} + 4$, where x is the number of hundreds of bushels of wheat, what is the consumer's surplus at $x = 7$, $p = 8.56$?

14.9   Integration by Parts (Optional)

Objective   ■ To evaluate integrals using the method of integration by parts

Formula 17 in Table 14.1 is the formula for **integration by parts**:

$$\int u\,dv = u\cdot v - \int v\,du.$$

This formula is very useful if the integral we seek to evaluate can be treated as the product of one function, u, and the differential of a second function, dv, so that the two integrals $\int dv$ and $\int v\cdot du$ can be found. Let us consider an example using this method.

EXAMPLE 1   Evaluate $\int xe^x\,dx$.

Solution   We cannot evaluate this integral using methods we have learned up to now. But we can "split" the integrand into two parts, setting one part equal to u and the second part equal to dv. This "split" must be done in such a way that $\int dv$ and $\int v\,du$ can be evaluated. Letting $u = x$ and $dv = e^x\,dx$ are possible choices. If we make these choices, we have

$$u = x \qquad\quad dv = e^x\,dx$$
$$du = 1\,dx \qquad v = e^x$$

Then

$$\int xe^x\,dx = u\cdot v - \int v\,du$$
$$= x\cdot e^x - \int e^x\,dx$$
$$= xe^x - e^x + C.$$ □

We see that choosing $u = x$ and $dv = e^x\, dx$ worked in evaluating $\int xe^x\, dx$ in Example 1. If we had chosen $u = e^x$ and $dv = x\, dx$, the results would not have been so successful.

How can we select u and dv to make integration by parts work? There are no general rules for separating the integrand into u and dv, but the goal is to select a dv that is integrable and will result in an $\int v\, du$ that is also integrable. There are usually just two reasonable choices, and it may be necessary to try both. Practice will increase your insight and lead to increasingly successful educated guesses. Consider the following examples.

EXAMPLE 2   Evaluate $\int x \ln x\, dx$.

Solution   Let $u = \ln x$ and $dv = x\, dx$. Then

$$du = \frac{1}{x}\, dx \qquad \text{and} \qquad v = \frac{x^2}{2}.$$

So

$$\int x \ln x\, dx = u \cdot v - \int v\, du$$

$$= (\ln x)\frac{x^2}{2} - \int \frac{x^2}{2} \cdot \frac{1}{x}\, dx$$

$$= \frac{x^2}{2} \ln x - \int \frac{x}{2}\, dx$$

$$= \frac{x^2}{2} \ln x - \frac{x^2}{4} + C.$$

Note that letting $dv = \ln x\, dx$ would lead to great difficulty in evaluating $\int dv$ and $\int v\, du$, so it would not be a wise choice.   □

EXAMPLE 3   Evaluate $\int \ln x^2\, dx$

Solution   It is frequently good practice to let expressions involving logarithms be part of u in integrating by parts, as the derivatives of logarithmic expressions are usually simple. In this problem, we can let $u = \ln x^2 = 2 \ln x$ and $dv = dx$ so $du = 2 \cdot \frac{1}{x}\, dx$ and $v = x$. Then

$$\int \ln x^2\, dx = x \ln x^2 - \int x \cdot \frac{2}{x}\, dx$$

$$= x \ln x^2 - 2x + C.$$

Note that if we write $\ln x^2$ as $2 \ln x$, we can evaluate this integral using formula 14.   □

Sometimes it is necessary to repeat the integration by parts more than once to complete the evaluation. As before, the goal is to produce a new integral that is simpler.

EXAMPLE 4   Evaluate $\int x^2 e^{2x}\, dx$.

Solution   Let $u = x^2$ and $dv = e^{2x}\, dx$, so $du = 2x\, dx$ and $v = \frac{1}{2}e^{2x}$. Then

$$\int x^2 e^{2x}\, dx = \frac{1}{2}x^2 e^{2x} - \int x e^{2x}\, dx.$$

We cannot evaluate $\int x e^{2x}\, dx$ directly, but this new integral is simpler than the original, and a second integration by parts will be successful. Letting $u = x$ and $dv = e^{2x}\, dx$ gives $du = dx$ and $v = \frac{1}{2}e^{2x}$. So

$$\int x^2 e^{2x}\, dx - \frac{1}{2}x^2 e^{2x} - \left(\frac{1}{2}x e^{2x} - \int \frac{1}{2}e^{2x}\, dx \right)$$

$$= \frac{1}{2}x^2 e^{2x} - \frac{1}{2}x e^{2x} + \frac{1}{4}e^{2x} + C$$

$$= \frac{1}{4}e^{2x}(2x^2 - 2x + 1) + C.$$

The most obvious choices for u and dv are not always the correct ones, as the following example shows. Integration by parts still requires some trial and error.

EXAMPLE 5   Evaluate $\int x^3 \sqrt{x^2 + 1}\, dx$.

Solution   Since x^3 can be integrated easily, it may appear that the new integral would be simplified if we let $u = \sqrt{x^2 + 1}$ and $dv = x^3$. But then du would be $\frac{1}{2}(x^2 + 1)^{-1/2}\, 2x$, making $\int v\, du$ more complicated than the original integral. But we can use $\sqrt{x^2 + 1}$ as part of dv; we can evaluate $\int dv$ if we let $dv = x\sqrt{x^2 + 1}\, dx$. Then $u = x^2$ and $dv = x(x^2 + 1)^{1/2}\, dx$, so $du = 2x\, dx$ and $v = \frac{1}{3}(x^2 + 1)^{3/2}$. Thus

$$\int x^3 \sqrt{x^2 + 1}\, dx = \frac{x^2}{3}(x^2 + 1)^{3/2} - \int \frac{2x}{3}(x^2 + 1)^{3/2}\, dx$$

$$= \frac{x^2}{3}(x^2 + 1)^{3/2} - \frac{2}{15}(x^2 + 1)^{5/2} + C$$

$$= \frac{1}{15}(x^2 + 1)^{3/2}[5x^2 - 2(x^2 + 1)] + C$$

$$= \frac{1}{15}(x^2 + 1)^{3/2}(3x^2 - 2) + C.$$

One further note about integration by parts. It can be very useful on certain types of problems, but not on all types. Don't attempt to use integration by parts when easier methods are available.

Exercise 14.9

Evaluate the following integrals.

1. $\int xe^{2x}\,dx$

2. $\int x\,e^{-x}\,dx$

3. $\int x^2 \ln x\,dx$

4. $\int x^3 \ln x\,dx$

5. $\int_4^6 q\sqrt{q-4}\,dq$

6. $\int_0^1 y(1-y)^{3/2}\,dy$

7. $\int x \ln(2x-3)\,dx$

8. $\int x \ln(4x)\,dx$

9. $\int q^3\sqrt{q^2-3}\,dq$

10. $\int \dfrac{x^3}{\sqrt{9-x^2}}\,dx$

11. $\int_0^1 x^2 e^x\,dx$

12. $\int x^3 e^x\,dx$

13. $\int_1^2 (\ln x)^2\,dx$

14. $\int x^3 \ln^2 x\,dx$

15. $\int \dfrac{x}{\sqrt{x-3}}\,dx$

16. $\int_0^4 x^3\sqrt{x^2+9}\,dx$

17. $\int \dfrac{\ln x}{x^2}\,dx$

18. $\int \dfrac{\ln(x-1)}{\sqrt{x-1}}\,dx$

19. $\int_0^2 x^3 e^{x^2}\,dx$

Review Exercises

Evaluate the following integrals.

1. $\int x^6\,dx$

2. $\int x^{1/2}\,dx$

3. $\int (x^3 - 3x^2 + 4x + 5)\,dx$

4. $\int (x^2 - 1)^2\,dx$

5. $\int (x^2 - 1)^2 x\,dx$

6. $\int (x^3 - 3x^2)(x^2 - 2x)\,dx$

7. $\int \dfrac{x^2\,dx}{\sqrt[3]{x^3-4}}$

8. $\int \dfrac{x^2\,dx}{x^3-4}$

9. $\int y^2 e^{y^3}\,dy$

10. $\int \dfrac{x^3 - 3x + 1}{x-1}\,dx$

11. $\int_0^5 (x^3 + 4x)\,dx$

12. $\int_{-2}^3 (x-1)^2\,dx$

13. $\int_{-2}^3 (x-1)\,dx$

14. $\int_2^3 \dfrac{x^2}{2x^3-7}\,dx$

Evaluate the integrals, using integral tables.

15. $\int \sqrt{x^2-4}\,dx$

16. $\int 3^x\,dx$

17. $\int x \ln x^2\,dx$

°18. Use integration by parts to evaluate $\int x^5 \ln x \, dx$.

19. Find the area between the curve $y = x^2 + 4$ and the x-axis from $x = 1$ to $x = 5$.

APPLICATIONS

20. If the marginal revenue for a month for a product is $\overline{MR} = 6x - 12$, find the total revenue from the sale of 4 units of the product.

21. A population of bacteria grows at the rate

$$r = \frac{100{,}000}{(t + 100)^2},$$

where t is time. If the population is 1000 when $t = 1$, write the equation that gives the size of the population at any time t.

22. If the marginal cost for a good is $\overline{MC} = 6x + 4$ and the related fixed costs are $\$1000$, find the total cost function for the good.

23. The demand function for a good under pure competition is $p = \sqrt{64 - 4x}$, and the supply function for the good is $p = x - 1$.
    (a) Find the market equilibrium.
    (b) Find the consumer's surplus at market equilibrium.
    (c) Find the producer's surplus at market equilibrium

° Problem is from the optional Section 14.9.

Warmup In this chapter you will need to work problems like the following. If you have difficulty with any problem, return to the section where that type of problem was introduced and refresh your memory before starting the chapter.

Problem Type	Introduced in Section	Used in Section	Answer
If $y = f(x)$, x is the independent variable and y is the _____ variable.	1.2 Functions	15.1	Dependent
What is the domain of $f(x) = \dfrac{3x}{x-1}$?	1.2 Domains	15.1	All reals except $x = 1$
If $C(x) = 5 + 5x$, what is $f(0.20)$?	1.3 Functional notation	15.1	6
(a) Solve for x and y: $\begin{cases} 0 = 50 - 2x - 2y \\ 0 = 60 - 2x - 4y \end{cases}$ (b) Solve for x and y: $\begin{cases} x = 2y \\ x + y - 9 = 0 \end{cases}$	2.6 Simultaneous solution of linear equations	15.5, 15.6	(a) $y = 5, x = 20$ (b) $x = 6, y = 3$
If $z = 4x^2 + 5x^3 - 7$, what is $\dfrac{dz}{dx}$?	11.3	15.2, 15.4, 15.5, 15.6	$\dfrac{dz}{dx} = 8x + 15x^2$
If $f(x) = (x^2 - 1)^2$, what is $f'(x)$?	11.5	15.2	$f'(x) = 4x(x^2 - 1)$
If $z = 10y - \ln y$, what is $\dfrac{dz}{dy}$?	13.4	15.2, 15.4	$\dfrac{dz}{dy} = 10 - \dfrac{1}{y}$
If $z = 5x^2 + e^x$, what is $\dfrac{dz}{dx}$?	13.5	15.2, 15.4	$\dfrac{dz}{dx} = 10x + e^x$
Find the slope of the tangent to $y = 4x^3 - 4e^x$ at $(0, 2)$.	11.2	15.2	-4

FUNCTIONS OF TWO OR MORE VARIABLES

Although we have been dealing primarily with functions of one variable, many real-life situations involve a variable that is a function of two or more variables. For example, the grade you receive in a course is a function of several test grades. The cost of manufacturing a product may involve the cost of labor, the cost of materials, and overhead expenses. The concentration of a substance at any point in a vein after an injection is a function of time since the injection t, the velocity of the blood v, and the distance the point is from the point of injection.

In this chapter we will extend our study to functions of two or more variables. We will extend the derivative concept to functions of several variables by taking partial derivatives, and we will learn how to maximize functions of two variables. We will use these concepts to solve problems in the management, social, and life sciences. In particular, we will discuss joint cost functions, marginal cost, marginal productivity, and marginal demand functions. We will use Lagrange multipliers to maximize functions of two variables subject to a condition that constrains the variables.

15.1 Functions of Two or More Variables

Objectives
- To find the domain and range of a function of two or more variables
- To evaluate a function of two or more variables given values for the independent variables
- To determine if a function of two or more variables is continuous

The relations we have studied up to this point have been limited to two variables, with one of the variables assumed to be a function of the other. But there are many instances where one variable may depend on two or more other variables. For example, the volume of a gas depends on the temperature and the pressure to which the gas is subjected. The universal gas law is $V = nRT/P$, where V is the volume, P represents the pressure, n represents the number of moles of gas, R is a constant, and T is the absolute temperature. (The constant R is called the universal gas constant.)

In economics, the demand function for a commodity frequently depends on the price of the commodity, available income, and prices of competing goods. Other examples from economics will be presented later in this chapter.

We write $z = f(x, y)$ to state that z is a function of both x and y. The variables x and y are called the **independent variables** and z is called the **dependent variable.** Thus the function f associates with each pair of possible values for the independent variables (x and y) exactly one value of the dependent variable (z).

The equation $z = x^2 - xy$ defines z as a function of x and y. We can denote this by writing $z = f(x, y) = x^2 - xy$. The domain of the function is the set of all ordered pairs (of real numbers) and the range is the set of all real numbers.

EXAMPLE 1   Give the domain of the function

$$g(x, y) = \frac{x^2 - 3y}{x - y}.$$

Solution   The domain of the function is the set of ordered pairs that do not give a 0 denominator. That is, the domain is the set of all ordered pairs where the first and second elements are not equal (that is, where $x \neq y$).   □

We graph the function $z = f(x, y)$ using three dimensions. We can construct a three-dimensional coordinate space by drawing three mutually perpendicular axes as in Figure 15.1. By setting up a scale of measurement along the three axes from the origin 0, we can determine the three coordinates (x, y, z) for any point P. The point shown in Figure 15.1 is $+2$ units in the x-direction, $+3$ units in the y-direction, and $+4$ units in the z-direction, so the coordinates of the point are $(2, 3, 4)$.

The pairs of axes determine the three *coordinate planes;* the xy plane, the yz plane, and the xz plane. The planes divide the space into eight octants. The point $P(2, 3, 4)$ is in the first octant.

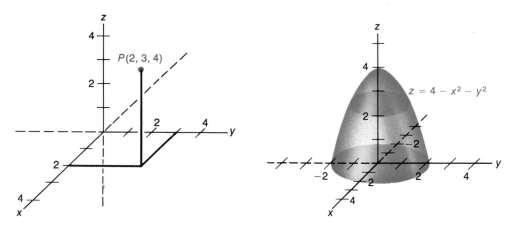

Figure 15.1   **Figure 15.2**

If we are given a function $z = f(x, y)$, we can find the z-value corresponding to $x = a$ and $y = b$ by evaluating $f(a, b)$.

EXAMPLE 2   If $z = f(x, y) = x^2 - 4xy + xy^3$, find
(a) $f(1, 2)$ (b) $f(2, 5)$ (c) $f(-1, 3)$

Solution   (a) $f(1, 2) = 1^2 - 4(1)(2) + (1)(2)^3 = 1$
(b) $f(2, 5) = 2^2 - 4(2)(5) + (2)(5)^3 = 214$
(c) $f(-1, 3) = (-1)^2 - 4(-1)(3) + (-1)(3)^3 = -14$ □

EXAMPLE 3   The cost of manufacturing a Wosh is given by

$$C(x, y) = 5 + 5x + 2y,$$

where x represents the cost of one ounce of material used and y represents the cost of labor in dollars per hour. If the material cost is $.20 per ounce and labor costs $3.50 per hour, what is the cost of manufacturing one Wosh?

Solution   The cost is

$$C(.20, 3.50) = 5 + 5(.20) + 2(3.50)$$
$$= \$13.$$ □

For a given function $z = f(x, y)$, we can construct a table of values by assigning values to x and y and finding the corresponding values of z. To each pair of values for x and y there corresponds a unique value of z, and thus a unique point in space. From a table of values such as this, a finite number of points can be plotted. All points that satisfy the equation form a "surface" in space. Since z is a function of x and y, lines parallel to the z axis will intersect such a surface in at most one point. The graph of the equation $z = -x^2 - y^2 + 4$ is a surface like that shown in Figure 15.2. The surface itself is like a bullet and is called a *paraboloid*.

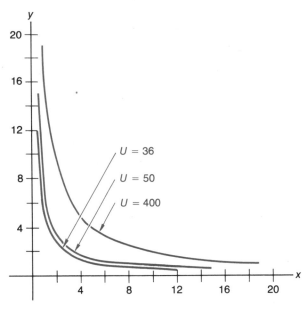

Figure 15.3

In practical applications of functions of two variables, we will have little need to construct the graphs of the surfaces. For this reason, we will not discuss methods of sketching the graphs. Although you will not be asked to sketch graphs of these surfaces, the fact that the graphs do *exist* will be used in studying relative maxima and minima of functions of two variables.

The properties of functions of one variable can be extended to functions of two variables. The precise definition of continuity for functions of two variables is technical, and may be found in more advanced books. We will limit our study to functions that are continuous and have continuous derivatives in the domain of interest to us. We may think of continuous functions as functions whose graphs consist of surfaces without "holes" or "breaks" in them.

Let the function $U = f(x, y)$ represent the **utility** (that is, satisfaction) derived by a consumer from the consumption of two goods, X and Y, where x and y represent the amounts of X and Y, respectively. Since we will assume the utility function is continuous, a given level of utility can be derived from an infinite number of combinations of x and y. The graph of all points (x, y) that give the same utility is called an *indifference curve*. A set of indifference curves corresponding to different levels of utility is called an *indifference map* (see Figure 15.3).

EXAMPLE 4   Suppose the utility function for two goods, X and Y, is $U = x^2y^2$ and a consumer purchases 10 units of X and 2 units of Y.
(a) If the consumer purchases 5 units of X, how many units of Y must be purchased to retain the same level of utility?

(b) Graph the indifference curve for this level of utility.

(c) Graph the indifference curves for this utility function if $U = 50$ and if $U = 36$.

Solution (a) If $x = 10$ and $y = 2$ satisfy the utility function, then $U = 10^2 \cdot 2^2 = 400$. Thus if x becomes 5, y must be 4.

(b) The indifference curve for $U = 400$ is $400 = x^2 y^2$. The graph for positive x and y is shown in Figure 15.3.

(c) The indifference map in Figure 15.3 contains these indifference curves. □

We can easily extend the concept of a function of two variables to that of a function of three or more variables. For example, $w = f(x, y, z)$ states that w is a function of the three variables x, y, and z. The implicit function relating the five variables x, y, z, w, and u is denoted by $f(x, y, z, w, u) = 0$.

In general, we can represent y as a function of n independent variables x_1, x_2, $x_3, \ldots, x_n$ by $y = f(x_1, x_2, x_3, \ldots, x_n)$. Of course it is no longer possible to "graph" the functions of three or more variables, since we would need more than three dimensions to represent the graphs. This does not imply that there is little use for functions of n variables. The applications in mathematics, science, and economics are numerous.

Exercise 15.1

Give the domain of the following functions.

1. $z = x^2 + y^2$

2. $z = 4x - 3y$

3. $z = \dfrac{4x - 3}{y}$

4. $z - \dfrac{x + y^2}{\sqrt{x}}$

5. $z = \dfrac{4x^3 y - x}{2x - y}$

6. $z = \sqrt{x - y}$

7. $q = \sqrt{p_1} + 3p_2$

8. $q = \dfrac{p_1 + p_2}{\sqrt{p_1}}$

Evaluate the following functions at the given values of the independent variables.

9. $z = x^3 + 4xy + y^2$; $x = 1$, $y = -1$

10. $z = 4x^2 - 3xy^3$; $x = 2$, $y = 2$

11. $z = \dfrac{x - y}{x + y}$; $x = 4$, $y = -1$

12. $z = \dfrac{x^2 + xy}{x - y}$; $x = 3$, $y = 2$

13. $C(x_1, x_2) = 600 + 4x_1 + 6x_2$; $x_1 = 400$, $x_2 = 50$

14. $C(x_1, x_2) = 500 + 5x_1 + 7x_2$; $x_1 = 200$, $x_2 = 300$

15. $q_1 = \dfrac{p_1 + 4p_2}{p_1 - p_2}$; $p_1 = 40$, $p_2 = 35$

16. $q_1 = \dfrac{5p_1 - p_2}{p_1 + 3p_2}; \ p_1 = 50, \ p_2 = 10$

17. Evaluate $w = \dfrac{x^2 + 4yz}{xyz}$ at $(1, 3, 1)$.

18. Evaluate $u = f(w, x, y, z) = \dfrac{wx - yz^2}{xy - wz}$ at $(2, 3, 1, -1)$.

APPLICATIONS

19. Suppose the utility function for two goods X and Y is given by $U = xy^2$, and a consumer purchases 9 units of X and 6 units of Y.
    (a) If the consumer purchases 9 units of Y, how many units of X must be purchased to retain the same level of utility?
    (b) If the consumer purchases 81 units of X, how many units of Y must be purchased to retain the same level of utility?

20. Suppose an indifference curve for two goods, X and Y, has equation $xy = 400$. If 20 units of X are purchased, how many units of Y must be purchased to remain on this indifference curve?

21. Suppose the number of units of a good produced, z, is given by $z = 20xy$, where x is the number of machines working properly and y is the average number of work-hours per machine. Find the production for a week in which
    (a) 12 machines are working properly and the average number of work-hours per machine is 30.
    (b) 10 machines are working properly and the average number of work-hours per machine is 25.

22. The Kirk Kelly Kandy Company makes two kinds of candy, Kisses and Kreams. The profit function for the company is $P(x, y) = 100x + 64y - 0.01x^2 - 0.25y^2$, where x is the number of pounds of Kisses sold per week and y is the number of Kreams. What is their profit if
    (a) they sell 20 pounds of Kisses and 10 pounds of Kreams?
    (b) they sell 100 pounds of Kisses and 16 pounds of Kreams?
    (c) they sell 10,000 pounds of Kisses and 256 pounds of Kreams?

23. The cost per day to society of an epidemic is

$$C = 20x + 200y,$$

where C is in dollars, x is the number of people infected on a given day and y is the number of people who die on a given day. If 14,000 people are infected and 20 people die on a given day, what is the cost to society?

24. An area of land is to be sprayed with two brands of pesticide, using x liters of brand 1 and y liters of brand 2. If the number of insects killed is given by

$$f(x, y) = 10,000 - 6500e^{-0.01x} - 3500e^{-0.02y},$$

how many insects would be killed if 80 liters of brand 1 and 120 liters of brand 2 were used?

25. Suppose a gas satisfies the universal gas law, $V = nRT/P$, with n equal to 10 moles of the gas and R, the universal gas constant, equal to 0.082054. What is V if $T = 10°K$ and $P = 1$ atmosphere?

15.2 Partial Differentiation

Objectives
- To find partial derivatives of functions of two or more variables
- To evaluate partial derivatives of functions of two or more variables at given points
- To use partial derivatives to find slopes of tangents to surfaces

We have used derivatives to find the rate of change of cost with respect to the quantity produced in Chapter 11. If cost is given as a function of two variables (such as material costs x and labor costs y), we can find the rate of change of cost with respect to *one* of these independent variables. This is done by finding the **partial derivative** of the function with respect to one variable, while holding the other one constant.

For example, suppose the cost of manufacturing a good is given by

$$C = 5 + 5x + 2y,$$

where x represents the cost of one ounce of material used and y represents the cost in dollars per hour. To find the rate at which the cost changes with respect to material used x, we treat the y variable as though it were a constant and take the derivative of C with respect to x. This derivative is

$$\frac{\partial C}{\partial x} = 0 + 5 + 0, \qquad \text{or} \qquad \frac{\partial C}{\partial x} = 5.$$

Note that the partial derivative of $2y$ with respect to x is 0 because y is treated as a constant. Because the partial derivative is a new type of derivative, we use a new symbol to denote it, $\partial C/\partial x$.

The partial derivative $\partial C/\partial x = 5$ tells us that the total cost C changes at a rate 5 times that of the cost of materials *if* labor costs remain constant. To see the rate at which total cost changes with respect to labor costs, we find $\partial C/\partial y = 0 + 0 + 2$, or $\partial C/\partial y = 2$. Thus if material costs are held constant, an increase of \$1 in labor costs will cause an increase of \$2 in the total cost of the good.

In general, if $z = f(x, y)$, we denote the partial derivative of z with respect to x as $\partial z/\partial x$ and the partial derivative of z with respect to y as $\partial z/\partial y$. Note that dz/dx represents the derivative of a function of one variable, x, and that $\partial z/\partial x$ represents the partial derivative of a function of two or more variables.

Other notations used to represent the partial derivative of $z = f(x, y)$ with respect to x are

$$\frac{\partial f}{\partial x}, \qquad \frac{\partial}{\partial x} f(x, y), \qquad f_x(x, y), \qquad f_x, \qquad \text{and} \qquad z_x.$$

If x is held constant in the function $z = f(x, y)$ and the derivative is taken with respect to y, we have the partial derivative of z with respect to y, denoted by

$$\frac{\partial z}{\partial y}, \qquad \frac{\partial f}{\partial y}, \qquad \frac{\partial}{\partial y} f(x, y), \qquad f_y(x, y), \qquad f_y, \qquad \text{or} \qquad z_y.$$

EXAMPLE 1   If $z = 4x^2 + 5x^2y^2 + 6y^3 - 7$, find $\partial z/\partial x$ and $\partial z/\partial y$.

Solution

$$\frac{\partial z}{\partial x} = 8x + 10y^2x$$

$$\frac{\partial z}{\partial y} = 10x^2y + 18y^2 \qquad \square$$

EXAMPLE 2   If $z = x^2y + e^x - \ln y$, find z_x and z_y.

Solution

$$z_x = \frac{\partial z}{\partial x} = 2yx + e^x$$

$$z_y = \frac{\partial z}{\partial y} = x^2 - \frac{1}{y} \qquad \square$$

EXAMPLE 3   If $f(x, y) = (x^2 - y^2)^2$, find
(a) f_x (b) f_y.

Solution   (a) $f_x = 2(x^2 - y^2)2x = 4x^3 - 4xy^2$
(b) $f_y = 2(x^2 - y^2)(-2y) = -4x^2y + 4y^3 \qquad \square$

EXAMPLE 4   If $q = \dfrac{p_1p_2 + 2p_1}{p_1p_2 - 2p_2}$, find $\partial q/\partial p_1$.

Solution

$$\frac{\partial q}{\partial p_1} = \frac{(p_1p_2 - 2p_2)(p_2 + 2) - (p_1p_2 + 2p_1)p_2}{(p_1p_2 - 2p_2)^2}$$

$$= \frac{p_1p_2{}^2 + 2p_1p_2 - 2p_2{}^2 - 4p_2 - p_1p_2{}^2 - 2p_1p_2}{(p_1p_2 - 2p_2)^2}$$

$$= \frac{-2p_2{}^2 - 4p_2}{p_2{}^2(p_1 - 2)^2}$$

$$= \frac{-2p_2(p_2 + 2)}{p_2{}^2(p_1 - 2)^2}$$

$$= \frac{-2(p_2 + 2)}{p_2(p_1 - 2)^2} \qquad \square$$

We may evaluate partial derivatives by substituting values for x *and* y in the same manner we did with derivatives of functions of one variable. For example, if $\partial z/\partial x = 2x - xy$, the value of the derivative at $x = 2$, $y = 3$ is

$$\left.\frac{\partial x}{\partial x}\right|_{(2,\ 3)} = 2(2) - 2 \cdot 3 = -2.$$

Other notations used to denote evaluation of partial derivatives with respect to x at (a, b) are

$$\frac{\partial}{\partial x} f(a, b) \qquad \text{and} \qquad f_x(a, b).$$

We denote the evaluation of partial derivatives with respect to y at (a, b) by

$$\frac{\partial z}{\partial y}\bigg|_{(a,\,b)}, \qquad \frac{\partial}{\partial y}f(a, b), \qquad \text{or} \qquad f_y(a, b).$$

EXAMPLE 5 Find the partial derivative of $f(x, y) = x^2 + 3xy + 4$ with respect to x at the point $(1, 2, 11)$.

Solution
$$f_x(x, y) = 2x + 3y$$
$$f_x(1, 2) = 2(1) + 3(2) = 8 \qquad \qquad \square$$

EXAMPLE 6 Suppose a company's sales are related to its television advertising by $s = 20{,}000 + 10nt + 20n^2$, where n is the number of commercials per day and t is the length of the commercials in seconds. Find the partial derivative of s with respect to n and use the result to find the instantaneous rate of change of sales with respect to the number of commercials per day, if they are currently running ten 30-second commercials.

Solution The partial derivative of s with respect to n is $\partial s/\partial n = 10t + 40n$. At $n = 10$ and $t = 30$, the rate of change in sales is approximately

$$\frac{\partial s}{\partial n}\bigg|_{\substack{n=10 \\ t=30}} = 700.$$

Thus increasing the number of commercials by one would result in approximately 700 additional sales. $\qquad \square$

We have seen that the partial derivative $\partial z/\partial x$ is found by holding y constant and taking the derivative of z with respect to x, using the usual differentiation rules. The formal definition of $\partial z/\partial x$ is as follows.

> The partial derivative of $z = f(x, y)$ with respect to x at the point (x, y) is
>
> $$\frac{\partial z}{\partial x} = \frac{\partial}{\partial x}f(x, y) = \lim_{h \to 0} \frac{f(x + h, y) - f(x, y)}{h}.$$

To find $\dfrac{\partial}{\partial y}f(x, y)$, we hold x constant, and use the formula

$$\frac{\partial z}{\partial y} = \frac{\partial}{\partial y}f(x, y) = \lim_{h \to 0} \frac{f(x, y + h) - f(x, y)}{h}.$$

We have already stated that the graph of $z = f(x, y)$ is a surface in three dimensions. The partial derivative of such a function may be thought of as the slope of the tangent to the surface at a point (x, y, z) on the surface *in the*

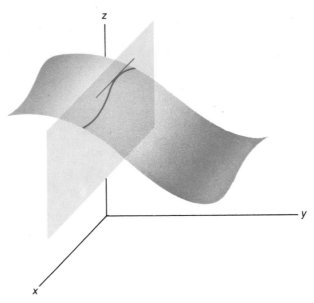

Figure 15.4

direction of the x-axis. That is, if a plane parallel to the x-axis cuts the surface, passing through the point (x_0, y_0, z_0), the line in the plane that is tangent to the surface will have a slope equal to $\partial z/\partial x$ evaluated at the point. Thus

$$\frac{\partial z}{\partial x}\bigg|_{(x_0, y_0)}$$

represents the slope of the tangent to the surface in the direction of the x-axis (see Figure 15.4).

Similarly,

$$\frac{\partial z}{\partial y}\bigg|_{(x_0, y_0)} = \frac{\partial}{\partial y} f(x_0, y_0)$$

represents the slope of the tangent to the surface at (x_0, y_0, z_0) in the direction of the y-axis (see Figure 15.5).

EXAMPLE 7   Find the slope of the tangent in the x-direction to the surface $z = 4x^3 - 4e^x + 4y^2$ at the point $(0, 2, 12)$ on the surface.

Solution
$$\frac{\partial z}{\partial x} = 12x^2 - 4e^x$$

Evaluating the partial derivative at the given point, we find the slope of the tangent.

$$\frac{\partial z}{\partial x}\bigg|_{(0, 2)} = 12(0)^2 - 4e^0 = -4$$

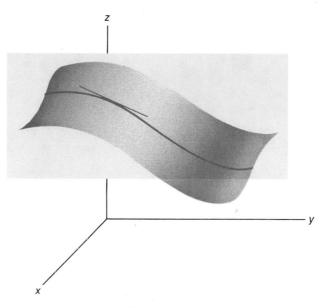

Figure 15.5

This tells us that z is *decreasing* at a rate of 4 units for each increase of 1 unit in x at this point. That is, the slope of the tangent to the surface in the x-direction is negative at $(0, 2, 12)$. □

EXAMPLE 8 Using the same function and point as that of Example 7, find the slope of the tangent in the y-direction to the surface at the point.

Solution
$$\frac{\partial z}{\partial y} = 8y$$

$$\left.\frac{\partial z}{\partial y}\right|_{(0,\,2)} = 8(2) = 16$$

So the slope of the tangent in the y-direction is increasing, at a rate of 16 units up in the z-value for each unit change in y. □

Up to this point we have considered derivatives of functions of two variables. We can easily extend the concept to functions of three or more variables. We can find the partial derivative with respect to any one independent variable by taking the derivative of the function with respect to that variable while holding all other variables constant.

EXAMPLE 9 If $u = f(w, x, y, z) = 3x^2y + w^3 - 4xyz$, find

(a) $\dfrac{\partial u}{\partial w}$ (b) $\dfrac{\partial u}{\partial x}$ (c) $\dfrac{\partial u}{\partial y}$ (d) $\dfrac{\partial u}{\partial z}$

Solution   (a) $\dfrac{\partial u}{\partial w} = 3w^2$ (b) $\dfrac{\partial u}{\partial x} = 6xy - 4yz$ (c) $\dfrac{\partial u}{\partial y} = 3x^2 - 4xz$ (d) $\dfrac{\partial u}{\partial z} = -4xy$ □

EXAMPLE 10   If $C = 4x_1 + 2x_1{}^2 + 3x_2 - x_1x_2 + x_3{}^2$, find

(a) $\dfrac{\partial C}{\partial x_1}$ (b) $\dfrac{\partial C}{\partial x_2}$ (c) $\dfrac{\partial C}{\partial x_3}$

Solution   (a) $\dfrac{\partial C}{\partial x_1} = 4 + 4x_1 - x_2$ (b) $\dfrac{\partial C}{\partial x_2} = 3 - x_1$ (c) $\dfrac{\partial C}{\partial x_3} = 2x_3$ □

Exercise 15.2

1. Find $\dfrac{\partial z}{\partial x}$ if $z = x^4 - 5x^2 + 4x + 3y^3 - 5y$.

2. Find $\dfrac{\partial z}{\partial y}$ if $z = x^5 - 6x + 4y^3 - y$.

3. Find $\dfrac{\partial z}{\partial x}$ if $z = x^2 - 5y + y$.

4. Find $\dfrac{\partial z}{\partial y}$ if $z = x^2 - 5y + y$.

5. If $z = x^3 + 4xy + 6y$, find z_y.
6. If $z = x^2 + 4xt + 6y$, find z_x.
7. If $z = 4x^2 - 5xy + 6y^2$, find z_y.
8. If $z = 4x^2 + 6xy^2 - y$, find z_x.
9. If $z = xy + y^2$, find z_x.
10. If $z = xy + y^2$, find z_y.

11. If $z = e^x + y \ln x$, find $\dfrac{\partial z}{\partial x}$.

12. If $z = e^x + y \ln x$, find $\dfrac{\partial z}{\partial y}$.

13. If $z = e^{xy}$, find z_y.
14. If $z = \ln(xy)$, find z_x.

15. If $z = (x^3 + y^2)^3$, find $\dfrac{\partial z}{\partial x}$.

16. If $z = \sqrt{x - y}$, find z_y.

17. If $f(x, y) = (xy + y)^2$, find $\dfrac{\partial f}{\partial y}$.

18. If $f(x, y) = x\sqrt{y - x}$, find $\dfrac{\partial f}{\partial x}$.

19. If $C(x, y) = 600 - 4xy + 10x^2y$, find $\dfrac{\partial C}{\partial x}$.

20. If $C(x, y) = 1000 - 4x + xy^2$, find $\dfrac{\partial C}{\partial y}$.

21. If $q = \dfrac{5p_1 + 4p_2}{p_1 + p_2}$, find $\dfrac{\partial q}{\partial p_1}$.

22. If $q = \dfrac{5p_1 + 4p_2}{p_1 + p_2}$, find $\dfrac{\partial q}{\partial p_2}$.

23. If $Q(x, y) = 1500 + x^2 + 4xy + y^2$, find $\dfrac{\partial Q}{\partial x}$.

24. If $Q(x, y) = 1500 + x^2 + 4xy + y^2$, find $\dfrac{\partial Q}{\partial y}$.

25. Find the partial derivative of $f(x, y) = 4x^3 - 5xy + y^2$ with respect to x at the point $(1, 2, -2)$.

26. Find the partial derivative of $f(x, y) = 3x^2 + 4x + 6xy$ with respect to y at $x = 2$, $y = -1$.

27. Find the slope of the tangent in the x-direction to the surface $z = 5x^3 - 4xy$ at the point $(1, 2, -3)$.

28. Find the slope of the tangent in the y-direction to the surface $z = x^3 - 5xy$ at $(2, 1, -2)$.

29. Find the slope of the tangent in the y-direction to the surface $z = e^{xy}$ at $(0, 1, 1)$.

30. Find the slope of the tangent in the x-direction to the surface $z = \ln(xy)$ at $(1, 1, 0)$.

31. If $u = f(w, x, y, z) = y^2 - x^2 z + 4x$, find

    (a) $\dfrac{\partial u}{\partial w}$ (b) $\dfrac{\partial u}{\partial x}$ (c) $\dfrac{\partial u}{\partial y}$ (d) $\dfrac{\partial u}{\partial z}$

32. If $u = x^2 + 3xy + xz$, find

    (a) u_x (b) u_y (c) u_z

33. If $C(x_1, x_2, x_3) = 4x_1^2 + 5x_1 x_2 + 6x_2^2 + x_3$, find

    (a) $\dfrac{\partial C}{\partial x_1}$ (b) $\dfrac{\partial C}{\partial x_2}$ (c) $\dfrac{\partial C}{\partial x_3}$

APPLICATIONS

Suppose the profit from the sale of Kisses and Kreams is given by

$$P(x, y) = 100x + 64y - 0.01x^2 - 0.25y^2,$$

where x is the number of pounds of Kisses and y is the number of pounds of Kreams. Answer problems 34 and 35.

34. Find $\partial P/\partial x$, and give the approximate rate of change of profit with respect to the number of pounds of Kisses if present sales are 20 pounds of Kisses and 10 pounds of Kreams.

35. Find $\partial P/\partial y$, and give the approximate rate of change of profit with respect to the number of pounds of Kreams that are sold if 100 pounds of Kisses and 16 pounds of Kreams are currently being sold.

Suppose the number of insects killed by two brands of pesticide is given by

$$f(x, y) = 10{,}000 - 6500e^{-0.01x} - 3500e^{-0.02y},$$

where x is the number of liters of brand 1 and y is the number of liters of brand 2. Answer problems 36 and 37.

36. What is the rate of change of insect deaths with respect to the number of liters of brand 1?

37. What is the rate of change of insect deaths with respect to the number of liters of brand 2?

38. Suppose the total cost of producing a good is $C(x, y) = 25 + 2x^2 + 3y^2$, where x is the cost per pound for material and y is cost per hour for labor. If material costs are held constant, at what rate will the total cost increase for each \$1 per hour increase in labor?

39. If, in Problem 38, the labor costs are held constant, at what rate will the total cost increase for each increase of \$1 in material cost?

40. If $U = f(x, y)$ is the utility function for goods X and Y, the *marginal utility* of X is $\partial U/\partial x$ and the *marginal utility* of Y is $\partial U/\partial y$. If $U = x^2y^2$,
   (a) find the marginal utility of X.
   (b) find the marginal utility of Y.

41. If the utility function for goods X and Y is $U = xy + y^2$,
   (a) find the marginal utility of X.
   (b) find the marginal utility of Y.

15.3 Applications of Functions of Two Variables in Business and Economics

Objectives
- To evaluate cost functions at given levels of production
- To find marginal costs from total cost and joint cost functions
- To find marginal productivity for given production functions
- To find marginal demand functions from demand functions for a pair of related products

Joint Cost and Marginal Cost

Suppose a firm produces two commodities using the same inputs in different proportions. In such a case the **joint cost function** is of the form $C = Q(x, y)$, where x and y represent the quantities of each commodity and C represents the total cost for the two commodities. Then $\partial C/\partial x$ is the **marginal cost** with respect to product x and $\partial C/\partial y$ is the **marginal cost** with respect to product y.

EXAMPLE 1   If the joint cost function for two products is

$$C = Q(x, y) = 50 + x^2 + 8xy + y^3,$$

(a) find the marginal cost with respect to x.
(b) find the marginal cost with respect to y.
(c) find the marginal cost with respect to x and y at $(5, 3)$.

Solution   (a) The marginal cost with respect to x is $\partial C/\partial x = 2x + 8y$.

(b) $\dfrac{\partial C}{\partial y} = 8x + 3y^2$

(c) $\dfrac{\partial C}{\partial x}\bigg|_{(5,\,3)} = 2(5) + 8(3) = 34$

Thus, if 5 units of product x and 3 units of product y are produced, the total cost will increase \$34 for each unit increase in product x if y is held constant.

$$\frac{\partial C}{\partial y}\bigg|_{(5,\,3)} = 8(5) + 3(3)^2 = 67$$

Thus, if 5 units of product x and 3 units of product y are produced, the total cost will increase \$67 for each unit increase of product y if x is held constant.   □

Production Functions

An important problem in economics concerns how the factors necessary for production determine the output of a product. For example, the output of a product depends on available labor, land, capital, material, and machines. If the amount of output z of a product depends on the amounts of two inputs x and y, then the quantity z is given by the **production function** $z = f(x, y)$.

EXAMPLE 2   Suppose it is known that z bushels of a crop can be harvested according to the function

$$z = (21)\frac{6xy - 4x^2 - 3y}{2x + 0.01y}$$

when $100x$ work-hours of labor are employed on y acres of land.
What would be the output (in bushels) if 200 work-hours were used on 300 acres?

Solution $z = f(x, y)$, so

$$f(2,300) = (21)\frac{6(2)(300) + 4(2)^2 - 3(300)}{2(2) + 3}$$

$$= (21)\frac{3600 + 16 - 900}{7} = 8148 \text{ (bushels)} \qquad □$$

If $z = f(x, y)$ is a production function, $\partial z/\partial x$ represents the change in the output z with respect to input x while input y remains constant. This partial derivative is called the **marginal productivity of x.** The partial derivative $\partial z/\partial y$ is the **marginal productivity of y,** and measures the rate of change of z with respect to input y.

Marginal productivity (for either input) will be positive over a wide range of inputs, but it increases at a decreasing rate, and may eventually reach a point where it no longer increases, and begins to decrease.

EXAMPLE 3 If a production function is given by $z = 5x^{1/2}y^{1/4}$,
(a) find the marginal productivity of x.
(b) find the marginal productivity of y.

Solution (a) $\dfrac{\partial z}{\partial x} = \dfrac{5}{2}x^{-1/2}y^{1/4}$

(b) $\dfrac{\partial z}{\partial y} = \dfrac{5}{4}x^{1/2}y^{-3/4}$

Note that the marginal productivity of x is positive for all values of x, but that it decreases as x gets larger (because of the negative exponent). The same is true for the marginal productivity of y. □

Demand Functions

Suppose that two goods are sold at prices p_1 and p_2, respectively, on a competitive market consisting of a fixed number of consumers with given tastes and incomes. Then the amount of each *one* of the goods demanded by the consumers is dependent on the prices of *both* goods on the market. If q_1 represents the demand for the first good, then $q_1 = f(p_1, p_2)$ is the **demand function** for that good. The graph of such a function is called a **demand surface.** An example of a demand function in two variables is $q_1 = 400 - 2p_1 - 4p_2$. Here q_1 is a function of two variables p_1 and p_2. If $p_1 = \$10$ and $p_2 = \$20$, the demand would equal $400 - 2(10) - 4(20) = 300$.

EXAMPLE 4 The demand functions for two goods are

$$q_1 = 50 - 5p_1 - 2p_2$$
$$q_2 = 100 - 3p_1 - 8p_2$$

What is the demand for each of the goods if the price of the first is $p_1 = \$5$ and the price of the second is $p_2 = \$8$?

Solution
$$q_1 = 50 - 5(5) - 2(8) = 9$$
$$q_2 = 100 - 3(5) - 8(8) = 21$$

Thus, if these are the prices, the demand for good 2 is higher than the demand for good 1. □

EXAMPLE 5 Using the demand equations in Example 4, find a pair of prices p_1 and p_2 such that the demands for good 1 and good 2 are equal.

Solution We want q_1 to equal q_2. Setting $q_1 = q_2$, we see that

$$50 - 5p_1 - 2p_2 = 100 - 3p_1 - 8p_2$$
$$6p_2 - 50 = 2p_1$$
$$p_1 = 3p_2 - 25$$

Now, any pair of values that satisfies this equation will make the demands equal. Letting $p_2 = 10$, we see $p_1 = 5$ will satisfy the equation. Thus the prices $p_1 = 5$ and $p_2 = 10$ will make the demands equal. The prices $p_1 = 2$ and $p_2 = 9$ will also make the demands equal. Many pairs of values (all those satisfying $p_1 = 3p_2 - 25$) will equalize the demands.   □

If the demand functions for a pair of related products, product 1 and product 2, are $q_1 = f(p_1, p_2)$ and $q_2 = g(p_1, p_2)$, respectively, then the partial derivatives of q_1 and q_2 are called **marginal demand functions.**

$\dfrac{\partial q_1}{\partial p_1}$ is the marginal demand of q_1 with respect to p_1.

$\dfrac{\partial q_1}{\partial p_2}$ is the marginal demand of q_1 with respect to p_2.

$\dfrac{\partial q_2}{\partial p_1}$ is the marginal demand of q_2 with respect to p_1.

$\dfrac{\partial q_2}{\partial p_2}$ is the marginal demand of q_2 with respect to p_2.

For typical demand functions, if the price of product 2 is fixed, the demand for product 1 will decrease as its price p_1 increases. In this case the marginal demand of q_1 with respect to p_1 will be negative; that is, $\partial q_1/\partial p_1 < 0$. Similarly, $\partial q_2/\partial p_2 < 0$.

But what about $\partial q_2/\partial p_1$ and $\partial q_1/\partial p_2$? If $\partial q_2/\partial p_1$ and $\partial q_1/\partial p_2$ are both positive, the two products are **competitive,** because an increase in price p_1 will result in an increase in demand for product 2 (q_2) if the price p_2 is held constant, while an increase in price p_2 will increase the demand for product 1 if p_1 is held constant. Stated more simply, an increase in the price of one of the two products will result in an increased demand for the other, so the products are in competition.

If $\partial q_2/\partial p_1$ and $\partial q_1/\partial p_2$ are both negative, the products are **complementary,** because an increase in the price of one product will cause a decrease in demand for the other product if the price of the second product doesn't change. Under these conditions, a *decrease* in the price of product 1 would result in an *increase* in the demand for product 2, and a decrease in the price of product 2 would result in an increase in the demand for product 1.

If the signs of $\partial q_2/\partial p_1$ and $\partial q_1/\partial p_2$ are different, the products are neither competitive nor complementary. This situation rarely occurs, but is possible.

EXAMPLE 6   The demand functions for two related goods, good 1 and good 2, are given by

$$q_1 = 400 - 5p_1 + 6p_2$$
$$q_2 = 250 + 4p_1 - 5p_2$$

(a) Determine the four marginal demands.

(b) Are good 1 and good 2 complementary or competitive?

Solution   (a) $\dfrac{\partial q_1}{\partial p_1} = -5$ $\dfrac{\partial q_2}{\partial p_2} = -5$

$\dfrac{\partial q_1}{\partial p_2} = 6$ $\dfrac{\partial q_2}{\partial p_1} = 4$

(b) $\partial q_1/\partial p_2$ and $\partial q_2/\partial p_1$ are both positive, so they are competitive.   □

Exercise 15.3

JOINT COST AND MARGINAL COST

1. The cost of manufacturing one item is given by

$$C(x, y) = 30 + 3x + 5y,$$

where x is the cost of one hour of labor and y is the cost of one pound of material. If the hourly cost of labor is $4, and the material costs $3 per pound, what is the cost of manufacturing one of these items?

2. The manufacture of one unit of a good is given by

$$C(x, y, z) = 10 + 8x + 3y + z,$$

where x is the cost of one pound of one raw material, y is cost of one pound of a second material, and z is the cost of one work-hour of labor. If the cost of the first raw material is $16 per pound, the cost of the second raw material is $8 per pound, and labor costs $8 per work-hour, what will it cost to produce one unit of the good?

3. The total cost of producing one unit of a good is

$$C(x, y) = 30 + 2x + 4y,$$

where x is the cost per pound of raw materials and y is the cost per hour of labor.

   (a) If labor costs are held constant, at what rate will the total cost increase for each increase of $1 per pound in material cost?

   (b) If material costs are held constant, at what rate will the total cost increase for each $1 per hour increase in labor costs?

4. The total cost of producing an item is

$$C(x, y) = 40 + 4x + 6y,$$

where x is the cost per pound of raw materials and y is the cost per hour for labor.

   (a) How will an increase of $1 per pound of raw materials affect the total cost?

   (b) How will an increase of $1 per hour in labor costs affect the total cost?

5. The profit from the sale of one unit of a good is given by

$$P(x, y) = 20x + 70y - x^2 - xy^2,$$

where x represents the cost per pound of raw materials and y represents the hourly rate for labor. The present cost for raw materials is $10 per pound and the present hourly rate for labor is $4.

(a) How will an increase of $1 per pound for raw materials affect the profit?

(b) How will an increase of $1 per hour in labor costs affect the profit?

6. The total cost from the sale of one unit of a good is given by

$$C(x, y) = 30 + 10x^2 + 20y - xy,$$

where x is the hourly labor rate and y is the cost per pound of raw materials. The current hourly rate is $5, and the raw materials cost $6 per pound.

(a) How will an increase of $1 per pound for the raw materials affect the total cost?

(b) How will an increase of $1 in the hourly labor rate affect the total cost?

7. The joint cost function for two products is

$$C = Q(x, y) = 30 + x^2 + 3y + 2xy,$$

where x represents the quantity of product X produced and y represents the quantity of product Y produced.

(a) Find the marginal cost with respect to x if 8 units of product X and 10 units of product Y are produced.

(b) Find the marginal cost with respect to y if 8 units of product X and 10 units of product Y are produced.

8. The joint cost function for products X and Y is

$$C = Q(x, y) = 40 + 3x^2 + y^2 + xy,$$

where x represents the quantity of X and y represents the quantity of Y.

(a) Find the marginal cost with respect to x if 20 units of product X and 15 units of product Y are produced.

(b) Find the marginal cost with respect to y if 20 units of X and 15 units of Y are produced.

9. If the joint cost function for two products is

$$C(x, y) = x\sqrt{y^2 + 1},$$

(a) Find the marginal cost (function) with respect to x.

(b) Find the marginal cost with respect to y.

10. If the joint cost function for two products is

$$C(x, y) = y \ln x,$$

(a) Find the marginal cost with respect to x.

(b) Find the marginal cost with respect to y.

PRODUCTION FUNCTIONS

11. Suppose the production function for a product is $z = \sqrt{4xy}$, where x represents the number of work-hours per month and y is the number of available machines.

(a) Determine the marginal productivity of x.

(b) Determine the marginal productivity of y.

12. Suppose the production function for a product is $z = \sqrt{x} \ln y$, where x represents the number of work-hours and y represents the available capital (per week).

(a) Find the marginal productivity of x.

(b) Find the marginal productivity of y.

DEMAND FUNCTIONS

13. The demand functions for two goods are given by

$$q_1 = 300 - 8p_1 - 4p_2$$
$$q_2 = 400 - 5p_1 - 10p_2.$$

Find the demand for each of the goods if the price of the first is $p_1 = 10$ and the price of the second is $p_2 = 8$.

14. The demand functions for two goods are given by

$$q_1 = 900 - 9p_1 + 2p_2$$
$$q_2 = 1200 + 6p_1 - 10p_2.$$

Find the demands q_1 and q_2 if $p_1 = \$10$ and $p_2 = \$12$.

15. Find a pair of prices p_1 and p_2 such that the demands for the two goods of problem 13 will be equal.

16. Find a pair of prices p_1 and p_2 such that the demands for the two goods of problem 14 will be equal.

17. The demand functions for two related goods, good A and good B, are given by

$$q_A = 400 - 3p_A - 2p_B$$
$$q_B = 250 - 5p_A - 6p_B.$$

   (a) Find the marginal demand of q_A with respect to p_A.
   (b) Find the marginal demand of q_A with respect to p_B.
   (c) Find the marginal demand of q_B with respect to p_B.
   (d) Find the marginal demand of q_B with respect to p_A.
   (e) Are the two goods competitive or complementary?

18. The demand functions for two related products, product A and product B, are given by

$$q_A = 600 - 4p_A + 6p_B$$
$$q_B = 1200 + 8p_A - 4p_B.$$

   (a) Find the marginal demand of q_A with respect to p_A.
   (b) Find the marginal demand of q_A with respect to p_B.
   (c) Find the marginal demand of q_B with respect to p_B.
   (d) Find the marginal demand of q_B with respect to p_A.
   (e) Are the two goods competitive or complementary?

15.4 Higher-Order Partial Derivatives

Objective   ■ To find and evaluate second and higher-order derivatives of functions of two variables

Just as each derivative of a function of one variable in turn may have second, third, and higher derivatives, partial derivatives may also have partial derivatives. A function of two variables, such as $z = f(x, y)$, has *four* second partial derivatives. The notations for these second partial derivatives follow:

$z_{xx} = \dfrac{\partial^2 z}{\partial x^2} = \dfrac{\partial}{\partial x}\left(\dfrac{\partial z}{\partial x}\right)$: Both derivatives taken with respect to x.

$z_{yy} = \dfrac{\partial^2 z}{\partial y^2} = \dfrac{\partial}{\partial y}\left(\dfrac{\partial z}{\partial y}\right)$: Both derivatives taken with respect to y.

$z_{xy} = \dfrac{\partial^2 z}{\partial y\,\partial x} = \dfrac{\partial}{\partial y}\left(\dfrac{\partial z}{\partial x}\right)$: First derivative taken with respect to x, second with respect to y.

$z_{yx} = \dfrac{\partial^2 z}{\partial x\,\partial y} = \dfrac{\partial}{\partial x}\left(\dfrac{\partial z}{\partial y}\right)$: First derivative taken with respect to y, second with respect to x.

EXAMPLE 1   If $z = x^3 y - 3xy^2 + 4$, find each of the second partial derivatives of the function.

Solution $$z_x = 3x^2 y - 3y^2 \text{ and } z_y = x^3 - 6xy;$$
then

$$z_{xx} = \frac{\partial}{\partial x}(3x^2 y - 3y^2) = 6xy$$

$$z_{xy} = \frac{\partial}{\partial y}(3x^2 y - 3y^2) = 3x^2 - 6y$$

$$z_{yy} = \frac{\partial}{\partial y}(x^3 - 6xy) = -6x$$

$$z_{yx} = \frac{\partial}{\partial x}(x^3 - 6xy) = 3x^2 - 6y \qquad \square$$

Note that z_{xy} and z_{yx} are equal for the function of Example 1. This will always occur if the derivatives of this function are continuous.

> If the second partial derivatives z_{xy} and z_{yx} of a function $z = f(x, y)$ are continuous at a point, they are equal there.

EXAMPLE 2   Find each of the second partial derivatives of $z = x^2 y + e^{xy}$.

Solution $$z_x = 2xy + e^{xy} \cdot y,$$
so

$$z_{xx} = 2y + e^{xy} \cdot y^2 = 2y + y^2 e^{xy}$$
$$z_{xy} = 2x + (e^{xy} \cdot 1 + ye^{xy} \cdot x)$$
$$\quad\ = 2x + e^{xy} + xye^{xy}$$

$$z_y = x^2 + e^{xy} \cdot x,$$
so

$$z_{yx} = 2x + (e^{xy} \cdot 1 + xe^{xy} \cdot y)$$
$$\quad\ = 2x + e^{xy} + xye^{xy}$$
$$z_{yy} = 0 + xe^{xy} \cdot x = x^2 e^{xy} \qquad \square$$

EXAMPLE 3   If $z = x^2y + \ln x$, find $z_{xy}|_{(1,\,1)}$.

Solution
$$z_x = 2xy + \frac{1}{x}$$
$$z_{xy} = 2x$$
$$z_{xy}|_{(1,\,1)} = 2(1) = 2 \qquad \square$$

We can find partial derivatives of order higher than the second. For example, $z_{xy} = 3x^2 - 6y$ in Example 1; we can find the following third-order partial derivatives from this second derivative:
$$z_{xyx} = 6x$$
$$z_{xyy} = -6.$$

EXAMPLE 4   If $z = x^3y^2 + 4 \ln x$, find z_{xyy}.

Solution
$$z_x = 3x^2y^2 + 4 \cdot \frac{1}{x}$$
$$z_{xy} = 3x^2(2y) + 0 = 6x^2y$$
$$z_{xyy} = 6x^2 \qquad \square$$

Exercise 15.4

1. If $z = x^2 + 4x - 5y^3$, find
   (a) z_{xx} (b) z_{xy} (c) z_{yx} (d) z_{yy}
2. If $z = x^3 - 5y^2 + 4y + 1$, find
   (a) z_{xx} (b) z_{xy} (c) z_{yx} (d) z_{yy}
3. If $z = x^2y - 4xy^2$, find
   (a) z_{xx} (b) z_{xy} (c) z_{yx} (d) z_{yy}
4. If $z = xy^2 + 4xy - 5$, find
   (a) z_{xx} (b) z_{xy} (c) z_{yx} (d) z_{yy}
5. If $f(x, y) = x^2 + e^{xy}$, find

   (a) $\dfrac{\partial^2 f}{\partial x^2}$ (b) $\dfrac{\partial^2 f}{\partial y\, \partial x}$ (c) $\dfrac{\partial^2 f}{\partial x\, \partial y}$ (d) $\dfrac{\partial^2 f}{\partial y^2}$

6. If $f(x, y) = y^2 - \ln xy$, find

   (a) $\dfrac{\partial^2 f}{\partial x^2}$ (b) $\dfrac{\partial^2 f}{\partial y\, \partial x}$ (c) $\dfrac{\partial^2 f}{\partial x\, \partial y}$ (d) $\dfrac{\partial^2 f}{\partial y^2}$

7. If $z = x^2 - xy + 4y^3$, find z_{xyx}.
8. If $z = x^3 - 4x^2y + 5y^3$, find z_{yyx}.
9. If $z = x^4 + x \ln y + y^2$, find z_{xyy}.
10. If $z = x^2y^3 + ye^x - y^2$, find z_{yxy}.

11. If $f(x, y) = x^3y + 4xy^4$, find $\dfrac{\partial^2}{\partial x^2} f(1, -1)$.

12. If $f(x, y) = x^4y^2 + 4xy$, find $\dfrac{\partial^2}{\partial y^2} f(1, 2)$.

13. If $z = x^4y + ye^{x^2}$, find $z_{yx}|_{(1,\,2)}$.
14. If $z = xy^3 + x \ln y^2$, find $z_{xy}|_{(2,\,1)}$.

15.5 Maxima and Minima

Objective
■ To find relative maxima, minima, and saddle points of functions of two variables

In the study of functions of one variable, we saw that for a relative maximum or minimum to occur at a point, the tangent line to the curve had to be horizontal at that point. For a surface whose equation is $z = f(x, y)$ to have a relative maximum or minimum at a point, we must have a horizontal *plane* tangent to the surface at the point (see Figure 15.6). But if the plane tangent to the surface at the point is horizontal, then all the tangent lines to the surface at that point must also be horizontal, for they lie in the tangent plane. In particular, the tangent line in the direction of the x-axis will be horizontal, so $\partial z/\partial x = 0$ at the point; and the tangent line in the direction of the y-axis will be horizontal, so $\partial z/\partial y = 0$ at the point. Thus we can determine the *critical points* for a surface by finding those points where *both* $\partial z/\partial x = 0$ and $\partial z/\partial y = 0$.

But how can we determine whether a critical point is a relative maximum or relative minimum, or neither of these? Finding that $\partial^2 z/\partial x^2 < 0$ and $\partial^2 z/\partial y^2 < 0$ is not enough to tell us we have a relative maximum. The "second derivative" test we must use involves all four second partial derivatives. To make the test easier, let us first define the value D as follows:

$$D = \frac{\partial^2 z}{\partial x^2} \cdot \frac{\partial^2 z}{\partial y^2} - \frac{\partial^2 z}{\partial x\, \partial y} \cdot \frac{\partial^2 z}{\partial y\, \partial x}$$

Or, assuming the second partial derivatives are equal (making $\partial^2 z/\partial x\, \partial y = \partial^2 z/\partial y\, \partial x$),

$$D = \frac{\partial^2 z}{\partial x^2} \cdot \frac{\partial^2 z}{\partial y^2} - \left(\frac{\partial^2 z}{\partial x\, \partial y} \right)^2 .$$

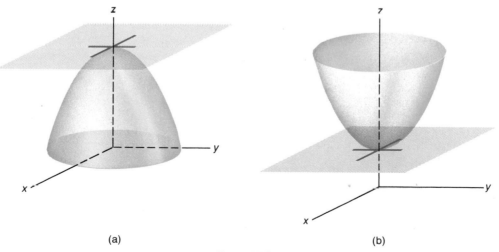

(a)   (b)

Figure 15.6

We shall state, without proof, the result that determines whether there is a relative maximum or minimum or neither at a point (a, b).

Test for Maxima and Minima If, at a point (a, b),

$$\frac{\partial z}{\partial x} = \frac{\partial z}{\partial y} = 0$$

for a function $z = f(x, y)$, and if all second partial derivatives are continuous there, and

$D = \frac{\partial^2 z}{\partial x^2} \cdot \frac{\partial^2 z}{\partial y^2} - \left(\frac{\partial^2 z}{\partial x \partial y}\right)^2$

(a) if $D > 0$, $\partial^2 z/\partial x^2 > 0$, and $\partial^2 z/\partial y^2 > 0$ at (a, b), then a relative minimum occurs at (a, b).

(b) if $D > 0$, $\partial^2 z/\partial x^2 < 0$, and $\partial^2 z/\partial y^2 < 0$ at (a, b), then a relative maximum occurs at (a, b).

(c) if $D < 0$, there is neither a relative maximum nor minimum at (a, b).

(d) if $D = 0$ at (a, b), then the test fails; the function must be investigated near the point.

We can test for relative maxima and minima using the following procedure.

PROCEDURE	EXAMPLE
To find relative maxima and minima of $z = f(x, y)$.	Test $z = 4 - 4x^2 - y^2$ for relative maxima and minima.
1. Find $\partial z/\partial x$ and $\partial z/\partial y$.	1. $\dfrac{\partial z}{\partial x} = -8x$; $\dfrac{\partial z}{\partial y} = -2y$
2. Find the point(s) that satisfy *both* $\partial z/\partial x = 0$ and $\partial z/\partial y = 0$. These are the critical points.	2. $\dfrac{\partial z}{\partial x} = 0$ if $x = 0$. $\dfrac{\partial z}{\partial y} = 0$ if $y = 0$. The critical point is $(0, 0, 4)$.
3. Find all second partial derivatives.	3. $\dfrac{\partial^2 z}{\partial x^2} = -8$; $\dfrac{\partial^2 z}{\partial y^2} = -2$ $\dfrac{\partial^2 z}{\partial x \, \partial y} = \dfrac{\partial^2 z}{\partial y \, \partial x} = 0$
4. Evaluate D at the critical point(s).	4. At $(0, 0)$, $D = (-8)(-2) - 0^2 = 16$.
5. Use the test for maxima and minima to determine if relative maxima or minima occur.	5. $D > 0$, $\partial^2 z/\partial x^2 < 0$, and $\partial^2 z/\partial y^2 < 0$. A relative maximum occurs at $(0, 0)$. The graph is shown in Figure 15.7.

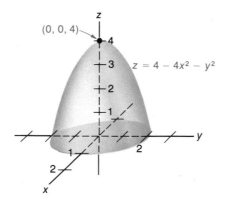

Figure 15.7

EXAMPLE 1   Test $z = x^2 + y^2 - 2x + 1$ for relative maxima and minima.

Solution   1. $\dfrac{\partial z}{\partial x} = 2x - 2;$ $\dfrac{\partial z}{\partial y} = 2y$

2. $\dfrac{\partial z}{\partial x} = 0$ if $x = 1$.

$\dfrac{\partial z}{\partial y} = 0$ if $y = 0$.

Both are 0 if $x = 1$ *and* $y = 0$, so the critical point is $(1, 0, 0)$.

3. $\dfrac{\partial^2 z}{\partial x^2} = 2;$ $\dfrac{\partial^2 z}{\partial y^2} - 2$

$\dfrac{\partial^2 z}{\partial x\,\partial y} = \dfrac{\partial^2 z}{\partial y\,\partial x} = 0$

4. At $(1, 0)$, $D = 2 \cdot 2 - 0^2 = 4$.
5. $D > 0$, $\partial^2 z/\partial x^2 > 0$, and $\partial^2 z/\partial y^2 > 0$. A relative minimum occurs at $(1, 0)$.
   (See Figure 15.8.)   □

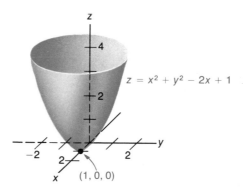

Figure 15.8

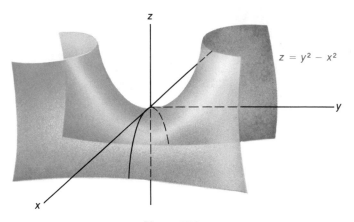

Figure 15.9

EXAMPLE 2   Test $z = y^2 - x^2$ for relative maxima and minima.

Solution   1. $\dfrac{\partial z}{\partial x} = -2x;$ $\dfrac{\partial z}{\partial y} = 2y$

2. $\dfrac{\partial z}{\partial x} = 0$ if $x = 0$.

   $\dfrac{\partial z}{\partial y} = 0$ if $y = 0$.

So both equal 0 if $x = 0$, $y = 0$. The critical point is $(0, 0, 0)$.

3. $\dfrac{\partial^2 z}{\partial x^2} = -2;$ $\dfrac{\partial^2 z}{\partial y^2} = 2$

   $\dfrac{\partial^2 z}{\partial x\, \partial y} = \dfrac{\partial^2 z}{\partial y\, \partial x} = 0$

4. $D = (-2)(2) - 0 = -4$
5. $D < 0$, so the critical point is neither a relative maximum or minimum. As Figure 15.9 shows, the surface formed may have the shape of a saddle. For this reason, critical points that are neither relative maxima or minima are frequently called **saddle points.**   □

As was stated in the test for maxima and minima, if $D = 0$, the test fails. When this happens, we must use the given conditions to determine if a relative maximum or minimum occurs. The following example involves a surface with two critical points.

EXAMPLE 3   Test $z = x^3 + y^3 + 6xy$ for relative maxima and minima.

Solution   1. $\dfrac{\partial z}{\partial x} = 3x^2 + 6y;$ $\dfrac{\partial z}{\partial y} = 3y^2 + 6x$

2. $\dfrac{\partial z}{\partial x} = 0$ if $0 = 3x^2 + 6y$; that is, if $y = -\frac{1}{2}x^2$.

$\dfrac{\partial z}{\partial y} = 0$ if $0 = 3y^2 + 6x$; that is, if $x = -\frac{1}{2}y^2$.

Since *both* conditions must be satisfied, we can substitute $-\frac{1}{2}y^2$ for x in $y = -\frac{1}{2}x^2$, getting

$$y = -\frac{1}{2}\left(-\frac{1}{2}y^2\right)^2,$$

or

$$y = -\frac{1}{8}y^4$$

$$y + \frac{1}{8}y^4 = 0.$$

So $y = 0$ or $y^3 - -8$; therefore $y = 0$ or $y = \quad 2$. If $y = 0, x = -\frac{1}{2}(0)^2 = 0$, so one critical point is $(0, 0, 0)$. If $y = -2, x = -\frac{1}{2}(-2)^2 = -2$, so the second critical point is $(-2, -2, 8)$.

3. $\dfrac{\partial^2 z}{\partial x^2} = 6x$; $\dfrac{\partial^2 z}{\partial y^2} = 6y$

$\dfrac{\partial^2 z}{\partial x\, \partial y} = \dfrac{\partial^2 z}{\partial y\, \partial x} = 6$

4. At $(0, 0)$, $D = 0 \cdot 0 - (6)^2 = -36 < 0$.
   At $(-2, -2)$, $D = (-12)(-12) - 36 = 108 > 0$.

5. At $(0, 0)$, $D < 0$, so a saddle point occurs at $(0, 0, 0)$. At $(-2, -2)$, $D > 0$, $\partial^2 z/\partial x^2 = 6(-2) = -12$, and $\partial^2 z/\partial y^2 = 6(-2) = -12$, so a relative maximum occurs at $(-2, -2, 8)$. □

EXAMPLE 4   Maximize the profit if the demand functions for products X and Y are $p_1 = 50 - x$ and $p_2 = 60 - 2y$, and if the joint cost function for the products is $C = 2xy$.

Solution   The profit function is $P = p_1 x + p_2 y - C$, so

$$P = (50 - x)x + (60 - 2y)y - 2xy,$$

or

$$P = 50x - x^2 + 60y - 2y^2 - 2xy.$$

To maximize P, we proceed as follows.

$$P_x = 50 - 2x - 2y \quad \text{and} \quad P_y = 60 - 4y - 2x.$$

Solving simultaneously $P_x = 0$ and $P_y = 0$, we have

$$\begin{cases} 0 = 50 - 2x - 2y \\ 0 = 60 - 2x - 4y \end{cases}$$

or $-10 + 2y = 0$, so $y = 5$. Thus $0 = 40 - 2x$, so $x = 20$. Now $P_{xx} = -2$,

$P_{yy} = -4$, and $P_{xy} = -2$, and

$$D = (P_{xx})(P_{yy}) - (P_{xy})^2 = (-2)(-4) - (-2)^2 = +4.$$

Since $P_{xx} < 0$, $P_{yy} < 0$ and $D > 0$, the values $x = 20$ and $y = 5$ yield maximum profit. Therefore, when $x = 20$ and $y = 5$, $p_1 = 30$, $p_2 = 50$ and

$$P = 600 + 250 - 200 = 650. \qquad \Box$$

Exercise 15.5

In the following problems, test for relative maxima and minima.

1. $z = 9 - x^2 - y^2$
2. $z = 16 - 4x^2 - 9y^2$
3. $z = x^2 + y^2 + 4$
4. $z = x^2 + y^2 - 4$
5. $z = x^2 + y^2 - 2x + 4y + 5$
6. $z = 4x^2 + y^2 + 4x + 1$
7. $z = x^2 + 6xy + y^2 + 16x$
8. $z = x^2 - 4xy + y^2 - 6y$

9. $z = \dfrac{x^2 - y^2}{9}$
10. $z = \dfrac{y^2}{4} - \dfrac{x^2}{9}$

11. $z = x^3 + y^3 - 6xy$
12. $z = x^3 + y^3 + 3xy$

APPLICATIONS

13. Suppose the profit from the sale of Kisses and Kreams is given by

$$P(x, y) = 100x + 64y - 0.01x^2 - 0.25y^2,$$

where x is the number of pounds of Kisses and y is the number of pounds of Kreams. Selling how many pounds of Kisses and Kreams will maximize profit?

14. The profit from the sales of two goods is given by

$$P(x, y) = 20x + 70y - x^2 - y^2,$$

where x is the number of units of good 1 sold and y is the number of units of good 2. Selling how much of each good will maximize profit?

15. A new food is designed to add weight to mature beef cattle. The increase in weight is given by $W = xy(20 - x - 2y)$, where x is the number of units of the first ingredient and y is the number of units of the second ingredient. How many units of each ingredient will maximize the weight gain?

16. The profit for a grain crop is related to fertilizer and labor. If the profit per acre is

$$P = 100x + 40y - 5x^2 - 2y^2$$

where x is the number of units of fertilizer and y is the number of work-hours, what values of x and y will maximize the profit?

17. Suppose $P = 3.78x^2 + 1.5y^2 - 0.09x^3 - 0.01y^3$ is the production function for a good with x units of one input and y units of a second input. Find the values of x and y that will maximize production.

18. Suppose x units of one input and y units of a second input results in

$$P = 40x + 50y - x^2 - y^2 - xy$$

units of a product. Determine the inputs x and y that will maximize P.

19. Suppose a manufacturer produces two brands of a product, brand 1 and brand 2. If the demand for brand 1 is given by $p_1 = 10 - x$ and for brand 2 by $p_2 = 40 - 2y$, and the joint cost function is $C = xy$, how many of each brand should be produced to maximize profit?

15.6 Maxima and Minima of Functions Subject to Constraints; Lagrange Multipliers

Objective

■ To find the maximum or minimum value of a function of two or more variables subject to a condition that constrains the variables

Many practical problems require that a function of two or more variables be maximized or minimized subject to certain conditions, or constraints, that limit the variables involved. For example, a firm will want to maximize its profits within the limits (constraints) imposed by its production capacity. Similarly, a city planner may want to locate a new building to maximize access to public transportation, yet may be constrained by the availability and cost of building sites.

We can obtain maxima and minima for a function $z = f(x, y)$ subject to the constraint $g(x, y) = 0$ by using the method of **Lagrange multipliers,** named for the famous eighteenth century mathematician Joseph Louis Lagrange. Lagrange multipliers can be used with functions of two or more variables when the constraints are given by an equation.

To find the critical values of a function $f(x, y)$ subject to the constraint $g(x, y) = 0$ we will use the new variable λ to form the objective function

$$F(x, y, \lambda) = f(x, y) + \lambda g(x, y).$$

It can be shown that the critical values of $F(x, y, \lambda)$ will satisfy the constraint $g(x, y)$ and will also be critical points of $f(x, y)$. Thus we need only find the critical points of $F(x, y, \lambda)$ to find the required critical points.

To find the critical points of $F(x, y, \lambda)$, we must find the points that make all the partial derivatives equal to 0. That is, the points must satisfy $\partial F/\partial x = 0$, $\partial F/\partial y = 0$, and $\partial F/\partial \lambda = 0$. Because $F(x, y, \lambda) = f(x, y) + \lambda g(x, y)$, these equations may be written as

$$\frac{\partial f}{\partial x} + \lambda \frac{\partial g}{\partial x} = 0$$

$$\frac{\partial f}{\partial y} + \lambda \frac{\partial g}{\partial y} = 0$$

$$g(x, y) = 0$$

Finding the values of x and y that satisfy these three equations simultaneously gives the critical values.

This method will not tell us if the critical points correspond to maxima or minima, but this can either be determined from the physical setting for the problem or by testing according to a procedure similar to that used for unconstrained maxima and minima. The following examples will illustrate the use of Lagrange multipliers.

EXAMPLE 1   Find the maximum value of $z = x^2 y$ subject to the condition $x + y = 9$.

Solution   The function to be maximized is $f(x, y) = x^2 y$.

The constraint is $g(x, y) = 0$, where $g(x, y) = x + y - 9$.

The objective function is

$$F(x, y, \lambda) = f(x, y) + \lambda g(x, y),$$

or

$$F(x, y, \lambda) = x^2 y + \lambda(x + y - 9)$$

Thus

$$\frac{\partial F}{\partial x} = 2xy + \lambda(1) = 0, \quad \text{or} \quad 2xy + \lambda = 0$$

$$\frac{\partial F}{\partial y} = x^2 + \lambda(1) = 0, \quad \text{or} \quad x^2 + \lambda = 0$$

$$\frac{\partial F}{\partial \lambda} = 0 + 1(x + y - 9) = 0, \quad \text{or} \quad x + y - 9 = 0.$$

Solving the first two equations for λ and substituting gives

$$\lambda = -2xy$$
$$\lambda = -x^2$$
$$2xy = x^2$$
$$2xy - x^2 = 0$$
$$x(2y - x) = 0.$$

So

$$x = 0 \quad \text{or} \quad x = 2y.$$

Now, $x = 0$ could not make $z = x^2 y$ a maximum, so we substitute $x = 2y$ into $x + y - 9 = 0$.

$$2y + y = 9$$
$$y = 3$$
$$x = 6$$

Thus the function $z = x^2 y$ is maximized at 108 when $x = 6$, $y = 3$, if the constraint is that $x + y = 9$. Testing values near $x = 6$, $y = 3$, and satisfying the constraint shows the function is maximized there. (Try $x = 5.5$, $y = 3.5$, $x = 7$, $y = 2$, and so on.)   □

EXAMPLE 2   Find the relative minimum of $z = x^3 + y^3 + xy$ subject to the constraint $x + y - 4 = 0$.

Solution   The function to be maximized or minimized is $f(x, y) = x^3 + y^3 + xy$.
The constraint function is $g(x, y) = x + y - 4$.
The objective function is

$$F(x, y, \lambda) = f(x, y) + \lambda g(x, y),$$

or

$$F(x, y, \lambda) = x^3 + y^3 + xy + \lambda(x + y - 4)$$

Then

$$\frac{\partial F}{\partial x} = 3x^2 + y + \lambda = 0$$

$$\frac{\partial F}{\partial y} = 3y^2 + x + \lambda = 0$$

$$\frac{\partial F}{\partial \lambda} - x + y - 4 = 0.$$

Solving the first two equations for λ and substituting gives

$$\lambda = -(3x^2 + y)$$
$$\lambda = -(3y^2 + x)$$
$$3x^2 + y = 3y^2 + x \qquad (1)$$

Solving $x + y - 4 = 0$ for y gives $y = 4 - x$. Substituting into equation (1) for y, we get

$$3x^2 + (4 - x) = 3(4 - x)^2 + x$$
$$3x^2 + 4 - x = 48 - 24x + 3x^2 + x$$
$$22x = 44 \qquad \text{or} \qquad x = 2.$$

Thus when $x + y - 4 = 0$, $x = 2$ and $y = 2$ give the minimum value $z = 20$.

□

EXAMPLE 3   Find the relative maximum of $z = 2xy - 2x^2 - 2y^2$ subject to the constraint $2x + y = 7$.

Solution   The constraint function is $g(x, y) = 2x + y - 7$, so the objective function is

$$F(x, y, \lambda) = 2xy - 2x^2 - 2y^2 + \lambda(2x + y - 7).$$

Then

$$\frac{\partial F}{\partial x} = 2y - 4x + 2\lambda = 0$$

$$\frac{\partial F}{\partial y} = 2x - 4y + \lambda = 0$$

$$\frac{\partial F}{\partial \lambda} = 2x + y - 7 = 0.$$

Solving the first two equations for λ gives

$$\lambda = -y + 2x$$
$$\lambda = -2x + 4y$$
$$-y + 2x = -2x + 4y$$
$$4x = 5y$$
$$x = \frac{5y}{4}.$$

Substituting for x in $2x + y - 7 = 0$ gives $\frac{5}{2}y + y - 7 = 0$, so the critical values are $y = 2$, $x = \frac{5}{2}$. Testing values near $x = \frac{5}{2}$, $y = 2$, shows the function is a relative maximum. $\square$

We can also use Lagrange multipliers to find the maxima and minima of functions of three (or more) variables subject to two (or more) constraints. The method involves using two multipliers, one for each constraint, getting an objective function $F = f + \lambda g_1 + \mu g_2$. We leave further discussion for more advanced courses.

We can easily extend the method to functions of three or more variables, as the following example shows.

EXAMPLE 4   Find the minimum value of $w = x + y^2 + z^2$, subject to the constraint $x + y + z = 1$.

Solution   The function to be maximized is $f(x, y, z) = x + y^2 + z^2$. The constraint is $g(x, y, z) = 0$, where $g(x, y, z) = x + y + z - 1$.

The objective function is

$$F(x, y, z, \lambda) = f(x, y, z) + \lambda g(x, y, z),$$

or

$$F(x, y, z, \lambda) = x + y^2 + z^2 + \lambda(x + y + z - 1).$$

Then

$$\frac{\partial F}{\partial x} = 1 + \lambda = 0$$

$$\frac{\partial F}{\partial y} = 2y + \lambda = 0$$

$$\frac{\partial F}{\partial z} = 2z + \lambda = 0$$

$$\frac{\partial F}{\partial \lambda} = x + y + z - 1 = 0.$$

Solving the first three equations simultaneously gives

$$\lambda = -1$$
$$y = \tfrac{1}{2}$$
$$z = \tfrac{1}{2}.$$

Substituting these values in the fourth equation (which is the constraint), we get $x + \frac{1}{2} + \frac{1}{2} - 1 = 0$, so $x = 0$, $y = \frac{1}{2}$, $z = \frac{1}{2}$. Thus, $w = \frac{1}{2}$. From the nature of the problem, we see that these values give us a minimum. □

EXAMPLE 5   Suppose the utility function for commodities X and Y is given by $U = x^2y^2$, where x and y are the amounts of X and Y, respectively. If p_1 and p_2 represent the prices of X and Y, respectively, and I represents the consumer's income available to purchase these two commodities, the equation $p_1x + p_2y = I$ is called the *budget constraint*. If the price of X is \$2, the price of Y is \$4, and the income available is \$40, find the x and y that maximizes utility.

Solution   The utility function is $U = x^2y^2$ and the budget constraint is $2x + 4y = 40$. The objective function is

$$F(x, y, \lambda) = x^2y^2 + \lambda(2x + 4y - 40).$$

$$\frac{\partial F}{\partial x} = 2xy^2 + 2\lambda, \qquad \frac{\partial F}{\partial y} = 2x^2y + 4\lambda, \qquad \frac{\partial F}{\partial \lambda} = 2x + 4y - 40$$

Setting these partial derivatives equal to 0 and solving gives
$$-\lambda = xy^2 = x^2y/2, \qquad \text{or} \qquad xy^2 - x^2y/2 = 0,$$
so
$$xy(y - x/2) = 0.$$

Thus $x = 2y$, so

$$0 = 4y + 4y - 40.$$

Thus $y = 5$ and $x = 10$.
   Testing values near $x = 10$, $y = 5$ shows these values maximize utility, at $U = 2500$. □

Exercise 15.6

1. Find the minimum value of $z = x^2 + y^2$ subject to the condition $x + y = 6$.
2. Find the minimum value of $z = 4x^2 + y^2$ subject to the constraint $x + y = 5$.
3. Find the minimum value of $z = 3x^2 + 5y^2 - 2xy$ subject to the constraint $x + y = 5$.
4. Find the maximum value of $z = 2xy - 3x^2 - 5y^2$ subject to the constraint $x + y = 5$.
5. Find the maximum value of $z = x^2y$ subject to the constraint $x + y = 6$.
6. Find the maximum value of $z = x^3y^2$ subject to the condition $x + y = 10$.
7. Find the relative maximum of $z = 2xy - 2x^2 - 4y^2$ subject to the condition $x + 2y = 8$.
8. Find the relative minimum of $z = 2x^2 + y^2 - xy$ subject to the constraint $2x + y = 8$.
9. Find the minimum of the function $z = x^2 + y^2$ subject to the condition $2x + y + 1 = 0$.
10. Find the minimum value of $z = x^2 + y^2$ subject to the condition $xy = 1$.
11. Find the minimum value of $w = x^2 + y^2 + z^2$ subject to the constraint $x + y + z = 3$.

12. Find the minimum value of $w = x^2 + y^2 + z^2$, subject to the condition $2x - 4y + z = 21$.

13. Find the maximum value of $w = xz + y$, subject to the constraint $x^2 + y^2 + z^2 = 1$.

14. Find the relative maximum of $w = x^2yz$ subject to $4x + y + z = 4$.

APPLICATIONS

15. Suppose the utility function for two commodities is given by $U = x^2y$ and that the budget constraint is $3x + 6y = 18$. What values of x and y will maximize utility?

16. Suppose the budget constraint in problem 15 is $5x + 20y = 80$. What values of x and y will maximize $U = x^2y$?

17. A firm has two plants, X and Y. Suppose the cost of producing x units at plant X is $x^2 + 1200$ and the cost of producing y units of the same good at plant Y is $3y^2 + 800$. If they have an order for 1200 units, how many should they produce at each plant to fill this order and minimize the cost of production?

18. Suppose the cost of producing x units at plant X is $(3x + 4)x$ and the cost of producing y units of the same good at plant Y is $(2y + 8)y$. If the firm owning the plants has an order for 148 units, how many should it produce at each plant to fill this order and minimize its cost of production?

19. On the basis of past experience a company has determined that its sales revenue is related to its advertising according to the formula

$$s = 20x + y^2 + 4xy,$$

where x is the amount spent in radio advertising and y is the amount spent in television advertising. If the company plans to spend \$30,000 on these two means of advertising, how much should they spend on each method to maximize their sales revenue?

Review Exercises

1. What is the domain of $z = \dfrac{3}{2x - y}$?

2. Evaluate $w = x^2 - 3yz$ at $(2, 3, 1)$.

3. Suppose an indifference curve for two goods, X and Y, has the equation $xy = 1600$. If 80 units of X is purchased, how many units of Y must be purchased?

4. Find $\dfrac{\partial z}{\partial x}$ if $z = 5x^3 + 6xy + y^2$.

5. If $z = e^{xy} + y \ln x$,

    (a) find $\dfrac{\partial z}{\partial x}$.   (b) find $\dfrac{\partial z}{\partial y}$.

6. Find the partial derivative of $f(x, y) = 4x^3 - 5xy^2 + y^3$ with respect to x at the point $(1, 2, -8)$.

7. Find the slope of the tangent in the x-direction to the surface $z = 5x^4 - 3xy^2 + y^2$ at $(1, 2, -3)$.

8. If $z = x^2y - 3xy$, find
   (a) z_{xx} (b) z_{yy} (c) z_{xy} (d) z_{yx}

9. Test $z = 16 - x^2 - 4y^2$ for maxima and minima.

10. Test $z = x^3 + y^3 - 3xy$ for maxima and minima.

11. Find the minimum value of $z = 4x^2 + y^2$ subject to the constraint $x + y = 10$.

12. Find the maximum value of $z = x^4y^2$ subject to the constraint $x + y = 9$.

APPLICATIONS

13. The joint cost function for two products is $C(x, y) = x^2 \sqrt{y^2 + 13}$.
   (a) Find the marginal cost with respect to x if 20 units of x and 6 units of y are produced.

   (b) Find the marginal cost with respect to y if 20 units of x and 6 units of y are produced.

14. The demand functions for two related goods, good A and good B, are given by

$$q_A = 400 - 2p_A - 3p_B$$
$$q_B = 300 - 5p_A - 6p_B.$$

   (a) Find the marginal demand of q_A with respect to p_A.
   (b) Find the marginal demand of q_B with respect to p_B.
   (c) Are the two goods complementary or competitive?

15. The profit from the sale of two goods is given by $P(x, y) = 40x + 80y - x^2 - y^2$, where x is the number of units of good 1 and y is the number of units of good 2. Selling how much of each good will maximize profit?

Appendix

Table I EXPONENTIAL FUNCTIONS

x	e^x	e^{-x}	x	e^x	e^{-x}
0.0	1.000	1.000	3.0	20.09	0.0498
0.1	1.105	0.9048	3.1	22.20	0.0450
0.2	1.221	0.8187	3.2	24.53	0.0408
0.3	1.350	0.7408	3.3	27.11	0.0369
0.4	1.492	0.6703	3.4	29.96	0.0334
0.5	1.649	0.6065	3.5	33.12	0.0302
0.6	1.822	0.5488	3.6	36.60	0.0273
0.7	2.014	0.4966	3.7	40.45	0.0247
0.8	2.226	0.4493	3.8	44.70	0.0224
0.9	2.460	0.4066	3.9	49.40	0.0202
1.0	2.718	0.3679	4.0	54.60	0.0183
1.1	3.004	0.3329	4.1	60.34	0.0166
1.2	3.320	0.3012	4.2	66.69	0.0150
1.3	3.669	0.2725	4.3	73.70	0.0136
1.4	4.055	0.2466	4.4	81.45	0.0123
1.5	4.482	0.2231	4.5	90.02	0.0111
1.6	4.953	0.2019	4.6	99.48	0.0101
1.7	5.474	0.1827	4.7	109.9	0.0091
1.8	6.050	0.1653	4.8	121.5	0.0082
1.9	6.686	0.1496	4.9	134.3	0.0074
2.0	7.389	0.1353	5.0	148.4	0.0067
2.1	8.166	0.1225	5.1	164.0	0.0061
2.2	9.025	0.1108	5.2	181.3	0.0055
2.3	9.974	0.1003	5.3	200.3	0.0050
2.4	11.02	0.0907	5.4	221.4	0.0045
2.5	12.18	0.0821	5.5	244.7	0.0041
2.6	13.46	0.0743	5.6	270.4	0.0037
2.7	14.88	0.0672	5.7	298.9	0.0033
2.8	16.44	0.0608	5.8	330.3	0.0030
2.9	18.17	0.0550	5.9	365.0	0.0027
			6.0	403.4	0.0025
			7.0	1097	0.0009
			8.0	2981	0.0003
			9.0	8103	0.0001

Table II   SELECTED VALUES OF $\log_e x$

x	$\ln x$	x	$\ln x$	x	$\ln x$
.002	−6.215	1.40	0.336	600	6.397
.004	−5.521	1.50	0.405	700	6.551
.010	−4.605	2	0.693	800	6.685
.015	−4.200	3	1.099	900	6.802
.018	−4.017	5	1.609	1000	6.908
.020	−3.912	7	1.946	1300	7.170
.023	−3.772	10	2.303	1600	7.378
.027	−3.612	20	2.996	2000	7.601
.030	−3.507	30	3.401	2300	7.741
.040	−3.219	50	3.912	2600	7.863
.045	−3.101	80	4.382	3000	8.006
.050	−2.996	100	4.605	3500	8.161
.080	−2.526	110	4.700	4000	8.294
.10	−2.303	130	4.868	4600	8.434
.20	−1.609	150	5.011	5100	8.537
.30	−1.204	170	5.136	5700	8.648
.40	−0.916	200	5.298	6300	8.748
.41	−0.892	230	5.438	6900	8.839
.48	−0.734	250	5.521	7500	8.923
.50	−0.693	280	5.635	8100	9.000
.52	−0.654	300	5.704	8700	9.071
.60	−0.511	350	5.858	9300	9.138
.70	−0.357	400	5.991	10000	9.210
.80	−0.223	410	6.016	11000	9.306
.90	−0.105	460	6.131	12000	9.393
1.00	0.0	500	6.215	13000	9.473
1.30	0.262	520	6.254	14000	9.547
1.35	0.300	580	6.363	15000	9.616

Table III   AREAS UNDER THE STANDARD NORMAL CURVE

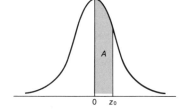

The value of A is the area under the standard normal curve between $z = 0$ and $z = z_0$, for $z_0 \geq 0$. Areas for negative values of z_0 are obtained by symmetry.

z_0	A	z_0	A	z_0	A	z_0	A
.00	.0000	.55	.2088	1.10	.3643	1.65	.4505
.01	.0040	.56	.2123	1.11	.3665	1.66	.4515
.02	.0080	.57	.2157	1.12	.3686	1.67	.4525
.03	.0120	.58	.2190	1.13	.3708	1.68	.4535
.04	.0160	.59	.2224	1.14	.3729	1.69	.4545
.05	.0199	.60	.2258	1.15	.3749	1.70	.4554

Table III (CONTINUED)

z_0	A	z_0	A	z_0	A	z_0	A
.06	.0239	.61	.2291	1.16	.3770	1.71	.4564
.07	.0279	.62	.2324	1.17	.3790	1.72	.4573
.08	.0319	.63	.2357	1.18	.3810	1.73	.4582
.09	.0359	.64	.2389	1.19	.3830	1.74	.4591
.10	.0398	.65	.2422	1.20	.3849	1.75	.4599
.11	.0438	.66	.2454	1.21	.3869	1.76	.4608
.12	.0478	.67	.2486	1.22	.3888	1.77	.4616
.13	.0517	.68	.2518	1.23	.3907	1.78	.4625
.14	.0557	.69	.2549	1.24	.3925	1.79	.4633
.15	.0596	.70	.2580	1.25	.3944	1.80	.4641
.16	.0636	.71	.2612	1.26	.3962	1.81	.4649
.17	.0675	.72	.2642	1.27	.3980	1.82	.4656
.18	.0714	.73	.2673	1.28	.3997	1.83	.4664
.19	.0754	.74	.2704	1.29	.4015	1.84	.4671
.20	.0793	.75	.2734	1.30	.4032	1.85	.4678
.21	.0832	.76	.2764	1.31	.4049	1.86	.4686
.22	.0871	.77	.2794	1.32	.4066	1.87	.4693
.23	.0910	.78	.2823	1.33	.4082	1.88	.4700
.24	.0948	.79	.2852	1.34	.4099	1.89	.4706
.25	.0987	.80	.2881	1.35	.4115	1.90	.4713
.26	.1026	.81	.2910	1.36	.4131	1.91	.4719
.27	.1064	.82	.2939	1.37	.4147	1.92	.4726
.28	.1103	.83	.2967	1.38	.4162	1.93	.4732
.29	.1141	.84	.2996	1.39	.4177	1.94	.4738
.30	.1179	.85	.3023	1.40	.4192	1.95	.4744
.31	.1217	.86	.3051	1.41	.4207	1.96	.4750
.32	.1255	.87	.3079	1.42	.4222	1.97	.4756
.33	.1293	.88	.3106	1.43	.4236	1.98	.4762
.34	.1331	.89	.3133	1.44	.4251	1.99	.4767
.35	.1368	.90	.3159	1.45	.4265	2.00	.4773
.36	.1406	.91	.3186	1.46	.4279	2.01	.4778
.37	.1443	.92	.3212	1.47	.4292	2.02	.4783
.38	.1480	.93	.3238	1.48	.4306	2.03	.4788
.39	.1517	.94	.3264	1.49	.4319	2.04	.4793
.40	.1554	.95	.3289	1.50	.4332	2.05	.4798
.41	.1591	.96	.3315	1.51	.4345	2.06	.4803
.42	.1628	.97	.3340	1.52	.4357	2.07	.4808
.43	.1664	.98	.3365	1.53	.4370	2.08	.4812
.44	.1700	.99	.3389	1.54	.4382	2.09	.4817
.45	.1736	1.00	.3413	1.55	.4394	2.10	.4821
.46	.1772	1.01	.3438	1.56	.4406	2.11	.4826
.47	.1808	1.02	.3461	1.57	.4418	2.12	.4830
.48	.1844	1.03	.3485	1.58	.4430	2.13	.4834
.49	.1879	1.04	.3508	1.59	.4441	2.14	.4838
.50	.1915	1.05	.3531	1.60	.4452	2.15	.4842
.51	.1950	1.06	.3554	1.61	.4463	2.16	.4846
.52	.1985	1.07	.3577	1.62	.4474	2.17	.4850
.53	.2019	1.08	.3599	1.63	.4485	2.18	.4854
.54	.2054	1.09	.3621	1.64	.4495	2.19	.4857

Table III (CONTINUED)

z_0	A	z_0	A	z_0	A	z_0	A
2.20	.4861	2.63	.4957	3.06	.4989	3.49	.4998
2.21	.4865	2.64	.4959	3.07	.4989	3.50	.4998
2.22	.4868	2.65	.4960	3.08	.4990	3.51	.4998
2.23	.4871	2.66	.4961	3.09	.4990	3.52	.4998
2.24	.4875	2.67	.4962	3.10	.4990	3.53	.4998
2.25	.4878	2.68	.4963	3.11	.4991	3.54	.4998
2.26	.4881	2.69	.4964	3.12	.4991	3.55	.4998
2.27	.4884	2.70	.4965	3.13	.4991	3.56	.4998
2.28	.4887	2.71	.4966	3.14	.4992	3.57	.4998
2.29	.4890	2.72	.4967	3.15	.4992	3.58	.4998
2.30	.4893	2.73	.4968	3.16	.4992	3.59	.4998
2.31	.4896	2.74	.4969	3.17	.4992	3.60	.4998
2.32	.4898	2.75	.4970	3.18	.4993	3.61	.4999
2.33	.4901	2.76	.4971	3.19	.4993	3.62	.4999
2.34	.4904	2.77	.4972	3.20	.4993	3.63	.4999
2.35	.4906	2.78	.4973	3.21	.4993	3.64	.4999
2.36	.4909	2.79	.4974	3.22	.4994	3.65	.4999
2.37	.4911	2.80	.4974	3.23	.4994	3.66	.4999
2.38	.4913	2.81	.4975	3.24	.4994	3.67	.4999
2.39	.4916	2.82	.4976	3.25	.4994	3.68	.4999
2.40	.4918	2.83	.4977	3.26	.4994	3.69	.4999
2.41	.4920	2.84	.4977	3.27	.4995	3.70	.4999
2.42	.4922	2.85	.4978	3.28	.4995	3.71	.4999
2.43	.4925	2.86	.4979	3.29	.4995	3.72	.4999
2.44	.4927	2.87	.4980	3.30	.4995	3.73	.4999
2.45	.4929	2.88	.4980	3.31	.4995	3.74	.4999
2.46	.4931	2.89	.4981	3.32	.4996	3.75	.4999
2.47	.4932	2.90	.4981	3.33	.4996	3.76	.4999
2.48	.4934	2.91	.4982	3.34	.4996	3.77	.4999
2.49	.4936	2.92	.4983	3.35	.4996	3.78	.4999
2.50	.4938	2.93	.4983	3.36	.4996	3.79	.4999
2.51	.4940	2.94	.4984	3.37	.4996	3.80	.4999
2.52	.4941	2.95	.4984	3.38	.4996	3.81	.4999
2.53	.4943	2.96	.4985	3.39	.4997	3.82	.4999
2.54	.4945	2.97	.4985	3.40	.4997	3.83	.4999
2.55	.4946	2.98	.4986	3.41	.4997	3.84	.4999
2.56	.4948	2.99	.4986	3.42	.4997	3.85	.4999
2.57	.4949	3.00	.4987	3.43	.4997	3.86	.4999
2.58	.4951	3.01	.4987	3.44	.4997	3.87	.5000
2.59	.4952	3.02	.4987	3.45	.4997	3.88	.5000
2.60	.4953	3.03	.4988	3.46	.4997	3.89	.5000
2.61	.4955	3.04	.4988	3.47	.4997		
2.62	.4956	3.05	.4989	3.48	.4998		

Answers to Selected Exercises

Exercise 0.1

1. $\in$ 2. $\notin$ 3. $\in$ 4. $\notin$ 5. Yes   6. No   7. No   8. No

9. (number line -6 to 10)   10. (number line -1 to 2)

11. $\sqrt{16} < 5$ 12. $-\sqrt{15} < -3$ 13. $\frac{3}{4} < \frac{5}{6}$ 14. $-3 + \sqrt{4} > -5$ 15. $-4 < -3$
16. $\pi > 3$ 17. 6 18. 5 19. -13 20. 3 21. -16 22. 0 23. 13 24. 5
25. -17 26. 1 27. 60 28. -36 29. 22 30. -4

Exercise 0.2

1. 2^4 2. x^2y^2 3. $1/2^3$ 4. $1/x^4$ 5. x/y^2 6. 1 7. x^7 8. a^6 9. x^{-2}
10. $y^{-27/5}$ 11. 2^7 12. a^3x^2 13. x^4 14. a^6 15. $1/y^2 = y^{-2}$ 16. y 17. x^2
18. $y^{-2} - 1/y^2$ 19. $x^{2/3}y^{2/3}$ 20. $8m^3$ 21. $16x^8y^4$ 22. $16/x^4$ 23. x^{10}/y^{15}
24. 4 25. $-2x$ 26. 125 27. -3, real   28. -9, real   29. Not real
30. $\sqrt{15}$, real   31. $1/9x^2$ 32. $3/64x^3$ 33. $1/8x^6y^3$ 34. $-6/my^2$ 35. $2/xy$
36. x^6y^3 37. $1/(2a)^{1/3}$ 38. $y^{3/4}$ 39. $(2x + 1)^2 - 1 = 4x^2 + 4x$
40. $(4x - 3) + 3 = 4x$ 41. $4x^{1/2} + 5x^{-3}$ 42. $2x^{-1} - \frac{1}{3}x^{1/3} + 1$ 43. $4x^{2/3} + \frac{2}{3}x^{-4}$
44. $\frac{4}{5}x^{-2} + \frac{7}{3}x^{-4/5}$ 45. $(x/y)^{-n} = x^{-n}/y^{-n} = y^n/x^n$

Exercise 0.3

1. $11x^2 + 19x - 6$ 2. $21pq - 2p^2$ 3. $7x^2y^2 - 4x^3$ 4. $m^2 - 7n^2 - 3$ 5. $a + 8b - c$
6. $35x^5$ 7. $-24x^5y^6$ 8. $3rs$ 9. $-3m^2/n^3$ 10. $2m^2x^3$ 11. $-5y^2$ 12. $9 + q$
13. $6x$ 14. $-12x - 4y$ 15. $2x + 2y$ 16. $2ax^4 + a^2x^3 + a^2bx^2$ 17. $6y^2 - y - 12$
18. $4x^2 - 13x + 3$ 19. $x^3 + 3x^2 + 6x + 4$ 20. $a^3 - 5a^2b + 7ab^2 - 2b^3$
21. $3 + m + 2m^2n$ 22. $(4x/y) + y + (2/y)$ 23. $3x^2 + 4x + 5$ 24. $a^2 + a + 4$
25. $x^2 - 3 + 4/(2x + 1)$

Exercise 0.4

1. $3b(3a - 4a^2 + 6b)$ 2. $4(2a^2b - 40x + bx^2)$ 3. $2x(2x + 4y^2 + y^3)$
4. $4yz(3y^2 + z - 2yz^2)$ 5. $(y - 4)(5 - x^2)$ 6. $(x + 5)(x - 3)$ 7. $(6 + y)(x - m)$
8. $(x + 4)^2$ 9. $(x + 4)^2$ 10. $(x + 4)(x + 2)$ 11. $(7x + 4)(x - 2)$ 12. $(3x + 2)(4x + 1)$
13. $(x - 5)^2$ 14. $(2y + 3)^2$ 15. $(5x + 2)(2x + 3)$ 16. $(2x - 1)(3x + 35)$
17. $(2x - 9)(5x - 1)$ 18. $3(x^2 + 2x + 3)$ 19. $3(2b - 1)^2$ 20. $x(x + 8)^2$ 21. $(2x + 3)^2$
22. $(x - y)^2$ 23. $2(x - 2)^2$ 24. $(x - 5y)^2$ 25. $7(3x + 2)(3x - 2)$ 26. $4(5x + 4)(5x - 4)$
27. $(7a + 12b)(7a - 12b)$ 28. $(4x - 5y)(4x + 5y)$ 29. $(x^2 + 3)^2$ 30. $(p^2 + q)(p^2 - q)$
31. $(y - 2x)(y + 2x)(y^2 + 4x^2)$ 32. $(x^3 + y^2)(x^3 - y^2)$

Exercise 0.5

1. $2y^3/z$ 3. $\frac{1}{3}$ 5. $(x - 1)/(x - 3)$ 7. $20x/y$ 9. $\frac{32}{3}$ 11. 12
13. $(16a + 15a^2)/12(x + 2)$ 15. $(2x^2 - 11x - 3)/(x - 5)(x - 4)(x - 1)$
17. $(85x - 39)/30(x - 2)$

Exercise 1.1

1. Conditional   2. Conditional   3. Conditional   4. Conditional   5. Conditional
6. Conditional   7. Identity   8. Identity   9. Identity   10. Conditional
11. Conditional   12. Conditional   13. Identity   14. Identity   15. True   16. False
17. False   18. True   19. True   20. False

21.

x	y
-2	-9
-1	-5
0	-1
1	3
2	7
3	11
4	15

22.

x	y
-2	-4
-1	-1
0	2
1	5
2	8
3	11

23.

x	y
-1	7
0	6
1	5
2	4
3	3
4	2
5	1
6	0
7	-1
8	-2

24.

x	y
-1	8
0	7
1	6
2	5
3	4
4	3
5	2
6	1
7	0
8	-1

25.

x	y
-2	-12
-1	-7
0	-2
1	3
2	8
3	13

26.

x	y
-2	-1
-1	2
0	5
1	8
2	11
3	14

27.

x	y
-2	-12
-1	-9
0	-6
1	-3
2	0
3	3
4	6

28.

x	y
-2	-20
-1	-15
0	-10
1	-5
2	0
3	5

29.

x	y
-3	-6
-2	$-\frac{16}{3}$
-1	$-\frac{14}{3}$
0	-4
1	$-\frac{10}{3}$
2	$-\frac{8}{3}$
3	-2

30.

x	y
-2	6
-1	$\frac{9}{2}$
0	3
1	$\frac{3}{2}$
2	0
3	$-\frac{3}{2}$

31. $y = 4x$

x	y
-2	-8
-1	-4
0	0
1	4
2	8

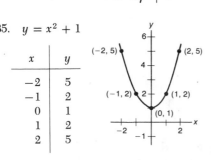

33. $y = 6x + 1$

x	y
-2	-11
-1	-5
0	1
1	7
2	13

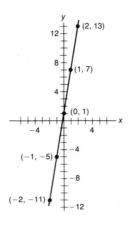

35. $y = x^2 + 1$

x	y
-2	5
-1	2
0	1
1	2
2	5

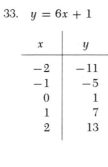

37. $y = x^3 + 1$

x	y
-2	-7
-1	0
0	1
1	2
2	9

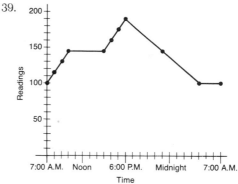

39.

Exercise 1.2

1. Yes   2. Yes   3. No   4. No   5. Yes   6. Yes   7. No   8. Yes   9. All reals
10. All reals   11. All reals except $x = 0$ 12. All reals except $x = 0$
13. All reals except $x = 4$ 14. All reals except $x = -3$ 15. D: all reals; R: $y > 4$
16. D: all reals; R: $y \geq -1$ 17. D: $x \geq 1$; R: $y \geq 0$ 18. D: all reals; R: all reals
19. D: all reals; R: $y \geq 1$ 20. D: $x > 2$ or $x \leq -2$; R: $y \geq 0$ 21. (a) Yes   (b) $v \geq -\frac{1}{4}$
(c) $v \geq 0$ 22. (a) Yes   (b) All reals except $t = -2$ (c) $t \geq 0$ 23. (a) Yes   (b) No

Exercise 1.3

1. (a) -10 (b) 6 (c) -34 (d) $8a - 10$ 2. (a) -3 (b) -11 (c) 17
(d) $1 + 4b$ 3. (a) -3 (b) 1 (c) 13 (d) $4x^2 - 3$ 4. (a) 21 (b) 33 (c) 8
(d) $3x^2 + 2x$ 5. (a) -2 (b) -5 (c) 0 6. (a) -1 (b) -9 (c) -4
(d) $x^3 + 3x^2h + 3xh^2 + h^3 - 8x - 8h - 1$ 7. (a) $x^2 + 2xh + h^2 - 3x - 3h$ (b) $2x + h - 3$
8. (a) Yes   (b) Yes   (c) No   (d) No   9. (a) $f(1) = 0.2533\ldots$ (b) $f(3) = 0.056$
11. (a) $P(100) = 1$ (b) $P(50) = 2$ (c) $P(10) = 10$ (d) Pressure increases
(e) Pressure decreases   13. (a) $N(2) = 48\frac{2}{3}$ (b) $N(10) = 248\frac{2}{51}$

Exercise 1.4

1. Yes   3. No   5. 2   7. 0   9. (a) $b = a^2 - 4a$ (b) $(1, -3)$, yes
(c) $(3, -3)$, yes   (d) 0, 4; yes

11.

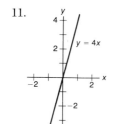

13.

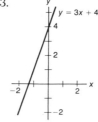

15.

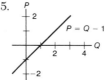

17.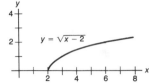

$y = \sqrt{x-2}$

19.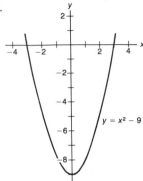

$y = x^2 - 9$

21.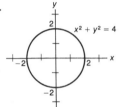

$x^2 + y^2 = 4$

23.

$3x^2 + y^2 = 3$

25.

$y = \sqrt{4t}$

Exercise 1.5

1. (a) $3 billion
   (b) $7.2 billion

   (c)

   $C = 3 + 0.7y$

3. (a) $5.6 billion
   (b) $14.6 billion

   (c)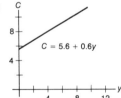

   $C = 5.6 + 0.6y$

5.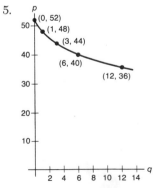

(0, 52)
(1, 48)
(3, 44)
(6, 40)
(12, 36)

7. (a)

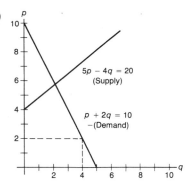

(c) $p = 2$, 4 units demanded, none supplied; therefore shortage

9. (a) $C(x) = 17x + 3400$ (b) $C(200) = \$6800$ 11. (a) $R(x) = 34x$ (b) $R(300) = \$10{,}200$
(c) $P(x) = 17x - 3400$ (d) $P(300) = \$1700$ (e) $x = 200$

Chapter 1 Review Exercises

1. Yes 2.

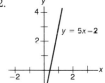

3.

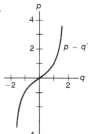

4. Yes 5. No 6. $-3 \leq x \leq 3$ 7. (a) $f(-3) = 2$ (b) $f(-x) = x^2 - 4x + 5$
8. $b = a^2 - 3a$

9.

10. (a) \$2 billion (c)
(b) \$6 billion

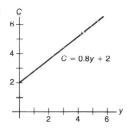

11. $q = 10$ 12. $p = \$475$ 13. (a) $R(x) = 4x$ (b) $C(x) = 2x + 500$ (c) $P(x) = 2x - 500$
14. $R(100) = 400$ 15. $C(100) = 700$

Exercise 2.1

1. $x = 9$ 3. $y = 10$ 5. $x = 4$ 7. $z = -1$ 9. $x = 5$ 11. $x = -\frac{5}{4}$ 13. $x = \frac{9}{2}$
15. $x = -\frac{5}{2}$ 17. $x = -6$ 19. $x = 5$ 21. $x = 40$ 23. $x = 1.7$ 25. \$31.88
27. \$85,000 29. $-40°$ 31. (a) 3333 approx (b) 15,873 33. \$246

Exercise 2.2

1.
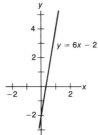
$y = 6x - 2$

3.
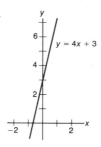
$y = 4x + 3$

5.
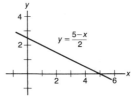
$y = \dfrac{5-x}{2}$

7.
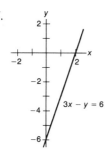
$3x - y = 6$

9.
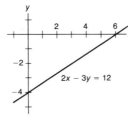
$2x - 3y = 12$

11.
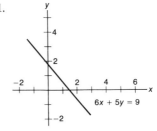
$6x + 5y = 9$

13.
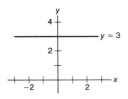
$y = 3$

15.
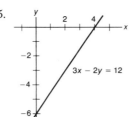
$3x - 2y = 12$

17.
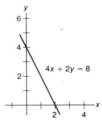
$4x + 2y = 8$

19.
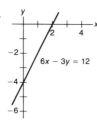
$6x - 3y = 12$

21.   See problem 19.
$$6x - 3y = 12$$
is equivalent to
$$2x - y = 4$$

23.   (a)
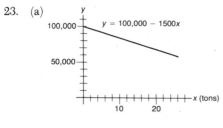
$y = 100,000 - 1500x$

(b)   73,750

25.
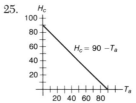
$H_c = 90 - T_a$

Exercise 2.3

1. $m = 2$ 3. $m = 3$ 5. $m = -5$ 7. $m = 2$ 9. $m = \frac{1}{13}$ 11. $m = 4, b = -6$
13. $m = \frac{1}{4}, b = 0$ 15. $m = 0, b = 3$ 17. $m = -\frac{1}{2}, b = -\frac{2}{3}$ 19. No slope, no y-intercept
(m undefined)   21. $m = 2, b = -3$ 23. $m = -\frac{2}{3}, b = 2$ 25. $\overline{MC} = 6$
27. (a) $R(x) = 84x$ (b) $\overline{MR} = 84$ 29. (a) $P(x) = 5x - 400$ (b) $\overline{MP} = 5$
31. (a) $m = 5, b = 250$ (b) $\overline{MC} = 5 = $ cost of producing each additional unit   (c) $FC = 250$
(d) Slope = marginal cost; C-intercept = fixed costs   (e) $5, $5   33. (a) 27
(b) $\overline{MR} = 27 = $ revenue received from the sale of one more item   (c) $27, $27   35. 0; they are
the same because if nothing is sold, no revenue is generated. Yes. This is the theoretical setting from
which revenue functions are formulated.   37. (a) $P(x) = 22x - 250$ (b) $m = 22$
(c) $\overline{MP} = 22$ (d) The profit from the sale of each additional item is $22, so produce and sell as
much as possible.

Exercise 2.4

1. $y = 3x - 2$

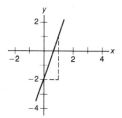

3. $y = \frac{1}{2}x + 3$

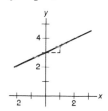

5. $y = -2x + \frac{1}{2}$

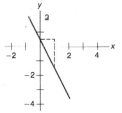

7. $y = -4$

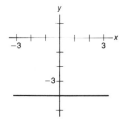

9. $y = \frac{1}{2}x - 1$

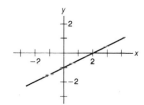

11. $y = -2x + 1$

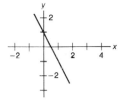

13. $y = -2x + 6$

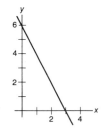

15. $y = 1$

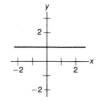

17.

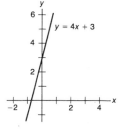

$y = 4x + 3$

19. $y = 2x - 4$ 21. $-x + 13y = 32$ 23. $y = 2$ 25. $C(x) = 27x + 3000$

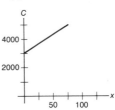

27. $P(x) = 10x - 6000$ 29. $n = 280\,\ell - 8000$ 31. $y = -\frac{1}{4}x + \frac{25}{2}$.

Exercise 2.5

1. $x = 1, y = 1$ 3. $x = 2, y = 2$ 5.   No solution   7. $x = 2, y = 5$ 9. $x = \frac{14}{11}, y = \frac{6}{11}$
11. $x = \frac{10}{3}, y = 2$ 13. $x = \frac{5}{2}, y = -\frac{3}{4}$ 15. $u = \frac{27}{11}, v = \frac{13}{11}$ 17. $x = -\frac{52}{7}, y = -\frac{128}{7}$
19.   Dependent   21. $x = 1, y = 7$ 23.   \$13,500 @ 5%; \$10,000 @ 6%
25.   A = 4 oz, B = $6\frac{2}{3}$ oz   27.   A = 4550, B = 1500   29.   Devel. = \$20,497.49,
promo. = \$12,049.75

Exercise 2.6

1.   (a) $C(y) = 0.6y + 8$ (b)   0.6   (c)   \$26 billion   3. $C(y) = 0.8y + 7$

5.

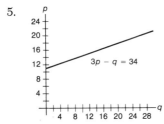

7. $q = 10, p = \$120$ 9. $q = 100, p = \$325$ 11. $x = 500$ units   13. $P(x) = 20x - 10,000$
15. $x = 22,000$ units

Chapter 2 Review Exercises

1. $x = 7$ 2. $x = \frac{31}{3}$ 3. $x = -13$ 4. $x = 1$ 5. $x = -\frac{1}{9}$ 6. $x = 10.05$

7.

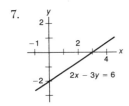

8.

9.

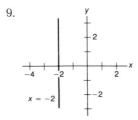

10. $m = -\frac{2}{5}, b = 2$ 11. $2y - x = 1$ 12. $y = -2x$ 13. $3x + 4y = 5$
14. $x = 2, y = 1$ 15. $x = 3, y = -2$ 16. (a) \$240   (b) 30   17. (a) \$4 billion
(b) \$8.8 billion   (c) $C(y) = 4 + 0.6y$

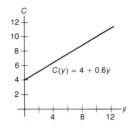

18. (a) $C(x) = 22x + 1500$ (b) $R(x) = 52x$ (c) $P(x) = 30x - 1500$ (d) $\overline{MC} = 22$
(e) $\overline{MR} = 52$ (f) $\overline{MP} = 30$ (g) $x = 50$ 19. $q = 300, p = \$150$

Exercise 3.1

1. A, C, D, F 3. No   5. $\begin{bmatrix} 9 & 5 \\ 1 & 7 \end{bmatrix}$ 7. $\begin{bmatrix} 0 & -2 & -1 \\ 4 & 2 & 0 \\ 2 & 3 & 7 \end{bmatrix}$ 9. 80   11. 86

13. $\begin{bmatrix} 80 & 75 \\ 58 & 106 \end{bmatrix}$ 15. A 17. $D = \begin{bmatrix} 10 & 4 \\ 7 & 2 \end{bmatrix}$

19. $\begin{array}{c} \\ \text{I} \\ \text{II} \\ \text{III} \end{array} \begin{array}{cc} \text{wt} & \ell \\ \begin{bmatrix} 140 & 5.5 \\ 151 & 5.7 \\ 141 & 5.5 \end{bmatrix} \end{array}$ or $\begin{array}{c} \\ \text{wt} \\ \ell \end{array} \begin{array}{ccc} \text{I} & \text{II} & \text{III} \\ \begin{bmatrix} 140 & 151 & 141 \\ 5.5 & 5.7 & 5.5 \end{bmatrix} \end{array}$

21. $\begin{bmatrix} 110 & 7 \\ 64 & 6.1 \\ 49 & 4.3 \end{bmatrix}$ or $\begin{bmatrix} 110 & 64 & 49 \\ 7 & 6.1 & 4.3 \end{bmatrix}$

Exercise 3.2

1. No   3. $\begin{bmatrix} 3 & 0 & 6 \\ 9 & 6 & 3 \\ 12 & 0 & 9 \end{bmatrix}$ 5. $\begin{bmatrix} 28 & 16 \\ 10 & 18 \end{bmatrix}$ 7. $\begin{bmatrix} 7 & 5 & 3 & 2 \\ 14 & 9 & 11 & 3 \\ 13 & 10 & 12 & 3 \end{bmatrix}$ 9. Impossible

11. $\begin{bmatrix} 29 & 25 \\ 10 & 12 \end{bmatrix}$ 13. No   15. $\begin{bmatrix} 13 & 9 & 3 & 4 \\ 9 & 7 & 16 & 1 \end{bmatrix}$ 17. $\begin{bmatrix} 17 & 0 & 14 \\ 8 & 2 & 11 \end{bmatrix}$

19. (a) $\begin{bmatrix} 13,500 & 12,400 \\ 10,500 & 10,600 \end{bmatrix}$ (b) A—from Kink; B—from Ace

21. (a) $\begin{bmatrix} 5 \\ 3 \\ 4 \\ 4 \end{bmatrix}$ (b) $[\$1,030,000]$ 23. (a) $\begin{bmatrix} 2.5 & 50 \\ 0.826 & 15.05 \\ 0 & 0 \end{bmatrix}$ (b) $\begin{bmatrix} 15 & 300 \\ 12.63 & 230.05 \\ 9.8 & 190 \end{bmatrix}$

Exercise 3.3

1. $\begin{bmatrix} 3 & 2 & 4 & | & 0 \\ 2 & -1 & 2 & | & 0 \\ 1 & -2 & -4 & | & 0 \end{bmatrix}$ 3. $\begin{bmatrix} 1 & -3 & 4 & | & 2 \\ 2 & 0 & 2 & | & 1 \\ 1 & 2 & 1 & | & 1 \end{bmatrix}$ 5. $\left. \begin{array}{l} x = 0 \\ y = -z \end{array} \right\} z = \text{free choice}$

7. $x = 1, y = -1, z = 1$ 9. $x = 1, y = 2, z = 2$ 11. $x = \frac{5}{7} + \frac{4}{7}z; y = \frac{3}{7} - \frac{6}{7}z$
13. No solution   15. $x_1 = 1, x_2 = 0, x_3 = 1, x_4 = 0$ 17. $13,500 @ 5\%, $10,000 @ 6\%$
19. $x_1 = 254, x_2 = 385, x_3 = 19$ 21. $x_1 = 3, x_2 = 2, x_3 = 1$ 23. Shipping $= $13,222.45$;
printing $= $12,224.49$ 25. A: $200 + x_4 = 100 + x_1$; B: $300 + x_1 = 200 + x_2$;
C: $200 + x_2 = 100 + x_3$; D: $500 + x_3 = 800 + x_4$ 26. $x_1 = 100 + x_4, x_2 = 200 + x_4, x_3 = 300 + x_4$
27. x_4 restricted to $0 \le x_4 \le 900$ and others accordingly

Exercise 3.4

1. Yes   3. $\begin{bmatrix} \frac{1}{3} & 0 & 0 \\ 0 & \frac{1}{3} & 0 \\ 0 & 0 & \frac{1}{3} \end{bmatrix}$ 5. $\begin{bmatrix} -1 & 1 & 0 \\ 1 & 0 & 0 \\ -1 & 0 & 1 \end{bmatrix}$ 7. $\begin{bmatrix} \frac{1}{3} & -\frac{1}{3} & \frac{1}{3} \\ -\frac{2}{3} & -\frac{1}{3} & \frac{7}{3} \\ \frac{1}{3} & \frac{2}{3} & -\frac{5}{3} \end{bmatrix}$ 9. $\begin{bmatrix} x \\ y \\ z \end{bmatrix} = \begin{bmatrix} 1 \\ 1 \\ 2 \end{bmatrix}$

11. $x = 2, y = 1$ 13. $x = 1, y = 1, z = 1$

Exercise 3.5

1. (a) 8, 8   (b) 40, 8   (c) Most—raw materials; least—fuels   (d) Agriculture
(e) Raw materials, manufacturing, service   3. Farm products $= 200$, Machinery $= 40$
5. Products $= \frac{7}{17}$ Households, Machinery $= \frac{1}{17}$ Households

7. $\begin{bmatrix} 24 \\ 96 \\ 24 \\ 120 \\ 492 \\ 3456 \end{bmatrix}$

Chapter 3 Review Exercises

1. $\begin{bmatrix} 6 & -1 & -9 & 3 \\ 10 & 3 & -1 & 4 \\ -2 & -2 & -2 & 14 \end{bmatrix}$ 2. $\begin{bmatrix} 3 & -3 \\ 4 & -1 \\ -2 & -6 \\ 1 & -2 \end{bmatrix}$ 3. $\begin{bmatrix} 8 & 8 & 4 & -10 \\ 12 & 6 & -2 & 0 \\ 0 & 0 & -6 & 10 \end{bmatrix}$ 4. $\begin{bmatrix} 12 & -6 \\ 15 & 0 \\ 18 & 0 \\ 3 & 9 \end{bmatrix}$

5. $\begin{bmatrix} 4 & 0 \\ 0 & 4 \end{bmatrix}$ 6. $\begin{bmatrix} 2 & -12 \\ -8 & -22 \end{bmatrix}$ 7. $\begin{bmatrix} 2 & 5 \\ 1 & 1 \end{bmatrix}$ 8. $\begin{bmatrix} 5 & 16 \\ 6 & 15 \end{bmatrix}$

9. $\begin{bmatrix} 2 & 37 & 61 & -55 \\ -2 & 9 & -3 & -20 \\ 10 & 10 & -14 & -30 \end{bmatrix}$ 10. $\begin{bmatrix} 43 & -23 \\ 33 & -12 \\ -13 & 15 \end{bmatrix}$ 11. $\begin{bmatrix} 10 & 16 \\ 15 & 25 \\ 18 & 30 \\ 6 & 11 \end{bmatrix}$ 12. Impossible

13. $\begin{bmatrix} 3 & 7 \\ 23 & 42 \end{bmatrix}$ 14. F   15. F   16. $\begin{bmatrix} 1 & 0 \\ 0 & 1 \end{bmatrix}$ 17. F   18. Yes

19. $x = -\frac{3}{2}, y = 7, z = -\frac{11}{2}$ 20. $x = 2 - 2z; y = -1 - 2z$

21. $x_1 = 1, x_2 = 11, x_3 = -4, x_4 = -5$

22. $\begin{bmatrix} -1 & -2 & 8 \\ 1 & 2 & -7 \\ 1 & 1 & -4 \end{bmatrix}$ 23. $\begin{bmatrix} 2 & 1 & -2 \\ 7 & 5 & -8 \\ -13 & -9 & 15 \end{bmatrix}$ 24. $\begin{bmatrix} -33 \\ 30 \\ 19 \end{bmatrix}$ 25. $\begin{bmatrix} 4 \\ 5 \\ -13 \end{bmatrix}$

26. $\begin{bmatrix} 250 & 140 \\ 480 & 700 \end{bmatrix}$ 27. $\begin{bmatrix} 1030 & 800 \\ 700 & 1200 \end{bmatrix}$

28. (a) Higher in June   (b) Higher in July   29. $X = \begin{bmatrix} 200 \\ 500 \\ 250 \end{bmatrix}$

30. $G = \frac{64}{93}H; A = \frac{59}{93}H; M = \frac{40}{93}H$

Exercise 4.1

1. $x < 2$ 3. $r \le -4$ 5. $r < 2$ 7. $x < -3$ 9. $x < \frac{3}{2}$
11. $x \le -1$

13. $x < -4$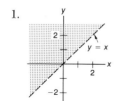

15. $x < 3$

17. $x \ge -\frac{7}{2}$

19. Closed

21. Open

23. Closed

25. Open

Exercise 4.2

1.   3. 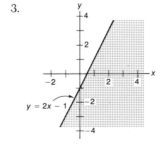   5.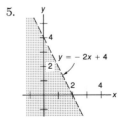

7.

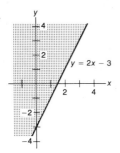

9.

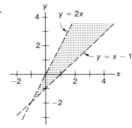

11.

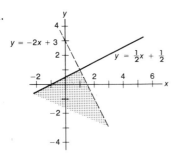

13.

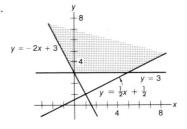

Exercise 4.3

1. Max $= 6$ at $(0, 2)$ 3.   Max $= 10$ at $(2, 4)$ 5.   Max $= 10,000$ at $(200, 100)$
7. Max $= 3000$ on line joining $(300, 0)$ and $(200, 100)$
9. Max $= 105$ at $(100, 130)$ 11.   Yes, on line joining $(100, 130)$ and $(120, 110)$

Exercise 4.4

1.
$$\left[\begin{array}{cccc|c} 2 & 4 & 1 & 0 & 24 \\ 1 & \boxed{1} & 0 & 1 & 5 \\ \hline 4 & 11 & 0 & 0 & f \end{array}\right]$$

3.
$$\left[\begin{array}{ccccc|c} 10 & \boxed{27} & 1 & 0 & 0 & 200 \\ 4 & 51 & 0 & 1 & 0 & 400 \\ 15 & 27 & 0 & 0 & 1 & 350 \\ \hline 6 & 7 & 0 & 0 & 0 & f \end{array}\right]$$

5. Complete: $x_1 = 11$, $x_2 = 9$; $f = 20$ 7.   Complete: $x_1 = 0$, $x_2 = 14$; $x_3 = 11$; $f = 525$
9. Not complete. New pivot circled

$$\left[\begin{array}{cccccc|c} 4 & 4 & 1 & 0 & 0 & 2 & 12 \\ \boxed{2} & \boxed{4} & 0 & 1 & 0 & -1 & 4 \\ -3 & -11 & 0 & 0 & 1 & -1 & 6 \\ \hline 3 & 3 & 0 & 0 & 0 & -4 & f - 150 \end{array}\right]$$

Either circled number may act as the
next pivot, but only one of them.

11. $x = 10, y = 38; f = 382$ 13. $x = 20, y = 10; f = 80$ 15. $x = 0$,
$y = 2, z = \frac{20}{3}; f = \frac{140}{3}$ 17. Ten speed = 10, Regular = 12; $P = 540$
19. 500 tomatoes, 1800 peaches; $P = 4100$ 21. 15 males, 20 females;
$f = 35$ animals

Exercise 4.5

1. $\begin{bmatrix} 4 & 1 & | & 11 \\ 3 & 2 & | & 12 \\ \hline 3 & 1 & | & g \end{bmatrix}$ transpose = $\begin{bmatrix} 4 & 3 & | & 3 \\ 1 & 2 & | & 1 \\ \hline 11 & 12 & | & g \end{bmatrix}$

3. $\begin{bmatrix} 4 & 1 & | & 12 \\ 1 & 1 & | & 9 \\ 1 & 3 & | & 15 \\ \hline 5 & 2 & | & g \end{bmatrix}$ transpose = $\begin{bmatrix} 4 & 1 & 1 & | & 5 \\ 1 & 1 & 3 & | & 2 \\ \hline 12 & 9 & 15 & | & g \end{bmatrix}$

5. $\begin{bmatrix} 1 & 3 & 0 & | & 1 \\ 4 & 6 & 1 & | & 3 \\ 0 & 4 & 1 & | & 1 \\ \hline 12 & 48 & 8 & | & g \end{bmatrix}$ transpose = $\begin{bmatrix} 1 & 4 & 0 & | & 12 \\ 3 & 6 & 4 & | & 48 \\ 0 & 1 & 1 & | & 8 \\ \hline 1 & 3 & 1 & | & g \end{bmatrix}$

7. Maximize $f = 11x_1 + 12x_2$
   Subject to $4x_1 + 3x_2 \le 3$
   $x_1 + 2x_2 \le 1$

9. Maximize $f = 12x_1 + 9x_2 + 15x_3$
   Subject to $4x_1 + x_2 + x_3 \le 5$
   $x_1 + x_2 + 3x_3 \le 2$

11. Maximize $f = x_1 + 3x_2 + x_3$
    Subject to $x_1 + 4x_2 \le 12$
    $3x_1 + 6x_2 + 4x_3 \le 48$
    $x_2 + x_3 \le 8$

13. $y_1 = 2, y_2 = 3; g = 9$ (min)
15. $y_1 = 1, y_2 = 8; g = 21$ (min)   17. $y_1 = \frac{2}{5}, y_2 = \frac{1}{5}, y_3 = \frac{1}{5}; g = 16$ (min)
19. Diet A = 4 servings, diet B = 10 servings; min = 1.42 oz
21. Food 1 = 4 g, food 2 = 3 g; $C = 15$ units (min)

Chapter 4 Review Exercises

1. $x \le 3$

2. $x \ge -\frac{20}{3}$

3. $x \ge -\frac{15}{13}$

4. (a) Closed   (b) Closed   (c) Open

5.

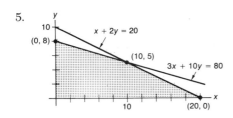

6.

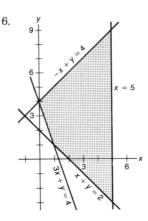

7. $f = 66$ at $(6, 6)$ 8. $f = 91$ at $(9, 2)$ 9. $f = 43$ at $(7, 9)$ 10. $f = 168$ at $(12, 7)$

11. $f = 260$ at $(60, 20)$ 12. $f = 360$ at $(40, 30)$ 13. $f = 270$ at $(5, 3, 2)$

14. $g = 32$ at $y_1 = 2$, $y_2 = 3$ 15. $g = 20$ at $y_1 = 4$, $y_2 = 2$ 16. $g = 7$ at $y_1 = 1$, $y_2 = 5$

17. $g = 16$ at $y_1 = \frac{2}{5}$, $y_2 = \frac{1}{5}$, $y_3 = \frac{1}{5}$ 18. $f = \dfrac{385{,}000}{13}$ at $\left(0, \dfrac{85{,}000}{13}, \dfrac{6000}{13}\right)$

19. $P = 590$ when smaller $= 75$, larger $= 110$ 20. $C = \$300{,}000$ when $\#1$
operates 30 days, $\#2$ operates 25 days   21. Cost $= \$5.60$; $A = 40$ lb, $B = 0$ lb

Exercise 5.1

1. $x^2 + 5x - 3 = 0$ 3. $x^2 - 6x + 2 = 0$ 5. $3x^2 - 4x + 0 = 0$

7. $y^2 - 3y - 2 = 0$ 9. $x^2 + 2x - 1 = 0$ 11. $x = \frac{2}{3}$, $x = 3$ 13. $x = 3$, $x = -1$

15. $x = 3$, $x = -7$ 17. $x = 1$ 19. $x = 5$, $x = -2$ 21. $x = 3$, $x = 1$

23. $x = -6$, $x = 2$ 25. $x = 2$, $x = -2$ 27. $x = -2$, $x = -5$ 29. $x = -\frac{1}{3}$, $x = \frac{1}{2}$

31. $x = \dfrac{9 \pm \sqrt{93}}{2}$ 33. No real zeros   35. $x = \dfrac{1 + \sqrt{7}}{2}$, $x = \dfrac{1 - \sqrt{7}}{2}$

37. No real zeros   39. $x = \dfrac{5 + \sqrt{37}}{2}$, $x = \dfrac{5 - \sqrt{37}}{2}$

41. (a) $v = 28\sqrt{30}$ (b) $v = 28\sqrt{70}$ (c) $\sqrt{\frac{7}{3}}$ 43. (a) $r = R/\sqrt{2}$
(b) $r = R\sqrt{3}/2$ (c) $v_r = 0$

Exercise 5.2

1. Vertex $(0, -4)$;
    zeros $(2, 0)$,
    $(-2, 0)$

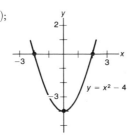

3. Vertex $(0, 18)$;
    zeros $(3, 0)$,
    $(-3, 0)$

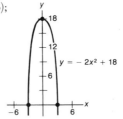

5. Vertex $(-2, 0)$; zeros $(-2, 0)$

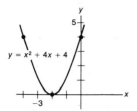

$y = x^2 + 4x + 4$

7. Vertex $(-\frac{1}{2}, 1\frac{3}{4})$; zeros: none

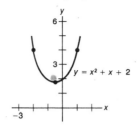

$y = x^2 + x + 2$

9. Vertex $(0, 4)$; zeros: none

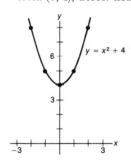

$y = x^2 + 4$

11. Vertex $(\frac{25}{12}, \frac{625}{24})$; zeros $(0, 0)$, $(\frac{25}{6}, 0)$

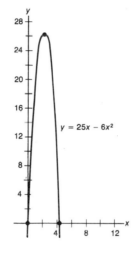

$y = 25x - 6x^2$

13.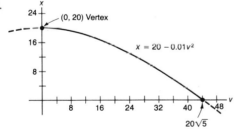

$(0, 20)$ Vertex

$x = 20 - 0.01v^2$

$20\sqrt{5}$

15.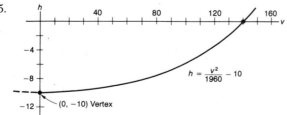

$h = \dfrac{v^2}{1960} - 10$

$(0, -10)$ Vertex

Exercise 5.3

1.

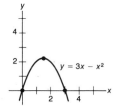

The graph shows curves labeled $p = q^2 + 8q + 3$ and $p = 4 - 4q - q^2$, with axes p (vertical, marked 2, 4, 6, 8, 10, 12) and q (horizontal, marked 2, 4, 6).

3. $p = \$27.08$, $q = 216\frac{2}{3}$ 5. $p = \$40$, $q = 30$ 7. $x = 40$ units, $x = 50$ units
9. $x = 28$ units, $x = 1000$ units   11. $x = 15$ units; reject $x = 100$
13. $x = 75$, $P = \$2025$ 15. Max revenue at $x = 625$; Max profit at $x = 57.5$.
Revenue does not incorporate the cost function.

Chapter 5 Review Exercises

1. $x = 0$, $x = -\frac{5}{3}$ 2. $x = 0$, $x = \frac{4}{3}$ 3. $x = -2$, $x = -3$
4. $x = (-5 + \sqrt{47})/2$, $x = (-5 - \sqrt{47})/2$ 5. No real roots
6. $x = \sqrt{3}/2$, $x = -\sqrt{3}/2$

7. Vertex $(0, -1)$; zeros $(1, 0)$, $(-1, 0)$

8. Vertex $(2, 1)$; no real zeros

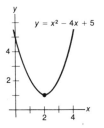

9. Vertex $(\frac{3}{2}, \frac{9}{4})$; zeros $(0, 0)$, $(3, 0)$

10. Vertex $(\frac{7}{2}, \frac{9}{4})$; zeros $(2, 0)$, $(5, 0)$

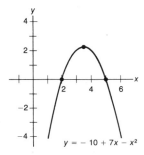

11. Vertex $(-1, 1)$; no real zeros

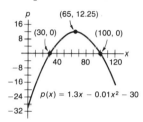

$y = x^2 + 2x + 2$

12. Vertex $(0, -1)$; no real zeros

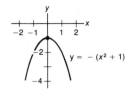

$y = -(x^2 + 1)$

13. $p = 400$, $q = 10$ 14. $p = 10$, $q = 20$ 15. $x = 46 + 2\sqrt{89}$, $x = 46 - 2\sqrt{89}$

16. $(15, 1275)$, $(60, 2400)$ 17. Max revenue $= \$2500$; max profit $= \$506.25$

18. Max profit $= 12.25$; break-even $x = 100$, $x = 30$

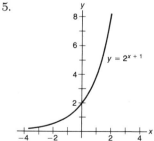

$p(x) = 1.3x - 0.01x^2 - 30$

Exercise 6.1

1.

$y = 4^x$

3.

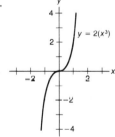

$y = 2(x^3)$

5.

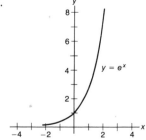

$y = 2^{x+1}$

7.

$y = e^x$

9.

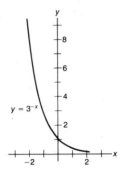

$y = 3^{-x}$

11.

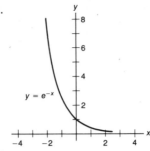

$y = e^{-x}$

13.

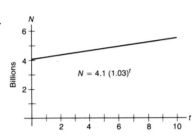

$N = 4.1\,(1.03)^t$

15.

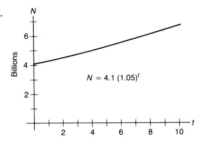

$N = 4.1\,(1.05)^t$

17.

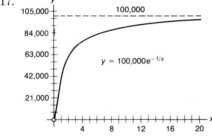

$y = 100{,}000e^{-1/x}$

Exercise 6.2

1. $2^4 = 16$ 3. $4^{1/2} = 2$ 5. $\log_2 32 = 5$ 7. $\log_4\left(\tfrac{1}{4}\right) = -1$ 9. 3 11. $\tfrac{1}{2}$

13.

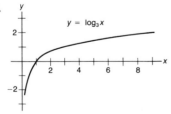

$y = \log_3 x$

15.

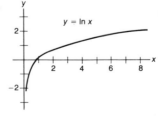

$y = \ln x$

17.

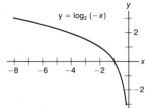

19. 4   21. x 23. 1   25. 1   27. x 29. 2   31. 1.0792

33. 0.5118   35. -2.4082 37. 8.319

39. $\log_a a^x = x$. Let $v = \log_a a^x$. In exp form: $a^v = a^x$; $\therefore v = x$.

41. $\log_a (MN) = \log_a M + \log_a N$. Let $u = \log_a M$; $v = \log_a N$. In exp form $a^u = M$ and $a^v = N$; $\therefore MN = a^u \cdot a^v = a^{u+v}$. In log form $\log_a (MN) = u + v = \log_a M + \log_a N$.

43. $pH = \log \left(\dfrac{1}{H^+}\right)$

   $- \log 1 - \log H^+$

   $= -\log H^+$

45.

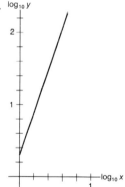

47. Straight line

Exercise 6.3

1. 128,402   3. (a) 600   (b) 2119   (c) 3000   (d)

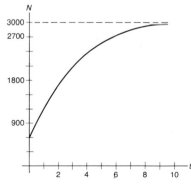

5. 1979   7. (a) 37   (b) 1.5 hours   9. (a) 52   (b) tenth   11. (a) 2038
(b) 4.9 months   13. (a) 69%   (b) 37,204 years (approx)   15. (a) $4.98   (b) 8
17. $502   19. (a) $333.81   (b) 147   21. $420.09   23. $2706.71

Chapter 6 Review Exercises

1.

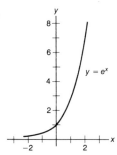

2.

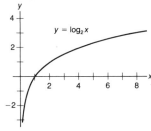

3.

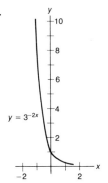

4.

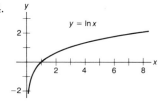

5.

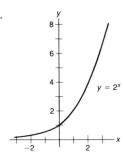

6.

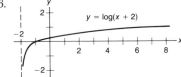

7. 1   8. 3   9. 0.6020   10. 0.6021   11. 1.8062   12. 1.8063
13. $\ln x + 2 \ln (2x + 1) - \frac{1}{2} \ln (x - 1)$ 14. (a) 3000   (b) 8603   (c) 10,000
15. (a) $27,440.58   (b) 12 weeks   16. $1366.19

Exercise 7.1

1. 3, 6, 9, 12, 15, 18, 21, 24, 27, 30   3. $\frac{1}{3}, \frac{2}{3}, 1, \frac{4}{3}, \frac{5}{3}, 2, \frac{7}{3}, \frac{8}{3}$ 5. $-\frac{1}{4}, \frac{1}{4}, -\frac{1}{4}, \frac{1}{4}, -\frac{1}{4}, \frac{1}{4}$
7. $-\frac{1}{2}, \frac{1}{4}, -\frac{1}{6}, \frac{1}{8}, -\frac{1}{10}, \frac{1}{12}$ 9. $-1, -\frac{1}{4}, -\frac{1}{15}, 0; a_{10} = \frac{1}{20}$ 11. 11, 14, 17
13. $\frac{15}{2}, 9, \frac{21}{2}, 12$ 15. $a_8 = 25$ 17. $a_8 = \frac{5}{2}$ 19. $a_6 = 15$ 21. $a_4 = 10$

Exercise 7.2

(Minor differences may occur if calculators are used)

1. 24, 48, 96, 192   3. 24, 16, $\frac{32}{3}$ 5. 320   7. $\frac{81}{4}$ 9. 40.5 ft
11. $4096   13. $14,326.78   15. $4774.55   17. $4755.03   19. $3661.54
21. $6483.12   23. $50.26 more at 8%   25. 8.24%   27. $502.47
29. 3 years   31. 4%

Exercise 7.3

1. 5   3. 3   5. $a_1 + a_2 + a_3 + a_4$ 7. 3   9. 53   11. 42   13. 50
15. 820   17. 7650   19. 1,368,650   21. 6.25   23. 100   25. 67.5
27. 30   29. 6   31. 2184   33. 2.625   35. 121   37. $\frac{422}{27}$

Exercise 7.4

(Minor differences may occur if calculators are used)

1. $12.58   3. $7328.22   5. $1072.97   7. $1074.82   9. $4775.14
11. $1216.57   13. $1357.77   15. $2115.07   17. $14,992.03

Exercise 7.5

1. (a) $2246.27   (b) $4236.68   3. (a) $1092.08   (b) $3149.43
5. $1008.24   7. $7950.50   9. $5236.10   11. $3720.83

Exercise 7.6

1. $1400/yr; 9.3%   3. (a) 2.8¢/unit   (b) $70,000   5. 1st: $18,250;
2nd: $9,125; 3rd: $4562.50; 4th: $2281.25   7. 1st: $1500; 2nd: $1000; 3rd: $500

Chapter 7 Review Exercises

1. 1, $\frac{1}{4}$, $\frac{1}{9}$, $\frac{1}{16}$ 2. 25   3. 8   4. $7\frac{17}{60}$ 5. $4\frac{1}{2}$ 6. $40\frac{4}{9}$ 7. $372.79
8. $1601.03   9. $1616.06   10. 8.24%   11. $1863.93   12. $77,217.35
13. $88.85   14. $6069.44   15. $9800/yr   16. 1st: $20,000; 2nd: $16,000;
3rd: $12,800; 4th: $10,240   17. 1st: $17,818.18; 2nd: $16,036.36; 3rd: $14,254.54;
4th: $12,472.73

Exercise 8.1

1. (a) $\frac{1}{6}$ (b) 0   (c) $\frac{1}{2}$ 3. $\frac{1}{4}$ 5. (a) $\frac{1}{13}$ (b) $\frac{1}{2}$ (c) $\frac{1}{4}$ 7. (a) $\frac{3}{10}$ (b) $\frac{1}{2}$

(c) $\frac{1}{5}$ (d) $\frac{3}{5}$ (e) $\frac{7}{10}$ 9. {HH, HT, TH, TT}; (a) $\frac{1}{4}$ (b) $\frac{1}{2}$ (c) $\frac{1}{4}$ 11. (a) $\frac{1}{12}$

(b) $\frac{1}{12}$ (c) $\frac{1}{36}$ 13. (a) $\frac{1}{2}$ (b) $\frac{5}{12}$ 15. $\frac{13}{31}$ 17. $\frac{1}{2}$ 19. (a) $\frac{1}{5}$ (b) $\frac{1}{14}$

(c) $\frac{13}{14}$ (d) $\frac{3}{7}$ 21. $\frac{1}{3}$ 23. $\frac{3}{8}$

Exercise 8.2

1. $\dfrac{1}{6} \cdot \dfrac{1}{6} = \dfrac{1}{36}$ 3. $\dfrac{3}{10} \cdot \dfrac{2}{10} = \dfrac{3}{50}$ 5. (a) $\dfrac{2}{5} \cdot \dfrac{2}{5} = \dfrac{4}{25}$ (b) $\dfrac{3}{5} \cdot \dfrac{3}{5} = \dfrac{9}{25}$ (c) $\dfrac{2}{5} \cdot \dfrac{3}{5} = \dfrac{6}{25}$

(d) 0   7. (a) $\dfrac{13}{52} \cdot \dfrac{13}{52} = \dfrac{1}{16}$ (b) $\dfrac{13}{52} \cdot \dfrac{13}{52} = \dfrac{1}{16}$ 9. $\dfrac{9}{18} \cdot \dfrac{5}{17} \cdot \dfrac{8}{16} = \dfrac{5}{68}$

11. (a) $\dfrac{4}{52} \cdot \dfrac{4}{51} = \dfrac{4}{663}$ (b) $\dfrac{4}{52} \cdot \dfrac{1}{51} = \dfrac{1}{663}$ 13. (a) $\dfrac{4}{52} \cdot \dfrac{4}{52} = \dfrac{1}{169}$ (b) $\dfrac{4}{52} \cdot \dfrac{3}{51} = \dfrac{1}{221}$

15. $(.95)^5 = .774$ 17. $.30 \cdot .20 = .06$ 19. He assumed the six events were independent, which they aren't.

Exercise 8.3

1. $\dfrac{1}{3}$ 3. $\dfrac{10}{17}$ 5. $\dfrac{2}{3}$ 7. $\dfrac{3}{4}$ 9. $\dfrac{2}{3}$ 11. (a) $\dfrac{5}{15} \cdot \dfrac{5}{15} = \dfrac{1}{9}$

(b) $\dfrac{5}{15} \cdot \dfrac{4}{15} + \dfrac{4}{15} \cdot \dfrac{5}{15} = \dfrac{8}{45}$ (c) $\dfrac{9}{15} \cdot \dfrac{9}{15} = \dfrac{9}{25}$ 13. (a) $\dfrac{1}{2} \cdot \dfrac{1}{2} \cdot \dfrac{1}{2} = \dfrac{1}{8}$ (b) $\dfrac{1}{2} \cdot \dfrac{1}{2} \cdot \dfrac{1}{2} = \dfrac{1}{8}$

(c) $\left(\dfrac{1}{2} \cdot \dfrac{1}{2}\right) \cdot \dfrac{1}{2} + \dfrac{1}{2} \cdot \dfrac{1}{2} \cdot \dfrac{1}{2} + \dfrac{1}{2}\left(\dfrac{1}{2} \cdot \dfrac{1}{2}\right) = \dfrac{3}{8}$ (d) $\dfrac{3}{8}$ 15. $\dfrac{30}{65} + \dfrac{29}{65} - \dfrac{8}{65} = \dfrac{51}{65}$

17. (a) $\dfrac{1}{3} + \dfrac{1}{5} = \dfrac{8}{15}$ (b) $1 - \dfrac{8}{15} = \dfrac{7}{15}$ 19. Pr(bad picture) $= .05 + .3 - .01 = .34$; Pr(good picture) $= 1 - .34 = .66$

Exercise 8.4

1. (a) $\dfrac{1}{2}$ (b) $\dfrac{2}{26} = \dfrac{1}{13}$ 3. (a) $\dfrac{2}{3}$ (b) $\dfrac{4}{9}$ 5. (a) $1 \cdot \dfrac{12}{51} = \dfrac{4}{17}$ (b) $\dfrac{12}{51} = \dfrac{4}{17}$

7. (a) $\dfrac{5}{9} \cdot \dfrac{4}{8} \cdot \dfrac{3}{7} = \dfrac{5}{42}$ (b) $\dfrac{5}{9} \cdot \dfrac{4}{8} \cdot \dfrac{4}{7} + \dfrac{5}{9} \cdot \dfrac{4}{8} \cdot \dfrac{4}{7} + \dfrac{4}{9} \cdot \dfrac{5}{8} \cdot \dfrac{4}{7} = \dfrac{10}{21}$ (c) $\dfrac{5}{9} \cdot \dfrac{4}{8} \cdot \dfrac{4}{7} + \dfrac{5}{9} \cdot \dfrac{4}{8} \cdot \dfrac{3}{7} +$

$\dfrac{4}{9} \cdot \dfrac{3}{8} \cdot \dfrac{2}{7} + \dfrac{4}{9} \cdot \dfrac{5}{8} \cdot \dfrac{3}{7} = \dfrac{4}{9}$ 9. $\dfrac{1}{3}$ 11. (a) $\dfrac{1}{2}$ (b) $\dfrac{2}{3}$ 13. .15   15. (a) $\dfrac{9}{20}$

(b) $\dfrac{2}{3}$ 17. .079

Exercise 8.5

1. 360   3. 151,200   5. 120   7. 24   9. 35,152   11. 24   13. $\dfrac{1}{120}$

15. (a) $\dfrac{1}{3}$ (b) $\dfrac{1}{3}$

Exercise 8.6

1. 15   3. 21   5. 252   7. 30,045,015   9. 792   11. 210   13. (a) .0005

(b) .002   15. (a) $\dfrac{1}{22}$ (b) $\dfrac{6}{11}$ (c) $\dfrac{9}{22}$ 17. $\dfrac{18}{35}$

Exercise 8.7

1. $\dfrac{15}{8}$ 3. $\dfrac{8}{3}$ 5. $10   7. $1.67   9. 1

11. $8\left(\dfrac{4}{52}\right) + 0\left(\dfrac{4}{52}\right) + (-1)\left(\dfrac{4}{52}\right) + (-2)\left(\dfrac{40}{52}\right) = -\dfrac{-52}{52} = -\$1.00$

13. If he buys 0, his profit is 0. If he buys 100, his expected profit is $3(100)(.25) + $3(50)(.20) + $3(10)(.55) + $(-1)50(.20) + $(-1)90(.55) = $62. If he buys 200, his expected profit is $3(180)(.25) + $3(50)(.20) + $3(10)(.55) + (-$1)(20)(.25) + (-$1)(150)(.20) + (-$1)(190)(.55) = $42. He should buy 100.   15. Without collision insurance, her expected cost per year is $1000(.08) = $80. With insurance, her expected cost per year is $100 + 100(.08) = $108. Thus she could expect to save money without collision insurance if she is as good as the average driver.
17. $E(x) = 0(.04) + 1(.35) + 2(.38) + 3(.18) + 4(.05) = 1.85$

Chapter 8 Review Exercises

1. $\dfrac{1}{3}$ 2. $\dfrac{1}{13}$ 3. $\dfrac{3}{4}$ 4. $\dfrac{2}{13}$ 5. $\dfrac{16}{169}$ 6. $\dfrac{2}{7}$ 7. $\dfrac{2}{13}$ 8. $\dfrac{7}{13}$ 9. $\dfrac{1}{2}$ 10. $\dfrac{1}{3}$

11. (a) $\dfrac{2}{9}$ (b) $\dfrac{2}{3}$ (c) $\dfrac{7}{9}$ 12. 26^3 13. $\dfrac{8}{15}$ 14. 30   15. (a) $\dfrac{3}{14}$ (b) $\dfrac{4}{7}$ (c) $\dfrac{3}{8}$

16. 2.4   17. $\dfrac{5}{8}$ 18. $\dfrac{58}{100}$ 19. $4! = 24$ 20. $_8P_1 = 1680$ 21. (a) $\dfrac{63}{2000}$ (b) $\dfrac{60}{63}$

22. $_{12}C_4 = 495$ 23. $_8C_4 = 70$ 24. (a) $\dfrac{(_{10}C_5)(_2C_1)}{_{12}C_6}$ (b) $\dfrac{(_{10}C_5)(_2C_1) + (_{10}C_4)(_2C_2)}{_{12}C_6}$

25. (a) $_{12}C_2 = 66$ (b) $_{12}C_3 = 220$ 26. $-50¢$

Exercise 9.1

1.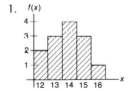

3.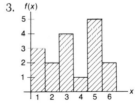

5.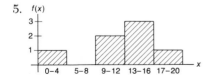

7.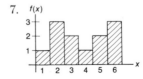

9.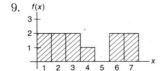

11.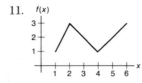

13.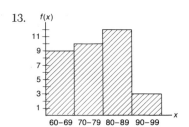

15.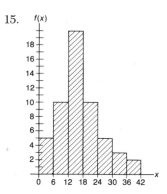

Exercise 9.2

1. 3   3. 13   5. No mode   7. 6   9. 39   11. 5   13. 12   15. 6   17. 8.5
19. 6   21. 4   23. 14   25. Mode = 2, median = 4.5, mean = 6   27. Mode = 17,
median = 18.5, mean = 23.5   29. Mode = 5.3, median = 5.3, mean = 5.32   31. (a) $30,000
(b) $18,000   (c) $16,000   33. Mean   35. Median

Exercise 9.3

1. 4, 8.5714, 2.9277   3. 14, 4.6667, 2.1602   5. 6, 24.2857, 4.9281   7. 8, 10.8571, 3.2950
9. $\bar{x} = \$7800$, $s = \$262.47$ 11. $\bar{x} = 6$, $s = 2.847$

Exercise 9.4

1. (a) $\dfrac{1}{64}$ (b) $\dfrac{5}{16}$ (c) $\dfrac{15}{64}$ 3. (a) 0.1382   (b) .9590   5. (a) $\dfrac{27}{64} = .4219$

(b) $\dfrac{27}{128} = .2109$ (c) $\dfrac{81}{256} = .3164$ 7. .2457   9. .0007

Exercise 9.5

1. (a)

x	0	1	2	3
$\Pr(x)$	$\dfrac{125}{216}$	$\dfrac{25}{72}$	$\dfrac{5}{72}$	$\dfrac{1}{216}$

(b) $3\left(\dfrac{1}{6}\right) = \dfrac{1}{2}$ (c) $\sqrt{3\left(\dfrac{1}{6}\right)\left(\dfrac{5}{6}\right)} = \dfrac{1}{6}\sqrt{15}$

3. $12\left(\dfrac{1}{6}\right) = 2$ 5. 15   7. $a^6 + 6a^5b + 15a^4b^2 + 20a^3b^3 + 15a^2b^4 + 6ab^5 + b^6$
9. $x^4 + 4x^3h + 6x^2h^2 + 4xh^3 + h^4$ 11. (a) $100(.10) = 10$ (b) $\sqrt{100(.10)(.90)} = 3$
13. (a) 60,000   (b) $\sqrt{24,000} = 154.919$ 15. 59,690

Exercise 9.6

1. 2   3. 1   5. .4641   7. .4641   9. $.4332 + .4821 = .9153$
11. $.4713 - .3643 = .1070$ 13. $.4987 - .4821 = .0166$ 15. .1915   17. .3944   19. .3944
21. .5381   23. .2957   25. (a) .3413   (b) .3413   (c) .6826   (d) .9546
27. $.4938 + .4938 = .9876$

Exercise 9.7

1. (a) Yes (b) 50 (c) 1   3. (a) 100 (b) 3 (c) No   5. (a) .9546
(b) $.5 - .4773 = .0227$ (c) .0454   7. Yes   9. Reject H_0. (The machine needs to be
repaired.)   11. Accept H_0. (1600 hours is a reasonable estimate.)

Exercise 9.8

1. $\widehat{y} = 3.7x - 3$ 3. $\widehat{p} = -2.9q + 317$ 5. $r = .97$ 7. $\widehat{y} = .57x - .11$
9. $\widehat{y} = 1.05x - .69$ 11. $r = .989$

Chapter 9 Review Exercises

1.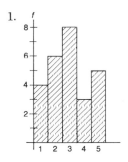

2. 3   3. $\dfrac{77}{26} = 2.96$ 4. 3   5. 15   6. 16   7. 15   8. $\overline{x} = 3.86$; $s^2 = 4.54$;

$s = 2.13$ 9. $\overline{x} = 2$; $s^2 = 2.44$; $s = 1.56$ 10. $\dfrac{32}{81}$ 11. $\mu = 4$, $\sigma = \dfrac{2\sqrt{3}}{3}$

12. $x^5 + 5x^4y + 10x^3y^2 + 10x^2y^3 + 5xy^4 + y^5$ 13. .9165   14. .1498   15. (a) .3413
(b) .6826 (c) .1360   16. (a) .9546 (b) .4773 (c) .1360   17. .297   18. .16308
19. Accept H_0; the machine appears to be working properly   20. $\widehat{y} = .68x + 23.8$
21. $r = .99$. Based on this very small sample, there is a mathematical relationship between the values
for these variables.

Exercise 10.1

1. 4   3. 3   5. 18   7. -1 9. 6   11. -4 13. 0   15. 6   17. 0
19. no limit ($\pm\infty$)   21. no limit ($\pm\infty$)   23.

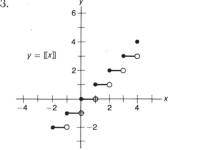

25. Does not exist since $\lim_{x \to 2^+} f(x) \neq \lim_{x \to 2^-} f(x)$ **27.** $3x^2$ **29.** (a) $2.00   (b) 3
(c) $3.00   (d) $3.50   (e) $2.00   (f) No limit

Exercise 10.2

1. Yes   **3.** Yes   **5.** No, $f(-3)$ undefined   **7.** No, $f(1)$ undefined   **9.** No, $f(-1)$ undefined
11. Yes   **13.** No, $\lim_{x \to 1^-} f(x) \neq \lim_{x \to 1^+} f(x)$ **15.** No, $\lim_{x \to 1^-} [\![x]\!] \neq \lim_{x \to 1^+} [\![x]\!]$
17. Continuous   **19.** Missing point discontinuity   **21.** Missing point discontinuity
23. Infinite discontinuity   **25.** Continuous   **27.** Jump discontinuity   **29.** (a) Yes
(b) No   (c) No   **31.** (a) Jump discontinuity at $x = 0$ (b) It changes from ice to water, or
from solid to liquid.

Exercise 10.3

1. 0   **3.** 1   **5.** $\frac{5}{3}$ **7.** 0   **9.** No limit $(+\infty)$ **11.** 3   **13.** $+\infty$ (no limit)
15. Undefined   **17.** 1

19. Asymptotes: horizontal $y = 0$,
vertical $x = 0$

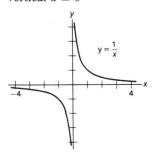

21. Asymptotes: horizontal $y = 1$,
vertical $x = 0$

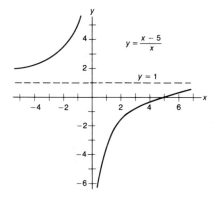

23. They are identical except at $x = 1$,
where $f(x)$ has a missing point
and $g(1) = 2$.

25.

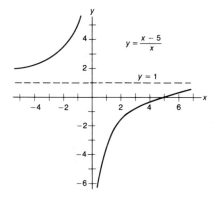

27.

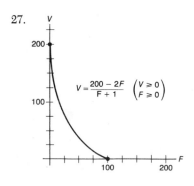

$$V = \frac{200 - 2F}{F + 1} \quad \begin{pmatrix} V \geqslant 0 \\ F \geqslant 0 \end{pmatrix}$$

29. No

Chapter 10 Review Exercises

1. 55   2. 0   3. -2 4. 6   5. No limit $(\pm\infty)$ 6. $-\frac{1}{2}$ 7. 0
8. Infinite discontinuity at $x = 5$ 9. Missing point discontinuity at $x = 2$ 10. Continuous
11. Jump discontinuity at $x = 1$ 12. Jump discontinuity at each integer
13. Asymptotes: horizontal $y = 2$,   14. Asymptotes: horizontal $y = 1$,
    vertical $x = 0$ vertical $x = 3$

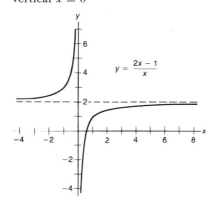 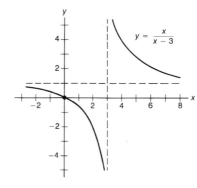

Exercise 11.1

1. $10x$ 3. $2x$ 5. $3x^2$ 7. 3   9. $8x - 2$ 11. 34   13. 14   15. 117
17. (a) 200   (b) 100   (c) 0   (d) It is neither increasing nor decreasing
19. 68 mph or 100 ft/sec

Exercise 11.2

1. (a) 1   (b) 1   3. (a) $f'(x) = 2x + 1$ (b) 5   5. 6   7. $y = 6x - 9$
9. $y = 6x - 2$

Exercise 11.3

1. 0   3. 1   5. $3x^2$ 7. $12x^2$ 9. $40q^7$ 11. 3   13. $18x^5 - 24x$ 15. $15q^2 + 8q$
17. $\frac{2}{3}x^{-1/3} = 2/3x^{1/3}$ 19. $-\frac{4}{5}x^{-9/5} = -4/5x^{9/5}$ 21. $\frac{1}{2}x^{-1/2} = 1/2\sqrt{x}$
23. $\frac{2}{3}q^{-1/3} = 2/3\sqrt[3]{q}$ 25. $-2x^{-3} = -2/x^3$ 27. $-3/x^4$ 29. $-1/3x^{4/3}$
31. $(3/2\sqrt{x}) + 9x^2$ 33. $x + 2x^{-4/3}$ 35. 19   37. 0   39. $y = 8x - 3$
41. $y = -4x + 1$ 43. $(2, -1)$ 45. (a) $v = 112 - 32t$ (b) $48 = v$ when $t = 2$; up
47. $dy/dt = 8t + 2$ 49. 70 gal/min   51. \$298.40

Exercise 11.4

1. $y' = 3x^2 + 2x - 6$ 3. $dp/dq = 9q^2 - 2q + 6$ 5. $f'(x) = 5x^4 + 12x^3 + 12x^2 - 2x - 3$
7. $R'(x) = 18x^2 - 4x + 300$ 9. $y' = (3x + 1)/(2\sqrt{x})$ 11. -8
13. $y' = (-x^2 - 1)/(x^2 - 1)^2$ 15. $dp/dq = (q^2 - 4q - 1)/(q - 2)^2$ 17. $dy/dx = 1$
19. $dp/dq = (2q^2 - 6q - 12)/(q^2 + 4q)^2$ 21. $y' = (2x^3 - 6x^2 - 8)/(x - 2)^2$ 23. $\frac{3}{4}$

25. $\frac{3}{5}$ 27. $(\frac{1}{3}, -\frac{50}{27})$ and $(1, -2)$ 29. $dy = (3x^2 + 8x + 5)\,dx$ 31. $ds = (3x^2 + 2x)\,dx$

33. $dC = (3x^2 + 2x - 1)\,dx$ 35. $dR/dn = r(1 - r)/[1 + (n - 1)r]^2$ 37. $S = 1000x - x^2$

39. $dP/dt = 10{,}000/(t + 10)^2$

Exercise 11.5

1. $6x(x^2 + 1)^2$ 3. $4(8x - 4)(4x^2 - 4x + 1)^3 = 16(2x - 1)^7$ 5. $-6x/(x^2 + 2)^4$

7. $-4(x + 2)(x^2 + 4x)^{-3}$ 9. $-3(2x + 3)(x^2 + 3x + 4)^{-4}$ 11. $-3(6x^2 + 3)/4(2x^3 + 3x + 5)^{7/4}$

13. $(x + 2)/\sqrt{x^2 + 4x + 5}$ 15. $(3 - 2x)/2\sqrt{3x - x^2}$ 17. $80x(x^2 - 3)^4$

19. $-96x/(4x^2 + 5)^3$ 21. $96{,}768$ 23. 2 25. $y = -3x + 4$ 27. $y = 300x - 475$

29. $x = 0, x = -2, x = 2$ 31. (a) $dy/dt = 4t(t^2 + 1)$ (b) 4040 33. $y' = kac/2\sqrt{cat}$

35. $dy/dx = (8k/5)(x - x_0)^{3/5}$ 37. (a) $C = (dQ/dt)/(dV/dt)$

(b) $dQ/dV = dQ/dt \cdot dt/dV = (dQ/dt)/(dV/dt)$

Exercise 11.6

1. 0 3. $15x^2$ 5. $3x^2 + 8x - 2$ 7. $10(3x^2 - 4)(x^3 - 4x)^9$

9. $(5x^3 + 3x^2 + 2)/2\sqrt{x^3 + 1}$ 11. $3(4q^3 + 3q^2 - 3)[(q + 1)(q^3 - 3)]^2$

13. $4x^2(4x + 9)[x^2(x^2 + 3x)]^3$ 15. $4(-2x^2 + 2x + 1)(2x - 1)^3/(x^2 + x)^5$

17. $2x(2x^2 + 19)/[3\sqrt[3]{(x^2 + 5)^2}(4 - x^2)^2]$ 19. $2(x - 1)(2x^2 - x + 1)$

21. $x(x^2 + 4)(7x^3 - 24x^2 + 12x - 32)$ 23. $(5x^3 + 2)/(2\sqrt{x^3 + 1})$

25. $(x^5 + 1)^2(17x^6 + 64x^5 + 2x + 4)$ 27. $(8x^4 + 3)(x^3 - 4x)^2(136x^6 - 352x^4 + 27x^2 - 36)$

29. $2x(x^2 - 4)^2(2x^2 + 7)/(x^2 + 1)^2$

Exercise 11.7

1. $\overline{MC} = 8$ 3. $\overline{MC} = 13 + 2x$ 5. $\overline{MC} = 3x^2 - 12x + 24$ 7. $\overline{MC} = 27 + 3x^2$

9. 10 11. 46 13.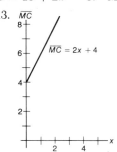

15. (a) $\overline{MR} = 4$

(b) The sale of each additional item brings in \$4 revenue at all levels of production.

17. (a) $\overline{MR} = 36 - 0.02x$ (b) 34 19. (a) $\overline{MR} = 36 - 0.02x$ (b) $x = 1800$

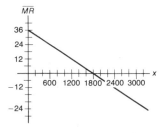

21. $\overline{MP} = 5$ 23. $\overline{MP} = 30 - 2x$ 25. (a) 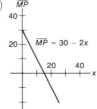   (b) $x = 15$

Chapter 11 Review Exercises

1. $20x^4 - 18x^2$ 2. $8x$ 3. 3 4. $1/2\sqrt{x}$ 5. 0 6. $-4/3\sqrt[3]{x^4}$
7. $-1/x^2 + 1/2\sqrt{x^3}$ 8. $9x^2 - 26x + 4$ 9. $15x^4 + 9x^2 + 2x$ 10. $2(1 - q)/q^3$
11. $(1 - 3t)/[2\sqrt{t}(3t + 1)^2]$ 12. $(9x^2 - 24x)(x^3 - 4x^2)^2$ 13. $6(30x^5 + 24x^3)(5x^6 + 6x^4 + 5)^5$
14. $(9x^2 - 24x)(x^3 - 4x^2)^2$ 15. $-(3x^2 - 4)/2\sqrt{(x^3 - 4x)^3}$ 16. $(2x^2 - 4)/\sqrt{x^2 - 4}$
17. $3/(1 - x)^4$ 18. $-2(2x - 3)/(x^2 - 3x + 1)^3$ 19. $-2(3x + 1)(x + 12)/(x^2 - 4)^2$
20. $-3x^2/(x - 1)^4$ 21. $y = 15x - 18$ 22. $y = 34x - 48$ 23. (a) $\overline{MC} = 6x + 6$
(b) 186 24. 53 25. (a) $\overline{MR} = 40 - 0.04x$ (b) $x = 1000$ units   26. 48
27. (a) $\overline{MR} = 80 - 0.08x$ (b) 72

Exercise 12.1

1. $(0, 0)$ max; $(2, -4)$ min

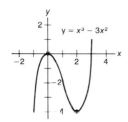

3. $(1, \frac{4}{3})$ HPI; no max nor min

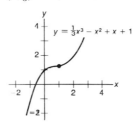

5. $(0, 0)$ HPI; $(3, -27)$ min

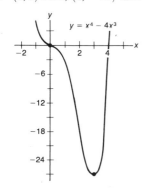

7. $(2, 0)$ min

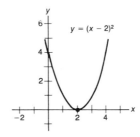

9. $(\frac{1}{2}, -\frac{27}{16})$ min; $(2, 0)$ HPI

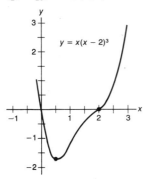

11. $(2, 0)$ min; $p = q^2 - 4q + 4$, is same as $p = (q - 2)^2$. Graph is identical to problem 7 with y replaced by p and x replaced by q.

13. $(\frac{4}{3}, -\frac{95}{27})$ min; $(-2, 15)$ max

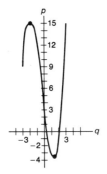

Exercise 12.2

1. No derivative at $x = 0$; no max, no min

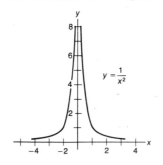

3. No derivative at $x = 1$; no max, no min

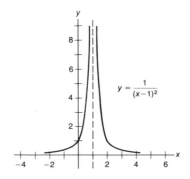

5. Min: $(0, -\sqrt[3]{4})$;
    derivative does not
    exist at $x = 2$, $x = -2$.

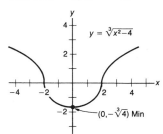

7.

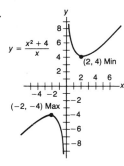

9. Domain: $x \geq 0$

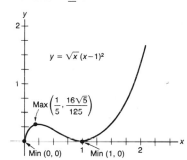

11. No derivative at $(2, 4)$

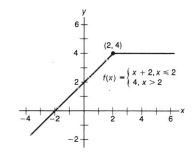

13. Absolute max $(0, 16)$ 15. Absolute min $(\frac{1}{4}, -\frac{1}{8})$; absolute max $(3, 15)$
17. Absolute max $(0, 16)$; absolute min $(3, 7)$ 19. Yes

Exercise 12.3

1. $v = a^2/4$; max when $x = a/2$ 3. $E = \frac{1}{2}$ at $t = 0$, max   5. 10^{-6} = hydrogen ion concentration
7. $x = 2$ 9. 3 weeks from now   11. $x = 500$ 13. $x = 250$
15. Max $R = \$50,176$ when $x = 28$ 17. 40 people   19. 25 plates

Exercise 12.4

1. $x = 5$ units   3. $x = 10$ units   5. 200 units $(x = 2)$ 7. No maximum;
produce as much as possible   9. $x = 15$ units   11. $x = 80$ units   13. $x = 10\sqrt{15} \approx 39$ units
15. $x = 1000$ units   17. rent = $\$220$

Chapter 12 Review Exercises

1.

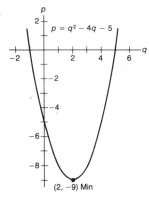

$p = q^2 - 4q - 5$

$(2, -9)$ Min

2.

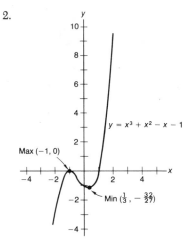

$y = x^3 + x^2 - x - 1$

Max $(-1, 0)$

Min $(\frac{1}{3}, -\frac{32}{27})$

3.

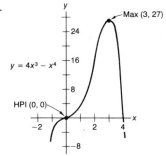

Max $(3, 27)$

$y = 4x^3 - x^4$

HPI $(0, 0)$

4.

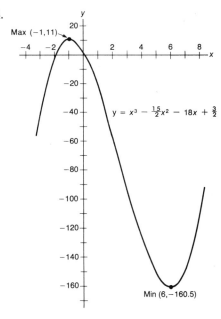

Max $(-1, 11)$

$y = x^3 - \frac{15}{2}x^2 - 18x + \frac{3}{2}$

Min $(6, -160.5)$

5.

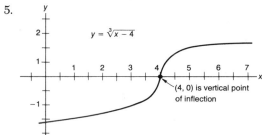

$y = \sqrt[3]{x - 4}$

$(4, 0)$ is vertical point of inflection

6. (a) (50;233,333) absolute max; (0, 0) absolute min (b) (64;248,491) absolute max;
(0, 0) absolute min 7. $x = 5$ units 8. $x = 1600$ units 9. $x = 1000$ units
10. $x = 7$ units 11. \$300 12. 10:00 A.M. 13. 325 in 1985 14. $x = 3$ units
15. selling 175 sets at \$425 each 16. $x = 152$ units

Exercise 13.1

1. $24x - 30$ 3. $60x - 2$ 5. $6x - 2x^{-3}$ 7. $6x + \frac{1}{4}x^{-3/2}$ 9. $20x^3 + \frac{1}{4}x^{-3/2}$
11. $-1/4(x - 1)^{3/2}$ 13. $4/(x^2 + 4)^{3/2}$ 15. $60x^2 - 96$ 17. $1008x^6 - 720x^3$
19. $-6/x^4$ 21. $3/8x^{5/2}$ 23. $3/8(x + 1)^{5/2}$ 25. 0 27. $-15/16x^{7/2}$ 29. 26
31. (a) $290x - 90x^2$ (b) $200, 60$ (c) $110, -250$ 33. -2 35. Decreasing
37. Decrease 39. $x = \frac{29}{18}$

Exercise 13.2

1. $(1, -2)$ 3. $(0, 0)$ 5. None 7. $(2, 0)$ 9. $(-2, -9)$ and $(1, \frac{3}{4})$ 11. $(3, -54)$

13. No points of inflection

15.

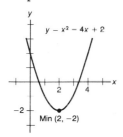

$$y = x^2 - 4x + 2$$

Min $(2, -2)$

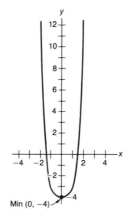

$y = 4x^3 - x^2$

Max $(0, 0)$

Min $(\frac{1}{6}, -\frac{1}{108})$

Flex $(\frac{1}{12}, -\frac{1}{216})$

17. Max $(0, 0)$; min $(2\sqrt{2}, -64)$,
$(-2\sqrt{2}, -64)$; pts of inflection
$(2\sqrt{6}/3, -320/9), (-2\sqrt{6}/3, -320/9)$

19. $y = x^4 - 4$; no points of inflection

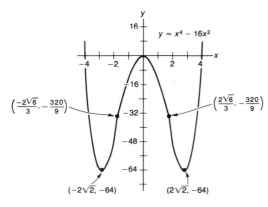

$y = x^4 - 16x^2$

$\left(\frac{-2\sqrt{6}}{3}, -\frac{320}{9}\right)$ $\left(\frac{2\sqrt{6}}{3}, -\frac{320}{9}\right)$

$(-2\sqrt{2}, -64)$ $(2\sqrt{2}, -64)$

Min $(0, -4)$

21. $f(y) = 3y^4 - 4y^3 + 1$;
     points of inflection: $(0, 1)$ and $(\frac{2}{3}, \frac{11}{27})$;
     min: $(1, 0)$

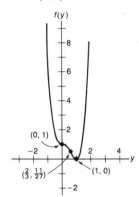

23. $w = z^2/8 - 1/z$;
     point of inflection: $(2, 0)$;
     min: $(-\sqrt[3]{4}, 3\sqrt[3]{16}/8)$;
     vertical asymptote: $z = 0$

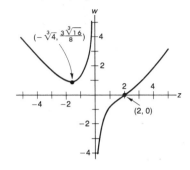

25. $p = 2q^2 + 4q$; no points of inflection

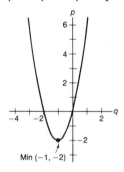

Exercise 13.3

1. $-x/2y$ 3. $-(2x + 4)/(2y - 3)$ 5. $-q/p$ 7. $-(2x + 3y)/3x$ 9. $-p/q$
11. $-x/y$ 13. $8\sqrt{p}$ 15. y/x or $\frac{1}{4}$ 17. 0 19. 0 21. $y = 2$ 23. $y = 0$
25. (a) Horizontal tangents at $(0, 1)$ and $(0, -1)$ (b) Vertical tangents at $(2, 0)$ and $(-2, 0)$

Exercise 13.4

1. $(1/x)\log_4 e$ 3. $1/x$ 5. $(3x^2 - 4)/(x^3 - 4x)$ 7. $[4/(4x - 1)] - 1/x$
9. $(3/x) + [1/2(x + 1)]$ 11. 0 13. $2q/(q^2 + 1)$ 15. $(-y \ln y)/x$ 17. -4
19. $(-1/H^+)\log e$ 21. A/B

Exercise 13.5

1. $4^x/\log_4 e$ 3. e^x 5. $3e^{3x}$ 7. $(2x + 3)e^{x^2+3x}$ 9. 1 11. $2x2^{x^2}/\log_2 e$
13. $xe^x + e^x$ 15. $x^2e^x + 2xe^x$ 17. $4e^{q^3}(3q^3 + 1)$ 19. 1 21. $-1/x$ 23. $-y/x$
25. $ye^x/(1 - e^x)$ 27. $y = -\frac{1}{3}x + 1$ 29. (a) 10 (b) 10 31. (a) 8.67 (b) 17.80
33. $100,000e^{-1/x}/x^2$

Exercise 13.6

1. 70   3. $200   5. (a) 60   (b) $570   (c) $9000   7. (a) 15   (b) $9450
9. $12 per item   11. $115 per item   13. (a) 1   (b) No change   15. (a) 84

(b) Revenue will decrease   17. 8   19. $\frac{1}{6}$ 21. $\frac{dR}{dp} = p \cdot \frac{dq}{dp} + q$; $e = 1 \Rightarrow \frac{dq}{dp} = \frac{-q}{p}$;

$\therefore \frac{dR}{dp} = p\left(\frac{-q}{p}\right) + q = -q + q = 0$ 23. $\frac{dR}{dp} = p\frac{dq}{dp} + q$; $e < 1 \Rightarrow \frac{-p}{q}\frac{dq}{dp} < 1 \Rightarrow \frac{dq}{dp} > \frac{-q}{p}$;

$\therefore \frac{dR}{dp} = p\frac{dq}{dp} + q > p\left(\frac{-q}{p}\right) + q = 0$ so $\frac{dR}{dp} > 0$

Chapter 13 Review Exercises

1. $12x^2 - 2/x^3$ 2. $-4/(x^2 - 4)^{3/2}$ 3. $96x$
4. $y = x^3 - 12x$; max: $(-2, 16)$; min: $(2, -16)$; point of inflection: $(0, 0)$

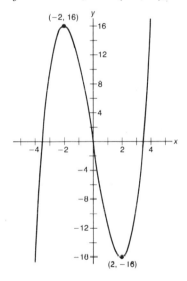

5. $p = q^3 - q^2 + 1$; max: $(0, 1)$; min: $(\frac{2}{3}, \frac{23}{27})$; point of inflection $(\frac{1}{3}, \frac{25}{27})$

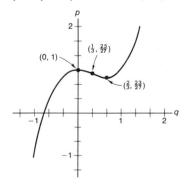

6. $x^2 e^x + 2xe^x$ 7. $2x$ 8. $1/q - [2q/(q^2 - 1)]$ 9. $\frac{5}{9}$ 10. $-y/x \ln x$ 11. 30
12. (a) 150 (b) $\$650$ 13. Yes   14. (a) 1 (b) No change

Exercise 14.1

1. $x^4 + C$ 3. $\frac{1}{7}x^7 + C$ 5. $\frac{1}{8}x^8 + C$ 7. $\frac{2}{5}x^{5/2} + C$ 9. $\frac{2}{3}x^{3/2} + C$ 11. $5x + C$
13. $\frac{5}{4}x^4 + C$ 15. $4x^{3/2} + C$ 17. $\frac{1}{5}x^5 - x^3 + C$ 19. $\frac{1}{4}x^4 - x^3 + 4x + C$
21. $\frac{1}{5}x^5 - x^2 + \frac{2}{3}x^{3/2} + C$ 23. $\frac{1}{3}x^3 + 5x^2 + 25x + C$ or $\frac{1}{3}(x + 5)^3 + C$
25. $\frac{16}{5}x^5 - \frac{8}{3}x^3 + x + C$ 27. $\frac{1}{7}x^7 + \frac{3}{5}x^5 + x^3 + x + C$ 29. $R(x) = 3x$
31. $R(x) = 2x^2 - 3x$ 33. $\$3700$ 35. $P(t) = \frac{1}{4}t^4 + \frac{4}{3}t^3 + 6t$ 37. (a) $x = t^{7/4}/1050 + C$
(b) 0.96 tons

Exercise 14.2

1. $\frac{1}{4}(x^2 + 3)^4 + C$ 3. $\frac{1}{3}(3x - x^3)^3 + C$ 5. $\frac{1}{8}(x^2 + 5)^4 + C$ 7. $\frac{1}{6}(x^4 + 6)^{3/2} + C$
9. $9x - 2x^3 + \frac{1}{5}x^5 + C$ 11. $\frac{1}{8}(x^2 + 1)^4 + C$ 13. $\frac{1}{10}(x^2 - 2x)^5 + C$
15. $\frac{3}{8}(x^2 + 2x)^{4/3} + C$ 17. $-1/3(x^3 - 1) + C$ 19. $-1/9(x^3 - 5)^3 + C$
21. $-1/8(x^6 - x^4)^4 + C$ 23. $-8/3(x^3 - 4) + C$ 25. $-1/8(x^4 - 4x)^2 + C$ 27. 3720
29. $R(x) = 60,000x + [40,000/(10 + x)] - 4000$

Exercise 14.3

1. $\ln |x^3 + 4| + C$ 3. $\ln |x^3 - 2x| + C$ 5. $\frac{1}{4}\ln |x^4 + 1| + C$ 7. $2 \ln |x^2 - 4| + C$
9. $\frac{1}{4}\ln |4z + 1| + C$ 11. $\frac{1}{3}\ln |z^3 + 3z| + C$ 13. $\frac{1}{3}x^3 + \ln |x - 1| + C$
15. $x + \frac{1}{2}\ln |x^2 + 3| + C$ 17. $e^{3x} + C$ 19. $-e^{-x} + C$ 21. $\frac{1}{4}e^{x^4} + C$ 23. $\frac{1}{2}e^{y^2} + C$
25. $\$1030.97$ 27. $n = n_0 e^{-Kt}$

Exercise 14.4

1. $C(x) = x^2 + 100x + 200$ 3. $C(x) = 2x^2 + 2x + 80$ 5. $\$3750$
7. (a) $x = 3$ units is optimal level   (b) $P(x) = -4x^2 + 24x - 200$ (c) loss of $\$164$
9. $C(y) = 0.4y + 0.6\sqrt{y} + 5$ 11. $C(y) = 0.3y + 0.4\sqrt{y} + 8$

Exercise 14.5

1. (a) 0.45 (b) 0.495 (c) $\frac{1}{2}$ (d) Answers in (a) and (b) are slightly smaller, but (c) is the
same   3. $\frac{20}{3}$

Exercise 14.6

1. 60 3. 33 5. 25 7. $12\sqrt[3]{25}$ 9. 98 11. $\frac{7}{3}$ 13. $12,960$ 15. 0
17. $8\sqrt{3} - \frac{7}{3}\sqrt{7}$ 19. 0 21. $\frac{1}{6}\ln\left(\frac{112}{31}\right)$ 23. $\frac{1}{6}$ 25. $\frac{1}{2}(e^9 - e)$ 27. Same absolute
values, opposite signs   29. 6 31. $K(\pi R^4/2)$ 33. 238

Exercise 14.7

1. $\$83.33$ 3. $\$161.89$ 5. $\$83.33$ 7. $\$11.50$ 9. $\$204.17$ 11. $\$2766.67$
13. $\$17,839.58$ 15. $\$133.33$ 17. $\$2.50$ 19. $\$103.35$

Exercise 14.8

1. $\frac{1}{8}\ln\left|\frac{4+x}{4-x}\right| + C$ 3. $\frac{1}{3}\ln\left[(3+\sqrt{10})/2\right]$ 5. $w(\ln w - 1) + C$

7. $\frac{1}{3} + \frac{1}{4}\ln\left(\frac{3}{7}\right)$ 9. $\frac{1}{3}\ln\left|3x + 1 + \sqrt{(3x+1)^2 + 1}\right| + C$

11. $\frac{1}{4}[10\sqrt{109} - \sqrt{10} + 9\ln(10 + \sqrt{109}) - 9\ln(1 + \sqrt{10})]$ 13. $\frac{1}{3}\ln\left|3x + \sqrt{9x^2 - 4}\right| + C$

15. $\frac{1}{8}\ln\left(\frac{9}{5}\right)$ 17. $-\frac{1}{6}\ln\left|7 - 3x^2\right| + C$ 19. $\frac{1}{32}\left\{\ln\left|4x^2 + 5\right| + [5/(4x^2 + 5)]\right\} + C$

21. $\$3391.10$

Exercise 14.9

1. $\frac{1}{2}xe^{2x} - \frac{1}{4}e^{2x} + C$ 3. $\frac{1}{3}x^3\ln x - \frac{1}{9}x^3 + C$ 5. $104\sqrt{2}/15$

7. $\frac{1}{2}x^2\ln(2x - 3) - \frac{9}{8}\ln(2x - 3) - \frac{1}{4}x^2 - \frac{3}{4}x + C$ 9. $\frac{1}{5}(q^2 - 3)^{3/2}(q^2 + 2) + C$ 11. $e - 2$

13. $2\ln^2 2 - 4\ln 2 + 2$ 15. $(x - 3)^{1/2}(\frac{2}{3}x + 4) + C$ 17. $-(1 + \ln x)/x + C$

19. $(3e^4 + 1)/2$

Chapter 14 Review Exercises

1. $\frac{1}{7}x^7 + C$ 2. $\frac{2}{3}x^{3/2} + C$ 3. $\frac{1}{4}x^4 - x^3 + 2x^2 + 5x + C$ 4. $\frac{1}{5}x^5 - \frac{2}{3}x^3 + x + C$

5. $\frac{1}{6}(x^2 - 1)^3 + C$ 6. $\frac{1}{6}(x^3 - 3x^2)^2 + C$ 7. $\frac{1}{2}(x^3 - 4)^{2/3} + C$ 8. $\frac{1}{3}\ln|x^3 - 1| + C$

9. $\frac{1}{3}e^{y^3} + C$ 10. $\frac{1}{3}x^3 + \frac{1}{2}x^2 - 2x - \ln|x - 1| + C$ 11. $\frac{825}{4}$ 12. $\frac{32}{3}$ 13. $-\frac{5}{2}$

14. $\frac{1}{3}\ln 20$ 15. $\frac{1}{2}x\sqrt{x^2 - 4} - 2\ln|x - \sqrt{x^2 - 4}| + C$ 16. $3^x\log_3 e + C$

17. $\frac{1}{2}x^2(\ln x^2 - 1) + C$ 18. $\frac{1}{36}x^6(6\ln x - 1) + C$ 19. $\frac{172}{3}$ 20. 0

21. $p = 1990.099 - 100{,}000/(t + 10)$ 22. $C(x) = 3x^2 + 4x + 1000$ 23. (a) $(7, 6)$

(b) $\$7.33$ (c) $\$24.50$

Exercise 15.1

1. $\{(x, y): x \text{ and } y \text{ are real numbers}\}$ 3. $\{(x, y): x \text{ is any real number and } y \text{ is any real number}$
except $0\}$ 5. $\{(x, y): x \text{ and } y \text{ are real numbers and } 2x - y \neq 0\}$ 7. $\{(p_1, p_2): p_1 \text{ and } p_2 \text{ are}$
real numbers and $p_1 \geq 0\}$ 9. -2 11. $\frac{5}{3}$ 13. 2500 15. 36 17. $\frac{13}{3}$

19. (a) $x = 4$ (b) $y = 2$ 21. (a) 7200 (b) 5000 23. $\$284{,}000$ 25. 8.2054

Exercise 15.2

1. $4x^3 - 10x + 4$ 3. $2x$ 5. $4x + 6$ 7. $12y - 5x$ 9. y 11. $e^x + y/x$

13. xe^{xy} 15. $9x^2(x^3 + y^2)^2$ 17. $2y(x + 1)^2$ 19. $-4y + 20xy$ 21. $p_2/(p_1 + p_2)^2$

23. $2x + 4y$ 25. 2 27. 7 29. 0 31. (a) 0 (b) $-2xz + 4$ (c) $2y$

(d) $-x^2$ 33. (a) $8x_1 + 5x_2$ (b) $5x_1 + 12x_2$ (c) 1 35. $\dfrac{\partial p}{\partial y} = 64 - 0.5y$; rate $= 56$

37. $70e^{-0.02y}$ 39. $4x$ 41. (a) y (b) $x + 2y$

Exercise 15.3

1. 57 3. (a) 2 (b) 4 5. (a) -16 (b) -10 7. (a) 36 (b) 19

9. (a) $\sqrt{y^2 + 1}$ (b) $xy/\sqrt{y^2 + 1}$ 11. (a) $\sqrt{y/x}$ (b) $\sqrt{x/y}$ 13. $q_1 = 188$;

$q_2 = 270$ 15. Any values for p_1 and p_2 that satisfy $6p_2 - 3p_1 = 100$ and that make q_1 and q_2
nonnegative, such as $p_1 = 10, p_2 = 21\frac{2}{3}$.   17. (a) -3 (b) -2 (c) -6

(d) -5 (e) Complementary

Exercise 15.4

1. (a) 2   (b) 0   (c) 0   (d) $-30y$ 3. (a) $2y$ (b) $2x - 8y$ (c) $2x - 8y$
(d) $-8x$ 5. (a) $2 + y^2 e^{xy}$ (b) $xye^{xy} + e^{xy}$ (c) $xye^{xy} + e^{xy}$ (d) $x^2 e^{xy}$ 7. 0
9. $-1/y^2$ 11. -6 13. $4 + 2e$

Exercise 15.5

1. Max $(0, 0, 9)$ 3. Min $(0, 0, 4)$ 5. Min $(1, -2, 0)$ 7. Saddle $(1, -3, 8)$ 9. Saddle
$(0, 0, 0)$ 11. Saddle $(0, 0, 0)$; min $(2, 2, -8)$ 13. $x = 5000$, $y = 128$ 15. $x = \frac{20}{3}$, $y = \frac{10}{3}$
17. $x = 28$, $y = 100$ 19. Brand $1 = 0$, brand $2 = 10$

Exercise 15.6

1. Min $(3, 3, 18)$ 3. Min $(3, 2, 35)$ 5. Max $(4, 2, 32)$ 7. Max $(3, \frac{5}{2}, -28)$
9. Min $(-\frac{2}{5}, -\frac{1}{5}, \frac{1}{5})$ 11. Min $x = 1$, $y = 1$, $z = 1$, $w = 3$ 13. Max $x = 0$, $y = 1$,
$z = 0$, $w = 1$ 15. $x = 4$, $y = 1$ 17. $x = 900$, $y = 300$ 19. $x = \$10,003.33$, $y = \$19,996.67$

Chapter 15 Review Exercises

1. $\{(x, y): x \text{ and } y \text{ are real numbers and } y \neq 2x\}$ 2. -5 3. 20   4. $15x^2 + 6y$

5. (a) $ye^{xy} + \dfrac{y}{x}$ (b) $xe^{xy} + \ln x$ 6. -8 7. 8   8. (a) $2y$ (b) 0   (c) $2x - 3$

(d) $2x - 3$ 9. Max at $(0, 0, 16)$ 10. Saddle at $(0, 0, 0)$; min at $(1, 1, -1)$ 11. Min at
$(2, 8, 80)$ 12. Max at $(6; 3; 11,664)$ 13. (a) 280   (b) $\frac{2400}{7}$ 14. (a) -2 (b) -6
(c) Complementary   15. $x = 20$, $y = 40$

Index

3 4 5 6 7 8 9